Politics in Georgia

Politics in Georgia

Third Edition

Robert M. Howard

Arnold Fleischmann

Richard N. Engstrom

The University of Georgia Press | Athens

© 2017 by the University of Georgia Press
Athens, Georgia 30602
www.ugapress.org
All rights reserved
Set in 10/13 Minion Pro

Most University of Georgia Press titles are
available from popular e-book vendors.

Printed digitally

Library of Congress Cataloging-in-Publication Data

Names: Howard, Robert M., 1956– author.
Title: Politics in Georgia / Robert M. Howard, Arnold Fleischmann, and
Richard N. Engstrom.
Description: Third Edition. | Athens, Georgia : The University of Georgia Press,
[2017] | Previous edition lists Arnold Fleischmann as the first author on the title
page. | "The first [edition] was published in 1997, the second [edition] in 2007, and
this third edition in 2017"—T.p. verso. | Includes bibliographical references and
index.
Identifiers: LCCN 2017019754| ISBN 9780820351766 (Hardback : alk. paper) |
ISBN 9780820352893 (Paperback : alk. paper) | ISBN 9780820351773 (Ebook)
Subjects: LCSH: Georgia—Politics and government.
Classification: LCC JK4316 .F54 2017 | DDC 320.4758—dc23 LC record available
at https://lccn.loc.gov/2017019754

Robert Howard dedicates this book
to the loving memory of his parents,
Amy and Bernard Howard.

Arnold Fleischmann is grateful to
Carol Pierannunzi, Tom Lauth,
and the late Susette Talarico for
giving life to this project.

Rich Engstrom dedicates his
contribution to all of his former
colleagues and students in Georgia.

CONTENTS

Introduction | ix

CHAPTER 1   State and Local Governments in the Federal System | 1

CHAPTER 2   The Setting for Contemporary Georgia Politics | 28

CHAPTER 3   Georgia's Constitution | 57

CHAPTER 4   Voting and Elections | 99

CHAPTER 5   Political Parties and Interest Groups | 122

CHAPTER 6   The Legislature | 149

CHAPTER 7   The Executive Branch | 181

CHAPTER 8   The Legal System | 208

CHAPTER 9   Local Government and Politics | 243

CHAPTER 10   Public Policies | 282

Notes | 339

References | 379

Index | 403

INTRODUCTION

This volume is the third edition of *Politics in Georgia*, with each edition appearing one decade apart. The first was published in 1997, the second in 2007, and this third edition in 2017. In the second edition of this book, the authors noted the emerging Republican takeover of the politics and political environment of the state. However, they hedged in calling it a complete takeover and instead stressed the still "purplish" nature of state politics. In 2007, the politics in Georgia remained in a state of flux, with most voters styling themselves as moderate, and Democrats still holding some statewide offices and some congressional seats.

Beyond politics, the second edition noted a few cultural and demographic changes over the previous decade, for example, the continued population growth in Georgia, the continued growth in corporate relocation and emergent businesses such as high technology, the continued growth in immigrant population in the state, and the changing racial demographics in Atlanta, the largest, most prominent (and capitol) city in Georgia. The second edition also noted that the African American population in Atlanta had declined as whites moved into the city and African Americans started to move into the mostly all-white and mostly all-Republican suburbs of Atlanta, often referred to by locals as the "doughnut around the hole."

So what has changed over the past decade, and what is our assessment of politics in Georgia for this third edition? First, there has been a change, albeit with some continuity, in authorship. Carol Pierannunzi, one of the two original coauthors, retired from Kennesaw State University as director of the Burruss Institute of Public Service and Research and took a position with the Center for Disease Control. Arnold Fleischmann remains as a coauthor. However, Fleischmann moved from his position at the University of Georgia to become the head of the Political Science Department at Eastern Michigan University. It has taken two new authors to replace Carol Pierannunzi. Robert Howard is a professor of political science at Georgia State University, where he has been a faculty member since 1998. Richard Engstrom was an assistant professor at Georgia State, moved on to become the associate director of the Burruss Institute at Kennesaw University, and is now the associate director for the Institute for Governmental Service and Research at the University of Maryland. Thus, while only one of us currently resides in the state of Georgia, all of us have extensive experience with the state and analyzing its politics.

The new edition reflects the research and teaching interests of the authors. Howard specializes in law and courts, judicial politics, and public policy. Engstrom has particular expertise in parties and electoral politics. Fleischmann specializes in urban politics, including economic development policies, zoning, annexation, and local elections. Although each author participated in the writing and development of the entire book, several of the chapters have been extensively revised because of the particular expertise of the author. For example, the chapters on the judiciary and policy are almost completely new.

In addition to the interests of the authors, political, economic, and demographic changes have also resulted in extensive changes to the book. In 2007, the authors of the second edition claimed that Georgia was more purple than red or blue. Georgia is now, at least at the state level, a red state dominated by Republicans. All statewide officeholders are Republicans, and both houses of the legislature are heavily Republican. Democrats hold only four of the fourteen congressional districts. All the congressional Democratic representatives are African American, and three are from the Atlanta area.

Since the second edition, Georgia has had three presidential election cycles and two midterm elections. In all of them, the Republican candidates dominated. In 2008 and 2012, while Barack Obama won the presidency by relatively large margins, the Republican presidential candidate easily won the state. In 2008, John McCain won 52.2 percent of the vote, while Barack Obama won 47 percent. The 47 percent won by Obama represents the highest percentage of any Democrat running statewide in this past decade. In 2012, Mitt Romney won 53.3 percent, compared to Obama's 45.5 percent. In the last presidential election, won by Donald Trump, Trump garnered 51.3 percent of the vote and Hillary Rodham Clinton won 45.6 percent, while the Libertarian candidate, Gary Johnson, won 3.1 percent. In the Senate race, the incumbent Republican Johnny Isakson easily won reelection with 55 percent of the vote, compared to Democratic newcomer Jim Barksdale's 40.8 percent.

These Democratic vote percentages match the 2014 midterms. Michelle Nunn, a daughter of former popular Democratic senator Sam Nunn, running for the Senate, garnered 45.2 percent of the vote, compared to David Perdue's 52.9 percent. Jason Carter, the Democratic candidate for governor and grandson of former president Jimmy Carter, received 44.8 percent of the vote, losing to incumbent governor Nathan Deal's 52.81 percent.

Thus, it appears that a Democratic candidate can expect to earn at most 47 percent of the vote in a statewide election. A popular Republican incumbent will get between 53 and 55 percent of the vote, while even the lowest total for a Republican candidate will be about 51 percent. This implies that Georgia is firmly a red state dominated by Republicans. Even so, some changes in the state allow us to predict the potential for a purple state over the next decade. Trump's 51 percent was the lowest for a Republican candidate running for president, the Senate, or governor this decade. Even more interesting, Clinton won some formerly Republican counties surrounding Atlanta. Cobb County and Gwinnett County have been dominated by Republicans and continue to be so at the local level, with Republicans occupying most of the county commissioner seats. In the 2016 presidential election, however, both counties voted for Clinton, solidifying the turn toward Democratic control of Atlanta suburbs. Clinton also won many of the counties surrounding the cities of Savannah and Columbus.

The Republican Party in Georgia continues to be a business-oriented party. Significant changes in tax policy—replacing a broad-based income tax with some form of consumption tax or a drastic reduction in overall corporate or personal tax rates—has so far not occurred in Georgia. Business leaders also led the opposition to divisive social policy considered by the legislature. While social conservatives are active in Georgia politics, the state has not adopted as large a share of their agenda as in other states. An attempt at a law limiting the rights of transgender persons was defeated. Concealed campus carry was vetoed by Governor Deal in 2016 but became law with his signature in 2017. State officials in Georgia complied with the U.S. Supreme Court's decision to overturn bans on same-sex marriage.

The political change is, in part, a result of the demographic changes. While the African American population has remained steady, the Hispanic and the Asian populations have grown over the past ten years. In addition, minority populations are no longer concentrated in Fulton County, DeKalb County, and the city of Atlanta but have settled in the neighboring suburban counties of Cobb, Gwinnett, Douglas, Henry, Newton, Rockdale, and Clayton. As noted in our second edition, the African American population in the city of Atlanta continues to decline, now down to about 54 percent from 61 percent at the beginning of this century. The state also continues to grow in population and business, including a revival in several central cities. Many corporations have emerged or relocated here, and these businesses tend to favor more moderate social and fiscal policy. On the flip side, rural areas continue to decline, particularly in South Georgia.

The Approach and Contribution of This Book

Thus, we present significant revisions to the second edition. For the most part, however, we have not revised the plan of the book or the methods of writing or presentation. This book is meant for many different audiences, and we write it to reach as many of them as possible. As the authors did in earlier editions, we draw on a wide variety of sources for this material, including scholarly literature, journalist accounts, and government and private document and data sources. We again follow a similar pattern of comparing Georgia to the federal government, to the other forty-nine states, and to itself as we examine changes over time.

The third edition makes, we believe, a significant scholarly addition to our understanding of politics in Georgia. Using new ideas and new measurements for political actors that were not available a decade ago, we offer new theories and new ideas on the political institutions and political actors in the state of Georgia. We think this latest edition makes a scholarly contribution to our understanding of Georgia politics, institutions, and political actors, and the book has important things to say about politics in the South, in demographically and politically growing and changing states, and in the United States. In some sense, one can argue that what happens in Georgia does not stay in Georgia.

We also intend for this book to reach as wide an audience as possible beyond the scholarly community, including undergraduate students taking courses in Georgia and American politics, journalists and political actors, and the general public. As such, we have kept academic jargon to a minimum and used graphs, charts, figures, and tables to present much of our information.

The Organization of This Book

Although we kept the basic structure of the second edition, we have made a few organizational changes. As previously, we start with an overview of the federal system, which divides power between the federal government and state governments. We then move to an overview of Georgia's history, politics, and economy. We, of course, provide updates to the second edition to reflect the changes that have occurred in the power balance between the states and the central government and the changes in Georgia over the past decade.

Chapter 3 provides an overview of the Georgia Constitution. We offer an overview of the U.S. Constitution, which we have extensively revised from earlier editions, and note the differences between it and the Georgia Constitution(s). We also provide a comparison between the Georgia Constitution and constitutions of the other forty-nine.

The next five chapters deal with voting and the political institutions of Georgia. One major change with the third edition is the elimination of a separate chapter on public opinion. This change does not indicate that we think public opinion is unimportant; in fact, we think quite the opposite. However, for ease of presentation we decided to interweave public opinion about these political institutions and political actors directly into the respective chapters about each actor and institution.

Chapters 4 and 5 focus on voting and elections and political parties. These chapters note the changing political affiliations of Georgians and the present dominance of the Republican Party. Chapter 4 provides an overview of voting and elections and the runoff system that is in use in Georgia, reviews election procedures and turnout, and offers a brief discussion of the 2016 presidential election. Chapter 5 reviews the basics of political parties and interest groups and shows the increasing power of interest groups over the past decade. The chapter also examines the growing vote share of the Republican Party in statewide and local elections. Again, these chapters provide comparisons to the federal government and to other states.

The next three chapters analyze the three branches of government—one chapter each for the legislative branch, the executive branch, and the judicial branch. Chapter 6 starts with an examination of the legislatures of the fifty states before focusing on Georgia. We discuss the mechanics of drawing districts and qualifications for office, the legislative session, and the demographic and political characteristics of the current and prior Georgia legislatures.

Chapter 7 examines the executive branch. We note that this branch of government extends beyond the governor and includes other statewide elected officials required by the constitution, as well as gubernatorial appointments, including powerful boards. We compare the power of the Georgia governor to that of other state governors and note that in the past decade websites and social media have become increasingly important to the operations and "power of persuasion" of the governor.

Chapter 8 looks at the legal system of Georgia. It first provides a broad overview of the U.S. legal system, including a primer on law and interpretation of law, before moving to the specifics of the Georgia legal system. This chapter, in particular, notes the changing demographics and political nature of the judicial system of Georgia, highlighting the increase in women and minorities and the recent domination of the judicial system by Republican appointees.

In chapter 9, we move beyond our state-level coverage to examine local politics and local government. We provide comparisons to other states' local governmental structure before reviewing the specifics of Georgia local government. We also consider the impact of the U.S. and state constitutions, as well as state law and action, on local government; review local elections; provide specific information on local initiatives and referenda; and describe the status of local government finances and services.

Our final chapter is devoted to policy. We have significantly added and revised this section of the previous edition. After providing an overview of public policy adoption and implementation and financing, we review several specific areas of policy, including transportation, the environment, education, social welfare, and public safety and security. We conclude the chapter with a look toward the future.

Politics in Georgia

CHAPTER 1

State and Local Governments in the Federal System

Americans often take their political system for granted. Indeed, they might not appreciate how creative the framers of the Constitution were in establishing federalism, an American invention that gives certain powers to the national government, others to the states, and some to both. Federal systems have also developed in countries such as Australia, Brazil, Canada, and Germany.

Federalism is very different from a unitary political system, as in Great Britain or France, where the national government possesses all authority and decides which powers and responsibilities lesser governments should have. It also contrasts with a confederation, where independent states turn over limited powers to a larger government, as was tried in the United States in the 1780s and the former Soviet Union and Yugoslavia in the early 1990s.

The dynamic character of American federalism has been instrumental in Georgia's political development. The fact that the federal system in the United States leaves a great deal of authority to the individual states has permitted Georgia to develop certain political institutions and practices that differ from the other states. At the same time, the federal government has also used its authority within the federal system to bring about significant changes in Georgia.

The Nature of Intergovernmental Relations

American federalism is a dynamic rather than a fixed set of relationships. The U.S. Constitution mentions only the state and national governments, which leaves it to the states to establish and control local governments. Given the diversity among different governments in the system, it should not be surprising that the distribution of power among the national, state, and local levels of government has been a constant source of debate. Indeed, governments in the United States are linked to one another by regulation, cooperation, and competition.

Regulation

The key elements in the national government's ability to regulate lower-level (often called subnational) governments are spelled out in the U.S. Constitution's supremacy clause, enumerated powers, elastic clause, and Fourteenth Amendment. The supremacy clause, which can be found in Article 6, declares that the Constitution and federal law are "the supreme law of the land." The federal government's power extends to the enumerated powers granted to Congress in Article 1—a long list that includes taxing and spending, regulating interstate commerce, establishing a postal system, and declaring war, among many others. Most critically, the federal government's authority has expanded over the years as a consequence of the elastic clause, which allows Congress to enact laws "necessary and proper" for carrying out its enumerated powers. What that phrase means in practice is often a source of conflict. In the 1960s, for example, Congress used its power to regulate interstate commerce to prohibit racially segregated public facilities such as bus stations and motels. Finally, the Fourteenth Amendment requires the states to guarantee "due process of law" and "the equal protection of the laws." In practice, this has meant that the U.S. Constitution, particularly the Bill of Rights, provides minimum protections for all Americans that states cannot violate, but each state can grant its own citizens more rights.

Below the national level, states have substantial power to regulate local governments. State constitutions and laws specify how local governments are created, what powers they have, how they can raise and spend money, the procedures for conducting their business, and a host of related requirements. Local officials often complain, though, about state mandates, which are standards and procedures imposed by the states, often without the allocation of state money to the local level to help meet the requirements (see chapter 9).

Cooperation

Governments also cooperate with one another to achieve goals. Many social welfare programs, for instance, have been established and supervised by the federal government, administered by the states, and funded by all three levels of government. The federal government, though, often "buys" the cooperation of state and local governments by making money available only under certain conditions. For example, the federal government does not set speed limits, but it responded to the energy crises of the 1970s by giving highway funds only to states adopting a fifty-five-mile-per-hour limit. Similar action pressured states to pass laws about the drinking age and seat belt use. States have a "choice" in such matters, but failing to do what the federal government wants can cost them many millions of dollars.

States have at times cooperated when economic connections cross their borders. For example, New York and New Jersey created an agency decades ago that operates bridges, tunnels, airports, and other services in both states to serve the huge metropolitan area centered on New York City. Similarly, Missouri and Illinois created an agency in 1949 that eventually provided bus service and light rail in St. Louis and its suburbs, which exist in both states on both sides of the Mississippi River.

States also work with lower-level governments in a wide array of fields through funding, technical assistance, training, and the like. For example, in 2013, states provided almost $489 billion to their local governments for various activities. In 2014, of the $617.6 billion in revenues collected by local school systems in the United States, 8.6 percent was from federal sources, 46.7 percent was from state sources, and the remaining 44.7 percent was local.[1] Local governments also cooperate with one another to share costs or resources, as when governments jointly build an airport or develop a landfill or when one government purchases services from another.[2]

Competition

Relations among governments can also be competitive—and disputes sometimes very heated. An example of competition between levels is the federal government's efforts to restrict the use of lands that it owns; states may see the same land as a source of economic growth and revenue if it were used for mining, logging, oil and gas drilling, grazing, or recreation. Another example of different levels of government competing occurred when more than twenty states challenged the authority of the federal government to implement the Affordable Care Act passed by Congress in 2010, more commonly known as Obamacare.[3] Those states, which included Georgia, objected to the federal government regulating the insurance industry, which has historically been regulated by states. That effort failed in the U.S. Supreme Court, however.[4]

Perhaps more common is competition between governments at the same level. The classic example is state and local governments using services, tax breaks, amenities, and other incentives to convince businesses to choose them when deciding where to locate.[5] For instance, several states courted BMW before the company's 1992 decision to build an automobile factory in South Carolina. The selection of Georgia as the site for a Kia assembly plant in 2006 also illustrates this point. Volkswagen picked Chattanooga as a plant site in 2008 over competitors in Alabama and Michigan, and Caterpillar picked a long-vacant site near Athens in 2012 for a major manufacturing plant.[6] Similar actions occur at the local level, where cities and counties compete for a company's operations, as when United Parcel Service sought land for its new headquarters when leaving Connecticut for metropolitan Atlanta.

State and local governments have remained important players in the evolution of American federalism. The remainder of this chapter establishes a context for examining Georgia's government and politics by describing the scope of subnational government and by analyzing state and local responses to recent economic, social, and political changes.

The Scope of Subnational Government

There are more than ninety thousand subnational governments in the United States—quite an array of states, counties, cities, villages, towns, school districts, and special districts. The number of states remained at forty-eight between 1912 and 1959, when Alaska and Hawaii achieved statehood, and the total since then has remained at fifty. Substantial changes have occurred at the local level, however (see table 1.1).

While the total number of local governments is about the same today as it was fifty years ago (over 90,000) and the number of counties has remained relatively stable, at slightly over 3,000, over 21,000 school districts disappeared between 1962 and 2012, as states forced the merger of school systems, especially in rural areas. There are also about 1,500 more municipal governments (cities) than fifty years ago, with many created as rural areas became suburbs of cities. The greatest percentage increase in governments occurred among special districts, which numbered only 18,323 in 1962, but grew by more than 20,000 over the past five decades. Most special districts are empowered by states to provide a single service such as water, medical care, or public transportation.

Despite the limited attention many Americans give to them, state and local governments are quite impressive in their size and activities. Table 1.2 presents a stark contrast among the three levels of government in terms of how they raise money and how they spend it. State spending in FY 2014 totaled just over $2 trillion, and local governments spent $1.7 trillion. Those amounts added together were slightly higher than what the federal government spent, although it is worth noting that part of state and local expenditures included federal money. As table 1.2 indicates, the three levels of government tend to get their revenues from different sources.

State and local data are from the Census Bureau and are based on statistical sampling rather than financial audits. The percentages do not total 100 because the table highlights the major categories found in any of the three levels of government. For instance, property tax revenues are included because local

Table 1.1. Number of Local Governments in the United States, 1962–2012

Type of Government	1962	1967	1972	1977	1982	1987	1992	1997	2002	2007	2012
Counties	3,043	3,049	3,044	3,042	3,041	3,042	3,043	3,043	3,034	3,033	3,031
Municipalities	18,000	18,048	18,517	18,862	19,076	19,200	19,279	19,372	19,429	19,492	19,519
Townships	17,142	17,105	16,991	16,822	16,734	16,691	16,656	16,629	16,504	16,519	16,360
School Districts	34,678	21,782	15,781	15,174	14,851	14,721	14,422	13,726	13,506	13,051	12,880
Special Districts	18,323	21,264	23,855	25,962	28,078	29,532	31,555	34,683	35,052	37,381	38,266
Total	91,186	81,248	78,188	79,862	81,780	83,186	84,955	87,453	87,525	89,476	90,056

Sources: U.S. Census Bureau 2011, table 426; 2013a, table 2.

Table 1.2. Government Finances, Fiscal Year 2014

	Federal	State	Local
Revenue ($ billions)	$3,021.5	$2,361.5	$1,772.1
Major Sources			
Federal Intergovernmental Revenue	N/A	23.4%	3.8%
State Intergovernmental Revenue	N/A	N/A	27.4%
Social Insurance and Retirement	33.9%	—	—
Individual Income Taxes	46.2%	13.2%	1.7%
Corporate Income Taxes	10.6%	2.0%	0.5%
Sales/Excise Taxes	3.1%	17.4%	6.0%
Property Taxes	—	0.6%	25.4%
Charges and Fees	—	8.1%	14.8%
Utility Revenue	—	0.6%	8.3%
Motor Vehicle Licenses	—	1.0%	0.1%
Insurance Trust Revenue*		25.4%	6.0%
Expenditures ($ billions)	$3,506.1	$2,048.5	$1,722.2
Major Functions			
Defense and International Affairs	18.5%	N/A	N/A
Intergovernmental Expenditures	16.5%*	24.3%	0.9%
Education	2.6%	13.9%	36.1%
Public Welfare/Income Security	14.6%	23.9%	3.1%
Health and Hospitals	11.7%	5.6%	8.2%
Law Enforcement, Fire, Corrections	1.4%	3.5%	9.5%
Transportation	2.6%	4.9%	5.3%
Natural Resources, Parks, Recreation	1.0%	1.2%	2.4%
Utilities, Sewerage, Solid Waste	—	1.4%	15.4%
Insurance Trust Expenditures†	38.9%†	13.6%	2.7%
Interest on General Debt	6.5%	2.2%	3.6%

Sources: U.S. Census Bureau, Annual Surveys of State and Local Government Finances, http:/www .census.gov/govs/local; U.S. Office of Management and Budget, "The President's Budget for Fiscal Year 2017," Historical Tables 2.1, 2.2, 3.2, and 12.2, https://obamawhitehouse.archives.gov/omb/budget /Historicals.

*Grants to state and local governments totaled $577 billion, but they are included in the other functional categories in the table. The largest share (73%) went to income security and health.

†Medicare and Social Security, 60.5% of which is off-budget.

governments derive significant revenue by taxing land and buildings, but the national government does not use this tax. The table combines all the states in one column and all local governments in the other, which masks important variations. For example, Alaska, Florida, Nevada, South Dakota, Texas, Washington, and Wyoming do not have an individual income tax; New Hampshire and Tennessee tax only individuals' dividends and interest. In contrast, Alaska, Delaware, Montana, New Hampshire, and Oregon do not have a state sales tax. Some states do not allow local governments to levy sales taxes. Georgia, however, allows its counties and school districts to adopt several types of sales taxes to raise revenue.

Perhaps the most worrisome thing for state and local officials is the extent to which they depend on higher governments for money, which is labeled "intergovernmental revenue" in the table. One can easily imagine the impact of a state legislature cutting back on funding for cities or school districts. Another striking difference is local governments' reliance on property taxes, charges (a wide array of fees), and utility revenue (e.g., water bills). States, on the other hand, draw major revenues from sales taxes, while the national government's major source is individual income taxes. For all three levels, though, certain revenues go into protected trust funds such as Social Security, Medicare, retirement plans, and unemployment insurance.

The three levels of government also spend funds on different things. The first thing to notice is the national government's spending on security. This expenditure totaled over $640 billion in 2014, which is not quite 19 percent of federal spending, a major reduction from wartime periods in the country's history. Despite national debates on education, the $91 billion in spending is a small share of the federal budget (2.6 percent). Meanwhile, state education spending exceeded $283 billion in 2014 (almost 14 percent of their budgets), $227 billion of it on higher education. Local governments, mainly independent school districts, spent another $620 billion on education (36 percent of all local expenditures). More than $579 billion went to elementary and secondary schools. Also noteworthy is the extent to which local governments spend significant amounts on the "boring" day-to-day services like transportation, water, sewers, and solid waste collections and disposal.

The scope of subnational government is impressive beyond the total number of units and sheer dollars involved. In 2006, just before the Great Recession, the federal government had almost 2,439,000 full-time civilian employees and almost 300,000 part-time workers. State governments had 4.25 million full-time employees and another 877,000 working part time; local governments had 10.66 million full-time employees and another 3.5 million working part time (the overwhelming share of part-time state and local workers was in education). In

2014, well after the recession had ended, the federal work force had grown by roughly 37,000 full-time civilian employees (1.5 percent). In contrast, full-time state employment was about 500,000 less than in 2006, but part-time workers had increased by almost 715,000. Among local governments, the number of full-time employees had declined by about 100,000 over the eight-year period, and part-time employment had shrunk by about 200,000 workers.[7] Still, despite the image of a large national government, state and local governments remain the sites where most public employees work in the United States.

Like government spending, employment data also capture the great diversity in what the three levels of government do. In 2014, about 27.5 percent of full-time federal employees worked on national defense and international relations; another 21 percent worked for the Postal Service. In contrast, the largest share of full-time state employees were in higher education (35 percent), followed by corrections (12 percent) and hospitals (9 percent). At the local level, 57 percent of the full-time employees worked in education, almost entirely in K–12 school systems. The next most common categories were police (7 percent), hospitals (5 percent), and fire protection (3 percent).

Subnational Governments' Recent Challenges and Responses

Overcoming challenges might be the hallmark of state and local governments. The past three decades have confronted officials with dramatic economic, social, and political issues. They have responded with a wide range of policy innovations, but they also face an array of worsening and new problems.

Economic Challenges

Significant Trends and Events. Subnational governments have always had to deal with general cycles of economic growth and decline, as well as longer-term shifts in the structure of the U.S. economy. Periods of economic growth normally increase revenues for state and local governments, possibly resulting in new or better services. In contrast, recessions generally mean a drop in tax revenues, increased spending for entitlement programs such as unemployment compensation, and pressure to cut costs. These conditions can be especially daunting because of states' requirements to balance their budgets.

The nation has enjoyed several periods of substantial growth in gross domestic product (GDP) in recent decades. After adjusting for inflation, relatively long economic expansions took place when annual GDP increases ranged between 3.5 and 7.3 percent during 1983–1989 and 2.7–4.8 percent during 1992–2000. GDP also grew between 2.8 and 3.8 percent annually in 2003–2006.

On the other hand, the United States has experienced eleven recessions since the end of World War II. Many of these have been brief, such as those in 1981–1982, 1990–1991, and 2001. The most recent challenge for subnational governments was the "Great Recession"—the worst recession since World War II—which lasted from December 2007 through June 2009 (eighteen months) and saw overall GDP decline 4.1 percent. Unemployment reached a high of 10 percent in October 2009, and GDP turned negative for two years, including −2.8 percent in 2008 and a whopping −7.8 percent in the fourth quarter of that year. Employment in construction, manufacturing, and financial services were especially hard hit. The Great Recession also included a banking crisis and the bursting of a "housing bubble," which led to large-scale mortgage foreclosures and substantial drops in the value of real estate. The recovery was especially slow: in November 2011, employment was more than 4 percent below its level at the start of the recession four years earlier.[8] For subnational governments, the drop in consumer spending dented sales tax revenues, and the bursting of the bubble meant a significant drop in the value of real estate, which supported property taxes.

Beyond cyclical changes, states and communities have confronted large-scale shifts among the leading sectors of the economy. During an earlier era, this change included the move from agriculture to manufacturing. More recent has been the shift from manufacturing to services. In 1985, the nation's 19 million manufacturing jobs accounted for 18.2 percent of nonfarm employment. By 2006, the last year before the Great Recession, manufacturing jobs had shrunk to 14 million (10.4 percent). With a slight uptick coming out of the recession, manufacturing jobs reached 12 million in September 2013 (8.8 percent of nonfarm employment). In contrast, the service sector grew during 1985–2013 from 57 million jobs (58.9 percent) to almost 96 million (70.2 percent).[9]

The service sector itself has changed over time. Projections for 2010–2020 showed the most rapid employment growth for personal-care aides (70.5 percent) and home health-care aides (69.4 percent), both of which paid about $20,000 in 2010. They were followed by biomedical engineers (61.7 percent growth), whose median pay in 2010 was more than $81,000. The remaining occupations in the top ten were projected to grow 44–60 percent: three categories of helpers in skilled trades with annual earnings under $30,000 in 2010, event planners ($45,260), iron workers ($38,430), veterinary technicians ($29,710), and physical therapy assistants ($49,690).[10]

In addition to these structural and cyclical changes in the U.S. economy is a pattern generally referred to as "globalization." Among other things, this trend covers production and investment across national borders, location of facilities and other assets among countries, and shipping between countries. As a result,

American states and communities compete no longer just with one another but with places and countries around the world. Globalization also includes a higher level of economic integration. For example, the Canadian company Bombardier manufactures the body of a corporate jet in Mexico, attaches wings made in Northern Ireland and engines produced in Canada, and finishes the plane in Wichita, Kansas, to be marketed worldwide.[11]

Economic change is uneven, however; it does not occur everywhere in the same way or at the same rate. For instance, states in the North lagged below the national growth rate during the 1970s and experienced severe problems during the recession of 1981–1982. Resource-rich states in the Southwest and West, on the other hand, experienced more rapid growth in the 1970s, while the eight states in the South Atlantic region, which includes Georgia, grew slightly faster than the nation as a whole. By the mid-1980s, the New England economy had rebounded and expanded faster than any other region, only to drop into a severe recession by the end of the decade.

Between 1990 and 2000, the nation's GDP expanded almost 72 percent, but states varied in their performance. Georgia's economy expanded 108.6 percent during the 1990s—only five states grew faster. In contrast, thirteen state economies grew by less than 60 percent, including Alaska at 10.4 percent, Hawaii at 26 percent, Wyoming at 32.5 percent, Louisiana at 44 percent (with Hurricane Katrina in 2005), and West Virginia at 47.1 percent. Among Georgia's five neighbors, North Carolina's economy expanded 95.6 percent, followed by Tennessee (84.4), Florida (82.8), South Carolina (71.7), and Alabama (60.7).[12]

Growth during the first decade of the twenty-first century was exhilarating until the Great Recession, when the nation's GDP shrank 1.7 percent between 2008 and 2009. GDP grew over 45 percent between 2000 and 2010, but patterns again varied among the fifty states. Georgia's economy had a difficult time, growing just 36.8 percent during the decade. That rate is below the nation as a whole but far better than the worst case, Michigan, which grew only 8.8 percent. The fastest growth was among energy-producing states. Indeed, the leaders were Wyoming (113.8 percent) and North Dakota (93.6 percent). Growth was also higher among Georgia's neighbors: Alabama (49 percent), Florida (51.3 percent), North Carolina (51.6 percent), South Carolina (40.6 percent), and Tennessee (42.8 percent).[13] Georgia's lackluster economic performance was attributed in large part to its dependence on construction, which dropped precipitously during the recession as housing starts plummeted and real estate foreclosures, bankruptcies, and bank failures rose dramatically.[14] Just as the economy recovered, though, oil and gas prices slid dramatically, in part because of the expansion of American production. As a result, energy-producing states such as Alaska, Louisiana, North Dakota, Oklahoma, and Texas saw their tax revenues shrink significantly.[15]

Similar patterns of uneven development occurred at the local level. Rural areas have witnessed a decline in the number of farms since World War II. More recently, a majority of farms were described as retirement or lifestyle types, which account for limited agricultural sales.[16] Following several decades of growth, the manufacturing sector in rural America contracted substantially during the 2000s, in large part because of a strong dollar and low-wage competition overseas.[17] The decline in manufacturing and agriculture has been exacerbated by the waning of the natural resources economy, including industries such as timber.[18]

Metropolitan areas also exhibit uneven economic growth and development.[19] During the 1970s and 1980s, central cities lost residents and businesses (especially manufacturing) and had aging infrastructure and deteriorating services. The manufacturing base had been important as the traditional means for unskilled workers to enter the economy. On the flip side, jobs moved increasingly to suburbs over the past few decades, but the suburbs became more diverse and more likely to include residents living below the poverty level. Surprising to many observers was the growth of central cities in the 1990s, particularly with jobs for immigrants and the young and educated people sometimes called "the creative class." Although the central city surge abated somewhat in the early years of this century, some analysts see a curtailing of America's love affair with suburban life and an eagerness among many to live in cities because of cultural amenities, a desire to avoid the costs of commuting, and the long-term decline in violent crime.[20] Harvard economist Edward Glaeser sees the city as critical to economic growth "because technological change has increased the returns to knowledge that is best produced by people in close proximity to other people."[21]

Beyond these general patterns, some metropolitan areas have done better than others economically. Between 2001 and 2012, for example, U.S. GDP rose 52.3 percent, and Georgia's GDP increased 42.2 percent. Among Georgia's metropolitan areas, though, it ranged from 14.2 percent in Macon to 127 percent in Hinesville, which benefited from its connection to the military. Similar variation occurred during the Great Recession. From 2008 to 2009, almost all of Georgia's metropolitan areas saw their GDP drop, with the largest in Dalton (−6.4 percent), due to its heavy reliance on manufacturing. Declines experienced by other metropolitan areas were all under 4 percent, while Albany, Athens, Columbus, Hinesville, Valdosta, and Warner-Robbins experienced modest GDP growth. Still, the recession's effect on Georgia's metropolitan areas was not nearly as severe as it was in manufacturing-based Detroit (−8.1 percent) and areas battered by the housing crisis such as Las Vegas and Phoenix, each of which had GDP drops of more than 6 percent.[22]

As this discussion suggests, changes in growth and decline depend heavily on an area's economic base. Thus, the rebound in manufacturing had a significant impact on smaller metropolitan areas, particularly in the Midwest. As the economic recovery continued in 2012, financial activities and professional services led to modest GDP growth in Macon, construction fueled 2.3 percent growth in the Brunswick area, manufacturing led Dalton's 2.4 percent growth, Savannah's growth benefited from hospitality and finance, and Atlanta's 2.6 percent GDP increase was thanks largely to finance along with business and professional services.[23]

State and Local Responses to Economic Challenges. How have states and communities dealt with these economic changes? Perhaps the most widespread and obvious are the efforts to promote economic development, which date back to the 1930s, when the goal was to attract factories, a strategy that was called "smokestack chasing." These efforts have come to include major infrastructure improvements (e.g., roads, buildings), tax breaks, loans and loan guarantees, free land, buildings, property improvements, job training, advertising and other promotional activities, and a variety of other initiatives. The use of these kinds of incentives intensified during the Great Recession. It is unclear, though, how much these efforts actually influence the decisions of businesses when more and more governments try the same things.[24]

Economic development efforts have changed over the years. Most states and communities have aimed to diversify so that they are not too dependent on one sector of the economy such as mining or a narrow type of manufacturing. Leaders now target the service sector and corporate headquarters, as with Boeing's 2001 decision to leave Seattle for Chicago after rejecting offers from Denver and Dallas–Fort Worth. There was even substantial competition for the new national headquarters of the United Church of Christ, the Presbyterian Church (U.S.A.), and the Evangelical Lutheran Church in America.[25]

State and local leaders have gotten more entrepreneurial.[26] They increasingly promote economic development by setting up public-private partnerships and foundations, which operate less in the public eye than government. They also promote investment from abroad and markets for their products in other countries. By 2013, for instance, forty-one states maintained overseas offices to promote trade and investment. Georgia is among the leaders in using this strategy and maintained eleven offices in 2015, in Canada, Mexico, Israel, plus three in Asia, two in Europe, and three in South America.[27]

Some analysts think that the Great Recession was substantially different from the earlier crises that state and local governments weathered. Subnational governments confronted economic hard times (and the tax revolt that began in the late 1970s) by developing new revenue sources, including a wide range of user fees, and relying more on the private sector, nonprofit agencies, and charities to provide services.

Economic conditions today could be far different because of the limits they place on leaders, especially at the local level. Some observers even see a "new normal" in which communities must survive in an increasingly globalized economy while confronting substantial revenue declines, greater pressure to rein in expenditures that have outpaced inflation and population growth for more than a decade, higher debt burdens, and substantial obligations for employee pensions, health care, and sick leave. This situation implies a future in which local governments have fewer resources, smaller work forces, and new ways of delivering services.[28] Some analysts believe there are few countervailing forces that will change this scenario. Many even fear that events like municipal bankruptcy in Detroit and elsewhere, along with fiscal stress in Illinois and other states, will become widespread even as the nation recovers economically.[29]

Social Challenges

Significant Trends and Events. Subnational governments have also had to cope with issues related to population movements, racial and ethnic change, education, and poverty. During the mid-1970s, the media, public officials, and scholars focused on dramatic population growth in the Sunbelt and the equally striking economic decline in the Frostbelt. During the 1980s, the rural states of Iowa, North Dakota, West Virginia, and Wyoming lost population. Another twenty-five states grew more slowly than the nation as a whole. At the other extreme, Nevada's population expanded 50 percent, while that of Alaska, Arizona, and Florida expanded by more than 30 percent, and Georgia registered an 18.6 percent increase (see table 1.3).

From 1990 to 2000, when the nation grew by 13.1 percent, every state added population, including North Dakota's meager 0.5 percent. Nevada grew by two-thirds, and Arizona's population expanded 40 percent. The South and the West continued to lead in population increases during the first decade of the twenty-first century, but the 2010 census suggests that the Great Recession put the brakes on the hyper-growth of the previous decade.

Growth also varied widely at the local level, which also means that population shifts within states can vary widely. Rural and metropolitan areas generally have moved in opposite directions. Rural counties accounted for 72 percent of the nation's land area in 2012 but only 15 percent of its population. Rural counties as a whole experienced their first population loss ever during 2010–2012. Areas based largely on recreation saw their growth slow during the recession, and ex-urban areas (the rural areas just beyond cities and their suburbs) actually lost residents.[30]

Metropolitan areas, which include a core city of at least fifty thousand residents and the counties economically connected to it, have gained residents since

Table 1.3. Population Changes in the States, 1980–2010

Percent Change	1980–1990	1990–2000	2000–2010
Negative	IA, KY, LA, MI, ND, WV, WY		MI
0–5	AL, AR, IL, IN, KS, MA, MS, MO, MT, NE, NY, OH, OK, PA, SD, WI	CT, ME, ND, OH, OK, PA, RI, WV	CT, IL, IA, LA, ME, MA, MS, NE, NJ, NY, ND, OH, PA, RI, VT, WV
5.1–10	CT, ID, ME, MN, NJ, OR, RI, TN, VT	HI, IL, IN, IA, KS, KY, LA, MA, MI, MO, NE, NJ, NY, SD, VT, WI, WY	AL, AR, CA, HI, IN, KS, KY, MD, MN, MO, MT, NH, OK, SD, WI
10.1–20	CO, DE, *GA*, HI, MD, NM, NC, SC, TX, UT, VA, WA	AL, AK, AR, CA, DE, MD, MN, MS, MT, NH, SC, TN, VA	AK, CO, DE, FL, *GA*, NM, NC, OR, SC, TN, VA, WA, WY
20.1–30	CA, NH	FL, *GA*, ID, NM, NC, OR, TX, UT, WA	AZ, ID, TX, UT
30.1–50	AK, AZ, FL	AZ, CO	NV
Greater than 50	NV	NV	
U.S. Change	9.8%	13.1%	9.7%

Source: U.S. Census Bureau 2012b, table 14.

the end of World War II, both in absolute numbers and as a percentage of the nation's population. In 2000, 82.8 percent of all Americans lived in metropolitan areas, a share that grew slightly to 83.7 percent in the 2010 census. Still, most of the nation's population growth in the early years of this century occurred in metropolitan areas, and more than one in every ten people lived in two metros—New York and Los Angeles. Within metropolitan areas, central cities enjoyed something of a rebound in the 1990s and first decade of the twenty-first century, but most of the population increases have occurred in outlying areas. In parts of the West, cities and suburbs alike have boomed. In some parts of the Northeast and the Midwest, both cities and their suburbs have witnessed population losses during recent decades. Growth was not as rapid in what the Census Bureau calls micropolitan areas, which are urbanized centers where the core city has a population between ten thousand and fifty thousand.[31]

Table 1.4 shows the population changes in Georgia's metropolitan areas and their core cities. Note that metropolitan areas are continually redefined by the U.S. Office of Management and Budget (OMB) as outlying counties become economically connected to them, which is why the number of counties is included in the table. For example, Metro Atlanta covered only five counties in 1970; by 2013, it encompassed twenty-eight. The original central city is used as

Table 1.4. Population of Georgia Metropolitan Statistical Areas, Number of Counties in Each Metro Area, and Core City Population

Metropolitan Area	1990			2000			2010		
	Metro Area	Counties	Core City	Metro Area	Counties	Core City	Metro Area	Counties	Core City
Albany	146,574	2	78,610	157,833 (7.7%)	2	76,925	157,308 (−0.3%)	5	77,434
Athens	136,025	4	86,553	166,079 (22.1%)	3	100,269	192,541 (15.9%)	4	115,452
Atlanta	3,069,425	18	393,962	4,263,438 (38.9%)	20	416,425	5,286,728 (24.0%)	28	420,003
Augusta	435,763	4	186,108	508,032 (16.6%)	5	195,182	564,873 (11.2%)	6	195,844
Brunswick			16,632	93,044		15,600	112,370 (20.8%)	3	15,383
Columbus	266,450	3	178,685	281,768 (5.7%)	4	186,291	294,865 (4.6%)	5	189,855
Dalton			22,535	120,031		27,921	142,227 (18.5%)	2	33,128
Gainesville			17,974	139,277		25,891	179,684 (29.0%)	1	33,804
Hinesville			22,951	71,914		30,446	77,917 (8.3%)	2	33,437
Macon	206,616	4	106,779	222,368 (7.6%)	5	97,255	232,293 (4.5%)	5	91,351
Rome			32,163	90,565		35,475	96,317 (6.4%)	1	36,303
Savannah	258,060	2	137,776	293,000 (13.5%)	3	133,412	347,611 (18.6%)	3	136,286
Valdosta			41,305	119,560		44,280	139,588 (16.8%)	4	54,518
Warner Robins			44,718	144,021		49,117	179,605 (24.7%)	1	66,588
Georgia	6,478,216			8,186,453 (26.4%)			9,687,653 (18.3%)		

Sources: Various tables available at the Census Bureau's "Metropolitan and Micropolitan Main" site, http://www.census.gov/population/metro/; County and City Data Book 2007, table c-1, http://www.census.gov/compendia/databooks/2010/tables/cc_C-01.pdf; and Census Bureau population estimates for the 1990s, http://www.census.gov/popest/data/cities/totals/1990s/tables/SU-99-04.txt.

Note: Figures in parentheses are percentage change from the previous census. Number of counties and percentage changes are left blank until the census when the area is officially a Metropolitan Statistical Area.

Table 1.5. Micropolitan Areas in Georgia, February 2013

Americus (Schley and Sumter Counties)	Milledgeville (Baldwin and Hancock Counties)
Bainbridge (Decatur County)	Moultrie (Colquitt County)
Calhoun (Gordon County)	St. Marys (Camden County)
Cedartown (Polk County)	Statesboro (Bulloch County)
Cordele (Crisp County)	Summerville (Chattooga County)
Cornelia (Habersham County)	Thomaston (Upson County)
Douglas (Coffee County)	Thomasville (Thomas County)
Dublin (Johnson and Laurens Counties)	Tifton (Tift County)
Fitzgerald (Ben Hill County)	Toccoa (Stephens County)
Jefferson (Jackson County)	Vidalia (Montgomery and Toombs Counties)
Jessup (Wayne County)	Waycross (Pierce and Ware Counties)
LaGrange (Troup County)	

the name of the urban area in the table, although the OMB has added larger suburbs to the names over time (e.g., the OMB uses the label Atlanta–Sandy Springs–Roswell Metropolitan Statistical Area). In addition, because metropolitan and micropolitan areas are economic and social—not political—clusters of counties, some areas extend across state lines. For example, Columbus is the hub of a metropolitan area that extends into Alabama, and the Augusta Metropolitan Area includes residents across the river in South Carolina. Other areas are redefined or created, as when Warner Robins became its own metropolitan area for the 2010 census; previously, it was considered part of Metropolitan Macon.

Micropolitan areas were first created as a category for the 2000 census and are defined by county boundaries. A micropolitan area can be thought of as a somewhat urbanized region with a small city as its commercial hub. Table 1.5 lists Georgia's 23 micropolitan areas as of 2013, when the United States had a total of 536. Together, Georgia's micropolitan areas had over 980,000 residents in the 2010 census, ranging from just over 23,000 in the Cordele area to more than 60,000 in the Jefferson, LaGrange, and Statesboro micropolitan areas.

Despite its rural heritage and imagery, Georgia has become highly urbanized. Not counting Georgia residents classified as part of Metropolitan Chattanooga, 82.6 percent of the state's population lived in metropolitan areas (mainly Metropolitan Atlanta), and 10.1 percent lived in micropolitan areas.

As in the nation as a whole, Georgia's urban areas have experienced uneven population changes. For instance, while the population in the Albany area remained largely unchanged over two decades, the city of Macon lost residents, while its metro area experienced modest growth. Metro Atlanta, on the other hand, expanded more rapidly than the state as a whole. Most of that population growth was in suburbs, however, especially on the fringe of the area. Indeed, less than 10 percent of the metropolitan area population has lived inside the Atlanta city limits since the 1990s, although Atlanta reversed a long period of population losses during the past two decades.

On top of sheer increases and decreases in population—some of them quite large—over the past few decades, state and local governments have encountered major changes in their racial, ethnic, age, and citizenship composition. Most notably, urban areas, especially suburbs, have become more diverse with growing numbers of Latinos, Asians, and the foreign-born. Many cities are also characterized by a rising share of the "dependent" population, namely, those under age eighteen and those sixty-five and older, who rely heavily on government services.[32]

As of 2010, there were 40 million foreign-born residents in the United States, which is just under 13 percent of the population. Of the total, 18 million were naturalized citizens, 11 million were legal noncitizens, and 11 million were estimated to be unauthorized immigrants, 59 percent of whom came from Mexico. By comparison, the historic low for foreign-born residents was 4.7 percent in 1970, although that increased to 6.2 percent in 1980, when a quarter of the foreign-born lived in California. Georgia's foreign-born population was almost 940,000 in 2010 (9.7 percent of the state's total population).[33]

Subnational governments have also had to contend with problems related to their residents' education and poverty. Complaints have focused on the quality of high school and college graduates (especially in comparison to other nations), the ways in which colleges and public schools are organized and run, the preparation of teachers, declines in funding (especially during the Great Recession), and myriad other ills. These problems are often cited as evidence of the weak skills of the American work force.[34]

Poverty in the United States has dropped noticeably over the past two generations, although, as one would expect, it tends to move upward during recessions. With the onset of the Great Recession, state and local governments increasingly had to address poverty and related problems such as homelessness. Like population change, poverty varies geographically, with the highest poverty rates as the economy recovered in 2012 in Mississippi, Louisiana, New Mexico, and Arkansas (more than 20 percent); the lowest poverty levels were in New Hampshire, New Jersey, Wyoming, and Alaska (10 percent or lower). Partly because of its visibility, poverty was once seen as a major problem only in big cities. It has spread, however, so that a majority of those living in poverty are actually in suburbs.[35]

State and Local Responses to Social Challenges. How have states and localities dealt with these demographic changes? Population change is rarely neutral in its effects. According to V. O. Key, in his classic book *Southern Politics in State and Nation*, "The growth of cities contains the seeds of political change for the South."[36] Key was undoubtedly right, given the rural bias in southern politics that lasted well into the 1960s (see chapter 2), but he could not have predicted the significant impact of American suburbanization that followed World War II and the growth of the South and the West that has continued almost unabated since the 1970s.

Places experiencing rapid growth have often been forced to spend large sums for improvements in roads, water and sewer, schools, and other basic services. Rapid growth can also pit newcomers against long-time residents, and in some places, antigrowth coalitions have formed to try to limit the pace or type of change.[37] On the flip side, areas losing population must contend with fewer residents, foreclosures, abandoned homes and businesses, declining property values, and a host of related problems—with Detroit probably the "poster child" for this dilemma. Policy responses to such problems often include wide-ranging efforts to promote economic development. More recently, cities have adopted policies to repurpose abandoned property and downsize, although that is far easier in metropolitan areas than in rural areas experiencing an exodus of people and businesses.[38]

In response to immigration, which is generally overseen by the national government, a number of states have passed their own laws to address illegal immigration and deny certain benefits such as drivers' licenses to undocumented immigrants. Some governments have responded with "English only" laws stipulating that government business be conducted in English. On the other side, some places have passed policies like the "Dream Act," which allows undocumented immigrants to attend college at in-state tuition rates. These measures have been supported by a variety of public colleges and universities, and fifteen states adopted such laws by the end of 2013.[39]

Between the 2000–2001 and 2009–2010 school years, the revenues of public school systems grew 20 percent. Perhaps more important than this growth in investment, though, were shifts in the roles of different levels of government. Notably, the state share of revenues dropped from 50 to 44 percent, while the federal share rose from 7 to 13 percent (mainly because of spending to counter the recession) and the local share hovered in the range of 43–44 percent. During the two academic years of the Great Recession (2008–2010), state spending actually dropped by $20 billion.[40]

State officials also have addressed concerns about K–12 education by adopting stiffer graduation requirements for students, as well as higher pay and standards for teachers. They have also promoted increased use of charter schools and education vouchers. Efforts to revamp America's schools have been common since the Reagan years and received a push with the "No Child Left Behind" law signed by President George W. Bush in 2001. During the Obama years, the associations representing the nation's governors and state school superintendents led an effort to adopt the Common Core Standards Initiative, which seeks a curriculum that will achieve internationally recognized benchmarks for success, especially in mathematics and English. This effort has proved controversial, however.[41]

At the postsecondary level, the bottom line for public colleges and universities during the past decade is rather simple: cutbacks in state spending have meant that tuition and fees have become a greater percentage of university revenues. That change has significant implications for universities chasing tuition dollars and students often relying on debt to attend college.[42] On the policy front, states have tried to improve higher education by promoting better access to college, faster times for completing degrees, online and other instructional alternatives, and funding tied to indicators of "success" rather than enrollment levels.[43]

Political Challenges

Significant Trends and Events. Not surprisingly, political developments have also had major effects on subnational governments. Especially notable are changes in federal policy, geographical shifts in political power, and major transformations in the context within which state and local politics are played out.

Changes in many national government policies during the past generation have reshaped American federalism. During the 1960s and 1970s, new programs and funds were added to a system of federal grants-in-aid that had been devoted largely to highways and public assistance. Aid to state and local governments grew from $10.9 billion in 1965 to $20.2 billion in 1969, $68.4 billion in 1977, and $91.5 billion in 1980. Such grants became an increasing share of both federal spending and the budgets of state and local governments, and they raised the issue of whether the national government was "coercing" or "bribing" lower-level governments into adopting policies they otherwise might not.

Programs adopted under President Johnson relied heavily on categorical grants, which are for narrow purposes and maximize the discretion of federal agencies dispensing the money. In contrast, the Nixon administration emphasized revenue sharing and block grants, which are given for broad purposes, use mathematical formulas to dispense funds, and increase the discretion of state and local officials in using federal money. The grant-in-aid system changed substantially during the 1980s. The Reagan administration proposed a "new federalism" to shift a wide range of joint federal-state programs entirely to one level of government or the other, although the more dramatic elements of this agenda were not enacted. Money for federal grants grew more slowly during the 1980s. Several programs were terminated, and federal grants slipped from 25.8 percent of state and local revenues in 1980 to 18.2 percent by President Reagan's last year in office.[44]

Grant levels rose between 9 and 12 percent annually under Presidents Clinton and George H. W. Bush. Especially after the Republicans took control of Congress in 1995, there was increased emphasis on turning programs over to the states and granting them greater flexibility. Pressure also mounted to "privatize" government enterprises (sell them to the private sector or contract out for them).[45] However, President Bush's "No Child Left Behind" law also carried severe penalties in educational funding for states that did not comply. Following the terrorist attack on the Twin Towers in 2001, the political environment also shifted, with implications for federalism. In 2004, concern for safety gave opportunities to the federal government for consolidation and coordination of law enforcement, a policy once left largely to the states. It also provided the states a new source of revenue, as funding for training became available through the 2003 Homeland Security bill.

Perhaps the federal policy that generated the most reaction at the state level was the 2010 adoption of the Affordable Care Act ("Obamacare"), with its series of requirements and incentives related to Medicaid expansion, health exchanges, and practices. Incentives exist for states to implement the law, but Republican opponents of the law have fought the law's implementation and advocated its repeal. Georgia is one of many states that took the matter to court, ultimately failing to have the law declared unconstitutional by the U.S. Supreme Court.

Political power has also shifted geographically, both among and within states. The federal census conducted in years ending in zero is used to reapportion the 435 seats in the U.S. House of Representatives among the fifty states. The effects are generally felt in the next election following the census. Today's political map looks vastly different from the one that existed following World War II, as political power has gravitated to the South and the West. In 1952, the Northeast and the Midwest accounted for 57 percent of the seats in the House, whose largest delegations were from New York (43 seats), Pennsylvania and California (30 each), Illinois (25), Ohio (23), and Texas (22). By 1982, the Northeast and the Midwest's 208 seats were just 48 percent of the membership in the House, and California had the largest delegation (45 members, compared to 34 for New York, 27 for Texas, 23 for Pennsylvania, 22 for Illinois, 21 for Ohio, 19 for Florida, and 18 for Michigan).

Recent population trends have accelerated the shift in political power (see table 1.6). The reapportionment of the House of Representatives is related to

Table 1.6. Changes in Seats in the U.S. House of Representatives, 1990–2010

Change in Seats	1990 to 2000	2000 to 2010*
+4		TX (36)
+3		
+2	AZ, FL, **GA**, TX	FL (27)
+1	CA, CO, NV, NC	AZ (9), **GA** (14), NV (4), SC (7), UT (4), WA (10)
No Change	AL, AK, AR, DE, HI, ID, IA, KS, KY, LA, ME, MD, MA, MN, MO, MT, NE, NH, NJ, NM, ND, OR, RI, SC, SD, TN, UT, VT, VA, WA, WV, WY	AL (7), AK (1), AR (4), CA (53), CO (7), CT (5), DE (1), HI (2), ID (2), IN (9), KS (4), KY (6), ME (2), MD (8), MN (8), MS (4), MT (1), NE (3), NH (2), NM (3), NC (13), ND (1), OK (5), OR (5), RI (2), SD (1), TN (9), VT (1), VA (11), WV (3), WI (8), WY (1)
−1	CT, IL, IN, MI, MS, OH, OK, WI	IL (18), IA (4), LA (6), MA (9), MI (14), MO (8), NJ (12), PA (18)
−2	NY, PA	NY (27), OH (16)

Source: U.S. Census Bureau, "Congressional Apportionment: 2010 Apportionment Results," http://www.census.gov/popuiation/apportionment/dataJ2010apportionmentresults.htm!.

*Figure in parentheses is the number of House seats the state had following the 2010 census.

the balance of power within the Electoral College used to choose the president. Each state has as many electoral votes as it has members in the House and the Senate combined (plus three votes for the District of Columbia), and virtually every state awards its votes on a winner-take-all basis, with 270 of 538 votes required to win. Counting Senate seats in the formula does have a small-state bias: seven states had three electoral votes in 2012 (Alaska, Delaware, Montana, North Dakota, South Dakota, Vermont, and Wyoming), but only Montana among those seven states had more residents than Georgia's most populous county (Fulton).

Following the 2010 census, New York had just twenty-seven House seats (and twenty-nine electoral votes, compared to forty-five in 1950), including a loss of four seats between 1990 and 2010. During the same twenty-year period, Arizona, Florida, Georgia, Nevada, and Texas gained a combined eighteen seats in the House (and votes in the Electoral College); five other states in the South and West added one seat each. Despite this overall trend, some southern states (Mississippi and Louisiana) lost seats, and some had no gain (Arkansas, Kentucky, Tennessee, and Virginia).

Although no region has a majority, the South's 168 electoral votes in 2012 were 62 percent of the 270 votes needed for a majority.[46] From the mid-nineteenth century until the 1960s, the South voted solidly for Democratic candidates at all levels, mainly because of the party's commitment then to maintaining the region's system of racial segregation. Since 1964, however, African Americans have moved almost completely to the Democratic Party, and large numbers of conservative whites in the South have shifted their allegiance to the Republican Party.[47] With the exception of elections when the Democratic candidate was from the South (Carter and Clinton), Republican presidential nominees have had a near lock on the region since the 1980s, although Florida and Virginia were very competitive in 2008, 2012, and 2016, as was North Carolina in 2008 and 2012.

Similar geographical changes have occurred within many states. Prior to the mid-1960s, some legislatures had not been reapportioned in several decades, rural areas were substantially overrepresented, and the population of a state's legislative districts often varied widely. Federal court decisions beginning in the early 1960s forced state legislatures to have districts with equal populations, which benefited suburban areas as they grew more rapidly than cities. The federal Voting Rights Act (VRA) of 1965 created great pressure in the South to improve the chances of minority candidates by drawing districts with concentrations of nonwhite residents. Creating minority districts, usually in cities, also meant large numbers of districts in rapidly expanding suburbs, which were often white, affluent, and ripe territory for the Republican Party.

At the local level, residents and federal officials applying the Voting Rights Act pressured for the replacement of at-large city councils and county commissions with members elected from districts.[48] Critics claimed that at-large systems were biased against minorities in white-majority areas because electing candidates city- or countywide meant that whites would usually win because voters tended to vote along racial lines.

Compared to twenty or thirty years ago, today's state and local officials are operating in a political environment with increased partisan and ideological polarization, rising hostility to government, heightened political activism, and infusions of vast sums of money into the political system at all levels. Polarization—and what many see as the resulting "gridlock" between the two major political parties—seems most evident in Washington, D.C. Analyses of congressional roll call votes indicate that since the 1970s the ideological distance between the two parties has grown, with Democrats becoming somewhat more liberal and Republicans becoming far more conservative. The same is true of party activists such as donors, convention delegates, and primary voters. The desire of politicians to score political points, sometimes at any cost and with a constant eye to the latest news cycle, has led to what congressional scholars Thomas Mann and Norman Ornstein call "the new politics of hostage taking," which is probably most evident in battles over federal finances and the shutdown of the national government. It is also related to the rise of the Tea Party and its influence on the Republican Party, especially in the 2010 midterm elections.[49]

Rising hostility to government has taken many forms. Perhaps the most passive is public opinion. The most daunting data here trace the decline in trust in government. The consolation for officials at the subnational level, though, is that while only 28 percent of the public in a 2013 national survey had a positive view of the national government, 57 percent had a positive view of state government, and 65 percent expressed a favorable view of local government. The positive federal rating spiked from under 40 percent to 82 percent after 9/11 but has been in decline ever since. Perhaps as a sign of partisanship, the rating of state government varied among survey respondents, with positive ratings from Democrats, Republicans, and independents when the two parties shared control of state institutions (divided government) to major gaps in support when one party controlled both the legislative and the executive branches (unified government).[50]

Antigovernment hostility manifests itself not only in people's attitudes but also in their actions. In the 1990s, it led to the adoption of term limits for legislators in several states as a way to keep incumbents from accumulating power. The movement took hold in 1990, when citizens in Colorado, California, and Oklahoma used the initiative process, which requires petitions to place an issue on the ballot for voters to decide, to put term-limit proposals on the ballot in their states. Fifteen states now employ term limits, although another six had them repealed by the legislature or state supreme court.[51]

The initiative is permitted in twenty-four states and has become common in Oregon, California, and Colorado.[52] Over the years, the process has been used to limit taxes and spending, as well as to decide a host of policy questions. In November 2012, voters in thirty-eight states were asked to choose a president and faced 174 ballot measures, most of which were submitted by legislatures, but 42 were initiatives submitted by citizens. The initiatives led to marijuana legalization in Colorado and Washington, the approval of tax increases in California, the ratification of same-sex marriage in Maine and Maryland, and the rejection of assisted suicide in Massachusetts.[53] The year 2014 saw another 146 ballot measures, 35 of which were the result of the initiative. Voters in Alaska, Oregon, and Washington, D.C., approved legalization of marijuana; five states ratified an increase in the minimum wage; voters also restricted government taxing ability; results to approve bonds had a mixed reception at the polls.[54]

Activism also extends to traditional interest groups. One study of interest groups identified three trends at the state level between the early 1980s and mid-2000s: significantly more groups trying to influence state government; a broader range of interest groups, including those devoted to a single issue, social issues, and the "public interest"; and more intensive and sophisticated lobbying. Some shifts occurred in political influence, with hospital and nursing home associations, along with the insurance industry, joining the "top ten" most effective lobbying groups across the most states. In more than thirty states, general business organizations were still the most powerful, followed by teachers' organizations. Other significant interests represented utilities, manufacturing, local governments, and lawyers. Noticeably less influential were colleges and universities, the gaming industry, state employee associations, banking, and labor unions.[55]

At the local level, business interests and public employees still exert strong political influence. Business groups have become especially active since the 1980s in promoting local economic development, either on their own or with the cooperation of government. The new force in local politics since the 1970s is the neighborhood organization. These groups are often pitted against developers over zoning and other land-use issues. In built-up communities, they are also active in trying to maintain neighborhood amenities, safety, and public services.[56]

The growing importance of interest groups at the state and local levels is also reflected in the rapid expansion of political committees and their campaign contributions. Much has been made of the role of "independent" spending in national elections—especially the amounts and limited disclosure—since the U.S. Supreme Court's 2010 decision in *Citizens United v. Federal Elections Commission*.[57] State laws governing political contributions have been more lenient than federal law for quite some time. For instance, thirty-four states allow direct contributions to candidates for state offices by unions, including seven with no limit, and twenty-nine states allow companies to make contributions, including five with no limit.[58]

While the Supreme Court's decision might have allowed multiple ways to skirt the former restrictions on money in federal elections, another concern is that state elections have been "nationalized" by outside money.[59] For example, of the $56.4 million spent on state supreme court elections in 2011–2012, 27.4 percent was spent by interest groups and 15.3 percent by political parties—and just 57.3 percent was spent by candidates themselves.[60] Another issue is the extent to which campaign money now flows through the national organizations of both political parties to states, often allowing donors to avoid certain restrictions and allowing organizations to pool money from multiple states to target specific races.[61] At the local level, suburban and other outside money has long been present in big-city elections.[62]

State and Local Responses to Political Challenges. In many ways, state and local officials have responded to what is often labeled "coercive federalism" by campaigning against it. There is a long-standing practice, federalism scholar John Kinkaid observes, that "the party not in power in Washington, D.C., uses its dominance in a majority or sizable number of states to challenge policies of the party in power in Washington."[63] This has included state actions regarding environmental regulations, immigration enforcement, abortion, election procedures, and perhaps most notably, the Affordable Care Act. More than two dozen states challenged the health care law, which the U.S. Supreme Court upheld in part in 2012.[64] The matter did not end there, however. Only fourteen states and the District of Columbia chose to operate their own health care exchanges that individuals had to use to choose a health insurance plan. State-run plans got off to a better launch, but the remaining states relied on a federal exchange characterized by poor implementation. Twenty-five states and the District of Columbia were implementing the law's Medicaid expansion by 2014.[65] There is every reason to expect the state-led challenges to continue.[66] Indeed, a dispute over the language regarding subsidies and health exchanges went all the way to the U.S. Supreme Court, which decided in 2015 that it did not matter whether exchanges were run by the states or the federal government in order for people to participate in the system.[67]

Partisan change, particularly in the South, has extended beyond the attitudes and affiliations of individual voters. Officials and candidates often have responded by switching political parties. Between 1980 and 2009, 251 Southern legislators switched political parties, more than 90 percent of them from Democrat to Republican, Democrat to independent, or independent to Republican. Several Republican governors, including Sonny Perdue of Georgia, began their legislative careers as Democrats before becoming Republicans.[68] In addition, as Republicans gained in the region, they also used the creation of Democratic districts packed with minority voters to draw other districts that benefited their party. David Lublin and Thomas F. Schaller call such racial gerrymandering an "accelerant" for Republican fortunes, which were already becoming more favorable in the South.[69]

Economic, social, and political pressures have also affected government at the local level. One obvious change over the years involves the numbers and types of governments, including a huge reduction in the number of school districts and dramatic growth in the number of special districts (see chapter 9). Changes in the number and activities of local governments are controlled by the states, which are not known for dealing with local and regional issues in a very comprehensive manner.[70] Most city elections are nonpartisan, meaning that candidates running for office do so without party affiliations on the ballot, so much problem solving can avoid wrangling between political parties. Seeing themselves as largely abandoned by the national and state governments in the current political climate, many local leaders have struck out on their own to promote development of their communities, often in partnerships with business, universities, foundations, and a wide range of other entities.[71]

Change, Stability, and Subnational Governments

The American federal system has witnessed dramatic changes over the past generation. Recent shifts in international and national politics suggest that state and local governments may become even more important. Yet certain characteristics of subnational government in the United States have remained quite stable. Government structure, as reflected in state constitutions and city charters, has changed little. The Republicans and the Democrats are the only two viable political parties, although their fortunes have shifted in various places, and their influence is increasingly challenged by interest groups. Money still plays a powerful role in elections and policy making. Unlike Congress, those elected to state and local offices are often not professional politicians and have limited staff and compensation for doing their jobs. Race and ethnicity still polarize citizens. Finally, much of state and local politics involves location: where to put highways or public buildings, which services get provided in different areas, where to draw the boundaries of cities or legislative districts, how to zone specific pieces of property, and many similar issues.

Nevertheless, important trends are reshaping states and localities, perhaps none more than the Great Recession of 2007–2009, which led to reduced taxes but higher demands for social services, lower property values, numerous abandoned homes, and layoffs of public employees. Even as the recovery advanced slowly, state and local governments still faced a future that probably includes less grant money from the national government, deteriorating infrastructure, reduced work forces expected to deliver services more efficiently, and substantial reductions in retirement benefits that were promised in much better economic times—and maybe with questionable estimates.[72] Population and economic changes will also affect this mix, particularly if states continue a "race to the bottom" to see which ones give away the most in tax and regulatory relief to attract investment.

The changing political climate could also make governing difficult at the state and local levels. If the spigot of campaign money runs through Washington, candidates might increasingly be forced to cater to nonlocal interests in order to fund campaigns. There could also be pressure to grandstand on a national stage rather than be effective in the statehouse or city hall, if officials try to score points nationally rather than making good local policy.

Georgia has not been immune from the developments described above. Although key trends are covered more extensively in the next chapter, it is worth noting them here. Georgia has diversified, strengthened, and internationalized its economy during the past thirty years. The state has a long history of uneven development, however, which is typified by rural poverty and tensions between North and South Georgia. The state's population is changing dramatically. Po-litically, new groups have arisen, the Republicans have eclipsed the Democrats, and the national government has brought about significant change in Georgia. How Georgia responds to these developments is still an open question.

CHAPTER 2

The Setting for Contemporary Georgia Politics

Many factors influence Georgia's political institutions and practices. As with any state, to understand politics today, it is necessary to consider the historical, social, and economic factors that have shaped the state's politics.[1]

The Historical Setting

Georgia's political development has not always been smooth; in fact, sometimes it has been downright tumultuous. A brief overview of seven periods demonstrates that events in Georgia history still affect the state's political culture and institutions.

European Settlement and the Colonial Period

The Creek and the Cherokee nations inhabited much of what is now Georgia before the advance of European settlers in the sixteenth and seventeenth centuries.[2] Names of major rivers reflect the native presence: Chattahoochee, Etowah, Ogeechee, and Ocmulgee. For a time, Georgia was claimed by Spain, France, and England, although no country held any permanent settlement in the region. It was not until 1727 that the English began to muster the resources necessary to control the area under the philanthropic philosophies of James Oglethorpe. Georgia's original charter, proposed in 1730, called for settlement of the lands between the Savannah and the Altamaha Rivers. Trustees were to govern the colony as a refuge for those suffering religious persecution at home and as a source of relief for hardworking, unemployed, even indebted Englishmen to provide for the Crown while creating new lives for themselves. The trustees, headed by Oglethorpe, were prominent men in English society who were not permitted to own property in Georgia and were granted wide powers by the king.

Because of an overwhelming number of applicants, the trustees seldom had to pick settlers who were debtors or societal outcasts. In fact, most were tradesmen and small businessmen. The colonists left England in 1732 with approximately 120 settlers and landed at the site of what is now Savannah, for which Oglethorpe set out the plans. Although Oglethorpe himself was opposed to slavery, the practice was introduced to the colony as early as the 1750s, prompting the development of plantation-like settlements rather than the smaller farms envisioned by the charter.

Georgia grew steadily following the permanent English settlement at Savannah. The first land cession by the Creeks was followed by many more, as English settlements spread westward, each organized around a church or parish. Georgia under Crown rule was much as it was under the trustees. The Commons House of Assembly, composed of nineteen men who owned at least five hundred acres of land each, was able to enact law within royal limitations and with the approval of an upper house of twelve men appointed directly by the king. In order to vote for the members of the Commons House, male citizens of the colony had to show that they owned at least fifty acres of land.

The governor had royal authority to dissolve the legislature or overrule the judicial decisions made by the upper house. Georgia's colonial governors were primarily concerned with three major policies: military defense of the colony, negotiations with Native Americans, and border disputes with neighboring colonies, British or otherwise. After the Treaty of Paris in 1763 ended the war with France and Spain, Georgia's borders became better defined and less prone to attack from European competitors.

Georgia during the American Revolution

Discontent with British rule existed throughout the colonies in the 1770s.[3] Yet Georgia probably had fewer reasons than the other colonies to separate from England. The colony was dependent on the British for most manufactured goods and profited from exporting raw materials to England. In response to what were deemed unfair acts by the British government, a group of citizens met in Savannah to protest the actions of Parliament. The Council of Safety, as it came to be called, was the first organized protest to British rule in Georgia. This first government by Georgians preceded the Declaration of Independence by six months and was widely accepted by the newly declared free citizens of the state. Legislative power was vested in a provincial congress composed of representatives sent from each parish. The president of this body served as the executive, and courts were established. Thus the first self-government in Georgia incorporated the idea of three branches of government.[4]

With the news of the signing of the Declaration of Independence, Georgia adopted a new constitution in 1777 that provided for three branches of government, guaranteed religious freedom, and established the first eight counties as local jurisdictions. Problems arose quickly as powerful men struggled to fill the vacuum left by the toppled colonial government. To assure citizen support for the new state, British loyalists were declared to be traitors, expelled from Georgia, and had their property confiscated. Political parties developed, mostly as factions within the Whig Party. Disharmony among the Whigs complicated the party's ability to govern and to fight the war effectively. Even after the successful conclusion of the war, factionalism within the Whig Party prompted new action on the part of the state to establish an effective government.

The Years Following the Revolution

After the war, the Articles of Confederation created the national government, which exerted little influence on the individual states.[5] The legislature was the dominant force in state government, whose major actions dealt with land cessions from Indian tribes, the migration of British settlers from Florida (which had been returned to Spain in the Treaty of Paris), and the sale of confiscated Tory property. The fledgling court system was still in the process of self-definition. Local government was established around counties, which were created by the state legislature and gradually assumed responsibility for roads, the poor, and their own elections.

After the Articles of Confederation failed, Georgia adopted a new state constitution in 1789 modeled after the U.S Constitution. This document provided for a bicameral legislature and a single executive. Georgia also laid claim to a vast western landholding and attempted to sell this land to the national government in exchange for badly needed revenue. Congress refused, however, and Georgia was eventually forced to give up this territory to the federal government with little or no reparation.

Georgia's leadership following the war was quite different from that of previous periods. Royal governors and trustees were wealthy, educated men, generally lawyers, who were selected by the king after distinguished careers as servants to the Crown. Following the war, Georgia's political leadership was likely to be drawn from the militia and had little training in government. Many of these individuals were illiterate, were born in frontier country, and had few material goods. The new state constitution reflected this political emergence, and the aristocratic notions of the royal governors gave way in rapid order to the new concept of government by the "common man."

Georgia's extensive landholdings were the basis for the most notorious political scandal of the time, the Yazoo Land Deal. The legislature contracted with land speculators for the sale of a tract of western land approximately the size of the current state of Georgia. Following charges of bribery, the legislature eventually passed laws to repeal the sale, but much of the land had been resold, and the matter eventually had to be settled in the federal courts. The Yazoo land fraud stirred many to the point of violence. Citizens were so incensed that they prompted the drafting of a new state constitution with the expressed purpose of voiding the sale of any western lands by the state.

A second major event in Georgia during the post–Revolutionary War years was the invention of the cotton gin, which replaced the manual separation of cotton seed from the lint of the cotton plant.[6] This innovation, at a time when much of the Piedmont section of the state was being settled, prompted the development of larger farms devoted to cotton. Profits from these larger plantations made slavery itself more profitable as owners could clean the cotton as fast as they had hands to pick it. Demand for land from Indian territory also increased as the white population moved westward.[7] Larger cities were built around merchandising rather than manufacturing, as Georgia was able to export large quantities of lumber, cotton, and other local resources. Transportation was a problem for manufacturers, although matters improved with the development of railroads in the 1830s. Banks were chartered during this period, and the state flourished economically.

Social and Political Life in Pre–Civil War Georgia

In the years preceding the Civil War, Georgians established a political culture and social order that came to represent a "southern way of life." Glorified today by oversimplification and the passage of time, this lifestyle implied a leisurely way of living in quiet, stately plantations. In fact, such leisure was not the lifestyle for the vast majority of Georgians.[8]

About thirty-five hundred white Georgians owned more than thirty slaves each. While only a few whites lived on plantations, many blacks did. Quality of life for slaves was determined by their length of time as slaves, their skills as craftsmen, or their work within white households. Despite laws prohibiting the education of slaves, many were highly trained as craftsmen, and many were leased out by their owners. Most white Georgians were subsistence farmers for whom life was not easy, and religion was the focus of most social occasions.

Antebellum political life was defined by a splintering within the Democratic-Republican Party between the followers of two men, John Clark and George Troup, who were opponents in the gubernatorial race of 1819. Although the legislature elected Clark by a narrow margin, the bitter factionalism based on the personalities of these two men continued, and Troup became governor four years later.

A major political crisis occurred when the Cherokees declared themselves an independent nation and sought negotiations with the federal government. President Monroe agreed that the Cherokees could not be forced to sell their lands to the state and refused Troup's requests for federal troops to remove the Indians. Later, a treaty between the Creeks and the federal government involving lands within Georgia was hotly protested by Troup, who declared that the federal government had overstepped its authority by making a treaty without the approval of the state and called out the Georgia militia to enforce his will to have the Indian land surveyed. Federal officials did not wish to pursue the Indian matter to the point of violence and eventually interceded by paying the Indians for their land. Troup displayed a strong defiance against the federal government and won a powerful political victory for his assertions of states' rights.

The Troup faction eventually organized as the States' Rights Party. Troup himself served two terms as governor and then returned to his old seat in the U.S. Senate. Most Clark supporters joined the less radical Union Party. As early as 1832, discussions of states' rights were leading to strong language favoring nullification of federal law, especially on issues regarding protective tariffs, which the South bitterly opposed. Yet Georgia was often less likely to radicalize these arguments into discussions of secession than was more polarized South Carolina. The political parties in Georgia during this period were less defined by individuals and became more crystallized around ideology. Regionalism was beginning to develop among the southern states, which had little in common with the more industrialized North. States' rights were important to citizens who felt that their way of life, prosperity, or autonomy was threatened by the government in Washington.

The Civil War Years and Reconstruction

The Georgia Whig Party evolved from the old Troup and States' Rights parties. It was affiliated with the national Whig Party, received most of its support from more established areas of the state, and was especially supported by those Georgians who owned slaves. Although the party did not represent the antitariff views of the States' Rights Party, its membership did retain the ideology of states' rights. The Georgia Democrats, who were largely former Clark-Unionists, also advocated states' rights but more in the context of southern regionalism. They quickly found an eloquent spokesman in John C. Calhoun of South Carolina. As Calhoun's rhetoric became more radical in the years immediately preceding the Civil War, Georgia Democrats also became radicalized. Acceptance of new states into the Union and national debate over the Missouri Compromise, which admitted some states as slave states and others as free, sharpened public opinion in Georgia.

Although Georgia was more moderate than some southern states, due in part to its economic prosperity, states' rights was an integral part of the local political culture. The 1860 nomination and election of Abraham Lincoln as president were more than even moderates in the state could bear, and the legislature quickly voted appropriations for an enlarged state militia. The governor, Joseph Brown, moved Georgia quickly toward war, and the state seceded on January 2, 1861. The Confederate Constitution was adopted in March of that same year, and a new state constitution was drafted quickly to reflect these changes.[9]

Governor Brown's lack of loyalty to a centralized war effort and his strict adherence to a states' rights philosophy undermined the military efforts of southern generals. Brown felt conscription of soldiers by the Confederacy was unconstitutional, and his resistance to allowing Georgia's militia to defend other southern states proved problematic. He opposed the use of private property for the common war effort, martial law in Atlanta in 1862, and the military use of the railroads. Nevertheless, Brown was highly popular and was elected governor for four terms. Georgia was also well represented within the Confederate government, which included Alexander Stephens, who served as vice president.

The war stimulated industry in Georgia. The northern blockade forced Georgians to produce goods that had previously been imported. Despite this expansion, manufacturing was unable to keep up with demand during the war years. Construction of railroads also accelerated, although many rail lines were destroyed as military targets. Many other infrastructure developments in the state also were destroyed during the final days of the Civil War.

The state government established under the Confederacy was declared void at the end of the war, and the first military governor of the Reconstruction period called for a convention to establish a new government.[10] Delegates met at Milledgeville in 1865 and repealed the ordinance of secession, abolished slavery, drafted a new constitution, and repudiated state debt. Although elections were set for the following November, only those men who had not participated in the war or who were willing to take an oath of allegiance to the Union were permitted to vote.[11] Congress declared that the state delegates must not only repeal the acts of secession but also declare them void. Moreover, Congress required that the state ratify the Thirteenth and Fourteenth Amendments to the Constitution before readmission into the Union. Until then, Georgia was occupied as a captured wartime territory.

Not until 1868, when a new state constitution was written and the state capital had moved to Atlanta, did the legislature comply with the federal conditions for readmission to the Union. Bitter political fighting followed as Georgia refused to recognize black elected officials in the state legislature, and Congress refused to seat elected officials from the state. Black politicians elected during the early years of Reconstruction were never permitted to govern effectively and gradually lost office. Black voters were also rare, and when they did vote, they would be terrorized or coerced into voting for a particular candidate. Thus neither black officials nor black voters were significant political forces within the state during that time.

A highly organized group within the Democratic Party, which came to be known as the Bourbon faction, sprang up after the war to control the electorate and produced one-party politics in the state. The Democrats, despite intraparty differences, maintained their political stronghold for decades based on the general view that Republicans were northerners and outsiders. Bourbon Democrats based much of their appeal on the "southern way of life," a phrase that came to stand for states' rights and racial segregation.

The state slowly changed economically during this period.[12] Georgia was largely agricultural before and after the war. While most blacks had been slaves before the Civil War and were unemployed after the war, large plantations still required the labor that slaves had provided. Tenant farming, or sharecropping, was common practice during these years. Tenant farmers, who leased land on which to live and grew crops in exchange for a portion of the harvest, replaced slaves as labor on large plantations. Most blacks and poor whites quickly found that participation in this system was the only way to make a living.

Railroads were gradually rebuilt, and the state itself became involved in the railroad construction industry. Northern investors, or "carpetbagger merchants," created a commodity market in the cities of Georgia, with Atlanta especially benefiting from this investment. Cotton and cotton milling remained important to the state's economy. Mining, along with fertilizer and lumber production, grew as an important source of economic recovery. However, Georgia's relative poverty compared to other states was worse in 1900 than it had been in 1860. Although manufacturing increased, the slower rate of development within the state caused it to lag even further behind other states, with many citizens still struggling with conditions of poverty.

1880–1945

The cycle of rural poverty in Georgia was well established in the early 1900s. Merchants would provide farmers with credit against the upcoming harvest. Sharecroppers would often go into debt in order to feed their families until harvest. Because this arrangement often represented a substantial risk to merchants, interest rates were high. One or two bad crop years could condemn a farmer to lifelong debt. Because the landlord, who provided the land, and the merchant, who provided requisite materials, were entitled to a share of the harvest, many good harvests would be necessary for a sharecropper to free himself from debt. A drop in cotton prices before the First World War and then again immediately after the war made life in rural Georgia even more difficult.[13]

Life in Georgia improved in some ways during this period.[14] Colleges were established, and public education was expanded, although black and white students did not attend the same schools. High schools were made a part of the state's educational system in 1911, although many private high schools had been established before that date. As might be expected, white schools were uniformly superior to schools for black children, and even as late as the 1960s, some school districts did not provide high school education for minorities. More fortunate African Americans were educated in several private black colleges founded in Atlanta (part of what are now labeled historically black colleges and universities, HBCUs). Blacks were mostly engaged in farming, although a few had been able to secure their own farms. Local law enforcement, however, was still used to provide black prisoners for forced labor in a variety of industries.[15] Lynching and other forms of intimidation were used to maintain the racial order, including a campaign during 1912 that forced nearly 1,100 African Americans out of Forsyth County.[16] Black women who worked outside the home were most often employed as domestics in white households.

Women—or at least white women—also took more active public lives. Conveniences such as canned foods and mass-produced clothing provided extra leisure time for many women. Child labor and the prison convict leasing system were important social issues of the day, and the advocates of reform in Georgia were often female.

The financial and social plight of many blacks and whites, especially those in rural areas, prompted the first real attempt at breaking the stranglehold of the Democratic Party in the state. Since Georgia had remained essentially a one-party state since Reconstruction, real political contests were held not at the time of the general election but earlier, during the selection of the party's nominees for office. Prior to 1898, these nominees were selected by the party membership at conventions, but the introduction of the statewide primary election provided for more grassroots support for candidates. Black and white farmers, if united as a voting bloc, could control the nomination process under the primary system. A young attorney, Thomas E. Watson, sold himself as champion of these farmers, and a political movement based on agrarian political empowerment grew up around this dynamic young man.[17]

Georgia Populists stood for low-interest loans for farmers and a graduated income tax. They were unique in that the party encouraged blacks to vote with whites on the basis of a common interest in improved economic conditions. Georgia Democrats responded by calling up images of the destruction of white society due to intermingling of the races. Democrats continued to intimidate blacks not to vote or to vote for Democratic candidates. Although the Populist movement did secure some seats in the legislature, Watson himself lost a bid for a congressional seat. Populists were more successful in later elections, as economic woes prompted more whites to vote for Populist candidates. However, in order to attract more white voters, Watson and his followers moved away from their biracial rhetoric, and Watson eventually called for the total disenfranchisement of black voters.

Watson himself was something of an enigma. At various points in his career, he campaigned for black votes, became staunchly anti-Catholic and anti-Semitic, defended Bolsheviks in Russia, opposed Georgia's convict leasing system, and rallied behind the causes of Eugene Debs and other socialists. Watson's life was as tumultuous as the political times in which he lived. The Watson candidacies and the brief appeal of Populists in Georgia displayed a deep division within the Democratic Party even though the Populists made few political gains in the state. The decline of Populism may best be attributed to the adoption of Populist values by the Democratic Party.

During the first decades of the 1900s, conflicts in Georgia politics were based on personalities within the Democratic Party, lower taxes, rural issues, and most of all, white supremacy.[18] Several people stand out as leaders in Georgia politics during this era. Perhaps the most influential was Richard Russell, who served in the state legislature, became governor in 1931, and in 1932 was elected to the U.S. Senate, where he served until his death in 1971.[19] Another important political figure was Eugene Talmadge, who was governor during 1933–1937 and 1941–1943; he also ran unsuccessfully for the U.S. Senate in 1936 and 1938. Talmadge became almost dictatorial as governor, calling out the state militia to enforce his executive orders when other branches of government opposed his policies. Ellis Arnall was also a strong leader and perhaps the most progressive force in state politics prior to the Second World War. He reorganized the state Board of Regents, brought about simplification of the state constitution (which had been amended more than three hundred times since its last revision), and called for stricter adherence to the Fourteenth Amendment by allowing blacks to vote in greater numbers.

Georgia politics during the years of segregation was based on appeals to rural voters. This occurred because Democratic candidates for statewide offices were chosen in primaries based on county-unit votes, which were comparable to the electoral votes used to elect a U.S. president. The system was used to select party nominees beginning in 1876 and became part of state law with the Neill Primary Act of 1917. Under this process, each county was given twice as many unit votes as it had seats in the Georgia House of Representatives, and candidates needed a plurality of unit—not popular—votes to win a primary. Since the Constitution of 1868, Georgia House seats had been assigned to counties using a 3-2-1 formula. Beginning in 1920, the eight largest counties in population had three representatives, the next thirty largest had two seats, and the remainder had one representative. Thus, Fulton County, which cast more than 6,000 popular votes in 1940, had 6 unit votes; Quitman and Chattahoochee Counties, which each had fewer than 225 votes cast the same year, had 2 unit votes. With a county's unit votes awarded on a winner-take-all basis, candidates devoted great attention to rural counties, which accounted for nearly 60 percent of unit votes. In 1946, for example, Eugene Talmadge finished second in the gubernatorial primary to James Carmichael by about 16,000 votes; yet Carmichael lost the nomination to Talmadge 242 to 146 in unit votes.[20]

The Postwar Years

The Second World War ushered in significant changes for Georgia.[21] Military bases became an important part of the state's economy, and employment shifted gradually from farming to manufacturing, including textiles, aircraft production, food processing, and lumber. The development of Georgia's cities accelerated, especially Atlanta, where growth was aided during the 1960s by the progressive policies of Mayor Ivan Allen.[22]

At the end of World War II, Georgia remained a one-party state controlled by Democrats. One incident in particular indicates the degree to which personalities rather than partisan differences once dominated the political agenda. In 1946, Eugene Talmadge made a bid to regain the governor's office after an absence of four years. Since the primary was determined by the number of county-unit votes, Talmadge aligned himself strongly with the interests of the more numerous rural counties, which responded well to his good-old-boy image and emphasis on white supremacy and the "southern way of life." Talmadge won the gubernatorial primary and general election, while M. E. Thompson ran a successful campaign to be Georgia's first lieutenant governor. However, Talmadge's health was failing, and many voters in the general election wrote in the name of his son, Herman.

When the elder Talmadge died before taking office, the 1945 constitution provided several opinions for who should succeed him. This was the so-called three governors controversy.[23] Thompson, the lieutenant governor-elect, believed himself legally to be the next governor. Ellis Arnall, the incumbent governor, refused to relinquish the office until Thompson was sworn in. Herman Talmadge argued that the General Assembly should elect a governor from the two candidates with the highest write-in totals. After maneuvering by those who had backed various candidates in the primary, the legislature elected Herman Talmadge on January 15, 1947. The anti-Talmadge forces did not relent: Thompson asserted his claim to the governorship after being sworn in as lieutenant governor. The Georgia Supreme Court finally resolved the dispute on March 17, when it decided that Thompson was governor, but Herman Talmadge legally attained the office a year later in a special election.

At the close of World War II, white supremacy was strong in Georgia, and all candidates sought the support of white voters, with many openly aligning themselves with the Ku Klux Klan.[24] Jim Crow laws, separating whites from blacks in most public and social settings, were rigidly adhered to. Northern black soldiers stationed at Georgia's military bases often found such social stratification unbearable, and many were arrested for failure to observe the system. Action at the national level, such as decisions by the U.S. Supreme Court, eventually prompted change in Georgia, but the civil rights movement relied heavily on support from outside the state and stimulated a backlash of so-called massive resistance.[25]

As the national movement toward integration gained momentum, the Georgia General Assembly produced an amazing array of legislation to prevent integration within the state.[26] At one point, all state aid was removed from any public school that was integrated, and direct payments were authorized to parents of children who attended segregated private schools. In order to prevent blacks from attending college in the state, particularly at the University of Georgia, requirements for admission were set to include letters of recommendation from two graduates of the institution to which a student was applying. Since no blacks had attended most of these institutions, such letters would be difficult to obtain. Most of the actions by the state legislature were found to be unconstitutional in federal courts, but segregation was largely maintained until the 1964 Civil Rights Act, and it continued in many respects long after that date. Atlanta's black population was eventually empowered by the fact that white families, many fearing integration of the schools, left the city for the suburbs, and the city itself attained a black majority. The first black mayor, Maynard Jackson, was elected in 1973, and in elections since then, most of Atlanta's mayoral candidates have been black.

Federal courts also brought about major changes in Georgia. In *Toombs v. Fortson*, the court ruled that reapportionment for the election of the General Assembly must be made on the basis of the population of the state, with districts having roughly the same number of residents, rather than by county or other political boundaries.[27] After four earlier challenges had failed, in *Gray v. Sanders* the U.S. Supreme Court struck down the county-unit system as a violation of the Fourteenth Amendment's "equal protection" guarantee because the system malapportioned votes.[28] *Wesberry v. Sanders* also led to the redrawing of congressional districts in the state.[29]

The adoption of the Voting Rights Act in 1965 gave the federal government a direct role in the conduct of elections, particularly the power to object to districts thought to dilute the voting power of minority groups. Legal battles accompanied redistricting in recent decades. Following the 1990 census, the U.S. Department of Justice objected to congressional redistricting by the state legislature. After two unsuccessful attempts to redraw districts, state lawmakers finally satisfied the guidelines established by the federal government to protect minority voting strength in the 1992 elections.[30] Ironically, those districts were ruled unconstitutional in 1995 because race was a "predominant factor" used in drawing the district lines.[31] The future of the VRA remains ambiguous, however, after the 2013 decision by the U.S. Supreme Court in *Shelby County v. Holder*.[32]

Similar conflicts continued as Georgia entered the twenty-first century. Following the 2000 census, district lines drawn by the legislature were challenged on a number of grounds in federal court and redrawn by the Georgia General Assembly after majorities had become Republican, but the controversy also pitted the Republican governor and the Democratic attorney general against each other.[33] Republicans had control of state government following the 2010 census, although there were conflicts over representation of regions as North Georgia, especially the Atlanta suburbs, grew far more rapidly than rural areas and South Georgia. The state took both routes to federal approval of the redistricting allowed under the VRA. The first was using the courts, potentially leading to a challenge of the law. The other route was getting approval from the U.S. Department of Justice, which signed off on the congressional and legislative maps by the end of 2011, giving Republicans an advantage in the 2012 elections.[34]

Perhaps the most far-reaching change in Georgia politics has been the transformation of the one-party system. From the end of Reconstruction in the 1870s through the 1960s, the Democratic Party dominated Georgia. This legacy of the Civil War had created a "southern wing" of the party that protected the system of racial segregation. In this system, African Americans were largely Republicans (the party of Abraham Lincoln).

One-party control by Democrats began changing throughout the South with the rise of the civil rights movement and the federal government's implementation of the Civil Rights Act of 1964 and the Voting Rights Act of 1965. When Democrat Lyndon Johnson was reelected overwhelmingly as president in 1964, Georgia and several other southern states went for Republican Barry Goldwater. Over time, states have not changed much in terms of their liberal or conservative tendencies. What has happened, especially in the South, is that conservative whites have shifted their allegiance to the Republican Party, which has grown substantially.[35]

Given Georgia's conservative leanings, a steady realignment toward the Republican Party included more competitive races in the 1980s and 1990s. Democrat Zell Miller was elected governor by less than 55 percent of the vote in 1990 and 1994. Democrat Roy Barnes was elected with 52.5 percent of the vote in 1998 but managed only 46.3 percent in losing to Republican Sonny Perdue in 2002. Republicans maintained their streak, winning the governorship in 2006,

2010, and 2014. Similar gains have occurred in other statewide offices and at the local level. The solid Democratic majority in the General Assembly also withered away, with Republicans capturing a majority in the Senate in 2002 and in the House in 2004.[36]

In terms of Georgia's presence in Congress, Mack Mattingly was the first Republican U.S. senator from Georgia since the 1870s when he was elected in 1980. Senate seats switched between the two parties in the 1980s and 1990s until Republicans held both seats with the election of Saxby Chambliss in 2002 and Johnny Isakson in 2004; each was reelected to a second term, and when Chambliss retired, Republican David Perdue won the seat in 2014. A similar pattern occurred in the U.S. House, with a few Republican representatives in the 1960s giving way to a GOP majority of the Georgia delegation beginning with the 1994 election.

The Social and Cultural Setting

Several social trends stand out in shaping contemporary Georgia politics, especially compared to the state's historical image and its characteristics in the first few decades after World War II. Most important are Georgia's significant population growth, its development as overwhelmingly urban, the large numbers of people migrating to—and within—the state, and the increasing diversification of the state's population. All these changes have the potential to clash with the state's long-standing conservative values and political leanings.

Population Growth and Urbanization

In recent decades, Georgia not only experienced phenomenal population growth, but it has become overwhelmingly urban. It took from 1900 to 1960 for the state's population roughly to double from 2 million to 4 million (see figure 2.1). Georgia's population expanded by about 1 million during the 1970s and 1980s. Georgia ranked thirteenth in population among the states in 1980 and eleventh in 1990. This was followed by even larger increases during the 1990s and the first decade of the twenty-first century—about 1.5 million more residents each decade. Despite the lingering effects of the Great Recession, Georgia grew an estimated 5.4 percent between 2010 and 2015, when the nation expanded more slowly (4.1 percent). This left Georgia with an estimated population of just over 10.2 million residents in 2015, making it the eighth-largest state, about 400,000 behind Ohio and 172,000 ahead of North Carolina.[37]

In addition to experiencing substantial population increases, Georgia has become an urban state, which might seem to run counter to its rural and small-town image. The U.S. Census Bureau has long tracked metropolitan statistical

Figure 2.1. Georgia Population, 1900–2010 Censuses

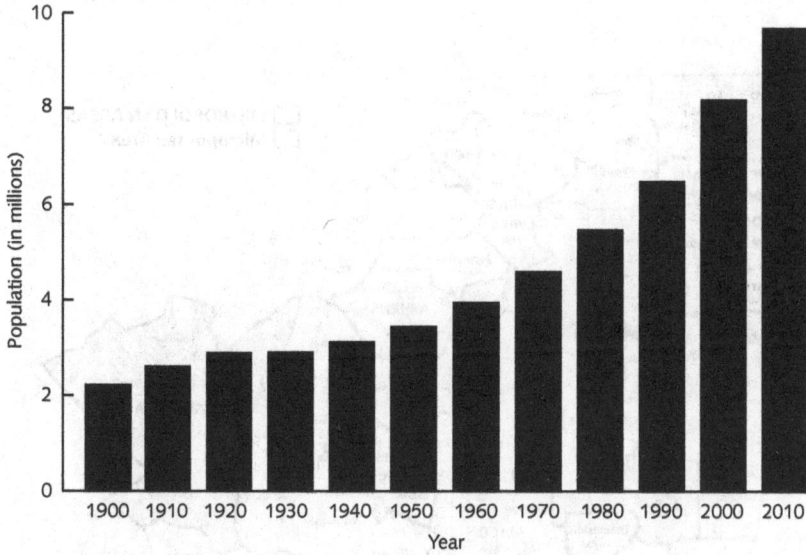

areas (MSAs), which are counties that develop around a core city (or cities) of at least fifty thousand people. Since 2000, the Census Bureau has also gathered data for what it calls "micropolitan" areas, which are counties centered on a city of at least ten thousand but fewer than fifty thousand residents. These smaller urban areas can be thought of as regional trading centers somewhat removed from MSAs. The number and boundaries of metropolitan and micropolitan areas in the United States are not fixed. In fact, they are adjusted in response to population changes.[38] Figure 2.2 is a map of Georgia's metropolitan and micropolitan areas as defined for the 2010 census. Especially noteworthy is the concentration of micropolitan areas in South Georgia and the large land area of Metropolitan Atlanta.

In terms of urbanization, roughly half of Georgia's population in 1970 lived in metropolitan areas, but that grew to 67 percent in 1990 and 81 percent in 2010.[39] This shift includes existing metropolitan areas' population increases and expansion over more territory, as well as the emergence of new MSAs. The most dramatic growth has occurred in Metropolitan Atlanta. In the 1970 census, the metropolitan area was just five counties: Clayton, Cobb, DeKalb, Fulton, and Gwinnett. With the area's booming growth, the number of counties considered part of Metropolitan Atlanta expanded to eighteen in 1990, twenty in 2000, and twenty-eight for the 2010 census, and twenty-nine with the addition of Morgan

Figure 2.2. Georgia Metropolitan and Micropolitan Areas, 2010 Census

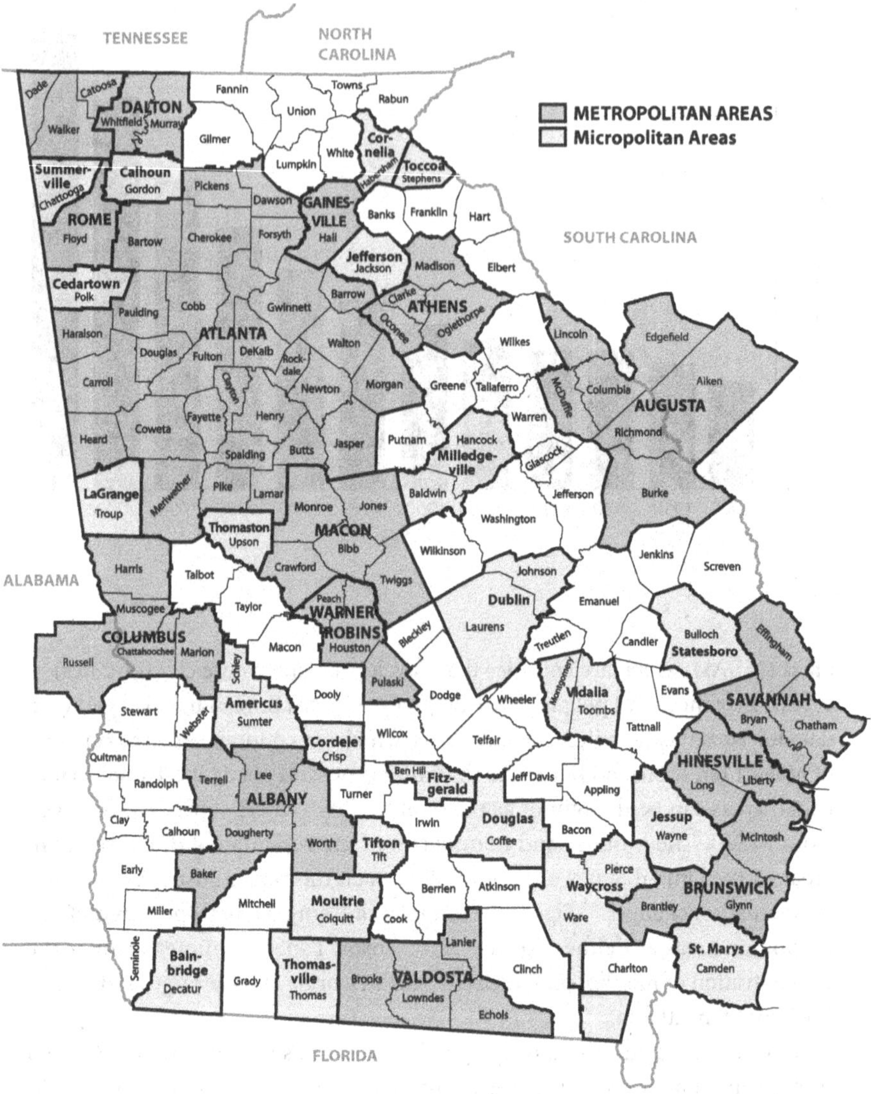

Source: U.S. Census Bureau, http://www2.census.gov/geo/maps/metroarea/stcbsa_pg/Feb2013/cbsa2013_GA.pdf.

County in 2013. The 2010 census revealed that nearly 5.3 million people lived in Metropolitan Atlanta—almost 55 percent of Georgia's 9.7 million residents.

Another 1.7 million Georgia residents in 2010 lived in metropolitan Albany, Athens, Augusta, Columbus, Macon, and Savannah, which had been classified as MSAs for the 1990 and 2000 censuses.[40] In response to Georgia's continued urban development, the federal government designated an additional seven metropolitan areas after the 2000 census: Brunswick, Dalton, Gainesville, Hinesville, Rome, Valdosta, and Warner Robins. Together, these fourteen MSAs (not counting residents of three North Georgia counties considered suburbs of Chattanooga, Tennessee) were home to 2.7 million people—28 percent of the state's population (see figure 2.3). These areas are built around major universities, medical centers, large corporations, retirement/tourist destinations, and military bases. The category of "micropolitan area" designates smaller, regional economic centers. In Georgia, this includes places such as Dublin, LaGrange, Milledgeville, Toccoa, and Waycross. These twenty-three areas grew 10 percent between 2000 and 2010, when they had over 981,000 residents—10 percent of the state's population.

While Georgia's overall population increases are extremely impressive, growth has not occurred evenly across the state. Population losses have occurred over many years in some areas: 53 counties, particularly in South Georgia, actually had fewer residents in 1990 than they did in 1930. During the booming 1990s, when Georgia's population expanded 26 percent, 8 counties actually experienced a decline, and another 42 grew by less than 10 percent. Between 2000 and 2010, when Georgia added nine hundred thousand people, 32 of the state's 159 counties lost population. However, three-fourths of these "declining" counties already had fewer than twenty thousand residents in 2000.[41] Aside from economic ramifications, such population shifts can enhance the political importance of growing areas in drawing legislative and congressional districts, securing government projects and spending, and influencing statewide elections.

A number of factors influenced urban development in Georgia. Among them were technologies that made agriculture less labor-intensive and caused the loss of many unskilled farm jobs, the development of manufacturing, the more recent growth in the service sector, the availability of services in urban areas, expanded interstate and international export of Georgia's products, and the wider availability of transportation, especially airlines and railroads.[42]

While farming continued to be important to the state's economy, many people left farms for more lucrative jobs in urban areas. In 1949, Georgia had 222,000 farming families; by 1969 that number fell to approximately 47,000. In 1930, a majority of the state's black citizens lived on farms, but by 1970 few black families remained on Georgia farms.[43] As tenant farms and sharecropping became

Figure 2.3. Distribution of Georgia's Population, 1960–2010 Censuses

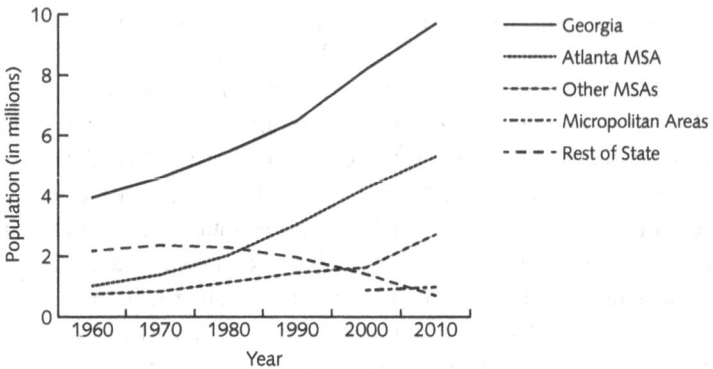

less available, blacks moved to the cities to find jobs, but economic conditions for black families still lagged significantly behind those of whites. Many blacks left the state to find employment in northern cities, and it was not until the 1970s that the number of blacks leaving Georgia fell below the number moving to the state.[44]

As more black residents began to enter Georgia cities, white reluctance to integrate and political maneuvering to avoid it prompted heated debates. In Washington, politicians from other regions who favored rapid social change in the South during the 1950s and 1960s were angered by actions of the Georgia General Assembly. Richard Russell, Georgia's senior U.S. senator, was so irritated by the federal government's insistence on integration that he presented several unsuccessful plans to "solve" the threats that he saw to the South. Arguing that the black population should be dispersed equally among the states, he proposed a bill to relocate black southerners to northern states, providing $1,500.00 to each black resident who chose to move. Russell later attempted to allocate funds to relocate southern blacks to Africa as a solution to problems of segregation and discrimination. He remained a strong defender of the "southern way of life" until his death in 1971.[45]

When the federal courts began to strike down laws that separated the races, whites in Georgia began to move as well. Perhaps the most unsettling action by the federal government was the integration of public schools. Although several actions by the Georgia General Assembly were struck down as unconstitutional, white parents were able to move to different school districts or to send their children to private academies that did not admit blacks. From 1963 to 1970, white enrollment in the city of Atlanta's public schools dropped by one half, and black students outnumbered white students by two to one by 1970. White enrollment declined each subsequent year, so that eventually there were few whites left in the school system to integrate the majority black schools.[46]

Widespread "white flight" to the suburbs was not unique to Georgia. This move was subsidized, even encouraged, by the federal government's tax break for mortgage interest and the increased availability of mortgages facilitated by the Veterans Administration and Federal Housing Administration. The interstate highway system, which gave suburban whites easy access to jobs in cities, was also an incentive to move to the suburbs for those who could afford it. Since many suburban areas did not want mass transportation, highways are often jammed during rush hours with autos carrying a single passenger. This pattern played out in Georgia, where several cities developed a significant nonwhite population.[47] Atlanta's black majority has elected black mayors from 1973 to 2013, although the city's governing elite could change if the city's racial and ethnic mix continues to include more whites and Hispanics. Savannah also has elected many black public officials, including several mayors, since the mid-1990s.

More recent patterns of migration have produced population shifts within urban areas. Many younger, more affluent, and smaller households are choosing to live in central cities. Many are drawn back due to frustrations with commuting from the suburbs, the unique architectural styles of older homes, or the proximity to cultural and social sites.[48] This may be noted in some larger cities in Georgia, especially Savannah and Atlanta, whose residents have restored in-town properties originally built decades ago. This process has increased demand for such homes, driven prices up, and moved some housing stock beyond the reach of lower-income residents. It has brought other controversies over the demolition of houses to build large estate-like homes that tower over their smaller neighbors.[49] Many cities, counties, and school districts responded to such development, which produced rising home values—and the subsequent higher property taxes—by exempting seniors from part of their property tax.[50] The flip side is that while whites might be returning to central cities, minority populations may be increasingly likely to move to suburbia.[51]

Interstate migration patterns have also had an impact on the population of the state. During the 1930s, 1940s, and 1950s, when more people left Georgia than moved to the state, population increased because the number of births greatly exceeded deaths. Beginning in the 1960s, though, the number of people moving to Georgia was higher than the total leaving. As older, more industrialized areas in the North experienced decline, southern metropolitan areas like Atlanta, Savannah, Augusta, and Columbus saw population and economic growth, although their trajectory was interrupted by the Great Recession, which started in 2008.

It is important to keep in mind that the United States has become a very mobile country. The Census Bureau's 2014 estimates revealed that a slight majority of Georgia residents had been born in the state (56 percent). Despite population movements, thirty-seven states had a native majority, although it varied widely. At the high end, more than 70 percent of the residents in Alabama, Iowa, Michigan, Mississippi, Ohio, Pennsylvania, and Wisconsin were born there. Over 60 percent were natives in Arkansas, Illinois, Indiana, Kentucky, Maine, Massachusetts, Minnesota, Missouri, Nebraska, New York, North Dakota, Oklahoma, South Dakota, Tennessee, and (perhaps surprisingly) Texas. At the other extreme, only 25.8 percent of Nevadans were born in the state, as were 36.1 percent of Florida residents and 41 percent of those living in Wyoming.

Where are the "new" Georgians coming from? The largest group was born in Florida (372,000), followed by New York (302,000), Alabama (221,000), Tennessee (192,000), and three other states sending over 150,000.[52] This pattern has continued despite the Great Recession. The impact of migration is even more striking for Metropolitan Atlanta, where only 47.5 percent of the residents were born in Georgia and 13.3 percent were foreign born.[53]

Population Profile: The 2010 Census and Beyond

Georgia's population was nearly 9.7 million in the 2010 census, which was roughly 1.5 million more than in 2000, and an estimated 10.2 million in 2015. Detailed data on the elements contributing to Georgia's growth are available for 2014. The "natural" increase of total births over deaths totaled just over 248,000. An increase of almost 152,000 people was due to "net migration"—the difference between the number of people moving to Georgia minus those leaving. Two-thirds of the migration gain was labeled international, which encompasses not just immigrants from other countries but also native-born Americans moving back to the state, including military personnel.[54]

Beyond the sheer numbers, Georgia's population has become more diverse racially and ethnically. The Census Bureau asks people to identify as one race or as two or more. As table 2.1 indicates, the largest groups were white (60.4 percent) and black (31 percent). These compare to 63.6 and 28.7 percent, respectively, in 2004. Those identifying as Hispanic or Latino were 9.1 percent in 2014. Hispanics can be of any race, which left those identifying as white but not Hispanic at 55 percent of Georgia's population in 2014.[55]

In terms of other characteristics, Georgia is relatively young compared to the nation as a whole, with 28 percent of all citizens age 19 or under and a median age of 35.8 years. Georgia remained below the national level in per capita income, and the statewide poverty rate was both higher than the level nationally and above the rate before the Great Recession.

Georgia's education levels remain somewhat low. While 29 percent of those

age twenty-five or older in 2014 had earned a bachelor's or advanced college degree, about the same as the nation as a whole, over 14 percent had not completed
high school. Both figures were improvements over a decade earlier, however,
and much higher than the previous generation, when 49.7 percent of Georgians
(versus 39.6 percent of all Americans) age twenty-five or older had not completed high school in 1960.[56]

Statewide data provide only a partial picture of Georgia's population. Concentrations of groups varied significantly across the state in 2014. For example, the percentage of the population with less than a ninth-grade education
exceeded 12 percent in Hall and Whitfield Counties—more than double the
percentage for the state. At the other end of the educational spectrum, more
than 40 percent of the population had a bachelor's degree or higher in five
counties—all of them in Metropolitan Atlanta—and another five counties had
more than 30 percent with such educational attainment (Chatham, Cherokee,
Clarke, Columbia, and Gwinnett). As one might expect, college and military
towns are much younger than the state as a whole. Five counties, including
Athens-Clarke, had a median age under 30. On the other hand, ten counties
had a median age over 45, including Towns County at 52.1 years. Most of these
areas were rural, although some in North Georgia have become retirement destinations.

There is also wide variation within the state regarding race and ethnicity.
While an estimated 31 percent of Georgia residents in 2014 identified as black or
African American, 23 of Georgia's 159 counties had black majorities. Most were
rural, but the list also included Bibb, Clayton, DeKalb, and Augusta-Richmond.
In contrast, African Americans comprised less than 10 percent of the population in 29 counties. Some were suburban counties near Atlanta (Cherokee, Forsyth) or Athens (Oconee). Most were in North Georgia, stretching all the way
to the Tennessee and North Carolina border—areas that historically were not
connected to the plantation system of agriculture. Similarly, Hispanics made
up an estimated 9.1 percent of Georgia's population, but 86 counties had almost
no Hispanic presence (under 5 percent of the population). Most of these were
concentrated in Middle and South Georgia, including less than 1 percent Hispanic in ten counties. At the other end, five counties were more than 20 percent
Hispanic: Whitfield (almost 33 percent), with an economy tied heavily to the
carpet industry around Dalton, along with Atkinson and Echols in Southeast
Georgia, Gwinnett in suburban Atlanta, and Hall in North Georgia, which has
had a long connection to agriculture, including the poultry industry.[57]

The bottom line is that Georgia's population displays three striking patterns:
continued growth, increasing diversity, and wide differences within the state.
Needless to say, all these characteristics can make for interesting politics at both
the state and the local levels.

Table 2.1. Georgia and U.S. Population Profiles

	Georgia	United States
Population, 2015 estimate	10,241,860	321,418,820
Change, 1980–1990	18.6%	9.8%
Change, 1990–2000	26.4%	13.1%
Change, 2000–2010	18.3%	9.7%
Change, 2010–2015	5.4%	4.1%
Georgia Native, 2014	55.6%	
Race and Ethnicity, 2014		
White	60.4%	73.8%
Black	30.9%	12.6%
Other	6.7%	10.7%
Two or More Races	2.0%	2.9%
Hispanic (can be any race)	9.1%	16.9%
Age, 2014		
19 and Under	28.2%	26.3%
20–44	34.9%	33.6%
45–64	25.5%	26.4%
65 and Over	11.4%	13.8%
Median Age	35.8 years	37.4 years
Highest Level of Education (age 25 or older), 2014		
Not a High School Graduate	14.4%	13.1%
High School Graduate	28.4%	27.7%
Some College	21.1%	21.0%
Associate's Degree	7.0%	8.2%
Bachelor's Degree	18.2%	18.7%
Advanced Degree	10.8%	11.4%
Per Capita Personal Income, 2014	$25,427	$28,555
Persons below Poverty Level, 2014	18.5%	15.6%

Source: U.S. Census Bureau, "American Fact Finder" estimates from the American Community Survey (multiple data sets), http://factfinder.census.gov/faces/tableservices/jsf/pages /productview.xhtml?pid=ACS_14_5YR_DP05&src=pt.

The Economic Setting

At the end of World War II, Georgia was still largely agricultural. Rural areas also depended heavily on textiles, the state's largest manufacturing industry. Plus Georgia had few nationally prominent firms before the 1970s. Today Georgia is a key player in the service sector, as well as the U.S. and world economies (see table 2.2).

The federal Bureau of Economic Analysis calculates gross domestic product (GDP) by state. In 2015, the value of goods and services produced in Georgia was nearly $500 billion. This ranked tenth among the states, slightly behind North Carolina and ahead of Virginia and Massachusetts. It might seem small relative to California's $2.5 trillion economy and the $1-trillion-plus economies of Texas and New York, but from another perspective, Georgia contributed 2.75 percent to the nation's GDP in 2015.

Georgia's economy grew rapidly during the late 1990s, but the pace slowed somewhat during 2001–2003 before hitting 4.1–6.6 percent before the Great Recession (see figure 2.4). Georgia's economy actually shrank 0.3 percent from 2007 to 2008 and another 1.1 percent from 2008 to 2009. Growth resumed in 2010–2013, but at a slower rate that never exceeded the rate of the nation as a whole. By 2015, though, the recovery was exceeding GDP growth for the nation.

The impact of the Great Recession is also reflected in Georgia's unemployment rate, as shown in table 2.2. Georgia reached its all-time high with 10.4 percent unemployment in January 2010. Unemployment dropped to 6.9 percent in December 2014, as compared to 5.4 percent nationally, and to 5 percent in mid-2016. As with many other characteristics, rates vary within the state. Labor markets around the United States were stronger in college and government centers. Similarly, unemployment in the Athens Metropolitan Area stood at 4.9 percent in December 2014. It was over 7 percent, though, in the Albany, Brunswick, and Hinesville–Fort Stewart areas. Metropolitan Atlanta registered 6.4 percent unemployment, which was slightly better than Detroit, but somewhat worse than Providence and Sacramento for areas with more than one million residents.

Although agriculture, forestry, fishing, and hunting contributed $4.5 billion to the state economy in 2015, the sector comprised about 1 percent of Georgia's GDP. Service industries were the largest segment of the economy, with 26 percent of the total. These sectors parallel the national economy, but Georgia was different in a few respects. Most noticeably, manufacturing was less significant in Georgia than in the United States as a whole. On the flip side, Georgia was slightly more dependent on transportation, sectors related to real estate, and wholesale and retail trade. It should not be surprising that companies in all these sectors, as well as trade associations representing them, can be quite active in state and local politics. The government category is rather broad. It includes

Table 2.2. Georgia and U.S. Economic Profiles

	Georgia	United States
Gross Domestic Product, 2015 (current $ billion)	$495.7	$18,036.6
State Rank	10	75.4%
Change, 2000–2015	62.1%	75.4%
Change, 2014–2015	5.0%	3.7%
Leading Components of Gross Domestic Product, 2015		
Services*	26.0%	25.5%
Finance, Insurance, Real Estate	19.3%	17.6%
Wholesale and Retail Trade	14.1%	10.1%
Government	12.7%	11.1%
Manufacturing	11.1%	18.9%
Information†	6.0%	5.0%
Transportation and Warehousing	4.1%	3.4%
Construction	3.7%	4.2%
Agriculture, Forestry, Fishing, Hunting	0.9%	1.4%
Nonfarm Employment by Industry, June 2016	4,384,100	144,172,000
Services*	38.6%	44.4%
Trade, Transportation, Utilities	21.2%	18.9%
Government	15.7%	15.4%
Manufacturing	8.8%	8.5%
Finance, Insurance, Real Estate	5.5%	5.7%
Construction	4.1%	4.6%
Unemployment Rate		
July 2006	4.8%	4.7%
July 2008	6.3%	5.8%
July 2010	10.2%	9.4%
July 2012	8.9%	8.2%
July 2014	7.1%	6.2%
July 2016	5.0%	4.9%

Sources: U.S. Bureau of Economic Analysis, http://www.bea.gov/index.htm; U.S. Bureau of Labor Statistics, http://www.bls.gov/.

* Includes business and professional services, education, health care, social services, arts, entertainment, hospitality, and other nongovernment services.

† Includes publishing, films and recording, telecommunications, broadcasting, data processing, Internet services, and related industries.

Figure 2.4. Georgia's Gross Domestic Product, 1997–2015
(current dollars, in millions)

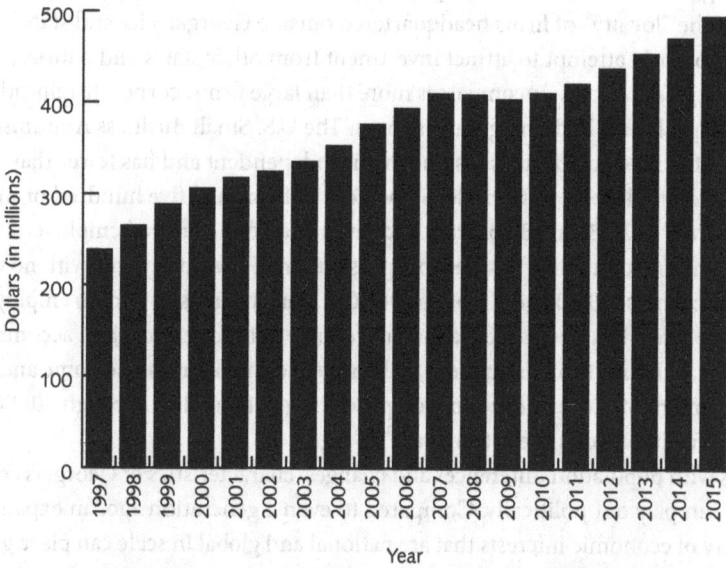

not just traditional state and local government workers but also federal workers in Georgia and the large numbers of people working for local school systems and public colleges and universities.

Georgia is also a player in the increasingly global economy. In 2015, the state was home to eighteen of the nation's five hundred largest companies, based on total revenues, as listed in *Fortune* magazine.[58] This was about the same number as a decade earlier, although there were a few changes. Perhaps the most visible new player in Georgia was NCR (originally known as National Cash Register), which moved from Ohio and was number 423 on the list. The top one hundred companies included Georgia firms recognized worldwide such as Home Depot, United Parcel Service, Coca-Cola, and Delta Air Lines. They were followed in the next one hundred by Aflac and the Southern Company. The remaining companies were somewhat less visible nationally but nonetheless among the country's five hundred largest.

Some critics have expressed concerns about the extent to which Georgia's economy is driven by firms based elsewhere that could have little interest in the state's well-being. As the economy emerged from the Great Recession in 2012, almost two hundred thousand workers in Georgia were employed by firms that were majority-owned by foreign companies, 63 percent of them European and another 20 percent based in Asian or Pacific countries. The state also reported that foreign firms invested $2.82 billion in 117 projects during 2012.[59] The issue of headquarters has arisen with the outside acquisition of banks, Turner Broadcasting, Scientific-Atlanta, Georgia-Pacific, and BellSouth.[60] Despite questions about the "loyalty" of firms headquartered outside Georgia, city and state leaders vigorously attempt to attract investment from other states and nations.

Georgia's economy encompasses more than large firms, corporate relocations and acquisitions, and foreign investment. The U.S. Small Business Administration defines a small business as one that is independent and has fewer than five hundred employees. In Georgia, 56 percent of firms had five hundred or more employees in 2013, and 32 percent had fewer than one hundred employees. It is worth noting that many business people set themselves up as firms with no employees: almost 800,000 of Georgia's 962,085 small businesses had no employees in 2013. Small businesses were a major presence in food services and accommodations, agriculture, construction, and real estate. Small firms also come and go: 79.5 percent of those opened in Georgia during 2013 made it through 2014 (the same survival rate as the U.S. average).[61]

As with population differences and changes, characteristics of Georgia's economy can play out politically. Compared to even a generation ago, an expanded variety of economic interests that are national and global in scale can place great demands on Georgia's political system at both the state and the local levels.

Stability, Change, and the Importance of Context

When V. O. Key published *Southern Politics* in 1949, he subtitled his chapter on Georgia's political leadership "The Rule of the Rustics." The state, he argued, was dominated by powerful whites who controlled the belt of heavily black counties running through the middle of the state. Key went on to analyze the virtual absence of a Republican Party in Georgia, a Democratic Party split into two factions by the candidacies of Eugene Talmadge, limited participation in elections, conflicts between the state's cities and rural areas, support for conservative policies by Georgians in Congress, and an enduring politics of race. Yet Key saw change occurring in the South: "Its rate of evolution may seem glacial, but fundamental shifts in the conditions underlying its politics are taking place. All these changes drive toward a political system more completely in accord with the national ideas of constitutional morality."[62] Times have changed, but in some ways, time has stood still.

The Sources and Consequences of Change

In comparison to the conditions and "glacial" shifts that Key witnessed in the 1940s, Georgia politics in the early twenty-first century might seem revolutionary, but Key might also recognize some features that have changed little. Change is often related to a wide range of external and internal factors. The broader trends affecting the state include national and international population movements, structural changes in the economy, and national political changes and events. Internally, change is influenced by the rise of new political leaders, changes in public attitudes, the mobilization of new or resilient groups, and key events. These developments occur, however, against the legacies of Georgia history and those benefiting from the political status quo.

Population trends have reshaped the Georgia that Key knew and can have substantial effects on politics.[63] Large numbers of migrants coming to Georgia, especially from outside the South, have brought different ethnic and religious backgrounds, as well as a wide range of views regarding political parties, taxes, public services, and similar matters. Adding new generations can also yield change if younger voters have different views than their elders. For example, voters amended the state constitution in 1992 to allow lotteries after years of having such "gambling" prohibited, and over one hundred communities voted in 2011 to allow alcohol sales on Sundays after the practice had been outlawed for decades.[64]

Population change can also undermine the stability of neighborhoods and entire communities. Rapid growth, for instance, can require substantial investments in new roads, schools, and other services, not to mention generating more traffic. All these factors can pit longtime residents against newcomers, especially if urban neighborhoods gentrify quickly.[65] Indeed, gentrification in Atlanta neighborhoods has been associated with declining voter participation among an area's long-term residents.[66] On the flip side, declining areas might experience lost jobs and businesses, lower home values, crime, and problems with local government finances and services.

Beyond population increases and decreases, changes in the makeup of a community can also have profound effects. For example, a city with a large number of retirees might require a different mix of businesses and government services compared to one with many young families, whose primary concern could be the quality of local schools. Similarly, an influx of people whose primary language is not English can pose challenges for schools, businesses, and local governments.[67] This issue emerged, for instance, in state-level debates over whether written exams for a Georgia driver's license should be available only in English.[68] Also, as Atlanta's population changed in the 1990s and 2000s, the city went from being two-thirds black to nearly equal numbers of black and white voters and an election for mayor in 2009 (the first with a viable white candidate since 1981) largely pitted white and black voters against each other.[69]

Population changes have had other effects. They have increased residential segregation, as well as animosity between cities and suburbs. This tension manifested itself in efforts to create new cities in suburban Atlanta, which, if successful, would shift key decisions such as control of land use in these areas from the county governments to the new cities. Growing and declining areas of the state often see themselves as competing with one another, and neighborhoods in many communities have fought development they dislike. "New" populations have become more organized and politically active during the past generation: Latinos, seniors, gays and lesbians, and the disabled.

Economic changes also have had significant impacts on Georgia. The state's leading industries and occupations are quite different from those of fifty years ago, and the economy is far removed from the role that farming and forestry played in the 1800s, with agriculture itself changing dramatically.[70] Investment capital is more mobile, and Georgia cannot divorce itself from what is now a global economy. Coming out of the Great Recession, foreign investment in Georgia totaled over $2.8 billion in 2012 and over $1 billion in 2013 and 2014, with new jobs reported at more than eighteen thousand. Similarly, the state had more than $38 billion in exports and nearly $88.7 billion in imports during 2015.[71] As with investment, Georgia competes with other states to promote its products and to be the destination for imports to the United States, in part through Atlanta's airport and the major seaports in Brunswick and Savannah.

It is critical to remember that change has also been imposed—or at least fomented—from outside the state. Beyond the three constitutions during the 1860s that took the state through secession, war, and Reconstruction, federal court decisions during the 1950s and 1960s, along with legislation such as the Civil Rights Act and the Voting Rights Act, imposed changes that influenced citizen behavior and attitudes, reduced the power of rural areas in the Georgia legislature, eliminated government-enforced segregation of businesses and government facilities, diversified the state and local government workforce, and removed decades-long barriers that prevented blacks from registering, voting, and running for public office.[72] Over the longer haul, such national political changes also shifted the makeup of the Democratic and Republican political parties.

The one-party rule by Georgia Democrats for most of the twentieth century that was familiar to Key has given way to one-party rule by Republicans (see chapters 4 and 5). The demographic makeup of the two political parties has changed since the 1960s. Most notably, conservative whites have not abandoned their ideological views; they simply have switched to the Republican Party.[73] The Republican Party developed a solid base, first in suburban and later in rural areas. Democrats fare better in cities, and Republicans maintain their strongholds in suburban areas. African Americans tend to vote loyally for the Democratic Party. Patterns based on ideology are still evident, with much of the rural and southern portions of the state maintaining their traditionally conservative voting patterns, often joined by suburbanites.

Republican presidential candidates have carried Georgia in every election but one since 1984. The party won the governorship for the first time in modern history in 2002. Republicans followed that gain by winning their first majority in the Georgia House in 2004, when they also increased their seats in the state senate, where they already held a majority. Georgia Republicans have been elected to the U.S. House of Representatives since the 1960s but have been dominant in the delegation in the twenty-first century. They gained control of both U.S. Senate seats with the election of Johnny Isakson in 2004 and Saxby Chambliss two years earlier.

Scenarios for the Future

Georgia has changed in many ways, but traditions and underlying conditions still make adaptation to change quite difficult. Perhaps the greatest political constant is racial conflict. Georgia obviously has ended the widespread violence familiar to Key in the 1940s, but random attacks, protests, and lawsuits have been used regularly by a wide variety of individuals, organizations, and government agencies to handle disputes. Conflicts have ignited over election procedures and symbols such as the state flag. As social issues like gambling and alcohol have receded, abortion, marriage, school curricula, and firearms have become prominent on the political agenda. These conflicts will likely continue for the foreseeable future since conservative attitudes remain dominant, which is consistent with Georgia's religious profile, but demographic and attitudinal changes will probably continue to generate opposition.[74]

The traditional white-black conflict described by Key will probably be transformed as Georgia's population diversifies. The growth in the Latino population in particular has spawned conflicts over language, access to public services, and political participation. There is little reason to think that these issues will become less salient in the future, especially as a wider range of minority groups and leaders join the political landscape and challenge the political status quo.[75]

Georgia politics also seems to have sustained its image of devoting significant attention to parochial interests.[76] Many state boards, including those for higher education and transportation, have seats assigned to specific regions. Similarly, the Georgia General Assembly considers numerous bills dealing with matters that in many states would be handled by local officials.

Certain aspects of political participation in Georgia still fare poorly, especially voting (see chapter 4). When Key examined voter turnout from 1920 to 1946, the share of Georgians of voting age who actually participated in general elections and most Democratic primaries hovered at or below 20 percent. Such low turnouts are not simply the result of segregation: turnout among white voting-age Georgians in Democratic primaries for governor averaged 30 percent.[77] The legacy of low turnout continued for quite some time, generally lagging by single digits during the 1990s. The gap between Georgia and the nation has narrowed, though, and the state now more closely resembles the United States as a whole. In the 2008 and 2012 presidential races, Georgia trailed the national level by just 1.3 percent. In the 2014 midterms, Georgia turnout was actually 0.6 percent above the national level of 33.2 percent among voting-age adults, and turnout was essentially the same for the November 2016 election.[78]

One form of political participation that remains high but is often viewed negatively is the involvement of interest groups in Georgia politics, which might not be surprising given the part-time nature of the state legislature (see chapters 5 and 6). Key noted the influence of Atlanta money in elections.[79] Until the 1990s, there were no limits on the amount of donations to candidates for state and local office, and lobbyists were virtually unregulated by the state. The number of lobbyists easily exceeded one thousand in recent years; they spent $1.4–1.8 million annually during 2008–2012, but $750,000 in 2014.[80] Critics have long complained about the lavish trips, preferential deals, campaign contributions, and other benefits that interest groups provide to legislators, as well as the limited reporting required of lobbyists and others trying to influence the legislature or state bureaucracy.[81] It is hard to imagine these connections and efforts diminishing.

It is difficult to say how much Georgia has become like the rest of the nation and how change might unfold in the short or long term. Economically, the state has moved well past its isolated position at the end of World War II to become an integral player in the changing world economy. Socially, Georgia's population has grown dramatically; it has also become more educated, urban, and diverse. Politically, much has changed since V. O. Key's time, and even since the 1960s. The dynamics of the American federal system almost guaranteed change. Yet some characteristics are so pervasive, some traditions and institutions so powerful, and some conflicts so deep-seated that certain aspects of life in Georgia have changed little. The remainder of the book will explore these developments by comparing contemporary Georgia to the state's past, to the other forty-nine states, and to the nation as a whole.

CHAPTER 3

Georgia's Constitution

This chapter examines Georgia's current constitution, compares it to its nine predecessors and other state constitutions, and explains its connection to the U.S. Constitution. Although most U.S. residents have some passing familiarity with the U.S. Constitution, each of the fifty states, including Georgia, has its own constitution. While the Georgia Constitution shares some similarities with the U.S. Constitution, there are many important differences.

Of course, this topic begs the question, what is a constitution? In the simplest sense, a constitution outlines the rules that provide a framework for the operation of government. David Easton, a famous political scientist, once defined politics as the authoritative allocation of the values of society. Just as drawing up or changing the rules can affect the outcome of a game, the particulars of constitutions can help determine the allocation of these values and thus who wins or loses politically. For this reason, constitutions should be thought of as political documents. This is especially true of state constitutions, which often include matters that seem like policy decisions better made by passing laws—as with Georgia's lottery. Yet putting such decisions in constitutions makes it harder for opponents to repeal or modify them. No matter what is in a state constitution, though, it cannot be at odds with provisions of the U.S. Constitution.

The U.S. Constitution: The Supreme Law of the Land

The U.S. Constitution has endured longer than any other document as a basis for government. The document's stability is due in large part to its broad but flexible grants of power and its reinterpretation in response to changing conditions. It is also difficult to amend. There have been only twenty-seven amendments to the U.S. Constitution as compared to seventy for the most recent version of the Georgia Constitution, which took effect in 1983. The U.S. Constitution specifically lists in Article 1 legislative powers given to the federal government. Such "enumerated" powers are adaptable to new situations by the so-called elastic clause in Article 1, Section 8, which permits Congress to do whatever it considers "necessary and proper" to carry out the powers listed elsewhere in the document. The elastic clause has allowed a broad interpretation of the federal government's powers within limits established by the courts. Article 6 reinforces the idea of a powerful national government by declaring that the Constitution and federal law are "the supreme law of the land."

It is important to understand two historical facts in relation to the development of the meaning of the Constitution throughout American history:

1. The new nation was a collection of mostly independent colonies, settled by different people for very different reasons in an age of limited travel, information, and education. These colonists became the first state residents. For the most part, their knowledge and allegiance was to their state, not a vaguely defined group of united states.
2. The country had just fought a revolutionary war, both upper and lower case, meaning that the American Revolution is the name assigned to this conflict, and the rulers were overthrown—a king, a strong central government, including a powerful judiciary, and a government with a power to tax.

Accordingly, the earliest government plan, the Articles of Confederation, reflected these two facts: Although the articles did create a central government out of a collection of states, central power was limited, there was no chief executive or judiciary, and the approval of nine out of thirteen states was required for the exercise of any national authority. Second, the national government derived its power from the states, not the people, and it had no power to directly tax the people nor compel states to provide money to the national government.

This system was very ineffective and caused major problems. The national government was broke; it could not pay its debts. Virginia, one of the largest debtor states (primarily farmers indebted to English merchants) refused to honor its debts; thus treaties with other nations had limited or no value. The states engaged in trading practices that hurt each other, acting more like separate countries than one nation. Thus there were significant problems concerning interstate commerce, taxation, war debt, and the military.

To remedy the problems in interstate commerce, delegates from five states (New Jersey, New York, Pennsylvania, Delaware, and Virginia) met in Annapolis in 1786. These delegates quickly realized that more states were needed in order to effectuate any sort of change, which led to a call for another meeting with participation of all the states. The new convention was to meet in Philadelphia in 1787 to amend the articles, although it quickly became a convention to adopt a new constitution.

Out of this new convention came the U.S. Constitution. Thus, the Constitution came about because of the ineffectiveness of the Articles of Confederation. In the end, it created an executive and a judicial branch, attempted to balance power between the states and the federal government, and shared power between the large and small states. Most tellingly, the preamble states that "we the people," rather than "we the states," adopt the Constitution. Early rulings by the Supreme Court, led by Chief Justice John Marshall, solidified the power of Congress, the Supreme Court, and the central government, stressing, among other factors, that power derives not from the states, but from the people.

Concern over the powers of the states caused great debate during the process of ratifying of the Constitution. Alexander Hamilton and James Madison argued (in *The Federalist*, nos. 17 and 45, respectively) that the national government would be highly dependent on the states. Madison claimed that state governments would be closer to the people and that many more people would be employed by government at this level. In addition, he asserted that with the Senate elected by the state legislatures and the president chosen by the Electoral College, concerns over the lack of states' rights were unfounded. Moreover, Madison argued that different political cultures within the states would provide a common bond for the citizens of each state, and that this commonality would overshadow the power of the federal government in the minds of the populace. Drawing on the ideals of the feudal system, Hamilton noted that people often had stronger loyalty to feudal lords than to a nation's king. He argued that states and localities, like feudal estates, would be closer to the people, and the people would respond to them rather than to the federal government. Amendment Ten addresses concerns that states would have too little authority by declaring that all powers not given to the federal government are "reserved to the states" or the people. However, the Constitution was clearly a document that gave power to the national government at the expense of state power.

The Constitution has seven articles and twenty-seven amendments, the last of which, adopted in 1992, provides that no change in the compensation paid to representatives can take effect until the next Congress sits. That amendment, by the way, was proposed in 1789 by James Madison. It languished for years until a University of Texas undergraduate made it the subject of a term paper and then a political cause. Michigan's ratification of the amendment, 230 years later, made it the thirty-eighth state to adopt it, thus finally providing the three-fourths of the states required to enact a constitutional amendment.[1] The Constitution provides two separate frameworks for government, both of which most of us are familiar with, at least in the terminology. One is the tripartite, or checks-and-balances system, among the executive, the legislature, and the judiciary, and the other is the federalism scheme allocating power between state and federal government.

Article 1 lays out the legislative power. It is the longest and most important section of the Constitution. Clearly the framers expected Congress to be the most important and powerful branch of the new government. Madison famously wrote in Federalist 51, "In republican government, the legislative authority necessarily predominates." To resolve disputes between the large and small states, the framers adopted what was known as the Virginia plan, which created a bicameral legislature. A lower house would be representative of the people, and an upper house would represent the state interests. Thus there would be a bicameral legislature that reflected these tensions. The House of Representatives would be apportioned on population and be subject to election every two years, while the Senate would have equal representation from all the states, two senators per state who would hold office for a six-year term.

As for powers, the Constitution contains seventeen specific clauses of enumerated powers and then an open-ended power known as the "necessary and proper"—often called elastic—clause. In addition, Congress was given authority over its own affairs and protection and independence from the executive and the judiciary.

Articles 2 and 3 are much less detailed than Article 1. Article 2 lays out executive powers. It provides that the executive powers shall reside in the presidency and delineates the method of election, the president's military and appointment powers and duties, the oath of office, the requirement of a state of the union, and the duty to see that the laws be faithfully executed. The Constitution offers little else concerning executive powers—and nothing to anticipate the vast lawmaking powers of the president through appointments to the bureaucracy and the issuance of executive orders.

The judiciary was created by Article 3; hence, the judiciary is sometimes referred to as the third branch of government. The Constitution only specifically mentions the Supreme Court. The size of the court, its location, jurisdiction (the court's authority to hear a case), and all other lower federal courts come from congressional statutes.

Articles 2 and 3 also provide checks on the power of each branch. For example, Congress passes the laws, but the president can veto the law, unless Congress overrides the veto by a two-thirds vote. Congress, on the other hand, has the power to investigate the president and authorize spending. The Supreme Court has the final say in interpreting the law, but the president appoints Supreme Court justices, who must be confirmed by Congress, and Congress creates all other courts besides the Supreme Court (the only court mentioned in the Constitution) and determines most of the jurisdiction of the courts. That is, with the exception of the limited jurisdiction given to the Supreme Court, Congress determines which cases federal courts can hear and on occasion has stripped federal courts, including the Supreme Court, of hearing certain types of cases and has threatened to do so on numerous occasions.

Madison and Hamilton, of course, did not account for the degree to which many citizens now move from state to state, nor could they have imagined the impact of mass communication, the legislative responsibilities of the president, or the growth of the bureaucratic state. Still, their views provide an understanding of what was expected of the states. Most people expected national supremacy to have little effect on government operations within states. However, the elastic clause has allowed federal intervention in state affairs. For example, transportation traditionally has been governed by the states, but federal funding has been withheld in instances where states did not adhere to federal mandates regarding speed limits and the legal drinking age.

Although the Constitution is difficult to alter, amendments have been made to it in response to these changes. We the people, not the state legislatures, directly elect senators since the passage of Seventeenth Amendment in 1913. Presidential and vice presidential candidates run as a unified ticket, instead of the vice presidency being awarded to the runner-up in the Electoral College. The Electoral College is now directly tied to the popular vote in each state, with most states awarding its electoral votes to the popular vote winner. Various other amendments have "tinkered" with these three articles, such as limiting the president to a maximum of two terms; placing the inauguration of the president in January, not March; providing a mechanism for the vice president to temporarily assume the powers of the president if the president is physically (or emotionally) incapacitated; ending slavery; giving African Americans, women, and eighteen-year-olds the right to vote; and establishing a direct income tax.

Thus the U.S. Constitution represents the ultimate authority: states may not pass legislation or implement policy that contradicts it. However, states can have constitutional provisions and laws, and state courts of last resort can issue rulings that are beyond the review of the U.S. Supreme Court and the federal government, and they often adopt laws to test the limits of decisions made by the federal government.

The former occurs through a doctrine known as "adequate and independent" state grounds. The U.S. Supreme Court has the power to review state court applications of federal law, but state supreme courts reserve the right to interpret state law authoritatively. Put more simply, as defined by the Supreme Court in the nineteenth-century case of *Murdock v. City of Memphis*,[2] state supreme court decisions based on state law independent of federal interpretation are outside the jurisdiction of the federal courts and, thus, are not reviewable by the U.S. Supreme Court.

In the context of civil liberties, incorporated federal rights provide a minimum level of protection from which states cannot subtract; therefore, deviations based on state constitutional law can only expand civil liberty guarantees. Each state retains the "sovereign right to adopt in its own Constitution individual liberties more expansive than those conferred by the Federal Constitution."[3]

Table 3.1. State Constitutions as of January 1, 2013

State	Number of Constitutions	Estimated Number of Words	Amendments
Alabama	6	388,882	892
Alaska	1	13,479	29
Arizona	1	45,910	152
Arkansas	5	65,700	102
California	2	67,048	529
Colorado	1	72,860	158
Connecticut	2	16,562	31
Delaware*	4	29,613	146
Florida	6	43,514	122
Georgia	10	42,100	75
Hawaii	1	21,498	113
Idaho	1	24,626	125
Illinois	4	16,401	14
Indiana	2	11,476	47
Iowa	2	11,089	54
Kansas	1	14,097	97
Kentucky	4	27,234	42
Louisiana	11	73,224	184
Maine	1	16,313	172
Maryland	4	43,198	230
Massachusetts	1	45,283	120
Michigan	4	31,164	30
Minnesota	1	11,734	120
Mississippi	4	26,229	126
Missouri	4	68,670	120
Montana	2	12,790	31
Nebraska	2	34,934	230
Nevada	1	29,895	138
New Hampshire	2	13,060	145
New Jersey	3	26,360	70
New Mexico	1	33,198	169
New York	4	44,397	227
North Carolina	3	17,177	32
North Dakota	1	18,895	156
Ohio	2	56,818	175

Table 3.1. (*continued*)

State	Number of Constitutions	Estimated Number of Words	Amendments
Oklahoma	1	81,666	196
Oregon	1	49,016	255
Pennsylvania	5	26,078	30
Rhode Island	2	11,407	13
South Carolina	7	27,421	500
South Dakota	1	27,774	118
Tennessee	3	13,960	43
Texas	5	86,936	491
Utah	1	20,320	118
Vermont	3	8,565	54
Virginia	6	21,899	49
Washington	1	32,578	106
West Virginia	2	33,324	72
Wisconsin	1	15,392	147
Wyoming	1	26,349	100

Source: Council of State Governments, Book of the States, 2016, 9–10.

* Amendments are not subject to voter approval.

In addition to "adequate and independent" state grounds, states often pass laws to test federal law. For example, states have attempted to restrict abortion practices following *Roe v. Wade* and related cases,[4] and more recently states have sought to avoid all federal oversight over gun ownership and record keeping. They do so despite the obvious limitations of the supremacy clause, which makes federal law supreme when there is a conflict between state and federal law.

States adopt their own constitutions as a framework for governance. One of the earliest state constitutions, the 1780 Constitution of the Commonwealth of Massachusetts, drafted by John Adams, is the world's oldest functioning written constitution and served as a model for the U.S. Constitution.[5] Many later state constitutions are modeled after the U.S. Constitution, although most are much more detailed and restrictive. State constitutions do not include implied powers such as those in the U.S. Constitution, although states are presumed to possess "police power," namely, the ability to promote public health, safety, morals, or general welfare. The police power is generally considered among the reserved powers of the states granted by the Tenth Amendment of the U.S. Constitution, and it predates federal power. Today much of the police power is delegated by states to their local governments.[6]

Unlike the U.S. Constitution, which has fewer than nine thousand words and has been amended only twenty-seven times since 1789, state constitutions are long and are frequently amended or replaced. Table 3.1 indicates the number, length, and amendments for each state constitution. The states vary widely in the detail within their constitutions and the manner in which they amend the documents. Many states have had only one constitution. The constitution of Massachusetts, for example, has endured since 1780. Georgia and Louisiana have had the most constitutions, with Georgia having ten and Louisiana eleven. Georgia's current constitution took effect in 1983, and it is the newest state constitution with the exception of Rhode Island's.

Basics of the Georgia Constitution

The current Georgia Constitution consists of eleven sections and in printed format runs to eighty-nine pages. Thus it is considerably longer and more complex than the U.S. Constitution. While it parallels the U.S. Constitution in that it has specific articles concerning the legislative, executive, and judicial branches of government and has its own bill of rights, it goes beyond the U.S. Constitution and adds provisions regarding taxation and finance, voting and elections, education, and counties and municipal corporations, and has a catch-all "Miscellaneous Provisions" article.

Article 1 of the Georgia Constitution allows state courts to determine whether laws or actions comply with the state or U.S. constitutions. This process of judicial review is similar to that at the national level. However, the U.S. Constitution does not specifically grant federal courts the power of judicial review; rather it has been assumed by courts since *Marbury v. Madison* (1803).[7] The power of judicial review is specifically given to Georgia courts. Any law or administrative rule in Georgia, whether adopted by the state or by local governments, may be challenged in court. Georgia courts may also, unlike federal courts, challenge private practices such as activities of businesses or individuals. Unlike the U.S. Constitution, in which most rights have been added as amendments, Georgia's constitutions since 1861 have included a bill of rights as an integral part of the document. Article 1 in the 1983 Constitution includes twenty-eight paragraphs covering "Rights of Persons."

Article 2 deals with voting and elections. The Georgia Constitution provides basic ground rules, such as the use of secret ballots and the establishment of eighteen as the minimum voting age (Georgia was the first state to adopt this minimum age, in the 1940s, predating the adoption of the Twenty-Sixth Amendment to the U.S. Constitution in 1971). Runoff elections and recalls are constitutionally established, as are procedures for removing and/or suspending public officials. However, the Georgia Constitution leaves most of the specifics regarding voter registration and election procedures to be decided by the General Assembly. This is a major difference from the U.S. Constitution in that election procedures are very vague and outlined in Article 1 (legislative powers) and Article 2 (executive powers).

Article 3 is the parallel to the U.S. Constitution's Article 1 and deals with the legislative branch. The Georgia legislature is officially named the Georgia General Assembly and is bicameral. The presiding officer of the Georgia House of Representatives is called the speaker and is chosen by the members, and the leader of the Georgia Senate is the lieutenant governor of Georgia and is elected independently of its members. All 236 members of the General Assembly are up for election every two years. The General Assembly also meets for a very limited time each year and lacks the salary and staff found in the U.S. Congress.

Articles 4, 5, and 6 cover the executive and judicial branches. Article 5 is called the "Executive Branch" and encompasses the governor, the lieutenant governor, and elected department heads. Article 4 covers constitutional boards and commissions, while Article 6 establishes the judicial branch. Similar to the federal structure, Article 6 provides for a high court of last resort, an intermediate appellate court structure, and a basic trial court. Georgia's high court of last resort is the Georgia Supreme Court, while the basic trial court is the Superior Courts of Georgia. Georgia has many lesser trial and specialized courts such as a probate court that deals with estates. Judges in Georgia are either elected or appointed and then subject to retention elections.

The other articles deal with education, taxation and finance, amendments, and miscellaneous areas. Some of these constitutional provisions exist because the issues fall under state, not federal, domain. For example, although the federal government plays a role in education, it is one that has traditionally been left to the states, and the major source of financing for education is usually local property taxes. Georgia, like almost every state, has a constitutional guarantee of a free public education. There are, of course, reasons beyond state responsibility for the greater specificity of the Georgia Constitution, and we examine this issue in the next section.

Politics and State Constitutions

Unlike the U.S. Constitution, the Georgia Constitution (and, indeed, most state constitutions) includes a wide range of very specific policies. Of course, legislatures normally enact policies by passing laws. In many states, however, including Georgia, state constitutions contain many very specific policy provisions that often benefit a very few individuals or interests. It is very difficult to amend the U.S. Constitution. Doing so requires a two-thirds vote of both houses of Congress and then ratification by three-fourths of the states. Given the vast regional, political, partisan, and ideological differences of the United States, amending the U.S. Constitution for specific policy purposes is unlikely. The Eighteenth Amendment, which led to the prohibition of the buying, selling, and use of alcohol, is perhaps the only instance when such an amendment was adopted. It was repealed by the Twenty-First Amendment, and the prohibition amendment is now considered a spectacular failure.[8]

However, it is much easier to amend state constitutions, including the Georgia Constitution, and there are at least four reasons for these frequent policy amendments: state police powers, political advantage, state court decisions, and the requirements of the national government. Georgia's constitution has numerous examples of these processes.

Police Power

The federal government is a government of limited powers. Although significant powers exist under the U.S. Constitution, there must be a specific constitutional basis for the assertion of federal power. Oftentimes this asserted power is premised on the commerce clause of the tax and spending power of Congress. States, however, have what is called a police power. That is, states have the power to regulate on behalf of the health, safety, welfare, and sometimes morals of the people. The leading Supreme Court case on this power is *Jacobson v. Massachusetts*.[9] In this case the court upheld the state's compulsory smallpox vaccinations program. The court noted that individual liberty is sometimes not as important as the common good, which in this case was public health. This police power is therefore vast, and it means that the state can legislate on many more areas than the federal government.

Examples of the extent of this power can be found in many state constitutions. Education, for example, falls under a state police power. Although the federal government does play a significant role in education, basic financing and education requirements are left to the states. The Georgia Constitution, like almost all other state constitutions, specifically enshrines this role for the state and specifies a payment process in Article 7, section one:

> The provision of an adequate public education for the citizens shall be a primary obligation of the State of Georgia. Public education for the citizens prior to the college or postsecondary level shall be free and shall be provided for by taxation. The expense of other public education shall be provided for in such manner and in such amount as may be provided by law.

Political Advantage

Enacting public policy through a constitutional amendment makes overturning the policy much more difficult than doing so with a policy enacted through ordinary legislation. In order to change a state constitution, one has to go through an amendment process, while for legislation, one only has to get a majority in both legislative houses to agree, which is a much simpler process. Thus, if a group is able to get its position on an issue included in a state's constitution, its opponents will have a more difficult time trying to repeal or change the policy. Such legitimate use of the state constitution is really a matter of exercising power through the "rules of the game." Georgia's constitution is riddled with such provisions. Various tax and spending provisions, such as those pertaining to education, gasoline, and alcohol, are dealt with through Georgia's constitution.

Earmarking. Like many state constitutions, Georgia's "earmarks" certain funds (identifies revenue sources that must be spent for designated purposes). The most significant are motor fuel taxes, which Article 3 requires to be spent "for all activities incident to providing and maintaining an adequate system of public roads and bridges" and for grants to counties. Moreover, this money goes for these purposes "regardless of whether the General Assembly enacts a general provisions Act."[10] Thus the constitution provides those groups interested in highway construction with guaranteed sources of funds. The 1992 amendment creating the lottery requires that net proceeds (after expenses and prizes) go to "educational programs and purposes" with the governor's annual budget, including recommendations for the use of these funds.[11] An amendment in 1998 further restricted these funds.

In other cases, the constitution merely permits the earmarking of funds. For example, the General Assembly can use taxes on alcoholic beverages for programs related to alcohol and drug abuse. The legislature is allowed to create a variety of trust funds for programs ranging from the prevention of child abuse to promotion of certain crops.

Tax Breaks. The constitution provides special tax treatment of various groups and activities over and above what the General Assembly enacts through tax laws. An example is the taxation of timber, one of Georgia's largest industries. An amendment approved by voters in 1990 requires that timber be taxed at fair market value only at the time of its harvest or sale.[12] Previously, it was taxed annually at market value. This change produced a major drop in property tax revenues for some counties and school districts. A tax break for blueberry farmers, which was offered as an amendment in 1994, was not ratified, however. The constitution also requires that certain agricultural land be assessed at 75 percent of its value, and it exempts part of the value of a disabled veteran's home from property taxes.[13] Other sections of the constitution authorize rather than require the General Assembly to provide certain types of tax preferences, as with taxes for homes on a historic register and heavy motor vehicles owned by nonresidents.[14]

Morality Issues. Various groups often attempt to use state constitutions to establish their position on controversial practices. This happened with the U.S. Constitution when the Eighteenth Amendment was added in 1919 to ban the sale of alcohol. It was repealed, however, by the Twenty-First Amendment in 1933. Similar provisions exist in the Georgia Constitution. The 1983 constitution contains a prohibition against whipping as a punishment for a crime. While some of those drafting the new document saw this as outdated, it was included out of fear that the General Assembly might pass bills permitting whipping in schools or prisons.[15]

The 1983 constitution prohibited lotteries, as had all its predecessors since 1868. Interestingly, this prohibition was in Article 1, which covers the "Origin and Structure of Government", and the bill of rights. After being elected governor in 1990, Zell Miller convinced the General Assembly to submit a proposed amendment to voters to create state-run lotteries whose proceeds must be spent on education. The amendment was ratified by a narrow margin in November 1992 following a strong campaign for passage by its supporters.

Another amendment proposed on a morality issue was the ban on same-sex marriage, which was ratified in 2004. By adding language to the state constitution itself, proponents of this amendment eliminated the possibility of a statute allowing same-sex marriage and have removed it as a question in Georgia courts. This change in the state constitution also prohibited local governments from recognizing same-sex marriages within the state of Georgia, for example, in the case of a couple moving to Georgia from a state with a different definition of marriage.

This amendment, however, demonstrates another reason that the Georgia Constitution needs amendment: it has to respond to court decisions. For example, the U.S. Supreme Court has issued several critical decisions on same-sex marriages, the first two bolstering the right of same-sex couples, and the final one abolishing all state prohibitions of same-sex marriage. In *Hollingsworth v. Perry*, the court overturned California's constitutional ban on same-sex marriages, while in the other, *United States v. Windsor*,[16] the court overturned a portion of the Defense of Marriage Act that banned federal benefits. The California case did not specifically rule on the constitutional ban but effectively overturned the ban on grounds of standing, while Windsor only applies to the federal government.

Although neither ruling specifically affected the Georgia constitutional ban on same-sex marriage, both had major implications for the future. The allowance of federal benefits to same-sex couples meant that federal workers in same-sex marriages, including military personal residing in Georgia, were eligible for federal, but not state, benefits. These decisions also raised issues of visitation, divorce, property and inheritance rights, and potentially child custody issues. Finally, the right to same-sex marriage itself was settled in 2015, when the Supreme Court ruled that it was guaranteed by the U.S. Constitution in *Obergefell v. Hodges*.[17] This reversed policy in fourteen states, including Georgia, that had a marriage ban. Both the governor and the attorney general issued statements of compliance with the ruling, and the state's probate judges, who issue marriage licenses in each county, were prepared for the ruling.[18]

Limits on Policy Making. Constitutions affect politics by deciding who makes decisions, limiting the discretion of government agencies, and allowing certain interests to be represented in the policy process. For example, Article 4 created six state boards and commissions, and Article 8 created two more for education. As noted earlier, the Georgia Constitution establishes important political ties between the State Transportation Board and the General Assembly, thereby reducing the power of the executive branch over highways. An example of constitutional limits on the discretion of government agencies is the requirement that veterans be given a preference in state civil-service employment.[19] Perhaps the most visible way that the Georgia Constitution represents certain interests is through residency requirements, as with membership from each congressional district on certain boards and commissions and the requirement that at least one member of the Board of Natural Resources be from one of the coastal counties.[20]

State Court Decisions

A second reason for including policies in a constitution is to respond to state court decisions. For example, the Georgia Supreme Court might hold that a state law or an action by a local government violates the Georgia Constitution. Almost the only way to undo the court's unconstitutionality ruling is to amend the state constitution. While difficult, this is much easier to do than amending the U.S. Constitution. A 1994 amendment permits local governments to prohibit alcohol sales at clubs with nude dancing. This amendment was a way to get around a Georgia Supreme Court ruling that nude dancing was expressive conduct protected by the Georgia and U.S. constitutions. Alcohol sales are not constitutionally protected, so regulating them is a way to try to drive nude dancing clubs out of business, which was subsequently considered allowable under the Georgia Constitution.[21]

The Federal Government and State Constitutions

A third way in which politics affect state constitutions is to satisfy some requirement of the national government. For example, the Georgia Constitution was amended in 1988 and 1992 to create a trust fund to provide medical services for the poor through the federal Medicaid program. Without the trust fund, money unspent at the end of the budgetary year would have to go to the state's general fund and could be used for any purpose, as specified elsewhere in the Constitution.[22] With the trust fund, the unspent money can be carried over to the next year to pay for medical care. Another example can be found in Article 3, which was written to satisfy federal court decisions about how legislative districts must be drawn.

Previous Constitutions of Georgia

Table 3.2 lists Georgia's constitutions along with some of their characteristics.[23] Each of these documents should be seen as a political response to some conflict, problem, or crisis. In addition to substantive differences, the documents also vary in the methods used to draft and approve them. Seven of Georgia's constitutions were written by conventions composed of elected delegates. Two were prepared by bodies whose members were either appointed or included because they held specific offices. The constitution of 1976 resulted from a request by Governor Busbee to have the Office of Legislative Counsel prepare an article-by-article revision of the constitution of 1945 for the General Assembly. It also is worth noting that the 1961 constitution was the first to be ratified by voters.

Eighteenth-Century Constitutions

Prior to its ten constitutions, Georgia had a temporary governing document in 1776. It was followed by three constitutions between 1777 and the end of the eighteenth century. The third had the longest life, lasting from 1798 to 1861.

The Rules and Regulations of 1776. Even before American independence in 1776, Georgians were asserting their independence from England. Colonial Georgia, dependent on imports for most manufactured items, was hard hit by the var-

Table 3.2. Georgia's Ten Constitutions

Year Implemented	Revision Method*	Major Characteristics
1777	Convention	Separation of powers, with most power in the hands of the unicameral legislature.
1789	Convention	Bicameral legislature, which chose the governor; no bill of rights.
1798	Convention	Popular election of governor; creation of Supreme Court; greater detail than predecessors.
1861	Convention	Long bill of rights; first constitution submitted to voters.
1865	Convention	Governor limited to two terms; slavery abolished; Ordinance of Secession repealed; war debt repudiated; some judges elected.
1868	Convention	Authorization of free schools; increased appointment power for governor; debtors' relief.
1877	Convention	More restrictions on legislative power; two-year terms for legislators and governor; no gubernatorial succession; most judicial appointments by legislature.
1945	Commission	Establishment of lieutenant governorship, new constitutional officers, new boards, state merit system; home rule granted to counties and cities.
1976	Office of Legislative Counsel†	Reorganization of much-amended 1945 constitution.
1983	Select Committee‡	Streamlining of previous document, with elimination of authorization for local amendments.

Source: M. Hill 1994, 3–20.

* Group responsible for proposing new document.

† State employees, attorneys.

‡ Almost exclusively leaders from the three branches of state government.

ious import taxes that had led to colonial protests. Public opinion in Georgia favored independence, and citizens mobilized to break with England. The first self-government in Georgia was defined by the Rules and Regulations of 1776, which were adopted before the signing of the Declaration of Independence. Because the document was written quickly, it was short and simple. All existing laws were maintained except those that conflicted with actions taken by the Continental Congress. It declared that governmental authority resided within the state, not with the monarchy, and that power originated from the governed. While this document was not officially a state constitution, many have noted that it served as one. The more formal separation from England represented by the Declaration of Independence prompted Georgians to adopt a more permanent state government and to write a new state constitution.

The Constitution of 1777. Georgia's first constitution included many now-familiar ideas such as separation of powers among the legislative, executive, and judicial branches of government; proportional representation on the basis of population; and provisions for local self-government. This constitution, like the Rules and Regulations of 1776, included little expressed protection of individual liberties. Despite this omission, Georgia's political culture at the time was more liberal than other states, and the constitution was written to empower the "common man," although only white males of twenty-one years who had paid property taxes in the previous year were permitted to vote. The Anglican Church was disestablished, and even people unfamiliar with law easily understood the language in the document. Those citizens of the state who still held loyalties to the British were encouraged or forced to move elsewhere, usually to Florida, which was controlled by Spain. Local control of the judiciary was ensured by the fact that no courts were established above the county courts.

The transition from the Rules and Regulations of 1776 to a new constitution in 1777 was little noted by citizens. This document governed the state until the downfall of the Articles of Confederation in 1788. Georgia ratified the U.S. Constitution in January 1788—the fourth state to do so—and redrafted the state constitution in 1788 to reflect this monumental change in national government.

The Constitution of 1789. This document provided for a bicameral legislature. Although some accommodations were made for representation on the basis of population in the House of Representatives, all legislative districts were drawn within counties, which could have from two to five representatives and one senator. Slaves were counted as three-fifths of a person, in accord with the U.S. Constitution and to meet the demands of landowners seeking to enhance representation for areas with large plantations. The state capital was moved to Louisville; provisions were included to mandate public education at the county level;

and new counties were created to be included in the legislature. In addition, the constitution authorized the legislature to elect the governor and most other state officials except the legislature itself. Restrictions on voting included race, gender, age, residence, and the payment of taxes in the previous year.

The short-lived tenure of this constitution can be attributed to a public scandal that took place in 1789. The state legislature, attempting to settle wartime debt, sold 15.5 million acres of land to speculators who had formed a number of companies named after the Yazoo River in South Carolina. The Virginia, South Carolina, Georgia, and Tennessee Yazoo Companies, among others, attempted to produce huge profits through land negotiations with several state legislatures. In Georgia, approximately 35 to 50 million acres of land were sold for about $500,000. When it was made public that these lands had been sold at a much lower price than expected and that many legislators held stock in the land companies, there was a great political outcry. Citizens also were angered by allegations that bribery within the legislature had preceded debate on the sale of these lands. In 1798 a convention was called to draft a new state constitution, which would include provisions to void the sale. Specific requirements on the sale of lands by the state legislature were established in this constitution.

The Constitution of 1798. This charter was written by a convention and retained much of the language of the previous document. However, it was much longer due to increased detail about the authority of the legislature. As time passed, this constitution was amended, among other reasons, to permit more democratic requirements for voting, establish executive offices to handle some of the duties of the legislature, outlaw foreign slave trade, and establish local governments. This constitution proved to be more enduring than its predecessors and was in effect until the formation of the Confederacy forced its dissolution in 1861.

The 1860s and 1870s: Four Constitutions in Short Order

The Constitution of 1861. Secessionist fever at the start of the Confederacy could hardly allow the state constitution to go untouched. T. R. R. Cobb, the main author of the Confederate Constitution, was also the author of the Georgia Constitution under the Confederacy. Permitting senators to represent more than one county reduced the size of the state legislature. Judicial review was institutionalized in this document, and state judgeships were established as elective offices. The population was too concerned with preparation for war to pay much attention to the document or the convention that produced it, and it was ratified with little fanfare. It should be noted, however, that the constitution of 1861 was the first to be submitted to the voters for approval in a referendum. This was also the first Georgia constitution with an extensive list of personal liberties, including freedom of thought and opinion, speech, and the press. However, citizens were warned that they would be responsible for "abuses of the liberties" given to them. Naturally, the Georgia Constitution under the Confederacy included ideals of states' rights, and the governor was greatly empowered.

The Constitution of 1865. Georgians drafted this document reluctantly in order to accommodate the mandates of Congress for readmission to the Union. Only those men who expressed moderate political beliefs before and after the war were permitted to work on the document, which included the abolition of slavery, repudiation of Civil War debt, and repeal of the acts of secession. This repeal was not met with great enthusiasm by the North, which had insisted that the ordinance of secession be declared void. Also absent was enfranchisement of the black population of the state, although this point was not as likely to stir northern animosity since blacks could only vote in six northern states at the time. These omissions put pressure on Georgia to rewrite the constitution just three years later in order to meet the requirements for reentry into the Union. Moreover, public opinion held that the constitution of 1865 was the work of northern "carpetbaggers" trying to make quick fortunes in the postwar South, or worse yet in the eyes of many, "scalawags"—southerners willing to cooperate with Yankees.

The Constitution of 1868. When the constitutional convention was called in 1867, it was boycotted by most of Georgia's popular leaders. The state capital, at that time in Milledgeville, refused to accommodate many of the delegates, some of whom were black. Therefore, the convention was held in Atlanta, and the new constitution, perhaps in retaliation for the inhospitable treatment by the city of Milledgeville, specified Atlanta as the capital. The constitution of 1868 met the requirements of Congress for readmission to the Union and, to the delight of most citizens, eliminated all debts incurred prior to 1865. Public education was also provided for, funded by poll and liquor taxes, although it was some time before this policy was implemented. Black citizens were ensured equal rights, at least on paper, and property rights for women were upheld. Moreover, some attempts were made to enhance the business climate, as the state was badly in need of a stronger tax base.

Due to high representation of poor and black citizens at this convention, the constitution of 1868 was a liberal document for the times, particularly for allowing black elected representatives to be seated in the General Assembly in 1870. Overall, the new constitution was widely unpopular due to its compliance with northern demands, which were enforced by the presence of northern troops until 1876. It remained a symbol of southern defeat until it was replaced in 1877.

The Constitution of 1877. The new document was a return to more conservative ideals. It reduced the authority of state officials and shifted power to counties, most of which were rural. Most noteworthy was its not-so-subtle disenfranchisement of blacks and poor whites through the mandate that only those who had paid all back taxes would be eligible to vote. As the constitution of 1877 was being drafted, factionalism within the ranks of the Democratic Party erupted. Many who were sympathetic to old southern culture were reluctant to compromise with those who called for economic development and progressive policies. An agreement was reached to comply with northern requirements for reconstruction, as well as demands from more industrialized northern states that the South continue to supply them with raw materials. This compromise stirred up a faction of the Democratic Party labeled Bourbons, who were dedicated to pre–Civil War agrarian economic and social norms, white supremacy, and local and state self-determination. The Republicans found that the compromise left them with little power, and it would be quite some time before the Republican Party reasserted itself in Georgia.

This constitution also codified the system of representation under which the six counties with the largest populations were represented in the lower house of the legislature by three members each, the next twenty-six most-populous counties by two each, and the remaining counties by one member. This 3–2–1 ratio became the basis for the Democratic Party's use of the county-unit system to elect statewide candidates—a custom that became state law in 1917 with passage of the Neill Primary Act. The Bourbon political philosophy produced little for the average Georgian but maintained the ideals of the past and persisted until after World War II.

The constitution of 1877 was not well suited to changing conditions. For example, it forbade public borrowing, thereby eliminating the possibility of large-scale improvements in transportation or education financed by the state. In a state badly in need of postwar construction, this provision hindered the state's development. The constitution eventually included 301 amendments, many of which were temporary or dealt with local, rather than statewide, issues. Other amendments made supreme court justices elected officials, established juvenile courts and a court of appeals, empowered an elected Public Service Commission (PSC) to regulate utilities, and modified the boards overseeing education.

The Constitutions of 1945 and 1976

The Constitution of 1945. The Constitution of 1877 lasted until 1945, albeit in much-amended form. Dissatisfaction with the 1877 constitution, a careful study of the document in the 1930s, and prodding by Governor Ellis Arnall led to the creation of a twenty-three-member commission to draft a new constitution. The use of a commission rather than an elected convention reflects the governor's wish to depoliticize the constitution and bring it up to date, as well as the General Assembly's previous failure to muster the two-thirds vote needed to call a convention.[24]

The new constitution included few substantive changes; its main effect was to condense its heavily amended predecessor. Perhaps the most notable changes were the creation of the office of lieutenant governor and new boards for corrections, state personnel, and veterans' services. One contested issue was the ban on governors succeeding themselves, which the General Assembly retained in the draft submitted to voters. Other controversies surrounded home rule for local governments and the poll tax. With a turnout of less than 20 percent of those registered, voters approved the document by slightly more than a three-to-two margin following an active campaign on its behalf. Within three years, though, the new constitution added its first amendments. In fact, 1,098 amendments were proposed between 1946 and 1974. Voters ratified 826, of which 679 (82 percent) were local in nature.[25]

The Constitution of 1976. An effort to revise the 1945 constitution occurred during the early 1960s, but a federal court ruling prevented voters from considering it during the 1964 general election. Another attempt died in 1970, when the house, but not the senate, approved a document for submission to the electorate.

After assuming office in 1975, Governor George Busbee asked the Office of Legislative Counsel to draft a reorganization of the 1945 constitution in time for the 1976 election. After some revision by the General Assembly, voters approved the document in November of that year. With no substantive changes in the new constitution, the General Assembly almost immediately set out to consider a more thorough revision, creating the Select Committee on Constitutional Revision during its 1977 session.[26]

The Constitution of 1983

Like its predecessors, Georgia's current constitution reflects the changing politics of the state yet maintains many characteristics considered traditional: conservative fiscal policy, small government, and deference to localities. However, the constitution of 1983 was neither easily written nor quickly adopted. In fact, it is a good example of how factionalism can play a role in state politics.

Adoption of the Constitution

Between 1946 and 1980, Georgians were asked to vote on 1,452 proposed amendments (1,177 of them purely local in nature) and ratified more than 1,100. This created an unwieldy document understood by only the most diligent of constitutional students. Because it so restricted the behavior of local governments, localities often were forced to amend the constitution before they could make changes in taxation or municipal codes. For example, voters in Muscogee County voted on three amendments in 1966 and one in 1968 that applied only to their local governments and paved the way for the merger of the city of Columbus and Muscogee County governments in 1970.[27] Voters became so annoyed with the large number of proposals that they began to vote them down. In 1978, the statewide ballot included more than 120 proposed changes in the state's constitution, one-third of which failed to pass.[28]

By the late 1970s, many citizens were pleased when Governor Busbee sought the rewriting of the constitution, although Busbee may not have realized the difficulty of such a task. The proposed constitution was debated for three years by the Select Committee on Constitutional Revision, whose members included the governor, the lieutenant governor, the speaker of the house, the attorney general, and eight other elected officials. The Select Committee began work in May 1977 and appointed committees with broader citizen membership to revise individual articles of the constitution for consideration by the General Assembly and the electorate. In November 1978, two articles were submitted to voters, who rejected them.[29]

Subsequent efforts by the Select Committee and the 1980 session of the legislature failed to produce a new constitution. During its 1981 session, though, the General Assembly created the Legislative Overview Committee on Constitutional Revision, with thirty-one members from each legislative chamber, to work with the Select Committee. These efforts produced a document that was approved in a 1981 legislative special session and modified at the 1982 session before being submitted to the electorate.

Like constitutional revisions generally, this one was quite political. Lobbyists and others representing specific interests were quick to get involved in the process, which former governor Ellis Arnall likened to "dancing with a grizzly bear."[30] Moreover, the process was a costly one, with some estimates of the tab for the 1981 special session at $30,000 per day.[31] A confrontation occurred between the speaker of the Georgia House of Representatives, Tom Murphy, and the governor over the powers to be granted to the legislature under the new constitution. This debate was fueled by the fact that under previous constitutions, the presiding officers of the House and the Senate, as well as most legislative committee and subcommittee chairs, were named by the governor. This intimidating power of the governor over the legislature had continued until the 1960s, when it was changed by constitutional amendment.[32] Murphy wanted these powers to be retained by the legislature, while Busbee favored the delegation of some powers to bureaucratic offices and state boards. The governor and the General Assembly also had disagreements over tax breaks and gubernatorial term limits. Some members of the legislature seemed more interested in having control over writing the new document than in its eventual passage. At one point, Busbee asked legislators to forget the proposal and spend the remaining days of the session on other topics.[33]

Voters reacted angrily to this potential loss of opportunity, and the members of the General Assembly returned after a weekend break determined to come to consensus. Agreement was eventually reached, and the resulting document was indeed much shorter than the previous state constitution. It also was written in gender-neutral and simpler language, making it easier for the average citizen to understand. Voters approved the new constitution in November 1982 by a nearly three-to-one margin. It took effect the following July. The new constitution was the product of long debate and the work of over two hundred people. It required more than 3,100 hours of work spread out over a three-year period. Thousands of Georgians appeared at public hearings to argue for or against provisions in the document. Although it can be argued that the new constitution was one of evolution rather than revolution, it made many noteworthy changes:[34]

1. Eliminated the requirement that local governments place changes in taxation, municipal codes, and employee compensation on the state ballot;
2. Established a unified court system, consolidating the duties of justices of the peace and small claims courts into magistrate courts, and strengthening the state supreme court;
3. Required nonpartisan election of state court judges;
4. Enhanced the power of the General Assembly to enact laws and set tax policy;
5. Gave the Board of Pardons and Paroles power to stay death sentences;
6. Incorporated an equal protection clause;
7. Reduced the total amount of debt that the state may assume;
8. Provided more open-to-the-public committee and legislative meetings; and,
9. Incorporated more formal separation of powers between the legislative and the executive branches.

Even this more-streamlined document has not closed the door on the amendment process. Between 1984 and 2014, a total of ninety-eight amendments were proposed, and seventy-five approved (see table 3.3). Because the Georgia Con-

Table 3.3. Proposed Amendments to the
Georgia Constitution

Year	Number of Amendments Submitted to Voters	Number Ratified
1984	11	10
1986	9	8
1988	15	6
1990	9	8
1992	8	7
1994	6	5
1996	5	4
1998	5	3
2000	7	6
2002	6	4
2004	2	2
2006	3	3
2008	3	2
2010	5	3
2012	2	2
2014	2	2
2016	4	3
Total	102	78

Sources: Galileo Scholar, Georgia Legislative Documents,
https://www.galileo.usg.edu/scholar/databases/zlgl/?Welcome.

stitution is so specific, amendments may be offered that affect only narrow interests, such as blueberry farmers or law enforcement officials. In many cases, voters skip those constitutional amendments that are unfamiliar to them.

Several proposals since the dawn of the new century highlight these extremes. In the November 2000 election, three amendments were approved to allow benefits for law enforcement officials, firefighters, public school employees, and state highway employees killed or disabled in the line of duty. One allowed members of the General Assembly to be removed from office after conviction for a felony rather than after exhausting all their appeals. Another amendment raised from five to seven years the amount of time that state court judges must have been able to practice law before they can begin their judicial service. Finally, voters approved a measure related to property tax relief.

The 2002 election included six proposed amendments. Of the four amendments approved by voters, two provided tax incentives for the redevelopment and cleanup of deteriorated or contaminated properties. Another amendment established a program of dog and cat sterilization funded by special license plates. Finally, voters approved a measure to prohibit individuals from holding state office if they have defaulted on their federal, state, or local taxes.

The November 2004 ballot included only two proposed amendments. One was a rather obscure question regarding the jurisdiction of the state supreme court. The other, however, was a contentious measure banning same-sex marriage, which attracted thirteen thousand more votes than the court measure.[35] All three amendments passed in 2006, including one that many considered symbolic, which added hunting and fishing rights to the constitution. Voters split on three amendments related to growth and development in 2008 and five proposals in 2010, including rejection of a ten-dollar vehicle tag fee to fund trauma care.

More-recent elections have included some proposals that appealed to conservative voters. One amendment ratified in 2012 made it easier to bypass local school boards to set up charter schools. Another passed in 2014 prohibited the legislature from raising the maximum income tax rate.[36]

From the voter's perspective, few of the amendments proposed over the past two decades seem like burning issues at the core of what government does or how it operates. Nevertheless, Georgia is like most states in that its constitution includes narrow topics that many people would expect to be addressed in laws or regulations.

Constitutional Distribution of Authority

Perhaps the most important aspect of the Georgia Constitution is the fact that it is better thought of as "a power-limiting document rather than a power-granting document."[37] That is, many provisions specify things that the state of Georgia and its local governments may not do. Like most states, Georgia includes the ideal of separation of powers adopted by the framers of the U.S. Constitution. There are important differences compared to the national government, however.

Legislative Branch. Although the U.S. Congress and the Georgia General Assembly are similar in some ways, there are important differences. Both are bicameral legislatures, with the presiding officer of the lower house chosen by its members and the leader of the senate elected independently of its members. However, while the entire U.S. House of Representatives runs for election every two years but only one third of the U.S. Senate is up for election, the entire Georgia General Assembly is up for election every two years. The General

Assembly also meets for a limited time annually and lacks the salary and staff support found in Congress.[38] As we detail in chapter 6, it is practices that have developed outside the respective constitutions that most distinguish Congress from the General Assembly, particularly the greater power of the presiding officers at the state level.

Executive Branch. Perhaps the most striking difference between the U.S. and the Georgia constitutions is the number of elected officials in the state executive branch. The most visible elected executives are the governor and the lieutenant governor, although the latter's primary duties are legislative, as the lieutenant governor is the presiding officer of the senate. While they may be compared to the U.S. president and vice president, the governor and lieutenant governor are not elected together and may represent different views and political parties. Georgia voters also elect to four-year terms their attorney general, secretary of state, superintendent of schools, and the "commissioners" who head the Departments of Labor, Insurance, and Agriculture.[39] The large number of elected officials has the effect of limiting the power and authority of the governor, in that independently elected officials have little reason to respond to the political needs of the governor. This arrangement is quite different from the national government, in which the heads of most agencies are nominated and may be fired at will by the president, with the only limitation being Senate approval of nominees. Of course, because Georgia has a part-time legislature, the governor has additional informal powers that the president of the United States lacks.

Article 4 of the Georgia Constitution also provides for six multimember boards and commissions whose responsibilities seem to be simultaneously legislative, administrative, and judicial. Perhaps the most important is the Public Service Commission, whose five members are elected statewide for staggered, six-year terms. The PSC is responsible for regulation of telephone services, utilities such as gas and electricity, communication networks, and transportation such as trucking and rail systems. Since the PSC holds public hearings and considers rates charged to consumers, it functions in part as a judicial agency. It also handles enforcement and employs inspectors and engineers, making the PSC appear to be an executive agency. Article 8 gives constitutional status to two other boards appointed by the governor: one for elementary and secondary education, and another with jurisdiction over the state university system (see chapter 7).

Judicial Branch. The 1983 constitution also maintained an independent judiciary. Unlike the federal legal system, in which federal judges are appointed by the president and confirmed by the Senate, the Georgia Constitution requires the election of state judges. Georgia's district attorneys, who are local officials responsible for criminal prosecutions, are also elected, unlike U.S. attorneys who are, like federal judges, presidential appointees. Thus, Georgia does not employ the same checks and balances as at the national level, where, subject to Senate confirmation, local prosecutors are presidential appointees under the authority of the U.S. Department of Justice, and judges are appointed for life. However, the governor is permitted to appoint people to vacant or newly created judgeships, subject to a later retention election, and quite often this practice ensures gubernatorial appointees end up with judicial positions.[40] Another practice not found at the national level is the ability of the attorney general to issue advisory opinions, which have the force of law in Georgia unless overturned in court (see chapter 7). Article 3 of the U.S. Constitution formally prohibits advisory opinions by the federal courts, mandating that federal jurisdiction requires, among other things, a "case and controversy."

Local Government. In addition to allocating authority among branches of state government, Georgia's constitution also establishes a framework for the operation of local government.[41] This is especially important because the U.S. Constitution says nothing about the matter (see chapter 9).

Procedures

Constitutional Amendments. Georgia's constitution outlines several important governmental procedures, some of which differ significantly from the U.S. Constitution, although they are similar to methods commonly used in other states (see table 3.4). The most fundamental difference may be the method for carrying out constitutional changes. In Georgia, the legislature can ask voters to create a convention to amend or replace the constitution. It can also propose amendments if they are approved by a two-thirds vote in the house and senate—a procedure like the one at the national level. While the U.S. Constitution requires ratification by three-fourths of the states, the Georgia Constitution requires approval by a majority of voters casting ballots on the amendment. This provision makes ratification of an amendment easier than in states requiring a majority of those voting in the election, which can be a problem when people vote for highly visible offices and skip proposed amendments that are complicated and further down the ballot.[42]

Lawmaking. The other major procedures outlined in the Georgia Constitution cover the legislative process and other legislative powers such as impeachment. Unlike the U.S. Constitution, Georgia's constitution differentiates between local bills and those of statewide applicability, grants the governor a line-item veto for appropriations bills, and requires the state to adopt a balanced budget.[43]

Table 3.4. Procedures for Amending State Constitutions

Legislative Vote to Submit Amendment*	Voter Ratification Required				
	⅔ on Amendment	⅗ on Amendment	Majority on Amendment	Majority in Election	No Voter Participation
¾ (1)†			CT‡		
⅔ (21)			17§	HI, TN, WY**	DE††
⅗ (10)	NH	FL	7	IL	
Majority (18)			17	MN	

Source: Council of State Governments, *Book of the States 2016*, 11–12.

* Eighteen states also allow citizens to use the initiative process to place amendments on the ballot.

† Number of state in parentheses.

‡ Requires ¾ approval in one legislative session but only a majority in two consecutive sessions.

§ Method used in Georgia.

** Hawaii allows a lower percentage for amendments approved in two legislative sessions. Tennessee requires a majority on first passage in the legislature but ⅔ on second passage.

†† Ratification requires ⅔ approval in two sessions of the legislature.

The Georgia Constitution in Practice: Rights and Liberties

Constitutions do more than establish governmental institutions and specify procedures. They also guarantee rights to individuals and regulate government's ability to interfere with people's liberties. Amending a constitution is normally a very difficult process. Therefore, including rights and liberties in a constitution is designed to protect them better than if such guarantees could be reduced or eliminated simply by passing a law.

State constitutions may not infringe on liberties and rights protected by the U.S. Constitution. As previously discussed, the Fourteenth Amendment to the U.S. Constitution provides a baseline or minimum standards of rights and liberties, but states are free to grant their citizens broader rights. The discussion below covers some of the major provisions in Georgia's bill of rights. Under each heading, the first section describes how Georgia courts have applied these guarantees in specific cases. This section is followed by a discussion of related federal court cases originating in Georgia. These cases, which are based on the U.S. Constitution, often brought about substantial changes not only in Georgia but in the nation as a whole.

Right to Life, Liberty, and Property

Life, liberty, and property are the first rights listed in the Georgia Constitution.[44] Like guarantees in the U.S. Constitution, they cannot be abridged "except by due process of law." State courts have found this guarantee to be broader than under the U.S. Constitution.[45] Georgia courts traditionally have found that the state has the power to regulate businesses so long as the regulation is applied equally to all who engage in the same types of businesses and has some "rational relationship" to a valid purpose. Only when litigants can show that their due process has been violated are they able to convince the courts that government regulation is "arbitrary" or "unreasonable." Thus laws regulating the licensing and training of professionals have largely been upheld as reasonable and not arbitrary. Similarly, the Georgia Supreme Court has held that a mandatory life sentence for a second drug conviction does not violate due process or equal protection and therefore is neither unreasonable nor arbitrary, despite statistical evidence that a larger percentage of black defendants end up serving life sentences under the law.[46]

The Georgia Supreme Court has taken a broad view of government compensation owed to the owners of private property that has been taken for public use. All states and the federal government have some power of eminent domain (the taking of private property for public use such as expanding a highway, constructing facilities, and laying water or sewer lines). While most Georgia court decisions have permitted government to determine the size and use of land taken, restrictions have been imposed on compensation for property. The courts also have applied the notion of "taking" to regulation of private property, that is, government regulation may be so restrictive that it has the same effect as seizing someone's land. In 2005, in *Kelo v. City of New London*,[47] the U.S. Supreme Court, relying on a clear line of precedent, upheld the taking of private property for private development as a justifiable taking under the Fifth Amendment. At issue was the desire of the local municipality to clear an economically depressed, or "blighted," area by using eminent domain and then selling the area for private development instead of erecting a school or a public highway.

In response, many states limited the use of eminent domain, including Georgia, which amended its constitution to allow only elected officials to invoke eminent domain and limits its use to economic development as described "by general law." Under the amendment, "small businesses and homes can no longer be taken by local government for economic development purposes." The legislation also tightened the definition of "blight," a term used to justify a government's taking of private property to convert it to a more productive use.

Equal Protection

Georgia Courts. The second paragraph in Georgia's bill of rights guarantees that "no person shall be denied the equal protection of the laws."[48] This language mirrors the Fourteenth Amendment to the U.S. Constitution. While the Georgia Supreme Court has held that the federal and state equal protection guarantees "coexist," the justices have acknowledged that the state may interpret the Georgia Constitution to offer broader rights than are available under the U.S. Constitution.[49]

A great deal of the controversy over equal protection involves government's classification of groups, with the courts being most vigilant regarding sex and race. In 1984, the Georgia Supreme Court found unconstitutional a law that provided benefits to children whose mothers were wrongfully killed but did not afford the same protection to children whose fathers were wrongfully killed.[50] The court also struck down Atlanta's program to set aside a share of contracts for minority- and female-owned businesses because the city failed to demonstrate the need for a race-conscious program.[51] Local governments have continued to adopt set-aside programs, however, after studies to determine the effects of prior discrimination. Such policies remain highly contentious and must operate within guidelines laid out by the U.S. Supreme Court, which has been increasingly skeptical of such initiatives.

Perhaps more controversial have been several Atlanta ordinances dealing with gay rights. In 1995, the Georgia Supreme Court held that Atlanta could create a registry of unmarried couples (both heterosexual and homosexual) and forbid discrimination based on sexual orientation. However, the court concluded that the city exceeded its authority by extending insurance benefits to the domestic partners of city employees.[52] The city also extended various protections based on sexual orientation, although the Georgia legislature intervened to limit their enforcement for private clubs.[53]

Federal Courts and Discrimination. The Fourteenth Amendment clearly prohibits discrimination based on race. Yet Georgia, like other southern states, used a number of strategies to disenfranchise black citizens from the 1870s to the 1960s and in effect treated blacks as second-class citizens. These strategies included voting restrictions such as the poll tax, the white primary, and other measures eventually eliminated by federal legislation and court decisions,[54] as well as de jure segregation in almost all public areas and arenas.

A poll tax requires citizens to pay an annual levy to be eligible to vote, thereby making it harder for the poor to vote. Georgia had used a poll tax earlier in its history, but it became particularly restrictive when the 1877 constitution made it cumulative, which meant that anyone falling behind in the annual tax had to

Table 3.5. Major Federal Cases on Discrimination

King v. Chapman 154 F.2d 450 (1946)	Building on a 1944 U.S. Supreme Court case covering Texas, the circuit court of appeals found that the rules of Georgia's Democratic Party, which restricted voting in primary elections to whites only, violated the equal protection guarantee of the Fourteenth Amendment.
Heart of Atlanta Motel v. United States 379 U.S. 241 (1964)	Upheld constitutionality of Title 2 of the Civil Rights Act of 1964, which prohibited racial discrimination in public accommodations.
Olmstead v. L.C. 527 U.S. 581 (1999)	The state's practice of involuntarily institutionalizing disabled individuals judged suitable to live in less restrictive settings violates the Americans with Disabilities Act of 1990.
United States v. Georgia 546 U.S. 151 (2006)	Court found that Georgia violated the Americans with Disabilities Act of 1990 because its prisons were not adequately equipped to accommodate paraplegic inmates.

make back payments. The poll tax was not repealed until 1945, when Governor Ellis Arnall made it a major issue during the legislative session. In other southern states, the poll tax lasted until the Twenty-Fourth Amendment to the U.S. Constitution banned it in 1964.

Perhaps the most blatant attempt to disenfranchise blacks was the white primary, which restricted voting in party primaries to whites only. Blacks could participate in the general election, but their votes were inconsequential because Republican opposition rarely appeared on the ballot. This essentially meant that whoever won the Democratic Party's primary automatically won the election to public office. White primaries in Georgia had been adopted in some counties by the 1890s. Beginning in 1900, only whites could vote in the Democratic Party's primary elections across the state. In a 1927 Texas case, the U.S. Supreme Court held that it was unconstitutional for state law to restrict primary voting on the basis of race. Virtually the entire South was controlled by the Democratic Party then, and party leaders thereafter used party rules to enforce the white primary. Unlike general elections, which are processes of government, primaries could be regarded as activities of political parties, which are "private" organizations.

Finally, in 1944 the U.S. Supreme Court held that party rules enforcing a white primary in fact abridged the right to vote based on race. Georgia's white primary was overturned the following year by a federal appeals court in *King v. Chapman*. Perhaps the most immediate effect of this decision was in Atlanta, where business and political leaders began developing a coalition with the city's large black middle class.[55]

Three other restrictions were included in the Disenfranchisement Act of 1908, which voters approved as an amendment to the Georgia Constitution by a two-to-one margin:

The literacy test required that voters be able to read and explain any paragraph of the federal or state constitution; while the property qualification required ownership of 40 acres of land or property assessed at $500. The grandfather clause enfranchised men who had served in the United States or Confederate military forces and their descendants; no one could register under that provision after 1914.[56]

Implementation of the literacy test was in the hands of local election officials, who exercised great discretion, especially their power to purge voter registration rolls of those judged to be unqualified.

Jim Crow, or de jure segregation laws, was a fact of life in the states of the old Confederacy until a series of Supreme Court decisions starting in the 1950s and the passage of the Voting Rights and Civil Rights Act by Congress in the mid-1960s. As the momentum grew to desegregate during the 1950s and 1960s, the Georgia General Assembly produced an array of legislation to forestall the process.[57] At one point, all state aid was removed from any integrated public school, and payments were authorized to parents of children who attended segregated private schools. In order to prevent blacks from attending college in the state, requirements for admission were set to include letters of recommendation from two graduates of the institution to which a student was applying. Since no blacks had attended most of these institutions, such letters would be difficult to obtain. Although most actions by the Georgia General Assembly were struck down as unconstitutional, white parents were able to move to different school districts or to send their children to private academies that did not admit blacks. Although the Civil Rights Act limited outright segregation, resistance to the federal mandates allowed it to continue in many respects long after that date. For example, the Chatham County school board's unsuccessfully tried to claim that integration would heighten black children's feelings of inferiority, mocking the very language of Brown v. Board of Education.[58]

However, since 1978 and the Regents of the University of California v. Bakke case,[59] the court has consistently held that the Fourteenth Amendment prohibits any sort of racial classification without a compelling state justification, meaning that affirmative action programs cannot be based solely on race.

As a result, many recent controversies have involved the use of affirmative action in admissions decisions at Georgia's public colleges and universities. This includes several years of litigation over policies at the University of Georgia. In 2003, the U.S. Supreme Court reaffirmed the Bakke decision and gave support to the limited use of affirmative action in college and graduate admissions in two cases involving the University of Michigan, ruling that diversity is a compelling justification. Although the strict scrutiny standard was affirmed in the most recent case, Fisher v. University of Texas,[60] the Supreme Court did uphold race-conscious admissions systems.

The Civil Rights Act of 1964 was designed to end discrimination in public accommodations (hotels, restaurants, transportation, etc.), even if privately owned. Because of its requirements for privately owned businesses, it could not be premised on the Fourteenth Amendment, which applies only to state action. This was made clear in a famous case involving the state of Georgia, *Heart of Atlanta Motel v. United States*. The U.S. Supreme Court, in demonstrating the act's constitutionality, took a broad view of the U.S. Constitution's commerce clause and upheld the Civil Rights Act as a valid exercise of Congress's authority. The court rejected the motel's claim that it was a local business. Because the motel served interstate travelers, its practice of refusing lodging to blacks was held to obstruct commerce, and the motel would therefore have to serve black customers.

Not all discrimination is premised on race, and not all discrimination is remedied by Supreme Court decisions finding Fourteenth Amendment violations. Congress has also passed laws dealing with discrimination based on religion, age, and disability, even where the Supreme Court has failed to expand the concept of Fourteenth Amendment discrimination to cover such areas. One of the leading cases regarding the disabled was based on the ways in which the Georgia Department of Human Resources had institutionalized people involuntarily after it was determined that such people could be placed in a community setting. In *Olmstead v. L.C.*, the U.S. Supreme Court held that such action violated the protection of the Americans with Disabilities Act of 1990.

Federal Courts and Equal Representation. Since the early 1960s, federal courts have become increasingly active in the process of drawing districts for legislative bodies. The courts have interpreted the equal protection guarantee of the Fourteenth Amendment to mean that one person's vote should have the same weight in an election as another person's; to do this requires election districts of roughly equal population. In *Toombs v. Fortson*, the court ruled that reapportionment for the General Assembly must be made on the basis of the population of the state rather than by county or other political boundaries. Each district must have roughly the same number of inhabitants. After four earlier challenges had failed, in *Gray v. Sanders*, the U.S. Supreme Court struck down the county-unit system as a violation of the Fourteenth Amendment's equal protection guarantee because the system malapportioned voters by underrepresenting urban residents. Other litigation also forced the General Assembly to redraw congressional districts in the state.[61]

Questions of representation have become increasingly linked to race since Congress passed the Voting Rights Act in 1965. The VRA suspended use of literacy tests, allowed for federal election examiners and observers, and required affected state and local governments to receive approval from the national government before making changes in their electoral systems. This "preclearance"

Table 3.6. Major Federal Cases on Representation

Gray v. Sanders 372 U.S. 368 (1963)	Held that Georgia's county-unit system violated the Fourteenth Amendment's equal protection guarantee because it malapportioned votes among the state's counties.
Fortson v. Toombs 379 U.S. 621 (1965)	Upheld a lower court's 1962 decision that the Fourteenth Amendment required seats in the General Assembly to be apportioned with districts of roughly equal population rather than being based on county or other political boundaries.
Miller v. Johnson 515 U.S. 900 (1995)	Invalidated Georgia's congressional redistricting following the 1990 census as a violation of the Fourteenth Amendment's equal protection clause because race was the predominant factor in drawing district boundaries. The General Assembly had created three black-majority districts, with the eleventh district having a very irregular shape.
Georgia v. Ashcroft 539 U.S. 461 (2003)	Held that courts reviewing redistricting under the Voting Rights Act have to consider all relevant factors affecting minority voters, not just the chance of electing minority candidates.

process pays close attention to changes that might dilute the voting strength of minority groups.

The U.S. Department of Justice objected to congressional redistricting by the Georgia General Assembly following the 1990 census. After two unsuccessful attempts to redraw districts, state lawmakers finally satisfied federal guidelines to protect minority voting strength in the 1992 elections.[62] Ironically, in 1995 those districts were ruled unconstitutional in *Miller v. Johnson* because race was a "predominant factor" used in drawing the district lines.[63] Similar litigation occurred following redistricting based on the 2000 census: in *Georgia v. Ashcroft*, the U.S. Supreme Court again required Georgia to consider factors other than race in drawing legislative districts.

A recent ruling by the U.S. Supreme Court, *Shelby County v. Holder*, calls into question some of the key provisions of the VRA, and this has significant implications for the state of Georgia.[64] The Voting Rights Act requires "preclearance" or preapproval of any changes to election law in the most of the states of the old Confederacy—Alabama, Georgia, Louisiana, Mississippi, South Carolina, Texas, and Virginia; Alaska and Arizona—and to scores of counties and municipalities in other states, including localities in New York, Michigan, Florida, and California. The court decision eliminates this preclearance requirement.

Rights Related to Expression and Association

Georgia's bill of rights includes a number of provisions designed to allow people to hold and express opinions, to associate with others, and to participate in the political process. These include two paragraphs on religion, as well as one on the press, another on the right to assemble and petition, and one on libel, which is not mentioned in the U.S. Constitution.

Georgia Courts and Freedom of Conscience and Religion. Religious freedom was the earliest liberty to be addressed by Georgia's constitution drafters.[65] Even the Rules and Regulations of 1776 included a provision for freedom of religion. The Georgia Constitution includes language that is somewhat different from the First Amendment to the U.S. Constitution. Perhaps the most striking difference is Georgia's limitation on religious practices: "but the right of freedom of religion shall not be so construed as to excuse acts of licentiousness or justify practices inconsistent with the peace and safety of the state."[66] Thus courts in Georgia have at times limited free exercise of religion, including a decision that freedom of religion does not include the distribution of literature in public.[67] Nor has the Georgia Supreme Court extended freedom of religion to the use of controlled substances.[68] The state has also been drawn into controversies over links between religion and public school science courses, usually in relation to "creationism" and "intelligent design."[69]

Georgia Courts and Freedom of Speech and the Press. Georgia courts have adopted a broad interpretation of freedom of speech.[70] For example, while the U.S. Supreme Court held that screening of movies was not in and of itself a violation of free speech, the Georgia Supreme Court found that an ordinance requiring approval of a censor before screening movies was unconstitutional in Georgia.[71] The court also held that it violated free speech to ban those between the ages of eighteen and twenty-one from premises with sexually explicit performances.[72]

Free speech, as interpreted by the Georgia courts, includes limits. Indeed, the Georgia Constitution says that people "shall be responsible for the abuse of that liberty," as in cases involving incorrect publication of delinquent debt, inaccurate information regarding criminal activity, or use of photographs for advertising without the subjects' permission. The Georgia Supreme Court has upheld an injunction against antiabortion protesters on the grounds that the protest was limited by reasonable restrictions regarding time, place, and manner.[73] The court has held, however, that picketing is not protected free speech when the protest includes an illegal strike. The court also upheld the state's "Anti-Mask Act," which targets groups such as the Ku Klux Klan by prohibiting intimidating or threatening mask-wearing behavior, despite a claim that the law violates a person's freedom of speech.[74]

Another difference between the United States and Georgia law is the protection of confidential press sources. The Supreme Court of the United States has repeatedly held that the First Amendment does not cover a member of the press's right to withhold information from law enforcement. The same is true under the Georgia Constitution.[75] However, under Georgia law, the media have been granted limited protection by a state shield law that, while it allows reporters to be forced to turn over information from confidential sources, states that the government must show that the evidence is material and relevant, is necessary for one of the parties to prepare a case, and cannot reasonably be gathered by other means.[76] In terms of other publications, the Georgia Supreme Court has held that it violates free speech for a city to prohibit the distribution of printed materials to homes.[77]

Controversies have swirled around language or behavior judged offensive by many people. For instance, the Georgia Supreme Court struck down as too vague and a violation of free speech a state law attempting to outlaw bumper stickers considered to be profane.[78] Even greater debates have involved sexually oriented communication, particularly after the Georgia Supreme Court ruled that nude dancing was protected expression and overturned local regulations banning such entertainment as too broad or outside the authority granted to local governments. To reverse this action, Georgia voters approved a constitutional amendment in 1994 to increase local governments' control over nude dancing through their power to regulate alcoholic beverages. A number of local governments subsequently adopted ordinances to prevent clubs with nude dancing from serving alcohol. The Georgia Supreme Court has held that such alcohol regulations do not violate the free speech rights associated with such entertainment.[79]

Federal Courts and Freedom of Speech and the Press. The U.S. Supreme Court has considered many cases during the past fifty years dealing with the First Amendment's guarantees regarding religion, speech, the press, and association. Two major cases on obscenity originated in Georgia. In the 1969 decision on *Stanley v. Georgia,* the court found that "the mere private possession of obscene matter cannot constitutionally be made a crime," which Georgia law had done. Police had a warrant to search Stanley's home for materials related to illegal gambling, but they found allegedly obscene material. The state claimed that certain types of materials should not be possessed or read, and that obscene materials may lead to sexual violence or other acts. The court rejected these claims, holding that the state asserted the "right to control the moral content of a person's thoughts . . . but it is wholly inconsistent with the philosophy of the First Amendment."

In the 1973 case *Paris Adult Theatre I v. Slaton,* the Supreme Court was asked to determine whether the state could ban a commercial theater from showing films considered obscene. Here the court reached a decision that was the op-

Table 3.7. Major Federal Cases on Freedom of Speech and the Press

Stanley v. Georgia 394 U.S. 557 (1969)	Overturned state law making private possession of obscene material a crime. The Georgia law was held to violate the First and Fourteenth Amendments to the U.S. Constitution.
Paris Adult Theatre I v. Slaton 413 U.S. 49 (1973)	Banning the showing of allegedly obscene films to consenting adults in a commercial theater was held not to violate the First Amendment or the right to privacy.
Cox Broadcasting Corp v. Colin 420 U.S. 469 (1975)	Overturned the Georgia law prohibiting publication of the name of a rape victim obtained from public records.
Forsyth County *v. Nationalist Movement* 505 U.S. 123 (1992)	Invalidated a local ordinance requiring participants to pay law enforcement costs for demonstrations and empowering the county administrator to determine how much to charge a group seeking a permit for a demonstration. The court found fault with the ordinance because it granted excessively broad discretion to the administrator, who was required to examine the content of a group's message in determining the fee to be charged for law enforcement protection.

posite of *Stanley*, holding that the state had an interest in "stemming the tide of commercialized obscenity." The court held that it did not make a difference that the films in question were shown only to consenting adults and the business posted warnings of the films' content and prohibited minors from entering. Instead, the court held that the state had a valid interest in "the quality of life and the total community environment, the tone of commerce in the great city centers, and, possibly, the public safety itself."

The U.S. Supreme Court also used a Georgia case involving white supremacists to limit restrictions on protest. Forsyth County was the scene of several marches by civil rights supporters and countermarches by the Ku Klux Klan during the 1980s. To manage these events, the county commission adopted an ordinance requiring those seeking a demonstration permit to pay a fee for law enforcement protection. The county administrator had discretion over the size of the fee, which could not exceed $1,000. One group refused to pay a $100 fee and sued the county. In *Forsyth County, Georgia v. Nationalist Movement*, the U.S. Supreme Court found that the county ordinance contained no standards for the administrator to follow and was thus unconstitutional because it "contains more than the possibility of censorship through uncontrolled discretion [and] the ordinance often requires that the fee be based on the content of the speech" of the group seeking the permit.

Cox Broadcasting Corp. v. Colin dealt with Georgia's law prohibiting publication of a rape victim's name. This case pitted the desire to protect the victim's privacy against the freedom of the press. The court held that prohibiting the publication of crime victims' names obtained from public records would violate freedom of the press.

Rights of Those Accused and Convicted of Crimes

The Georgia Constitution includes several provisions to protect people in dealing with the state's legal system.[80] These include conditions regarding searches, seizures, and warrants by law enforcement officials; access to the courts and the use of juries; the right to an attorney to cross-examine witnesses in criminal cases; the right to avoid self-incrimination; protection against excessive bail and "cruel and unusual" punishment; and a prohibition against double jeopardy. Most of these guarantees parallel those in the U.S. Constitution's Bill of Rights, although Georgia has added other guarantees. For instance, the state bill of rights explicitly prohibits whipping and banishment from the state as punishment for crimes, imprisonment for debt, and being "abused in being arrested, while under arrest, or in prison."[81]

Georgia Courts. One of the most notable distinctions between the U.S. Constitution and Georgia's is that the state offers more protection to defendants against unreasonable searches and seizures by law enforcement authorities. In addition, Georgia has long recognized the right of indigents to have a lawyer appointed, although this right does not extend to civil cases.[82] A major problem with providing attorneys to poor criminal defendants has been appropriating sufficient funds to make the guarantee work well.

Arguments often are made that certain punishments are "cruel and unusual." Georgia courts have held that punishment exceeding the crime is, in some cases, constitutional. For example, fines larger than amounts taken by theft have been permitted. In some instances, defendants have been banished from certain counties, but the Georgia Supreme Court has not upheld banishment from the state as a whole. Georgia's use of the death penalty was found to be unconstitutional in 1972 by the U.S. Supreme Court because the state did not have standards to protect against the unequal application of capital punishment. Currently, Georgia law lists the conditions under which the death penalty may be sought and is in line with later U.S. Supreme Court rulings permitting executions. The Georgia Supreme Court has ruled that it is not cruel and unusual punishment to sentence someone to life in prison for a second conviction for selling cocaine.[83] The justices reached the opposite conclusion in 1989, however, about executing someone who is mentally disabled—well before a 2002 U.S. Supreme Court decision banned the practice nationally as cruel and unusual punishment.[84] Georgia courts have also grappled with concerns that prosecutors may be discriminatory when exercising their discretion in requesting sentences for a crime.[85]

Federal Courts and Search and Seizure. Georgia has produced few major federal cases related to the search and seizure rights of criminal defendants found in the U.S. Constitution's Fourth Amendment. In 1997, however, the U.S. Supreme Court overturned a Georgia law requiring candidates for state office to pass a drug test, which the General Assembly had passed as part of its antidrug efforts during the 1980s. Walker Chandler filed to run as Libertarian Party candidate for lieutenant governor in 1994 but refused to take the drug test. In *Chandler v. Miller*, the court held that the drug tests did not fall within the category of constitutionally permissible suspicionless searches. Indeed, the court found that the test was essentially "symbolic" rather than being directed at some identifiable problem that might demand such a search.

Federal Courts and the Rights of Criminal Defendants. The U.S. Constitution's Sixth Amendment includes the right to a fair trial, which is not spelled out in detail. Therefore, the courts have had to define what that right means in practice. Some of these cases have dealt with the size of trial juries and whether they must reach a unanimous decision. In a 1973 Florida case, the U.S. Supreme Court had permitted six-member juries in civil cases. In *Ballew v. Georgia*, however, the court ruled in 1978 that Georgia's use of five-person juries in misdemeanor cases violated the right to a fair trial, in part because of the reduced deliberation and bias in favor of the prosecution regarding hung juries. Georgia's current constitution allows the General Assembly to permit six-member juries in misdemeanor cases or in courts of limited jurisdiction.[86]

Federal Courts and the Death Penalty. Two appeals to the U.S. Supreme Court from Georgia during the 1970s became the landmark cases regarding the use of capital punishment in the United States. *Furman v. Georgia*, in 1972, effectively ended executions throughout the country. Four years later, *Gregg v. Georgia* allowed the state's rewritten capital punishment law to stand, thereby opening the door for states to resume executions.

How did these two cases differ? The members of the U.S. Supreme Court had a range of views regarding capital punishment, but the major concern was how the death penalty was applied. In *Furman*, the court was concerned with both the lack of guidelines to use in deciding when to impose a death sentence and the wide variation in its use for similar crimes. The states then began revising their laws, and the court decided several cases in 1976 based on the new statutes. In *Gregg*, the court upheld Georgia's new capital punishment law, in part

Table 3.8. Major Federal Cases Affecting Those Accused or Convicted of Crimes

Chandler v. Miller 520 U.S. 305 (1997)	Held that Georgia's requirement that candidates for state office pass a drug test violated the Fourth Amendment protection against suspicionless searches.
Ballew v. Georgia 435 U.S. 223 (1978)	Held that a criminal trial using a jury of fewer than six members violated the Sixth Amendment guarantee to a fair trial.
Furman v. Georgia 408 U.S. 238 (1972)	Held that Georgia's methods of administering the death penalty violated the Eighth Amendment's guarantee against cruel and unusual punishment. The decision effectively ended executions in the United States for more than a decade.
Gregg v. Georgia 428 U.S. 153 (1976)	Upheld Georgia's revised law on capital punishment, which limited the crimes for which the death penalty could be imposed and specified the factors to be considered and procedures to be used in deciding when to impose capital punishment.
Coker v. Georgia 433 U.S. 584 (1977)	Found that Georgia's imposition of the death penalty for the crime of rape was grossly disproportionate and thus a violation of the Eighth Amendment's ban on cruel and unusual punishment.
McCleskey v. Kemp 481 U.S. 279 (1987)	Rejected the claim that racial differences in the imposition of the death penalty violated the equal protection guarantee of the Fourteenth Amendment and amounted to cruel and unusual punishment in violation of the Eighth Amendment.
Georgia v. Randolph 547 U.S. 103 (2006)	Police cannot search a home without a warrant when one occupant grants permission but another physically present occupant refuses to permit the search.
Ali v. Federal Bureau of Prisons 552 U.S. 214 (2008)	When items are detained, all officers are protected through sovereign immunity. It is not excluded to customs and excise officials only.
Dean v. United States 556 U.S. 568 (2009)	It is not required for the court to have proof of whether a firearm was accidentally discharged during the course of another crime to give a harsher sentence.
Moncrieffe v. Holder 569 U.S. __ (2013)	If the difference between federal and state drug laws is unclear, the court must categorically follow federal law before following state law.

because it required specific findings by the jury regarding the facts of the crime and the character of the defendant; it also had a process for appellate courts to review death penalty cases.

Two other cases tested the constitutionality of the conditions under which Georgia imposed the death penalty. In *Coker v. Georgia*, the U.S. Supreme Court held that the death sentence for the crime of rape was grossly disproportionate to the offense and thus violated the Eighth Amendment ban on cruel and unusual punishment. In *McCleskey v. Kemp*, the court confronted the issue of bias in imposing the death penalty. Warren McCleskey presented a study showing that the use of the death sentence in Georgia was statistically related to the race of the murder victim and, to a lesser extent, the race of the defendant. This pattern, he argued, violated the Eighth and Fourteenth Amendments. The Supreme Court rejected these claims, citing appellate courts' review of cases with facts similar to McCleskey's case.

The Right to Privacy

Georgia Courts. Like the U.S. Constitution, Georgia's does not mention a right to privacy. In 1904, though, Georgia became the first state to recognize a privacy right when the Georgia Supreme Court found this right in natural law and the guarantees of liberty found in the U.S. and state constitutions.[87] Privacy has been extended to the right of a prisoner to refuse to eat, even to the point of starvation, and a person's right to refuse medical treatment even if doing so was certain to lead to death. In *Powell v. State of Georgia*, the Georgia Supreme Court overturned the state's law banning sodomy on right to privacy grounds.[88]

Federal Courts, Dual Citizenship, and the Right to Privacy. The U.S. Supreme Court first recognized a right to privacy in a 1965 Connecticut case dealing with government regulation of contraception. Since then, the courts have been forced to define the limits of privacy rights. These debates include two Georgia cases. *Doe v. Bolton* is all but forgotten today, but it was the challenge to Georgia's abortion law decided in 1973 along with *Roe v. Wade*, the more widely known Texas case in which the Supreme Court held that the right to privacy included a woman's right to abortion.

The second Georgia case was *Bowers v. Hardwick*. In this case, Michael Hardwick challenged Georgia's criminal sodomy law as a violation of the right to privacy insofar as it applied to consensual sexual conduct. He also argued that as a homosexual he faced constant threat of arrest and prosecution. The U.S. Supreme Court rejected Hardwick's claim and upheld Georgia's sodomy law, which prohibited certain acts but did not specify the gender or sexual orientation of the participants.

Table 3.9. Major Federal Cases on the Right to Privacy

Doe v. Bolton 410 U.S. 179 (1973)	This is the less famous Georgia case decided along with *Roe v. Wade*. It overturned Georgia's ban on abortions as a violation of a woman's right to privacy.
Bowers v. Hardwick 478 U.S. 186 (1986)	Held that the right to privacy did not protect consensual homosexual sex from prosecution under Georgia's sodomy law.

Georgia's sodomy law provides a good example of the way in which dual citizenship can produce different rights under the U.S. and state constitutions. The Georgia Supreme Court reinforced the *Hardwick* decision in 1996, when it ruled, in *Christensen v. State*, that the state's sodomy law did not violate Georgia's right to privacy.[89] However, that changed in 1998, when the Georgia Supreme Court overturned the state antisodomy law, effectively overruling *Hardwick* at the state level. Ironically perhaps, the incident involved a heterosexual, not homosexual, couple. In *Powell*, the Georgia Supreme Court held that, "insofar as it criminalizes the performance of private, non-commercial acts of sexual intimacy between persons legally able to consent, [the sodomy law] 'manifestly infringes upon a constitutional provision' . . . which guarantees to the citizens of Georgia the right to privacy."[90] However, the court later rejected the claim that Georgia's right to privacy also protected commercial sexual activity.[91]

Thus, while any given state's law criminalizing sodomy would not violate the federal right to privacy as applied in *Bowers v. Hardwick*, state courts around the country could consider such a law in violation of broader rights guaranteed in their state constitutions. That possibility changed rather dramatically in 2003, however, when the U.S. Supreme Court's *Lawrence v. Texas* decision overturned sodomy laws in those states that still had them.[92]

The most recent frontier in battles over privacy rights deals with medical treatment. For instance, a 1997 U.S. Supreme Court decision left the door open for states to either ban or allow doctor-assisted suicide. This produced a conflict when former U.S. attorney general John Ashcroft attempted to keep Oregon from implementing its law allowing the practice, a case in which the court sided with Oregon in a January 2006 decision.[93] Although major federal cases on this subject have not originated in Georgia, disputes will undoubtedly continue in the face of breakthroughs in medical treatment and research.

The Continuing Significance of Georgia's Constitution

A constitution is not some kind of sacred or unchanging blueprint for government. Constitutions are essentially political documents, which is why individuals, businesses, political parties, and interest groups often fight vigorously about interpreting and amending constitutions. For instance, lawsuits have attacked as racially biased the methods of selecting Georgia's judges and juries.[94] By approving an amendment to create a state-sponsored lottery in 1992, voters gave the governor, the legislature, and the bureaucracy millions of dollars to distribute to programs and individuals. They also paved the way for firms to profit from the production, sale, and marketing of lottery tickets. Another amendment granted a property-tax break for growing timber,[95] although voters rejected a similar proposal for blueberries in 1994. The 1992 amendment requiring that local school board members be elected and superintendents be hired allows boards to recruit superintendents from anywhere. Under the old system of electing school superintendents in some counties, only local residents could run for the office.[96]

As the preceding examples demonstrate, constitutions help distribute political and economic power. Constitutions also adopt policies that under other circumstances might be made simply by passing a law. Given the extensive detail in the Georgia Constitution, voters undoubtedly will face proposed amendments every election year as various interests try to modify the document to achieve their ends. Indeed, the popularity of the HOPE scholarship program seems to have given birth on a regular basis to proposed amendments supposedly designed to protect the program—and enhance the image of the Republicans and the Democrats who support them.[97]

If a large number of amendments are ratified by voters, the constitution might become unwieldy and difficult to interpret. A second possibility is that Georgians will become so annoyed with proposals on the ballot that they rebel by voting no on amendments. Finally, interest groups, political parties, and members of the General Assembly might regularly use constitutional change as just another way to achieve their political ends. If so, Georgians might treat amendment battles as just an ordinary part of the election process even though they are not on the same scale as the initiatives proposed in western states. None of these scenarios bodes well, however, for the durability of the 1983 Georgia Constitution.

CHAPTER 4

Voting and Elections

Before discussing the details of elections in the state of Georgia, we should consider why we hold elections at all. One of the most important concepts in government involves the question of a government's *legitimacy*. Governments, including Georgia's state government in Atlanta, are powerful entities that can exert a great deal of control over individuals. Governments establish laws and tax systems and create organizations that enforce them. Failure to obey a Georgia law can lead to a person being fined, imprisoned, or (in certain cases) even put to death.

An important question is, what gives officials in Washington, D.C., or Atlanta the right to regulate behavior and the power to punish individuals? In democracies the answer is that the right to govern stems from the will of the people. The people of the United States (in the case of the national government) and the people of Georgia (in the case of Georgia's state government) select those who make laws, and they have the power to unselect those who make laws. This selection process takes place through elections.

Elections in Georgia

Georgia, like all democracies, relies on elections to establish its government's legitimacy. But knowing that the state holds elections does not tell us much because democratic governments can take many forms. Georgians elect a large number of public officials—in fact, Georgia has more elected public officials than any other state! While other states turn to different selection methods for many public offices (appointment by the governor, for example), Georgia's democracy is the most reliant on its population to decide who serves in government. This reliance on elections is curious given the fact that Georgia has one of the nation's lowest voter turnout rates.

Types of Statewide Elections

General Elections. All states have general elections, which typically get the most attention in the media. General elections involve party nominees running against each other to see who will win elected office (though there are usually methods for independent candidates running without the support of a party to qualify to appear on the general election ballot as well). Like most states, Georgia's statewide elections usually involve the nominees of the two major parties, the Democratic Party and the Republican Party, competing against one another to win more votes than their opponent. In most states, including Georgia, voters select party nominees from a group of potential candidates in a primary election. Some states also use party conventions to nominate candidates for certain offices.[1]

Primaries. Primary elections determine which candidates will represent political parties in the general election. States hold several different types of primaries. The two most common are labeled "closed" and "open." Twenty-eight states hold closed primaries, which require voters to register as a member of a particular party to participate in the party's primary election.

However, twenty-one states, including Georgia, hold open primaries, in which those who are eligible to vote in the general election may vote in either party's primary. In Georgia and ten other states, party primary voters simply tell workers at the polling place which party's ballot they wish to use in the primary election. The other nine states with open primaries permit voters to choose one party's ballot in secret.

Open primaries give voters the opportunity to decide which party's nomination contest they would like to cast a vote in. They also permit people to vote strategically. For instance, members of one party with few contested offices could vote in the opposite party's primary, casting votes for the weakest candidates in the other party's primary.[2] These "strategic voters" are not supporting their preferred candidates but rather are trying to get weak, beatable candidates nominated by the opposing party. There is nothing illegal about strategic voting, but some critics argue that open primary states like Georgia should change their election rules to prevent this sort of behavior.

Georgia holds two party primary elections in presidential election years, a March presidential preference primary and another primary in July to determine party candidates in elections for state and local offices.

Georgia's presidential primary in 2016 was on March 1, approximately midway through the primary season. On the Democratic ballot, Hillary Clinton defeated Bernie Sanders 71 percent to 28 percent. Five candidates appeared on the Republican ballot (though only four were still actively seeking the nomination by the time the Georgia primary took place: Donald Trump, Marco Rubio, Ted Cruz, and John Kasich). Donald Trump, the eventual nominee, won the state's Republican primary with 38.8 percent of the vote. Marco Rubio barely beat Ted Cruz for second place, 24.4 percent to 23.6 percent.

The outcome of each political party's presidential primary is used to select delegates to its national convention, where its presidential nominee is formally chosen. Georgia law allows each party's state executive committee to determine the method for selecting delegates, who are required to vote at the convention for the candidate whom they are pledged to support unless the candidate gets less than 35 percent of the delegate votes or releases delegates from their obligation. In any case, delegates are not legally bound beyond the second ballot for president in the event that a convention proves competitive.[3] The process of awarding delegates to the conventions begins well before the primary. The national party approves each state's methods for selecting delegates, although they generally are assigned in proportion to each candidate's share of the vote in the primary.

Runoffs. When discussing elections, we often say that the winner is the person who receives the majority of the votes. This is not always the case, however. In most states, the individual who receives the most votes in an election is declared the winner, even if that person receives less than a majority of the votes cast. For example, a three-person contest might result in Candidate A receiving 20 percent of the vote, Candidate B receiving 45 percent of the vote, and candidate C receiving 35 percent of the vote. Candidate B would be said to have won a plurality of the votes but not the majority of the votes (which would require more than 50 percent of the votes cast). In most states, Candidate B would be declared the winner of the election, having received the most votes.

Georgia's election rules, however, require that the winner of a primary or general election receive a majority of the vote in order to win elected office. It is one of eleven states that hold a second, "runoff," election if no single candidate is able to capture 50 percent of the vote. A runoff election requires that the two candidates receiving the most votes face off in a second election, the winner of which will win. Because only two candidates compete in a runoff, the winner of that election must receive the majority of the votes (the closest of elections between two candidates will always mathematically result in the winner having at least 50 percent + 1 of the electorate's votes).

The logic behind the runoff system is based, in part, on the assumption that elections should reflect the will of the majority of the electorate. In states where there is a tradition of one-party politics, candidates have faced their strongest opposition in the primaries. If only a plurality were required in such states, it would be possible to achieve elected office by finishing first in a primary with many candidates and receiving much less than 50 percent of the vote. The run-off was intended to prevent that occurrence. Not surprisingly, most of the states currently using runoffs are southern states with a history of one-party domination.[4]

The questions of whether the runoff is necessary or if it discriminates against female and minority candidates have been frequently debated. There have even been several legal challenges over the continued use of the runoff in southern states. Many argue that the 1964 Georgia version of the runoff was intended to dilute black voting strength and prevent black candidates who led in the primary from making it to the general election.[5] In primary runoffs for state and federal offices in the South between 1970 and 1986, there was virtually no difference in the success rate of the primary leader when the two candidates were of the same race. When the candidates were of the opposite race, however, black front-runners in the primary won the runoff only 50 percent of the time they faced a white opponent. In contrast, white leaders defeated black runners-up 90 percent of the time. Similar results exist in runoffs for county offices in Georgia from 1970 to 1984, where black front-runners defeated white opponents in runoffs 50 percent of the time, but white primary leaders beat black runners-up 84 percent of the time.[6]

Some critics of the runoff argue that the Solid South no longer exists and that primaries are no longer the determinant of who will hold office. Thus other arguments against the runoff note the cost and confusion surrounding so many elections, as well as the related concern that divisive primary and runoff campaigns may weaken a party's ultimate nominee in the general election.[7] Despite the criticism of primary runoffs, the U.S. Supreme Court permitted their continued use in 1999, when it refused to hear an appeal of a Georgia case.[8]

One study found that in the 215 runoffs held in Georgia between 1970 and 1986 for Congress, the legislature, and statewide offices, the leader in the primary won 69 percent of the time in the runoff. This success rate contradicts a popular impression that a weakened front-runner generally loses to a coalition of voters who backed other candidates in the primary. The record was worse, however, for the eighty-three incumbents in those 215 runoffs. Just 48 percent of the incumbents who led in the primary went on to win their runoffs; of those incumbents who finished second, only 20 percent were runoff victors. The same study reported that at the county level from 1970 to 1984, the primary leader won the runoff 71 percent of the time.[9] A more recent, national study found that even though front-runners in primary elections do end up losing their runoffs approximately one-third of the time, runoff election rules still do not change outcomes very often since the vast majority of primary election outcomes in runoff states produce winners with more than 50 percent of the vote.[10]

Referendum, Initiative, and Recall. States also conduct elections in which candidates are not running for office. The most common are referenda, in which legislative bodies place issues on the ballot for public approval. Critics often complain, though, that asking people simply to vote yes or no on a question is not a good way to decide complex policy issues. Georgia voters are accustomed to referenda on whether to amend the state constitution. In their communities, they are often asked to decide whether local governments should levy sales taxes or be permitted to go into debt to pay for public improvements such as roads and buildings.

In some states, citizens may place issues on the ballot through a petition process, without any required input from elected officials. Over 2,400 initiatives have been on statewide ballots since the first initiatives in Oregon in 1904, with 41 percent passing. Such citizen initiatives are now permitted in twenty-four states as a method to amend constitutions or adopt laws. Between 2000 and 2016, there were 592 statewide initiatives, 269 of which (45 percent) passed. As has been true historically, Oregon and California were the most active states.[11] Georgia's constitution does not permit initiatives, although the General Assembly studied the matter in 1995.[12]

In recent years, regulatory changes in many states have made it more difficult for citizens to put initiatives on the ballot. As a result, ballot measures are not nearly as common as they were as recently as the first decade of the twenty-first century. Only 35 measures appeared on statewide ballots in 2014, and even fewer (28) appeared in 2015.[13] There was an uptick in 2016, however, with 76 initiatives certified for the ballot across sixteen states. Voters were even busier in November of that year, with over 150 total ballot measures in thirty-five states.[14]

Recalls are special types of elections that remove public officials from office before their terms have expired. Recall of state officials is allowed in Georgia and eighteen other states; recall of local officeholders is more widely permitted.[15] Some states exempt certain officeholders, usually judges, from the recall process. In Georgia, all persons who occupy elected state or local offices, even if they were appointed to fill unfinished terms, are subject to removal by recall. Recall elections are placed on the ballot through a petition process.[16] For statewide office, petitions must include valid signatures totaling 15 percent of the number of citizens registered to vote at the last election that included the office in question; at least one-fifteenth must be obtained in each congressional district. Those wishing to circulate such petitions must first meet requirements to begin the process; they then have a limited time to complete the petitions once they are issued by election officials—ninety days for statewide office and thirty to forty-five days for lesser officials, depending on the number of signatures required. When enough signatures of eligible voters have been obtained, recalls are placed on a ballot, with voters simply choosing yes or no in deciding whether to remove the official. The public official has the right to challenge the recall, which is typically handled by a Georgia Superior Court judge. The judge reviews the petition to determine if legal grounds exist for the recall. Public officials can only be recalled if the officer has been found to engage in malfeasance, to violate the oath of his or her office, to engage in misconduct, to fail to perform his or her legally required duties, or to misappropriate funds or property. If a judge determines that grounds for a recall exist, the collection of signatures with the goal of holding a recall election can continue.

If an office becomes vacant through recall, a special election is held to fill the position. The special election can take the usual form of elections in Georgia: party primaries, possible runoff elections if candidates fail to win a majority in the primary, general election, possible runoff election when no nominee gets a majority of the vote in the general election. However, the governor can choose to hold one primary in which all candidates wishing to hold office, regardless of their party affiliation, run at once. If no candidate wins a majority in this "jungle primary," the top two candidates compete in a runoff election. This process is less expensive and less time consuming than the normal election process and is therefore commonly used in special elections to fill vacant elected offices.

Recall elections are rare in Georgia, and the process to implement one is very difficult to complete. In 2012 an attempt to recall Athens mayor Nancy Denson was unsuccessful when recall supporters were unable to collect even one hundred of the seventeen thousand signatures necessary to trigger a recall election.[17] Recall attempts were thrown out due to a lack of legal grounds in a 2014 attempt to recall a Warwick city councilman and in a 2012 attempt to recall the McIntosh County Commission chairwoman.[18]

Election Procedures

In addition to deciding the rules of an election system, states must make other important decisions such as voter eligibility standards, redistricting, timing, and election administration. These can have a substantial impact on elections. Much of American political history is a story of removing barriers to voting, and the same can be said of Georgia.

The Right to Vote. Changes in registration requirements may alter turnout or promote certain election outcomes. Historically, such laws included the poll tax, which required citizens to pay an annual levy to be eligible to vote, thereby making it harder for the poor to vote. Georgia had used a poll tax earlier in its history, but it became particularly restrictive when the 1877 constitution made it cumulative, which meant that anyone falling behind on his annual tax had to make back payments. The poll tax was not repealed until 1945, when Governor Ellis Arnall made it a major issue during the legislative session. In other southern states, it lasted until the 1960s.[19]

Throughout the South, the most infamous limits on voting were designed to restrict participation by blacks after Reconstruction. V. O. Key argued that during the 1870s, whites did not need "disfranchising measures" to gain power, which they had already gained through "force and threat of force."[20] Even though most blacks were Republicans, by 1890 competition among white Democratic factions for black votes led to efforts to thwart black voting.[21]

Perhaps the most blatant attempt to disenfranchise blacks was the white primary. Unlike general elections, which are processes of government, primaries could be regarded as activities of a political party, which is a "private" organization. Throughout the South, Democratic Party bodies adopted rules restricting primary voting to whites only. White primaries in Georgia had been adopted in some counties by the 1890s. The state Democratic Party began using primaries rather than conventions to select statewide nominees in 1898, and beginning in 1900 only whites could vote in the party's primary elections. Blacks could participate in the general election, but with almost no Republican candidates, their votes were inconsequential. A Texas law prohibiting blacks from voting in Democratic primaries was ruled unconstitutional in 1927, but southern Democratic parties continued applying their rules as "private" organizations to limit primary voting to whites, which the court held to be constitutional. Not until 1944 did the U.S. Supreme Court hold, in another case from Texas, that party rules enforcing a white primary also abridged the right to vote based on race.[22] Georgia's white primary was overturned in the federal courts soon thereafter in *King v. Chapman*. Perhaps the most immediate effect of this decision was in Atlanta, where the city's business and political leaders began developing a coalition with the black middle class.[23]

Three other important voting restrictions existed in Georgia's past, all of which were the core of Hoke Smith's campaign for governor in 1906. In office, he called for passage of the Disenfranchisement Act of 1908, establishing "literacy," "property," and "grandfather" requirements to vote. Later that year, voters approved an amendment to the Georgia Constitution by a two-to-one margin: "The literacy test required that voters be able to read and explain any paragraph of the federal or state constitution; while the property qualification required ownership of 40 acres of land or property assessed at $500. The grandfather clause enfranchised men who had served in the United States or Confederate military forces and their descendants; no one could register under that provision after 1914."[24] Implementation of the literacy test was in the hands of local election officials, who were given the power to purge voter registration rolls of those they judged to be unqualified.[25]

The last legal hurdles to enfranchising blacks were removed by the Voting Rights Act (VRA), which Congress passed in 1965 and has renewed several times since then. The law suspended use of literacy tests, allowed for federal election examiners and observers, and required affected state and local governments to receive approval from the federal government before making changes in their electoral systems. This "preclearance" process by the U.S. Department of Justice, or a federal court, was especially attentive to changes that might dilute the voting strength of minorities.

The effects of the VRA were not immediate. A 1966 Supreme Court decision turned back a challenge to the law's basic provisions by the state of South Carolina. Litigation over application of the law has been frequent, however. In Georgia, the estimated percentage of blacks registering to vote rose from 27 percent in March 1965, before passage of the VRA, to 53 percent in September 1967. During the same period, however, white registration rose from 63 to 80 percent. Many observers also credit the act with aiding the election of black officials. The number of blacks elected to state and local offices in Georgia rose from 21 in 1968 to 266 in 1981. By 2000, Georgia's number of black elected officials had grown to 582, the vast majority of which were city council and school board members, and over 30 percent of whom were female.[26]

Though the overall trend has been toward increased access to the election system, other changes have occurred that arguably could make it more difficult for some citizens to participate meaningfully in elections. In 2006, the state tightened its voter identification rules, requiring that voters present picture ID cards in order to be allowed to vote. In 2013, the Supreme Court rolled back the Voting Rights Act requirement that changes to voting laws and practices be precleared by the federal government, ruling that requiring states like Georgia to submit their election system changes to the review process was an undue burden and constitutionally impermissible.[27]

In other extensions of the franchise, Georgia became the first state to reject the Nineteenth Amendment to the U.S. Constitution in 1919. Its ratification by enough other states, however, meant that Georgia's white women voted for the first time in 1920. Georgia was more of a leader regarding age, however, as voters ratified a state constitutional amendment in 1943 that made Georgia the first state to grant the franchise to eighteen-year-olds.[28]

Redistricting. Prohibiting certain groups from voting is an obvious way to influence elections, but more subtle means of affecting election outcomes also exist. A method that has received much attention, particularly in Georgia, is redistricting. States redraw district boundaries for their legislatures and the U.S.

House of Representatives following each U.S. census. Every representative represents the residents of a geographic area within the state. Gerrymandering, or the practice of drawing districts in order to achieve political outcomes, is one method by which some candidates can be given a set of constituents that is more likely to vote for them. By carefully influencing the redistricting process to produce favorable districts, incumbents may protect their political careers, minority political parties may be prevented from gaining legislative seats, rural or urban districts may dominate, or the voting strength of minority groups may be diluted. Since the 1960s, several factors have influenced redistricting in Georgia, especially actions by the federal courts, implementation of the Voting Rights Act, and the rise of the Republican Party.

Although it did not originate in Georgia, the U.S. Supreme Court's 1962 decision in *Baker v. Carr* affected the state.[29] This landmark ruling and its progeny forced states to draw legislative districts on the basis of population rather than political boundaries such as county lines. The "one person, one vote" standard requires districts of equal population, although slight variation is tolerated. In Georgia, a string of federal court decisions eliminated the county-unit system, the rotation of state senate seats among the counties in a district, and rural over-representation in the General Assembly.[30] In addition to pressures regarding black representation, redistricting in Georgia has been complicated by a shift in party control of the legislature. When the Democratic-controlled General Assembly drew legislative and congressional districts, Republicans were highly critical of what they believed to be gerrymandering to ensure Democratic electoral victories. Since the Republicans have taken control of the General Assembly, district lines have been redrawn several times to undo the advantages to Democratic candidates and to appease the U.S. Department of Justice.

Redistricting is a difficult and politically entangling process. Interest groups such as the ACLU and the NAACP are often actively involved, and politicians concerned for their careers are often not pleased by the results. Party competition and local elites complicate the process. Legislatures today are assisted in the redistricting process by computers and map-writing software. While these technical advancements may make some aspects of the job easier, they certainly do not make it less controversial.

The General Assembly faced a particularly difficult task of redistricting after the 2000 census. Blacks and Republicans felt they had much to gain in the redistricting process, which covered the U.S. House, as well as the General Assembly's 180 house and 56 senate seats. Due to population growth, Georgia's number of U.S. representatives grew from 11 to 13, and its electoral vote thus went from 13 to 15. Some of the districts drawn were oddly shaped, while others generally followed boundaries of counties or other jurisdictions. Republicans, who obtained the majority in the General Assembly after the first round of redistricting, wanted to change the boundaries again. The controversy grew complicated, and district lines for congressional and state legislative seats changed in every election from 2002 to 2006. The controversy spilled over to include a challenge of authority between the state attorney general, a Democrat, and Governor Sonny Perdue, a Republican. The attorney general argued that he had state constitutional authority to challenge district lines in federal court, while the governor argued that he should make the decision about when the state would bring issues to the federal courts. Eventually Thurbert Baker, the attorney general, won the argument, but the courts also ruled that the lines drawn by the Republican-dominated General Assembly would be allowed to stand.[31]

Georgia has also had an unusual history with the use of multimember districts (where more than one representative was elected). Because multimember districts are generally more expensive for campaigns, they tend to favor candidates who are incumbents or who have strong financial backing. When multimember districts were eliminated, it was considered a benefit to minority candidates. Between 1971 and 1981, blacks had already increased their seats in the Georgia House from thirteen to twenty-one through the elimination of some multimember districts.[32] The shift of the state's electorate prompted Democrats to reintroduce multimember districts. This time, many districts in suburban areas were drawn to be represented by multiple representatives, who ran for specific, numbered seats within each district. This would require candidates to campaign across a wider area than candidates running in single-member districts, thereby increasing the costs of campaigning. The multimember districts were short lived, however, and by 2004, the General Assembly no longer included multimember district representatives.[33]

Following the 2000 census, Georgia maps were reviewed by the U.S. Justice Department and contested in federal courts before the districts were approved. In 2004, after partisan control of the General Assembly shifted to Republicans, and the governor and the attorney general entered the fray, a panel of federal judges drew the districts that the state legislators could not. As the 2006 General Assembly elections approached, district lines for the General Assembly changed—midway through the decade—in part for political gains. Multiple changes in district lines after a census is likely to confuse voters, but the state has to adjust to shifting standards of compliance with the Justice Department and federal courts, not to mention political parties, interest groups, and incumbents seeking political advantages.[34]

The 2010 redistricting cycle began with the Republican majority changing the procedures used to redraw the state's congressional, state house, and state senate districts. Rather than rely on technical experts at the University of Georgia, the legislature set up its own office to handle the technicalities of map creation and demographic analysis. The Redistricting Committee's proposal was approved by the state legislature in a special session and signed into law by Governor Nathan Deal. The redistricting plan was then precleared, with a few minor revisions, by the U.S. District Court.

Timing. Length of terms and the related scheduling of elections can also have important consequences. This impact is most apparent in comparing turnout in presidential and congressional races. Nationally, turnout in presidential elections has hovered around 50 to 55 percent of the voting-age population since 1968.[35] In contrast, turnout in off-year congressional elections has been less than 40 percent since 1974.[36] In 2014, it was 36.3 percent.[37]

The Georgia Constitution requires that members of the General Assembly be elected for two-year terms in even-numbered years. The governor and other statewide officeholders have four-year terms and are elected in even-numbered years between presidential elections. Although Georgia's governor has been elected for a four-year term ending in the "off year" since 1942, this practice has become the norm nationally since the 1960s as state political parties have tried—apparently with success—to protect gubernatorial nominees from association with unpopular presidential candidates.[38]

Municipal elections in Georgia are not held at the same time as major state and national races, which affects their outcomes. With a handful of exceptions, they also are nonpartisan. With no party identification of candidates on the ballot, voters must rely on other cues, such as name recognition. Many people argue that nonpartisan elections discourage participation, especially when they are not held with elections for higher offices, and favor candidates who are more organized or spend more to advertise during the campaign.[39]

Election Administration. The U.S. Constitution leaves administration of elections in the hands of the states, which has produced interesting differences in voter registration, voter information and outreach efforts, and rules for polling places and absentee ballots.[40]

The requirements for registering can limit participation in elections. During the struggles for black franchise, states required voters to register months ahead of scheduled elections. However, starting in the early 1970s registration deadlines began to ease. The earliest deadline now is thirty-one days before a general election. Georgia requires registration twenty-eight days in advance of the election; Colorado, Idaho, Iowa, Maine, Minnesota, Montana, New Hampshire, Wisconsin, and Wyoming even permit voters to register on Election Day; and North Dakota does not require registration.[41] Some states removed voters from the registration list for failure to vote for a specified number of years, but this practice was outlawed by Congress in 1993. Even though later deadlines may facilitate registration, the locations and times for registering may deter would-be voters. Information campaigns using the media, direct mail, and toll-free phone numbers also may increase voter registration and turnout. The same is true of registration drives targeted to specific groups such as students and outreach efforts such as multiple registration sites, candidate forums, and distribution of sample ballots.[42]

Debates over voter registration intensified during 2005–2006, when the General Assembly changed the procedures regarding the types of identification that would be accepted at polling places. Arguments focus on whether the law targets certain groups and the impact the procedures might have on voter fraud. Two voter ID laws were overturned in federal court for being too restrictive.[43] Currently, Georgia voters must show one of six acceptable forms of identification; acceptable ID cards include a Georgia driver's license (including an expired license), any federal or state photo ID, a U.S. or Georgia government-issued photo ID, a valid U.S. passport, a valid military photo ID, or a valid tribal photo ID. If a Georgia resident does not have one of these photo IDs, that person can acquire a free Voter Identification Card at his or her local county registrar's office or Department of Driver Services office.[44]

Rules governing polling places and absentee ballots can affect election results—not to mention stir up controversy. Whenever ballots are improperly marked, such as when a voter selects more than one candidate or votes both a straight party ticket and for a candidate of the opposing party for a specific office, ballots are declared void. Georgia became the first state to adopt electronic ballots statewide, eliminating many of these voting errors. In the 2000 presidential election, only some of the counties had adopted electronic voting procedures, but by 2004 all counties were using this technology. Comparing voting accuracy in the two elections reveals that voting errors due to "undervoting" (failing to vote in the presidential race) or "overvoting" (voting for more than one candidate in a single race) were drastically reduced. Undervoting rates, for example, went from 3.5 percent in 2000 to 0.39 percent in 2004.[45] However, new voting technologies have not convinced some election observers that the machines are foolproof, and some citizens express concern over the lack of paper ballots to back up electronic voting data. Despite the concerns of these citizens, polls show that most Georgians have been pleased with the new voting technologies.[46]

Changes in Georgia's absentee balloting have also generated controversy. With anyone allowed to vote by absentee ballot without having to state a reason, critics argue that this flexibility has led to voting fraud, particularly with elderly voters and the dead, and in some rural counties. Early or advance voting is a relatively recent change in the voting process in Georgia. Early voting is strictly for the convenience of voters, and no reason is required for advance voting in the state. Polls remain open at centralized county locations beginning on the fourth Monday before the election until the Friday before Election Day. Early voting has grown in popularity. In the November 2004 election, over 422,000 voters cast ballots before Election Day (13 percent). By the November 2012 election, that number had grown to over 1.9 million early votes (49 percent).[47]

Turnout in Georgia Elections

For most of the past century, Georgia's voter turnout was extremely low. Between 1920 and 1946, less than 20 percent of voting-age adults (less than 30 percent of voting-age whites) voted in Georgia's Democratic primaries for governor and U.S. senator. Turnout was not much different in presidential elections—which is not surprising given the Democratic lock on the South's electoral votes during the period. Several factors account for this pattern. Poll taxes and literacy tests were barriers to voting by blacks and poor whites. Few candidates ran as Republicans, given the party's association with the North and Reconstruction. The real political contests were in Democratic primaries, in which only whites were permitted to vote until the mid-1940s. Within this context, incumbents held office for long periods of time, and voters were apathetic.[48] Many of these conditions have changed in recent years, but the state continues to be dominated by one political party and to have relatively low rates of voter turnout.

General Elections

Voting changed with the rise of partisan competition and the civil rights movement. Turnout in presidential elections in the South through 1948 hovered between 20 and 25 percent of the voting-age population—roughly the same rate as in Democratic primaries for governor and five to ten points above turnout in gubernatorial general elections. Turnout in presidential and other elections rose sharply beginning in 1952, and by the mid-1960s gubernatorial contests had also changed in the South, with general election turnout exceeding that for the Democratic primary.[49] In Georgia, 62 percent of those registered voted in the 1962 gubernatorial primary, but only 23 percent of registered voters cast ballots in the general election. The pattern reversed in 1966, when 45 percent of those registered voted in the primary and 54 percent voted in the general election.

Obviously, turnout is affected by the prestige of the offices on the ballot. Georgia has traditionally been one of the states with the lowest turnout, although the state began to look more like the nation during this century. Figure 4.1 compares turnout in Georgia to the United States as a whole. These data are from the United States Elections Project and cover turnout for the highest office on the ballot among voting-eligible adults, which is the voting-age population minus those not eligible to vote plus eligible voters living overseas.[50]

Between 1960 and 2004, Georgia ranked among the bottom five states in turnout of eligible voters in every presidential election. Even the placement of Georgian Jimmy Carter on the ballot in 1976 and in 1980 did not raise voters' interest enough to bring large numbers to Georgia's polling places, and Georgia placed forty-ninth in turnout in both those elections. By 1992, turnout in Georgia rose to 49 percent, which still left the state far below a nationwide rate of 58 percent. In 2004, turnout in Georgia exceeded 50 percent for the first time and lagged the United States by just under 4 percent. Beginning in 2008, though, turnout in Georgia edged ahead of the national level.

Georgia's turnout in off-year elections is also rather anemic, generally in the range of 30–35 percent and again among the lowest states. Off-year turnout grew closer to 40 percent beginning in 2010 and exceeded national turnout in 2014. One factor affecting turnout may be Georgia's historic lack of party competition up and down the ballot. Between 1982 and 1986, only two states had less competitive races for their legislatures. Modern Georgia has been a virtual lock for the Republican Party at all levels of elected office, though some argue that demographic changes might make the state competitive again between the two parties.

Turnout also varies among groups within the population. The Georgia secretary of state collects registration and turnout data by race/ethnicity and gender. The coalitions that support the Democrats and the Republicans tend to differ, and modern campaigns often target different campaign messages to specific groups, for example, Latinos or suburban women. Figure 4.2 tracks turnout by racial or ethnic group in Georgia from 1996 through 2016. Note that these turnout rates include only registered voters and are therefore higher than in figure 4.1, which is based on the larger number of people who could register, whether they voted or not. Also, data on Asians and Hispanics were not collected separately until 2004.

The most obvious pattern in the figure is the drop in turnout in the off-year elections, when the presidency is not on the ballot. In addition, turnout for whites is uniformly higher than for other groups. That gap is larger when compared to Asians and Hispanics than it is relative to African Americans. However, the black-white gap was narrowest in 2008 and 2012, when President Obama was on the ballot. White—and Hispanic—turnout also surged to record highs during this twenty-year period in 2016.

The secretary of state's data also tally registered voters by gender; thus table 4.1 provides more detail than figure 4.2 for recent elections. The table includes the 2012 and 2016 presidential elections, along with the 2014 midterm election, when the governorship and other statewide offices, the entire legislature, and a U.S. Senate seat were on the ballot.

Figure 4.1. Voter Turnout in Georgia and the United States, 1980–2016

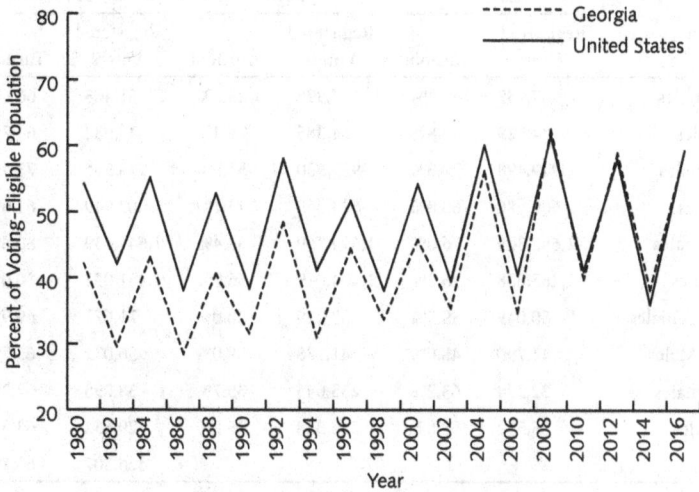

Source: State and national turnout of voting-eligible population from Professor Michael McDonald's United States Elections Project, http://www.electproject.org/home /voter-turnout/voter-turnout-data.

Figure 4.2. Georgia Voter Turnout by Race/Ethnicity, 1996–2016

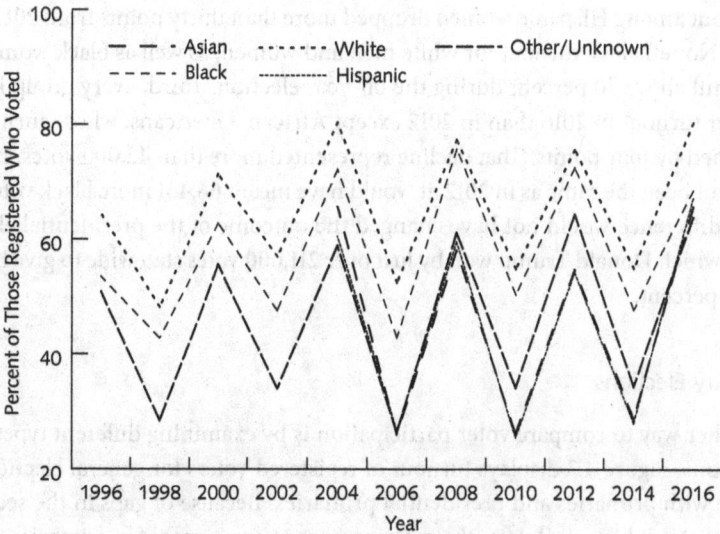

Source: Georgia Secretary of State, "Voter Turnout by Demographics," http://sos.ga.gov/index .php/Elections/voter_turn_out_by_demographics.

Table 4.1. Georgia General Election Turnout of Registered Voters by Race and Gender

Population Group	2012 Registered Voters	Turnout	2014 Registered Voters	Turnout	2016 Registered Voters	Turnout
Asian Females	37,957	55.8%	37,996	28.2%	51,463	66.6%
Asian Males	34,523	48.8%	34,385	29.4%	45,982	64.7%
Black Females	949,498	77.3%	929,530	51.0%	978,555	73.4%
Black Males	660,486	65.8%	624,269	43.1%	662,949	61.6%
White Females	1,685,309	76.0%	1,594,769	53.4%	1,642,639	80.8%
White Males	1,485,658	75.3%	1,404,019	56.7%	1,451,033	80.0%
Hispanic Females	50,049	59.5%	52,229	28.0%	71,675	69.9%
Hispanic Males	41,790	48.0%	41,788	28.0%	56,071	63.7%
Other Females	32,274	63.2%	235,045	35.7%	38,295	67.2%
Other Males	25,552	58.8%	216,358	36.8%	29,652	63.5%
Unknown					426,307	63.7%
Total	5,003,096	73.8%	5,170,388	50.2%	5,453,347	74.8%

Source: Georgia Secretary of State, "Voter Turnout by Demographics," http://sos.ga.gov/index.php/
Elections/voter_turn_out_by_demographics.

Several points in the table are worth highlighting. First is the overall gap of more than twenty points between the 2014 off-year election and the presidential years before and after it. Second, the gaps are not the same across groups. Turnout among Hispanic women dropped more than thirty points from 2012 to 2014. Nonetheless, turnout for white men and women, as well as black women, was still above 50 percent during the off-year election. Third, every group had higher turnout in 2016 than in 2012 except African Americans, whose turnout declined by four points. That decline represented more than 42,000 votes. Had turnout been the same as in 2012, it would have meant 66,461 more black voters. That difference would not have changed the outcome of the presidential election, which Donald Trump won by just over 211,000 votes statewide to give him 51.05 percent.

Primary Elections

Another way to compare voter participation is by examining different types of elections. Figure 4.3 displays turnout of registered voters for general elections, along with primaries and presidential primaries. Because of gaps in the secretary of state's historical data, there are no bars in some years for primaries and presidential primaries. Georgia has jockeyed for a nationally significant date for

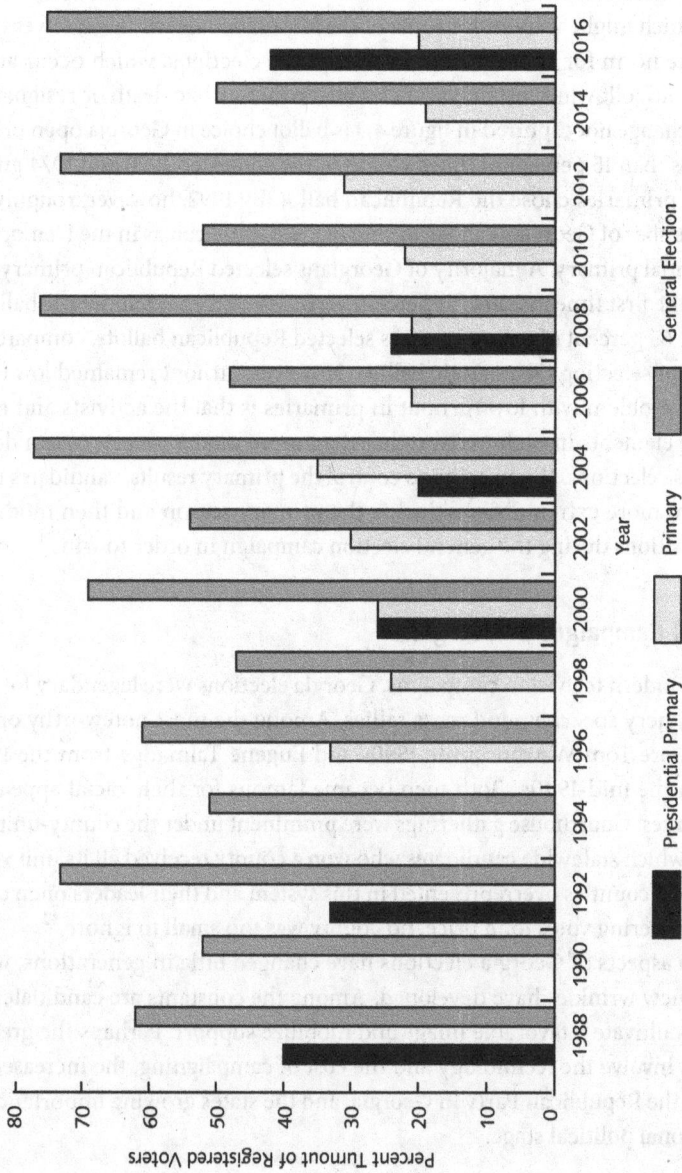

Figure 4.3. Turnout in Primary, Presidential Primary, and General Elections, 1988–2016

Sources: Georgia Secretary of State, "Voter Turnout by Demographics," http://sos.ga.gov/index.php/Elections/voter_turn_out_by_demographics; "Voter Registration Statistics," http://sos.ga.gov/index.php/Elections/voter_registration_statistics; and "Current and Past Election Results," http://sos.ga.gov/index.php/Elections/current_and_past_elections_results.

its presidential primary, and it has generally been in the second wave of major states, including others in the South. The Republican and Democratic primaries for state and local offices have been in the middle of the summer (July or August), which might account for some of the low turnout levels. Even lower turnout is the norm for runoff elections and special elections, which occur at unusual times following certain vacancies due to factors like death or resignation.

One change not captured in figure 4.3 is ballot choice in Georgia open primaries. Less than 15 percent of those voting in the contested 1970 and 1974 gubernatorial primaries chose the Republican ballot. By 1992, however, roughly the same number of Georgians chose to vote in the Republican as in the Democratic presidential primary. A majority of Georgians selected Republican primary ballots for the first time in 2004 (51 percent versus 49 percent Democratic ballots). By 2016, 65 percent of primary voters selected Republican ballots, compared to 35 percent selecting Democratic ballots. However, turnout remained low overall. One problem with low turnout in primaries is that the activists and more extreme elements in each party, rather than more moderate voters, can dominate these elections. When activists control the primary results, candidates must appeal to more extreme views during the primary season and then moderate their positions during the general election campaign in order to win.[51]

Political Campaigns in Georgia

Before modern television campaigns, Georgia elections were legendary for corruption, fiery speeches, and mass rallies. Among the most noteworthy on the stump were Tom Watson in the 1890s and Eugene Talmadge from the 1920s through the mid-1940s. Both men became famous for their racial appeals to rural whites. Courthouse gatherings were prominent under the county-unit system, in which statewide candidates who won a county received all its unit votes. With rural counties overrepresented in this system and their leaders often capable of delivering votes for a price, no county was too small to ignore.[52]

Some aspects of Georgia elections have changed little in generations, while several new wrinkles have developed. Among the constants are candidates' efforts to cultivate a favorable image and mobilize support. Perhaps the greatest changes involve the technology and the cost of campaigning, the increased vitality of the Republican Party in Georgia, and the state's growing importance on the national political stage.

Campaign Costs

Running a statewide campaign is expensive. This is true nationally, not just in Georgia. One analysis estimated that the average gubernatorial campaign between the 1970s and early 1990s cost $8.6 million per state, or $3.87 per registered voter (adjusted for inflation to 1993 dollars). Georgia ranked nineteenth during that period, with an average cost per campaign of $7.7 million. That translates to $2.42 per registered voter, which was below the figure for thirty-three other states. Cost for gubernatorial elections spiked sharply beginning in 1999, and overall costs have jumped 119 percent since 1977.[53] In his 2002 unsuccessful bid for reelection, Roy Barnes raised a record $20 million. His opponent, Sonny Perdue, raised and spent under $5 million. Given that slightly over two million votes were cast in that election, the estimated cost per vote had risen to $12.28.[54] Even in 2004, without a governor's race at the top of the ticket, candidates for statewide, state legislative, and state judicial races raised an average of $11.46 per vote cast.[55] In that year, candidates who planned to run in 2006 for governor collected more than $5 million, and Governor Perdue raised another $10.4 million during 2005 for his reelection.[56] The cost of running for office has remained high in Georgia; in 2014 Republican governor Nathan Deal raised $14.7 million in his race against Democrat Jason Carter, who collected $7.7 million.[57]

In most cases, funds come from large corporate and individual contributors or from large corporations through political parties. Corporations often create political action committees (PACs) to contribute to candidates. PACs may also be created by candidates to raise and spend money on their behalf. PACs are especially important in campaigns for federal offices because corporations and unions cannot give directly to candidates. Instead, a PAC solicits donations from an organization's members. In state and local races, however, Georgia law permits corporations and unions to donate their own funds directly to candidates. As explained in chapter 6, the 1992 General Assembly tightened regulation of campaign contributions, stipulating that legislators cannot receive contributions directly while the legislature is in session and commissioners cannot receive money from utilities and organizations that they regulate. This was affirmed and extended by the Georgia Government Transparency and Campaign Finance Act of 2010.[58]

Campaign contribution limits for candidates for statewide office are set at $6,600 for each primary and general election. A $3,900 limit is set for runoffs following primaries and/or general elections. Candidates for the Georgia General Assembly and other offices that do not have statewide constituencies are limited to $2,600 for primary and general elections and $1,400 for runoffs from any single donor.[59] Contributors are also restricted to $2,500 on a statewide referendum such as a constitutional amendment. These regulations do not inhibit lobbyists and legislators. For example, although lobbyists may not provide money for campaigns during the legislative session, they may entertain legislators during that period.

Though Georgia has fairly restrictive legal limits on political donations from individuals, loopholes in the contribution limits exist. Children and spouses of donors may also contribute. Friends and family members can coordinate their contributions. In many instances, several checks for the maximum contribution arrive in one envelope, a process often referred to as "bundling." According to some political analysts, this practice has the effect of a single contribution.[60] Moreover, there are no limits on contributions to political parties.[61] Candidates may also use their personal funds to finance their own campaigns.

Candidates can accrue campaign donations for future elections, and many collect relatively large sums even when they are running unopposed. A large accumulation of campaign contributions, often called an official's "war chest," may discourage future opponents or prepare an incumbent for future campaigns for higher office. Candidates can also contribute campaign funds to other candidates in their party. Some observers may criticize such practices, but candidate-to-candidate giving has a long history in the state and is within legal mandates.[62]

Campaign contributions often flow to those most in power. For many years, Republican candidates faced an uphill battle to raise campaign funds, since donors were more likely to contribute to the Democratic governors, Democratic committee chairs, and party leaders who could help them gain access to the policy makers with the most influence over legislation, implementation, and oversight. By 2004, however, Republicans were in the governor's office and in control of the legislature, so their candidates for the General Assembly were able to outpace their Democratic opponents for the first time. Since then, the Republican fund-raising advantage has been sustained, and Democratic candidates have had a hard time keeping up with Republican fund-raising.

The 2008 and 2012 Presidential Elections in Georgia

Georgia's Electoral College votes have been reliably cast for Republican presidential candidates for over twenty years. In 2008 Democratic candidate Barack Obama's campaign did target early resources at Georgia, thinking that they might be able to swing the state into the Democratic column. However, those early efforts were not sustained, and both presidential candidates focused their campaign resources on swing states like Ohio, Florida, and Pennsylvania. That year Senator John McCain won Georgia's fifteen Electoral College votes, 52.1 percent to 46.9 percent, over Senator Barack Obama. Interestingly, two Georgians ran for the presidency that year as minor party candidates: former U.S. representative Bob Barr received 0.73 percent of the Georgia vote as the Libertarian Party's presidential candidate, and Cynthia McKinney won 0.01 percent of the Georgia vote as the Green Party candidate.

Georgia's 2008 election results were typical for a presidential election: Senator Obama's support was concentrated in the Atlanta metropolitan area (notably heavily populated Fulton and DeKalb Counties) and many of the central Georgia counties with high numbers of African American voters. Senator McCain won the more rural areas of the state and the more populated Cobb and Gwinnett Counties in Atlanta's suburbs. That recipe led, once again, to a Republican victory in the state.

In 2012, President Barack Obama won reelection but was still unable to win over a majority of Georgia's voters, who supported his opponent, Governor Mitt Romney, who won the state 53.3 percent to 45.5 percent (a slightly more Republican result than four years earlier). Georgia's voting patterns remained markedly similar to the 2008 results. In fact, only two counties flipped party majorities. Early County, previously a McCain-supporting county in the southwest part of the state, cast a majority of votes for the Democrat, President Obama, in 2012, and Chattahoochee County, in central Georgia near Columbus, supported the Republican, Governor Romney, after having backed Obama in 2008. Again, very little effort was spent by either campaign in the state, as both campaigns knew that Georgia's sixteen Electoral College votes (which had increased from fifteen after the 2010 congressional reapportionment process gave Georgia an additional member of the U.S. House of Representatives) could be counted on to support the Republican candidate.

Recent Gubernatorial Campaigns

The two terms in the governor's office served by Sonny Perdue (2003–2011) and Nathan Deal's election to a second term in 2014 reflect the story of the decline of the Democratic Party and the rise of the Republican Party in the state. Both governors began their political careers as Georgia Democrats as state senators, and Deal moved on to the U.S. House of Representatives as a Democratic congressman. Deal switched to the Republican Party in 1995, and state senator Purdue switched in 1998; both won reelection to their seats as Republicans after switching parties.

In the 2002 gubernatorial election, state senator Sonny Perdue defeated incumbent governor Roy Barnes 51 percent to 46 percent (Libertarian candidate Garrett Michael Hayes won a little over 2 percent of the vote) and became the first Republican governor of Georgia since Reconstruction. He handily defeated his Democratic opponent, former lieutenant governor Mark Taylor, 58 percent to 38 percent in 2006 (the Libertarian candidate won almost 4 percent of the statewide vote). This victory solidified the idea that the state had transitioned from Democratic stronghold, to a brief time as a competitive state, to a reliably Republican state.

U.S. congressman Nathan Deal faced former governor Roy Barnes in his 2010 bid to succeed Sonny Perdue, but as was true in the past when Georgia was a solidly Democratic state, the most competitive part of the 2010 gubernatorial election was the party primary. Deal faced six other candidates running for the Republican nomination, and he finished second to Secretary of State Karen Handel, winning 23 percent of the vote to Handel's 34 percent. Georgia law calls for a runoff election if no candidates wins a majority of the vote, so Handel and Deal faced each other in a second primary election to determine the Republican nominee. Deal defeated Handel in a remarkably close election: 50.2 percent to 49.8 percent. The general election was anticlimactic, with Deal defeating Barnes by 10 percentage points (53–43 percent). Deal won reelection in 2014, winning 53 percent of the vote to Democratic state senator Jason Carter's 45 percent.

The 2016 Elections

In 2008 and 2012, while Barack Obama won the presidency by relatively large margins, the Republican presidential candidate easily won the state. John McCain in 2008 won 52.2 percent of the vote in Georgia, while Barack Obama won 47 percent, which represents the highest percentage of any Democrat running statewide since 1980 (see chapter 5, table 5.1). In 2012, Mitt Romney won 53.3 percent in Georgia, as compared to Obama's 45.5 percent. Donald Trump, the Republican candidate, won the 2016 election in Georgia by a similar, if smaller, margin: 51.05 percent of the vote versus 45.9 percent for Hillary Rodham Clinton and 3.06 percent for Gary Johnson, the Libertarian candidate. Trump garnered 211,000 more votes statewide than Clinton.

Trump's 51 percent was the lowest for a Republican candidate running for president, U.S. Senate, or governor this century. Even more interesting, Clinton won some formerly Republican counties surrounding Atlanta. Cobb County and Gwinnett County have been dominated by Republicans and continue to be so at the local level, with Republicans occupying most of the county commissioner seats. In the 2016 presidential election, both counties voted for Clinton, solidifying the turn toward Democratic control of Atlanta suburbs. Clinton also won urban centers such as Augusta, Columbus, Macon, and Savannah. Trump, as he did nationwide, dominated rural areas and won most of Georgia's counties, even if many of those counties are sparsely populated. In fact, Clinton performed better in Georgia than she did in Ohio, a state where both candidates campaigned very heavily. Georgia did not see much of a national effort by either party.

Republicans dominated the Senate and most of the local races, with most Republicans outpacing Trump in percentage and raw vote totals. The only other statewide race on the ballot was the U.S. Senate seat, which pitted the incum-

bent Johnny Isakson against Democrat newcomer Jim Barksdale. Isakson easily won reelection with 55 percent of the vote as compared to Barksdale's 40.8
percent. Democrats did pick up one seat in the state House of Representatives.

With this smaller presidential margin and the potential for a Democratic
takeover of Atlanta and suburban Atlanta, it does appear that the state is trend-
ing "purplish." However, whether this shift will happen by the next midterm
election in 2018, the next presidential election in 2020, or beyond is unknown
at this point.

CHAPTER 5

Political Parties and Interest Groups

Most Americans assume that political parties and organized interest groups have always been an integral part of the political system. Both institutions aggregate public preferences and assert those preferences during the policy-making process. It is important to remember, however, that both have been viewed with suspicion by those concerned about effective democratic government. The earliest and most vocal critics of parties and interest groups included the drafters of the U.S. Constitution, who designed the American political system to control what James Madison labeled "the mischiefs of faction." Madison worried about the many factors that "divided mankind into parties, inflamed them with mutual animosity, and rendered them much more disposed to vex and oppress each other than to cooperate for their common good."[1] America's founders imagined a political system that fostered cooperation more than conflict, and those founders saw parties and interest groups as forces that would divide, as opposed to unify, democratic citizens. Nonetheless, political parties developed during George Washington's tenure as the nation's first president, and interest groups have been with us virtually as long.

Political parties and interest groups are formal organizations that connect citizens with public officials. Thus, they are often labeled "linkage" institutions and are treated as fundamental components of any understanding of American democracy. Georgia's parties and interest groups are a product of the state's environment and are similarly essential to understanding how democracy has functioned and developed in the state.

Political Parties in the United States

The Many Meanings of "Political Party"

Political parties can generally be thought of as coalitions that aim to win elections and control government. The goal of winning elections has led parties to perform a wide range of functions: recruiting and supporting candidates, propagandizing, mobilizing voters, providing citizen access to government officials and processes, and forging coalitions on issues. Parties may also exercise power after elections by pressuring officials to maintain the party position on issues, influencing executives and legislatures to place loyal party members in positions of power, and threatening to withhold support in coming campaigns.

Political parties operate at three levels: as formal organizations, in government, and among the electorate.[2] In the United States, these three components operate relatively independently from one another. As formal organizations, the national and state parties exist as both permanent and temporary entities. The permanent apparatus includes party officials, committees, and workers. The two major national parties, as well as most of their counterparts at the state level, have headquarters, budgets, and paid staff that function on a permanent basis, not just during campaigns. The temporary features include caucuses, primaries, and conventions used during election years to choose candidates and party leaders, develop platforms, and establish rules to govern the party.

The party in government consists of candidates and officeholders using a given party label. In the United States, unlike in many democracies, it is almost impossible to force such leaders to adhere to party positions on issues. This is the case because candidates pick the party label they use, although at one time in American history party leaders chose candidates. Moreover, candidates now cultivate their own loyal followers, build their own campaign organizations, and raise the funds for their election contests. Nevertheless, party affiliation remains quite important when elected executives appoint officials to important government jobs and legislatures choose presiding officers and committees.

The party identification in the voting electorate is a somewhat elusive concept since few requirements exist for calling oneself a member of a political party in the United States. Although some states require citizens to identify their party or call themselves "independent" when registering to vote, what is known about the composition of American parties is based on public opinion surveys that ask people to name the party (if any) with which they identify. Most surveys also try to determine how strong or weak a person's ties are to a given party. The detail and history of such surveys have allowed scholars to examine how Americans' identification with the two major parties is related to other conditions, including a president's popularity and the performance of the economy. The bottom line remains, however, that party identification in the United States is simply a person's feeling of loyalty.

Dynamics of the American Party System

Americans may take for granted or criticize the options offered them by the current two-party system, yet political parties in the United States have displayed historical and geographical variation.[3] A number of political parties arose and disappeared by 1860, but the major issues that divided them were fairly constant and quite volatile: the power of the national government versus the states, economic interests, and slavery. Even though the Democrats and the Republicans emerged from the Civil War as the nation's dominant parties, they have experienced challenges from a variety of minor parties that formed because of ideology, issues, or support for individual leaders. These include the Populists in the 1890s, Theodore Roosevelt's "Bull Moose" candidacy in 1912, and segregationist challenges to Democratic presidential candidates in the South in 1948 and 1968. Minor parties are on the ballot in most states today. In Georgia, the Libertarian Party places candidates for statewide offices on most ballots. Although their share of the vote in most elections seldom exceeds 5 percent, they can drain off enough support from Democratic or Republican candidates to affect the outcomes of elections.[4]

In addition to external challenges, the Democrats and the Republicans have had to cope with shifts in their core groups of supporters.[5] For instance, blacks have moved overwhelmingly to the Democratic Party, which has also developed strong support among women and Jews. Republicans, on the other hand, have gained support over the past thirty years among white southerners and white ethnics in northern urban areas, both of whom were key members of the Democratic coalition that began with Franklin Roosevelt's New Deal of the 1930s. Today the Democratic Party's membership has become more associated with liberal ideology, while ideological conservatives have become an increasingly large majority of the Republican Party. Many of these shifts have been associated with controversial issues such as the Vietnam War, civil rights, government taxing and spending, and abortion.

Perhaps the most enduring characteristic of American parties has been their lack of centralized control, which is quite different from their counterparts in Europe. This decentralization has been especially true since the 1830s, when the selection of presidential candidates by party members in Congress was replaced with conventions of delegates chosen at the state and local levels. A generation ago, V. O. Key emphasized the decentralized nature of American political parties, particularly their lack of tight organization at the national level and the great differences among them from state to state.[6] Today, while national parties may be thought of as collections of state parties, they are also important players in financing campaigns, recruiting congressional candidates, polling and other research, and training political operatives.

The states of the former Confederacy have occupied an important position within the decentralized party system. The region's unusual features include a long period of domination by the Democratic Party and the resultant differences with the remainder of the nation, southern support for Republican presidential candidates beginning after World War II, growing competition between the two major parties at the state and local levels, and the dramatic shifting of support from the Democratic to the Republican Party in recent years. Georgia has not been immune from these developments, which have had profound effects on the state's politics.

Partisan Change in Georgia

Georgia has a long history as a Democratic stronghold, but changes in elections beginning in the 1980s have clearly shown that the state is no longer bound by this tradition. Trends include changes in the composition of the parties, stronger support for Republican presidential candidates, and dramatic Republican gains in local and state elections.

The Solid South and Democratic Factionalism

The idiosyncrasies of southern politics have long been the subject of research and popular discussion. V. O. Key's 1949 classic, *Southern Politics*, argues that the region's politics were hampered by the electorate's noninvolvement, the problems of a largely agrarian society within the world's major industrial nation, and the nagging burdens of racial strife and political corruption. It is ironic that in more recent times the Democratic Party has come to represent support for civil rights—the issue that traditionally was the foundation for Democratic rule in the South based on maintaining segregation.

Prior to the Civil War, the Whig Party represented the views of states' rights advocates, and the Republican Party was more closely allied with a strong unionist ideology. After the Civil War, the Republican Party forced its will on the people of the vanquished Confederacy. To Georgians and other white southerners, Republicans were associated with the "carpetbagging Yankees," who profited from southern misfortunes in the Reconstruction years. Newly enfranchised blacks were more likely to ally themselves with the Republican Party in the post–Civil War South, while white voters were strongly held within the ranks of the Democratic Party by antiblack rhetoric. White supremacy and African American disenfranchisement were essential to Democratic dominance.

Those who attempted to tie the races together based on shared issues, as the Populists tried with farming interests, found that fear of black empowerment was stronger than any other bond that might sway whites.[7]

Key noted that the lack of party competition within the South produced politics that were essentially party-free. Since all candidates were Democrats, the real contests developed in the Democratic primary, not the general election. This is not to say that differences did not exist among candidates, but factions formed within the Democratic Party, and personal loyalties to individuals became of paramount importance. This arrangement produced some rather flamboyant political personalities, notably the Longs of Louisiana, George Wallace in Alabama, and the Talmadges of Georgia.

The historical lack of party competition in Georgia was associated with strong factions within the Democratic Party. Following Reconstruction, a faction known as the Bourbons held power within the party based on white supremacy, local self-governance, and resistance to national policies. Stability was more the goal than was sound government. Thus, the Bourbons provided little in the way of policy but were able to hold office under leaders such as Governor Alfred Colquitt. Other Bourbons fared well with political rhetoric emphasizing that they had fought in the war, represented the South, and were strong supporters of white supremacy. They included Joseph Brown, who served as U.S. senator and governor; John Gordon, who became a U.S. senator; and Henry Grady, who is best known as editor of the *Atlanta Constitution*. Unlike most other Bourbons, Grady did advance some new ideas, among them the value of manufacturing in the Georgia economy.[8] However, Grady and his peers never strayed far from what they considered traditional southern values. In fact, it would have been politically unwise not to support such widely held views.

At times, true ideological differences divided the party, as with the Arnall-Talmadge struggle for power in the 1940s. The Talmadge dynasty (Eugene and his son, Herman) was particularly important because it clearly divided Democrats into Talmadge and anti-Talmadge forces. Eugene Talmadge was perpetually a candidate in the Democratic primaries of Georgia, appearing on every ballot from 1926 until 1946, when his death led to the controversy with three people claiming to be governor. Despite a temporary setback, Talmadge's son, Herman, reclaimed the governor's office for the family in a 1948 special election.[9] The Talmadges were particularly strong in rural areas, where class and race appeals were well received. Ellis Arnall represented a break from traditional Georgia politics when he was elected governor in 1942. His administration included establishment of the Board of Regents to insulate the university system from political control, repeal of the poll tax, and establishment of a state merit system of employment. Arnall served only a single, four-year term. Herman Talmadge, on the other hand, remained a powerful figure until, amid scandal, he lost his last bid for reelection to the U.S. Senate in 1980.

Democratic presidential candidates were careful to attend to the racial concerns of the South if they hoped to win the party nomination and the region's solid bloc of Electoral College votes. One way to maintain control of the party nominating process was to restrict those who could participate. Among states in the Southeast, only Florida held presidential primaries. Delegates to the national conventions from other southern states were chosen by party caucuses or the state Democratic Party committee (as was the case in Georgia), not by the general population. National party platforms carefully avoided civil rights, which might alienate southern whites. Moreover, New Deal policies in the 1930s and 1940s benefited the economy of the South, furthering ties to the Democratic Party.[10]

It can be argued that the social programs of the 1930s were part of the reason that black voters began to join the Democratic Party in the South, and the party came under increasing pressure nationally to adopt civil rights as a core of its platform in later years. As early as 1948, with Harry Truman as its candidate, the Democratic Party began to voice mild support for broadening civil rights. While this strategy prompted the abandonment of the party by some rural white voters and the loss of some electoral votes to the States' Rights Party, the Democrats cultivated stronger support for civil rights. With the elimination of barriers to black enfranchisement, the Democrats tapped into a loyal bloc of black voters in southern states. Together, these developments sowed the seeds of change in the two major parties—change that became more evident in the 1980s and 1990s.

Party Coalitions

In 1968, blacks attending the Democratic national convention accounted for 10 percent of all southern delegates. By 1988, this share had increased to one-third of the region's delegates—higher than the overall proportion of blacks in the South. Blacks made up 44 percent of Georgia's delegation in that year.[11] Today, black voters are far more likely to identify with the Democratic Party than with the Republican Party, especially in the South. On the flip side, the Democratic Party in the South has seen a wholesale loss of white voters.[12] Analysis of black turnout in Georgia primaries illustrates the reliance of Democratic candidates on their votes. In 1996, 33 percent of all Democratic primary ballots were cast by black voters. By 2004, that figure had risen to 47 percent, making black voters virtually essential to winning contested Democratic primaries.[13] An analysis of census data that measured population change in Georgia between 2000 and 2010 affirmed the growing importance of minority voters, finding that 81 percent of newcomers to Georgia in that period were nonwhite.[14]

Racial differences are also seen in electoral outcomes. Almost all of the state's black members of the General Assembly are Democrats, as were the blacks elected as attorney general and labor commissioner during the 1990s. Georgia's

Republican leaders have made efforts to attract black voters, however. The state's first Republican governor in more than century, Sonny Perdue, appointed a black jurist to the Georgia Supreme Court, and the election of the first two black Republicans in the state legislature was proclaimed by Republican legislative leadership as a historic event. However, both of these representatives were elected in majority-white districts, and few would debate that the Democratic Party retains the loyalty of a large majority of black voters in the state. Alan Abramowitz, an elections expert at Emory University, reports that Democrats usually receive the support of 90 percent of African Americans who go to the polls.[15]

Following the 2004 elections for the Georgia General Assembly, Republicans held the majority in both the Georgia House and Senate for the first time in 130 years. The Republican majority could be attributed in part to several members of the General Assembly who switched from the Democratic Party to the Republican Party, including some who changed right after the election. The Republican Party systematically courted newly elected members to ensure their majority. Party switching by elected officials in Georgia, while relatively new, has been a pattern in the South since the 1990s.[16] Both Sonny Perdue and Nathan Deal, the state's first Republican governors since the Reconstruction period, began their political careers as Democrats.

Patterns of change also took place within the electorate, though the transition from Democratic Party to Republican Party in partisan identification (the party with which eligible voters say they most identify) lagged behind how Georgians cast their votes. In Gallup tracking polls measuring party identification in 2008, 45.4 percent of Georgia respondents stated that they identified with the Democratic Party, while only 41.3 percent claimed to be Republicans. By 2015 more Georgians were claiming Republican Party identification, 43.7 percent to 39.8 percent.[17]

Support for Republican Presidential Candidates

In recent years, Republican presidential candidates have enjoyed support from the South. As table 5.1 shows, Georgia has backed recent Republican candidates even in losing efforts. Georgia has been less likely to cast electoral votes for Republican candidates than its neighbors do, due partly to the support given to a Georgian, Jimmy Carter, as the Democratic nominee in 1976 and 1980, and support for fellow southern candidate Bill Clinton in 1992, but it is a rare presidential election that includes Georgia in any list of "battleground states" in which the election is close. Democratic presidential candidates' difficulty in attracting southern votes is due in part to the conservative bent of the region and the lack of appeal Democratic candidates nominated in recent presidential races have for southern voters. Democratic candidates such as Michael Dukakis

Table 5.1. Georgia Presidential Vote Distribution, 1956–2012

Year	Republican Candidate	Percent	Democratic Candidate	Percent
1956	Eisenhower	33.3	Stevenson	66.4
1960	Nixon	37.4	Kennedy	62.5
1964	Goldwater	54.1	Johnson	45.9
1968	Nixon	30.4	Humphrey	26.7
1972	Nixon	75.0	McGovern	24.6
1976	Ford	33.0	Carter	66.7
1980	Reagan	41.0	Carter	55.8
1984	Reagan	60.2	Mondale	39.8
1988	Bush, G. H. W.	59.8	Dukakis	39.5
1992	Bush, G. H. W.	42.0	Clinton	44.3
1996	Dole	47.5	Clinton	46.1
2000	Bush, G. W.	55.0	Gore	43.2
2004	Bush, G. W.	58.0	Kerry	41.9
2008	McCain	52.1	Obama	46.9
2012	Romney	53.3	Obama	45.5

Sources: Georgia Presidential Election Results, http://www.historycentral.com/elections/states/Georgia.html.

in 1988 and John Kerry in 2004 often took more liberal stands on issues than the southern electorate or even southern Democrats. Georgia did cast its electoral votes for Bill Clinton in 1992, but prior to the Clinton victory Georgia had not supported a Democratic presidential candidate since Jimmy Carter in 1980; the state and has not supported one since. Both elections for George W. Bush were clear victories, and both elections for Barack Obama were clear losses in Georgia.

Increases in Republican Officeholders

The 1994 elections ushered in dramatic changes throughout the United States, as Republicans, who had slim majorities in the U.S. Senate several times during the 1980s, won control of both houses of the U.S. Congress for the first time since 1953. Yet, Georgia had a legislature that remained heavily Democratic and was the last former Confederate state—in 2002—to elect a Republican governor following Reconstruction. However, in recent years the Republican Party has come to dominate elections in the state and gained the same kind of power wielded by Democrats since the end of the nineteenth century.

Statewide Offices. There was no Republican opposition to the Democratic nominee for governor in Georgia before the mid-1960s. However, Republican Barry Goldwater carried Georgia while being defeated soundly for the presidency in 1964, which seemed to give a shot in the arm to the state's Republicans. In 1966, the Republican Party nominated Congressman Bo Callaway for governor. He finished first but did not receive over 50 percent of the vote. Under a law requiring the General Assembly to select a governor when no candidate is able to get a majority, Democratic candidate Lester Maddox was selected. Despite this setback, five constitutional officers switched to the Republican Party in 1968. None ever won elective office again.[18]

Republican fortunes remained pallid until 1990, when Johnny Isakson received 45.7 percent of the votes for governor in his loss to Democrat Zell Miller. The two parties also ran a tight race in 1994 and 1998, as Guy Milner, a well-financed Republican candidate, sought the office in two election cycles (see table 5.2). In 2002, Republican challenger Sonny Perdue unseated the incumbent Democrat, Governor Roy Barnes. In 2006, Lieutenant Governor Mark Taylor, despite previous success in statewide elections, failed to win the governorship back for Democrats. Subsequent Democratic candidates who were expected to be formidable (former Governor Roy Barnes in 2010 and Jimmy Carter's grandson, state senator Jason Carter, in 2014) both won less than 45 percent of the vote in their respective elections.

Other races also indicate that the Republican Party now has a loyal voting base. Republicans have held a majority of the seats on the Public Service Commission since the 1990s. By 2004, Republicans held not only majorities in both chambers of the General Assembly and the governor's office but also the offices of state superintendent of schools and insurance commissioner. Democratic candidates in 2004 held on to the offices of lieutenant governor, secretary of state, agriculture commissioner, attorney general, and labor commissioner. In 2006, when Democrats Cathy Cox and Mark Taylor both decided to run for governor, their decision left the offices of secretary of state and lieutenant governor open, and Republican candidates took both. In the race for lieutenant governor, state senator Casey Cagle became the first Republican to attain that office. Cagle faced Jim Martin, a former state legislator and commissioner of the state's Department of Human Resources. Although one might argue that Martin had more statewide name recognition, Cagle won with 54 percent of the vote. In the secretary of state race, Fulton County commissioner Karen Handel defeated her Democratic opponent, state legislator Gail Buckner, by the same margin.[19] No Democrat has been elected to an open statewide seat in Georgia since 2002.

The General Assembly. Elections for the state legislature have also become more likely than ever to produce Republican victories. As late as 1950, Republicans in

Table 5.2. Georgia Gubernatorial Vote Distribution, 1966–2014

Year	Republican Candidate	%	Democratic Candidate	%
1966	Callaway	46.7	Maddox	46.2
1970	Suite	40.7	Carter, James	59.3
1974	Thompson	30.9	Busbee	69.1
1978	Cook	19.3	Busbee	80.7
1982	Bell	37.2	Harris	62.5
1986	Davis	29.5	Harris	70.5
1990	Isakson	45.7	Miller	54.3
1994	Milner	47.1	Miller	52.9
1998	Milner	44.1	Barnes	52.5
2002	Perdue	51.4	Barnes	46.3
2006	Perdue	57.9	Taylor	38.2
2010	Deal	53.0	Barnes	43.0
2014	Deal	52.8	Carter, Jason	44.8

Sources: Scammon and McGillivray 1993; Georgia Secretary of State, http://www.sos .state.ga.us/elections/election_results/default.htm.

the Georgia General Assembly numbered under 2 percent of the total. By 1971, only 12 percent of the House and 15 percent of the Senate were Republican, and in 1984 the numbers remained relatively unchanged.[20] In actual numbers, Georgia Republicans built a strong beachhead in 1992. The GOP won 15 of the 56 Senate seats (27 percent), gaining four new members; the number of Republicans in the house jumped from 34 to 52 of the 180 members (29 percent). These gains may have been due in part to redistricting, but they were extended in the summer of 1993, when Republicans won special elections for two vacant senate seats.

The GOP chipped away further at the Democratic majority in the General Assembly in the 1994 elections. The House of Representatives changed to 114 Democrats and 66 Republicans, while the Senate grew to 21 Republicans and 35 Democrats. The election produced key Democratic losses. Democrats still held 63 percent of the seats in the General Assembly, which was higher than the party's 52 percent share of seats in the forty-nine state legislatures using partisan elections, but it also represents continued erosion of Democratic control. By 2004, Republicans had taken over the majority in the Georgia General Assembly by taking 99 of the 180 seats of the house and 34 of the 56 seats in the senate.

Changes in Georgia reflected changes in the South as a whole. Between 1990 and 1994, the GOP gained almost two hundred seats in southern legislatures.[21]

Republican majorities were achieved in at least one chamber of the state legislatures of Virginia, South Carolina, North Carolina, and Florida in 2004.[22] In
that same year, Republican candidates captured five U.S. Senate seats formerly
held by southern Democrats. In 2016, Georgia Republicans held what some call
a legislative "trifecta": when one party controls both chambers of the state legislature and the governorship. Eight of the ten states of the former Confederacy
shared this status, meaning that lawmaking in those states was dominated by
one political party, the exceptions being Louisiana and Virginia (both elected
Democratic governors).

In Georgia, the members of each party in the General Assembly form a caucus to plan strategy, select party members to serve on legislative committees,
and determine who will serve as legislative leaders. Recent changes in partisanship have enhanced the power of the Georgia Republican Caucus. Republicans
hold power by chairing all committees, and Democrats find themselves in the
historically unusual position of minority party. Members of the minority party
often attempt to offer unified opposition to the majority party, but that means
that Georgia Democrats must be able to get over differences based on urban and
rural representation. For example, urban and rural Democrats demonstrated
differences of opinion on a vote to ban homosexual marriage, with many rural
Democrats voting with Republicans.[23]

Congress. Republican candidates for the U.S. Senate and House of Representatives had limited success in Georgia until the 1990s. Mack Mattingly, the
first Republican elected statewide since Reconstruction, lost his Senate seat in
1986 after only one term. Many argued that Mattingly's one victory was due in
large part to anti-Talmadge sentiment, yet Mattingly did well in many areas of
the state, notably suburban Atlanta. One pollster estimates that Mattingly was
able to attract only 9 percent of the black vote and was soundly defeated in the
black-majority counties of southwest Georgia. Mattingly also had little appeal
and party organization in rural areas.[24]

Even though Mattingly lost to Democrat Wyche Fowler in 1986, Paul Coverdell recaptured the seat for the GOP in 1992. Fowler was able to achieve only 49
percent of the vote to Coverdell's 48 percent; a Libertarian candidate garnered
3 percent. Under Georgia law requiring at least 50 percent of the vote in order
to attain office, a runoff election was held to determine who would hold the
Senate seat. Turnout in the runoff was the key to success, and Republican voters turned out in greater numbers than did Fowler supporters, thereby winning
the seat for Coverdell. The Democrats did regain Coverdell's seat in 2000, but
only because Democratic governor Roy Barnes appointed former governor Zell
Miller to the seat upon Coverdell's death. Miller, after winning a special election,

served the remainder of Coverdell's term in office. When the seat again came up for election in 2004, Republican Johnny Isakson easily defeated Democrat Denise Majette 58 percent to 40 percent. Both of Georgia's Senate seats have been in Republican hands ever since.

Before the 1992 election, only a few Republicans from Georgia had been elected to the U.S. House of Representatives. Bo Callaway rode Barry Goldwater's coattails to a victory in 1964. Pat Swindall was elected to the House from the Fourth District during the 1980s but lost his seat amid public scandal over money laundering. Newt Gingrich held a seat in the 1980s, but he defeated his Democratic opponent by only one thousand votes in 1990, and in 1992 he faced strong opposition within the Republican Party. His tight margins of victory were particularly noteworthy given his prestige within the U.S. House of Representatives, first as minority whip and later as speaker of the House.

The partisan pattern we have seen for other elected offices (Democratic dominance replaced by Republican dominance) also repeated itself in House races. By the late 1990s, Republicans were able to win a majority of congressional seats, but many races were competitive. Following the 2000 census, Georgia gained two seats to send thirteen representatives to the House. Democratic House candidates continued to be competitive through 2008, when six of Georgia's representatives were Democrats and seven were Republican. However, Republican gains have continued, and the 2014 elections sent nine Republicans and only four Democrats to the U.S. House of Representatives. Of course, nine Republican seats represent 69 percent of the available seats. What is notable is that generally statewide Democratic candidates garner about 45 percent of the vote. The congressional balance, therefore, does not represent the proportional statewide vote.

Local Offices. Republicans are becoming more numerous at the local level in Georgia as well. The party's actual strength is somewhat unclear, however, because almost all cities elect their officials on a nonpartisan basis. Republican strongholds at the local level in Georgia include not only rural areas but also several Atlanta suburbs such as Cobb, Gwinnett, and Fayette Counties. These areas have high numbers of new residents—many from more traditionally Republican parts of the country. However, the growing number of black and Latino registered voters in suburban Atlanta counties could shift the balance. All congressional districts in metropolitan Atlanta experienced a rise in the number of black voters in the early twenty-first century,[25] a trend that has not reversed. Party activists keep a close watch on demographic change and will move quickly to push for advantageous districts and policy positions that ensure partisan electoral success.

The Future of Party Politics in Georgia

When V. O. Key examined politics in the South during the 1940s, he concluded that one-party politics was a detriment to the region's development. Two generations after Key's assessment, one-party politics continues in Georgia, but only because Georgia Republicans have thoroughly replaced the long-dominant Democratic Party. Table 5.3 shows how dramatic and quick the takeover has been; after a period of competition in the early years of this century, what was once a 100 percent Democratic set of governing institutions in 1960 has become a 100 percent Republican in 2012. There are many who predict a long, one-party dominance in Georgia—by Republicans—based on these changes and the South's conservative traditions.[26]

However, as times change it is not clear that those traditions will continue to be as dominant as they have been in the past. Indeed, recent studies indicate that projected demographic changes in Georgia will lead to an increase in both minority (Georgia is projected to be a majority-minority state by 2060) and urban residents, suggesting that Democrats will become more and more electorally competitive as these trends play out.[27] A counterargument to this prediction is that the state saw both increasing minority and urban populations throughout the 1990s and 2000s, and those changes did not work to the Democratic Party's favor in those decades as Republicans became more and more successful in elections. In fact, victory margins for Republicans since the year 2000 are at the highest point in over a century, despite yearly reports of demographic changes supposedly favorable to Democrats. In presidential races, despite the demographic trends, Democratic candidates have not targeted Georgia as a worthwhile battleground state and have spent their general election media and campaign budgets in more promising states such as Florida, Virginia, North Carolina, and Colorado. Given these signs, it is tempting to see Georgia as simply and reliably Republican for some time to come.

Yet it is difficult to imagine that majority-minority, increasingly urban voters (who will eventually replace the ideologically conservative generation that elected conservative Democrats and then conservative Republicans) will never change the overall partisan makeup of the state. The Democratic Party has every incentive to put resources into candidate recruitment, voter registration, and get-out-the-vote initiatives. If and when it does, it is unlikely that Republicans will cede the state to the Democratic Party without a fight. Republicans have a strong incentive to work hard against losing their advantage in the state: Georgia plays a very important role in the party's presidential election strategy. In both the 2008 and 2012 elections, Georgia was the second most populous state to support the Republican nominee, providing 16 Electoral College votes (behind Texas's 38). The Republican path to the 270 Electoral College votes requires

Table 5.3. Party Change in Georgia Elections, 1960–2012

Political Parties in Georgia	1960	1964	1968	1972	1976	1980	1984	1988	1992	1996	2000	2004	2008	2012
State Offices														
Governor	D	D	D	D	D	D	D	D	D	D	D	R	R	R
Lieutenant Governor	D	D	D	D	D	D	D	D	D	D	D	D	R	R
Secretary of State	D	D	D	D	D	D	D	D	D	D	D	D	R	R
Commissioner of Labor	D	D	D	D	D	D	D	D	D	D	D	D	D	R
Attorney General	D	D	N/A	N/A	N/A	D	R	R	D	R	R	R	D	R
School Superintendent	D	D	D	D	D	D	D	D	D	R	R	R	D	D
Commissioner of Agriculture	D	D	D	D	D	D	D	D	D	D	D	D	D	R
Commissioner of Insurance	D	D	D	D	D	D	D	D	D	R	R	R	R	R
State Senate	53D 1R	50D 4R	46D 7R 1/I	50D 6R	51D 5R	51D 5R	49D 7R	46D 10R	45D 11R	36D 20R	34D 22R	*30R 26D*	*34R 22D*	*38R 18D*
State House	202D 3R	203D 2R	183D 22R	173D 22R	155D 24R	160D 20R	156D 24R	153D 27R	144D 36R	114D 66R	102D 78R	107D 72R 1 Ind	*106R 74D*	*116R 63D 1/I*
Other Important Offices														
U.S. Senate	D/D	D/D	D/D	D/D	D/D	D/R	D/D	D/R	D/D	D/R	*R/D*	*R/R*	*R/R*	*R/R*
U.S. House	10D	10D	8D 2R	8D 2R	10D	9D 1R	9D 1R	8D 2R	9D 1R	*8R 3D*	*8R 3D*	*8R 5D*	*7R 6D*	*9R 5D*
Electoral College Votes	D	R	I	R	D	D	R	R	D	R	R	R	R	R

Note: For the U.S. and state House and Senate, italic entries indicate a Republican majority; all others are Democratic majority.

Republican candidates to win Georgia, the loss of which would be devastating to its chances of winning the presidency. Given the important role that Georgia plays in the Republican Party's presidential strategy, one can expect it to devote considerable resources to keep Georgia in the Republican column.

The future of partisan politics in Georgia is likely to be exciting and contentious, given both the demographic patterns that incentivize Democrats to make a play for Georgia and the strategic needs that incentivize Republicans to retain it. It seems unlikely that the state will remain a safe and reliable "Red" Republican fixture, or that the state will simply follow demographic trends and transition suddenly to a "Blue" Democratic one.

Interest Groups

Interest groups provide an avenue for influence in addition to those available from elections and other forms of participation. Unlike political parties, the goal of interest groups is not necessarily to win elections and control government. Nor are they composed of the diverse membership typical of political parties. Rather, they are made up of like-minded individuals who pursue favorable public policies. Those who join groups in the United States tend to have higher incomes and education levels than the general population, which should not be surprising given the amount of time, money, and skills that can be required for membership. Unlike voting, where one person's vote is given the same weight as another's, interest groups allow people to act on the strength of their concern about an issue by investing varying amounts of time and money.[28]

Most interest groups are organized to further economic goals. Examples include labor unions, groups representing professions such as doctors and real estate agents, and industries like oil and cotton production. Other types of groups have proliferated since the 1970s, including social welfare, educational, ethnic, religious, and public affairs organizations. Also increasingly common are single-issue groups such as those dealing with abortion and the environment. So, too, are law firms, consultants, and others who offer services as lobbyists for hire. Not everything interest groups do is strictly political, however; they also do things such as provide training and information for their members.[29]

Interest Group Strategies

Lobbying. Perhaps the most widely recognized—and criticized—activity of interest groups is lobbying, which is the process of communicating information to officials in order to influence policy. Those engaged in such endeavors include contract lobbyists hired by a client for a fee, in-house lobbyists who work for an organization or business, those representing government agencies, citizen volunteers who promote causes on an unpaid basis, and private individuals acting on their own behalf. While their activity is often discussed in terms of legislatures, interest groups can also lobby the executive branch. Beyond the testimony, office visits, and research or reports provided by traditional lobbyists, lobbying also can include mobilizing grassroots members of an organization and using the media to promote goals.[30]

Donations. Another frequent strategy of interest groups is the distribution of money and other benefits (trips, skyboxes, etc.) to public officials. Although public attention is occasionally focused on scandals related to monetary benefits for public officials, such as the 2006 case of Washington lobbyist Jack Abramoff, there is little evidence of officials exchanging their action for such benefits. In fact, groups often reward candidates both for their past support and to make sure that such "friends" have sufficient campaign funds to get reelected. Some groups even give donations to candidates competing for the same office, especially when there is no incumbent running. The goal of such donations is to influence policy by trying to place supportive people in key positions. Corporations and unions cannot give money directly to candidates for federal offices, so they form PACs, which solicit contributions from individuals and donate the pooled money to candidates' campaign committees. Practices and regulations regarding nonfederal offices differ substantially among the states.[31]

The Courts. Many groups also use the legal system to promote their interests. Such efforts include action to influence the selection of judges and prosecutors. Most state and local judges and district attorneys are chosen by public election, which has prompted groups to recruit, endorse, and fund such candidates. Just because the federal government's legal officials are appointed, however, doesn't mean that politics isn't involved in the selection process.

Interest groups can also file lawsuits and submit legal briefs in cases, even when they are not one of the parties, in order to shape the way that courts apply the law to a particular type of case. Evidence suggests that since the mid-1960s these amicus curiae briefs have increased and involve a wide array of interests, although this varies among the states.[32] There is also evidence from the middle years of the first decade of the new century that, though the use of such briefs is still on the rise, most do not influence the reasoning applied to judicial decisions.[33]

Other Strategies. Beyond these conventional methods of influencing policy, interest groups also engage in protests, which can be either legal or illegal. Also in the illegal category are strategies such as violence and bribery. Protest and violence often are designed to get public attention and support for a group that has not achieved its goals using other means.

Interest Groups in the States

Although scholars, the media, and the public have devoted great attention to the proliferation and activities of interest groups in national politics, such organizations are important at the state and local levels as well. Traditionally, business, labor, education, agricultural, and local government groups have been cited as the most active in the states. Since the 1970s, a larger and more diverse set of interest groups has developed, including those involved in social issues, as well as individual companies and local governments lobbying on their own despite belonging to general membership organizations. The interest group environment in the United States continues to evolve; research conducted during the 1990s found that associations representing schoolteachers were the most influential groups in forty-three states, followed by general business organizations (e.g., chambers of commerce), bank associations, manufacturers, labor unions, and utilities,[34] while a similar study during the early years of this century determined that the business associations had taken the lead, followed by schoolteachers, utility companies, lawyers, and hospital associations.[35] A study comparing the policy preferences held by members of different groups to policy outcomes, conducted during the second decade of the current century, found that business interests have become most effective at influencing policy by a wide margin.[36]

Discussions of general patterns can cloud important differences among the states. Ronald J. Hrebenar and Clive S. Thomas have studied state interest-group activities for many years. Their studies have produced a method of state comparison presented in table 5.4. The Hrebenar-Thomas classification divides state interest group activities into five categories: dominant, where interest groups retain an overwhelming influence over state policy making; dominant-complementary, where interest groups have a strong policy influence; complementary, where interest groups share influence with other political forces; subordinate-complementary, in which interest groups supplement other, more dominate, political forces; and subordinate, in which interest groups have a minor role in policy making. Hrebenar and Thomas have never categorized any of the fifty states in the subordinate category; Georgia is categorized with twenty-five other states in the dominant-complementary group, and among those twenty-five are every southern state with the exceptions of Florida and Alabama (which they estimate are "dominant" systems). In their decades of

Table 5.4. Classification of the Fifty States According to the
Overall Impact of Interest Groups in 2002

Dominant	Dominant-Complementary	Complementary	Subordinate-Complementary	Subordinate
5 states	26 states	16 states	3 states	none
Alabama	Alaska	Colorado	Michigan	
Florida	Arizona	Connecticut	Minnesota	
Montana	Arkansas	Delaware	South Dakota	
Nevada	California	Hawaii		
West Virginia	Georgia	Indiana		
	Idaho	Maine		
	Illinois	Massachusetts		
	Iowa	New Hampshire		
	Kansas	New Jersey		
	Kentucky	New York		
	Louisiana	North Carolina		
	Maryland	North Dakota		
	Mississippi	Pennsylvania		
	Missouri	Rhode Island		
	Nebraska	Vermont		
	New Mexico	Wisconsin		
	Ohio			
	Oklahoma			
	Oregon			
	South Carolina			
	Tennessee			
	Texas			
	Utah			
	Virginia			
	Washington			
	Wyoming			

Source: Nownes, Thomas, and Hrebenar 2008, 121.

studies, Hrebenar and Thomas have never noted changes in the degree to which interest groups dominate the policy process in Georgia.[37]

More-recent studies have noted that interest-group environments in states develop independently of one another,[38] and the differences among states may be especially true in the South, where the historical lack of competition among political parties helped to nurture particularly strong networks of influential interest groups. Interest groups in southern states like Georgia have changed during the past three decades with the decline of rural political control, the rise of the Republican Party, racial change, and economic and population growth. More diversity among interest groups has replaced a system dominated by agriculture, local governments, and churches. There are now more groups involved in the policy-making process in state capitals: public employees and state agencies have become important political participants; groups have developed more elaborate tactics, including more extensive and sophisticated lobbying; most states have seen a rise in the use of contract lobbyists; and interest groups have received more attention, both from the media and in the form of increased regulation. As one might expect, Georgia has not been immune to these changes.[39]

Interest Groups in Georgia

Interest groups are nothing new to Georgia politics. During the 1940s, V. O. Key concluded that organized interests were few, and those that existed represented Georgia's major corporations, which included utilities such as Georgia Power, other companies regulated by the state, firms opposed to Franklin Roosevelt's New Deal, and Atlanta's business elite.[40] For much of the 1950s and 1960s, political disputes centered on racial and urban-rural issues. Although racial change was not easy, Georgia's business leaders, especially those often described as Atlanta's "business elite," promoted moderation as a means of achieving economic growth. They also promoted the state as an active player in development. From this base, the number and types of groups have expanded as state government has grown and economic issues have taken center stage.[41]

Getting a firm grip on the history of Georgia's system of interest groups is somewhat difficult because legal requirements for reporting their activities were extremely lax until the 1990s. Nevertheless, all analyses seem to agree with Key's assessment that business interests dominate Georgia's interest-group ecosystem. Studies from the 1960s through the 1990s all note the primary position of business in influencing Georgia's policy-making process, and few would challenge that assessment today.[42]

The number of lobbyists working to influence policy in Georgia has also risen steadily. In the early 1970s, roughly 300 people were registered to lobby the General Assembly. One tally of lobbyists during the 1990s found 1,059 registered lobbyists.[43] By 2016, the number had risen to over 1,400 lobbyists representing over 6,000 clients.[44]

Regulation of Interest Groups

It may be a gross understatement to say that Georgia has seldom been a leader in regulating interest groups.[45] Until 1992, Georgia was one of the only two states not requiring lobbyists to report their activities, although lobbyists did have to register and wear an identification badge while in the Capitol. Certain actions, such as getting paid based on the outcome of specific bills and discussing pending matters on the floor of the house and senate during the session, were illegal.

During 1991 and 1992, Secretary of State Max Cleland and some of the media, particularly the Atlanta daily newspapers, campaigned for ethics reform—laws governing the behavior of interest groups and public officials.[46] The issue was quite controversial, but the General Assembly amended the "ethics in government" law in 1992. The new procedures transferred lobbyist registration from the secretary of state to the State Ethics Commission, set an annual registration fee (except for government and nonprofit organizations), and required those registering to wear a badge labeled "Lobbyist" while in the capitol. The law also mandated that lobbyists disclose their expenses, the public officials on whom money is spent, and the specific bill about which they were lobbying; they are not required to disclose their compensation. Reports are filed monthly when the General Assembly is in session and two other times during the year.[47] There are no limits on how much legislators can accept in the way of meals, gifts, trips, or similar benefits.

Passing lobbyist regulation is not the same as enforcing it, and critics complain that the General Assembly gives the Georgia Government Transparency and Campaign Finance Commission insufficient staff and budget to monitor lobbying. Critics contend that lobbyists frequently fail to list specific legislators or bills when filing reports. One tally found that only 138 of the 3,800 reports covering the 1993 legislative session listed a bill or general subject discussed at events paid for by registered lobbyists. Only 7.5 percent of the expenditures were reported as directed to a specific legislator.[48] A 2014 audit conducted by the Georgia Department of Audits and Accounts found that the commission was not adequately monitoring political committee activities, was not accurately tracking ethics compliance form submissions, was not consistently enforcing penalties for late submissions, and had not implemented a system to ensure that investigations into violations were conducted consistently. The commission also has a history of failing to investigate alleged violations in a timely manner. A 2014 investigation by reporters at the *Atlanta Journal-Constitution* found that

Table 5.5. Georgia Campaign Donation Limits, 2016

Type of Election	Type of Office	Donation Limit
Primary	Statewide	$6,600
Primary Runoff	Statewide	$3,900
General Election	Statewide	$6,600
General Election Runoff	Statewide	$3,900
Primary	All Other	$2,600
Primary Runoff	All Other	$1,400
General Election	All Other	$2,600
General Election Runoff	All Other	$1,400

Table 5.6. Top Ten PAC Contributors to Statewide,
State Legislative, and State Judicial Campaigns in 2016

Georgia Trial Lawyers Association	$1,232,424
Georgia Dental Association	$899,850
Georgia Association of Realtors	$760,275
Georgia Optometric Association	$609,535
Georgia Hospital Association	$558,330
Georgia Medical Association	$558,200
Automobile Retail Dealers of Georgia	$456,581
Georgia Apartment Association	$435,250
Independent Insurance Agents of Georgia	$425,542
Coca-Cola	$419,933

Source: followthemoney.org.

one-fourth of open Ethics Commission cases involved complaints so old that any enforcement would be impossible due to statutes of limitations on prosecution.[49]

As with lobbying, Georgia placed few limitations on contributions to candidates' campaigns until the 1990s. Unlike laws governing federal elections, state law permits companies and unions to donate directly to candidates' campaigns. Disclosure of donations has been required since the 1970s, but no limits on such amounts were set until 1990. Campaign contribution limitations as of 2016 are presented in table 5.5. Of course, many companies and individuals contribute to more than one candidate, and there are no limits on the amounts of their own money that candidates can spend on their campaigns.

As table 5.6 indicates, some sectors are notably heavy contributors. Of the top ten PACs contributing to statewide, state legislative, and state judicial races in 2016, the single largest contributor was the Georgia Trial Lawyers Association, providing over $1 million to political campaigns.[50] Business and medical interests are also represented on the list. A careful review of contributors shows that organizations contribute to more than one candidate in the same race. For example, the Georgia Trial Lawyers Association's two largest recipients for its donations are the Georgia Democratic Party and the Georgia House Republican Trust.[51]

Lobbying

Lobbyists, especially the more professional and experienced ones, are active between legislative sessions, although the pace quickens when the General Assembly is meeting.[52] Interest groups do a variety of things to press their points of view: testifying at hearings, dispensing information, providing favors, and sponsoring events. Some of these actions are aimed at securing the passage of legislation. Others are defensive—designed to defeat bills that a group opposes. Some seek to foster general "goodwill" for the organization. All seek to build winning coalitions of interests, which is not always easy.

Information. The use of testimony and other information can be very useful to interest groups and public officials alike in a state such as Georgia, where legislators are part-time officials who receive low pay and limited staff support. Providing facts about pending legislation and mobilizing members of a group are not always sufficient for success, however. The willingness of officials to listen and defer to the judgment, expertise, or power of a group and its lobbyist is also important. There are even customs about where certain lobbyists position themselves in the halls of the Capitol to talk to representatives and senators during the legislative session.[53]

Favors. Interest groups also make use of events and favors, such as receptions, dinners, seminars, trips, tickets, and other gifts. For example, lobbyists spent $1.1 million entertaining Georgia lawmakers during 2005.[54] Critics claim that such tactics buy access and influence in legislative and executive branch decisions. Some of these gifts are generally available to members of the General Assembly during the legislative session, for instance, soft drinks provided by Coca-Cola, newspapers supplied by Delta Air Lines, hotel hospitality suites furnished with food and beverages, the annual "Wild Hog Supper" sponsored by various agricultural interests, and a doctor on call provided by the Georgia Medical Association. Similar benefits throughout the year include tickets to professional and college sporting events and buffets for legislators held before a University of Georgia football game. Beyond favors that seem general in nature, others appear targeted at those with substantial influence. For instance, Georgia Power offered inexpensive leases on its lakefront property to state officials until 1991.[55]

Lobbying is not limited to business interests. During 2006, the Georgia Municipal Association registered eight lobbyists, Emory University had seven, and the Association County Commissioners and the state Department of Transportation had thirteen registered lobbyists each.[56] Although the Board of Regents of the University System of Georgia had only one registered lobbyist in 2004, the University of Georgia and Georgia Tech have provided executive and legislative leaders with seats to football games. Other groups use the political system to promote policies consistent with certain ideologies, values, or ways of life. These include groups on both sides of debates over firearms regulation, as well as religious groups.[57]

Relationships. The success of interest groups depends in part on building strategic relationships, and critics complain about the extent to which legislators serve on committees related to their occupations. For instance, the ten members of the Senate Banking and Financial Institutions Committee in 1993 included one who chaired a bank board of directors and another who represented a lending company as part of his law practice. While these senators had special expertise regarding banking, they were chided in some quarters for favoritism.[58]

Those representing government also try to build useful alliances. One study of state agencies found that they benefit in the General Assembly because of their "insider" status, which requires less courting of legislators than private lobbyists must do. They are also in a favorable position to keep legislators informed. Agency influence varies, however. The most effective agencies are those with substantial discretion and resources that make them capable of providing benefits to legislators' districts and constituents—not surprisingly, other lobbyists identified the Department of Transportation as the most influential with legislature.[59]

While building alliances is important, the proliferation of groups can pit some interests against others. For example, lawyers, doctors, and insurance companies were very active in the 2005 legislative debate on medical malpractice tort reform. Disagreements among particular industries may be especially troublesome for organizations representing a diverse membership, for example, the Georgia Chamber of Commerce, which is the leading group promoting the general concerns of business. The same can be said of the Georgia Municipal Association (GMA), which includes scores of cities that often have competing interests. The GMA also can find itself in conflict with groups representing county governments and school boards.

In many ways, newspaper headlines often suggest that interest groups seduce public officials. It is worth noting, though, that the relationship is a two-way street. Spending by groups is not necessarily directed toward passive officials; lobbyists' largesse and politicians' power mean that some interests may fear *not* providing favors. Indeed, one former lobbyist wrote to a newspaper arguing that a culture existed "for far too many years" in which legislators "openly demanded" favors from lobbyists.[60]

Campaigns

As Georgia's electorate expands, the scope of state government grows, and the two major parties remain competitive, the cost of campaigns undoubtedly will rise. Because $30 million may soon become the low end for combined spending by the major parties' gubernatorial candidates, some observers expect that successful gubernatorial candidates will have to raise large sums of money early in their campaigns, primarily in Metropolitan Atlanta. This necessity, in turn, could strengthen ties between politicians and interest groups. There have long been concerns about whether campaign contributors "buy" political access or favors with their donations to candidates. This problem was highlighted in 1996, when the press obtained a memo from state school superintendent Linda Schrenko directing her chief of staff to give priority to campaign contributors when scheduling appointments.[61]

Concerns have been raised about campaign fund "loopholes." One complaint is that companies cannot give to the campaigns of elected officials whose agencies regulate them, but their employees can do so as individuals. For instance, recent insurance commissioners have been chided for accepting—and soliciting—campaign contributions from people whose business their office regulates. Critics have also questioned candidates' use of leftover campaign money for personal purposes. Finally, donations to political parties are essentially unregulated. In 2004, over $13 million was donated to party committees, an amount equal to over one-fourth of all political contributions at the state level for that year. This absence of regulation may allow donors to route large sums of money to campaigns over and above the amounts they give to candidates, which are limited under state law.[62] Similarly unregulated are donations to committees tied to officials, as with a fund connected to house speaker Glenn Richardson, a Republican. During 2005, the fund collected more than $175,000, much of it from interest groups and their lobbyists, with funds used for polling, personnel, technology, and similar support. House speaker David Ralston maintained a similar arrangement, and interest groups did indeed make contributions to his leadership committee that exceeded regular campaign contribution limits. The tobacco company Altria, for example, contributed $2,500 to Ralston's campaign fund, but then gave another $10,000 to his leadership fund.[63] The existence of these funds is not new, and recent leadership committee funds are similar to those maintained by Democratic officials in the past.[64]

Interest groups are also involved in elections where there are not candidates: referendum campaigns. Georgia does not have an initiative process permitting citizens to circulate petitions placing policy questions on the ballot. Thus the referenda most familiar to Georgians are proposed amendments to the state constitution, local votes to adopt a sales tax or to use debt financing for public projects, and questions tied to local bills passed by the General Assembly (e.g., consolidating the Athens and Clarke County governments).

Interest groups can be very active in referendum campaigns when they have substantial financial stakes in the outcome. For instance, the state's voters approved a constitutional amendment in 1990 that substantially reduced the local property tax burden of timber and agricultural land. The amendment was promoted as environmentally responsible because lower taxes could encourage forest preservation and planting. Major timber companies were significant backers of the amendment, including a reported contribution of $32,000 by Georgia Pacific. The amendment produced a tax saving for these companies, but other taxpayers in a number of counties had to pay more to make up for the lost revenue.[65] Similarly, the campaign supporting a 2012 sales tax referendum that financed an expansion of the state's transportation infrastructure was heavily financed by the concrete and construction industry.[66]

Grassroots Pressure

Traditional lobbying and the use of campaign money are not the only strategies employed by interest groups. Some also use the "grassroots" by mobilizing their members to write or call public officials. Groups such as the National Rifle Association and AARP (originally known as the American Association of Retired Persons) have a reputation for being very effective with such efforts. Groups also use media campaigns to promote their goals and images. They "go public" by rating legislators according to roll call votes; in such cases, a group identifies bills it considers important and then rates legislators according to the percentage of bills on which they voted "correctly."

A similar tactic during campaign years is to rate candidates according to their answers on questionnaires about issues important to a group. Opponents are often saddled with derogatory labels, as when an environmental group calls those twelve legislators with the lowest ratings "the dirty dozen." Ratings sometimes carry the subtle threat of a group's members voting en masse against candidates who do not measure up to a group's standards.

Many grassroots organizations also attempt to influence policy by registering voters. The 2004 gay marriage controversy prompted not just supporters of the proposed ban but also opponents of the ban, such as Georgia Equality, to reach out to voters through registration drives. One representative of that group estimated that political mobilization against the ban on gay marriage would cost $1 million.[67] Despite their efforts, the constitutional amendment to ban gay marriage passed by over 76 percent.

Litigation and Protest

Interest groups outside the political mainstream often have few resources to achieve their policy goals through normal legislative and executive channels. In fact, they often have to defend themselves against laws or bureaucratic decisions. Under such conditions, groups use other avenues to achieve their policy goals. One important strategy is to turn to the courts, federal and state. Civil rights organizations used the federal courts, for instance, to eliminate state actions that restricted blacks' right to vote.[68] Groups such as the American Civil Liberties Union exist primarily to initiate litigation against the state on behalf of particular interests. Some of these cases can be quite controversial, however, as when the ACLU successfully represented a student seeking to eliminate prayers before high school football games as a violation of the U.S. Constitution's prohibition against the "establishment" of religion. A similar lawsuit by a public employees' organization challenged a state law requiring mandatory drug tests for all state and local government job applicants. The law was declared unconstitutional in the federal courts in 1990 as a violation of both the guarantee against unreasonable search and seizure and the right to privacy.

Groups also use protests to dramatize their position or create political pressure. This was the case during much of the 1960s, when civil rights groups used peaceful protest to turn public opinion in the United States against racial segregation in the South. Both sides in the abortion debate use a variety of protest strategies, such as picketing. Worker organizations such as unions have limited influence in Georgia, so they have held rallies at the Capitol to dramatize what they argue are inadequate payment levels from the fund set up to compensate workers injured on the job.[69]

Supporters and opponents of the 2004 constitutional amendment banning gay marriage in Georgia used court action and protest to further their agendas. Opponents of the ban attempted to block its placement on the ballot through the courts and organized protests at the state Capitol. Supporters of the amendment also worked with legal representation to make sure that the language of the amendment would not prevent its placement on the ballot and organized "Family Day" at the state Capitol, which was in part a demonstration of support for passage. Ultimately litigation succeeded for opponents of the ban, and the amendment was declared unconstitutional in 2015 as a result of the U.S. Supreme Court's ruling in *Obergefell v. Hodges*.

Political Participation and the Future of Georgia Politics

Some observers might argue that little has changed since V. O. Key described Georgia politics in the 1940s. Although the Democratic dominance that lasted through the 1990s gave way to a recent Republican dominance, business interests have maintained the substantial influence over the policy process that Key noted decades ago. However, demographic changes suggest that partisan competition may return to Georgia elections, and Democratic Party candidates may have cause to be optimistic about the future. Republicans, on the other hand, have the advantage of incumbency and a national party that will not relinquish the state easily. There are far more interest groups in Georgia politics than a generation ago, and their ability to use resources—primarily money—may be more important than ever in the electoral and policy processes. Georgia's past as a reliable, one-party state that attracts little attention in national elections may not, in fact, look anything like its future.

CHAPTER 6

The Legislature

The framers of the U.S. Constitution expected legislatures to be the branch of government closest to the people. In Jefferson's view, legislators were to be citizen lawmakers who applied the values of the community to government without placing themselves above average citizens.

The U.S. Congress and many states have left behind the idea of the citizen-legislator in favor of the professional politician. The Georgia General Assembly, however, may be characterized as a citizen legislature in that members must maintain other sources of income, districts are relatively small, and most members do not have ambitions for higher office. Yet the General Assembly, like other legislatures, is not a mirror reflection of the people it purports to represent.

The Fifty State Legislatures

State legislatures have much in common.[1] For example, they are charged with the duties of representing the people of their districts, reapportioning districts following the census, enacting laws, adopting taxing and spending measures, overseeing enforcement of current laws, and interceding for constituents. Every state, except Nebraska, has a bicameral legislature, elects its legislature on a partisan basis, and has an upper chamber called the senate. Forty-one states call their lower chamber the house of representatives, and forty-four states hold annual legislative sessions.

Differences do exist among legislatures, especially in terms of provisions in state constitutions and statutes (see table 6.1). Among the formal distinctions, size varies from a low of 49 in Nebraska's unicameral legislature to a high of 424 in the small state of New Hampshire. Georgia, with 236 members, has the third-largest legislature. Qualifications such as minimum age, terms of office, length of residence, and term limits also vary. Georgia is one of twelve states

Table 6.1. State Legislatures

Characteristics	Minimum	Maximum	Georgia
Length of Term (Years)			
Lower House	2 (44 states)	4 (5 states)	2
Senate	2 (12 states)	4 (38 states)*	2
Total Members	49 (NE)	424 (NH)	236
Lower House	40 (AK)	400 (NH)	180
Senate	20 (AK)	67 (MN)	56
Annual Salary, 2016	$200 (NH)†	$100,113 (CA)	$17,342
Number of Committees, 2016‡			
Lower House	6 (ME)	46 (MS)	38
Senate	5 (MD, ME)	43 (MS)	30
Republican Percent of Seats, 2016			
Lower House	13.7% (HI)	85.0% (WY)	65.0%
Senate	4.0% (HI)	86.6% (WY)	69.6%

Source: Council of State Governments, *Book of the States*, 2016, 56–57, 68–70, 113–114.

* Nebraska's unicameral legislature is the Senate, whose members serve four-year terms. Senators in Illinois and New Jersey are included in this total, although some serve for two years.

† Another seven states only reimburse legislators at a daily rate during the legislative session.

‡ Excludes states relying primarily on joint committees for most substantive work.

using only two-year terms; thirty-two states elect their upper chamber to a four-year term and their lower chamber for two years. Regular legislative sessions range from off-year limits of thirty calendar days in New Mexico and Virginia and twenty legislative days in Wyoming to unlimited length for annual sessions in fourteen states. Leadership, procedures, and compensation also differ widely.

In addition to the characteristics imposed by state constitutions and laws, legislatures also differ in their informal traits. One of these has been labeled "legislative professionalism," which refers to career patterns. According to an often-used distinction, state legislative bodies can be professional, hybrid, or citizen legislatures. Professional legislatures are composed largely of career politicians who devote large portions of their time to legislative work and who may not hold another job. For many of these persons, election to the legislature is a means of achieving other goals, as well as an accomplishment in its own right. Professional legislatures have high compensation levels, long legislative sessions, and large numbers of staff members to assist legislators. One classification includes nine states in this category.[2]

At the other extreme are citizen legislatures, which have short sessions, low levels of pay, and very limited staff support. Members generally have outside careers, often in business or law, although they can use legislative service as a springboard to run for higher office. Georgia is among the sixteen states with a citizen legislature. The remaining twenty-five states are classified as hybrid because their combination of compensation, session length, and staff fall between the two extreme categories. One study of forty-one legislatures with data available in 1998 found that in thirty-one of them, at least 60 percent of members had outside careers. These ranged from a high of 93 percent in Indiana to a low of just 27 percent in California. Georgia's 62 percent ranked thirtieth from the top in the percentage of members with outside careers.[3]

Legislators tend to be fairly similar. Most are males, have lived in their state or district long term, hold professional occupations, and are of higher socioeconomic status than the state population as a whole. They also tend to be well educated and are generally highly involved in local and community organizations. Diversity has increased, although it varies widely among the states. By 2015, more than 24 percent of legislators in the fifty states were women, as opposed to 4 percent in 1969. Similarly, 9 percent of legislators were black, which compares to 2 percent in 1971.[4]

The Georgia General Assembly: Constitutional Provisions

Georgia's legislature, officially named the Georgia General Assembly, has been operating continuously since Georgia became one of the thirteen original states in 1777. It consists of two chambers, called the House of Representatives and the Senate. All Georgia legislators are elected to two-year terms in November of even-numbered years. Should a seat become vacant during the legislative session, a special election is held to fill the position.

Legislative Districts

Since Georgia's earliest legislatures were based on county representation, the General Assembly initially had at least one representative for each county. As the number of counties grew to 159, the legislature became relatively large. Moreover, as local population grew at different rates, county-based representation proved problematic when small, sparsely populated counties were represented equally with larger ones. In addition, Senate districts were drawn to include three counties, and each seat rotated among its three counties at the end of each term. Thus the real power in the legislative branch was concentrated in the House, where members could hold unlimited tenure.[5]

Redrawing legislative districts occurs following the U.S. census held every ten years. In the 1960s, federal courts ruled that all representation within state legislatures must be based on population rather than county. Since then, Georgia has eliminated the rotation system for state senators, all 56 of whom are now elected from single-member districts. With the adoption of the Constitution of 1983, the Senate has been restricted to *not more than* 56 members, while the House has been required to have *at least* 180 members. Thus the legislature could enlarge the number of representatives in the House or decrease the size of the Senate, as long as the constitutional mandates on size are upheld.

The House of Representatives has employed a combination of single-member and multimember districts over the years. Multimember House districts provide for election of candidates to a "post," or position, within the district. Imagine, for example, a district ("A") that elects three members to the House. District A would have three times the population of a single-member district. Candidates would file to run for one of the three posts within the district. Thus someone running for the House in District A, Post 3, does not compete with candidates for District A, Post 1, although the electorate consists of the same voters. Multimember House districts were done away with following the 1990 census, but the General Assembly reinstated them after the 2000 census. Those multimember districts were eliminated following a series of lawsuits, however, and all 180 members of the House now represent single-member districts. Based on Georgia's population of almost 9.7 million in the 2010 census, each member of the House has roughly 53,800 constituents, and each Senate district has approximately 173,000 residents.

The General Assembly used a special session to draw new districts following the 2000 census. The session was expected to be quite interesting because it included not only the General Assembly's own districts but also Georgia's seats in the U.S. House of Representatives, which increased from eleven to thirteen as a result of population growth. As in most instances of redistricting, the majority party, in this case the Democratic Party, drew maps designed to ensure the election of its party's candidates. Two federal lawsuits were filed that affected Georgia's new districts. In the first, two dozen Republicans argued that the new plan violated "one person, one vote" principles. In an unrelated case, the U.S. Supreme Court established new standards for redistricting that required a new review of the 2001 districts for the Georgia Senate. The confusion surrounding the maps resulted in districts shifting before and after the 2002 elections, with final maps drawn not by the General Assembly but by a federal court, just three months prior to the 2004 state primaries. Candidates who had represented districts for many years found that they no longer lived in their home districts and could not move in time to meet the twelve-month residency requirements for the 2004 elections. Additional changes to the State Senate district map were adopted in 2006, despite strong opposition from Democrats.

Redistricting controversies also affected the balance of power between the governor and Georgia's attorney general. Governor Sonny Perdue, a Republican, asked that a court case filed by the state regarding state Senate districts be withdrawn. Attorney General Thurbert Baker, a Democrat, refused to withdraw the suit, stating that it was the attorney general, not the governor, who had the authority to make legal decisions for the state. The dispute ended up in court, and the Georgia Supreme Court decided in favor of Attorney General Baker in September 2003.[6] The 2010 round of redistricting was much less contentious, as the Republican-controlled plans for U.S. House districts, state House districts, and state Senate districts were approved by the U.S. Justice Department, and no judicial ruling or mid-decade changes created the legal and political dilemmas that were common during the early years of this century.

Qualifications of Members

The Georgia Constitution requires that persons seeking office in the General Assembly be registered voters, U.S. citizens, and Georgia citizens for at least two years.[7] It also requires that representatives live within their districts for at least one year, which may force incumbents to run against each other after districts are redrawn. Those elected to the Senate must be at least twenty-five years old, whereas members of the House must be twenty-one or older. Persons may not simultaneously run for more than one office or in the primaries of two political parties. Also ineligible are persons on active military duty, those who hold other elected or civil offices within the state (unless they resign), and convicted felons. Therefore, members of the Georgia General Assembly are not permitted to hold other state or county offices, nor may they be employees of the state or faculty at state colleges and universities. However, it is permissible to hold office on local school boards and to run for a seat in the General Assembly. Under a 1990 state law, candidates were required to pass a drug test until it was ruled unconstitutional by the U.S. Supreme Court in 1997.[8]

Legislative Sessions

The legislature in Georgia meets annually in regular session for forty legislative (not calendar) days, beginning on the second Monday of January.[9] If the House and Senate leadership schedule many consecutive workdays early in the session, it can reach the forty-day threshold in mid-March; however, if the leadership allows for many nonworking days, the legislative calendar can run through late April. The General Assembly may be called into special session by the governor, who sets the agenda, or by agreement of three-fifths of the membership of each chamber. Special sessions may be called to deal with unexpected crises, such as natural disasters, budgetary shortfalls, or other state emergencies. Special sessions may not last longer than forty legislative days and generally cannot be used for matters unrelated to the official agenda.

Compensation

The Georgia Constitution allows members of the General Assembly to set their own salaries by law, although any raise cannot take effect until the term of office after the raise is approved. Setting salaries by law is the procedure in most states, although some states set salaries in their constitutions, and others use compensation commissions, at least in part, to set salaries or other compensation of legislators.[10]

When the National Conference of State Legislatures compared compensation in 2016, members of the General Assembly were paid $17,341 per year, plus mileage and expense allowances. Twenty-seven states had annual legislative salaries higher than Georgia's. This included $100,113 per year in California, $71,685 in Michigan, and $79,500 in New York. On the other end of the spectrum were states that provided legislators only token payments. Seven states pay less than $15,000 per year. New Hampshire legislators were compensated only $200 for their two-year term. Six states paid a fixed amount for each day or week that the legislature is in session rather than an annual salary. That was only $10 per day in Alabama, although members did have expense allowances.[11] Georgia legislators' salaries are tied to raises for state workers, with the lawmakers receiving half the percentage increase given to state employees. Thus legislators set their own salaries indirectly for coming years when they include employee pay raises in the state budget.

Like all but five states, Georgia pays a per diem to legislators for expenses. In 2016, members of the General Assembly received $173 per day during the legislative session and for committee service when the legislature was not in session. Long-distance telephone expenses are free, clerical help is provided, and each legislator receives an additional amount for general expenses.

The Georgia General Assembly: Characteristics of Members

There are nearly 7,400 state legislators in the United States (1,971 senators and 5,411 members of lower houses). Among the significant characteristics of legislatures are turnover in membership, demographic characteristics, and partisan makeup. All of these have changed to some degree during the past generation, especially in Georgia.

Membership Turnover

State legislatures are relatively stable institutions, although turnover is higher in elections following redistricting. Vacancies can occur for several reasons, including death, resignation, retirement (for a host of reasons), defeat in a primary, and loss of a general election. One study discovered that lower-house turnover averaged 21 percent between 1984 and 1990. That research also found that 54.4 percent of new members in lower houses in 1979–1980 were still in office by 1983–1984, but only 27.1 percent remained as long as 1989–1990. In state senates, 62.2 percent remained through 1983–1984, and 33.6 percent served through 1989–1990.[12]

In 1994, most turnover nationally occurred because legislators did not seek reelection. In only five bodies did less than 80 percent of incumbents running for reelection lose: Missouri Senate (69 percent), Nevada Senate (75 percent), North Carolina House (74 percent), Washington House (74 percent), and Wyoming Senate (78 percent). Similarly, 20 percent of the seats in state legislatures changed between 1994 and 1996, although turnover was 30 percent or higher in Arizona, California, Idaho, Louisiana, Maine, New Hampshire, New Mexico, Oregon, and South Dakota. Redistricting occurred after the 2000 census, and of all seats up for election in 2002, turnover reached 26 percent, although most legislators did not lose seats at the ballot box.[13]

One of the major factors affecting turnover in many states since the 1990s, but not Georgia, has been term limits. Beginning in 1990, when voters approved initiatives in California, Colorado, and Oklahoma, a total of twenty-one states eventually limited the number of terms that people could serve in their legislatures. However, courts overturned term limits in four states, and they were repealed in Idaho and Utah. Thus, by 2005, term limits remained in just fifteen states. Still, term limits have shaken up the political landscape. They were first applied in 1996, when 26 of 151 House members and 4 of 35 senators in Maine could not seek reelection; in California, 22 of the 80 members of the Assembly (the lower house) had to relinquish their seats. In 1998, term limits forced the retirement of 50 of the 100 members in the Arkansas House and 63 of 110 members in the Michigan House. In 2000, half of the lower houses in Michigan and Florida were ineligible for reelection. For the 2002 election, 322 legislators in eleven states had to give up their seats; in 2004, the total was 262, including significant numbers of legislative leaders and committee chairs. Republicans scored major gains in the 2010 and 2014 midterm elections, which contributed to turnover of 14 percent in state senates in 2015 and 15.6 percent in lower houses.[14]

Longevity has been somewhat higher in the Georgia General Assembly than in other state legislatures. Georgia has never adopted term limits for its 236 legislators. In 1979 66 percent of the twenty-nine House freshmen in 1979 were still in office during 1983–1984, as were 55.2 percent in 1989–1990. In the Senate, 5 of the 6 freshman senators in 1979 were still there in 1983–1984, but only 1 remained by 1989–1990.[15]

In Georgia, turnover has been associated with both partisan change and re-

districting. Democrats maintained control of the General Assembly in the elections of 1998 (34–22 in the Senate, 102–78 House) and 2000 (32–24 Senate,
104–74 House), but the new century has accelerated change, especially given redistricting. In 2002, 10 of Georgia's 56 state senators were not on the November
ballot, and another 6 lost in the general election. Those 16 new members represented a 29 percent turnover. Aided by the party switching of four senators,
Republicans took control of the Senate (30–26) in 2003 for the first time since
Reconstruction. In the Georgia House, 40 of the 180 representatives did not
make it to the general election in 2002, because they either gave up their seats
or lost a primary. The remaining 140 incumbents all won reelection, however,
producing a turnover of 22 percent—a surprisingly low figure for a redistricting
year.

One factor in turnover in Georgia is the constant redistricting process. In
2000, 2002, and 2004 (as well as 2006 for some state senators), incumbents
faced different districts than those that had elected them in the previous election cycle. For some incumbents, this meant that they no longer even lived
within district boundaries. Following last-minute changes in 2002, candidates
were caught off guard by the requirements on length of residency, and it was
too late to move into the districts that they had represented in the past. Other
incumbents realized that they would have to face off in elections with colleagues
of their party. Faced with changing their residence or rebuilding a base in a new
district, many incumbents chose to retire. In 2004 alone, fifty seats were left
open by retiring incumbents.

Demographic and Occupational Characteristics

In addition to more freshmen, the 2004 elections brought other changes to the
General Assembly (see figure 6.1). In the House, the 180 members included
thirty-four women in 1993 and thirty-six in 1995. A decade later, that number
had increased only to thirty-seven (21 percent). In the Senate, there were seven
women after the 2004 election—the same as after the 1994 election. Thus, 18.6
percent of the General Assembly was female in 2005, slightly below the national
figure of 22.5 percent. Trends shown in figure 6.1 point to continuing increases
in female representation in the Georgia General Assembly, and in 2015 Georgia
had fifty-six women legislators in the state House and state Senate, constitut-
ing 23 percent of total seats, compared to a high of 41 percent in Colorado and
Vermont and 15 percent or lower in eight states, including a low of 12 percent
in Louisiana.[16]

In terms of race, the number of blacks in the Senate remained unchanged at
nine following the 1992 redistricting and elections but increased to thirty-one in

Figure 6.1. Composition of the Georgia General Assembly,
by Race and Gender, 1990–2016

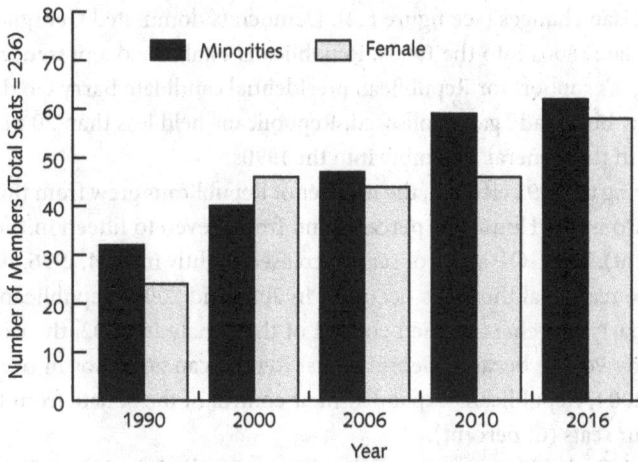

Sources: Center for American Women and Politics and publications from the
Georgia General Assembly and the Georgia Official and Statistical Register.

the House. After the 1994 elections, blacks added one seat in each chamber, for
a total of ten senators (18 percent) and thirty-two representatives (18 percent).
Following the 2014 election, blacks held twelve seats in the Senate (21 percent)
and forty-one in the House (23 percent).

At least one constant remains, though, in the composition of Georgia's legislature: the presence of lawyers. In 1985, 46 of the General Assembly's 236 members were attorneys (19 percent); the next largest occupations were farmer (27
members) and real estate (26 members). The 1995 General Assembly included 45
lawyers (33 percent); 25 retirees; 13 members associated with real estate sales, development, construction, and contracting; and 16 working in insurance. In 2005,
there were at least 32 lawyers in the General Assembly (14 percent). That number
was exceeded by the 60 (25 percent) who identified themselves as business owners, CEOs, or self-employed. The presence of business is probably much larger,
but the reporting system treats separately professions such as consulting, while
some members reported their field of work (e.g., insurance) without indicating
their ownership status. In 2012, the number of lawyer-legislators in the Georgia
General Assembly was 41, a little over 30 percent of the total. The share of attorneys in 2015 was 15 percent—about the same as nationally, where it ranged from
3 percent in Alaska and New Hampshire to 30 percent in New Jersey.[17]

Partisan Composition: The Rise of Georgia Republicans

Perhaps more startling than demographic shifts in the General Assembly have been partisan changes (see figure 6.2). Democrats dominated Georgia politics from the late 1800s into the 1980s. Republicans established a presence following Georgia's support for Republican presidential candidate Barry Goldwater in 1964. Slow but steady gains followed. Republicans held less than 20 percent of the seats in the General Assembly into the 1990s.

Following the 1992 election, the number of Republicans grew from thirty-four to fifty-two in the House (29 percent) and from eleven to fifteen in the Senate (27 percent). The GOP share of seats increased slightly in 1994, 1996, 1998, and 2000. The real breakthroughs occurred in 2002 and 2004. Republicans, aided by four party switchers, gained control of the Senate in 2002, the same year that Sonny Perdue became Georgia's first Republican governor in over a century. In 2004, Republicans expanded their control of the Senate from thirty to thirty-four seats (61 percent).

Going into the 2002 election, Democrats controlled the House 105–74 and saw almost no erosion in their share of seats. However, perhaps a harbinger of things to come was the general election defeat of Tom Murphy, the Democratic speaker of the House since 1974. In the 2004 election, the Republicans recorded

Figure 6.2. Partisan Affiliation, Georgia General Assembly, 1976–2016

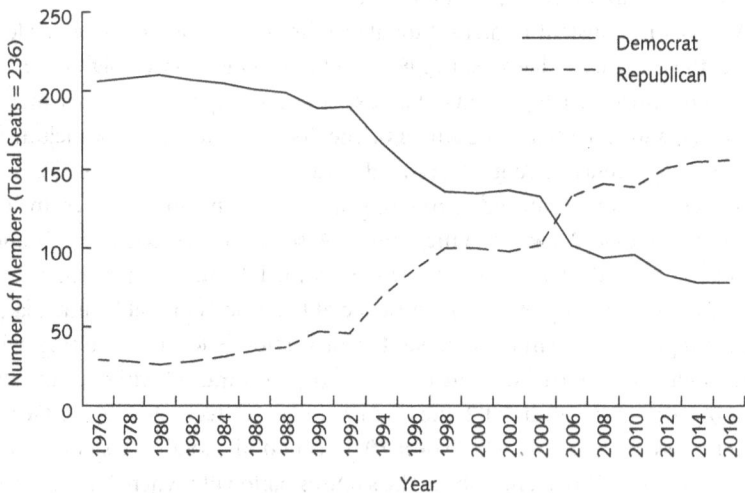

Source: Council of State Governments, Book of the States, 1976–2016.

huge gains to take control of the House, winning ninety-six seats and adding two party switchers, thereby gaining control of both houses of the legislature to complement a Republican in the governor's mansion. Republicans have continued to build on their success through the first two decades of this century, and Democrats continue to see their percentage of the legislature decline. In fact, many observers note that Georgia may be one of the strongest Republican states in the union.[18]

Legislative Leadership

The Georgia Constitution provides for the selection of presiding officers in each chamber.[19] In the Senate, the lieutenant governor serves as president, just as the vice president of the United States is formally the presiding officer of the U.S. Senate. Thus the presiding officer of the Senate is chosen by Georgia's voters in a statewide election, although the winner is elected independently from the governor. The Georgia Senate also elects one of its members as president pro tempore should the need arise to replace the presiding officer. In the House, the representatives elect a speaker from among their members along with a speaker pro tempore.

Legislative leadership in Georgia is similar to most states. Forty-five states have a lieutenant governor, with twenty-six elected on a ticket with the governor and seventeen elected independently. Two other states, Tennessee and West Virginia, do not have direct elections for lieutenant governor. In these two states whoever is elected the president of the state senate is the de facto lieutenant governor. All lieutenant governors are first in line to succeed to the governorship in their states, but their power in the legislative branch varies. Twenty-nine states in addition to Georgia (including Nebraska's unicameral legislature) make the lieutenant governor the presiding officer of the Senate. In the remaining twenty-four states, the Senate chooses its own presiding officer.[20] Like Georgia, the lower house in the other forty-eight bicameral legislatures elects one of its members as speaker. Twenty-five of these forty-eight states also elect a speaker pro tempore; the other twenty-three legislatures either have no such position or have their speaker appoint someone.

Informal norms sometimes guide leadership selection. One study that examined legislative leadership in the states over almost fifty years found that twenty-eight lower houses and thirty-three senates had a norm of one or two terms for leaders from 1947 until 1968. From 1968 through 1980, three or four terms became more common in both chambers. From 1981 to 1992, twelve lower houses had a norm of presiding officers serving five or more terms; the same was true of eighteen senates. Georgia is one of a handful of states where long service as a presiding officer was a norm from 1947 to 1992.[21]

Party Caucuses

In reality, decisions on leadership positions generally are made by party membership before the session begins. A meeting of Republican legislators in each chamber—the House Republican Caucus and the Senate Republican Caucus—elects its party's leaders. Democratic caucuses do likewise for their House and Senate leadership. For example, Republican senators chose their leadership for the 1995 session the week of the November 1994 elections, while House members picked their leaders the week after the election—roughly two months before the General Assembly convened. In 2002, when Republicans won control of the Senate, the long-time Democratic speaker of the House, Tom Murphy, was defeated for reelection. Although behind-the-scenes campaigning with caucus members occurred, in less than two weeks after the November 5 election, House Democrats had chosen their leaders, with Representative Terry Coleman officially elected speaker after the House began its new session the following January. In the Senate, Republicans also moved quickly to choose their leaders for the session that would start two months later.[22]

Members of each caucus are expected to remain loyal to their party nominee when floor votes are taken for presiding officers. Thus, a nomination by the majority party caucus is tantamount to election on the floor. Party caucuses also meet to discuss official positions on major issues and to set priorities. Leaders of the caucuses exert influence over the agenda of the legislature by devising strategies, promoting party positions on bills, and using the media to promote their goals.

Leadership in the House of Representatives

The Speaker. The speaker of the House has broad powers going beyond those officially granted to the office. They include the ability to change the order of bills appearing on the calendar and to control floor debate through recognition of members, suspension of debate, and decisions about the appropriateness of amendments. The speaker may also maintain order on the floor, require attendance by members in order to maintain a quorum, and control activity in the visitors' galleries. In addition, the speaker is second in line to succeed the governor, after the lieutenant governor.

Perhaps the greatest power of the speaker is the ability to appoint the membership of the committees that will review and draft legislation. The speaker also determines the committee to which a bill is sent for review. These powers are strong incentives for members of the House to cooperate with the speaker. The speaker may attend any and all committee meetings as an ex officio member and is a voting member of the powerful Rules Committee. In general, the speaker does not vote on bills as do other members of the House. In four instances, a speaker may vote during the floor debate. They occur when the House is tied on any floor vote, a requirement for a two-thirds or three-fifths vote is short by one additional vote, the speaker's vote would cause a tie, or the House is holding an internal election.

Longevity can increase the unofficial power of the speaker, as in the case of Thomas B. Murphy, who was first elected to the House from Haralson County in 1960 and became speaker in 1973. The House changed dramatically during Murphy's tenure, and he had to withstand several attacks on his power and prerogatives, especially in the early 1990s. Opponents accused him of being both dictatorial and vengeful. Supporters viewed him as someone who maintained order and stability in the 180-member House as the institution and the state developed over the years. These concerns were heightened at the end of the 1994 legislative session when the seventy-year-old speaker suffered a heart attack. He finally lost power when his constituents turned him out of office in 2002 by nine hundred votes.

In the speaker's absence, the speaker pro tempore, who is elected by the membership of the House, presides. The speaker may appoint other members to preside temporarily over the House as needed. Whenever presiding over the House, the speaker pro tempore or other representatives hold the same powers of debate regulation that the speaker does.

Other Leadership Positions. Another powerful office is that of majority leader, who is chosen by the party caucus. The majority leader and caucus officers may also assist the speaker in determining the party's position on important issues. Party whips are elected to assist in this process and may be instrumental in convincing other party members to vote along party lines.

The minority leader, caucus officers, and minority party whip are chosen by the caucus and perform much the same duties as their majority-party counterparts. Naturally, the minority party does not exert as much influence within the chamber as does the majority party.

Unlike the lack of formal links between the U.S. president and Congress, one member in each chamber serves as liaison to the governor's office. The administration floor leader in the House is picked by the governor and may introduce or sponsor legislation from the governor's legislative agenda.

Leadership in the Senate

The Lieutenant Governor. The leadership in the Senate is in many ways similar to that of the House, but there are important differences, which can be attributed to the smaller size of the Senate and its constitutional mandates. Unlike the speaker of the House, the lieutenant governor is elected not from a district within the state but by statewide election, which makes the position fairly visible to the electorate. As presiding officer, the lieutenant governor is referred to as a president of the Senate. Unlike the speaker, the president of the Senate may not vote under any circumstances.

The long dominance of the Democratic Party once guaranteed that the presiding officer and the majority of members in the Senate came from the same political party. The duties of the lieutenant governor included assigning senators to committees, referring bills to committee, and controlling debate and order on the Senate floor. However, the authority of lieutenant governors in the states is a combination of constitutional provisions, laws, and senate rules. This became painfully obvious to Georgia lieutenant governor Mark Taylor following the November 2002 elections. The new Republican majority changed Senate rules to remove the lieutenant governor's control over committee assignments and diminish his authority in other ways. In 2005, after they also gained a majority in the House, the new Republican speaker also denied Taylor the traditional role of presiding over the joint session of the House and the Senate that hears the governor's annual state-of-the-state speech.[23]

Other Leadership Positions. The president pro tempore, who is elected from the majority party, can fill in as presiding officer. The Senate also has positions of majority and minority leaders, as well as majority and minority whips. As in the House, these positions are selected by the party caucuses, which also select a senator to chair the caucus, develop their party's positions on important issues, and try to persuade senators to vote the party line on bills. As in the House, the administration floor leader designated by the governor introduces the governor's legislative agenda in the Senate.

Legislative Staff

Staffing is quite different in state legislatures compared to Congress. The fifty states had just over 26,000 permanent staff members in 2015, which compares to similar totals in 1996 and 2003, but is 53 percent higher than the almost 17,000 permanent staffers in 1979. The flip side of this growth is a decline in session-only staff in the states—from slightly more than 10,000 in 1979 to 5,547 in 2015. Altogether, state legislatures used 31,678 staff members in 2015, ranging from a high of 2,865 in New York to a low of 92 in Vermont. Staff totals were less than 200 in another seven states and more than 1,000 in four more.[24]

The Georgia General Assembly furnishes its members with limited staff support. Both the House and the Senate are assisted by personnel who provide a wide variety of services. This staff includes messengers, clerks, and doorkeepers. They generally are assisted by student interns during the legislative session. These "housekeeping" duties are not taken lightly. The clerk of the House and the secretary of the Senate are charged with filing all papers necessary for the proper functioning of the chambers. They compile the House and Senate journals after the close of the session and manage other necessary clerical functions.

There are also professional positions designed to deal with the complex duties and diverse policy questions that come before the General Assembly. This expertise is concentrated in research and budget offices in each chamber. Staffing was also affected by the 2002 election results. The new speaker in the Democratic-controlled House added a press secretary, policy analyst, and administrator to his staff. After the Republicans won their first majority in the Senate in more than a century, they created their own budget office rather than share one with the Democratic House. Republican Senate leaders added other staff positions as well. All these changes reflect both new leaders and efforts by the two parties to bolster their ability to contend with each other. In the end, the National Conference of State Legislatures reported that the General Assembly had 525 permanent staff, as well as 210 session-only staff, in 2015. This ranked Georgia twelfth among the states in the total number of legislative staff. The 2015 total of 735 staff members compares to 823 in 2003, 742 in 1996, 679 in 1988, and 600 in 1979.[25]

The Committee System

Comparing the Fifty States. Committees have become key parts of the way modern legislatures organize to do their work. Beyond that, there are substantial differences among the states. In 2015, the number of Senate committees ranged from five to forty-three, while House committees varied between six and forty-six. Six states use standing committees made up of House and Senate members. These joint committees are a major reason that several legislatures have very few standing committees in each chamber. Committee systems also vary in how members and chairpersons are selected. Senates have a range of other procedures for appointing committees, with under one-third having the presiding officer make such decisions. In three-fourths of the lower houses, the speaker appoints committee members. The remainder rely on one or more of the following: committees, shared responsibility between the speaker and the minority leader, party caucuses, and seniority. There was slightly less variation in the methods for choosing which members would chair committees. Sixteen of the senates have their presiding officer pick committee chairs, while forty-one of the forty-nine lower houses have given this responsibility to the speaker.[26] This system displays the unusual power of presiding officers in state legislatures, which could be based in part on the need to get work done during limited sessions and the desire of parties to promote an agenda when they are in a majority.

Georgia: Types of Committees. In Georgia, the constitution permits each chamber of the General Assembly to set its own procedures. It would be difficult for each member to be highly prepared on every issue that comes before the legislature and impossible to conduct debate on issues with everyone to be included in all discussions. This is especially true given the General Assembly's large number of members and the brief sessions. Therefore, standing (permanent) committees have been established to deal with issues that require regular attention. In 2015, the House operated with thirty-eight committees, and the Senate had thirty (see table 6.2). House committees are generally larger, with the Appropriations Committee having ninety-seven members in 2015; Senate committees have an established size of four to twenty-eight members. Senators serve on four to six committees; representatives normally are assigned to three or four committees.

Occasionally the entire membership of the House or Senate may have interest in an upcoming piece of legislation or other important matter. In this instance, the entire chamber may relax parliamentary procedure and meet as one large committee. The Committee of the Whole permits relaxed procedures and more-open discussion. At the other extreme, a committee-of-one may be appointed to permit a single legislator to receive a per diem allowance while conducting research on a bill, writing a report, or other official business, even when the legislature is out of session. Committees-of-one are temporary assignments.

Some committees include members of both the House and the Senate. These are joint committees and may be standing or ad hoc. Georgia has fewer joint standing committees and relies on them less than do other states, but they are used on occasion to reduce confusion between the chambers and iron out differences between standing committees before legislation is drafted. Joint committees are especially useful in the budget process, in which time is an important factor. Conference committees are temporary joint committees formed when bills passing the House and the Senate differ in language or intent. In such cases, compromises must be made to ensure that each chamber will consider the exact same bill for final passage.

Committee Membership and Leaders. Members of House and Senate committees generally retain their assignments until they request another or vacate their seats. Leadership within the committees is not guaranteed, however, and is appointed in the House by the speaker. When Republicans gained control of the House in the 2004 election, they adopted several innovations to the committee

Table 6.2. Standing Committees of the Georgia General Assembly, 2016

Senate	House of Representatives
Administrative Affairs	Agriculture and Consumer Affairs
Agriculture and Consumer Affairs	Appropriations
Appropriations	Banks and Banking
Assignments	Budget and Fiscal Affairs Oversight
Banking and Financial Institutions	Code Revision
Economic Development and Tourism	Defense and Veterans Affairs
Education and Youth	Economic Development & Tourism
Ethics	Education
Finance	Energy, Utilities, and Telecommunications
Government Oversight	Ethics
Health and Human Services	Game, Fish, and Parks
Higher Education	Governmental Affairs
Insurance and Labor	Health and Human Services
Interstate Cooperation	Higher Education
Judiciary	Human Relations & Aging
Judiciary Non-Civil	Industry and Labor
MARTOC	Information and Audits
Natural Resources and the Environment	Insurance
Public Safety	Interstate Cooperation
Reapportionment and Redistricting	Intragovernmental Coordination
Regulated Industries and Utilities	Judiciary
Retirement	Judiciary Non-Civil
Rules	Juvenile Justice
Science and Technology	Legislative and Congressional Reapportionment
Special Judiciary	MARTOC
State and Local Governmental Operations	Motor Vehicles
State Institutions and Property	Natural Resources and Environment
Transportation	Public Safety and Homeland Security
Urban Affairs	Regulated Industries
Veterans, Military and Homeland Security	Retirement
	Rules
	Science and Technology
	Small Business Development
	Special Rules
	State Planning & Community Affairs
	State Properties
	Transportation
	Ways and Means

Sources: Georgia House of Representatives, "House Committees List," http://www.house.ga.gov /Committees/en-US/CommitteeList.aspx; Georgia Senate, "Senate Committees List," http://www .senate.ga.gov/committees/en-US/SenateCommitteesList.aspx.

system designed to enhance the power of their leadership. Perhaps the most visible and controversial was speaker Glenn Richardson's authority to designate an unlimited number of "hawks." Like the speaker, the speaker pro tempore, the majority leader, and the majority whip, hawks were considered ex officio members of all House committees and subcommittees. All these party leaders had committee voting rights with the exception of the speaker, who was allowed to vote only in the Rules Committee. Thus, if legislation favored by party leaders was in trouble in committee, they could mobilize the hawks to achieve their ends. As one might expect, House Democrats reacted negatively to this flexible definition of committee membership.[27] Ultimately, Richardson's successor eliminated the hawk system and returned committees to their usual voting structure.

The lieutenant governor lost the authority to control committee appointments as president of the Senate in 2003, when Democrat Mark Taylor faced the new Republican majority. The selection of committee members and leaders is now made by the Committee on Assignments, which includes the lieutenant governor. However, the other two members are the president pro tempore and the majority leader—an arrangement that left the Republicans with a two-to-one majority on this crucial committee.[28] Committee leadership is exercised by a chairman, a vice chairman, and a secretary (the important exception here is the House Appropriations Committee, which operated with six vice chairmen in 2005). Committee and subcommittee chairs are aware that their positions depend on continued good relations with the chamber leadership.

Besides standing committees, other committees may be formed to deal with issues on an ad hoc basis. These temporary committees may be formed to watch over the implementation of a new bill or to deal with a one-time-only project such as the 1996 Olympics. Interim committees are established between sessions to investigate issues or write reports that will be presented to the entire chamber when it is again in session. These committees disband when their tasks are complete, and members are not guaranteed continued assignment on future committees.

Committees and Legislators' Goals. Committees do more than allow legislatures to work more efficiently. They also provide a way for legislators to pursue reelection, issues that are important for their districts, policies they consider important, and a variety of other goals. Although committee assignments allow members to develop expertise, specialization has been criticized on occasion as a conflict of interest when members sit on committees related to their occupations or businesses. Committee work can also help legislators obtain campaign funds from interest groups. Committees permit legislators to use "pork barrel" politics—legislation that can provide benefits for specific constituencies. Traditional examples of this practice are public works projects such as highways.

Consider the example of the House Higher Education Committee, which has jurisdiction over the colleges and universities in the University System of Georgia, the campuses under the Department of Technical and Adult Education, and the HOPE Scholarship Program. In 2005–2006, the committee had seventeen members (nine Republicans and eight Democrats). Perhaps more interesting than the partisan makeup of the committee was its geography. The Democrats came from districts that included Georgia Tech, the University of Georgia, Valdosta State University, Georgia Southwestern State University, Columbus State University, and Augusta State University. The Augusta representative's district was next to one that included the Medical College of Georgia. In addition, the Democrat from Jonesboro had a district next to one that included Clayton State University, and another's district included a private institution (Emory University).

The nine Republicans represented districts without large institutions. The committee chairman came from Douglasville, home to one of the four campuses of West Central Technical College. One member's district included North Georgia College & State University, another represented a district with Waycross College, and the vice chairman's district was home to South Georgia College. The remaining Republicans included one from Cobb County, one from Rockdale County, and two from Gwinnett County. These four members may not have had readily apparent interests within their districts, but their areas had important technical colleges. In addition, the General Assembly approved legislation in 2005 to create a state college at a site in Gwinnett County where several state institutions were offering programs and degrees. Moreover, students from Cobb and Gwinnett counties were major beneficiaries of HOPE Scholarship dollars. The ninth Republican member was from Griffin, where the University of Georgia's College of Agricultural and Environmental Sciences had a campus for many years and started offering degrees in 2005.[29]

Types of Legislation

Like other legislatures, the Georgia General Assembly spends significant time considering bills introduced by its members in hopes that they will be passed and become part of state law. Bills before the General Assembly can be classified as a resolution, general legislation, or local legislation. All currently enforceable statutes are published in the *Official Code of Georgia Annotated*, which is updated periodically to include both new laws and legal opinions on implementation of current law.[30]

Resolutions. Much of what is considered by the General Assembly is not intended to be implemented as statute. Some of the items brought up for consideration are statements of legislative opinion and may be enforceable only on the membership of the legislature itself. For example, the legislature may wish to honor an individual or a sports team, in which case the General Assembly might pass a resolution describing their achievements. Resolutions also might be used to create special committees, determine compensation for citizens who have been injured or suffered damages by state actions, or set requirements for legislative staff. The resolution would have little impact on other citizens of the state. It does, however, express the approval of the state government.

Resolutions might be passed to require the General Assembly itself to behave in a specific manner, as with rules of conduct, scheduling, or agreements on budgetary matters. In some cases, resolutions are passed by only one chamber to establish rules only for the membership of that body, but joint resolutions require passage through both chambers, as in the case of budgetary resolutions. Resolutions *generally* do not require the signature of the governor since they do not require implementation outside the legislature itself, although they might be passed in much the same way as other legislation. However, joint resolutions that are enforceable as law do require the governor's signature and may be vetoed.

Proposed amendments to the state constitution are special cases of joint resolutions for which two-thirds of each chamber must vote in favor. They are then placed on the ballot for public approval by a majority of the voters. The governor has no formal role in this process, but he may be influential in proposing amendments and mobilizing public opinion before the referendum.

General Legislation. General legislation has application statewide. Laws regarding election procedures or speed limits on state highways are examples. Local governments may not pass ordinances that contradict general law. Most general legislation intended to change existing law will specify exactly which statutes will be changed, but any new legislation supersedes past legislation. For this reason the passage date may be important. Only the most recently *passed* legislation is applicable.

Local Legislation. Local legislation refers to those laws passed by the Georgia General Assembly that apply only to specific cities, counties, or special districts within the state. The General Assembly retains the power to govern localities through the passage of local legislation, which may not contradict general legislation and may not be used to change the tenure of particular local officials.[31] It can, however, be used to create or change political boundaries.

The passage of local legislation differs in some ways from the passage of gen-

Table 6.3. Bills Introduced and Passed in Regular Sessions of the Georgia General Assembly, 1980–2016

Year	Total Number of Bills Introduced	Number of General Bills Passed	Number of Local Bills Passed	Total Number of Bills Passed	Local Acts as Percent of Total Bills Passed
1980	1,817	419	347	766	45.3
1981	1,598	353	486	839	57.9
1982	1,891	358	395	753	52.5
1983	1,199	310	273	583	46.8
1984	1,658	385	398	783	50.8
1985	1,429	344	430	774	55.6
1986	1,893	381	532	913	58.3
1987	1,574	352	456	808	56.4
1988	1,781	427	266	693	38.4
1989	1,542	404	310	714	43.4
1990	1,316	437	332	769	43.2
1991	1,556	374	234	608	38.5
1992	1,497	507	363	870	41.7
1993	1,559	327	305	632	48.3
1994	1,239	354	300	654	45.9
1995	1,575	298	222	520	42.7
1996	1,121	338	225	563	40.0
1997	1,515	298	213	511	41.7
1998	2,117	306	218	524	41.6
1999	1,386	219	242	461	52.5
2000	1,836	333	170	503	33.8
2001	1,290	205	191	396	48.2
2002	2,014	256	365	621	58.8
2003	1,437	199	215	414	51.9
2004	2,038	208	186	394	47.2
2005*	N/A	N/A	N/A	N/A	N/A
2006	1,937	274	235	509	46.2
2007	1,226	209	188	397	47.4
2008*	N/A	N/A	N/A	N/A	N/A
2009	1,160	194	158	352	44.9
2010	1,287	239	122	361	33.8
2011	958	152	105	257	40.9
2012	1,556	208	309	517	59.8

Table 6.3. Bills Introduced and Passed in Regular Sessions of the Georgia General Assembly, 1980–2016 (*continued*)

Year	Total Number of Bills Introduced	Number of General Bills Passed	Number of Local Bills Passed	Total Number of Bills Passed	Local Acts as Percent of Total Bills Passed
2013	974	184	153	337	45.4
2014	1,250	190	132	322	41.0
2015	955	184	128	312	41.0
2016	1,282	195	128	323	39.6
Total	52,463	10,421	9,332	19,753	47.2

Sources: Georgia General Assembly, Legislative Services Committee and Office of Legislative Counsel, Summary of General Statutes Enacted, 1980–2016

* Data from 2005 and 2008 were not officially published by the Georgia Legislative Services Committee or the Office of Legislative Counsel.

eral law. Local bills must be preceded by a period of advertisement in which citizens of the jurisdiction concerned are notified of the potential law. This notification most often occurs in local newspapers. Legislators from the district(s) involved generally speak on the floor, and other lawmakers normally defer to them because the bill typically affects only the districts of members sponsoring the local bill. This pattern of local courtesy is reciprocal. For this reason, most local legislation passes without dissent. Unlike the required three readings of general bills, local legislation requires only one reading, and sometimes only the title is read. Because so little debate takes place, the General Assembly at times votes on several local matters at once.

The Georgia General Assembly is notable for its involvement in local matters and limited grant of authority to local governments (see chapter 9). As a result, local legislation comprises a large share of the statutes adopted by the legislature (see table 6.3). The legislature's workload is a bit higher than suggested by table 6.3 because the table does not include resolutions. Still, Georgia ranks just below the middle of the states in workload. In comparison to the 955 bills in the Georgia General Assembly in 2015, thirty-four legislatures had more bills introduced that year, including over 14,000 in New York, more than 9,000 in New Jersey, and almost 7,000 in Massachusetts.[32]

How a Bill Becomes a Law

Assuming that a bill begins in the House of Representatives, the following section describes the path from introduction to enactment as law. Not all legislation will follow all the steps outlined below. In fact, most legislation is stopped early in the process, but all contingencies are covered here in order to provide a complete description.[33]

Introduction and Referral

Initially, legislation is an idea conceived by legislators or brought to them by lobbyists, other politicians, private citizens, corporations, or interest groups. Only members of the General Assembly may introduce legislation. Bills generally are written by several persons and may be sponsored by multiple legislators. The legislative staff (the Budget and Research Office in the House of Representatives and the Senate Research Office in the Senate) may assist in drafting a bill. In some instances, legislation passed by other states may be used as models for Georgia. Bills may be introduced in either chamber of the General Assembly or at the same time in both chambers. One exception is proposed legislation dealing with public revenues or appropriation of public money, which is constitutionally mandated to begin in the House of Representatives.

Bills to be introduced are filed with the clerk of the House of Representatives. Bills must adhere to a specific format dictated by the constitution and observed procedures. Each bill begins "BE IT ENACTED BY THE GENERAL ASSEMBLY OF GEORGIA" and has a summary title that describes the bill's intent. The title of the bill must directly relate to the content of the proposed legislation, and bills are constitutionally restricted to no more than one purpose. The state constitution mandates that all bills be read three times from the floor on three separate days. Because the title is required to be a summary of intent, reading the title only is substituted for reading the entire bill. A second reading of the bill, which occurs on the second day after introduction, will also be of the title only. The constitution forbids the introduction of bills that deal with specific individuals or that might limit the constitutional authority of the General Assembly. Population bills (those that apply to jurisdictions of a certain population) are also forbidden, as are bills that would have the effect of limiting business competition or creating monopolies within the state.[34]

Once a bill is introduced in the House, the speaker determines which committee will review the proposal. Because committee jurisdictions overlap to some degree, the speaker has some influence on the outcome of the bill by deciding which committee gets it. The speaker may choose to give a bill to a committee that is likely to receive it favorably, amend it in certain ways, or even kill it.

Committee Action

Once assigned to a committee, the bill may be referred to a subcommittee, where a smaller number of legislators might have more time to devote to its content. Not all bills are referred to subcommittees, however. Whether a committee or subcommittee works on the legislation, a number of courses may be followed at this stage. Public hearings may be held on the proposed legislation. Lobbyists or other interested parties may testify about the potential impact of the bill or the need for more legislation in a particular area. The media may follow the bill at this stage, and according to the state constitution, they must be permitted entry into committee meetings. Such "sunshine laws" are designed to allow public scrutiny at this stage of lawmaking, which is generally not held up to public view.[35] The committee or subcommittee may determine that further study is necessary, or members may decide that the legislation is unnecessary or undesirable, in which case it will not be acted on further. They may also recommend a bill be passed or amended. In some instances, the bill will go forward from the committee with a recommendation that it not be passed by the full chamber. A bill reported unfavorably indicates some disagreement within the committee, and that at least one legislator is confronting the majority. Such action would not be taken lightly, as it might have negative political consequences.

On occasion, members of the chamber who are not on the committee considering a bill might have an interest in its passage. In such instances, a motion may be made on the floor of the House to bring the bill to a floor vote, even over the objections of the committee. These motions represent a clear challenge to the decisions made by committee leadership holding the bill and, under rule 59, must be supported by at least two-thirds of the members present. Forcing a bill out of committee does not ensure its passage, and bills sent to the floor may simply be referred to other committees, in which case the process could begin again. The Senate does not permit such floor challenges, and committees may choose not to act on any bills in their jurisdiction.

Scheduling Floor Debate

Once a bill has made its way out of committee, it must be placed on the calendar to receive attention on the floor. In the first half of the legislative session, placement of a bill on the calendar is achieved through the general calendar of the clerk of the House, but as the session progresses, time on the floor is more strictly guarded. During the final twenty days of the session, the Rules Committee of the House meets daily to determine which bills will be discussed on the floor that day. This scheduling is called the rules calendar. The Rules Committee may select any bill for daily consideration that has been reported favorably by standing committees. Thus the Rules Committee may decide that a particular piece of legislation is never acted on by the House, even if a standing committee favors it. Members of the Rules Committee therefore hold substantial power over all legislation, especially since most committees do not finish work early enough in the session on many bills to place them on the general calendar. The chairs of the rules committees in both chambers are strong political forces in the General Assembly, as little legislation that does not meet their approval is likely to be passed. It should be remembered that in the House the speaker is a voting member on the Rules Committee. Attendance by the speaker at Rules Committee meetings is a clear indication that the speaker wants certain bills to appear on the calendar.

Floor Action

Once on the calendar and called up for discussion, bills are read on the floor for the third time. At this point, members are free to propose amendments and debate various issues relative to the bill's content. Debate is controlled by the presiding officer of each chamber. Restrictions on debate time are set by rules of the House and the Senate, and there is no provision for filibuster. Those legislators who wish to speak on the merits or disadvantages of a bill must obtain permission from the presiding officer, who may allow questions from the floor. The chair of the committee that reported the bill is given a special allocation of time to discuss the bill, and dissenting opinions are also permitted floor time prior to voting on the bill.

Bills are passed by a simple majority of the entire membership of each chamber, although there are several exceptions to this rule. Tax legislation, proposed amendments to the constitution, veto overrides, punitive action taken against a member of the General Assembly, or motions to change the order of business require two-thirds majorities. Procedural changes may only require a majority of those members present. In most instances, votes are taken using electronic voting boxes located on the desks of the legislators. At other times, votes are taken by voice or a show of hands. Generally, voice votes are used for less controversial issues, as are votes by hand counts. In some cases, a roll call vote may be taken in which legislators are individually called on to respond "yea" or "nay." For important voting procedures, such as a veto override, both electronic and roll call voting may be used. Once a bill has achieved a majority vote in one chamber, it must be passed in identical form by a majority vote in the other chamber in order to continue on the path to becoming a law.

Bills are transmitted from one chamber to another after careful proofreading. Transmittal is a formal procedure governed by strict rules and normally takes several days. During the more frantic days of the session, transmittal of bills may be expedited. In one famous effort to beat the deadline for the end of the session, a legislator hung from the balcony in 1964 to stop the hands of the clock just before midnight. Although he did not fall, his precarious position caused him to knock the clock off the wall and break it, thus allowing debate to continue. In later interviews, one of his colleagues admitted, "We'd been imbibing."[36] To prevent a logjam of legislation in the final days, the Senate will not accept House bills after the thirty-third day of the session. The House has no such constraint, but its rules recognize the need to deal with the Senate's limitation. This date is known as "crossover day" because it is the last time a bill can cross over between the two chambers for a first reading in order to be considered during the session.[37]

In most cases, bills passed by the Senate and those passed by the House are similar but not exactly the same. A conference committee is then brought together by the presiding officers of the House and the Senate to work out the differences between their respective versions of the bill. This committee may be made up of members of the standing committees that had jurisdiction over the bill earlier, but it must be composed of legislators who had voted in favor of passage of the bill. Conference committees may recommend substantial changes in the bill but may not deviate from the bill's original intent. They also must act quickly and may not report a bill back to either floor of the General Assembly with an unfavorable recommendation.

When a conference committee has worked out the final language of a bill, it must once again be voted on by each chamber and receive a majority. This final passage must produce an identical bill passed by a majority of the House and a majority of the Senate. The final version is then certified by the clerk of the House and the secretary of the Senate prior to being sent to the governor. Failure by either chamber to pass the conference committee's version of a bill generally spells its death. In some cases, the conference committee may again be asked to rework the bill for further consideration.

The Governor

The governor has authority to act on legislation passed by the General Assembly that would have the effect of law, except for changes in the state constitution.[38] If the governor signs the bill, it becomes law on a specified date, usually with the start of the fiscal year on July 1. If the governor fails to act on a bill, it will become law following a six-day waiting period for bills passed during the first thirty-four days of the session or following a forty-day waiting period for bills passed during the final six days of the legislative session. Thus bills may sit on the governor's desk after adjournment of the legislature and become law even if the governor does not sign them. In some cases, the governor will veto legislation. If the governor vetoes a bill after the adjournment of the General Assembly, the next legislative session may take up action on the veto.

Like forty-four other states, Georgia provides for two types of vetoes, full and item (often called line-item veto), although the item veto in Georgia applies only to appropriations bills.[39] A full veto is a rejection of an entire bill. The governor will transmit a vetoed bill back to the legislature with an explanation of the objections to it. The General Assembly is then free to either modify the bill to meet the expectations of the governor or try overriding the governor's veto with a two-thirds majority in each chamber. Veto overrides are not easily accomplished, and the General Assembly has not been able to override the full veto of any governor since 1974. That was even the case with Governor Deal's controversial 2016 vetoes of a "religious liberty" bill and one allowing guns to be carried on college campuses.[40]

Item vetoes are rejections of specific passages in appropriations bills. Reconsideration of bills in which specific funding has been vetoed is not necessary, and the governor's actions officially reduce the appropriation. Thus the line-item veto can be a tool to enhance a governor's power vis-à-vis the legislature. For example, Governor Miller vetoed a line item for $479,479 in 1992 that was listed under the Department of Education's budget for "special projects." Miller indicated that the vague entry left him unable to determine how the money was to be used. Subsequent investigation of this expenditure revealed that the speaker of the House and other key legislators had maintained control of approximately $2.5 million in public money for a six-year period. Much of the money had been spent in the home districts of these legislators without approval by the governor. While the media attention surrounding this disclosure labeled it a "slush fund," no legal action was taken by the attorney general's office.[41]

As is true in the legislature, the end of the session is a busy time for the governor, with many pieces of legislation reaching the governor's desk at the same time. At the end of the 1992 session, Governor Miller signed more than one hundred pieces of legislation in a single day, almost half of the total for that session.[42] Once a bill has been signed into law, it takes precedence over previous legislation. Exceptions to the July effective date for laws are bills that specify another date, local bills, constitutional amendments, or resolutions that deal with the operation of state government agencies or budgets.

Factors Influencing the Legislative Process

The legislative process involves more than constitutional or legal requirements. Of the many actions that can affect the legislative process, two of the important ones are the pressures brought to bear by lobbying and the norms that affect the behavior of legislators.

Lobbying

Interest groups have an important role in the political process (see chapter 5). All interest groups have the same goal: to create and maintain policy in accord with their objectives. They can do this in all three branches of government. An organization's ability to influence public policy depends on the number of people or other resources it possesses, how it is organized, how cohesive it is, and other factors.

Lobbying got its name from the fact that many policy advocates would wait outside the floor of legislature chambers to speak to legislators before they cast votes. Although lobbyists are not permitted on the floor of the Georgia House or Senate, one can still find representatives from organized groups waiting to speak to legislators in the Capitol's corridors. The lobbying process has carried a rather negative connotation and was declared unconstitutional in Georgia until a new constitution was implemented in 1983. The definition of what should be considered lobbying was left up to the legislature, and the practice existed despite its supposed unconstitutionality.

Lobbyists in the Georgia Legislature. In Georgia, lobbyists were divided for many years into two camps: urban and agricultural interests. By the 1990s, a coalition interested in economic development blurred some of the barriers between these two groups, and an economic growth lobby became a driving force in Georgia politics. Economic development is so widely accepted as a function of government that it may be impossible to separate the interests of government and economic growth. It is not uncommon for business groups to hold ties to the legislative committees that regulate them.[43] Recent actions suggest that this business coalition remains quite successful in the legislative process.

Some observers argue that the growth of the economic development lobby is beneficial because it has diminished urban-rural and racial divisions. Those representing other interests might not evaluate the political scene so optimistically. For instance, social welfare lobbyists are less likely to be successful in Georgia's political climate for a number of reasons. First, Georgians are often wary of social welfare spending by government. Second, Georgia's constitution requires a balanced budget, and programs that operate on public funds are in tight competition for budgetary allocations. Finally, social welfare groups have traditionally been less successful at building coalitions with legislators than have economic development lobbyists. Environmental groups have faced similar obstacles to success.

Government agencies also have a vested interest in public policy. For example, the Department of Corrections has a strong interest in decisions regarding the staffing, funding, and operation of prisons. Agencies lobby for policy through their interaction with lawmakers, their influence on the information available to the legislature, and their prestige as experts and government officials. Some evidence suggests that agencies are more influential when they can provide services or projects for legislators' districts or help with constituent concerns.[44]

Success for lobbyists depends in part on effective use of time, money, and information. In general terms, that fact has translated into campaign contributions and other benefits to legislators. Such established relationships permit long-term lobbyists a head start on their competition. One analysis found that interest groups spent more than $900,000 lobbying the legislature in 2004. That included over $780,000 for entertainment and nearly $30,000 for tickets to sporting events. Efforts included individual meals and huge social events, not to mention free food and beverages at the Capitol provided by the Georgia Association of Convenience Stores. During 2004, the Georgia Chamber of Commerce, the Georgia Soft Drink Association, and Coca-Cola each spent more than $20,000 on lobbying; Georgia Power spent almost $44,000; and the Savannah Chamber of Commerce emerged as the big spender, at $50,024. Entertainment spending has been complemented in recent years by more grassroots mobilization, including by educators, environmentalists, and Christian conservatives. With limited staff resources, legislators often rely on lobbyists and interest group members for information.[45]

Lobby Regulation. Lobbyists who are attempting to influence public policy in Georgia must register for each legislative session and pay a filing fee to the five-member Georgia Government Transparency and Campaign Finance Commission, which was created by the 1986 Ethics in Government Act. While in the state Capitol, lobbyists must wear badges that identify them as lobbyists and disclose their organization. Statements must be filed to delineate an organization's purposes and expenses.

Critics have expressed concern over practices such as providing meals, entertainment, and travel for legislators. Others have complained about the "revolving door" through which former officials turn to lobbying when they leave government service. However, prior to the 1992 session, Georgia's lobbying laws were among the least restrictive in the fifty states. Media reports linked a bill passed in the legislature to international money laundering and a Georgia-based bank. This coverage and efforts by then-secretary of state Max Cleland helped lead to increased control of lobbying. These initiatives received strong support from "good government" groups and some members of the media. Lawmakers were greatly divided, however, and despite objections by House speaker Tom Murphy, an ethics bill was passed. It limited campaign contributions by lobbyists, clarified the state's bribery laws, and for the first time required lobbyists to disclose what they spent to influence legislation.[46]

Even with the changes adopted in 1992, Georgia remained among the least restrictive states in terms of lobbying regulation. One study covering the years 1990–2003 compared states in terms of lobbying definitions, prohibited activities, and disclosure requirements. On a 0–18 scale of regulation, Georgia moved from a score of 1 in 1990–1991 to 8 in the mid-1990s, where it remained through 2003. At the other end were the eighteen states with scores between 12 and 17. Another thirteen states had scores of 11 or 12.[47] More recently, Governor Sonny Perdue promoted more stringent ethics legislation after his election in 2002 but met with limited success, even after his fellow Republicans controlled the General Assembly.[48]

Legislative Norms

It is sometimes argued that norms of behavior are necessary in order to achieve stability and efficiency within legislatures, whether at the state or the federal level. Norms may be quite simple (a consistently friendly manner toward those in positions of power) or very complex (practices adopted toward committee chairs or deference to colleagues on local legislation).

Several norms appear to further the interests of individual legislators as they pursue policy goals or influence within the General Assembly. Since some traditions of behavior have no written guidelines, norms are often noted subjectively by observers or adhered to by participants. In other cases, norms of behavior may be based in part on written bylaws of the legislature. Major norms in the Georgia General Assembly include behavior toward colleagues on and off the floor, patterns of reciprocal voting, and the use of loyalty and limited seniority in committee assignment and leadership positions.

Collegiality. Rules of the House and Senate prohibit disruption of activity on the floor. While total silence is not observed, and side conversations are more the rule than the exception, members do not applaud or hiss at comments made from the floor. Members nonetheless often move freely around each chamber during debate. In the Senate, members are forbidden from passing between the speaker and the presiding officer. While on the floor, members speak to one another only through the presiding officer. Thus someone wishing to ask a question would first ask the presiding officer whether the speaker would yield the floor for a question. Direct address is not permitted, and legislators have long referred to one another in formal language such as the "gentleman from the Seventy-Second District" or by Mr., Mrs., or Ms.[49]

Legislators also are forbidden by rule from making disparaging remarks about the General Assembly or other members. This institutional loyalty officially governs only remarks made on the floor or in the House and Senate journals. However, it is generally practiced outside the chambers as well.

Work and Reciprocity. Members are expected to do their share of the work. Since all members of the Georgia General Assembly are required to vote on all legislation unless excused before the vote is called, they are expected to be informed on most issues coming up for votes. While it is not possible to be fully informed on all matters, the committee system provides a means for members to rely on one another for information and support. In the General Assembly, as in most other legislatures, members are expected to defer to the work of a committee when its bills come to the floor for votes. In turn, members of other committees expect the same deference when their bills are voted on. Thus the norm of reciprocity is apparent in the behavior of members of the House and the Senate. While procedures are available to bring a bill to the floor without the approval of the relevant committee, legislators risk alienation from their peers with such a violation of reciprocity.

Once bills receive committee recommendations and are presented for floor votes, it is assumed that most of the debate has already taken place. Bills that would divide the members are not likely to get that far in the lawmaking process. Therefore, unanimous or nearly unanimous floor votes are not uncommon. This is not to say that no debate takes place on the floor or that close votes do not sometimes occur, but members generally avoid the public display of divisiveness that such debate would produce. Compromises are reached in more private settings, such as committees or even behind the scenes. The cohesiveness of the membership may be explained in a number of ways. It may be an indication that members are concerned about the public appearance of such debate and believe it violates the stability of the institution. Moreover, a publicly voiced debate would certainly have a loser as well as a winner, and no member looks forward to the possibility of losing a public debate. Finally, the short length of the session and limited time permitted for debate also force members and leaders to build consensus if they hope to pass any legislation regarding a particular matter.

Seniority and Loyalty. Those members who have attained positions of power within the chamber generally retain them until they are no longer in office or the presiding officer removes them. Positions such as committee chair, vice chair, and secretary are generally awarded based on some combination of loyalty and the number of years served on a committee (seniority). However, seniority is not in and of itself a guarantee of chairing a committee. For example, Bobby Lawson and Ken Poston lost committee positions in 1993 after backing an unsuccessful bid to unseat Tom Murphy as speaker of the House.[50] Some legislators have built successful public careers despite violating traditional norms and being considered outsiders. Cynthia McKinney was considered by many to be a political outsider during her tenure in the Georgia General Assembly. She nonetheless was elected to the U.S. House of Representatives in Georgia's newly created Eleventh District in 1992, the first black female to represent Georgia in Congress.

The New Face of the General Assembly

As noted throughout this chapter, the Georgia General Assembly is in a state of transition. Redistricting following the 1990, 2000, and 2010 censuses has changed the balance of power to allow the election of more suburban, black, and Republican members. Norms of behavior are also in a state of flux, especially given the restrictions of new ethics legislation and recent calls for ever-tighter regulation of lobbying. In addition, the state's electorate is growing and changing, in part due to recent migrants from other states. More Georgians have aligned with the Republican Party; new interest groups have appeared on the scene; and partisan change will affect the way lobbyists and candidates conduct political activity. Sponsorship of legislation, floor debates, and roll call votes may be increasingly conflictual as the two parties attempt to stake out an agenda that differentiates them more clearly from each other in the eyes of voters. The Republican Party's new status as the established majority party has given it the tools of power, but intra-Republican disputes are becoming as important to policy making as intra-Democratic disputes were in the past. Georgia's General Assembly has a long history of weathering political change, and its institutions are designed to adjust to the political realities of the day so that it can do the work of representing the state's people in its representative democracy.

CHAPTER 7

The Executive Branch

With Kristina LaPlant

The governor is, of course, the leader of the executive branch of Georgia. However, the governor is only one part of the executive branch of government. In this chapter we will examine the qualifications, selection mechanisms, and powers of the various officeholders of this branch of government. First, we will focus on the governor and then examine the other elected cabinet-level officials. Throughout the chapter, we also compare the power and efficacy of the governor and the other department heads to those of other states.

Some aspects of the Georgia political system enhance the power of the governor, for example, having a part-time legislature. However, other things detract from the governor's power. For example, unlike the federal system, where the president uses appointment power to fill almost all the executive branch offices, Georgia, like most states, provides elections to fill these roles, thus diluting the power of the state executive.

This division of power among elected executive branch offices is quite common. Most notable is the separate election of the governor and the lieutenant governor. Unlike the election for the presidency of the United States, where the candidates for president and vice president run as a unified ticket, in Georgia separate elections are held for governor and lieutenant governor, so the governor and next in line can be from different political parties and have different policy goals and agendas.

The division of authority of executive powers among elected department heads is known as a "plural executive" (see table 7.1). Voters around the country choose just over three hundred executive officials in statewide elections. Ten states also elect members to multimember boards. There are, of course, a few exceptions to this system of dissipated authority. For example, voters in Maine, New Hampshire, New Jersey, and Tennessee only elect a governor, while Alaska and Hawaii voters choose only a governor and a lieutenant governor. Virginia elects these two officers and an attorney general.[1] Georgia elects the governor,

Table 7.1. Executive Branch Officials in the States

	Number of States Electing	Method of Selection in Georgia
Governor	50	Elected Statewide
Lieutenant Governor	43	Elected Statewide
Secretary of State	35	Elected Statewide
Attorney General	43	Elected Statewide
Agriculture Commissioner	12	Elected Statewide
Insurance Commissioner	11	Elected Statewide
Labor Commissioner	4	Elected Statewide
Education Superintendent	12	Elected Statewide
Utilities Commissioners	6	Elected Statewide*
Treasurer	36	Appointed by Board†
Auditor	23	Chosen by Legislature

Source: Council of State Governments 2014, Selected State Administrative Officials: Methods of Selection.

* Georgia's Public Service Commission consists of five members elected to six-year terms.

† Appointed by the State Depository Board.

the lieutenant governor, the secretary of state, the secretary of agriculture, the attorney general, the insurance commissioner, the state school superintendent, and the labor commissioner.

Many members of these plural executives are required to be elected by state constitutions; others are provided for by law. Their tasks vary significantly, and advocates of this system see it as promoting accountability to voters and furthering checks on the power of other officials. Financial monitoring, for instance, is assigned to elected auditors, comptrollers, and treasurers, as well as appointed officials. Spreading around this control over money made eminent sense to constitution drafters in the 1800s as a way to prevent corruption. The same might be said of attorneys general, whose independence in investigating and prosecuting could be a check on other state officials. Nevertheless, the 1900s saw increased centralization in the states, both in terms of the states increasing their power relative to their local governments and governors gaining authority relative to legislatures.[2]

The Governor

Even under the plural executive, governors are generally the most powerful political figures in their states, and the Georgia governor has much power relative to other political actors in the state and sits in the middle rankings of power relative to other state governors. This power derives from formal authority in the state's constitution as well as several other sources of power, including laws, the media, public opinion, ties to political parties and interest groups, and personal characteristics.

Institutional Powers

Formal authority derives from several structures of state government as outlined in each state's constitution and laws. A University of North Carolina scholar, Thad Beyle, listed several factors of formal power: the number of separately elected officials, the tenure of the governor (potential time in office), appointment power, budget power, veto power, and control of the state legislature by the governor's party.

Informal authority derives from factors outside the constitution and develops from such things as public opinion and elections. Beyle cites the election mandate of the governor (margin of victory in the last election), the governor's political ambition, the personal future of the governor (for example, "lame duck" status), and job performance rating as sources of informal power rank.

Beyle developed a scoring system on a 1–5 scale that ranks governors based on these two types of power: institutional and personal. These scores are then averaged separately for the items comprising institutional and personal power, and the two averages can then be added to produce a measure of total power with a 1–10 range.[3]

Except for party control, institutional power is fixed. Personal power varies depending on many factors beyond the control of any individual. It is also important to keep in mind that formal power can be vastly different from a politician's willingness and ability to use it, which means that power can vary significantly from one governor to another. A system of institutional and personal power still omits informal powers, which, if exercised, make the power of the Georgia governor rank very much above the average or median power of all governors.

We can use Beyle's system to rank and update the formal power scores from 1998 through 2014 to include the first term of Georgia governor Nathan Deal (see figure 7.1). As the figure indicates, power has not been static. Indeed, the power of the Georgia governor has moved from a low of 3.0 (2.955) in 1998 to a high of 3.5. In 2007, the average and the median for institutional power in the fifty states was 3.7. The Georgia governor's power was scored as 3.5, slightly less than average and below the median. Seven states scored 4.0 or higher in 2007, while five states scored less than 3.0. The remaining 38 states scored between 3.0

Figure 7.1. Formal Power of Georgia's Governor

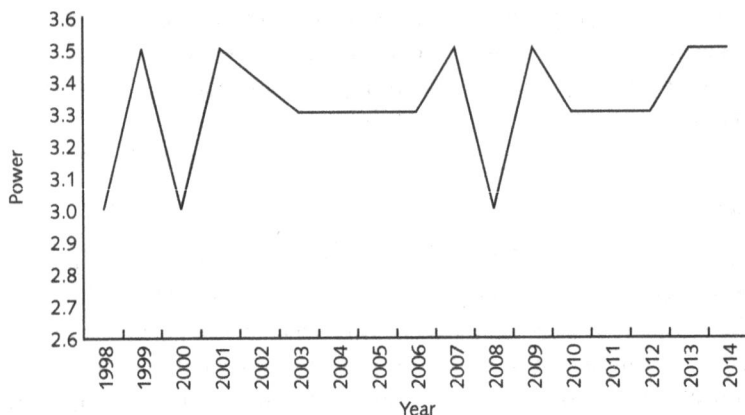

and 3.9, including Georgia at 3.2 (up from 2.8 in 2002). Along with three other states, Georgia scored 2.8 in institutional power, just ahead of the low score of 2.7 registered by Alabama.

The main reason for the lower Georgia ranking vis-à-vis other states is the large number of separately elected officials and the governor's very weak appointment power. Though the number of separately elected officials has remained the same over the past decade, the governor's power to appoint has increased. Furthermore, the Georgia governor has always had strong budgetary and veto authority.

Two factors can account for much of this increased power. The first is the election process. The governor is limited to two terms; power decreases as the governor approaches an election and is at its nadir when the incumbent is in his final year, a situation that occurred in 1998 with Zell Miller about to leave office. The second is party control of the legislature. The period 1998 to 2014 encompasses the change from Democratic control to Republican dominance. The power of Republican governors has increased as the Republican Party increased its control of both houses of the legislature.

Tenure. One source of power is the length of the gubernatorial term. Most states from the beginning of the republic limited the power of the governor, an outgrowth of mistrust of centralized power and rule by the British monarchy.[4] In fact, of the original thirteen states, ten limited the governor to one term. Eleven states allow governors to have unlimited four-year terms. There is no specific geographic logic to gubernatorial term limits, which have been set in northeastern states such as Connecticut and Massachusetts, western states such as Washington and Utah, midwestern states such as North Dakota and Minnesota, as well as Texas. New Hampshire and Vermont have no term limits, but governors must run for reelection every two years. The majority of states, including Georgia, limit the executive to two four-year terms. The most extreme is Virginia, which does not allow governors to succeed themselves.[5]

Reflecting this movement from suspicion to acceptance of centralized gubernatorial power, the term of the Georgia governor has changed over the years. The 1877 constitution limited the governor to two consecutive two-year terms. A 1941 constitutional amendment provided for a four-year term but prohibited governors from succeeding themselves in office. This, in turn, was changed in 1976 to permit successive terms but limited tenure to two terms. The constitution implemented in 1983 permitted two consecutive four-year terms with no lifetime restriction on the time of a governor's service. The governor is the only statewide-elected official with a constitutional limit on the number of consecutive terms.[6]

Veto Power. The veto—or even the threat of using it—is one of the strongest powers possessed by a governor because it allows significant legislative influence. Gubernatorial veto power is often classified as strong or weak. A chief executive can use four different vetoes: the basic or package, the line item, the amendatory, and the pocket. In addition, governors confront different override possibilities. Most legislatures, forty-four in all (and the Congress in overriding the veto of the president of the United States), require a supermajority of votes to override the veto, either three-fifths or two-thirds, while the remaining legislatures can override by a simple majority.

A package veto (basic veto) permits a governor to veto an entire bill and all its provisions. A line-item veto allows the governor to veto specific lines in appropriations bills. Congress attempted to give the president line-item veto authority, but the U.S. Supreme Court declared the law unconstitutional in 1998.[7] Nineteen states even allow the item veto for a broader range of bills than just appropriations. Amendatory vetoes allow a governor to veto a bill and send it back to the legislature with recommended amendments. Finally, a pocket veto (possessed by the president of the United States) allows the governor to kill a bill simply by failing to sign the bill into law after the legislative session has ended.

The governor's veto power in Georgia is considered very strong (5 out of 5 points) because it includes the standard veto of bills and substantial legislative majorities to override the veto. This is not unusual; under the Beyle scoring system, thirty-nine states allow strong veto provisions. In Georgia, the governor's veto power is included in the legislative article of the constitution, which describes the process for enacting laws. Under these provisions, the governor has six days to act on a bill while the General Assembly is in session. If the General Assembly has adjourned for the session or for more than forty days (like a recess), the governor has forty days after adjournment to act. When vetoing a bill, the governor is required to return it to the chamber where it originated within three days during the session or sixty days after adjournment. Once the General Assembly has received a veto message, the originating chamber may consider the vetoed bill immediately. A bill becomes law if the governor does nothing—neither approves nor vetoes it.[8]

In Georgia, overriding the governor's veto so that a bill can become law requires two-thirds of the actual membership of each chamber—not just those present to vote. If an override fails in either house of the Georgia General Assembly, a bill is dead, but those bills vetoed during adjournment can be overridden during the next legislative session. Finally, the authority to veto specific items within a bill is limited to appropriations bills, which gives the governor the power to kill spending for specific projects without having to veto an entire budget. Twenty-five states make it easier to override a gubernatorial veto: six require only a majority of those elected; six mandate three-fifths of those elected; and thirteen specify three-fifths or two-thirds of those present for the override vote.

The Budget. Power over the budget is the power to shape the spending plan for the state, which is a key way that elected officials determine policy priorities. For most states, this authority is shared between the governor and the legislature. Under the Beyle system, the average for all states is 3.1, and the median is 3.0. Maryland exclusively rates at 5.0, and only New York and Nebraska receive a 4.0 score. Beyle rates Georgia's governorship a 3 in terms of budget-making authority. The Georgia legislature dominated the budgetary process until 1931. The executive's position was strengthened in 1962, when what was then called the Budget Bureau was placed under the governor with a budget director and staff support. The constitution directs the governor to prepare the state's annual budget and submit it to the General Assembly during the first five days of the regular session. Agencies submit their requests to the Office of Planning and Budget (OPB), which reports to the governor. The OPB, in turn, develops the draft appropriations bill, which is the starting point for budget debates in the legislature. This increased power is again part of the movement toward greater executive authority. However, the legislature has virtually unlimited power to change the budget submitted by the governor.[9]

Elected and Appointed Officials. Beyle assigns Georgia the lowest score possible for two indicators related to a governor's ability to control or manage the bureaucracy: the number of competing elected officials and the power to appoint officials in six key areas: health, education, highways, corrections, public utilities regulation, and public welfare. In each of the six major policy areas, top officials are chosen by voters or by boards. In the case of one board (Transportation), the governor does not even appoint the members; they are chosen by the General Assembly.[10] Like the majority of states, Georgia elects a lieutenant governor, an attorney general, and a secretary of state. Georgia is among the few states, however, that allows voters to choose the state school superintendent and the agriculture, insurance, and labor commissioners, as well as the five members of the Public Service Commission, which regulates utilities.

However, Beyle's system underestimates the appointment power of Georgia's governor, in part because the governor's influence is indirect, primarily through his power to appoint boards and propose the budget. In addition, the increasing dominance of the Republican Party in the Georgia legislature bolsters the governor's power. Finally, Georgia has a part-time legislature. This allows the governor to dominate both the Republican Party and state governance since during much of the year, there is no official legislative response to gubernatorial actions.

Political commentators and politicians acknowledge evidence of increased appointment power.[11] Although gubernatorial control over boards and commissions is nominally weakened because terms are long and staggered, the governor is not shy about forcing out recalcitrant members. Between these forced resignations and two terms (eight years) in office, over time a Georgia governor can dominate the boards.

Consider the Board of Regents, over which the governor has staggered appointment authority. The Board of Regents adopts policies and selects administrators for Georgia's public colleges and universities. Members serve staggered seven-year terms, which would appear to make it difficult for a governor to alter the board's composition and policies; however, Governor Deal was able to appoint sixteen members to the Board of Regents before the midpoint of his second term. The governor has used his appointment power in similar fashion over the Georgia Ports Authority and the Board of Natural Resources. In fact, as noted during the 2014 election, the governor appointed members to these boards who contributed nearly $1.3 million to Deal's campaign and PAC.[12]

Georgia's governor has the power to appoint members to an even larger number of state boards and authorities, ranging from regulatory boards for the construction industry, athletic agents, opticians, and nursing home administrators to agencies with significant budgets and policy-making authority. The latter include entities such as the Board of Education and the Georgia Lottery Corporation. In addition, the legislature and constitutional amendments have allowed the governor greater appointment authority over what had been traditionally local areas such as education. A constitutional amendment passed in the general election of 2012 created the State Charter Schools Commission, which functions under the auspices of the State Board of Education. Subsequent legislation specified that the state would have the power to seize control over failing schools and convert them into charters or shut them down. The district's superintendent, who would report to the governor, would have the power to fire the schools' principals, transfer teachers, and change what students learn. In essence, the governor and the General Assembly have created a "backdoor" method for approving school charters even if local school boards originally denied their charter application.[13]

Perhaps the most important appointment power of Georgia governors is their constitutional authority to fill vacancies in the executive and judicial branches without Senate confirmation. Obviously, a governor's impact is greatest when appointing the first members to a new board or commission, as Governor Perdue did with the Georgia Land Conservation Council in 2005.[14] In the case of elected positions, the appointment power allows the governor to pick someone who immediately becomes the incumbent in the next campaign. This power can be especially important in appointing judges, who tend to be reelected quite handily. Governor Perdue appointed ten judges to trial courts during his first year in office. He had the ultimate opportunity in 2005, when he appointed his top legal adviser to a vacancy on the Georgia Supreme Court.[15]

Gubernatorial Party Control. For 126 years (1877–2002), the governorship in Georgia was a position exclusively held by Democrats.[16] All of that changed in 2002, however, with the election of Sonny Perdue, Georgia's first Republican governor since Reconstruction.

While Perdue governed with a Republican Senate, he faced a Democratic House in his first two years. In Georgia, unified party control came full circle with the election of 2004, when Republicans won a majority in the House, which gave the party control of the legislature and governorship for the first time in more than a century.

Personal Powers

Richard Neustadt, the famed presidential scholar, has argued that the chief power of the president is the power to persuade. That is, beyond the formal authority of the office, the president's real authority comes from his ability to convince others to follow his policy preferences.[17] The same holds true for chief executives of states.

Formal authority is only part of a governor's political power. Personal power, which is essentially the power to persuade, forms a large part of the power of Georgia's governor. Under the scale we have been using, the informal authority of governors derives from the size of their electoral mandate, the degree to which they have moved up a state's political ladder, the potential time they could remain in office, and their ratings in public opinion polls. Obviously, these fac-

Figure 7.2. Informal Power of Georgia's Governor

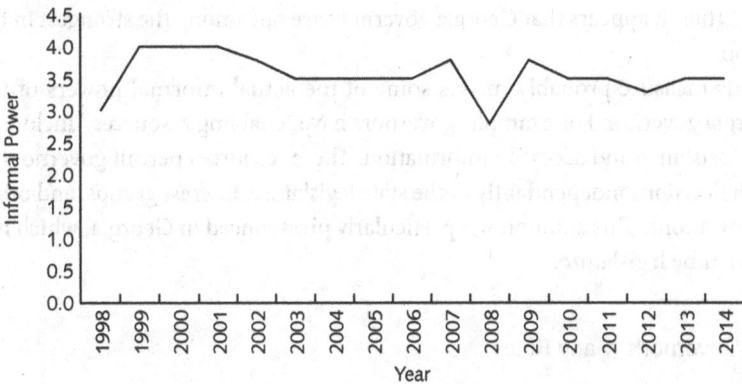

tors vary both among governors and over the course of an individual governor's time in office. In fact, well into his second term, Governor Deal remained
personally very popular. According to the *New York Times*, he had an approval
rating of 58 percent, compared to a disapproval rating of 27 percent. This 31
percent net favorability rating placed Deal fifteenth among all U.S. governors.[18]
These favorability ratings are most likely highly correlated with perceptions of
the strength of the state's economy. In a ranking by *Governing* during the same
period, Georgia's economy was also ranked fifteenth.[19]

In 2003, Beyle's measure of personal power rated Georgia at 3.7, the same as
the fifty-state average of 3.7. In 2007, the rating was 3.8. Again using these factors, we have scored the Georgia governor's informal authority through 2014
(see figure 7.2).

Despite the end of Democratic dominance in the governorship, succeeded
by a resurgence of fully unified government under the GOP since the 2004
election, the informal power of the Georgia governor has remained static and
pales in comparison to gubernatorial power in other states. To some degree,
this situation reflects the second-term victories by Perdue and Deal, which were
substantial, but Deal's election was not a landslide. In 2006, Perdue beat Mark
Taylor by an almost twenty-point margin of victory. In 2010, Deal beat former
governor Roy Barnes by ten points.

Of course, as the tenure of an incumbent governor continues, power begins
to ebb, although governors can position themselves for other offices. However,
Georgia's governors have largely failed to advance to national office. There are
two noticeable exceptions. The first is Jimmy Carter, who served one term as
president (1977–1981). The second is Zell Miller, who was appointed to a vacant
Senate seat (due to the death of Paul Coverdell) by then-governor Roy Barnes.

Because of this limited mobility, the informal powers of the governor during these years rank both below the median (4.3) and below the national average (3.9). Thus, it appears that Georgia governors are not among the strongest in the nation.

This measure probably misses some of the actual informal powers of the Georgia governor. For example, governors have "enabling resources," including staff assistance and access to information. These resources permit governors to reach decisions independently of the state legislature, interest groups, and other organizations. This autonomy is particularly pronounced in Georgia, which has a part-time legislature.

The Governor's Many Roles

One study has found that the nation's governors increased their resources between the late 1970s and early 1990s.[20] In addition, the staffing resources of the governor place the Georgia governor above the national median and right at the national average. Personal power, enabling resources, and a variety of individual characteristics are important in governors' leadership ability, which is often discussed in terms of the way they perform certain roles or functions. Political scientist Alan Rosenthal has identified four key roles that governors must play: policy maker, chief legislator, manager of the executive branch, and symbolic leader.[21]

Policy Maker. The president of the United States and the nation's governors have the ability to set the public agenda.[22] Several methods are available to a governor to set the agenda, including media attention, public addresses, press releases, and introduction of legislation by legislative floor managers.

Some state issues are perennial, namely, they occur year after year, often because addressing them annually is required. At the beginning of a new legislative session, the governor gives a State of the State address, similar to the president's State of the Union. At the same time, the governor sends his proposed budget and policy agenda to the legislature. The budget, which ostensibly outlines revenue and spending proposals, is really the primary policy document of the state. How a state chooses to raise revenue (e.g., sales tax, income tax, bonds, title and registration fees), and the allocation of the revenue (e.g., education, health and medical, agriculture, transportation, welfare) determine the policy priorities of the state. Given its brief annual session and limited staff, the General Assembly historically has produced a budget within 1–2 percent of the governor's recommendation, although there are modifications in the relative share appropriated to various programs.[23]

States also face cyclical issues, which grow in public concern and then decline without ever going completely away, such as health care, other issues determined by national legislation, and the redistricting that occurs every ten years. Governors also must confront transitory issues, which appear suddenly and then vanish after they are dealt with. Examples include ethics reform following a scandal, changing the drinking age in response to federal law, or the response to a natural disaster. It is worth noting that concern over an issue can vary widely among the states at the same time. It is also possible for issues to shift in type among transitory, cyclical, and perennial over time. This may be especially true of economic development, which gained great significance during the recession of the early 1980s. Most states had adopted a wide range of financial incentives, training programs, and similar tactics by the end of the decade.[24] The same might be said of the Great Recession of this century.

Governors have several methods available to set the public agenda. In addition to traditional media, governors now use social media devices such as Twitter and Facebook and personal websites to communicate directly with the public. For example, the Governor Nathan Deal's office uses several Twitter "handles": @GovernorDeal, @NathanDeal, @GovNathanDeal, and @GeorgiaGov. The first lady of the state, Sandra Deal, has her own twitter account, @GaFirstLady, and the Governor's Press Office set up its own Twitter account, @PressGovDeal. Of course, the governor also has his own Facebook page, https://facebook.com/GovernorDeal. Typically, someone in the governor's office updates the Facebook account or issues "tweets." Political figures, with the notable exception of President Trump, rarely do their own social media updates, instead relying on a staff member such as a social media director.[25]

Interestingly, Governor Deal does not post videos to YouTube or photos to other social media photo outlets. However, extensive photos and video are posted to the Georgia governor's website, http://gov.georgia.gov/. The website also contains all executive orders, press releases, newsletters, updates on legislation, as well as biographical information on the governor and the first lady.

All these strategies, including staged events such as speeches to groups, allow governors to promote their policies directly to the public without the intervention or commentary of traditional news media outlets. While this type of communication allows unfettered access without any filter, it also allows the governor to avoid any extensive media scrutiny or analysis. In short, it allows governors to present their "side" of events without any context or criticism by the media.[26] This approach is deliberately pursued by public officials and candidates, but it has potentially disturbing implications for democracy because in our country we rely on the media to act as an aggressive watchdog on the power of the government. This role for the press was noted as one of paramount importance in a democratic system of government by the Supreme Court in its landmark decision *Near v. Minnesota*.[27]

In terms of traditional roles, perhaps the most visible is the State of the State address to the General Assembly at the beginning of a new legislative session. The prestige of the office usually assures the governor of coverage by the state's television stations and daily newspapers.[28] The State of the State address allows the governor to set his budgetary and legislative priorities; strategically, the address also allows the governor to set the agenda for the legislative session and frame the political landscape for the media and the public.

Another practice is the use of commissions to study issues and report their findings and recommendations to the governor, who can then use these results to propose major policy changes. Such commissions can be composed of officials and private citizens, which can yield several advantages in agenda setting. First, these commissions tap the talents of individuals and organizations outside government. Second, appointment of prominent and well-connected citizens can increase the visibility and acceptance of commission conclusions. This helps upstage other proposals in the same policy area, lends an air of objectivity compared to proposals made by governors on their own, and includes representatives of affected groups in the commission's work. Third, depending on its composition and links with various other leaders, a commission can help formulate compromises or other proposals that have a high likelihood of passing the General Assembly. Indeed, a commission may be useful in pressuring legislators to adopt the governor's proposals. Finally, a commission's report can alert officials, interest groups, and the public to a problem and mobilize these people to support a specific remedy.

Georgia governors have used study commissions to consider policy changes that have the potential to generate significant opposition from legislators, agencies, local officials, and interest groups. For example, the Growth Strategies Commission was created in 1987 to deal with land-use planning, building codes, and permit systems. To minimize opposition by local leaders, the thirty-five-member commission, appointed by Governor Harris, worked with business leaders and representatives of Georgia's cities and counties to establish a system of long-term planning that starts at the local level and works its way through regional and state approval. In addition, the process was phased in slowly after the planning legislation was enacted in 1989.[29]

One of Governor Zell Miller's earliest actions was the appointment of a commission in 1991 to consider a perennial issue, the performance of the state bureaucracy. Miller touted the commission in statements about his achievements and agenda. Less than four years later, however, Miller set up the Governor's Commission on Privatization to identify services to be turned over to the private sector as a means of saving the state money.[30] Shortly after he took office in 2003, Sonny Perdue launched a similar effort to improve efficiency in state government by appointing eighteen leaders in business and other fields to his Commission for a New Georgia.[31]

Governor Deal also used these tactics. One of the most prominent was his urging and subsequent legislative adoption of an education reform commission. The stated purpose of the commission was to "study the state's education system, including its funding formula, and provide recommendations intended to improve the system, increase access to early learning programs, recruit and retain high-quality instructors and expand school options for Georgia's families."[32]

Chief Legislator. The notion of a governor being the chief legislator is somewhat ironic in that a governor is a state's chief executive, entrusted with enforcing and executing the laws, not enacting them. Nevertheless, in modern state governments, a governor is in fact the legislator in chief. The National Governors Association and scholarly literature identify several legislative powers, including budget and appropriations, state legislation, executive and judicial appointments, oversight of executive functions, and veto power.

In addition to the budget and the policy-making strategies discussed above, Georgia governors have several other methods of initiation. One is submission of bills to the General Assembly, where the governor selects one member in each chamber to serve as the administration's floor leader. Another is support for ideas proposed by legislators, agencies, or interest groups. A third is calling a special session of the legislature to address some issue or problem that the governor deems important, at least symbolically.

The governor's power of rejection is substantial. In Georgia, the legislative powers of the governor are augmented by the part-time nature of the Georgia legislature. Thad Kousser and Justin H. Phillips, two prominent researchers on state government, have found that part-time legislators hold other full-time jobs

> to which they must return soon after the legislative session. These individuals pay high opportunity costs if their governor vetoes their budget and calls them in to a special session. These costs make "citizen" legislators less patient, relative to the governor and their counterparts in more-professionalized legislatures, and give the governor a bargaining advantage.[33]

In addition, the governor has full and line-item veto authority. The governor can also benefit from the fact that most major bills are not passed until the end of the legislative session, which provides more time for review before (and politicking after) deciding to veto a bill. Georgia governors have exercised their veto power sparingly, as indicated in table 7.2.

For the most part, this is because of one-party control. The same party has controlled the governorship and both houses of the legislature for most of the twentieth and now twenty-first centuries. However, even during a few early years of this century, when Governor Perdue faced a Senate controlled by his

Table 7.2. Gubernatorial Vetoes of Bills, 1981–2014

Legislative Session	Governor	Full Vetoes	Item Vetoes	
			Number	Dollar Amount of Vetoes
1981	Busbee	12	3	$0
1982	Busbee	12	2	0
1983	Harris	12	2	0
1984	Harris	16	4	0
1985	Harris	4	4	8,000,000
1986	Harris	6	4	0
1987	Harris	9	5	0
1988	Harris	9	6	0
1989	Harris	10	4	0
1990	Harris	18	7	70,000
1991	Miller	13	10	5,000
1992	Miller	27	16	38,595,089
1993	Miller	16	10	0
1994	Miller	4	11	9,864,199
1995	Miller	14	14	9,042,422
1996	Miller	18	7	342,500
1997	Miller	15	11	9,417,245
1998	Miller	13	8	3,950,520
1999	Barnes	6	4	0
2000	Barnes	11	4	1,500,000
2001	Barnes	7	5	76,000
2002	Barnes	10	7	55,000
2003	Perdue	19	6	403,000
2004	Perdue	19	9	288,135
2005	Perdue	15	15	9,243,226
2006	Perdue	19	0	0
2007	Perdue	40	31	18,026,379
2008	Perdue	16	18	14,026,379
2009	Perdue	15	3	192,980
2010	Perdue	31	5	1,152,252
2011	Deal	9	11	3,645,704
2012	Deal	8	2	390,276
2013	Deal	5	0	0
2014	Deal	10	0	0

Sources: Georgia General Assembly, Legislative Services Committee and Office of Legislative Counsel, *Summary of General Statues Enacted*, 1981–2014; Governor Press Releases, 2006–2014; and Governor's Office of Planning and Budget, *Budget in Brief*, 2006–2014

Note: Data cover only bills and regular legislative sessions. One resolution was vetoed in 1984, 2007, 2008, and 2009; two resolutions were vetoed in 1991; and five item vetoes occurred during the 1991 special session. Amended Fiscal Year (AFY) line item vetoes are not included.

fellow Republicans and a House controlled by Democrats, he still used the veto sparingly, vetoing just 19 of the 1,944 bills and resolutions enacted by the General Assembly in 2004 (1 percent). This is more than Governor Deal, who has vetoed 32 bills during 2011–2015.

Georgia has seen limited use of the item veto. Other states have made it more difficult for governors to use the item veto because their legislatures have combined larger appropriations into fewer lines. Thus, a governor vetoing a large lump sum would have to kill a whole range of programs in addition to the one targeted with the veto.[34] Governor Deal used the line-item veto for only two provisions in 2013 (2014 fiscal year budget) and only one time in 2015 (2016 fiscal year budget).

Several factors allow governors to succeed in enacting their legislative agenda. In assessing a governor's prior experience, Alan Rosenthal concludes that "the years spent in the house or senate, the time served in gubernatorial office, and future tenure prospects do make a difference" in a governor's legislative success.[35] Experience does not automatically provide power, but it can furnish governors with connections, favors, and knowledge that further their influence in a state legislature. Beyle examined the career paths of the 225 individuals who served as elected governors in the states between 1970 and 1994. Only 8 percent held no prior political office. The state legislature was the most important starting point: 38 percent of all governors were members of their state legislature when elected.[36]

Kousser and Phillips have examined the influence of governors in pushing legislation in a variety of policy domains and analyzed the factors leading to gubernatorial success. First, they note that two recent governors of Georgia, Roy Barnes and Sonny Perdue, were very successful in passing their legislative agenda. They find that Barnes and Perdue in 2001 and 2006, respectively, and despite their party differences, won passage for nearly 90 percent of their proposals. This was the highest success rate for any state chief executive in those years.[37]

Kousser and Phillips argue that a key question they analyze is, "who is more influential—legislators or governors—when they bargain over the size of American state budgets?"[38] Using a variety of measures, they find that legislative professionalization is a key component in tempering the power of the governor. Of course, Georgia has a part-time legislature, thus ensuring that the governor has significant power in the budget process. Kousser and Phillips offer a slightly more complex statistical model, but they again find that legislative professionalism as defined by length of legislative sessions is a predictor of success: the longer the legislative session, the less likely the governor is to achieve both policy and budgetary success. Party control of the legislature also matters. Interestingly, they also find that governors have the most success in their "legacy year," that is, the last year of the term. Given these factors, it is not surprising that Georgia's governors do very well. Georgia has a part-time, nonprofessional legislature, and most often the party that controls the governor's office controls both houses of the legislature.

While these two scholars did not factor in political experience, Georgia governors have seldom lacked political expertise. Of the thirteen men who took office between 1947 and 2011, only Lester Maddox might be considered a political outsider. That was not for lack of trying, however: Maddox was defeated in his run for mayor of Atlanta in 1957 and 1961 and for lieutenant governor in 1962 before becoming governor in 1967. The other governors served in the General Assembly or some statewide elected position. In the case of Herman Talmadge, he was heir to a family political legacy.[39]

The power of unity refers to a governor's ability, as a single individual rather than part of a collective body, to take action and gain the attention of the public and the media. This gubernatorial power can be limited, though, by competition with other elected officials. With no limit on reelection, Georgia's lieutenant governor can build power and visibility to compete with the governor. The same is true of other members of the plural executive, who can undercut a governor's legislative program.[40]

The last three gubernatorial powers identified by Rosenthal—provision, publicity, and popularity—seem closely linked. Provision refers to the ability of governors to "fulfill members' needs."[41] Governors can bestow some benefits on legislators directly: appointing or hiring people, attending events, and writing or phoning on their behalf. Somewhat more indirectly, providing benefits for a member's district can aid both the legislator and the governor. This benefit can be achieved by including specific items in the state budget, such as the long-standing practice of making allocations from the governor's emergency fund.[42]

Publicity surrounding major policy initiatives, especially in election years, may enhance a governor's popularity. For instance, after launching his reelection campaign, Governor Zell Miller announced proposals to distribute unanticipated revenues from the state lottery, adopted a modest income tax cut, and shifted his emphasis on two hot issues, the state flag and welfare reform.[43]

In summarizing governors' many powers in the legislative process, Rosenthal concludes:

> Each of these powers alone is not sufficient to make a governor "chief legislator." But taken in combination, they are impressive. Together they allow the governor to persuade legislators—directly and personally, and indirectly through the media—that what he or she wants by way of policy, expenditures, and operations is what they ought to grant, in their own interests. . . . Given their advantages, it is a wonder that governors ever lose. But the fact

is that legislatures have significant power of their own and the will to use that power.[44]

It is worth noting, too, that success is affected by other participants in the political process, particularly interest groups. It can also vary with the formal power of legislatures, as well as their "professionalism," which ranges from part-time status in some states to full-time, well-paying jobs in others.

Combining these factors, the governor of Georgia is very successful in pushing through his legislative agenda. This holds true whether the governor is a Republican or a Democrat. In fact, given the part-time nature of the Georgia legislature, Beyle's measure might underestimate the power of the Georgia governor.

Manager of the Executive Branch. The governor is at least formally the state's chief administrator. It is difficult, though, to speak of governors "managing" the bureaucracy in the same way that executives in the private sector issue orders, change policies, or hire and fire subordinates. This is true in part because of the plural executive, civil service protection for state employees, and political constraints. Thus, governors often are left with indirect influence such as appointments and the budget.[45]

One way that some states have chosen to increase a governor's ability to manage the bureaucracy is through the power of reorganization in their constitution or statutes. Twenty-seven states, including Georgia, permit their governor to reorganize the bureaucracy by issuing executive orders. The remaining states require their legislatures to enact laws to reorganize the executive branch. The last such effort in Georgia occurred in the early 1970s, when the General Assembly responded to Governor Jimmy Carter's proposal to overhaul the executive branch.[46]

The nation's governors also vary in their salaries and staffs. When the Council of State Governments compared governors in December 2004, only eighteen states paid their chief executive less than $100,000. In 2014, the number was down to six. Georgia's governor was paid $127,303 in 2004, but that grew to $139,339.00 in 2015, which is slightly above the national average and right at the median. Eight states have gubernatorial salaries of at least $170,000, including a high of $187,000 in Pennsylvania. In terms of staff resources, the Georgia Governor's Office had a staff of fifty-six people in 2014. This number was reduced from eighty-seven in 2004. Governors in eight states had office staffs of fewer than twenty people, while those in Texas and Florida have staffs of over two hundred, and those in New York and New Jersey employed more than one hundred people.[47]

Governors also use pressure against agencies. In 1996, for instance, the appointed state school board had been feuding for some time with Linda Schrenko, the Republican who was elected state school superintendent in 1994. To end the conflict, Democratic governor Zell Miller called on the entire board to resign. Similarly, Sonny Perdue pressured members of the school board to resign before he had been sworn in as governor. Perdue also got resignations from the head of the Department of Human Resources and the chairman of the powerful transportation board, both of whom were already in office when he was sworn in as governor.[48]

Symbolic Leader. The last gubernatorial role is the symbolic one of defining a state's image. Governors may be pressured in several ways in terms of which policies to emphasize and how to portray them. During desegregation conflicts in the 1950s, for instance, Governor Marvin Griffin played to white voters at home in opposing desegregation, but he was viewed negatively outside the South. His actions also contrasted with local officials in Atlanta and elsewhere who adopted more moderate positions on race in hopes of promoting their communities to outsiders, especially investors.[49]

As Georgia grew after the desegregation battles, governors played a major role in promoting the state as both a place to invest and a source of products and services. Governor Jimmy Carter made several promotional trips within the United States, including a session to persuade movie industry leaders to film in Georgia. He also visited Latin America, Europe, and Israel. His successors did likewise, extending gubernatorial visits to Japan, South Korea, and Canada in addition to the traditional ventures in Europe. Governor Miller scheduled a trip to Russia his first year in office, and Governor Perdue made several trips abroad, including to Canada.[50] Governor Deal targeted the film industry, generating $5.1 billion dollars in FY 2014.[51] He also completed trade missions to emerging countries like Brazil, as well as more significant trade partners like China and Canada.[52]

Constitutional Officers

As table 7.1 indicates, Georgia's constitution requires the statewide election of seven officials in addition to the governor and the lieutenant governor: secretary of state, attorney general, state school superintendent, commissioner of insurance, commissioner of labor, commissioner of agriculture, and commissioner of utilities. These elected department heads must have reached the age of twenty-five, have been a U.S. citizen for at least ten years, and have been a Georgia resident for at least four years upon assuming office. The attorney general is also required to have had seven years as an active-status member of the State Bar of Georgia, which supervises the legal profession in the state.

The constitution leaves it to the General Assembly to spell out the power and duties of these officers, to determine their salaries, and to fund their agencies.[53] There is also a procedure under which four of the eight constitutional officers can petition the Georgia Supreme Court to hold a hearing to determine if a constitutional officer is permanently disabled and should be replaced.[54]

Even though they are members of the executive branch of government, constitutional officers possess power independent of the governor. They do so because of the prerogatives of their offices and ties to constituencies they serve. This makes Georgia (and many states) very different from the federal government, where the various branches of government are under the direct control of the president.

The attorney general, for instance, exercises great discretion regarding the handling of litigation to which the state is a party. Although that is also true of the U.S. government, the president could "fire" the attorney general if he or she fails to follow presidential policy directives. Such dismissal cannot occur in Georgia. In addition, the attorney general's office issues advisory opinions on the legality or constitutionality of actions taken by the state.[55] Similarly, the insurance and agriculture commissioners have substantial power to regulate certain types of businesses. However, they are sometimes seen as advocates of the industries they oversee, as when the agriculture commissioner participates in programs sponsored by food producers or processors.[56]

The narrow focus of their offices also means that constitutional officers' natural constituencies—for votes and campaign money—are the interests affected most directly by their decisions.[57] For example, Ralph Hudgens, the insurance commissioner, was first elected in 2010 and received the largest share of donations from the insurance, finance, and real estate sectors for his 2014 reelection campaign; furthermore, the insurance industry was the single greatest industry contributing to his campaign.[58] Donations to Agriculture Commissioner Gary Black follow a similar pattern. The agriculture sector is the single largest sector that donated to his campaign, with crop production and agricultural services being the largest donors of any industry.[59]

In addition to having conflicts with the governor, constitutional officers may do political battle with one another. Such a conflict occurred in 1995, when Insurance Commissioner John Oxendine refused to collect a premium tax on church-owned insurance companies providing coverage to churches, which he argued was unconstitutional. A fellow Republican, Attorney General Michael Bowers, filed suit against Oxendine to force him to collect the tax unless the legislature passed a law exempting such companies. Oxendine relented before a hearing in court.[60]

Boards and Commissions

States commonly assign decision making in certain policy areas to multimember boards rather than departments headed by individuals. Georgia is no exception, and its boards and commissions vary in their origin, authority, organization, operations, and political power. A few have their authority spelled out in the Georgia Constitution; many others have been created by law or executive order.

Constitutional Board and Commissions

The constitution provides for eight boards and commissions, as highlighted in table 7.3. These are among the most powerful agencies in Georgia, in part because any changes in their basic authority and membership require a constitutional amendment rather than passage of a law by the General Assembly. Their power is also reflected in the resources they control. In 2015, for instance, the University System Board of Regents had a state appropriation of roughly $1.9 billion. Some funds are earmarked in the Constitution: Article 3, for example, requires that state motor-fuel taxes, which were expected to total more than $849 million in fiscal 2015, must be spent for "an adequate system of public roads and bridges." That requirement provides substantial power to the Department of Transportation, which also received $1.3 billion from the federal government.[61]

The constitution insulates these boards from political pressure to some degree by providing relatively long terms that are staggered. In the case of the State Board of Education and the University System Board of Regents, the governor is specifically prohibited from being a member. This stipulation is in reaction to events in the 1940s, when Governor Eugene Talmadge, whose office entitled him to a seat on the board, conducted a purge of administrators accused of promoting racial integration. His action led to a loss of accreditation for Georgia's public colleges and universities.[62] The Public Service Commission was originally created by statute in 1879 to regulate railroads. Over time, its reach was extended to other utilities, and its membership was enlarged and made subject to election. The commission was given constitutional status in 1943, after voters approved an amendment.[63] In contrast to such arm's-length relationships, the State Transportation Board may seem like the essence of pork-barrel politics. One member is chosen for each congressional district by the state legislators whose districts overlap it—and benefit from highway construction.

Most constitutional boards and commissions use some geographical representation. Assigning one seat per congressional district has the effect of assuring South Georgia seats on boards that otherwise might be dominated by people

Table 7.3. Constitutional Boards and Commissions

Board/Commission	Number of Members	Membership Selection
Education	14*	One member per congressional district; appointed by the governor to seven-year terms, subject to Senate confirmation.
Natural Resources	19*	One member per congressional district plus five at-large members (at least one of whom must be from a coastal county); appointed by the governor to seven-year terms, subject to Senate confirmation.
Pardons and Paroles	5	Appointed by the governor to seven-year terms, subject to Senate confirmation.
Personnel	5	Appointed by the governor to five-year terms, subject to Senate confirmation.
Public Service	5	Elected statewide on a partisan ballot for six-year terms.
Regents	19*	One member per congressional district, plus five at-large members; appointed by the governor to seven-year terms, subject to Senate confirmation.
Transportation	14*	One member per congressional district; elected by a majority vote of the General Assembly members whose respective districts are embraced or partly embraced within such congressional district to five-year terms.
Veterans Services	7	Appointed by the governor to seven-year terms, subject to Senate confirmation.

Source: *Constitution of the State of Georgia*, art. 8, sec. 2; art. 8, sec. 4; art. 4, secs. 1–6.

* Membership varies along with Georgia's number of seats in the U.S. House of Representatives, which increased to fourteen following the 2010 census and reapportionment.

from the Atlanta area. It also means that the size of a board can change as Georgia acquires additional seats in the U.S. House of Representatives.

Statutory and Executive Boards

Beyond the small number of constitutional boards and commissions are many more created by law or executive order, including more than three dozen examining boards for professionals ranging from accountants to librarians to wastewater treatment plant operators. There are well over one hundred more boards and commissions established by statute that oversee, study, or make recommendations for various agencies and programs. Examples include the Council on Aging, the State Forestry Commission, the Lake Lanier Islands Development Authority, the Teachers Retirement System, and the World Congress Center Authority. Finally, governors can create commissions, boards, and task forces to advise them on various issues; they are usually dissolved once they have completed their mission.

Critics have long attacked the operation of Georgia's boards and commissions, including licensing boards' infrequent disciplining of professionals they oversee. They have also faulted the quality and background of gubernatorial appointees, the decisions and expenses of board members, and the use of outside consultants.[64]

The Bureaucracy

Public bureaucracies face a variety of competing goals and pressures. Their very creation represents a departure from the pristine separation of powers formula that supposedly governs the national and state governments. Of course, the main reason for their creation is the complexity of modern life and the need for specialization that are beyond the ability of nonspecialist legislatures.

Another reason is the lack of time. Legislatures, particularly part-time legislatures, have so much to do in the modern era that it is difficult to research complex issues, debate them, and then decide on appropriate action.

Today, most bureaucratic agencies are part of the executive branch of government. Accountability is a problem because the elected legislature delegates powers to unelected officials. Citizens want government to be efficient, yet they also expect it to be open and fair, responsive to their demands, and accountable for its actions. Unlike the relationship between private firms and their customers, how public bureaucracies operate is often decided through the political process. These tensions affect agencies and public employees who must interact with clients, the governor, the legislature, courts, interest groups, and the media.

State Employees

Most states have struggled for years with ways to set up personnel systems that promote efficient and effective government while also protecting government workers from partisan politics. Georgia has used various approaches and now operates with several personnel systems. Georgia emulated other states and in 1943 established a "civil service" system in which permanent employees are hired and rewarded on the basis of qualifications and performance, not party or personal loyalties. These workers were hired under the State Merit System—they constitute what the public normally thinks of as "bureaucrats." That system changed, however, when the legislature followed Governor Zell Miller's recommendation and closed the Merit System to employees hired after July 1, 1996. Employees no longer have the protections of the Merit System, and agency managers have more flexibility in rewarding, disciplining, and terminating state workers. Other employees remain under separate systems, including many upper-level management jobs or positions in the governor's office, the Georgia Lottery, the attorney general's office, the legislature, most authorities, and the University System of Georgia.[65]

The U.S. Census Bureau conducts its Census of Governments every five years. The 2010 census revealed that full-time-equivalent state employment in Georgia was 128,445. This compares to 123,000 in 2000—an increase of 4.3 percent. By way of comparison, state government employment nationwide grew 3.9 percent over the same ten years. Georgia had 129 state workers for every 10,000 residents in 2010, slightly below the national average of 137 and down from 143 ten years earlier (a reduction of over 10 percent).

Such comparisons can be hazardous because states differ significantly in the distribution of responsibilities among state and local governments, the private sector, and nonprofit organizations. The relative size of Georgia's public payrolls seems larger when factoring in local government employment (cities, counties, school districts, authorities), which reached 352,000 in 2002. This total is 22 percent higher than ten years earlier. It also equals 411 employees per 10,000 residents, which ranked tenth among the states. It is worth remembering that Georgia's population expanded 26.4 percent between 1990 and 2000, and another 6 percent from 2000 to 2003. In the end, Georgia had 554 state and local workers per 10,000 residents in 2002, as opposed to a national average of 542. Critics have blasted this level of public employment as excessive, although some see it as a result of the state's large number of counties. Debates have also focused on the composition of the state work force, especially regarding gender and race.

State Agencies

In 1991, the Governor's Commission on Effectiveness and Economy in Government identified 258 agencies: 8 interstate agencies, 35 major executive departments, 40 examining and licensing boards, 42 authorities and public corporations, 57 nondepartment agencies with executive functions, and 76 advisory boards.[66] There is little reason to believe that this wide range of agencies has changed much. A majority of state workers were employed outside Metropolitan Atlanta, however, including at public colleges, universities, and technical schools.

Size and Budget. As one might expect, agencies differ in the resources they control. Table 7.4 lists the funds and positions awarded to departments with state appropriations of $500 million or more in the 2005 fiscal year, when the state budget was more than $16.3 billion. It is important to remember that an agency's appropriations do not necessarily correspond to the size of its workforce. The

Table 7.4. State Funds Appropriated for Major Agencies, Fiscal Year 2015

Agency	Appropriation (in $ million)	Percentage of Total State Appropriation
Department of Education	7,944.5	38.1
Department of Community Health	3,068.6	14.7
University System of Georgia	1,939.1	9.3
Department of Corrections	1,148.5	5.5
Department of Transportation	864.1	4.1
Student Finance Commission	682.5	3.3
Department of Human Resources	523.9	2.5
Department of Revenue	177.7	.8

Source: Georgia Governor's Office of Planning and Budget 2015, 19.
Note: Total state funds appropriations for fiscal year 2015 equaled $20.837 billion.

Department of Education has only a modest number of staff members, but its large budget is the result of its mission to distribute substantial sums to Georgia's local school districts for a wide variety of purposes. Other departments receive substantial amounts from the federal government or other sources.

Organizational Change. State bureaucracies are not as immutable as many critics contend. Over the years, most states have created, abolished, or altered agencies. Some of these changes occurred because of political conflicts between different branches of government, governors' efforts to gain greater control over the bureaucracy, increased public concern over certain issues, or interest group pressure.

Like most states, Georgia has modified its executive branch on a somewhat regular basis. Two major reorganizations stand out: during the single term of Governor Richard Russell, when the General Assembly increased the power of the governor in 1931, and the reorganization in 1972 under Governor Jimmy Carter, which reduced the number of departments to twenty-two. These two changes increased the governor's ability to manage the bureaucracy through budgeting, better coordination and planning, and appointments.[67]

Many states have created agencies in response to actions taken by the federal government or growing public concern over certain issues. In Georgia, the Council for the Arts was established in 1964 as federal funding in this area expanded. The Office of Consumer Affairs was created in 1969 when such issues became more prominent in the United States. Neither of these agencies was present in three-fourths of the states until the 1970s. Georgia's 1972 reorganization followed a pattern established in most states of creating comprehensive departments to manage major policy areas: human resources (a range of agencies serving the poor), transportation (to take a broader view than its predecessor, the Highway Department), and natural resources (a series of departments that had dealt separately with conservation issues since the 1940s). Most states also created a separate department to deal with local governments—Georgia's Department of Community Affairs was spun off from existing agencies in 1977.

The 1980s were a decade when Georgia mirrored other states by establishing agencies to manage public radio and television resources (1981), improve coordination among the numerous organizations in the criminal justice system (1981), and cope with a range of environmental problems (1986). During the 1990s, changes in the state bureaucracy were tied to both pressing issues and changes in federal policy, including the creation of PeachCare, Georgia's part of a program established by Congress in 1997 to help states provide low-cost health insurance for the children of the working poor. PeachCare was originally part of what was the Department of Medical Assistance. With the rising costs of health care to the state—including PeachCare, Medicaid, and medical care for state employees—the legislature adopted a proposal by Governor Roy Barnes to reorganize Georgia's many health programs in a new Department of Community Health.[68] In 2005, the Department of Driver Services was created, encompassing most of the duties of the former Division of Motor Vehicles (DMV). Other DMV services were transferred to the Departments of Public Safety, Revenue, and Transportation, as well as the Public Service Commission. Governor Perdue made these changes to respond to critics of the services offered by the DMV, and the changes have continued under Governor Deal.

Managing Public Agencies. Public management can be difficult for a wide variety of reasons. Unlike the simple goal of profit in the private sector, agency objectives can be vague or even in conflict with one another. Beyond the question of goals is the dilemma of assessing achievement. How does one decide, for instance, if schools are producing an acceptable "product" for the state? Many agencies, in fact, furnish processes—renewing licenses, checking tax forms, or registering voters—where workers' accuracy and efficiency can be monitored. Yet the problem remains of deciding what indicators to use in evaluating agencies, as well as interpreting what can be considered "success."[69] Many of these matters are, of course, open to competing political interpretations.

In addition to multiple goals and performance measures, public sector managers typically must respond to multiple "bosses." Department heads must work closely with the governor, the legislature, and interest groups. Gubernatorial influence will be highest with managers whose selection requires the governor's approval. In contrast, department heads elected by voters or appointed by boards without the governor's consent normally will be more concerned with influencing the legislature, whose members frequently call to get information about programs, discuss regulations, complain about service delivery, request a project or service for their district, or seek jobs or contracts for constituents.[70] The General Assembly also earmarks some agency funds for projects in members' districts—what critics often call "pork barrel" spending—such as classroom buildings, museums, sewer improvements, senior centers, and similar spending.[71]

Given this complex administrative environment, government leaders often look for new and better ways to provide services. During the 1990s, this effort was associated with the "Reinventing Government" movement, which aimed to reshape public management to be more results oriented, entrepreneurial, and customer driven.[72] By the end of the decade, a major effort to evaluate management by state governments was funded with a grant from the Pew Charitable Trusts. Research teams at Syracuse University's Maxwell School of Citizenship and Public Affairs and at *Governing* magazine analyzed the states in five areas: financial management, capital management, human resources, managing for results, and information technology.

The Pew Government Performance Project issued grades between 1999 and 2008. Georgia received a B− in the first four categories in 2001 and a C+ for information technology, leaving the state with an overall grade of B−. In 2008, the criteria were reduced to four categories (capital management and management for results were combined into an infrastructure category), and Georgia improved its grades across the board. Most notably, Georgia increased a whole letter grade for human resources (A−) in areas such as retaining employees, training and development, and strategic workforce planning. Only a few states received grades of A− or A: six for information, four for human resources/people, five for money, and four for infrastructure. For the average grade over the four categories, only four states received an A: Michigan, Utah, Virginia, and Washington.[73] A second study, which characterizes the above five categories as "top-down" change, focused more on "bottom-up" changes in state management. Georgia was third among the states during 1998 in the latter study.[74]

As in other states, Georgia's citizens and officials undoubtedly will continue to look for ways to make government more efficient and responsive. This will not be easy, as James Q. Wilson reminds us: "The greatest mistake citizens can make when they complain of 'the bureaucracy' is to suppose that their frustrations arise simply out of management problems; they do not—they arise out of governance problems."[75]

Limits on Executive Power

Although granted extensive authority, Georgia's executive branch faces a variety of constraints on its power. Some of these are legal limitations; others might be labeled "political." Legal constraints include Georgia's constitution, laws, and courts. The nature of American federalism means that the executive branch is also constrained by the U.S. Constitution and federal law. The executive branch also confronts political limits. This may be especially true of governors' efforts to push proposals through the General Assembly. As chapter 5 indicates, interest groups can influence the executive branch's ability to propose and implement policies. Agencies also face constraints from public opinion, especially if it is coupled with citizen action.

Even though Georgia's executive branch has grown in size and power over the past generation, it still faces significant external challenges to its authority. It also must deal with internal tensions among the governor, elected department heads, the permanent bureaucracy, and the established procedures and norms of agencies.

CHAPTER 8

The Legal System

Change and Continuity: Georgia and the American Legal System

In this chapter we examine the legal system of Georgia. We do so first through a brief introduction of the American legal system and the types of laws that courts encounter. We then examine the court and judicial system of Georgia, focusing on the various courts and other parts of the system. We will see that although the Georgia legal system has undergone vast change, there is a significant continuity to the actors and the behaviors of those involved in the Georgia legal system.

The American legal system is a complex set of institutions and participants. It includes courts, judges, prosecutors, lawyers, and a wide range of others, among them supporting agencies such as corrections systems and law enforcement (covered in chapter 10, in the section "Law Enforcement in Georgia"). Complexity also occurs because of American federalism. Federalism is a unique feature and integral part of American constitutional politics and the administration of public affairs. What does it mean? In the simplest sense it is the "principle of government that provides for the division of powers between a national government and a collection of state governments operating over the same geographical area."[1]

Because of their fear of a powerful judiciary, the framers of the U.S. Constitution disputed the need for an independent federal judiciary, and although a federal judiciary was created, federal court jurisdiction was limited. Since Americans are citizens of both the United States and a state, their dual citizenship places them under the jurisdiction of two constitutions and two sets of laws. In effect, there is one legal system operated by the national government and a parallel set of legal systems in the fifty states.[2]

The vast majority of law and court decisions and litigation is left to the states under the concept of police power, which is the power to legislate for the health, safety, welfare, and sometimes morals of the people. Thus the laws we live and deal with from birth to death—education, health, marriage, divorce, safety, transportation—are state matters and state laws, and most legal practice involves state legal work.

The matter is also complex because of the many types of law. One can categorize the system through a hierarchy, with the U.S. Constitution and laws derived from the constitution sitting at the top.

The U.S. Constitution is the basic framework of government. It etches two different structures. The first framework creates the branches of government and is known as the separation of powers. The powers, duties, and responsibilities of the legislative, executive, and judicial branches are defined as the terms and procedures for taking office for each branch, whether by direct or indirect election or nomination and appointment. The constitution enumerates the specific and implied powers of each branch and the constraints on each branch of government imposed by the other branches.

The Constitution also has a clause known as the supremacy clause. Federal law is supreme, and any conflict with state law will be decided in favor of federal legislation, rule, or regulation. Of course, federal law must also adhere to the Constitution. Thus, first and foremost, no state or federal law can conflict with the Constitution of the United States. After meeting constitutional requirements, federal law is supreme, followed by regulations promulgated by federal regulatory and administrative agencies and executive orders. Regulations and executive orders have the full force and effect of law until superseded by federal statute. Next in importance comes state law, followed by state regulations and any orders promulgated by the governor, as well as city and town ordinances. Finally comes something known as case or common law.

Case law or common law is the law developed by judges through decisions of courts, as opposed to statutes adopted through the legislative process or regulations issued by the executive branch. It evolved out of medieval England and the idea that the law as handed down from the different English courts assumed jurisdiction over disputes previously decided by local or manorial courts. This consolidation of jurisdiction became the framework for the modern American judicial system.

Common-law courts base their decisions on prior judicial pronouncements, called precedents, rather than on legislative enactments. Common-law judges rely on their predecessors' decisions of actual controversies, rather than on codes or texts, to guide them in applying the law. Under the U.S. Supreme Court decision of *Erie Railroad Co. v. Tompkins*,[3] there is no federal common law.

Types and Categories of Law

In addition to the distinctions between federal and state law and constitutional law, statutory law, regulatory law, executive orders and common law, there are other distinctions in the types of law dealt with by the courts of Georgia. First is the distinction between private law and public law. Both affect residents of Georgia, but in the former, a court acts as an intermediary helping to settle disputes between private parties, for instance, matters involving contracts and torts. The state is involved as the referee. Public law involves the state enforcing or acting on matters of public policy and using the courts as an enforcement mechanism against private entities. This type of law governs relationships between the government and private entities, which could involve IRS tax suits, the regulation of foreign policy, and criminal justice.

The state and its pursuit of criminal justice is another divide of the law—the difference between civil and criminal law. Private law is always civil law, while criminal law is always public law because it involves the state, although often public law involves civil law suits. Criminal law involves the state seeking to impose a sanction or penalty on a party because that person has threatened or actually harmed public safety or welfare. The sanction can involve monetary fines, loss of liberty through incarceration, or even loss of life through the application of the death penalty. Criminal actions involve the state (e.g., the state of Georgia) against an individual. The state in a criminal proceeding has a very high burden of proof—it must prove every element of a crime beyond a reasonable doubt.

Civil law involves redress for some injury suffered by the complaining party known as the plaintiff. He or she alleges an injury due to the wrongdoing of the other party, known as the defendant, and seeks relief. This typically involves damages payable by the injuring party. Sometimes the plaintiff seeks something known as specific performance. That is, rather than money damages, the plaintiff asks the court to order the defendant to perform a certain action, such as sell a particular parcel of real estate to the plaintiff. No state sanction or penalty is imposed. The standard of proof in a civil case is borne by the plaintiff, who must show that the defendant was wrong by a preponderance of evidence—a much less burdensome standard than needed for criminal cases.

Examples of civil actions include claims for breach of contract, torts, such as automobile accidents and medical malpractice, as well as securities and real estate actions. In a contract lawsuit, a plaintiff might allege that the defendant's failure to adhere to the terms of the contract caused the plaintiff to pay a higher price for a good or service or miss an opportunity to make money. In these cases, the plaintiff will seek compensation for the difference in the price paid due to the breach of the contract. In an automobile case, the plaintiff alleges that the negligent operation of a moving vehicle by the defendant caused the plaintiff injury. The plaintiff then sues to be "made whole," and that amount often includes the damage of "pain and suffering."

The Georgia Legal System

State and local governments are major players in the American legal system despite rhetoric from politicians and interest groups calling on the national government to do more, especially regarding crime and private lawsuits. Most "law" occurs at the state level. Most lawyers are engaged in state, not federal, practices, and most civil litigation and most criminal actions occur at the state level.

Like most states, Georgia provides substantial resources to its legal system. In FY 2012, the General Assembly appropriated almost $2 billion to the major agencies in the legal system, which includes agencies such as the Georgia Bureau of Investigation and the Office of the Public Defender. This appropriation included almost $190 million for the judicial branch and more than $1.8 billion for the major executive agencies, with the largest single allocation to the Department of Corrections at more than $1.1 billion. Interestingly, the allocation to the court system increased little over this time, but significantly more was allocated to the agencies and the penal system. City and county governments also have major roles, primarily in law enforcement.[4]

Georgia's Court System

Georgia has an elaborate system of trial and appellate courts. It is more complex with more layers than the federal system but less elaborate than other state court systems. A simplified version of the Georgia court system is presented in figure 8.1. At the bottom of the court hierarchy are the trial courts. Trial courts apply laws to the facts in specific cases, as when they render a verdict of guilt or innocence in a criminal case. Appellate courts, on the other hand, review the actions of trial courts to determine questions of law—whether statutes or constitutional questions were interpreted or applied correctly. Unlike the U.S. Constitution, which grants Congress broad authority regarding the legal system, the Georgia Constitution includes substantial detail about the operation of trial and appellate courts, the selection and conduct of judges, the election and performance of district attorneys, and a range of procedures.

Trial Courts. At the lowest levels are the hundreds of local courts, primarily municipal and small county courts dealing with traffic matters, local ordinances,

Figure 8.1. The Georgia Court System

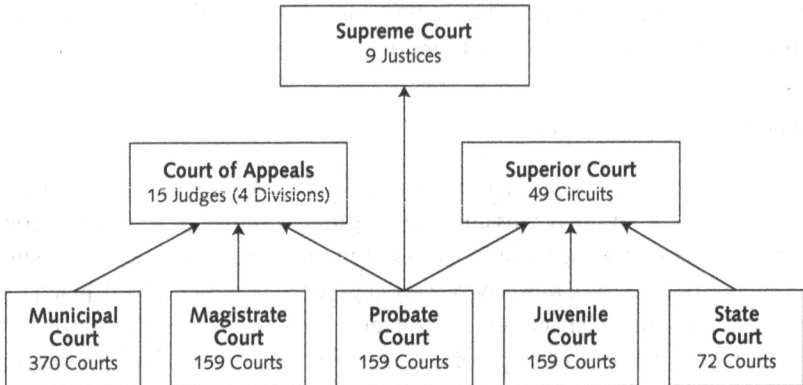

and other misdemeanors. They also process warrants and may conduct preliminary hearings to determine "probable cause" in criminal cases. Local acts passed by the General Assembly determine the qualifications and selection method for municipal court judges.

Georgia also has "specialized" courts. Most trial courts are courts of general jurisdiction, meaning that many different types of cases can be filed and heard in these courts, ranging from civil cases to criminal cases. Specialized courts are established to deal with specific areas of the law. The Georgia Constitution requires a probate court in each county. These courts are headed by an elected judge and deal primarily with wills and estates but also handle marriage licenses, appoint guardians, and oversee involuntary hospitalization of individuals. Probate courts may also issue warrants in some cases.

Juvenile courts are another type of specialized court designed to deal specifically with minors and the problems associated with minors, including deprived and neglected children under eighteen years of age; delinquent and unruly offenses committed by children under seventeen years of age; and traffic violations committed by juveniles. The juvenile courts also hear cases involving consent to marriage for minors, enlistment of minors in the military, and procedures for return of a runaway child resident who is taken into custody in another state. These courts have been established in each of Georgia's 159 counties. Juvenile court judges are chosen by superior court judges in each circuit. In smaller counties, juvenile court judges may serve part time or superior court judges may serve in juvenile court. There are no jury trials in juvenile courts, and records are generally sealed to protect minors. Occasionally minors are tried in state or superior courts if a jury trial is warranted. As of July 2014, almost 150 judges were serving juvenile courts in Georgia: 59 full-time juvenile courts judges, 35 part-time juvenile court judges; 9 full-time associate juvenile court judges, and 12 part-time associate juvenile court judges; 13 pro tempore judges; 4 superior court judges exercising juvenile court jurisdiction; and 15 senior judges.

Magistrate courts in each county deal with bail, misdemeanors, small civil complaints, and search and arrest warrants. They also handle civil suits with claims of $15,000 or less. As in juvenile courts, magistrate courts do not hold jury trials. Overlap may be a problem in counties that have state courts because superior courts hold concurrent jurisdiction. There are 159 magistrate courts staffed by 159 chief magistrates and a total of 354 magistrates.

The state constitution designates superior courts as Georgia's trial courts of general jurisdiction. The state is divided into forty-nine circuits with over two hundred superior court judges. The superior courts vary in population and size. Each county has its own superior court, but judges may handle cases in more than one county within a circuit. They exclusively hear divorces and felonies, land title cases, and equity cases. Most hear almost all important cases involving civil disputes. Jury trials are not held in many cases. They have some limited appellate jurisdiction to hear cases from lower limited-jurisdiction courts.

Georgia Court of Appeals. After a trial, the losing party (except the state when a criminal defendant is acquitted at trial) may appeal the case to a higher court, asserting some sort of error at the lower court level. The higher, or appellate court, may not take new testimony and can only review the facts as established at the trial court level. If appealed, these facts established at the trial provide the record of appeal along with the written and oral arguments of the losing party's attorney.

Like many states, but not all (forty-four have intermediate courts of appeal), Georgia has two levels of courts to hear appeals. Members of both courts are elected to six-year terms on a nonpartisan ballot. Cases decided at lower levels may be appealed to the Georgia Court of Appeals, except in cases where the Georgia Supreme Court has exclusive appellate jurisdiction. The court of appeals was created in 1907 to relieve some of the burden on the supreme court and can hear appeals on all cases except those involving constitutional questions, land title disputes, the construction of wills, murder, election contests, habeas corpus, extraordinary remedies, divorce and alimony, and instances when the original appellate jurisdiction lies with the superior courts, such as appeals from juvenile courts.

Judges are elected to six-year terms on a nonpartisan ballot. Initially the Georgia Court of Appeals consisted of one court of three judges; in 1960 the number of judges was increased to seven, and in the following year, the General

Assembly added two more judges and divided the court into three divisions of three judges each, one of which was to handle all criminal cases. The court was later expanded to twelve judges, and legislation passed in the 2015 session will now expand the Georgia Court of Appeals to fifteen judges, giving Governor Deal an unprecedented opportunity to influence future rulings for many years.[5]

The assignment of criminal cases to a single division was not eliminated until 1967.[6] The number of judges remained at nine until 1996. In 1984, the first woman, Dorothy Toth Beasley, and the first African American, Robert Benham, were named to the court. Benham was later appointed to the Georgia Supreme Court. In 2013, the first Asian American, Carla McMillan, was appointed by Governor Nathan Deal. In 1996, the number of judges on the court was increased to ten, and in 1999, the court expanded to twelve judges in four divisions; the 2016 legislative session increased the number to fifteen. In all, seventy-nine judges have served on this court, and this number will soon increase.

All three judges on the panel must agree before a case is disposed, and if one dissents, the case may be heard by a panel of seven members of the court of appeals.[7] Table 8.1 lists all the appointments to the Georgia Court of Appeals since 1907.

Since its creation in 1907, the court's responsibilities have remained constant, but that stability masks significant demographic and political change. The number of minorities, women, and Republicans serving the court have all increased, reflecting Georgia's demographic and political changes. The pace of change began to accelerate in the later part of the twentieth century, with the greatest rate of change occurring since the turn of the new century. In figures 8.2–8.4, we chart this change, examine the period beginning in 1970 through the present day. We use this period for several reasons: Prior to 1970 Georgia was essentially a one-party state—Democratic—and what political scientists term "southern Democratic," meaning a very conservative party, very different from its northern Democratic counterparts. Many Republican officeholders in the North were far more ideologically liberal than southern Democrats.

Change began in the 1970s. Jimmy Carter represented the new type of Democrat—much more moderate to progressive on many social issues, particularly race. With the end of state-mandated segregation, African Americans began to participate in the political process and legal profession, including running for political office and seeking various judicial positions.

As African Americans began to participate in the Democratic Party, many Democrats began to switch party affiliation, leading to the rise of the Republican Party in Georgia, which eventually led to Georgia becoming a Republican-dominated state. Likewise the rise of the women's movement led to much greater participation by women in the political process and legal profession, leading to an increase in women seeking and obtaining judicial positions.

Table 8.1. Judges Serving on the Georgia Court of Appeals

Judge	Years	Governor
Benjamin Harvey Hill	1907–1913	Hoke Smith
Richard Brevard Russell	1907–1916	Hoke Smith
Arthur Gray Powell	1907–1912	Hoke Smith
James Robert Pottle	1912–1914	Joseph M. Brown
Leonard S. Roan	1913–1914	John M. Slaton
Peyton L. Wade	1914–1919	John M. Slaton
Nash Rose Broyles	1914–1947	John M. Slaton
Robert Hodges	1916	Nathaniel E. Harris
Oliver Hazzard Bartow Bloodworth	1917–1932	Nathaniel E. Harris
Walter Franklin George	1917	Nathaniel E. Harris
Roscoe Luke	1917–1932	Nathaniel E. Harris
William Franklin Jenkins	1917–1937	Nathaniel E. Harris
Frank Harwell	1917–1918	Nathaniel E. Harris
Alexander William Stephens	1918–1943	Hugh M. Dorsey
Charles Whitefoord Smith	1919–1920	Hugh M. Dorsey
Benjamin Harvey Hill	1920–1922	Hugh M. Dorsey
Reason Chesnutt Bell	1922–1932	Thomas W. Hardwick
I. Homer Sutton	1932–1954	Richard Russell Jr.
Frank A. Hooper Jr.	1932	Richard Russell Jr.
Hugh James MacIntyre	1932–1952	Richard Russell Jr.
John Benjamin Guerry	1933–1940	Eugene Talmadge
Jule Wimberly Felton	1937–1969	Eurith D. Rivers
Bernard Clay Gardner Sr.	1940–1960	Eurith D. Rivers
David Monroe Parker	1944–1949	Ellis Arnall
John Murphy Clagett Townsend	1947–1961	Melvin E. Thompson
Charles William Worrill	1949–1953	Herman Talmadge
Ira Carlisle	1952–1963	Herman Talmadge
Joseph Dillard Quillian	1953–1960	Herman Talmadge
Horace Elmo Nichols	1954–1966	Herman Talmadge
John Sammons Bell	1960–1979	Ernest Vandiver
John Eccleston Frankum	1960–1967	Ernest Vandiver
Robert Henry Jordan	1960–1972	Ernest Vandiver
Homer Christian Eberhardt	1961–1974	Ernest Vandiver
Robert H. Hall	1961–1974	Ernest Vandiver
William Vance Custer Jr.	1961–1962	Ernest Vandiver
Robert Lee Russell Jr.	1962–1965	Ernest Vandiver

Table 8.1. Judges Serving on the Georgia Court of Appeals (*continued*)

Judge	Years	Governor
Charles Adams Pannell	1963–1976	Carl E. Sanders
Braswell D. Deen Jr.	1965–1990	Carl E. Sanders
J. Kelley Quillian	1966–1984	Carl E. Sanders
George Stanley Joslin	1967	Lester Maddox
George Price Whitman	1967–1972	Lester Maddox
Randall Evans Jr.	1969–1976	Lester Maddox
H. Sol Clark	1972–1977	Jimmy Carter
Irwin W. Stolz Jr.	1972–1977	Jimmy Carter
Julian Webb	1974–1979	Jimmy Carter
Thomas O. Marshall	1974–1977	Jimmy Carter
William Leroy McMurray Jr.	1976–2000	George Busbee
George T. Smith	1976–1980	George Busbee
Arnold Shulman	1977–1984	George Busbee
Harold R. Banke	1977–1991	George Busbee
A. W. Birdsong Jr.	1977–1998	George Busbee
Norman L. Underwood	1979	George Busbee
George H. Carley	1979–1993	George Busbee
John W. Sognier	1980–1992	George Busbee
Marion T. Pope Jr.	1981–2002	George Busbee
Robert Benham	1984–1989	Joe Frank Harris
Dorothy Toth Beasley	1984–1999	Joe Frank Harris
Clarence Cooper	1990–1994	Joe Frank Harris
Gary Blaylock Andrews	1991–Date	Zell Miller
Edward H. Johnson	1992–2010	Zell Miller
G. Alan Blackburn	1993–2010	Zell Miller
J. D. Smith	1993–2011	Zell Miller
John H. Ruffin Jr.	1994–2008	Zell Miller
Frank M. Eldridge	1996–2004	Zell Miller
Anne Elizabeth Barnes	1999–Date	Roy Barnes
M. Yvette Miller	1999–Date	Roy Barnes
John J. Ellington	1999–Date	Roy Barnes
Herbert E. Phipps	1999–Date	Roy Barnes
Charles B. Mikell	2000–2012	Roy Barnes
A. Harris Adams	2002–2012	Roy Barnes
Debra Bernes	2005–2010	George E. "Sonny" Perdue
Sara L. Doyle	2009–Date	George E. "Sonny" Perdue

Table 8.1 (*continued*)

Judge	Years	Governor
Keith R. Blackwell	2010–2012	George E. "Sonny" Perdue
Stephen Louis A. Dillard	2010–Date	George E. "Sonny" Perdue
Christopher McFadden	2011–Date	Nathan Deal
Michael P. Boggs	2012– 2016	Nathan Deal
William M. Ray II	2012–Date	Nathan Deal
Elizabeth L. Branch (Lisa)	2012–Date	Nathan Deal
Carla McMillian	2013–Date	Nathan Deal
Charlie Bethel	2016–Date	Nathan Deal
Tripp Self III	2017–Date	Nathan Deal

Source: http://www.gaappeals.us/history/roster.php.

Figure 8.2 shows the increase in the number of minority positions for the Georgia Court of Appeals. Since the number changed during this period from nine to twelve judges, we show the percentage of minority membership, which includes African Americans and Asian Americans. As one can see, minority representation has significantly increased since 1970, and the increase has continued even with the ascension of Republican dominance of the electoral system. The percentage of minority judges does not quite mirror the combined African American (31.4) and Asian American (.05) percentage of the population in Georgia, and of course to date there are no Hispanic or Latino (9.2 percent of the population) judges on the court, but the trend is increasing minority participation, except for the years 1994 to 1998, when minority members were not on the bench.

Figure 8.3 examines the percentage of women on the Georgia Court of Appeals, which also shows a significant increase since 1970. While the first woman was not appointed until 1984, by 2014 five of the twelve judges were female, representing 42 percent of the bench. This is, of course, still smaller than the percentage of females living in Georgia (51.3 percent).

Finally, we examine the growing strength of the Republican Party in Georgia and its relationship to the Georgia Court of Appeals. It is not as straightforward to obtain party identification for judges as it is to calculate the percentage of women or minorities. Georgia voter registration is done on a nonpartisan basis, and judicial elections are also nonpartisan. However, occasionally a retirement or other vacancy on the bench allows the governor to appoint a judge, who then runs in the subsequent election as an incumbent. Using standard political-science measures, we generally classify this judge as a Republican or a Democratic depending on the party of the appointing governor. We can also deter-

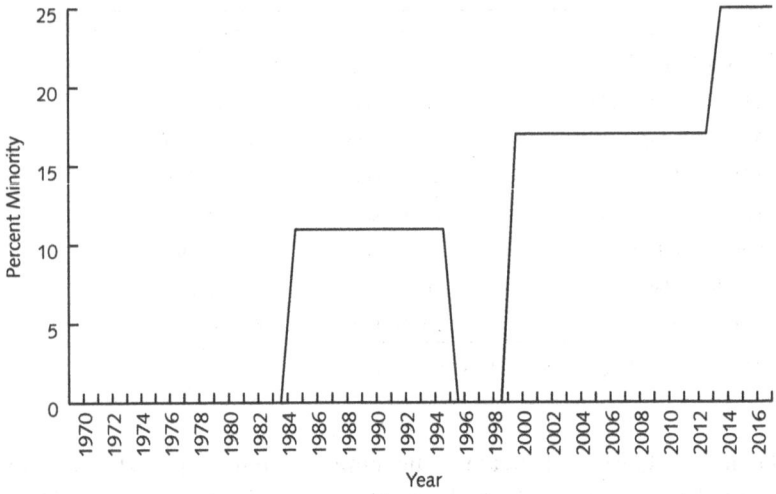

Figure 8.2. Percent Minority Members of the Georgia Court of Appeals, 1970–2017

Source: http://www.gaappeals.us/history/roster.php.

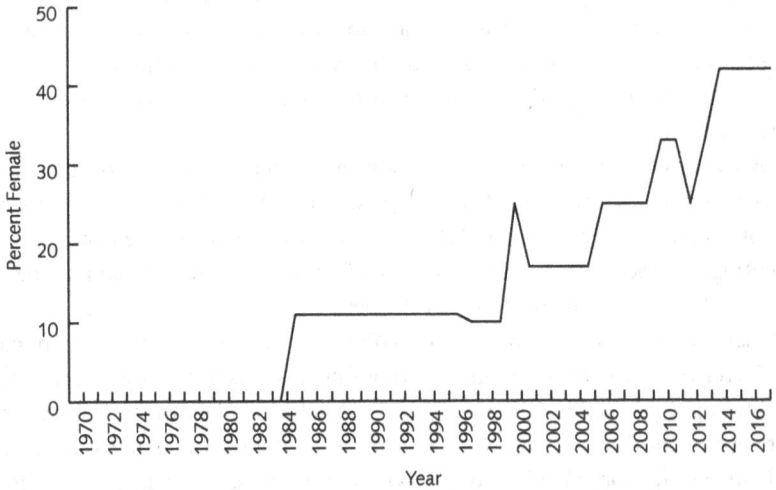

Figure 8.3. Percent Female Members of the Georgia Court of Appeals, 1970–2017

Source: http://www.gaappeals.us/history/roster.php.

Figure 8.4. Percent Republican Members of the
Georgia Court of Appeals, 1970–2017

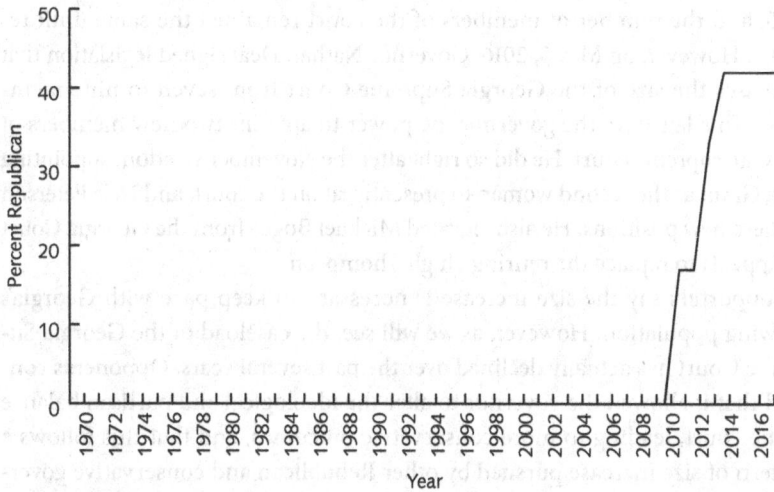

Source: http://www.gaappeals.us/history/roster.php.

mine partisan affiliation through political donation records, groups to which
the judge belongs, and endorsements to fill in the appointed gaps. Figure 8.4 is
based on these data and indicates the percentage of Republicans or Republican-
appointed members on the Georgia Court of Appeals. As we can see, it took
much longer for a Republican to join the court than for the court to include
women or minorities. This difference reflects decades of Democratic Party dominance. However, as the Republican Party started to control electoral politics,
the percentage of Republicans on the court of appeals has steadily grown, mirroring the rise of the Republican Party elsewhere in the state.

Georgia Supreme Court. The Georgia Supreme Court was created in 1845, and its
first session was held at Talbotton on January 26, 1846. Three judges sat on the
first court, and their salaries were set at $2,500 per year. At the time of the cre-
ation of the supreme court, Georgia's population stood at approximately eight
hundred thousand. The state was divided into eleven superior court circuits,
and the judges of the Georgia Supreme Court, similar to those of the early U.S.
Supreme Court, rode "circuit." That is, they traveled the state, holding court in
nine different localities during the course of the year. The hardships involved in
riding the circuit lasted until shortly after the Civil War, when the constitution
of 1855 provided that the court would sit at the seat of government.

The constitution was amended in 1896 to provide for the addition of three justices to the court and to stipulate that justices and the chief justice would be elected by the people. A seventh justice was added by the constitution of 1945, and the number of members of the court remained the same until recently. However, on May 3, 2016, Governor Nathan Deal signed legislation that increases the size of the Georgia Supreme Court from seven to nine members.[8] This law gave the governor the power to appoint two new members of the state supreme court. He did so right after the November election, appointing Britt Grant as the second woman to presently sit on the court, and Nels Peterson to these new positions. He also elevated Michael Boggs from the Georgia Court of Appeals to replace the retiring Hugh Thompson.

Supporters say the size increase is necessary to keep pace with Georgia's growing population. However, as we will see, the caseload of the Georgia Supreme Court has actually declined over the past several years. Opponents contend that it allowed the governor to alter the ideological and partisan balance of the court, leading to more conservative outcomes, and that this follows a pattern of size increase pursued by other Republican and conservative governors throughout the country.[9] Even with these changes, seven state supreme court justices are the norm for most states, and New York, California, and Florida—states with much larger populations than Georgia—all use seven-member courts. Of course, the demographic, political, social, and economic composition of the court has changed significantly.

From 1945 to 2016, the Georgia Supreme Court had been composed of seven justices. With recent legislation, the supreme court now consists of nine justices. The supreme court is charged with hearing all cases regarding the Georgia Constitution, the U.S. Constitution (as it applies within the state), the constitutionality of a law, and elections. It also may hear cases on appeal from the court of appeals or may be called on to decide questions of law from other state or local courts. It has authority to hear all cases in which a sentence of death may be given. The justices choose whether to hear appeals from lower courts through the process of certiorari, or request for information, from lower courts. The supreme court is also involved in administering the state court system and regulating the legal profession. Thus bar admission requirements and lawyer discipline are the province of the Georgia Supreme Court.

Table 8.2 lists all the justices who have sat on the Georgia Supreme Court, their years of service, and whether they assumed the role of chief justice.

As discussed in chapter 3, because of the U.S. Supreme Court case of *Murdock v. City of Memphis*, which announced the concept of "adequate and independent state grounds," the Georgia Supreme Court is the final interpreter of state law and as such has significant authority and power in the state as a coequal

Table 8.2. Justices of the Georgia Supreme Court

First Name	Last Name	Chief	Start Year	End Year
Joseph H.	Lumpkin		1845	1863
E. A.	Nisbet		1845	1853
H. L.	Benning		1853	1859
E. A.	Starnes		1853	1855
C. J.	McDonald		1855	1859
Richard F.	Lyon		1859	1865
Linton	Stephens		1859	1860
C. J.	Jenkins		1860	1866
I. L.	Harris		1866	1868
D. A.	Walker		1866	1868
Joseph E.	Brown	C	1868	1870
H. K.	McCay		1868	1875
O. A.	Lochrane	C	1871	1872
W. W.	Montgomery		1872	1873
Hiram	Warner	C	1872	1880
R. P.	Trippe		1873	1875
M. J.	Crawford		1880	1883
W. A.	Hawkins		1880	1880
James	Jackson	C	1880	1887
Alex M.	Speer		1880	1882
Samuel	Hall		1882	1887
M. H.	Blandford		1883	1890
Logan E.	Bleckley	C	1887	1894
Samuel	Lumpkin		1891	1903
S. R.	Atkinson		1894	1897
T. J.	Simmons	C	1894	1905
Andrew J.	Cobb		1897	1907
William H.	Fish		1897	1905
Henry T.	Lewis		1897	1902
William A.	Little		1897	1903
Samuel B.	Adams		1902	1902
John S.	Candler		1902	1906
Marcus W.	Beck		1903	1937
Joseph R.	Lamar		1903	1905
Henry C.	Turner		1903	1904
Beverly D.	Evans		1904	1917

Table 8.2. Justices of the Georgia Supreme Court (*continued*)

First Name	Last Name	Chief	Start Year	End Year
Joseph H.	Lumpkin II		1905	1916
Samuel C.	Atkinson		1906	1942
Horace	Holden		1907	1911
H. Warner	Hill		1911	1934
S. Price	Gilbert		1916	1937
Walter F.	George		1917	1922
James K.	Hines		1922	1932
Richard B.	Russell	C	1923	1938
John B.	Hutcheson		1934	1938
Warren	Grice		1937	1945
W. Henry	Duckworth		1938	1948
Charles S.	Reid	C	1938	1943
Samuel D.	Hewlett		1942	1942
William Y.	Atkinson		1943	1953
Lee R.	Wyatt		1943	1960
Thomas S.	Candler		1945	1966
T. Grady	Head		1945	1965
R. C.	Bell		1946	1949
W. Frank	Jenkins	C	1946	1948
L. C.	Groves		1948	1948
Bond	Almand		1949	1969
J. Harold	Hawkins		1949	1960
Charles W.	Worrill		1953	1954
Homer	Sutton		1954	1954
Joseph D.	Quillian		1960	1966
J. Eugene	Cook		1965	1967
John E.	Frankum		1967	1970
Jule W.	Felton		1969	1972
Peyton	Hawes		1970	1973
William B.	Gunter		1972	1977
Carlton	Mobley	C	1972	1974
G. Conley	Ingram		1973	1977
Benning M.	Grice	C	1974	1975
Robert H.	Hall		1974	1979
Harold N.	Hill		1975	1982
Jesse G.	Bowles		1977	1981

Table 8.2 (*continued*)

First Name	Last Name	Chief	Start Year	End Year
Thomas O.	Marshall		1977	1986
Robert H.	Jordan	C	1980	1982
H. E.	Nichols		1980	1980
Hiram K.	Undercofler		1980	1981
Hardy	Gregory, Jr.		1981	1989
George T.	Smith		1981	1991
Richard	Bell		1982	1992
Carol W.	Hunstein		1992	2009
Leah Ward	Sears	C	1992	2009
Harold G.	Clarke		1992	1994
Charles L.	Weltner	C	1992	1992
Willis B.	Hunt	C	1994	1995
Hugh P.	Thompson		1994	2016
Harris	Hines		1995	
Robert	Benham		2001	
Norman S.	Fletcher	C	2001	2005
Harold D.	Melton		2005	
David E.	Nahmias		2009	
Keith R.	Blackwell		2012	
George H.	Carley	C	2012	2012
Britt	Grant		2017	
Nels	Peterson		2017	
Michael	Boggs		2017	

Source: http://www.gasupreme.us/court-information/history/.

branch of government. As we noted for the Georgia Court of Appeals judges, as Georgia has undergone political, demographic, and social change, so has the Georgia Supreme Court. The number of minorities, women, and Republicans sitting on the court has increased, reflecting Georgia's demographic and political changes. The pace of change began to accelerate in the latter part of the twentieth century, with the greatest rate of change occurring since the turn of the new century. In the figures 8.5–8.9, we chart this change, examining the period beginning in 1960 through the present day. We go back ten more years than we did for the Georgia Court of Appeals to take advantage of some ideological measurements available for the members of the Georgia Supreme Court.

Figure 8.5. Minority Percentage of Georgia Supreme Court Justices, 1960–2017

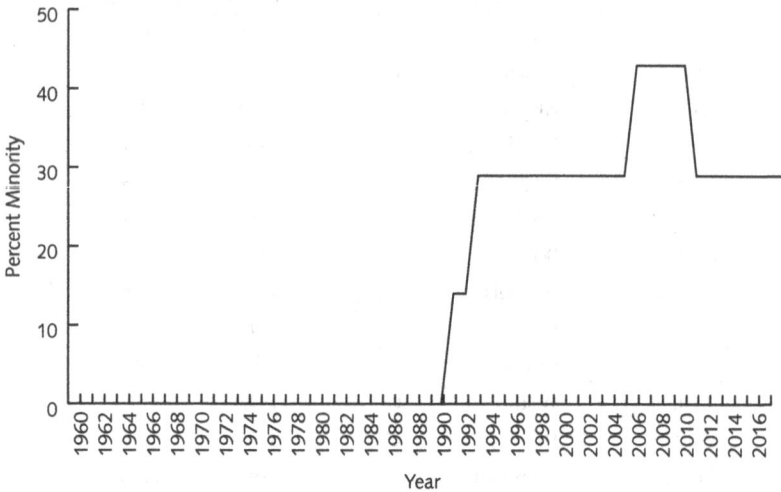

Source: http://www.gasupreme.us/court-information/history/.

Figure 8.5 shows the increase in the number of members of minority groups on the Georgia Supreme Court. Unlike the court of appeals, the number of justices has remained constant at seven. However, like the court of appeals, the percentage of minority membership has increased.

As we can see, minority representation, following the pattern of the Georgia Court of Appeals, has significantly increased. This increase has continued even with the ascension of Republican dominance of the electoral system. Minority representation, however, came more slowly on the Georgia Supreme Court, with the first minority justice, Robert Benham, not coming on the court until 1992, and then followed by Leah Sears in 1992. While three African American justices were on the court for a few years, now there are two, or close to the percentage of African Americans (31.4) in the state. Robert Benham was the first African American chief justice on the court and Leah Sears the second.

Figure 8.6 examines the percentage of women on the Georgia Supreme Court. As we saw with minority representation, female representation on the Georgia Supreme Court took longer than for the Georgia Court of Appeals. The first women, Leah Sears and Carol Hunstein, were both appointed in 1992. Justice Sears was also the second African American on the court and the first female chief justice. With the recent appointment of Britt Grant joining Hunstein on the state supreme court, two of the nine justices now on the bench are

Figure 8.6. Female Percentage of Georgia Supreme Court Justices, 1960–2017

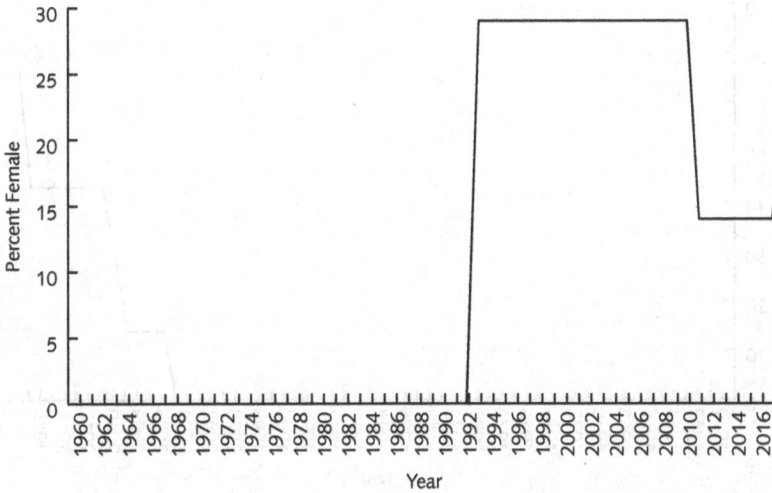

Source: http://www.gasupreme.us/court-information/history/.

women. That percentage of female supreme court justices is much lower than the state percentage of females living in Georgia (51.3).

We also examined the growing strength of the Republican Party in Georgia and its relationship to the Georgia Supreme Court. Again, as we did for the Georgia Supreme Court, using standard political-science measures, we generally classify this judge as a Republican or a Democrat depending on the party of the appointing governor or the judge's partisan affiliation as evidenced in political donation records, groups to which the judge belongs, endorsements, and the like.

Based on these data, figure 8.7 examines the percentage of Republicans on the Georgia Supreme Court. Mirroring the Georgia Court of Appeals, we can see it took much longer for a Republican to join the Georgia Supreme Court than for the court to have women or minorities, again reflecting decades of Democratic Party dominance. However, as the Republican Party started to control electoral politics, the percentage of Republicans on the Georgia Supreme Court has steadily grown, mirroring the rise of the Republican Party elsewhere in the state. With new appointments, the court now has nine Republican members and only three Democratic justices.

Because we have much more data on the Georgia Supreme Court than other courts, we can also examine ideological changes and continuity. Using a mea-

Figure 8.7. Republican Percentage of State Supreme Court Justices, 1960–2017

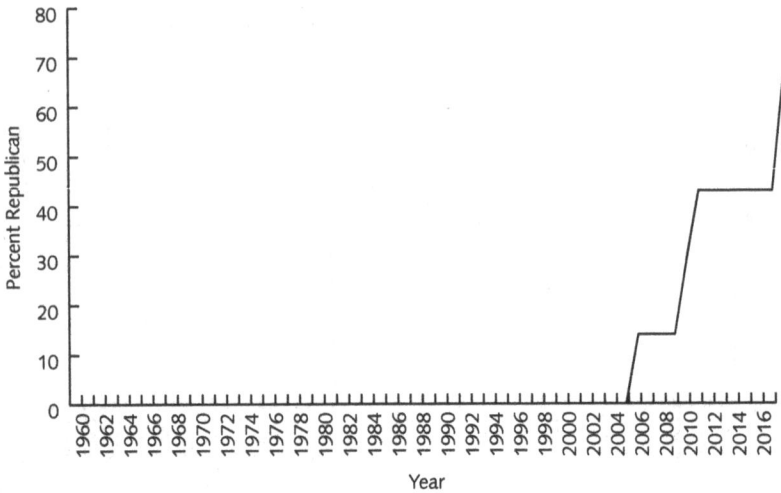

Source: http://www.gasupreme.us/court-information/history.

sure developed by political scientists known as PAJID scores, we can measure the changes in the average ideology of the Georgia Supreme Court from 1960 until the present day. PAJID is a measure of ideology for state supreme court justices developed by political scientists Paul Brace, Laura Langer, and Melinda Gann Hall and stands for Party-Adjusted Justice Ideology (PAJID).[10] It is a proxy, or indirect, measure imputed from the state elite and citizen ideological scores developed by another group of political scientists, which are in turn imputed from interest group ratings of each state's congressional delegation by the group Americans for Democratic Action.[11] While by no means perfect, these scores can be used to track the ideology the Georgia Supreme Court using a scale from 0, the most conservative, to 100, the most liberal (see figure 8.8). Georgia, a southern state, has always been politically conservative. We can see that only recently has the court averaged a score near 50, or the midway point between liberal and conservative ideological preferences. The recent upsurge represents several years of moderate Democratic governors such as Zell Miller and Roy Barnes, who were able to appoint justices to vacant positions, thus making them incumbents for election purposes. Thus, even though the state was Democratic dominated, the court showed that it represented a southern conservative Democratic Party until the demographic and political changes started to occur in the 1970s. Even so, it remains a moderate court, and Repub-

Figure 8.8. Average Ideology of Georgia Supreme Court Justices, 1960–2014

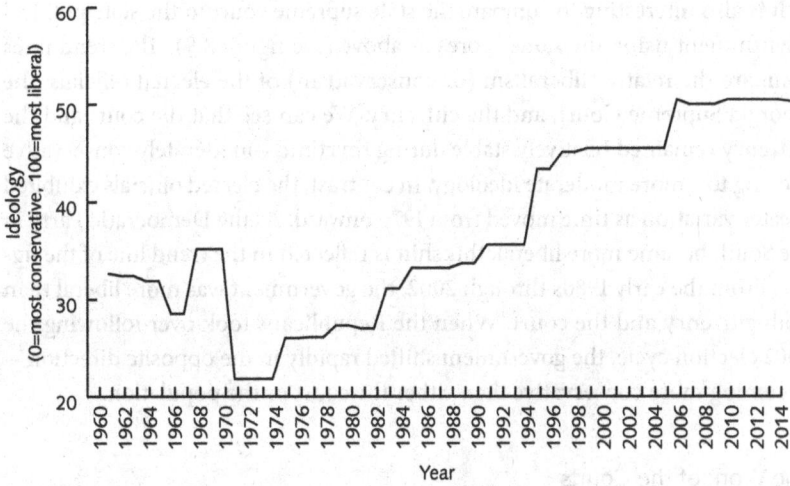

Source: Brace, Langer, and Hall 2000.

Figure 8.9. Average Ideology of Georgia Citizens, Elected Officials, and Supreme Court Justices, 1960–2014

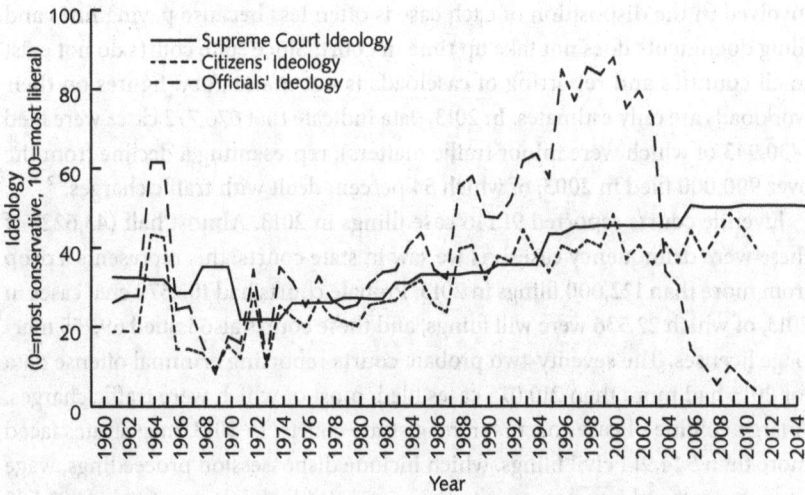

Source: Richard Fording, State Ideology Data, https://rcfording.wordpress.com/state-ideology-data/.

lican dominance of state government has not made the court more conservative because of the length of terms for each individual justice.

It is also interesting to compare the state supreme court to the state political environment using the same scores as above (see figure 8.9). The trend lines compare the relative liberalism (or conservatism) of the elected officials, the Georgia Supreme Court, and the citizenry. We can see that the court and the citizenry remained relatively stable during this time—moderately conservative moving to a more moderate ideology. In contrast, the elected officials exhibited greater variation as time moved from 1970 onward. As the Democratic Party in the South became more liberal, this shift is reflected in the trend line of the figure. From the early 1980s through 2002, the government was more liberal than both citizenry and the court. When the Republicans took over following the 2002 election cycle, the government shifted rapidly in the opposite direction—becoming more conservative than either the court or the population.

The Work of the Courts

Trial Court Dockets. In 2013, more than 440,000 cases were filed in Georgia's superior courts. This compares to 354,000 filings in 2003. The vast majority of filings are civil cases, and most of the civil cases involve domestic relations (e.g., child custody, divorce). As figure 8.10 shows, the workload has increased since 2003, but total filings have decreased in the past six years. Criminal filings have increased slightly but been offset by a drop in civil cases.

Lower-level courts have more cases filed than superior courts, but the time involved in the disposition of each case is often less because paying fines and filing documents does not take up time in court. Since state courts do not exist in all counties and reporting of caseloads is not mandatory, figures on their workloads are only estimates. In 2013, data indicate that 676,772 cases were filed (430,943 of which were minor traffic matters), representing a decline from the over 900,000 filed in 2003, of which 54 percent dealt with traffic charges.[12]

Juvenile courts reported 91,146 case filings in 2013. Almost half (43,622) of these were delinquency cases. As we saw in state courts, this represents a drop from more than 122,000 filings in 2013. Probate courts had 102,579 civil cases in 2013, of which 22,536 were will filings, and these courts also issued 69,755 marriage licenses. The seventy-two probate courts reporting criminal offense data for 2013 had more than 210,075 cases filed, most of which were traffic charges. A large volume of cases occurs in magistrate courts. In 2013, magistrates faced more than 544,914 civil filings, which include dispossession proceedings, wage garnishment, and foreclosures. On the criminal side there was a total of 395,602 warrants and filings, with these courts issuing 133,360 felony warrants and 167,696 misdemeanor warrants. Finally municipal courts deal with many traf-

Figure 8.10. Georgia Superior Court Filings, 2007–2013

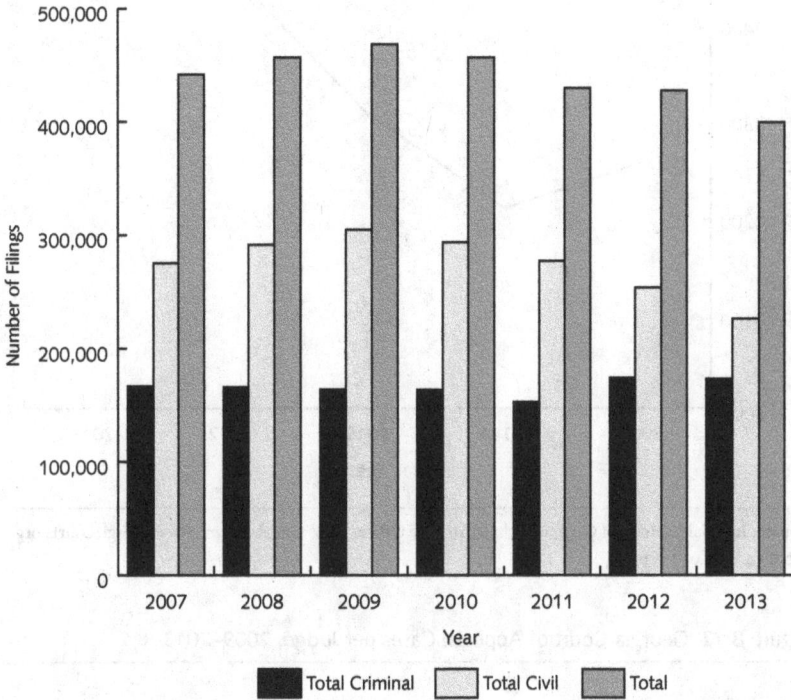

Source: Judicial Council of Georgia, Administrative Office of the Courts, http://www.georgiacourts.org
/content/caseload-reports.

fic matters. These courts reported 1,134,742 traffic filings in 2013 and disposed
of 67,133 misdemeanor cases in 2013.

Appellate Court Workloads. Cases heard at the appellate level are time consuming and receive much media attention. The Georgia Court of Appeals had 3,432
cases filed during 2013, more than 2,500 of them being direct appeals. The court
issued more than 900 published opinions and disposed of more than 2,500
cases. Figures 8.11 and 8.12 show a general upward trend in filings and caseload
per judge since 2009, although there was slight drop in 2013.

The Georgia Supreme Court disposed of over 1,900 cases in 2013 but issued
fewer than 300 formal opinions, which represents a drop from previous years
(see figure 8.13). As we can see, the caseload of the court varies over time and obviously does not depend on population growth or trials and dispositions of lower
court matters. This is also confirmed by examining the number of opinions issued

Figure 8.11. Georgia Court of Appeals: Total Filings 2009–2013

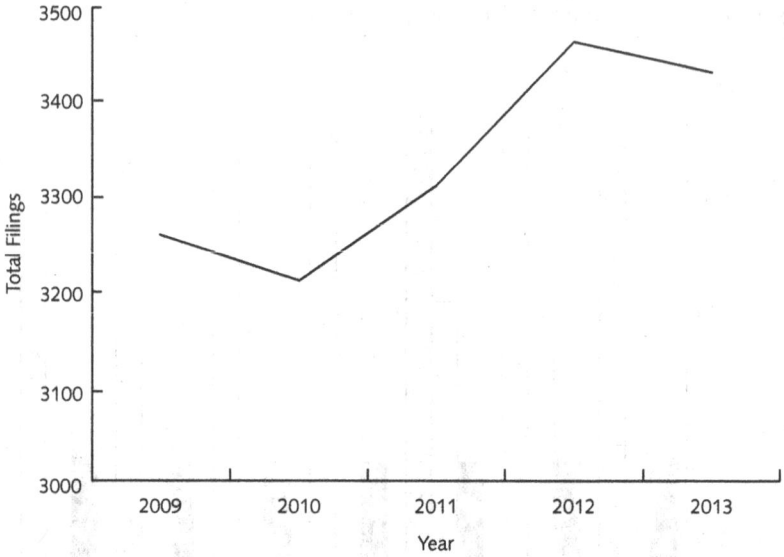

Source: Judicial Council of Georgia, Administrative Office of the Courts, http://www.georgiacourts.org
/content/caseload-reports.

Figure 8.12. Georgia Court of Appeals: Cases per Judge, 2009–2013

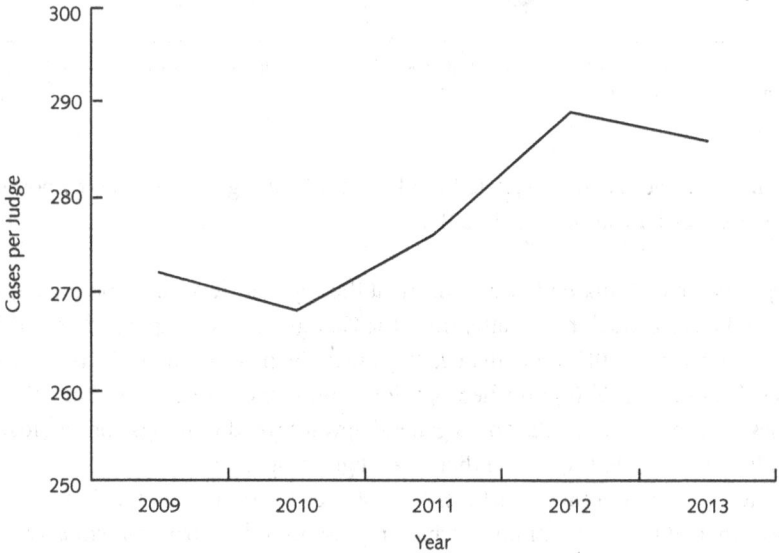

Source: Judicial Council of Georgia, Administrative Office of the Courts, http://www.georgiacourts
.org/content/caseload-reports.

Figure 8.13. Georgia Supreme Court Workload: Filings, 2008–2014

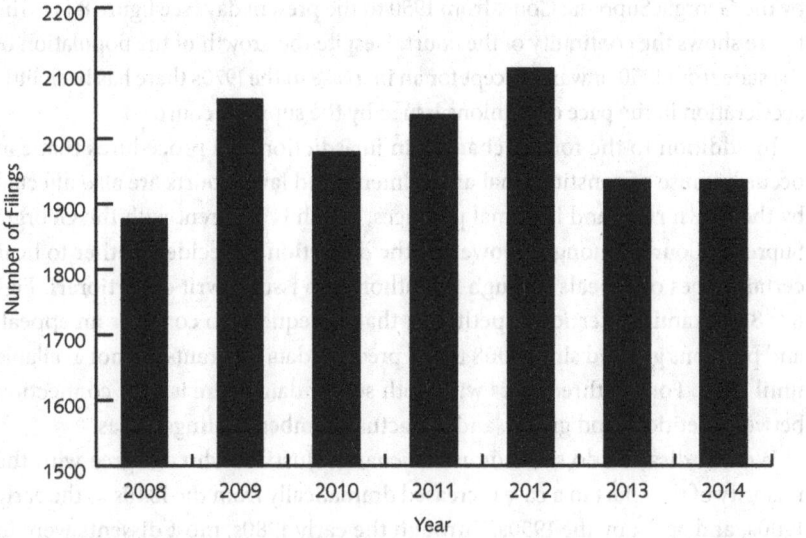

Source: Judicial Council of Georgia, Administrative Office of the Courts, http://www.georgiacourts.org
/content/caseload-reports.

Figure 8.14. Georgia Supreme Court Workload: Opinions Issued 1950–2014

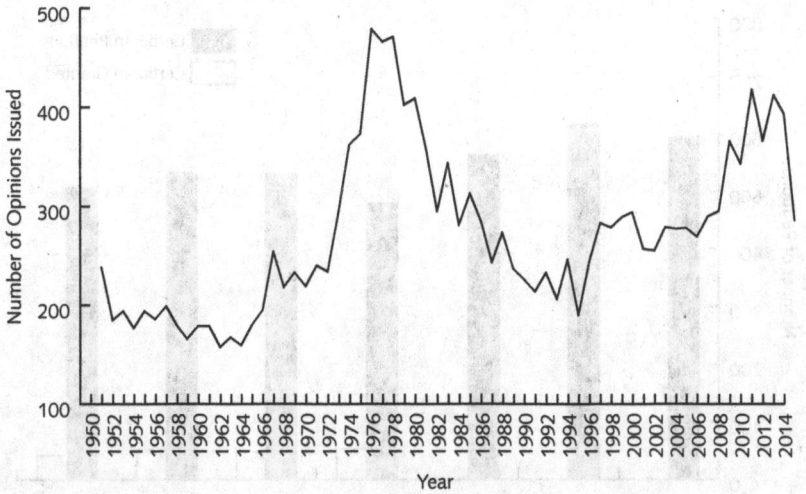

Source: Judicial Council of Georgia, Administrative Office of the Courts, http://www.georgiacourts.org
/content/caseload-reports.

by the Georgia Supreme Court from 1950 to the present day (see figure 8.14). The figure shows the continuity of the court. Despite the growth of the population of the state from 1950 onward, except for an increase in the 1970s there has been little acceleration in the pace of opinions issued by the supreme court.

In addition to the formal changes in jurisdiction and procedures that can occur because of constitutional amendments and laws, courts are also affected by their own rules and informal practices, which is apparent with the Georgia Supreme Court. Among its powers is the discretion to decide whether to hear certain types of appeals through its authority to issue a writ of certiorari. Figure 8.15 examines certiorari petitions, that is, requests to consider an appeal, and petitions granted since 2008 to the present (data on grants are not available until 2011). For the three years with both sets of data, there is little connection between petitions and grants, and the actual number of filings varies.

Written dissents do show dramatic change. Justices who disagree with the majority of the court in a case increased dramatically from the 1840s to the early 1900s, and again by the 1950s. Through the early 1980s, most dissents were in civil cases. By the beginning of the new century, dissents were almost equally split between civil and criminal cases. Moreover, by 2001, only about one-third

Figure 8.15. Georgia Supreme Court Workload: Certiorari Petitions and Petitions Granted, 2008–2014

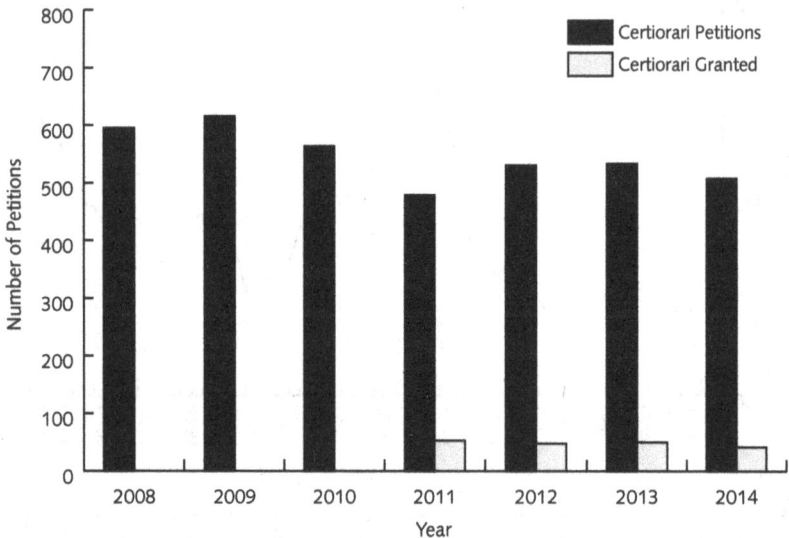

Source: Judicial Council of Georgia, Administrative Office of the Courts, http://www.georgiacourts.org/content/caseload-reports.

of the dissents in cases were by a single justice, as compared to just over 50 percent in the early 1900s and as late as the 1950s.[13] The supreme court has also altered its habits in issuing per curiam opinions, which do not identify their author. From the 1840s through the early 1980s, most per curiam opinions merely affirmed decisions by the court of appeals in civil cases. By 1998–2001, though, 90 percent dealt with the disciplining of attorneys.[14]

One study of dissent rates among the fifty states noted the differences in dissent rates between cases involving mandatory jurisdiction, that is, where the court must take the case, and discretionary jurisdiction, that is, where the court can decide on whether it wants to hear the case.[15] The U.S. Supreme Court, for example, has almost complete discretion over its docket. Some observers theorize that dissent will be greater in discretionary jurisdiction, and the data bear this out for Georgia. In 2003, for example, almost 19 percent of cases had at least one dissent, while in mandatory cases the dissent rate dropped to 11.7 percent. General dissensus rates (cases in which there are both dissenting and concurring opinions) also increased in discretionary, as opposed to mandatory, cases. The dissensus rate for discretionary cases was 24.5 percent as compared to 15.8 percent in mandatory cases. Considering that the court in 2004 had one Republican, the data show that partisan identification in Georgia masked significant policy differences.

Judicial Agencies

A modern, complex judicial system needs administration and management. Several organizations perform these functions for Georgia's legal system.[16] One of the major agencies is the Judicial Council; created in 1973, it is composed of twenty-four members of the judiciary. The chief justice of the Georgia Supreme Court chairs the council. The council evaluates the need for new courts, court circuits, and personnel. It also may conduct studies of other aspects of the judicial system. Several other councils provide support and research for different types of courts. For instance, the Council of Superior Court Judges uses several committees to study various aspects of the workings of superior courts.

Another key agency is the Administrative Office of the Courts (AOC), which was created in 1973 and reports to the Judicial Council. The AOC provides administrative support and research to the judicial branch. It also serves as a public information office, disseminating information on caseloads, judges, and the like to interested officials and citizens. The AOC works with various organizations providing training and education, such as those for court administrators, reporters, and interpreters. The Institute of Continuing Judicial Education holds seminars and conferences to train judges, clerks, judicial secretaries, and other court personnel.

The Judicial Qualifications Commission, created in 1972, sets standards for judicial conduct and holds hearings to determine whether judges are guilty of misconduct.[17] It consists of two judges appointed by the state supreme court, three lawyers appointed by the State Bar of Georgia, and two citizens appointed by the governor.[18] Judicial quality and judicial ethics have been a concern recently. In 2007, the Judicial Qualifications Commission decided to more aggressively police judicial conduct. By the middle of 2015, this increased vigilance led to more than seventy judges resigning from the bench, including some who have been convicted, arrested, or had charges brought against them.[19] However, it appears that the commission has overstepped its mandate. The legislature adopted a resolution calling for the creation of a seven-member committee to subpoena witnesses and documents and take sworn testimony to investigate.[20] Another resolution called for a constitutional amendment to abolish the existing Judicial Qualifications Commission by creating a new one that would eliminate the power of the state bar to make appointments. The ammendment passed in 2016.[21]

Providing attorneys for the poor in criminal cases has remained controversial since a series of U.S. Supreme Court decisions during the 1960s.[22] Historically, complying with such decisions was a decentralized matter in Georgia, with the state's counties choosing several methods of providing counsel to indigent defendants. In 2001, about half of Georgia's counties used a system in which judges appointed attorneys, with compensation varying by county. In another fifty-nine counties (38 percent), indigent defense, like many local government services, was put out for bid by firms. In the remaining twenty-one counties (13 percent), the county funded and staffed a public defender's office to represent poor defendants just as it would any county government agency. The state did provide some financial support for indigent defense. However, debates over the different approaches to indigent defense led the Georgia Supreme Court to create a commission in 2000 to study the issue.[23]

The commission's work became more critical as the federal courts expanded the conditions under which indigents were entitled to an attorney, including a 2002 case from Alabama in which the U.S. Supreme Court ruled that someone who receives a probated or suspended sentence that could lead to imprisonment had the right to legal representation. The General Assembly responded to these demands in 2004 and created a statewide system with a public defender office in each judicial circuit. The system was expected to cost more than $40 million annually and is paid for by increases in court fees, fines, and bail bonds. It is under the supervision of the Georgia Public Defender Standards Council, which can permit certain counties to opt out of the system if they have an adequate system of their own.[24]

In addition to these agencies, the Attorney General's Office serves as prosecutor for capital felony cases at the state level, as well as counsel for the state and its agencies. The attorney general is an elected official, but lawyers may be hired as assistant attorneys general to work in this office as in any other state agency. Qualifications for attorney general are set by the state constitution and include a requirement that the candidate be a member of the state bar for seven years preceding election.

Most criminal cases are handled at the local level by district attorneys, with one elected in each of the judicial circuits for a four-year term on a partisan ballot. Each serves as prosecutor for the state in superior court and must have been a member of the state bar for three years prior to election.

Judges, Juries, and Lawyers

In addition to establishing courts, the states oversee key participants in the legal system. The most important regulations include qualifications, selection, and procedures for judges, juries, and attorneys.

Judicial Qualifications and Selection

Judicial Selection in the States. Unlike the national level, where judges are nominated by the president and confirmed by the Senate, the states employ five methods of choosing judges. Some elect judges in partisan elections, while other states hold nonpartisan elections. Still others require that judges be appointed by the governor. Three states have at least some judges elected by the legislature. Others allow for the selection of judges under a merit system of screening by nominating commissions that submit candidates to a state's governor. Once in office, such judges stand periodically for election and often confront retention elections. While most are routinely reelected, some are defeated over contentious issues. For instance, the Iowa Supreme Court unanimously voted in 2009 to strike down a state law banning marriage between same-sex partners. In 2010, three of the judges were defeated in a retention election.[25] Given the presence of several selection methods in some states, one recent tally listed eight states with partisan election of judges, thirteen with nonpartisan elections, fifteen relying exclusively on merit appointment through a nominating commission, four employing gubernatorial appointments, and two (Virginia and South Carolina) with legislative election of judges. Another nine states combined merit selection with other methods of selecting appellate and general trial court judges.[26]

Each selection method has its detractors and advocates. Henry Glick, a judicial scholar, notes that state selection systems do not make much difference in determining who becomes a judge.[27] Gubernatorial appointment has existed since colonial times, but election became common by the 1820s. Some research suggests that appointment systems improve gender diversity on state supreme courts.[28] Critics of elections complain about judges who may be too political; opponents of appointment argue that judges are not accountable to the public. Since the 1940s, states have increasingly adopted merit plans, although such an approach does not mean that no politics is involved. State nominating commissions tend to have "elite" backgrounds compared to the public, include some members loyal to the governor, and reflect splits within the legal profession. Only a small percentage of judges selected under merit plans get voted out of office. More generally, one study found that only 20 percent of state supreme court races between 1980 and 1995 were close (defined as the winner getting less than 55 percent of the vote). Elections were more likely to be close, however, in nonpartisan contests without an incumbent running and in partisan races, where more than one-third were close, even with incumbents on the ballot.[29]

Underlying all these debates is the growing public recognition that courts not only enforce laws but also make policy themselves. At the trial level, research findings are mixed on whether judges' race, ethnicity, or gender are associated with disparities in the sentences they hand down to various types of defendants.[30] One study, however, has found that black trial judges are harsher than their white counterparts when imposing sentences.[31] Some evidence also suggests that limits on judges' flexibility can reduce racial disparities in sentencing.[32]

Appellate courts are important policy makers, in part because they define the scope of rights under state constitutions, can create or expand important legal doctrines, and use a variety of factors in deciding individual appeals.[33] For instance, state appeals courts have been drawn into debates over controversial issues such as same-sex marriage. Judicial discretion is one reason governors try using court appointments to change policies; it is also a reason that judicial elections have become more contentious in recent years, especially as rules governing judicial campaigns have gotten looser. Judicial elections have become more partisan, increasingly aggressive, more like other media-based campaigns, and more costly. In 2004, candidates spent more than $39 million in forty-four contests. Candidates for a state supreme court seat in West Virginia raised $2.8 million, while interest groups spent another $4.5 million; two candidates in Illinois spent a combined $9 million, to which interest groups and political parties added another $4.4 million.[34] One study comparing the states found that spending in state supreme court elections between 1990 and 2000 was highest for races in which no incumbent was running, where the terms were longer, where the number of seats on the ballot was low, and the volume of tort cases was high.[35]

Judicial Selection in Georgia. Georgia has a long-standing commitment to electing judges, although there are some requirements regarding age, residence in counties or circuits, and membership in the state bar.[36] Georgia's constitution specifies that members of the Georgia Supreme Court and the Georgia Court of Appeals be elected in statewide elections on a nonpartisan ballot for six-year terms and must have been authorized to practice law seven years prior to election. The justices of the supreme court choose a chief justice from among themselves.

In terms of trial courts, superior court judges are also elected in nonpartisan elections but serve four-year terms and are elected by voters who live within their circuits. State court judges are elected in nonpartisan countywide elections for four years. Juvenile court judges are appointed by the superior court judges of the counties in which they serve their term.

Most probate judges are elected in partisan county elections, but in seventeen counties they are elected on a nonpartisan ballot. In counties with more than ninety-six thousand residents, probate judges are required to meet age and other qualifications not applied to probate judges in other counties. Magistrates may be appointed or elected in Georgia, depending on the county. In some cases, chief magistrates are elected in partisan county elections and appoint other magistrates to serve terms concurrent with their own. Qualifications, selection, and terms of office for municipal court judges vary widely and are set by the cities in which the judges serve.

Judicial elections are usually low-key affairs, with incumbents seldom facing challengers. That situation is changing, however. In 1996, a candidate for the Georgia Court of Appeals ran a thirty-second television commercial criticizing the incumbent for writing an opinion overturning a conviction in a child molestation case. Georgia's judicial conduct rules prohibit judicial candidates from announcing their views on disputed issues. The Georgia Judicial Qualifications Commission criticized the ad but did not attempt to remove it from the air.[37]

Despite the requirement that judges be elected, appointment is still important for filling vacancies and new judgeships, especially since most judges are reelected easily. Except in magistrate, probate, and juvenile courts, the Georgia Constitution authorizes the governor to appoint a replacement to serve the remainder of a judge's term when a position becomes vacant for any reason. This gives the governor substantial power in shaping the composition of the judiciary. The Judicial Nominating Commission assists the governor in making such appointments, although the selection process includes input from political leaders and members of the legal profession.[38] One study calculated that 66 percent of superior court judgeships were filled by appointment between 1968 and mid-1994.[39] A concern is that those appointed to judicial vacancies are chosen because of political connections. For instance, going into his 2002 reelection campaign, Governor Roy Barnes had filled 53 judgeships. Of the 173 finalists considered for these posts, 60 of the 120 not chosen had contributed a total of $136,400 to Barnes's campaign. Moreover, 44 of the 53 chosen as judges gave a total of $165,300; some of their relatives and associates also made contributions.[40] Similarly, when a vacancy occurred on the Georgia Supreme Court in 2005, Governor Sonny Perdue appointed his personal legal advisor to fill it.[41]

All judges, whether appointed or elected, are subject to recall under the Georgia Recall Act of 1989. Judges may also be removed from office, disciplined, or forcibly retired by the seven-member Judicial Qualification Commission. This censure may occur if a judge is guilty of willful misconduct while in office, is convicted of a crime, willfully and persistently fails to perform duties, is habitually intemperate, engages in prejudicial conduct that brings the judicial office into disrepute, or becomes disabled to the extent that it seriously interferes with the performance of judicial duties. The commission's findings and recommendations are subject to review by the Georgia Supreme Court.

Juries

There are two types of juries on which citizens may be chosen to serve: trial (also known as petit) juries and grand juries. While trial juries are better known to the public because of media coverage of some criminal cases, grand juries are important in determining how and if a case will proceed against a defendant.

Members of trial and grand juries are chosen in each county by a board of jury commissioners, which is required to develop jury pools that are "a fairly representative cross section of the intelligent and upright citizens of the county." They do this by relying on drivers' licenses or similar state-issued identification, voter registration lists, or other lists of residents.[42] Once called, jurors must serve or face contempt of court, and employers must excuse jury-related absences. Arguments have been made over the years about the fairness of the size and composition of the pools of potential jurors in various counties. Both the General Assembly and the courts have stepped in to deal with such problems, including a 2002 Georgia Supreme Court decision, which held that Hispanics were to be treated as a distinct group when considering whether juries include a fair cross-section of a county.[43]

Trial Juries. Trial juries in civil and criminal cases vary in size according to the level of the court and the laws of the jurisdiction. Juries are used at the option of the defendant, who can choose to have the judge rather than a jury render a verdict in a case. Juries are ultimately the decision-making institution for a court case but must operate within the confines of the law and the evidence presented to them within the courtroom. Juries may be influenced by many factors, including formal influences, such as the charges and instructions given by a judge, or informal ones, such as the appearance of a defendant or witnesses.[44]

With rare exceptions, citizens tried for criminal offenses are entitled to trial by jury under the U.S. Constitution.[45] Anyone who could receive punishment of more than six months' imprisonment must have the option of a jury trial, but the size of the jury may vary from twelve (as it is in federal cases) to as few as six, depending on the state. Some states require unanimous jury decision, as does the federal government, while other states require a specific majority of a twelve-person jury. The U.S. Supreme Court has required states to use unanimous decisions with six-person juries.[46]

Juries are not required for all court decisions in Georgia, but the size of the jury is determined by the level of the court. Since appellate courts review the actions of lower courts and do not hold trials, juries are not used. Magistrate courts and juvenile courts never hold jury trials, and other lower courts are not likely to use juries. State courts have six-member juries, while superior courts juries have twelve members. Juries in civil cases consist of six or twelve members, depending on the dollar amount of damages sought and whether either party in state court requests a jury of twelve rather than six members. In Georgia, unanimous decisions are required in criminal cases but not in civil trials.[47]

The size of a jury pool for a case may vary by county in Georgia. The state has set a minimum number of thirty for felonies and forty-two for capital cases; other pools are generally twice the size of the trial jury. The pool is reduced in three ways to arrive at a trial jury. First, the judge may excuse someone from service due to family emergencies, work schedule conflicts, or other unavoidable hindrances. Such excuses usually only postpone service rather than permanently excuse the juror. Both sides in a case then question potential jurors—a process known as voir dire. Second, if an attorney can convince the judge that a potential juror cannot be impartial, the person is removed from the pool "for cause." The number of such challenges is not limited. Those excused or struck for cause are replaced in order to maintain the required size of the pool.

Third, each side is then allowed a limited number of peremptory strikes, for which the attorneys do not have to give a reason for removing a potential juror from the pool. The number of peremptory strikes depends on the required size of the jury. Thus when all the strikes are used by both sides, a jury of six or twelve is left. Prior to 2005, the defense got twice as many strikes as the prosecution in a criminal case. With the change in the law, each side gets fifteen strikes in a death penalty case, nine each in other felony cases, and three each in misdemeanor trials.[48] In civil cases, the plaintiff and the defendant continue to get an equal number of strikes. Attorneys generally use peremptory strikes to try to shape a jury in their favor. In a very recent case from Georgia, the U.S. Supreme Court overturned a Georgia Supreme Court decision and severely limited the ability of litigants to remove potential jurors on the basis of race.[49]

Grand Juries. Grand juries are used by over half the states to issue indictments in criminal cases. All other states make grand jury indictments optional, with the prosecutor filing a document that is called an "information" in order to enter a formal charge against someone. Four states (New Jersey, South Carolina, Tennessee, and Virginia) require grand juries for all indictments. Georgia is one of fifteen states that require a grand jury for felony indictments. Six states require grand jury indictments for capital crimes, and Pennsylvania does not empower the grand jury to indict.

Grand juries in most states consist of eighteen to twenty-three citizens selected in the same manner as trial juries. Grand juries may be used to determine whether enough evidence exists to bring a case to court. In this instance, they serve the same function as preliminary hearings in determining whether there is "probable cause" to support an indictment. A grand jury and a preliminary hearing differ in the degree of influence the prosecuting attorney can exert in the process. Since it is the charge of the grand jury to determine whether sufficient evidence exists, only the prosecution is heard, business is conducted in secret, and the defense has no right to cross-examine witnesses. Also, decisions by the grand jury need not be unanimous. Many have argued that these characteristics make grand juries unnecessary and merely a rubber stamp for the prosecutor.[50]

Grand juries in Georgia consist of sixteen to twenty-three members and issue presentments in addition to indictments. Grand juries selected school boards in some counties until the state constitution was amended in 1992; evidence suggests that the process was begun in the 1870s to minimize the influence of black voters. Grand juries also have broad powers to study the records and activities of county governments, issue reports, and make certain decisions.

Lawyers

According to the American Bar Association, there were almost 1.4 million active lawyers in the United States in 2016.[51] Women represented 35 percent of the total, blacks constituted 5.0 percent, and Hispanics made up 4.0 percent.[52] The nation's law schools have been adding to the total by conferring almost forty thousand degrees in 2015, although this figure represented a drop since 2010, due to the tightened legal market.[53]

Legal services generally are provided in exchange for a fee. This practice is controversial because costs may prevent those who are less well off from having access to lawyers. A series of court cases has guaranteed free legal representation to poor criminal defendants in cases where they could receive a jail sentence, although each state sets up its own system for providing attorneys (see the discussion of indigent defense above). The national government and the states also provide some legal assistance to the poor in civil matters.[54]

Legal Education. Training lawyers generally occurs in two ways. The first involves the formal education provided by law schools. The other covers ongoing education for practicing attorneys. Although some are for-profit entities, most law schools are within universities, including many public institutions, which use tax money to train professionals in a variety of fields besides law. Law schools are accredited nationally by the American Bar Association. Georgia's five accredited programs in 2015 included two funded by the state at the University of Georgia and Georgia State University, as well as three at private institutions, Emory and Mercer, with both schools affiliated with their respective universities, and John Marshall, a recently accredited stand-alone law school.

Law schools prepare students to pass the state bar exam, which is a prerequisite for practicing law. This preparation usually consists of a three-year program of study. In his widely adopted text on the legal system, Henry Glick has summarized this training: "Law schools put heavy premiums on business law, with relatively little emphasis on other areas such as consumer law, civil rights, or environmental law. The major thrust is learning the basics of business problems and serving business clients."[55] Lawyers' education need not end with law school and the bar exam, however. Continuing education also is available, usually through publications, formal courses, and seminars at professional conferences. Lawyers in Georgia are required to attend at least twelve hours of continuing legal education annually under the supervision of the Commission on Continuing Lawyer Competency. A wide range of programs is also run by the Institute of Continuing Legal Education (ICLE), which is sponsored by the State Bar of Georgia and the state's accredited law schools.[56]

Regulation of the Legal Profession. It is surprising to many people that the training and regulation of lawyers are left largely to the states and the legal profession itself. Oversight of any profession or industry can often become controversial, which may be especially true at the state level, where there may be few organized interests representing consumers or others affected by the regulated industry. Glick describes this situation for lawyers: "One of the important characteristics of a state-regulated profession is that it has the authority to do work that is prohibited of others. . . . Despite internal differences that frequently occur among lawyers, protecting the profession is the one issue on which most lawyers close ranks."[57] This undertaking is more difficult for lawyers than doctors, Glick adds, because lawyers have lower status than do medical professionals, have less control over their clients, and perform work that is often not easy to separate from routine procedures conducted by nonlawyers. For example, requiring attorneys for certain property transactions can bring lawyers into conflict with another powerful interest regulated by the states, real estate groups. Critics have charged that state bar associations limit the size and activities of the legal profession, thereby increasing the cost of legal services. Competition has increased in recent years, however, as the U.S. Supreme Court outlawed certain regulations and lawyers have begun advertising.

At the national level, the American Bar Association sets rules regarding ethical conduct in the legal profession. Enforcement is left to the states, usually through their supreme court and bar association. This is the case in Georgia, where the state bar association functions as a self-governing administrative arm of the Georgia Supreme Court. According to the state bar, there were 3,224 requests for grievance forms during the 2014–2015 bar year. The number of grievances actually submitted to the Office of the General Counsel was 1,997, a slight increase over the 1,857 received the previous year.[58] Additionally, the Consumer Assistance Program (CAP) fields thousands of inquiries each year, about 80 percent of which are resolved without having to file a grievance under the disciplinary procedure.[59]

The Future of Georgia's Legal System

Elected officials, police, prosecutors, the courts, and corrections agencies are under pressure to solve a host of problems—many of which may not be soluble. Politically, this pressure has translated into efforts to criminalize more behavior and stiffen penalties. Indeed, it seems that every candidate for public office tries to create a tougher image than the next. In 2011, 28 percent of Americans polled by the Gallup Organization reported "a great deal" or "quite a lot" of confidence in the criminal justice system—a decrease from 34 percent in 2003.[60]

State courts have been drawn into this maelstrom. They are being asked to improve their efficiency, in part through technological improvements and alternatives to traditional lawsuits. They are also on the front line of debates over biases in the law, the legal profession, and the judiciary. Changes over the past few decades, plus growing interest group involvement in judicial elections, suggest that Georgia's legal system will no longer be a relatively invisible part of state government. In fact, it might become even more visible as it grapples with controversial issues and becomes more politicized.

CHAPTER 9

Local Government and Politics

Georgia had more than 1,300 local governments in 2012. These counties, cities, and special districts provide a wide range of basic services, including police, fire, water, roads, and schools. Georgians expect local officials to be accessible and responsive to their concerns, yet the effectiveness of any local government is influenced by how it is organized, constraints and rewards imposed by the state and national governments, and the actions of other communities. This chapter considers the crucial role of the state in controlling local governments, describes the organization and functions of local governments, and examines citizen participation and policy making in Georgia communities.

The Foundations of Local Government

Each state's system of local government is different. Georgia's local governments include counties, cities, and special districts. Unlike many states in the Midwest and New England, Georgia does not have townships providing services in rural areas; instead, counties assume such responsibilities. Counties and cities are considered general-purpose local governments because they provide a wide range of services and have been granted broad authority by the state. Rhode Island and Connecticut do not have counties. In Georgia, like most states, counties serve as "administrative arms" of the state, performing tasks such as prosecuting people and running courts, providing public health services, processing vehicle license plates, and maintaining necessary records such as those for real estate and marriage. Special districts are limited to a single service or a narrow range of functions. Probably the most visible examples are school districts, although others exist for hospitals, airports, water, and other services.

Local government changed as the nation grew after World War II. The number of local governments in the United States dropped 23 percent between 1952 and 2012, primarily due to the elimination of more than fifty thousand school

Table 9.1. Number of Local Governments in the
United States and Georgia, 1942–2012

| | United States | | Georgia | |
| | | Percent | | Percent |
Year	Total	Change	Total	Change
1942	155,116		946	
1952	116,807	−24.7	976	3.2
1957	102,392	−12.3	1,121	14.9
1962	91,236	−10.9	1,219	8.7
1967	81,299	−10.9	1,204	−1.2
1972	78,269	−3.7	1,244	3.3
1977	79,913	2.1	1,264	1.6
1982	81,831	2.4	1,269	0.4
1987	83,237	1.7	1,287	1.4
1992	85,006	2.1	1,298	0.9
1994	87,504	2.9	1,345	3.6
2002	87,576	0.1	1,449	7.7
2007	89,527	2.2	1,440	−0.6
2012	90,056	0.6	1,378	−4.3

Source: U.S. Census Bureau, *2012 Census of Governments*,
"Government Units by State: Census Years 1942 to 2012," http://
factfinder.census.gov/faces/tableservices/jsf/pages/productview
.xhtml?src=bkmk.

districts, particularly in the Midwest and the Plains states (see table 9.1). Special districts almost tripled during the same period, however, as states created more governments for services such as parks, airports, hospitals, water, fire protection, libraries, and highways—even cemeteries.

The trend was different in Georgia, where the number of local governments actually increased 41 percent from 1952 to 2012. Georgia's 1,378 local governments might seem like many, but it is well below the total in Illinois, with 6,963 local governments, including more than 1,400 townships and over 3,200 special districts. After Illinois, the states with the most local governments are Texas (5,147), Pennsylvania (4,897), California (4,425), and then six states with more than 3,000. Last was Hawaii, with only 21 local governments.

Georgia has also witnessed a change in the mix of government types (see table 9.2). The number of counties has remained constant at 159 since the 1930s. Only Texas has more counties (254). The federal Census of Governments, which is conducted every five years, counts merged cities and counties as cities. They will be counted as counties here, however, because they still conduct county func-

Table 9.2. Number and Type of Local Governments in Georgia, 1942–2012

Year	Counties	Municipalities	School Districts	Special Districts
1942	159	470	222	94
1952	159	475	187	154
1957	159	508	198	255
1962	159	561	197	301
1967	159	512	194	338
1972	159	529	189	366
1977	159	529	188	387
1982	159	531	187	390
1987	159	531	186	410
1992	159	534	183	421
1997	159	532	180	473
2002	159	528	180	581
2007	159	530	180	570
2012	159	529	180	510

Source: U.S. Census Bureau, *2012 Census of Governments*, table constructed from "Number of Governments" menu at http://www.census.gov/govs/go/index.html.

tions and elect county officers such as sheriffs. The number of cities increased from 470 to 529 from 1942 to 2012 (12.6 percent), while the total for school districts has held fairly steady since the 1970s. The major change occurred among special districts, which have increased to more than 500. Compared against the total of 154 in 1952, this was a 231 percent increase. These special districts perform functions such as housing and community development (191), hospitals (96), soil and water conservation (37), health (32), and airports (20).[1]

Critics have often taken aim at the substantial number of small local governments in Georgia. The General Assembly responded in 1993 by passing legislation that used grants and rules to encourage consolidation and elimination of smaller jurisdictions. As a result, 188 cities had their charters revoked on July 1, 1995, because they did not provide three of eleven listed services, hold regular meetings, or conduct elections.[2] In the end, Georgia ranked twenty-third among the states in 2012 in the number of local governments.

The U.S. Constitution and Local Governments

The U.S. Constitution says nothing about local governments, but it does refer to states, and that language and federal laws have been extended to governments created by the states. The basic responsibility for establishing and regulating local governments, then, rests with the fifty states, each of which has created a distinct system of local government. That does not mean, however, that the national government does little to influence things at the local level. Indeed, Congress, the executive branch, and federal courts have used grants, regulations, and legal action to affect local politics and policies.

The legal doctrine underlying state-local relations is known as Dillon's Rule, which treats local governments as "creatures of the state" with only those powers explicitly granted to them, clearly implied from explicitly granted powers, or essential to meeting their responsibilities.[3] This doctrine can restrict the discretion of local officials and means that the authority of local government is often open to interpretation, debate, and—not surprisingly—litigation.

State Methods for Limiting Local Governments

States restrict local governments in their charters, by regulating local government boundaries and territory, and by imposing a wide range of mandates (requirements). A local government's charter is comparable to a constitution. The process by which a new municipal government is created and granted a charter is known as incorporation, and states grant charters to local governments in much the same way they establish procedures for private companies and nonprofit organizations to incorporate. Municipal charters typically cover the organization of the government, procedures for selecting officials and conducting public business, powers of taxing and spending, requirements for providing public services, and other basis features.

A second constraint is state control over local governments' territory. The boundaries of a city are set at the time that it incorporates. However, states also control annexation (the power of a city to extend its boundaries to add unincorporated territory on its fringe that is not in another city) and consolidation (the merger of two or more local governments).

A third way that states limit the discretion of local officials is with mandates—standards, functions, procedures, or other rules that impose obligations or prohibitions. Examples include requirements for public meetings, a list of services that must be provided, standards and testing procedures for drinking water, eligibility for holding elected office, taxing and spending limits, and certification criteria for teachers, police officers, and other employees (discussed later in this chapter). States justify mandates in terms of setting minimum standards for local governments throughout the state. In contrast, local officials often complain that mandates substitute state priorities for local decisions and impose significant costs on local governments.

The Georgia Constitution and Local Governments

The Georgia Constitution is very detailed regarding local government. In fact, Article 9, which is devoted to counties and municipalities (cities), comprises more than 15 percent of the document. Local government is also treated in parts of Article 8 ("Education") and several other sections. The constitution's major provisions about local governments cover their organization and authority, the use of home rule, and their finances.

Local Government Organization and Authority

The constitution is somewhat more specific regarding counties than cities and special districts. Article 9 even restricts the number of counties to no more than 159, although no such limit applies to other types of local government. However, that restriction has not prevented efforts in the affluent northern part of Fulton County to break away and re-create Milton County, which was absorbed by Fulton during the Great Depression of the 1930s.[4] The constitution also requires all counties to have certain elected officials. These "constitutional officers" include a clerk of the superior court, judge of the probate court, sheriff, and tax commissioner (or tax collector and tax receiver), each of whom is elected to a four-year term. The constitution leaves it to state law to spell out the characteristics of local legislative bodies such as county commissions and city councils.

Article 6, which covers the judicial branch, prescribes the procedure for electing the various judges and the district attorney in each judicial circuit, which can include one or more counties. Every county, however, must have at least one superior, magistrate, and probate court.

Georgia's constitution goes to some length to prohibit counties from taking actions that would affect local school systems or any court. It also lists functions that cities and counties may perform if they choose, including public transportation, health services and facilities, libraries, and enforcement of building codes. This provision is especially important to counties, which were first authorized to provide urban services by a constitutional amendment ratified in 1972. Article 9 also allows counties and cities to use planning and zoning, take private property, make agreements with one another, and consolidate. Other sections cover intergovernmental relations, local taxation and debt, and various types of districts.[5]

Home Rule

The constitution also provides home rule. In most states, this means that a local government is granted broad powers to write and amend its charter and to take any action not prohibited by the state. Home rule has proven more limited in

Georgia than in many states, however. Georgia has a long-standing reputation for not granting much authority to its cities and counties to determine their form of government. However, it has granted local governments flexibility in carrying out their functions. Unlike the majority of states, Georgia does not divide its cities into "classes" (usually based on population), with different levels of authority granted to each class.[6]

A major reason for this limited local power is the constitution itself, which places many restrictions directly on counties and cities. It also permits the legislature to adopt local laws, which some state constitutions prohibit. While general laws are applied throughout the state, a local law applies to the city, county, or special district specified in the bill. Local laws cannot conflict with general laws, however. The General Assembly passes local bills on a wide range of topics. For example, local laws established procedures for citizens to vote on merging the governments in Athens-Clarke County in 1990 and Augusta-Richmond County in 1995.

A significant share of all legislation adopted by the General Assembly is local (see chapter 6). For local bills to be reported from committee, they must have the support of state legislators from the affected city or county. An unofficial norm of "local courtesy" then dictates that the rest of the House or the Senate should defer to the judgments of the delegation from the city or county named in the bill. The dilemma is that communities must depend on the General Assembly to determine their future. Moreover, there is nothing to stop state legislators from doing something without formally involving local officials or residents.[7]

Financial Constraints

The constitution generally leaves the question of how local governments can raise and spend money to the General Assembly.[8] In contrast, the constitution covers debt in substantial detail. Georgia employs two major restrictions common among the states. One is that debt cannot exceed 10 percent of the assessed value of taxable property within the jurisdiction. The other requires that voters approve new debt by a simple majority in an election. However, these provisions only apply to general obligation debt—borrowing in which the local government pledges tax revenues to pay off bonds sold to raise money. The constitution also places an annual limit on the amount that can be borrowed on a short-term basis.

There are many loopholes in the requirement for voter approval of debt. Revenue bonds are the major exception to the required voter approval and debt limitation. Revenue bonds are backed not by taxes but by revenues from projects being financed by the bonds. Airport bonds, for example, are generally paid off with parking revenue, aircraft landing fees, rents from airlines and concession-aires, and the like. With all types of local government borrowing, though, the real limit is the willingness of investors to buy bonds based on the risk and the interest rate. Especially since the Great Recession, counting on income from local government bonds is not a sure thing, as evidenced by the recent bank-ruptcies of Detroit; Jefferson County, Alabama; and several cities in California, as well as the ongoing financial problems of other local governments.[9]

Georgia Law and Local Governments

State control does not stop with the constitution. The General Assembly has wide latitude to pass laws that regulate local governments, including territory and mandates dealing with services, personnel, finances, and procedures.

Territory

The state's major focus regarding territory is procedural and is based on long-standing differences between counties and cities in the United States. At least until World War II, municipal governments served built-up areas need-ing a wide range of services, while counties provided minimal services in rural locations. Thus, as areas became urbanized, they would form their own city governments or become part of existing municipalities. While this remains the pattern in many states, Georgia counties have been allowed to provide urban services since the 1970s.

Creating New Local Governments. Georgia originally had only two counties. By 1832, there were 32 counties. In two periods counties proliferated significantly: 37 were created between 1850 and 1860, bringing the total to 132; another 24 were added in the early twentieth century, which enhanced rural political power under the county-unit system. Fulton County's merger with two less-well-off counties during the 1930s reduced the total to its present level of 159, which is the maximum allowed by the constitution.[10]

More common has been the creation of municipalities and special districts. Like other states, Georgia uses its general laws to specify guidelines for incorpo-rating a municipal government, but granting a charter to a city requires a local law.[11] To incorporate, a new municipality must have at least two hundred resi-dents and a minimum density of two hundred people per square mile, cannot be closer than three miles from an existing municipality, and must have at least 60 percent of its area subdivided into lots used for nonagricultural purposes.

While some smaller city governments in rural parts of Georgia have disap-peared in recent years, political battles have been fought over the creation of new suburbs in Metropolitan Atlanta. Some of the controversies have had partisan, racial, and class overtones. The move to incorporate had been long-standing in parts of northern Fulton County, where many residents claimed that the county government was not responsive to their needs and was taxing them to provide services to other areas. General law made this difficult, though.

Incorporation became easier once Republicans took control of the state legislature and supported local laws making it easier to incorporate. The biggest change was the 2005 incorporation of Sandy Springs after many years of trying. The city stood out for having almost no employees and hiring private contractors for almost all its services.[12] Additional cities followed, including Johns Creek, Milton, Chattahoochee Hill Country, Dunwoody, and Peachtree Corners. The city of Atlanta also annexed a few square miles of unincorporated Fulton during 2003–2010, mainly to the southwest.[13]

Battles over territory extended east into DeKalb County in the second decade of the present century, including incorporation of Brookhaven in 2012. Such efforts accelerated amid corruption cases involving county officials.[14] Residents in several unincorporated areas promoted incorporation, and existing cities promoted annexation of additional territory. Following disagreements among residents, businesses, and even the House and the Senate, the General Assembly passed bills on the last day of the 2015 session to allow voters in areas to be called LaVista Hills and Tucker to decide whether to incorporate as cities. Several other areas lost out on such an opportunity, and Atlanta, Decatur, Clarkston, and Avondale Estates were rebuffed in their efforts to annex more territory. Voters eventually approved incorporation for Tucker but narrowly rejected the proposal for LaVista Hills. Given the ongoing resident, intergovernmental, and partisan wrangling, it is unclear how efforts to incorporate and annex in DeKalb and Fulton Counties will shake out in coming years.[15]

Special districts are permitted by the Georgia Constitution and general laws. Perhaps the most important characteristic of special districts is their relative independence from county and city governments, especially in the case of Georgia's local school systems. In contrast, various authorities and districts maintain ties to general-purpose local governments. The legislature can either create such districts by local law or authorize cities and counties to establish them.[16] One of the most visible might be the Metropolitan Atlanta Rapid Transit Authority (MARTA). Despite its name, MARTA provided bus and subway service only in Fulton and DeKalb counties when it began operating in the early 1970s. Following a November 2014 referendum in which Clayton County voters agreed to a 1 percent sales tax, MARTA extended bus service to that county in March 2015.

Annexation and Consolidation. The state also sets ground rules for changing the boundaries of local governments. General law includes procedures to change a county's boundaries, but such events are virtually nonexistent. Annexation and consolidation efforts are much more frequent.

Annexation is a city's addition of adjacent territory that does not have its own municipal government—the area's only government in Georgia is its county. Municipalities can annex through local acts of the General Assembly, passage of a resolution by a city with a subsequent referendum in the area proposed for annexation, or two petition processes. One method permits cities to annex adjoining territory if requested in a petition signed by the owners of 100 percent of its acreage. The other process allows the petition to be signed by the owners of 60 percent of the property and 60 percent of the voters in the area under consideration. Under both processes, the city must hold a public hearing and pass an ordinance to complete the annexation. The state has also authorized cities to annex unincorporated areas of fifty or fewer acres—islands—that they surround.[17]

Annexation can be an incremental change in boundaries, but consolidation—the merger of governments—appears more radical because it can eliminate some governments altogether. Merger of two or more cities is almost unheard of in Georgia, but Georgia stands out among the states for its many efforts to consolidate cities and counties. General law for merging cities with counties in Georgia is quite brief, and each consolidation is considered by the General Assembly on a case-by-case basis using local laws. Consolidations require majorities in each of the governments being merged. This requirement can be troubling to consolidation backers, as when Rockdale County voters approved a merger with Conyers (the only municipality in the county) in 1989, but the consolidation failed in Conyers.[18]

Georgia has had more than thirty proposals to merge cities and counties on local ballots since 1933 (see table 9.3). Nevertheless, by 2015, voters had approved only seven mergers. Three involved small cities and counties, but the other four were in metropolitan areas: Columbus and Muscogee County (1970), Athens and Clarke County (1990), Augusta and Richmond County (1995), and Macon and Bibb County (2012). Adoption by voters in these larger counties was not easy, however. It took five tries in Augusta-Richmond County and Macon-Bibb County; Athens-Clarke County voted four times starting in 1969; the Columbus-Muscogee merger passed on the second attempt.[19]

Politics and Local Government Boundaries. Drawing the boundaries of local governments might seem like a mundane matter, but such changes can be hotly debated because of their effects. For instance, adding territory can provide city officials a larger tax base, additional federal or state funds, more utility customers, affluent areas with lower demand for services, and even supportive voters. Such moves can also pit governments against one another, as with Atlanta's

Table 9.3. City-County Consolidation Elections in Georgia

Location	Year	Result
Macon-Bibb County	1933	Failed
Albany-Dougherty County	1954	Failed
Albany-Dougherty County	1956	Failed
Macon-Bibb County	1960	Failed
Columbus-Muscogee County	1962	Failed
Athens-Clarke County	1969	Failed
Brunswick-Glynn County	1969	Failed
Columbus-Muscogee County	1970	Passed
Augusta-Richmond County	1971	Failed
Athens-Clarke County	1972	Failed
Macon-Bibb County	1972	Failed
Savannah-Chatham County	1973	Failed
Augusta-Richmond County	1974	Failed
Augusta-Richmond County	1976	Failed
Macon-Bibb County	1976	Failed
Athens-Clarke County	1982	Failed
Tifton-Tift County	1984	Failed
Lakeland-Lanier County	1986	Failed
Brunswick-Glynn County	1987	Failed
Augusta-Richmond County	1988	Passed*
Conyers-Rockdale County	1989	Failed
Athens-Clarke County	1990	Passed
Metter-Candler County	1994	Failed
Ellaville-Schley County	1994	Failed
Augusta-Hephzibah-Richmond County	1995	Passed
Griffin-Spalding County	1997	Failed
Rome-Floyd County	1998	Failed
Hawkinsville-Pulaski County	1999	Failed
Waycross-Ware County	2000	Failed
Cusseta-Chattahoochee County	2003	Passed
Preston-Weston-Webster County	2008	Passed
Macon-Payne-Bibb County	2012	Passed
Hawkinsville-Pulaski County	2013	Passed

Source: Georgia General Assembly, *Acts and Resolutions of the Georgia General Assembly: 2014*, vol. 3, *Local and Special Acts and Resolutions*, pp. 265A–365A.

* Voided by the courts under the federal Voting Rights Act.

conflicts with Fulton County and the Atlanta Public Schools over the city's annexation attempts. Similarly, by incorporating a new city government, its residents secure greater political influence than if they were only part of their larger county government, especially in matters like land-use regulation. Developers, manufacturers, and other property owners can also use boundary changes to obtain better infrastructure or lower development costs and regulation. When annexation and consolidation add population, it allows boosters to portray a place as larger and growing. Indeed, one of the first reactions to the 1995 Augusta-Richmond County consolidation vote was that its larger size would "put Augusta on the map." Race and class divisions also characterize many incorporation, annexation, and consolidation debates, particularly when affluent, white suburbanites and black city residents anticipate changes in their political power or social and economic conditions. Such debates became more common in Georgia during the 1990s and continued into the new century with conflicts such as the incorporation of a new city of Sandy Springs north of Atlanta in 2005, along with subsequent incorporation efforts in several areas of Fulton and DeKalb Counties.[20]

Services

The state plays a key role in trying to guarantee that Georgians, no matter where they live, receive local government services that meet certain minimum standards. For example, various local services affecting environmental quality are under the supervision of the Georgia Department of Natural Resources. Requirements include certification of supervisors of local water and sewer systems and reports to the state of results from periodic tests of water samples. Local governments must also meet standards regarding the disposal of waste.

Other state actions are designed to encourage public safety and health. They include minimum standards for full-time and volunteer fire departments, as well as the licensing and inspection of local emergency medical services. There are statewide building codes, although local governments can adopt stricter requirements. The state also sets standards and provides funds for county boards of health. The state uses financial incentives to encourage local governments to provide certain types of services, as with the requirement that counties without an emergency management organization would not be eligible for disaster assistance.

Personnel

Georgia sets standards for public servants in the constitution, state law, and agency rules. These rules cover those elected to office, as well as hired and appointed officials. Requirements cover minimum qualifications to hold an office, while others regulate behavior once in a position.

Elected Officials. Those elected at the local level in Georgia must satisfy very few state requirements.[21] To run for most city and county offices, candidates must file a notice with local election officials. They cannot have been convicted of certain crimes, including election law violations. The state has set thirty days as the minimum time candidates must reside within the area in which they would be elected. In partisan elections, candidates can compete for only one political party's nomination. The state permits local governments to charge a filing fee within certain limits. Beyond such minimum standards for candidates, new city council and county commission members have been required since 1990 to attend a training and education course to prepare them for their "positions of public trust."[22] Additional standards are applied to officials expected to have some specialized knowledge, such as county coroners.[23]

Appointed Officials. Some appointed officials exercise substantial authority on their own; others are members of boards that make decisions collectively. Appointed executives such as city managers can be fired almost any time that a majority of the city council wants to do so. This is usually true as well for officials such as the city attorney or the city clerk. The state still sets standards for such jobs, however. Since the early 1990s, full-time city clerks must complete a training course at the expense of their employer.[24] This mandate might seem trivial until one considers that the clerk maintains government records, keeps minutes of various public meetings, publishes and distributes a wide range of official notices, and performs similar tasks that must meet numerous legal requirements. Similarly, municipal court judges, who are not necessarily lawyers, have been required since 1991 to complete a training course and annual training thereafter in order to remain certified.[25]

Local governments also include citizens appointed to various boards, commissions, authorities, and advisory groups. Some appointed bodies have substantial power to shape public policy, and seats on them are highly coveted. For instance, builders, developers, and neighborhood activists frequently compete over appointments to planning commissions, which review land-use plans and zoning cases.[26] Citizens also serve on boards that govern airports, hospitals, convention centers, park systems, museums, and similar facilities. Such board members often spend time raising private funds, recruiting volunteers, and promoting their organizations. This is also true of advisory boards such as beautification commissions and councils on aging.

Public Employees. The state allows local governments to establish civil service systems with hiring, evaluation, and promotion based on "merit," but it does set some minimum qualifications. In the area of public safety, for example, the state requires minimum levels of training for peace officers, full-time firefighters, and police chiefs. None of these requirements applies to county sheriffs, who are elected officials.[27]

School-system personnel are regulated heavily by the state, which, for example, provides rules regarding the qualifications, selection, and performance of local superintendents. Teachers must satisfy certification requirements and meet certain standards to advance their careers. Local school personnel also must teach required materials, complete reports mandated by the state, and satisfy regulations regarding student discipline.[28]

Finances

Other than the constitutional limits on debt, most financial constraints on local governments are found in general laws. The most basic is the requirement that local governments "operate under an annual balanced budget."[29] The state also restricts revenues. Counties and municipalities can use several sources but rely most heavily on sales and property taxes. Most school districts have relied historically on property taxes as their overwhelming source of local revenue. However, dissatisfaction with property taxes, particularly among homeowners, prompted the General Assembly to place a proposed constitutional amendment on the November 1996 ballot to allow schools to use a 1 percent sales tax if approved by local voters. Voters ratified the amendment, although it passed by only 50.8 percent—just over 28,000 votes out of more than 1,869,000 ballots cast. This narrow margin suggested that local school boards would have a difficult time convincing voters to approve an additional sales tax. The tax quickly proved popular, however. In March 1997, for instance, voters in sixty-three of the sixty-seven school districts with a sales tax referendum on the ballot approved the measure.[30]

User fees are especially important to special districts and authorities, as with the payments made to hospital authorities, fares paid to transit systems, and landing fees paid by airlines to airport authorities. Cities and counties have increasingly turned to user fees as a revenue source, especially for utility services such as water, after the Great Recession, which began in 2008, reduced property values.

Georgia, like most states, limits local taxes.[31] In addition to property taxes, counties are allowed to levy a 1 percent sales tax on top of the 4 percent state sales tax. Counties cannot levy the tax without the approval of their voters, however. Disputes arise on occasion over the agreements that a county and its cities must reach over their respective shares of the taxes collected.[32] Counties also have been permitted since 1985 to use a 1 percent special-purpose local-option sales tax (SPLOST). This tax is temporary, must be approved in a referendum, and must finance specific projects. It has proven quite popular with voters. State law allows local governments to employ an income tax, but referendum requirements are so severe that it is not used.

The state also restricts how taxes are administered. For example, the property tax is applied to 40 percent of a residential property's market value, not 100 percent. Related requirements deal with standards for determining the market value of property, the training of assessors, and certification of each county's tax digest (overall valuation of taxable property). In addition, general law prevents the taxation of property owned by various charitable, religious, nonprofit, and governmental organizations. State law reduces the tax burden of agricultural, timber, conservation, and historic property. The General Assembly also passes many local laws allowing cities and counties to vote on a "homestead exemption." This reduces a homeowner's property taxes by exempting a certain share of its value from being taxed. These tax breaks are usually targeted to certain groups, for example, seniors and those with low incomes. General law also forbids application of the sales tax to services, certain transactions involving government agencies and nonprofit organizations, and a list of consumer goods that includes water sold through mains, animals used for breeding, and Bibles. In 1996, the General Assembly passed a law to phase out the state sales tax on groceries, which are still subject to local sales taxes.

Finally, general law regulates budgetary practices.[33] Local governing bodies are required to adopt an annual budget detailing revenue sources and expenditures for the upcoming fiscal year. They must hold a hearing on the budget after publishing notices announcing it. Most transfers of funds within departments can be done administratively, but changes in amounts appropriated in the budget can be made only by the governing body. Most local governments must submit to audits by state agencies, make an annual report on their finances to the Georgia Department of Community Affairs, and have an annual audit of their finances. The most important function of such audits is to verify that funds have been collected and spent in accordance with legal requirements and accounting standards.

Procedures

The legislature has passed a number of general laws that can be viewed as attempts to promote fairness in public decision making. Many apply to all governments in Georgia, not just those at the local level. Like many states, Georgia mandates that elected and appointed bodies conduct their business in meetings open to the public. The exceptions to such "government in the sunshine" include discussions of future real estate acquisitions and the hiring, evaluation, or dismissal of an employee. Even then, officials must first meet with a quorum in a public session and vote (with each member's vote recorded) to meet behind closed doors. Still, disputes arise over unofficial gatherings and retreats by elected officials. Likewise, the state requires notification and public hearings before certain action is taken, as when cities and counties buy land and consider the rezoning of property.[34]

State law also limits the ability of officials to withhold information from the press or the public. Citizens are guaranteed the right to inspect public records and to make copies for no more than twenty-five cents per page. Certain items are exempt from the law, and litigation has occurred to determine whether specific documents and computer records are "public."[35]

Other statutes require disclosure of information related to the use of political influence. Candidates are required to disclose all campaign contributions and expenditures of $101 or more. Also, financial disclosure statements must be submitted during campaigns by all candidates and annually by elected county, municipal, and school officials.[36]

Similar requirements cover policy making. For instance, city council members, county commissioners, and those appointed to planning and zoning commissions are required to disclose interests in property affected by a rezoning proposal and must disqualify themselves from voting on the matter. Those applying for a rezoning must disclose certain gifts and campaign contributions to local officials considering their application.[37] Ironically, the committees required by state law to advise cities and counties on impact fees for development must have a minimum of 40 percent of their members from "the development, building, or real estate industries."[38]

The General Assembly also has adopted other laws dealing with the issue of biased decision making. To avoid conflicts of interest, city council members are "ineligible to hold any other municipal office" during their term.[39] Appointed board members of certain types of authorities are not to participate in decisions in which they have a "substantial interest or involvement." They also are required to disclose such interest.[40]

Local Government Structure

The organization of local government has been especially controversial during two periods in American history. The first occurred in the early twentieth century—the Progressive Era—when reformers sought to eliminate the power of political "machines." Reformers tried to weaken these local political party organizations with procedural changes such as the nonpartisan ballot, at-large elections (choosing council members citywide rather than from districts), majority vote requirements with the use of runoffs, laws aimed at eliminating vote fraud, use of civil service to hire and promote people based on merit rather than political connections, and the council-manager form of government with a hired executive rather than an elected mayor running a city on a day-to-day basis. Among other effects, these "reforms" are associated with lower turnout in local elections and the success of incumbents.[41]

The second reform effort began with the civil rights movement of the 1960s and actually sought to reverse many changes made during the Progressive Era. Critics argued that at-large elections and majority vote requirements were biased against nontraditional candidates. The problem, they asserted, involved more than a lack of resources. The tendency of people to vote along racial lines meant that whites would control at-large governing bodies of communities where they outnumbered minorities. Requiring the winner of an office to get a majority vote, detractors claimed, meant that candidates such as minorities and women could get a plurality in the first election but lose a seat after powerful and traditional groups united to defeat them in a runoff between the top two finishers.

Research supports many of these claims. Most studies indicate that blacks clearly win seats closer to their share of a community's population when elections are conducted by district rather than at large. The evidence is not so convincing regarding the fate of Hispanics and women under at-large systems. Results are also ambiguous concerning runoffs. Activists of the second reform era frequently found an ally in the U.S. Department of Justice, which used the provisions of the Voting Rights Act to force changes in local electoral systems. When such changes are made, minority candidates generally see major improvements in the proportion of seats they hold on local governing bodies. Even with district elections, there are often battles over where to draw the boundaries of each district, which can affect who wins and loses.[42] Both waves of reform, along with other factors, have left an imprint on local government structure in Georgia,[43] although that could be diminished by the U.S. Supreme Court's 2013 blow to the Voting Rights Act in *Shelby County v. Holder*.

Counties

It is difficult to speak of "administering" county government in Georgia. First, an elected commission in each county has "governing authority" to enact ordinances, adopt a budget, and the like. These legislative bodies range in size from one to twelve members, but the structure often has no clearly identified executive. Second, several department heads—called constitutional officers because they are required in the Georgia Constitution—are chosen by voters even though the county commission approves their budgets and is legally liable for their actions. Their position is comparable to the plural executive at the state level. These officials include a sheriff, a tax commissioner, a superior court clerk, and a judge of the probate court. They can include a treasurer, a coroner, and a surveyor, although under certain conditions these offices can be abolished. Elected department heads and court officials deal directly with the county commission rather than reporting to an executive. Critics argue that such jobs are administrative and should be filled by hiring the best-qualified person rather than electing someone locally to fill the position.[44]

Georgia's 159 counties use five forms of government (see figure 9.1). One type exists only in Georgia and combines legislative and administrative power in a single county commissioner rather than a board. As late as 1988, there were twenty-four sole-commissioner counties, mostly in small, rural counties where supporters argue that a larger board is expensive and unnecessary. Citizens in several counties have voted in recent years to abandon the sole commissioner in favor of multimember boards. Lawsuits also have attacked the sole-commissioner system. In 1992, a federal appeals court ruled that the single-commissioner system in Bleckley County, 22 percent of whose residents were black, violated the Voting Rights Act. In a five-to-four decision in June 1994, however, the U.S. Supreme Court overturned this decision, which left the sole commissioner in place. The number of sole-commissioner counties in Georgia was reduced to eleven in 2003 and eight by 2005, six of them in North Georgia, but the system has remained controversial.[45]

The second form of government, the traditional county commission, lacks a chain of command with an executive to whom departments report. Instead, the commission exercises executive authority as a group, although the chair may take the lead in coordinating county services and trying to build consensus on policy decisions. Some counties place more responsibility in the hands of their commission chairperson by making the job full time. Thirty counties used this system in 2015, including twenty-one with fewer than twenty thousand residents. The remainder included a few large counties in Metropolitan Atlanta (Carroll, Clayton, Rockdale, and Walton).

The commission-manager and commission-administrator forms were used in 121 Georgia counties in 2015. The major difference between the two is that county managers are hired by the commission and have authority to appoint and remove key department heads, prepare and propose the budget for the commission, and oversee day-to-day operations. Most county administrators come up short on one or more of these key characteristics, particularly with personnel decisions. Still, both types of officials generally can be fired whenever the county board of commissioners wants.[46] The number of counties using these two forms of professional administration has increased substantially over the past two decades. Most of this change is due to abandoning the traditional county commission, which was used in 93 counties in 1993.

The final form of county government in Georgia is the elected executive.

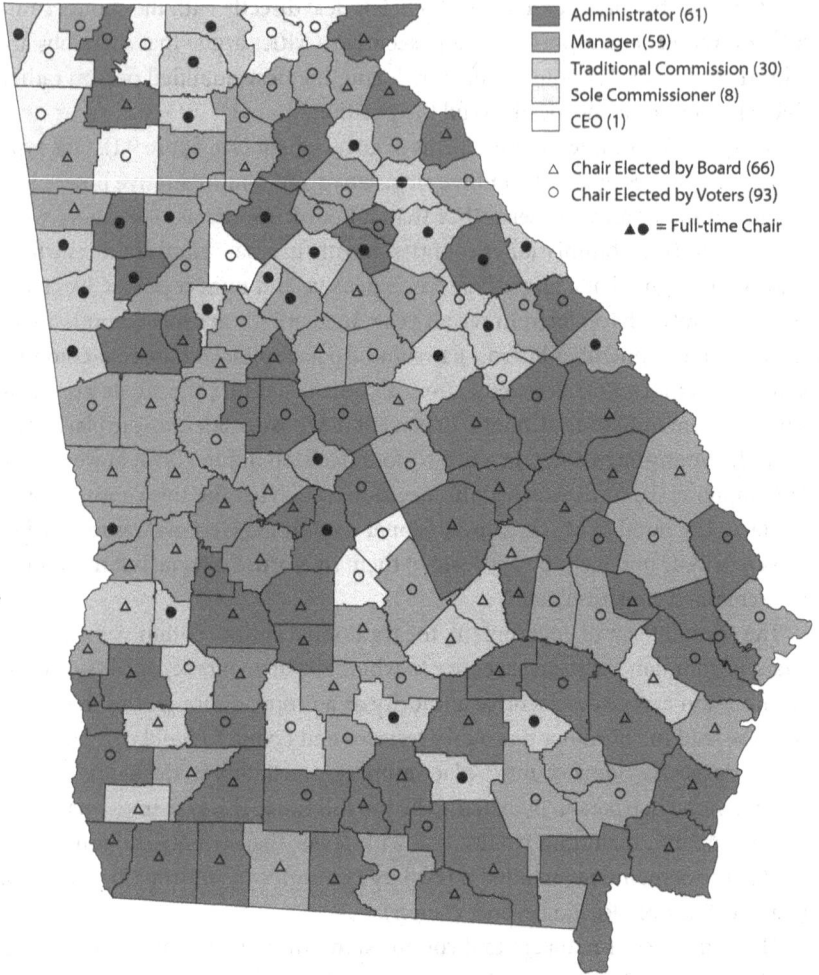

Figure 9.1. Structure of Georgia County Governments

Administrator (61)
Manager (59)
Traditional Commission (30)
Sole Commissioner (8)
CEO (1)

△ Chair Elected by Board (66)
○ Chair Elected by Voters (93)
▲● = Full-time Chair

This structure exists only in DeKalb County, where the executive has authority to appoint department heads, prepare the annual budget, and veto ordinances adopted by the county commission.[47]

Municipalities

Georgia's municipalities essentially use four forms of government, although they are organized very differently from those of counties.[48] The most common is a mayor-council form of government, which has two variants. The strong mayor form comes closest to a separation of legislative and executive powers. Policy making is the responsibility of the city council. The mayor is elected separately and usually prepares the budget, appoints and removes department heads, and often has veto power. Under the weak mayor form, there is less distinction between the powers of the council and those of the mayor. The mayor normally presides over city council meetings but has limited budgetary power, no veto, and limited control over the selection of department heads.

A third system is the commission form of government in which voters elect a mayor and other members, who frequently are designated to head specific departments. This system in effect merges executive and legislative responsibilities. Popular in the early 1900s, it has almost disappeared in Georgia and the rest of the states as council-manager government gained wide acceptance.

The fourth type is the council-manager form of government. This system vests policy making with the city council. The mayor normally presides over the council, which hires a professionally trained manager to run the city on a day-to-day basis. City managers generally have authority to hire and fire most department heads. This system resembles the structure of a corporation, with voters akin to shareholders and the council like a board of directors.

A 2016 survey of city governments by the Georgia Department of Community Affairs (DCA) had 504 responses but did not include consolidated city-county governments. This response rate is very good relative to the more than 529 municipalities (not counting consolidated governments) included in the U.S. Census Bureau's 2012 *Census of Governments*. Of the 504 municipalities, only 4 (0.8 percent) reported using the commission form of government (see table 9.4), which is consistent with national patterns. The DCA data indicate that almost half of city governments in the state use the strong-mayor system, while roughly a quarter each have the weak-mayor system and the council-manager form.[49]

Among the strong-mayor-council cities is Atlanta, as well as smaller places like Hiawassee, Jonesboro, St. Marys, and Warner Robins, where the community has vested executive authority in the mayor rather than a hired administrator. Smaller cities like Douglasville and Monroe retained the weak-mayor

Table 9.4. Structure of Georgia City Governments, 2015

Form of Government	Number of Cities	Percentage of Cities
Strong Mayor	237	47.0
Weak Mayor	130	25.8
Council-Manager	128	25.4
City Commission	5	1.0
Other	4	0.8

Source: Georgia Department of Community Affairs 2016.
Total = 504 municipalities.

system, but so did the large Atlanta suburb of Roswell. Government structure is not carved in stone, however, and voters can modify their charters as conditions change. For example, the International City/County Management Association (ICMA) noted that 7 percent of cities in their national survey reported an effort to change government structure between 2006 and 2011, most commonly to add a hired administrator or to change city councils by altering the number of members or the method of electing them.[50]

Special Districts

The structure of special districts in Georgia varies widely. Perhaps the most visible are the state's 180 public school systems, where policy making is the responsibility of the local school board, while the superintendent is charged with administration of the schools. With the ratification of a constitutional amendment in November 1992, all members of Georgia's local school boards must be elected, and all superintendents are hired (and can be fired) by their school board. Previously, two-thirds of the county superintendents and 85 percent of the boards were elected by voters. Surprisingly, eighteen systems had elected superintendents but appointed school boards. School boards appointed by grand juries date back to the end of Reconstruction and were quite numerous at one time. Elected superintendents in office on January 1, 1993, were allowed to serve out their terms.[51]

The U.S. Census Bureau counted 510 special districts in Georgia in 2012. These governments exist to provide services as varied as public hospitals, libraries, water, public housing, downtown development, cultural and convention centers, fire protection, and airports. One example is the Metropolitan Atlanta Rapid Transportation Authority (MARTA), which provides bus and subway service. Others, often called business improvement districts, provide a range of services to assist the development of certain sections of cities and counties. Special districts often appear more like a private firm than a local government because their boards are generally appointed for fixed terms by the city council or county commission. Most of Georgia's special districts do not have the power to levy property taxes; instead, they tend to rely on sales taxes, fees charged for services, and revenue from the sale of bonds. Due in part to the indirect selection of boards and executives, there is concern that special districts are not as accountable to the public or as well managed as the traditional city and county departments that report directly to a chief executive and an elected governing body.[52]

Participation in Local Politics

Political participation in the United States, especially voting, tends to be lower at the local level than it is in the states or for the national government. This tendency may seem surprising because participating should be easier at the local level, where the time, effort, and other costs of getting involved can be relatively low. Local politics can also be more informal and personal since officials are more readily accessible.

Several factors might explain limited participation in local politics. Virtually all city elections are nonpartisan, which means that political parties are not very active in mobilizing voters. Voter interest and knowledge may be low because media attention to local campaigns is less extensive than coverage of national and state elections. Unlike the social and economic issues that dominate national politics, local governments devote much of their effort to very basic services. Research does suggest that even though citizens do not vote often in local elections, they frequently contact local government agencies with service complaints and requests. Moreover, scandals and issues like crime, schools, traffic, land use, and pollution always have the potential to activate citizens locally, at the ballot box or in other ways.[53]

Elections

Voter Participation. Local elections in the United States are notorious for low turnout. The percentage of adults voting in municipal elections is in the range of 20–30 percent, or about half the level of national elections. It is not unusual, though, for turnout in some local elections to drop to single digits. Like other elections, turnout at the local level has declined over the past generation.

Turnout at the local level varies with the timing of elections, the use of or absence of party labels on the ballot, the offices up for election, the competitiveness of individual contests, and the salience of issues at a given time. J. Eric Oliver's analysis of almost five hundred municipalities in fifteen states found average turnout of 18 percent of registered voters when local elections were not held the same date as the 2006 state and national midterm election, but turnout rose to 76 percent when local officials were chosen simultaneously with the 2004 presidential election.[54] Turnout at the local level also tends to be higher when the mayor's office is on the ballot. This trend is consistent with the general pattern that turnout tends to be higher in mayor-council than in council-manager cities, and in cities using a partisan ballot, where political parties might be active in mobilizing voters. Party labels also provide messages to voters about candidates' views, but these cues are lacking in nonpartisan races.[55]

Turnout also varies among different groups of voters. Not surprisingly, Oliver discovered that those most likely to vote in municipal elections are homeowners, longer-term residents (ten or more years), the better educated, and the middle-aged (forty–sixty-five). Some renters were more involved than others, however. Turnout was higher for renters living in a city at least five years versus newer residents, and for renters with at least some college versus those who were less educated. Indeed, the differences in voting were almost two to one.[56]

Compared to voting for president or governor, media coverage is often low for down-ballot contests, offices are less visible, and voters may feel less informed or concerned. Several Georgia examples illustrate both the variation in turnout among different types of elections and the tendency for voters to skip items on the ballot. In the November 2012 presidential election, 67 percent of Athens-Clarke County's 60,266 registered voters cast ballots in the presidential race between Barack Obama and Mitt Romney. In contrast, just under 10 percent of those registered voted in November 2011, when the major issue was adoption of a sales tax for the school district.

These differences show up in ballot rolloff, namely, the extent to which people skip races as they move down the ballot from "greater" to "lesser" offices or issues. In the November 2, 2010, general election, more than 47 percent of those registered in Clarke County voted in the contests for U.S. Senate and governor, and 46 percent voted in the mayor's race. However, only 35.8 percent cast votes in the contest for a seat on the Georgia Supreme Court. Similar patterns prevail in runoffs, which occur when no candidate in a crowded field gets a majority and the two highest vote getters then face each other a few weeks later. The 2010 runoff was held four weeks later in Athens—around Thanksgiving—and 22 percent voted in the mayor's race (less than half the turnout in the first round), while 18–19 percent voted in runoffs for statewide judgeships.[57]

Similar patterns occur around the state. In the 2009 Atlanta city elections, the mayor's office was open, with a field of competitive candidates and a likelihood that people would vote heavily along racial lines. Turnout in the nonpartisan election was 30.5 percent of those registered. Four years later, when Mayor Kasim Reed ran for reelection virtually unopposed, turnout dropped to 19 percent. In March 2015, when the only thing on the ballot was whether to borrow $250 million for infrastructure improvements, just 7.5 percent of Atlanta's registered voters went to the polls.[58]

In Chatham County, elections for mayor and city council in several small cities were held in November 2013, with turnout ranging between 17 and 46 percent of registered voters. With no elections in Savannah, turnout for a countywide vote to adopt a special sales tax was 19 percent. This compares to November 2011, when Savannah voters had to choose a new mayor, and turnout reached 32.8 percent. There was very little ballot rolloff for three referendum questions, including one on package sales of alcohol and a sales tax for schools. Turnout in the December runoff for mayor dropped only slightly, to 29.8 percent. In the November 2014 general election, with all statewide offices on the ballot, turnout in Chatham County reached 51 percent of registered voters, although roughly 20,000 fewer votes were cast for the only county office on the ballot (coroner) compared to governor and U.S. senator. At the high end, 72.6 percent of registered voters cast ballots in the November 2012 general election. As one might expect with the presidency and state legislature on the ballot, there was some rolloff for county offices. With roughly 109,000 votes cast for president, competitive races for sheriff, district attorney, clerk of superior court, and county commission chair drew 5,000–7,000 fewer votes. In contrast, those running unopposed for three county offices (tax commissioner, surveyor, and coroner) each attracted fewer than 80,000 votes.[59]

Local Campaigns. Local elections in Georgia vary significantly in their scale, competitiveness, and cost. At one end of the scale are at-large offices in large cities and counties. There campaigns for mayor, county executive or commission chair, sheriff, and similar offices can be expensive, media-driven efforts that focus on candidates' personal characteristics and management style as much as their positions on issues. District elections in large places can also be competitive and expensive.

In Atlanta's October 1989 city elections, Maynard Jackson raised almost $2 million to regain the mayor's seat he gave up in 1982 because of term limits. The incumbent city council president, who ran unopposed for his at-large office, raised $122,500 in donations. The eighteen winners of city council seats received a combined $762,350 in money and in-kind contributions, including $305,370 donated to eight candidates who ran unopposed. Donations to council candidates ranged from a few dollars to a $38,000 contribution by one development firm. Of the $3.3 million in donations greater than $100 to all candidates in 1989, only 51 percent came from contributors in Atlanta, 26 percent came from suburban donors, and 22 percent came from outside Georgia.[60]

Such patterns have continued. When Shirley Franklin ran successfully for Atlanta mayor in 2001, she secured support from the Atlanta Federation of Teachers and the Atlanta Labor Council, endorsements from two of the largest mainline Protestant congregations in Atlanta, and the backing of political establishment leaders such as Maynard Jackson, Andrew Young, and U.S. representative John Lewis. Franklin highlighted her management and leadership experience, which she hoped would appeal to Atlanta's new middle-class arrivals, whose votes were effectively up for grabs. Atlanta votes heavily Democratic in state and national elections, and Franklin tried to inject partisanship into the race using radio spots with former mayors Jackson and Young, including ads that labeled Franklin a "life-long Democrat," in contrast to her opponent.[61]

In 2005, Mayor Franklin and City Council president Lisa Borders cruised to reelection. A few weeks ahead of the November 8 election, Franklin had received almost $1.2 million in contributions, while Borders had raised over $700,000. Two unopposed candidates for at-large city council seats had raised a combined $580,000.[62]

In the November 2009 mayoral election, in which Franklin could not run because of term limits, the three leading candidates had spent more than $4 million by election day.[63] The contest included Mary Norwood, the first viable white mayoral candidate in nearly thirty years, who got 46 percent in the general election; her two leading black opponents garnered 38 and 14 percent. With no one achieving a majority, Norwood faced Kasim Reed in a runoff, which he won by fewer than eight hundred votes. The campaign included partisan appeals, such as efforts to paint Norwood as a Republican.[64]

Expensive campaigns have not been limited to Atlanta. In Columbus-Muscogee County (just over two hundred thousand residents), Jim Wetherington defeated the incumbent mayor in 2006. He decided not to seek reelection in 2010, but he still had a campaign war chest of over $172,000. His successor, Teresa Tomlinson, raised over $230,000 when she won with a runoff in 2010. For her reelection bid in 2014, Tomlinson raised over $235,000 in contributions, effectively scaring off major opponents.[65]

At the other extreme are small municipalities and counties, where it is often difficult to attract candidates for office, campaigns can be personal, and little money is spent to win elections. In 1995, eight cities in Gwinnett County had contested races in the November municipal elections, but five others canceled elections when only one person qualified to run for each city council seat. Jonesboro, in Clayton County, had a different quandary: three city council seats but only two candidates. Local contests for judgeships and district attorneys are also notorious for their lack of competition.[66]

Contentious local issues can motivate people to run for office and to vote. Statewide voter turnout in the July 1996 primary election was 27 percent. It reached 44 percent in Oconee County, though, as candidates in the Republican primary for school board chair debated the role of religion in the schools.[67] In the May 2016 primary, only 59 of Georgia's 159 counties had turnout above 10 percent, with the highest rates in counties with fewer than 10,000 registered voters. In DeKalb County, with more than 375,000 registered voters and a string of corruption cases, turnout exceeded 15 percent, and a Democratic runoff in July for a county commission seat topped 11 percent. In the process, the district attorney and a county commissioner were defeated, and the interim chief executive decided not to seek reelection.[68] Similarly, raising crime as an issue in Savannah's 2015 elections helped several candidates, including one who defeated the incumbent mayor.[69]

Voting Patterns. Elections in Georgia changed significantly when the rights of black voters were expanded in 1946, following the elimination of the white primary, and in 1965, when Congress passed the Voting Rights Act. This was especially true in Atlanta, where white business leaders who dominated local politics in the 1940s and 1950s forged an alliance with moderate black leaders to promote incremental and peaceful racial change along with the city's growth. This coalition essentially wrote off poor whites, who formed a solid bloc favoring racial segregation. Voting during the 1960s and 1970s was polarized along racial and class lines. In municipal and Democratic primary contests, where candidates were not differentiated by party, blacks and higher-status whites tended to vote together for moderate or liberal candidates. In presidential elections, higher-status whites shifted some of their votes to the Republican nominee, while less-affluent whites were more likely to join with blacks in support of the Democrat. Racial polarization tended to be higher for more-visible local offices, such as mayor of Atlanta, than for lesser positions, and when a black candidate was running.

Atlanta voting patterns also changed over time. Racial polarization jumped after passage of the 1965 federal Voting Rights Act but declined by the mid-1970s. Moreover, polls indicated that after the election of Atlanta's first black mayor in 1973, blacks maintained their level of trust in local government, while whites' modest decline in trust was similar to general trends in the nation. A 1981 poll suggested that it was unusual for voters to support someone of their own race if that candidate disagreed with them on issues. When Maynard Jackson was returned to the mayor's office with 79 percent of the vote in 1989, however, he won by building a coalition that cut across racial and class lines. As Atlanta's demographic makeup shifted during the 1990s, class differences became more pronounced, particularly in elections with major candidates of the same race, and gay and lesbian voters became an important voting bloc citywide and an even more significant force in certain city council districts.[70]

Elected Officials. One of the most notable changes in local politics in Georgia is the increased presence of black, female, and Republican officeholders. In 1971 26 blacks held elected city and county offices in Georgia. By 1993, 371 blacks had been elected to city and county offices. In 2002, the total reached 413; only

Alabama and Mississippi had more.[71] Reliable data on municipal officials no longer exist, but in mid-2015, African Americans accounted for 176 of the 812 county commissioners in Georgia (21.7 percent), while whites held 544 seats (67 percent), and the remaining 11.3 percent were vacant, of different ethnicity, or unknown.[72]

In 1981, women held 183 city council and mayoral positions in Georgia. Another 22 were county commissioners. By 1985, 251 of Georgia's mayors or city council members were women; 28 held county commission seats in 1988. The share of women on county commissions rose from 5.1 percent in 1981 to 7.4 percent in 1991. Over the same ten-year period, the share of women on school boards went from 15.5 to 22.7 percent. Atlanta had its first female mayor during Shirley Franklin's two terms (2002–2010), and in 2015, women were mayors in Albany, Athens, Columbus, and Savannah.[73] Also in 2015, 116 women were serving as county commissioners (15 percent), a modest change over two decades earlier.[74]

As they have at the state level, Republicans have made major inroads in local government, although the degree of partisan change is difficult to measure because many local elections are nonpartisan. In 1981, 96 percent of county commissioners were Democrats, 3.8 percent were Republicans, and 0.2 percent were independents. By 1991, 87.6 percent were Democrats, 10.3 percent were Republicans, and 2.1 percent were independents. By mid-2015, the GOP held 419 of the 812 county commission seats in Georgia (51.6 percent), while Democrats occupied 311 (38.3 percent). The remaining positions were vacant, won by independents, elected on a nonpartisan ballot, or unknown. Excluding counties with a sole commissioner, consolidated city-county governments using a nonpartisan ballot, and commissions with vacant seats, thirty counties had all-Republican commissions in mid-2015, while seventeen had only Democrats. The Republican strongholds were concentrated in North Georgia, mainly suburban areas of Atlanta and Athens, as well as mountain counties, with only seven GOP counties south of Macon. On the flip side, the all-Democrat commissions included some suburban areas south and east of Atlanta (Clayton, Rockdale) and counties in the area traditionally viewed as the Black Belt. This trend does not mean that all the remaining counties were two-party competitive, however, as forty-one counties with boards larger than three seats had just one member from the "out" party or an independent.[75] Demographic changes might make Democrats more competitive in other suburban Atlanta counties, including Gwinnett.[76]

Republican gains were especially pronounced in metropolitan areas. In Metropolitan Atlanta, Republicans held 45.1 percent of county commission seats by 1991—a sharp rise over the 12.3 percent ten years earlier.[77] Following the 2012 and 2014 elections, Republicans held 105 seats on county boards of commissioners (72 percent), as opposed to 40 for Democrats. Republicans did better the farther one traveled from Atlanta, especially in the northern suburbs. Democrats, on the other hand, dominated Clayton and DeKalb counties. Some inner suburbs, which used to be considered solidly Republican, have become competitive between the two parties (Douglas) or even shifted Democratic (Rockdale, Spalding) as their populations changed.[78]

In Georgia's other metropolitan areas, Republicans made up 15.8 percent of county commissioners in 1991.[79] Change had occurred by the early twenty-first century, though. Core urban counties maintained a Democratic edge, but suburban areas were often Republican strongholds. In Bibb County (Macon), Democrats enjoyed a 4–1 control of the county commission following the November 2012 elections. In suburban Jones and Monroe counties, Republicans held the boards by a 3–2 margin, while Democrats controlled Twiggs County 4–1. In Metropolitan Savannah, Democrats had a 6–3 edge on the Chatham County Commission. In suburban Bryan and Effingham counties, in contrast, Republicans won all twelve seats during the 2012 and 2014 election cycles.[80]

Referenda. Local elections often involve more than choosing among candidates. In a referendum, Georgians are asked to vote yes or no on a public policy question. Some of these elections are required by general law, as with the sale of general obligation bonds or the adoption of a SPLOST. Other referenda are held under local acts passed by the General Assembly. Between 2000 and 2013, citizens voted in 458 referendum elections in communities throughout the state. The largest share covered homestead exemptions for property taxes, but others dealt with the structure of local government, incorporation of new cities, the powers of local governments, term limits of elected officials, and similar matters.[81] A third type of referendum includes questions put on the ballot by city or county officials as "advisory" rather than binding.

Referenda generally do not attract many voters. In the first thirty-two counties voting on a SPLOST in 1985, nineteen had turnout of 25 percent or less, and only three counties exceeded 40 percent turnout.[82] Low turnout can be attributed at times to the scheduling and low-key nature of referendum elections. Indeed, some public officials have been accused of holding tax referenda on dates when voters are likely to pay attention—and oppose—new taxes. In September 2005, for instance, only 12 percent of Cobb County voters cast ballots in a special election proposal to adopt a SPLOST to increase the local sales tax from 5 to 6 percent.[83] Local voters are often asked to decide referenda on controversial issues such as the sale of alcohol—a strategy that allows officials to avoid making the decision themselves. Support for Sunday sales and liquor by the drink often comes from business and political leaders who tout alcohol sales as a way to attract hotel and restaurant chains and to generate sales tax revenues.

In some cases, a community feels forced to approve alcohol sales because neighboring cities already do.[84]

Recall Elections. Similar to a referendum is a recall, which permits citizens to vote on whether to remove an elected official from office. Georgia permits the recall of anyone holding an elective state or local office. In order for a recall vote to be held, there must first be a valid petition whose required number of petition sponsors, signatures, and time limit vary. The major hurdle is quickly getting signatures equal to 30 percent of the total number of registered voters at the last election when the office was on the ballot.

Petition sponsors also must demonstrate that the official they want to remove committed misconduct or some other serious breach of responsibility. Unlike the state law struck down as unconstitutional in 1988, merely being unhappy with an official's judgment or performance is not sufficient grounds for a recall. If a petition is valid, citizens vote yes or no on removing the official named. If more than half of those voting cast their ballots in favor, the official is removed immediately and a special election is held to fill the vacancy. Since it took effect in April 1989, Georgia's new recall statute has been used sparingly, although recall efforts have occurred in smaller Atlanta suburbs, where elected officials do not serve full time and professional staff support is limited.[85]

Interest Groups in Local Politics

Like their state and national counterparts, local groups lobby, endorse candidates, make campaign contributions, try to influence public opinion, and use other tactics. Many national and state groups, such as chambers of commerce, unions, teachers groups, and environmental organizations, have local affiliates. Nonetheless, local interest groups operate on a smaller scale, in terms of both geographical area and number of members. Unlike groups operating in a state capital or Washington, D.C., those at the local level often have few resources except the ability to mobilize large numbers of people. As a result, groups arise and disappear over specific issues.

Among the most prominent and effective local interest groups are those in the business community. In smaller places, business leadership is often concentrated in the local chamber of commerce, although professionals such as attorneys and those involved in real estate, along with executives of major local firms can also be influential because such firms have the staff to monitor and deal with local government. For example, one study found that officials of chambers of commerce and banks were among the most likely to attend economic development meetings in Georgia's rural counties and small towns.[86] Local chambers of commerce and similar groups often promote their communities to outside investors and tourists, sometimes with subsidies from city and county governments. For example, the Athens Convention and Visitors Bureau got over 31 percent of the local hotel room tax in 2015 to promote Athens as a destination.[87] Local service organizations such as the United Way also provide a means for bringing together leaders from business, government, and nonprofit groups.

In larger communities, numerous business organizations may have substantial budgets and full-time staffs. These groups can even compete with one another. The Atlanta area, for example, has multiple chambers of commerce with thousands of member firms. In the city of Atlanta, other organizations have promoted downtown, conventions and tourism, and the Midtown and Buckhead areas.[88] Politicians often respond to such economic power by helping to promote a wide range of development plans favored by business leaders. Individual companies (especially large ones) can also have political clout because they pay substantial taxes, employ many workers, and can have many locational options, although the state will often get involved with major firms, as with the decision by Mercedes-Benz to relocate its U.S. headquarters to Sandy Springs from New Jersey.[89] With such investment, the state could care little where a company locates as long as it is in Georgia.

Perhaps especially crucial to a city's fortunes are developers, whose projects can transform entire neighborhoods and can add substantial value to a community's property-tax base. This often puts them in a strong bargaining position with local officials, as with the proposed development of Fort McPherson by movie producer Tyler Perry. However, developers are often "the enemy" for many neighborhood and historic preservation groups.[90]

City and county officials worry, though, as the number of locally headquartered companies decreases. They express concern about the lack of commitment to a community by outside owners in terms of civic engagement, jobs, and leadership. This was the case as Georgia-based banks disappeared following mergers, and some observers lamented the diminishing presence of Turner Broadcasting in Atlanta in the years following its acquisition by Time Warner, which is headquartered in New York City.[91]

Government employees also can be powerful interest groups in local politics. In many small counties, in particular, a substantial percentage of all jobs can be in local government. In larger places, police officers, firefighters, public school teachers, and health care workers can be politically important groups.

Perhaps the most unusual interest groups at the local level are neighborhood organizations, which tend to be all-volunteer and lack permanent structure, staff, and financial resources. Even though membership and activity can fluctuate, neighborhood organizations can exert substantial political clout, especially when development can affect an area's property values and quality of life. In established parts of metropolitan Atlanta, groups representing middle-class and affluent homeowners testify and appear in large numbers at planning commission rezoning hearings, attend meetings of city councils and county commissions, contact elected officials, endorse candidates, picket, and even file lawsuits. For example, action by neighborhood groups forced almost a decade worth of delays and changes in a highway that the state built between downtown Atlanta and the Carter Presidential Center. Organizations of homeowners also have cropped up in newer suburban areas to fight commercial development, traffic, and apartments.[92]

The Local Policy Process

Many factors influence policies adopted by local governments, including constraints imposed by the state constitution and laws, the structure of local government, the types of political participation discussed above, and the actions of other governments. Many key decisions revolve around government services, taxing and spending, and a community's physical characteristics and quality of life.

Services

Service decisions are complicated and often controversial. Local leaders must decide about the types and level of services they provide. They also choose who will furnish services—government, the private sector, nonprofit organizations, or volunteer groups—as well as how to pay for services.

Table 9.5 details nineteen services commonly provided directly by local governments in Georgia during 2014. The data are from an annual survey of local governments conducted by the Georgia Department of Community Affairs. The completed questionnaires cover 151 of Georgia's 159 counties and 484 of 529 city governments.[93]

It is worth noting that the surveys asked local governments only whether they provide a service; they did not ask how widely available a service is, how much is spent on it, or similar measures of performance. For instance, the counties providing public transit do not necessarily have big fleets of buses—this category includes services such as paratransit vans for the disabled or the elderly. Moreover, just because a government does not provide a service itself does not mean that it is not available—it could be supplied by another government or by contract with a company or nonprofit organization.

The table highlights historic differences between cities and counties. Cities are more likely to provide the wide range of water and solid waste services one might expect in built-up, more densely populated communities. Such services are less necessary in rural areas. Counties must serve as "administrative arms

Table 9.5. Services Provided by Georgia Cities and Counties, 2015

Service	Percentage Providing Service	
	Cities (484)	Counties (151)
Animal Control	21.1	62.9
Building Inspection	38.4	73.5
Building Permits	59.1	89.4
Construction and Code Enforcement	47.7	84.1
Emergency Medical Services	3.3	57.6
Emergency 911 Service	5.0	79.5
Fire Protection	56.6	81.5
Health Screening Services	0.4	18.5
Jail	3.5	90.1
Law Enforcement	69.4	99.3
Planning	64.0	74.8
Public Hospital	305	2.0
Public Transit	1.4	35.1
Senior Citizen Program	13.0	57.0
Telecommunications	8.7	8.6
Wastewater Collection	56.6	17.9
Wastewater Treatment	50.8	14.8
Water Distribution	78.1	29.1
Water Supply	72.1	26.5
Water Treatment	70.0	24.5
Storm Water	52.1	35.8

Sources: Georgia Department of Community Affairs 2015a, section 2; 2015c, section 2.

of the state" in providing courts, public records, a variety of social services, and other functions. Thus jails are essentially a county function. Because counties administer a number of social welfare programs for the state, it should not be surprising that they are more likely than cities to run health and senior programs. The substantial county role in emergency services could be a function of their greater geographical size and economies of scale.

Some services differ substantially by the size of the local government. For instance, twenty-two of the twenty-four counties in the survey with more than one hundred thousand residents provide animal control; it is provided by another organization in one county and another government in the other. In contrast, sixteen of the smallest twenty-nine counties (fewer than ten thousand residents) have no animal control service. This reflects in part the power counties were given in 1972 to provide urban services, which means that citizens did not need to live inside a city to get services such as garbage pickup, county police, water distribution and treatment, zoning, animal control, health screening, and similar services.[94]

Comparable differences exist between larger and smaller cities. In Southwest Georgia, for example, Albany (more than seventy-five thousand residents) provides sixteen of the twenty-two services in table 9.5. It relies on an independent authority for hospital care; other governments for EMS, the jail, and health screening; and a nongovernmental organization for senior citizen programs. In nearby Morgan (population under two thousand), the county seat of Calhoun County, the city government provided nine of the twenty-two services, including all six related to water. Four other services are not available, with the remainder available from the county or other providers.[95]

Beyond the simple decision to provide certain services, local officials must deal with the needs and demands of different neighborhoods. Savannah addressed this problem with a program that began in the 1970s to provide higher service levels to neighborhoods in greater need. By taking this approach rather than furnishing every area the same level of street paving, inspections, flood control, and other services, officials attempted to promote equality of conditions.[96] Paying for services can also generate controversy, as with Cobb County's practice of diverting part of the money that users paid in their water bills to fund other services.[97]

Local Government Finances

A substantial part of local policies revolve around finances. As one might expect, government decisions about how to raise and spend money can be controversial. Participation by citizens and interest groups can influence these patterns, but so do other factors, including state and federal mandates. Table 9.6 provides an overview of revenue and expenditures among Georgia's local governments.

As with services, local budgets highlight differences between Georgia's cities and counties. On the revenue side, counties depend more heavily on property and sales taxes. In contrast, city revenues are often tied to enterprise funds, which are restricted to specific utility-type services such as water and sewer systems, solid waste, electric and gas supply systems, and airports. Enterprise funds operate almost as if they were businesses that generate revenue by charging for their services: water, natural gas, and electric bills; airport parking and landing fees; solid waste collection and disposal charges; and similar fees. They are normally separated from the general revenues that a local government spends on services such as police, fire, parks, and libraries.

Table 9.6. Georgia City and County Finances, Fiscal Year 2014

	Cities (458 of 529)	Counties (148 of 159)	Consolidated Governments (8 of 8)
Total Revenues	$7.87 billion	$9.08 billion	$1.05 billion
Percentage of Total			
General Revenue	46.1	83.1	78.5
Property Taxes	12.9	40.1	22.8
Local Option Sales Taxes	6.2	6.6	13.6
Special Purpose Sales Taxes	4.3	11.0	8.3
Excise/Special Use Taxes	8.2	4.6	8.8
Licenses/Permits/Fees	2.7	1.7	3.0
Intergovernmental Revenue	4.8	5.7	6.1
Service Charges/Other	6.9	13.4	15.8
Enterprise Fund Revenues	53.9	16.9	21.5
Total Expenditures	$8.25 billion	$8.48 billion	$1.06 billion
Percentage of Total			
General Expenditures	41.0	79.4	68.2
Administration	8.4	15.0	9.5
Courts	0.7	7.2	4.7
Public Safety	14.9	25.0	25.7
Community Development	2.0	1.8	3.5
Health and Human Services	0.5	5.7	2.5
Leisure Services	2.4	3.7	3.6
Public Works	0.5	0.6	0.3
Highways/Streets/Drainage	3.6	5.3	4.0
Capital Expenditures	6.2	10.6	12.2
Other	1.7	4.5	2.1
Enterprise Fund Expenditures	53.2	17.4	27.0
Debt Service (interest)	5.9	3.2	4.8

Source: Georgia Department of Community Affairs 2015b.

Note: Most of those not reporting were small counties and municipalities.

On the spending side, as one would expect from the revenue patterns, cities devote a significant proportion of their funds to services operated through enterprise funds. If one considers only general expenditures, both cities and counties devote the largest share to public safety, which includes police and fire protection. Counties spend a larger percentage, in part because they operate jails, usually under the county sheriff, while few cities have their own jails. Counties also devote a larger portion of their spending to courts, which reflects the tasks they perform on behalf of the state. Courthouse protection is also a typical function of the county sheriff. The eight consolidated governments in table 9.6 share characteristics of both cities and counties, which is reflected in their revenue and spending.

The table omits data on debt. At the end of FY 2014, the counties in the table collectively owed more than $5.7 billion, or $612.21 per resident. Most of this debt (58.2 percent) consisted of revenue bonds, while just 22.9 percent was general-obligation debt backed by taxes. For cities, debt totaled $10.4 billion ($3,048.99 per resident), with 74.6 percent being revenue bonds. This reliance on revenue bonds should not be surprising given the extent to which they are connected to services like water and sewer systems, which use fees to pay for debt, physical improvements and maintenance, and daily operations.[98]

It is also important to note that table 9.6 does not include local school systems, which are independent of Georgia's city and county governments and depend heavily on state revenues. Nor does the table include independent authorities, which many cities and counties set up to oversee public hospitals, industrial development, airports, downtown development, and similar ventures.

Regulation

Regulation is among the more important actions of local governments. Cities and counties license a variety of businesses, inspect restaurants and other establishments in the interest of public health and safety, and regulate taxi, trash collection, cable television, and similar services sold to the public.

Perhaps the most controversial type of local regulation concerns land use. Cities and counties in Georgia are allowed to adopt subdivision regulations, which control how large tracts of land can be divided into smaller parcels. Cities and counties also perform zoning, which includes several elements. The most important are the adoption of a map specifying the land use permitted for each piece of property and an ordinance spelling out zoning procedures. At a minimum, communities are divided into agricultural, residential, commercial, and industrial zones. Most places have more detailed categories. Zoning ordinances also control the size and location of buildings in each type of zone. The types of land use are arranged in a hierarchy with farmland and open space, which have the most restrictions, at the upper end and moving down to residential, commercial, and industrial uses at the bottom. It is usually harder politically to move down the hierarchy, for example, rezoning an area of single-family homes to allow a shopping center or factory.

Landowners wanting a different use for their property may apply for it to be rezoned. Following public notices of the requested change and reviews by the city or county planning staff, a planning commission made up of appointed citizens holds a public hearing and makes a recommendation to the city council or county commission, which has the final authority to reclassify the property's allowable land use by amending the zoning ordinance.

Zoning and subdivision regulation can be extremely controversial because of their effects on density, economic development, neighborhood characteristics, traffic, and property values. In Atlanta, citizen participation in rezoning increased and had greater effect during the 1970s after the city established a system of formal neighborhood involvement.[99] In the mid-1980s, most rezoning requests in the Atlanta metropolitan area involved only the applicant and local government officials. Substantial citizen opposition existed in some cases, mainly in established neighborhoods in cities like Atlanta. Still, only 21 percent of all applications were denied, while another 7 percent were tabled or withdrawn. The rest were approved, usually with compromises. In the end, planning commissions reached unanimous decisions over 75 percent of the time, as did city councils and county commissions, which adopted two-thirds of the recommendations made by their staff and 75 percent of those from planning commissions. Thus, by the time a rezoning application reached elected officials, compromise was often the result, although some decisions still led to lawsuits.[100]

Economic Development

Planning, zoning, and regulation obviously affect the physical development of a community, as well as the social fabric of neighborhoods. Local leaders also dedicate significant effort to promoting economic development, often by trying to attract new employers and helping existing companies expand. Economic development generally requires close collaboration between political and business leaders. In many communities, the local chamber of commerce takes a leading role. Some areas also have specialized organizations such as a convention and visitors bureau.[101] Many communities have also relied on semiautonomous authorities to promote development. In 2015, for instance, the state Department of Community Affairs had an inventory of over 450 authorities created for development, including 63 for industrial development and 153 for downtown development, with many of them being efforts by multiple governments.[102]

Economic development efforts include a broad arsenal of strategies, including tax breaks, loans, land and buildings, marketing assistance, job training, and infrastructure improvements such as roads, water, sewers, and even traffic lights. For instance, when Caterpillar announced plans to build a major manufacturing plant on the outskirts of Athens, the local government incentives to the company, including land, were expected to cost $30 million over twenty years.[103] In other cases, promotion involves repurposing old industrial sites or promoting development around existing transit nodes.[104]

Economic development involves more than manufacturing. Some communities use their freeway access as a selling point for warehouse and distribution facilities. Others use facilities, natural resources, and amenities to promote retirement, recreation, tourism, and entertainment. These things were part of the strategy in the Atlanta Braves' move from Turner Field to suburban Cobb County. Baseball games were part of a larger project that includes housing, retail, office, and restaurant development. This project was anticipated to include $300 million in stadium costs paid by Cobb County. The development was not without controversy, however, as some taxpayers complained about the county government's subsidy to the Braves, while others worried about the potential transportation problems at an already busy junction of two interstate highways without any public transit.[105] The public outcry over officials' deals with the Braves eventually cost the Cobb County Commission chairman his job when he lost to a Republican primary challenger in 2016.[106]

Intergovernmental Relations

As discussed in chapter 1, intergovernmental relations include both dealings that are horizontal (i.e., governments at the same level, such as local-to-local or state-to-state connections) and those that are vertical (governments at different levels, as when states regulate what local governments do). Moreover, these relationships can involve competition, conflict, and cooperation.

Dealing with the State and National Governments

Cities, counties, and special districts are always wary about what higher-level governments might do to them. Laws, court decisions, bureaucratic rules, and other actions—especially by the state—can affect local governments' budgets, authority, organization, and priorities.

Local leaders promote their interests and those of their communities in several ways. Most Georgia cities and counties have an agenda that they ask their local legislators to promote each year in the General Assembly. Local governments also maintain regular contact with state agencies such as the Department of Community Affairs and Department of Transportation, as well as various regional bodies. They also lobby in the legislature. During 2015, for instance, the city of Atlanta had several registered lobbyists, while the city council had another lobbyist and the city council president hired his own, who also represented other interests, including the city of Albany. Other lobbyists represented cities as varied as Kennesaw, Savannah, College Park, Conyers, Hinesville, Bainbridge, Lumpkin, Sandy Springs, and both Dunwoody and Marietta.[107] These services are not necessarily cheap—when Fulton County ended its use of outside lobbyists in 2013, it reportedly saved $400,000.[108]

Local interests are also represented by professional organizations. These organizations include the Georgia Municipal Association (GMA), which represents the interests of cities, and the Association County Commissioners of Georgia (ACCG). Other groups represent the interests of employees and officials such as sheriffs, teachers, school superintendents, and police officers. These groups publish newsletters, issue reports, hold conferences for their members, and pass policy recommendations that are forwarded to the General Assembly. In 2015, for example, the ACCG and the GMA had multiple lobbyists, most of whose expenditures went for meals.[109]

Why devote so much effort to lobbying? Aside from the effects of the state budget on local governments, cities and counties often lobby to defend local prerogatives. For example, during the 2015 session, several local governments worked with various interest groups to prevent the General Assembly from passing a law that would prevent local bans on plastic bags, a measure that was pushed by bag manufacturers and other business interests in response to bans in Athens and Tybee Island.[110]

There are also efforts to resist orders from state and local governments, including the courts. For example, federal courts intervened for eleven years to force Fulton County to improve conditions at its jail.[111]

Local Competition and Cooperation

Competition among local governments is fairly common, including efforts to outdo other communities in attracting new businesses, securing state and federal grant money, or just creating a better image. For example, leaders from several cities and counties in Metropolitan Atlanta tried a variety of tactics to attract the headquarters of United Parcel Service when the company relocated to Georgia from Connecticut. The same thing occurred when NCR moved from Ohio to suburban Atlanta in 2009. Ironically, the company stood to secure benefits from both the state and the city of Atlanta when it announced in 2015 that it was moving from the suburbs to a new location near the Georgia Tech campus.[112]

Relations among local governments are not necessarily competitive or antagonistic. In fact, several factors promote cooperation, including institutions designed to coordinate the activities of governments within an area or promote their shared interests. The state has established regional development centers whose functions include assisting local governments and playing a key role in long-term planning. Each of these agencies is governed by a board composed largely of officials from the cities and counties within its region.

A second stimulus for intergovernmental cooperation is the work of professional organizations. Groups such as GMA, the ACCG, the Georgia City-County Managers Association, organizations representing other types of officials (clerks, zoning administrators, etc.), and units of the University System of Georgia facilitate information sharing and professional development among local government officials.

A third basis for cooperation is a desire either to improve the quality or cost of services or to address problems that are regional in scope. This might be especially true for large-scale projects. For instance, Athens-Clarke County joined with Barrow, Jackson, and Oconee Counties to form the Upper Oconee Water Basin Authority, which developed the Bear Creek Reservoir to supply all four counties with water. Macon and Bibb County combined some operations, including planning, to improve efficiency and effectiveness in service delivery before their residents ultimately voted to consolidate in 2012.[113]

Fourth, cooperation can be forced by high-level governments. For instance, under the threat of losing federal highway money because of Atlanta's pollution levels, the legislature created the Georgia Regional Transportation Authority to promote policies that improved transportation and air quality. The legislature also adopted a law in 1997 forcing all governments in a county to agree on plans for providing services in order to reduce duplication and competition.[114] Local problems can also invite scrutiny from above. In 2015, for example, the federal courts lifted supervision of the Fulton County jail after eleven years of trying to rectify poor conditions at the facility.[115]

Finally, media, business, and other leaders often promote regionalism to address problems that are not confined to a single city or county. These include transportation, economic development, fiscal and economic disparities between communities, and efficient service delivery.[116]

The Future of Local Government in Georgia

Like much of Georgia, local government and politics have changed dramatically during the past generation. One of the most apparent changes is the increased number of cities and special districts. Another is the growth in local government responsibilities and budgets, especially among Georgia's urban counties. More startling during the past fifty years are the declining influence of white "courthouse gangs" in rural areas and the growing clout of black voters and local officials. Many observers would also be surprised by the partisan changes that have occurred at the local level, including large numbers of consistently "red" (Republican) and "blue" (Democratic) communities found on a map of the state.

Despite significant changes, local government in Georgia faces major challenges during the twenty-first century. Many of these issues relate to land use and natural resources, including transportation, water supply, and waste disposal; others deal with human resource problems such as education. Many rural and central city areas face problems of economic decline, while suburban communities must contend with rapid growth.

One view of the future argues that Georgia's communities must have more flexibility to organize and operate their local governments. That was the primary message in 1992 from the Governor's Local Governance Commission, which called for the removal of constitutional limitations on local government and a reduction in the General Assembly's involvement in local concerns. Little change has resulted from the commission's recommendations, however. Even with reform, the state's local officials still face many difficult problems.

CHAPTER 10

Public Policies

This chapter draws from the rest of the book and other research to examine the policy process in Georgia state government. It also makes comparisons to earlier periods, contrasts Georgia with the federal government and other states, and concludes with a discussion of the future of Georgia politics. Following an overview of the different stages in the policy process and the factors affecting actions at each stage, the remainder of the chapter examines different policies.

Policy Making in Georgia

Policy can be defined as a government's course of action in response to a perceived problem. It is important to remember that policies may be contradictory. Perhaps the most obvious example is the federal government's history of subsidizing tobacco growers and also trying to discourage people from smoking. Government inaction also constitutes a policy, as with the federal government's nonresponse to AIDS in the mid-1980s and lack of action in the face of genocide in Rwanda during the 1990s.

Descriptions of the policy process typically include several steps (see figure 10.1). The earliest stages include identifying a problem and formulating alternative responses to it. Together, they result in agenda setting, which often narrows the possible outcomes. The next step is the adoption of a policy, which could involve any combination of the executive, legislative, and judicial branches. Thus, this step might be a new law, a court decision, or some rule or other action by the executive branch. With the policy in place, it still must be implemented, which could be by a government agency, businesses, nonprofits, or others. A policy does not "end" once it is put in place because policies have impacts, not all of which have been intended or anticipated. The impacts may prompt action by those dissatisfied enough to try modifying or eliminating an existing policy, thereby starting the process all over again.[1] This general description of policy

Figure 10.1. The Policy Process

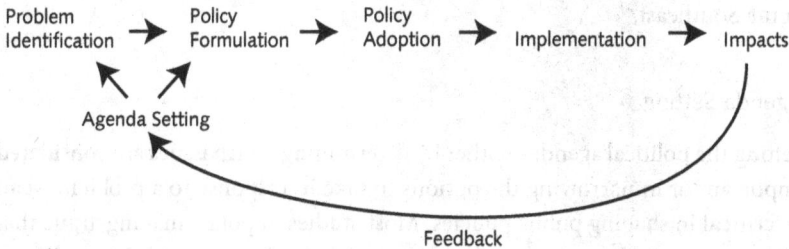

```
Problem          Policy           Policy
Identification → Formulation →   Adoption →   Implementation →   Impacts

         ↖  ↗
      Agenda Setting

                          Feedback
```

making can be applied to Georgia, although the process differs in some ways from that of the national government and other states.

Policy making today also departs from earlier periods in Georgia politics. It is unlikely that V. O. Key would recognize the policy process in Georgia today, although he noted in the mid-1940s that the South's "rate of evolution may seem glacial, but fundamental shifts in the conditions underlying its politics are taking place."[2] The formal rules of politics have changed significantly since he made his astute observations; so have the participants. The same can be said if one looks back to Georgia in the 1960s and the 1980s.

Perhaps the most noticeable difference is the policy agenda itself. In both the 1940s and the 1960s, politics in Georgia (like the rest of the Deep South) was dominated by the politics of race. Obviously, racial conflict has not disappeared in Georgia, but the policy agenda has shifted more to economic development, education, and a range of new issues.[3]

Participants and procedures have changed, too. The most significant of these involve Georgia's relationship with the national government. Change in Georgia was undeniably hastened by federal action beginning in the 1960s, particularly the Civil Rights Act and the Voting Rights Act. The battles among factions in a state dominated by Democrats in Key's day gave way to a competitive two-party system and then to Republican domination. Unlike the 1940s and 1960s, the policy process includes organized ideological, social, and religious groups. Moreover, these changes have occurred after the death of the county-unit system and the shift of electoral power from rural to suburban areas. Perhaps most startling to Key would be Republican control of state government in the twenty-first century.

Policy making in Georgia is not entirely a story of change, however. Policies are still enacted within a system characterized by low levels of voter turnout. Money and the influence of lobbyists are still important components of elections and policy making. Localism is alive and well in the General Assembly.

Still, although not often thought of as a policy innovator, Georgia has adapted to change and is constantly pressured to keep pace with other states, especially in the Southeast.

Agenda Setting

Setting the political agenda—either by determining which issues are considered important or in narrowing the options to take in response to a problem—can be critical in shaping public policies. Most studies of policy making argue that interest groups, the governor, agencies, legislative leaders, and the media are influential in agenda setting. Events, especially if seen as crises, can also shape the policy agenda.[4]

The preeminent agenda setter in Georgia is the governor, due to the formal powers of the office and the ability to use the media (see chapter 7). The governor's agenda-setting capacity may be diminished, however, by the plural executive. During agenda setting, Georgia's legislative leaders, particularly the presiding officers in the two chambers, are more powerful than their counterparts in Congress and more professionalized legislatures. Indeed, for many years critics berated leaders for their control over committee assignments and the flow of legislation, the use of behind-the-scenes deals, and "punishment" of legislators with whom they disagreed.[5]

The media role in agenda setting varies. The federal government is covered by multiple television and radio networks, interest-group publications, and Washington reporters working for a wide range of big-city newspapers and television stations. In larger states, especially those with full-time legislatures, state government usually receives more thorough media coverage, as with New York City newspapers and television stations covering state government in Albany, and the Los Angeles and San Francisco media reporting regularly on events in Sacramento. Overall, however, the number of full-time newspaper reporters covering state capitols dropped more than one-third from 2003 to 2014. About half of all statehouse reporters are full time, with newspapers far more significant than television. The rest of the reporters are part time, cover only the legislative session, or are students. Wire services, especially the Associated Press, are key providers of news, but recent growth has occurred among nontraditional sources such as all-digital sites and nonprofit organizations.[6]

In Georgia, the legislative session is short, and the media can seldom afford to have a large staff that specializes in the legislative process or specific policy areas. The Pew Research Center reported fewer than twenty journalists covering the Georgia Capitol full time in recent years.[7] Probably the premier media players are Atlanta's television stations and daily newspaper. One measure of their influence in agenda setting was the passage of ethics legislation by the General

Assembly in 1992 under what may have seemed a barrage of newspaper stories and editorials. They also reported extensively on the scandals involving cheating on student standardized tests in Atlanta's public schools in 2015 and corruption charges in DeKalb County government, which culminated in criminal convictions.[8] The *Atlanta Journal-Constitution* has also adapted to social media by having several of its reporters provide regular political blogs.

Among the non-Atlanta media, local television and radio stations can use satellite and other technology to broadcast reports from the Capitol. Some of the larger daily newspapers also send a reporter to the Capitol during the legislative session or for major events hosted by the governor. Even those newspapers, like smaller ones, rely on news services such as the Associated Press. Georgia newspapers that are part of Morris Communications, which is based in Augusta, enjoy economies of scale. Morris is a broad-based media company with significant holdings outside Georgia, and it owns daily newspapers in Athens, Augusta, Savannah, and Jacksonville (though based in Florida, the newspaper provides extensive coverage of Southeast Georgia). It also operates Atlanta-based Morris News Service, which can supplement local reporting. In fact, the company maintains a "capital bureau" in Georgia and four other states in its newspaper and radio markets.[9] Original coverage is somewhat more limited in other daily newspapers such as the *Macon Telegraph*, the *Rome News-Tribune*, the *Columbus Ledger-Enquirer*, the *Gainesville Times*, and the *Marietta Daily Journal*.

The final participants usually cited as influential in agenda setting are interest groups. Not all groups are created equal, however. As chapter 5 argues, the lack of a professional legislature and the long history of limited party competition have heightened the influence of organized interests in Georgia, particularly several professions and major Atlanta firms. Unlike in national politics, the influence of citizen groups (e.g., seniors, women) in Georgia is seldom felt compared to that of more numerous and resource-laden business lobbyists. Georgia incorporates local interests in policy making in part through the large volume of local bills and legislative allocation of grants to their districts—what many describe as providing "pork" to the folks back home.

As one might expect in the digital age, national groups have also extended their reach in Georgia. Perhaps the most controversial is the American Legislative Exchange Council (ALEC). Unlike long-standing groups with a nonpartisan image such as the National Governors Association and the National Conference of State Legislatures, ALEC is an organization of legislators and business interests promoting conservative public policies, including providing conferences and draft legislation for supportive lawmakers.[10]

States can also learn from one another, as well as from their local governments, which might be especially important in terms of formulating alternative solutions to a problem. In fact, there is a significant body of research on which states are more innovative in adopting policies and how policies spread among governments—a process called diffusion. Some of the earliest research on this topic labeled large states in the Northeast and the West as the most innovative, with other states following their lead.[11]

In some circumstances, states "learn" from problems and responses among their peers. For example, it took a series of well-publicized events and court cases for many states to adopt legislation beginning in the mid-1970s about the use of living wills affecting the terminally ill. Even then, the policy responses to this problem were not uniform, as many states chose somewhat different policies from those adopted earlier.[12] States also "copy" one another out of competition, as with tax incentives for economic development. States frequently respond to policy initiatives by their local governments, sometimes adopting a statewide policy to avoid wide discrepancies at the local level or to restrict local governments—known as preemption—as with local regulation of smoking, efforts to ban plastic bags or fracking, and setting a minimum wage higher than state or national rates.[13]

Policy Adoption

The policy adoption stage is one in which legislatures, courts, and agencies are considered most influential. It is worth remembering, though, that the procedures of these institutions vary significantly.

The way policies are adopted in Georgia differs somewhat from general descriptions of the policy process. Legislative committees and those who chair them seem less powerful than those in Congress, in part because of the control over committee assignments by party leaders in the Georgia House and Senate. Perhaps the major exception is the House Rules Committee, which is as powerful in killing bills as was the comparable congressional committee a generation ago. The presiding officers' influence is heightened, as in some other states, by the brevity of the sessions, legislative rules, the part-time nature of the job, and the lack of staff support. These features of an "amateur" legislature also give the governor and interest groups a prominent role in policy adoption. Preparation of the budget, use of administration floor leaders in each chamber, and the threat or use of the veto also enhance the governor's power.[14]

Courts are also key players in the adoption of policies—particularly appellate courts, whose decisions provide guidance to lower courts and often target the policies of other government officials. For instance, landmark cases decided by the U.S. Supreme Court have reshaped legislative representation, racial segregation, marriage, and the use of the death penalty (among other policies) in Georgia. State courts, especially the Georgia Supreme Court, can also adopt important policies.[15]

Policy Implementation

Finally, seeing that policies are carried out is usually the task of state agencies, although this responsibility can be turned over to lower-level governments, nonprofit organizations, or the private sector through contracting, grants, subsidies, vouchers to clients, and several related approaches.[16] Implementation can also be influenced by legislative oversight of agencies, as well as court decisions. As with policy formulation, implementation in Georgia can be complicated by the plural executive. In addition, state laws placing additional burdens on cities, counties, and school districts have become an especially sore point with local officials, who frequently object to such "unfunded mandates."[17]

The remainder of this chapter examines developments in several major policy areas: the budgetary process, economic development, transportation, environmental policies, education, social welfare, and public safety and security.

Politics, Policy, and the State Budget

There are several ways to examine policy change. One involves the state budget, particularly its overall growth and the components of its revenues and expenditures. Budgets themselves are statements of both policy and political priorities. Adopting a budget is a complex task, and the successes and failures of those involved in the process are related directly to political power within the state Capitol.

The budget is probably the most important piece of legislation considered by the Georgia General Assembly during its annual session. Budgets generally begin with the agencies that will eventually spend funds. Agencies predict coming expenditures based on a number of factors: past expenditures, new projects, changes in the number or circumstances of clients being served, one-time-only expenditures (e.g., outlays for buildings or new equipment), revenue from other sources, and changes in inflation or other economic trends. The budgetary requests of the agencies are often quite detailed, listing expenditures in areas such as salaries, equipment, travel, supplies, and capital improvements.

Requests for the upcoming fiscal year are collected by the various departments that house the agencies and are sent by September 1 to the Governor's Office of Planning and Budget (OPB).[18] The OPB has only a few months before the governor submits the budget in January, and the fiscal year starts on July 1. The OPB will scrutinize requests carefully at this point and often serves as a budget cutter. Some people argue that agencies pad their budgets in order to limit the effects of this process. Those programs that have the full support of the governor are less likely to feel the budget ax, but all agencies are aware that cuts take place at this stage. Before the onset of the Great Recession, Governor Sonny Perdue submitted a proposed budget for FY 2007 in January 2006 that included a combination of cuts and increases to agency requests, reflecting both the governor's priorities and improvements in Georgia's economy. Governor Perdue recommended spending more than $18.6 billion in state funds. Total proposed spending exceeded $34 billion, in large part because of the addition of federal money. Economic conditions subsequently worsened, and state revenues declined 0.5 percent in FY 2008, another 9.9 percent in 2009, and 8.9 percent in 2010 before growing again in FY 2011. The legislature amended the FY 2009 budget by cutting more than $2 billion. As the recovery proceeded, it was not until FY 2016 that the budget of $21.8 billion exceeded the one in FY 2009.[19]

Once the OPB has revised the budget to reflect the political viewpoints of the governor, it is introduced as a bill in the legislature, which has the final say in how much is appropriated to each agency—and for what purposes. The budget generally will be reviewed during the entire legislative session after being introduced in January. Each chamber has an appropriations committee, which will conduct hearings, debate, and determine the wording of the final bill. Since many groups are interested in the continued funding of government programs or money for new policy areas, lobbying the House and Senate Appropriations Committees is common. Moreover, the task of drafting the legislative budget is so important politically that senators and representatives compete fiercely for seats on the appropriations committee in each chamber.

The legislative role in the budgetary process is to modify and ultimately adopt the budget. The legislature may support items that the OPB reduced or deleted from agency requests. Cuts are also possible but less likely at this stage. The governor is relatively outside the budgetary process at this juncture, at least in formal terms. Governors may exert influence over the activities of the legislature, or they may try swaying public opinion to influence the budget indirectly as it weaves its way through the General Assembly. Interest groups also will attempt to affect the budget, both directly by testimony in public hearings and indirectly through the manipulation of public opinion and mobilization of their members. Many lobbyists who engage in these formal methods note that they are ineffective without established ties to legislators. For example, the Medical Association of Georgia long ago set up a list of doctors who have personal friendships with legislators and could intercede in the policy process.[20]

It should be remembered that the budget is a piece of legislation and must be passed like any other bill. House and Senate versions of the budget must be identical before being sent to the governor. Because the process examines expenditures in such detail, it is quite time consuming. The budget is often not completed until the final days of the legislative session. In many cases, the budget is the final bill passed before adjournment. The last-minute passage of the budget would make it difficult for a veto to be overridden. Georgia's governor is not likely to veto the budget but is likely to use the line-item veto (see chapter 7). However, the governor may not add to the budget and can only delete from it. In FY 2016, Governor Deal item-vetoed only one expenditure, totaling just over $800,000.[21]

There are, of course, winners and losers in the budgetary process. Those interests that represent large groups of mobilized voters are likely to be successful. So are major firms and business organizations that make important campaign contributions. Also, many agencies are protected by the presence of earmarked (dedicated) funds. The Georgia Department of Transportation (GDOT) is one agency protected to some degree because taxes collected on motor fuel throughout the state must be spent on roads. This restriction provides the GDOT somewhat greater freedom from the whims of the legislature than other departments that must fight for a piece of the budgetary pie. More than $866 million came from state motor fuel taxes in FY 2016, and the legislature added almost $24 million from general revenues. Still, almost $1.6 billion of the agency's $2.57 billion budget came from federal funds.[22]

The budget process thus has many stops and starts in which a variety of political players can have input. The result, it often seems, is that the budget is too complicated for average citizens to understand, and no one person has total control over the process. In Georgia, as in many other states, however, the governor has more formal control over budget outcomes than any other single individual. In recent years, when Georgia faced tight budgets and increased demands for services, the legislature has been supportive of most governors' requests for cuts and new sources for funding.

Georgia's Spending Patterns

One common way to examine policy is to consider the ways that governments allocate their resources. Without question, the state budget has grown substantially over the years. Figure 10.2 captures changes in state appropriations approved by the General Assembly and signed by the governor. Four points are worth emphasizing. First, the data cover fiscal years, namely, the state's budgetary year from July 1 through the following June 30, for example, FY 2016 ran from July 1, 2015, through June 30, 2016. Second, when the legislature convenes in January, it often amends the current budget, which had been adopted almost a year earlier. This makes sense as economic conditions and the state's revenue picture change over time.[23]

Third, the figure includes two lines. The top one captures spending included in the appropriations bill (current dollars). The bottom line represents "constant" dollars, namely, what the spending would be in 1980 dollars after sub-

Figure 10.2. State Appropriations in Current and Constant Dollars, 1980–2016

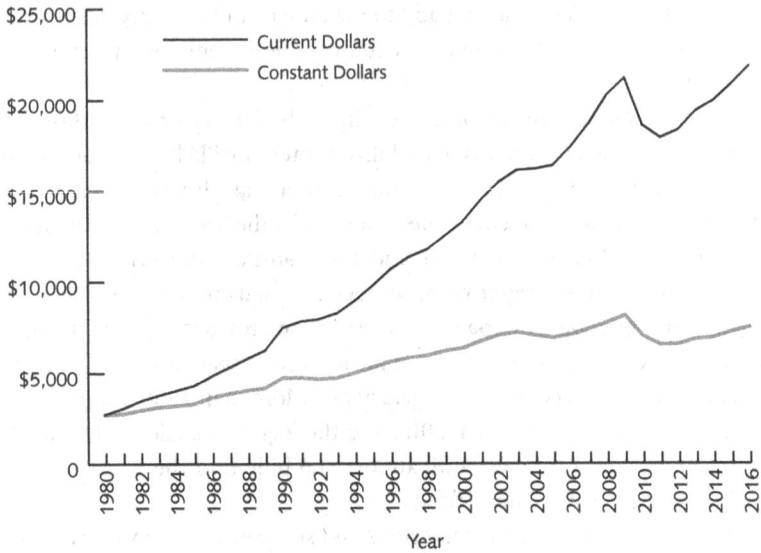

Source: Governor's Office of Planning and Budget 2016b, 34.

tracting the level of inflation that had occurred since then. In this case, the calculation is based on the U.S. Bureau of Labor Statistics' Consumer Price Index Calculator.[24] In a sense, the gap between the two lines represents how much of the growth in spending merely reflects increases in the price of goods and services rather than a decision to spend "new" money. This can also be illustrated with an example. Inflation was relatively high in the early 1980s. When the state increased spending from $2.7 billion in FY 1980 to $3 billion in 1981, it appears as a 12 percent jump. After factoring out inflation, though, it is really only 1.6 percent.

Fourth, the money that the General Assembly appropriates is not all the spending that the state devotes to various activities. Figure 10.3 covers only general funds that the state raises on its own. Substantial amounts come from the federal government for the state to use, often for fairly explicit purposes, while the state also gets restricted funds such as those from the lottery. In FY 2016, for example, the state appropriated almost $1 billion in lottery revenues and over $13 billion in federal funds, almost $7 billion of which went to health and nursing home programs and $1.6 billion went for transportation.[25]

The first billion-dollar budget occurred in 1967. State expenditures rose somewhat steadily until the 1970s, after which growth accelerated, which was

Figure 10.3. State Spending by Purpose, Fiscal Year 2016

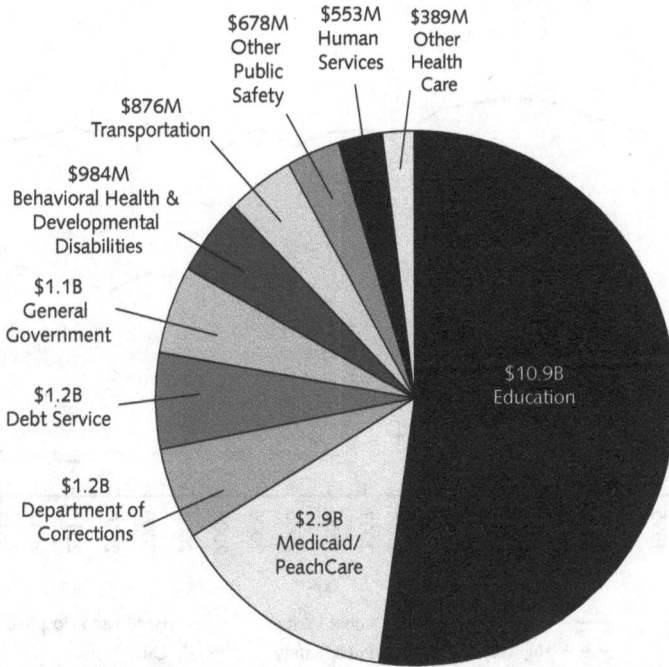

Source: Georgia Governor's Office of Planning and Budget 2016b.

due in part to increased federal aid and efforts to keep pace with inflation. As the figure indicates, budgetary growth seems less steep when adjusted for inflation. There were occasional dips as well, as during the recession of the early 1990s and the Great Recession, which began in 2008.

The budget for FY 1996 reached almost $10.7 billion, while the one for FY 2006 totaled $17.8 billion and then grew to $20.5 billion in FY 2008 before stagnating during the Great Recession, when the legislature cut spending 12 percent in FY 2009 and another 8.8 percent the following year. Expenditures did not reach $20 billion again until the FY 2014 budget was amended. With the state emerging from the economic slowdown, the budget increased, and Governor Deal proposed a budget for FY 2017 of $23.7 billion.[26]

The lion's share of state spending goes for education and health (see figure 10.3). As Georgia's budget has grown, there have been few shifts in the relative shares going to major functions (see figure 10.4). The data in the figure include

Figure 10.4. Percentage of Total State Expenditures Spent on Different Functions, 1995–2014

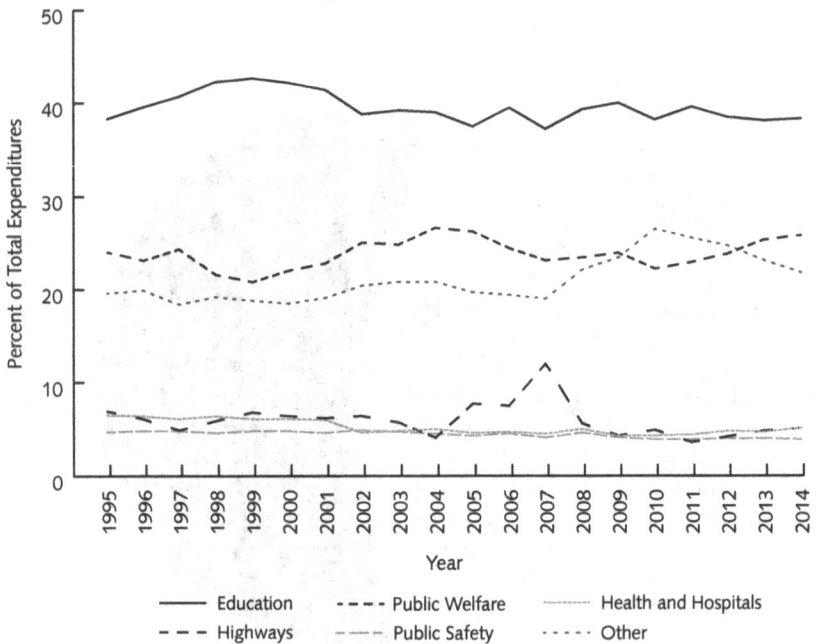

Source: U.S. Census Bureau, State Government Finances (annual), http://www.census.gov/govs/state /historical_data.html.

both money that the state spent directly and funds that it distributed to local governments such as school districts. Education, including K–12 and higher education, remains the "big ticket" item in Georgia's budget. It has commanded 40 percent or more of state spending since 1964, although it has trended lower since FY 2002. This drop is not due to regular cuts in education spending. Rather, education expenditures increased until FY 2011, but they were several hundred million dollars lower the next two years. Plus, spending in other areas fluctuated. For example, spending on highways dropped more than $400 million from 2003 to 2004 and then rose over $1.3 billion in 2005, when it reached $2.7 billion. Two years later, it jumped to $5 billion, but dropped back to $2.3 billion in FY 2008.

The "other" category includes a wide range of modest expenditures, including parks, recreation, and interest payments on debt. The only one that consistently exceeds $1 billion is trust fund payments, which include items such as unemployment compensation, retirement payments, and workers compensation. Some of the changes in figure 10.3 reflect shifting political priorities of governors and legislative leaders; others reflect pressures from interest groups and the features of existing or new federal programs.

The Georgia Constitution requires a balanced budget, but that does not mean that the state has no debt. States do their budgets differently from the national government, which finances its deficits by selling bonds to investors. States, on the other hand, do not go into debt to finance their overall operations. Rather, they sell bonds for long-term capital investments such as bridges, buildings, and major equipment, and they pay off the bonds over an extended period by building annual principal and interest payments into the state budget like any other expenditure. This is almost like a family living on its income but building mortgage payments into its budget until the house is paid for. For instance, the state appropriated $1.2 billion to fund general obligation debt in FY 2016.[27] States also set aside reserves, usually called "rainy day" funds, that can be used during difficult times. Georgia had over $1.5 billion in reserves in FY 2007. As the Great Recession worsened and the state drew on the reserves, the fund shrunk to barely over $100 million in FY 2009 and 2010. An improved economy allowed the fund to be replenished to over $862 million in FY 2014 and continue growing thereafter.[28]

Georgia's Revenue Sources

In addition to the annual decisions about spending on programs, the governor and the legislature face tough questions about how to raise revenue, which can have significant long-term fiscal and political consequences. To raise funds, Georgia's state government relies on taxes, fees, revenues from other governments, and borrowing (debt). In developing tax policies, states must consider what to tax, how to tax it, and at what rate. Like most states, Georgia once relied heavily on taxes applied to property, but the General Assembly adopted the individual and corporate income taxes in 1929 and the general sales tax in 1951. That made Georgia one of the earlier states to use an income tax but one of the later states to adopt a general sales tax. States are varied in their revenue systems, however. Five states (Alaska, Delaware, Montana, New Hampshire, and Oregon) do not have a general sales tax, although most state sales taxes exempt food and prescription drugs. Seven states do not use an individual income tax, and another two apply an income tax only to dividends and interest earned.[29]

Georgia's tax system has been regarded as somewhat regressive, that is, it takes a greater percentage from those with low incomes than from those with higher incomes. Progressive tax systems do just the opposite. Regressivity was due at one time to the application of the sales tax to necessities, particularly gro-

Figure 10.5. State Government Revenue Sources, 1995–2014

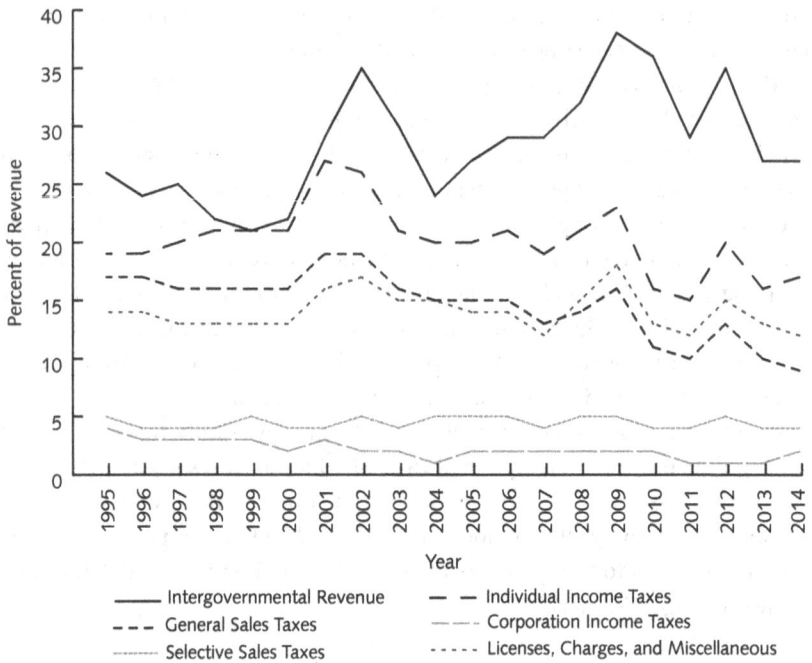

Source: U.S. Census Bureau, State Government Finances (annual), http://www.census.gov/govs/state/historical_data.html.

ceries. This criticism of the regressive tax system was a primary reason that the General Assembly passed a law in 1996 that phased out the sales tax on food by 1998, although the decision obviously resulted in a loss of revenue to the state. The income tax is not considered very progressive because the flat rate of 6 percent is applied to all income over $7,000 for individuals, and above $10,000 for couples, as opposed to having higher rates for six-figure and larger incomes.[30]

Today, Georgia derives most of its own revenues from the individual income tax and general sales tax (see figure 10.5). The latter was increased from 3 to 4 percent in 1989, with local governments having several options for increasing sales taxes with voter approval, which means that sales taxes can differ somewhat from place to place in Georgia. These revenue sources pale by comparison, though, with the share of funds coming from the national government.

The relative distribution of revenue shows some variation over time, especially swings in federal aid and the changing position of sales taxes and income taxes. This is most apparent during FY 2008–2012. Federal aid grew from $12.8

billion to $16.2 billion between FY 2009 and 2010. Meanwhile, as the economy worsened, individual income tax revenue dropped more than $1.8 billion between FY 2008 and 2010. Needless to say, federal money helped to plug this gap.

Georgia's tax system has been criticized for several reasons over the years in addition to being regressive. One is the degree to which it has been built on an ad hoc basis, sometimes as a result of short-term political considerations. Another target for discussion is the limited coverage of the sales tax, which applies to commodities but few of the personal and professional services that comprise a significant share of today's economy. Nor does it cover the full range of electronic commerce that competes with traditional retailers.[31]

The property tax has also been attacked on at least two grounds. First, critics argue that using the property tax to fund schools is both inefficient and unfair, particularly to those with no children in local public schools. Second, many complain that people wind up paying excessive taxes just because their property increases in value, even if the tax rate does not change. This can be especially burdensome for homeowners with fixed incomes, particularly seniors. Some local governments have responded to this dilemma by "freezing" homeowners' tax bills until they sell their property.[32]

Other criticisms are directed at tax breaks for certain activities or groups (e.g., the film industry, senior citizens). These provisions are known as "tax expenditures" because, while they are not a direct payment to an individual or company, they cost government lost revenue by allowing the taxpayer to keep more income than if the break did not exist. The Fiscal Research Center at Georgia State University prepares an annual report listing tax expenditures and estimates their magnitude. For example, the December 2015 report estimated that the film tax credit would cost the state $308 million in FY 2017.[33] Other research has found little relationship between business tax cuts and economic performance in the fifty states.[34]

A related issue is the degree to which the state has a diverse enough revenue base to weather a recession. Together, these issues pose potential problems for the state, although it remains to be seen whether governors and legislators are prepared to consider them systematically and carefully.[35]

Economic Development

State government leaders often see the promotion of economic development as one of their top priorities—if not their most important task. The major players in shaping development policy in most states are business groups and governors.[36] Policies to boost the private economy are often sold as essential to a state government's fiscal soundness. Generating business and job growth can also be important to politicians' reelection. However, critics often question how effective such efforts are and the extent to which policies do little to help small businesses and favor some industries over others.[37]

States compete intensively for new jobs and businesses. This practice may be especially true of the South, where financial incentives designed to lure manufacturers were pioneered decades ago. These include a variety of tax breaks, land, methods to reduce companies' loan costs, and a range of infrastructure improvements such as sewer and water, streets, and buildings. In general, the South has sold itself as a place of cheap labor and land, few labor unions, low levels of regulation, and generous government financial support—what many observers simply call "a good business climate." The trouble is that many states with such business climates also have low education and income levels. Moreover, rankings of states and localities often tell only part of a region's economic story. Indeed, firms might actually prefer and benefit more from lower tax rates rather than trying to qualify for selective incentives.[38]

Adopting incentives has often been compared to an "arms race" in which states try to outbid their neighbors in the incentives game. Indeed, states have tended to copy one another's policies. Perhaps the most seemingly fruitless use of incentives involves the movement of companies between the Missouri and Kansas sides of the border running through Metropolitan Kansas City.[39] As table 10.1 indicates, Georgia has actively sought to promote economic growth. The table has limitations, however. First, it does not include the level of commitment in dollar terms for each state. It is hard to quantify costs since data are often proprietary, with many incentives administered through the tax code. Second, the table omits local governments, which have extensive economic development policies of their own.

In addition to incentives, Georgia's efforts include the symbolism of renaming its lead agency the Department of Economic Development in 2004. In addition to trying to lure outside investment to the state, Georgia has increased its emphasis on helping existing businesses expand and promoting Georgia products overseas. By the mid-1990s, for instance, Georgia had provided training for over 165,000 workers at 2,300 companies during the previous thirty years, including employees of a large credit card processing facility in Columbus. The state also added infrastructure such as improvements to the ports in Savannah and Brunswick, as well as adding inland "ports" that serve as distribution centers for railroads, which ship containers directly from coastal docks to the centers rather than having a tractor-trailer drive each container inland.[40]

As the table suggests, Georgia has avoided a few riskier strategies, particularly using general obligation bonds, which guarantee the use of tax revenue to pay off the debt sold to investors buying the bonds. In contrast, Georgia uses revenue bonds, which are paid off with funds from the company benefiting from the state aid. However, many activities not supported with direct aid from the

Table 10.1. State Economic Development Policies, 2015

Type of Policy	Number of States Using Policy	Used in Georgia?
Financial Assistance		
State Industrial Development Authority	45	Yes
Private Development Credit Corporation	40	Yes
State Revenue Bond Financing	48	Yes
State General Obligation Bond Financing	29	No
State Loans for Building Construction	40	Yes
State Loans for Equipment/Machinery	42	Yes
State Loan Guarantees for Building Construction	28	Yes
State Loan Guarantees for Equipment/Machinery	31	Yes
State Financing Aid for Existing Plant Expansion	48	Yes
State Incentive for Industry in High Unemployment Areas	42	Yes
Tax Incentives		
Corporate Income Tax Exemption	41	Yes
Personal Income Tax Exemption	39	Yes
Excise Tax Exemption	30	Yes
Exemption/Moratorium on Land/Capital Improvements	42	Yes
Exemption/Moratorium on Equipment/Machinery	46	Yes
Inventory Tax Exemption on Goods in Transit (free port)	49	Yes
Tax Exemption on Manufacturers' Inventories	49	Yes
Sales/Use Tax Exemption on New Equipment	49	Yes
Tax Exemption on Raw Materials Used in Manufacturing	50	Yes
Tax Incentive for Creation of Jobs	46	Yes
Tax Incentive for Industrial Investment	46	Yes
Tax Credits for Use of Specialized State Products	8	No
Tax Stabilization Agreements for Specialized Industries	12	No
Tax Exemption to Encourage Research and Development	42	Yes
Accelerated Depreciation of Industrial Equipment	41	Yes

Source: "State Incentive Programs," *Site Selection Magazine*, November 2015, http://siteselection.com /issues/2015/nov/images/1511IncentivesChartswNotes.pdf.

state benefit from tax breaks. They can also receive financial support from local governments. Some policies provide benefits that vary geographically, as with Georgia's tax credit (reduction in income taxes) for companies that create jobs: the size of the credit depends on the economic condition of the county where the firm is located.

In 2015, Georgia maintained several international offices to promote investment in the state and to help Georgia firms export their products or services: Brazil, Canada, Chile, China, Colombia, Germany, Great Britain, Israel, Japan, Korea, and Mexico.[41] International efforts often include trade missions to significant countries, with the governor often being the symbolic head of the group.[42]

Many economic development efforts involve multiple incentives, especially in cases involving large firms. For instance, the state's failed efforts to get Daimler-Chrysler to build an automobile manufacturing plant near Savannah involved land, tax breaks, job training, highway improvements, and other benefits.[43] In 2006, Korean auto manufacturer Kia Motors chose Georgia for its first American facility. The plant was projected to cost $1.2 billion, employ roughly 2,500 workers at its Troup County site, and stimulate growth in related businesses. The state and local government incentives for Kia were reported at roughly $400 million, including state purchase of the site, road and other infrastructure improvements, a railroad spur, property tax abatements, tax credits for job creation, and job training. All told, the package was thought to cost $160,000 in incentives per new job, with workers' earnings averaging about $50,000 annually, plus benefits.[44] The state was also successful in capturing Mercedes-Benz's U.S. headquarters in Metropolitan Atlanta and a major Caterpillar factory in the Athens area. Georgia lost out to South Carolina, though, in attracting Volvo's first U.S. manufacturing facility and courted GE when the company reconsidered its Connecticut headquarters but eventually chose Boston.[45]

Local governments and business groups (e.g., chambers of commerce, convention and visitors bureaus) also compete with one another by using incentives and marketing their areas as locations for manufacturing, transportation, tourism, retirement, and other industries. However, a dilemma arises if communities compete by offering deals to firms that might have located or expanded in Georgia anyway. For example, Georgia attracted NCR's headquarters from Ohio only to have it move from Gwinnett County to Midtown Atlanta, which earned the company additional tax breaks.[46] In other cases, corporate investment might occur seemingly apart from state and local efforts, as with CNN reshaping its Atlanta presence and the pressure from the gaming industry to bring casinos to Georgia, possibly in the face of substantial opposition.[47]

Research suggests that financial incentives have limited effects on firms' location decisions, which are based primarily on market factors. Companies have become what many call "footloose"—having little local involvement or loyalty and willing to move, seemingly at the drop of a hat. As an example, Newell Brands moved to Georgia from Illinois in 2003, but it announced a relocation of its headquarters to New Jersey in 2016 following acquisition of another company and $16 million in incentives from the New Jersey Economic Development Authority.[48] Thus, neighboring states or communities may end up competing on a "level playing field," but each of them might have given away more financially than was necessary to attract a firm. Indeed, one research organization has raised concerns that Georgia is giving away too much tax revenue in exchange for questionable economic gains—a trade-off they called "Don't tax and they will come?"[49] Moreover, it is unclear whether development policies can exert much influence on states' economic conditions.[50]

Transportation

Georgia has a complex system of transportation, particularly in the Metro Atlanta region, with often overlapping authority that impedes responsibility for maintenance and development. Georgia has 473 airports (105 of which are commercial facilities), including Hartsfield Jackson International Airport, the nation's busiest airport; 5,000 miles of railways; almost 120,000 miles of public highways; and two major seaports and two inland ports.[51] There are fourteen urban and two rural transportation systems with the largest counties and cities operating more extensive systems, including Fulton, DeKalb, and Clayton counties' MARTA system and commuter bus systems such as the CCT in Cobb County, Gwinnett County Transit, and the recently opened Atlanta streetcar.[52] Finally, the state boasts thousands of miles of bicycle and pedestrian trails, including the developing BeltLine, which eventually will encircle the city of Atlanta with walking and bike trails as well as proposed public transportation.[53]

For most Georgians, discussions of transportation center on the time it takes to journey to work. In this respect, Georgia does not compare well to other states. Georgians take an average of twenty-seven minutes to commute to work, placing it among the eight worst states in the country. Some commuters in the metro Atlanta area have commute times in the forty-minute range, and in fact Atlantans average thirty minutes for their commutes.[54] In addition, those in the Metro Atlanta area have the longest average commuting distance in the entire country, averaging more than twelve miles to get to work.[55] While the percentage of commuters who carpool in Atlanta (10.4 percent) on average is higher than in other metropolitan areas (9.4 percent), the percentage of solo drivers (77.7 percent) is also higher than the national average for other cities (76 percent).[56]

Another aspect of transportation setting Georgia apart from other states is its major airport. Located ten miles from the center of Atlanta's business district,

Hartsfield-Jackson Atlanta is the largest airport in the world in both passenger and aircraft traffic. In 2015, 101 million people traveled through the airport. The airport offers air service to over 150 U.S. destinations and more than 80 international destinations in fifty-two countries, with over 2,700 arrivals and departures daily. The Maynard H. Jackson Jr. International Terminal opened in 2012, providing international travelers with a dedicated terminal building.

The airport serviced 636 tons of cargo in 2015.[57] It is the largest single location of work for employees in Georgia, with 58,000 people reporting to work at the airport, and a total payroll of $2.4 billion. The economic impact of the airport is estimated at $32.5 billion.[58] Clearly, the airport represents a significant contribution to transportation in the state. This role will continue in the years ahead with a $6 billion expansion to update the domestic terminal and concourses, introduce new features such as a hotel, and eventually add another concourse and runway.[59]

Railroads in Georgia are dominated by two large private companies, CSX and Norfolk Southern. Rail passenger service in the state is provided by Amtrak, with stations located in Atlanta, Gainesville, Jesup, Savannah, and Toccoa.

The Georgia Department of Transportation

In Georgia, the Department of Transportation (GDOT) has authority to plan, construct, and maintain highways and bridges. It also has some planning and financial responsibilities for airports, ports, railways, public transportation systems, and even bike paths and trails.[60] The GDOT as it is currently organized was created out of the existing state highway commission by then-governor Jimmy Carter in 1972. The GDOT's mission is to make transportation safe and efficient throughout the state.

The GDOT is most visible to Georgia residents as it maintains and upgrades Georgia's highways. Georgia has over 1,200 miles of interstate highway and 20,000 miles of federal and state highways.[61] The GDOT maintains a database of traffic patterns across the state, and specific information on almost 22,000 intersections and roadways is recorded by the department for planning use.[62] Information and data on construction and accidents is available on both state maintained and private Internet sites.[63]

The GDOT is governed by a board, which is elected by a caucus of the membership of the Georgia General Assembly for each of Georgia's U.S. congressional districts. Board members are elected in staggered five-year terms, with two to three members coming up for election each year. The board is assisted by a commissioner, who oversees the nine divisions of the department.

The GDOT maintains seven district offices throughout the state, which oversee the department's six thousand employees and $2.5 billion operating budget.[64] In addition to in-house employees, the GDOT offers contracts to private companies for much of the work to plan, construct, and maintain highways under the jurisdiction of the department. Unlike some of Georgia's other departments, which rely predominately on state appropriations, the GDOT has a strong supplemental revenue base provided by the federal government, the state's motor fuel tax, and other highway-use taxes and fees. The motor fuel tax is collected from individual drivers as a portion of the amount paid for fuel at regular gas retailers. In addition, the GDOT often receives funds through the U.S. Department of Transportation. These funds often are earmarked for special projects, such as those described below. Competition among private vendors for GDOT contracts is intense, and a system of sealed bidding is used to determine which vendor will receive contracts.

Transportation and transportation funding remains a serious and complicated issue for the state of Georgia. Infrastructure issues and growth, combined with a policy aversion to broad based tax increases and lack of any dominant regional planning, have all led to problems. Georgia primarily funds its transportation needs with a combination of state motor fuel taxes and federal funds. However, as a 2014 report of the joint study committee on critical transportation infrastructure funding noted, "This funding model, particularly its reliance on motor fuel taxes levied at both the state and federal levels, creates numerous and serious challenges in meeting Georgia's transportation needs."[65] Forty-eight percent of state-maintained roads and bridges are considered in poor or fair condition. A recent *AJC* article on transportation noted that "Metro Atlanta has been ranked 91st out of 100 among major metro regions nationwide for access to transit. Atlantans have one of the worst commutes in the nation, with the average driver wasting on average over $900 in fuel per year sitting in traffic. Prospective businesses rank our transportation woes and our inability to address them among of their chief concerns about moving to metro Atlanta."[66]

The report notes that the gas tax and declining federal spending leaves the state short of funds for critical transportation needs. The report goes on to observe that Georgia currently ranks forty-ninth in terms of state spending per capita on roads, and its investment in road construction and maintenance is relatively small compared to some peer states with similarly sized populations or road systems. Given that Georgia's population is estimated to grow to almost fifteen million by 2030 (a growth rate of almost 50 percent from 2010),[67] transportation funding will be critical.

MARTA and the Atlanta streetcar are additional indicators of the difficulties Atlanta confronts. Until 2015 with the passage of HB 213, MARTA had to use 50 percent of its revenues for operations, with the rest going toward infrastructure maintenance. The limitation went back to the 1965 law creating MARTA. This severely limited the ability of MARTA to grow or meet current challenges. The

Atlanta streetcar has its own set of issues and problems. The city of Atlanta and MARTA share responsibility for the $98 million system that runs in downtown Atlanta. Under the arrangement, Atlanta owns and operates the system, while MARTA provides "active management" and expertise, at least until the city has the technical capabilities to take the reins. Thus, no one authority has overall responsibility for maintenance and operation. This has led to numerous complaints including lack of leadership and staffing issues.

The Future of Transportation Policy in Georgia

Despite these issues, some change has occurred. In 2015 the legislature enacted a package of tax reforms to generate about $900 million in additional money for Georgia's roads and bridges in the first year. That total includes $170 million shifted over from Georgia's general fund each year, with the remainder consisting of new revenues. Among other things, the bill raised the gasoline tax on cars and levies an annual fee on electric, propane, and natural gas-powered vehicles of $300 for commercial vehicles and $200 for noncommercial vehicles. In 2016, the state legislature allowed the city of Atlanta to pursue a $2.5 billion expansion of MARTA. The MARTA expansion, which is likely to include a long-hoped-for light rail system along the BeltLine, would be funded with a 0.5 percent sales tax increase that Atlanta voters first have to approve.[68]

Coordination between MARTA and the city of Atlanta is not the only transportation management problem in the state. In most cases, even the GDOT is required to coordinate transportation planning with a multitude of other agencies and departments. For example, the Georgia Ports Authority operates all Georgia ports, and the National Transportation Safety Board (NTSB), the National Highway Traffic Safety Administration of the U.S. Department of Transportation are stakeholders in establishing transportation policy in the state. Although some argue that the GDOT is too powerful, it is clear that the fragmentation of policy in this area contributes to sometimes slow reaction of the state to problems in transportation.

While Atlanta dominates the Atlanta region, the city itself is only one member of a greater metropolitan area. Atlanta's population is less than half a million and that represents less than 10 percent of the entire region. Several of the counties opted out of MARTA at its creation and operate their own independent transportation systems.

There has been some effort in recent years to plan transportation in Georgia in a more systematic manner. The Georgia Regional Transportation Authority (GRTA) was established to coordinate transportation planning in the thirteen Georgia counties of Metro Atlanta in order to address mobility, air quality, and land use and how they relate to the transportation needs of Metro Atlanta, including both roads and public transit. It came about in large part because the numerous cities and counties in the region could not effectively (or would not at all) work with one another to achieve a comprehensive solution to the area's traffic woes and increasing summertime smog problems. However, it is clear that the Georgia Department of Transportation dominates the planning process statewide, and any attempts to coordinate transportation regionally must include the GDOT.

Problems and issues still remain. Georgia remains one of the bottom five states in highway spending. Regional distrust remains. One effort to raise taxes for transportation through a special local option sales tax (T-SPLOST) was voted down 63 to 37 percent along suburban and urban lines. "Voters in Atlanta's urban core strongly supported T-SPLOST, while it was defeated in the suburbs by people reluctant to support projects outside of their community."[69] Many argue that (mostly white) suburban counties reject connecting with the larger regional community.[70]

Environmental Policy

The environment and environmental concerns have played a major role in American political life for much of the latter part of the twentieth century and through the first two decades of the twenty-first century. Environmental policies impact all residents. They are also the result of a variety of influences by the private sector and from government at all levels. Nonprofit and nongovernmental organizations also seek to make themselves heard in the environmental debate, making it one of the most contentious policy areas. Recent controversies focus on whether market solutions may be beneficial to address some environmental problems, and to what degree property rights permit land use that may not be in the best interests of communities as a whole.

Congress created the U.S. Environmental Protection Agency (EPA) in 1970, a national agency dedicated to protecting environmental resources. The EPA was, by executive order, "reorganized" from parts of the Executive Branch by transferring units from existing organizations into a new independent agency. Control of air quality, among other things, was transferred from the Department of Health, Education, and Welfare, while control of water quality came from the Interior Department; radiation protection standards came from the Atomic Energy Commission and the Federal Radiation Council.

States have taken an increasingly active role in environmental policy, as is evidenced by their increased spending over time. In 2003, states spent $15.1 billion on the environment. By 2013 that total had increased to almost $20 billion, and states were spending $51 per capita on environmental programs.[71] Georgia spent over $207 million on the environment for FY 2013 and predicts an increase the coming fiscal year.

The states are the primary sources of environmental data, collecting information on water, air, and land quality. Much of the budget of the states is spent on data collection and monitoring of the environment, often in collaboration with federal agencies, universities, and nonprofit organizations. It is estimated that only one-third of all spending on the environment comes from federal sources, and the federal government has cut back on environmental spending since even before the recession of 2008.[72]

While several states have cut back on environmental spending, Georgia has not, although the increase has been small, with an overall 3.4 percent increase from 2011 to 2013. The 2016 budget and 2017 projected budget continue to increase spending on the environment. However, this small increase stands in marked contrast to many of Georgia's neighbors. In a similar time span, Florida decreased environmental spending by 38 percent, and Louisiana decreased spending by 4 percent.

Enforcement of environmental regulations and law is under the authority of the Georgia Environmental Protection Division, and it works in concert with and is a division of the Georgia Department of Natural Resources.[73] The division is composed of three branches, air protection, land protection, and watershed protection, and has the responsibility for implementing state and federal environmental laws on air, land, and water resources.

Air Protection

The Federal Clean Air Act requires each state to meet federal standards for air pollution. Under the Federal Clean Air Act, the U.S. Environmental Protection Agency oversees national air-quality standards. Individual states can enact stricter air standards if they choose, though each state must adhere to the federal plan. States implement federal air standards through an EPA-approved state implementation plan.

State implementation plans are generally required for an area of the state that has been designated a nonattainment zone. Many metropolitan areas, including Atlanta, do not comply with federal air quality standards as set forth in the Clean Air statutes.[74] Policies in these jurisdictions are required by federal law to have no negative impact on ozone and fine particulate matters such carbon monoxide, lead, or other particulate levels. Most Georgia residents encounter these policies through the promulgation and regulation of auto emission standards by Georgia's Clean Air Force.[75] The standards vary according to the area of the state in which cars are registered. However, these policies also have an impact on corporations. Air permits are issued under these standards, and new companies must explain how their businesses will control emissions to comply with the standards. One recent controversy is the potential opening of a coal-burning electrical production facility in the middle of Georgia. Although such a facility might add one hundred new jobs, some residents were concerned about the air emissions from the plant and aimed to block its opening.

Land Quality and Property Rights

One challenge facing Georgia's environmental future is the growth in population and corresponding demand for development. The Georgia Planning Act, enacted in 1989, remains the law governing land use and planning.[76] Included in the provisions are regulations regarding development of wetlands, water basins, and mountains. The Georgia Land Conservation Council (formerly the Georgia Community Greenspace Program adopted in 2000) requires that rapidly growing counties set aside 20 percent of all undeveloped land to be preserved. This program is funded in part through state allocations and in part from donations from individuals and nonprofit organizations.

The Georgia Department of Community Affairs, through its office of Planning and Environmental Management, oversees and works with communities to develop land and property. Services include assistance with solid waste management and recycling as well as regional and local planning and development.

The state also has a number of other programs for land conservation, including a Solid Waste Trust Fund, which is financed by a one-dollar fee paid by residents purchasing tires. This fund is to be spent on cleanup of illegal dump areas in the state. However, state officials have used the fund for other purposes. As of 2012, of the $57,624,708 raised in fees since 2004, $37,584,317, or over 65 percent, has been redirected to other agencies.[77] Recently, new legislation has sought to protect the fund.[78] Other recent initiatives include the reclamation of unused rail lines to provide park space or walking/biking trails, such as the highly popular Silver Comet Trail in Cobb County and the ongoing development of the Beltline Park in the city of Atlanta.[79]

One controversial issue related to land regulation is eminent domain. Eminent domain is the taking of private property for public use, and federal, state, and local governments are permitted to condemn property and take ownership for such a purpose. However, the Fifth Amendment to the U.S. Constitution specifically requires that property owners in eminent domain cases be awarded just compensation following due process for the taking of their land. Just compensation is usually determined by market analyses of property values.

In some instances, property owners have also been compensated when nearby public-use facilities, such as a landfill or an airport, negatively impact property values. The debate over just compensation is generally limited to property owners in specific disputes and generally settled on individual bases by the courts. Two debates over the meaning of the takings clause have been litigated before the U.S. Supreme Court. One concerns the meaning of public use. Traditionally, courts have given great deference to legislative determinations of public use, allowing for example, condemnation of blighted urban areas to be sold to a private developer.[80]

However, hostility to such actions has intensified since a June 2005 decision by the U.S. Supreme Court upholding such a condemnation in Connecticut.[81] Recent controversies over eminent domain in Georgia focus on whether governments can take property from homeowners to use for economic development. In some cases, homeowners have found that local governments attempted to take property that is then developed by private interests rather than for a more general public purpose such as roads, parks, or schools. In 2006, Georgia's voters by a vote of 83 percent endorsed a constitutional amendment requiring that elected officials formally vote for or against each use of eminent domain in their communities. This amendment complemented property rights protections passed earlier in the year by the state legislature.[82]

Water

Water quality and usage are arguably the single most important issue of environmental policy in the state, at least in terms of dollars spent, legislative debate, and judicial intervention. Fueled in part by the explosive growth of the Metropolitan Atlanta area, Georgia, Florida, and Alabama have a long-standing dispute over the Chattahoochee River, both in terms of water quality and the use of water from the river. While neighboring states continue to blame metro growth for the damage to quality and quantity, Atlanta has reduced its water consumption over the past decade. The local water district estimates that the region will use 25 percent less water by 2050 than was estimated in 2009.[83]

To deal with this specific litigation and other issues, in 2014 Georgia governor Nathan Deal established a new state office for the management of water resources in the state led by a "water czar," Judson Turner, a lawyer and the director of Georgia's Environmental Protection Division. According to the governor's office, the agency is "an office for interagency coordination and management of water resources."[84]

To date, significant issues still remain. The ongoing litigation with neighboring states remains, and the special master appointed by the Supreme Court to oversee the case warned that his decision will leave neither side totally satisfied and urged Georgia and Florida to seek a settlement. Much of the necessity of the litigation is a result of Georgia's dependency on the Chattahoochee for its water supply. Water consumption and lack of reservoir capacity remain an issue. The

Water Supply Program remains far from its goal of increasing the state's water supply.[85]

The debate about the Chattahoochee appears to be one of appropriate usage. Besides drinkable water, the river is also used to produce electricity at downstream facilities, to make the river navigable for barge traffic, for recreation, to maintain wildlife ecosystems, and to support industries dependent on water, such as Florida's oyster industry. In addition, the source of the litigation is more than just Metro Atlanta. Agriculture actually uses most of the water between North Georgia and Florida. Georgia's cotton and peanut farmers use the Flint River and underground aquifers to water their produce. The Flint River empties into the Chattahoochee just north of the Florida state line.

Already the litigation has had an impact. For example, a suit forced the city of Atlanta to overhaul its sewer system at a cost of more than $2 billion, paid for in part by a sales tax increase.[86] In addition, widespread replacement of inefficient toilets, improved detection and repair of leaks, and tiered pricing that charges higher rates for heavy users have reduced consumption. Some attempts to co-ordinate water use have been made, notably the Metro Atlanta Water District and the newly formed Middle Chattahoochee Water Coalition. Coastal areas of the state have different concerns, including saltwater intrusion, while farming areas are more focused on agricultural runoff. In urban areas, wastewater and construction runoff are additional topics of concern. Statewide water planning is also under way and will be crucial to the success of any water plan.

One suggested policy for water quality is the use of "trading water rights," by which persons or organizations that have water use permits can sell all or portions of their water use rights to other parties. Many argue that such a system would create market efficiencies and better define water use limitations. Others argue that market approaches will result in reduced regulation of water quality and overuse of water resources.[87] Another controversial issue related to transfer of water rights is the transfer of water from one basin to another. Water basins are defined naturally by the direction of water runoff and groundwater flow. So-called interbasin transfers allow areas of high use to take water from other water basins where demand is not as high. Interbasin transfers often are a result of one community pumping water from a nearby basin into its water system. Proponents of interbasin transfer note that such water use encourages more uniform growth and land development, as well as making efficient use of water resources.[88] Critics argue that this adversely affects downstream water use for natural and manmade communities.[89] This debate is complicated by the fact that many communities are located in more than one basin. Interbasin transfers are used in many Metro Atlanta counties, but new provisions for such use are certain to generate debate.

The Future of Environmental Policy

In the years ahead, environmental policy in Georgia will rely on new technologies for air, water, and land quality. Proposals for testing auto emissions as cars drive by monitors are already being discussed, and new methods for passive water and air quality testing are in use and proposed for the future.[90] It is also likely that the state legislature, which has deferred to regulatory agencies in the past, will take up environmental planning more in the future. Water planning districts are being institutionalized, and the General Assembly has begun to provide state fiscal resources for planning.

Essential to success are more statewide coordination and regional planning with neighboring states. The so-called water wars between Alabama, Georgia, and Florida are nonproductive and slow efforts by all three states to control pollution. Market approaches may also be an important trend for the future of environmental policy in Georgia.[91]

Education

Education plays a key role in American society. James Madison famously noted that "a well instructed people alone can permanently be a free people."[92] Almost 150 years later, Chief Justice Warren echoed this sentiment in *Brown v. Board of Education* (1954). He wrote that "education is perhaps the most important function of state and local governments. . . . It is the very foundation of good citizenship. . . . It is doubtful that any child may reasonably be expected to succeed in life if he is denied the opportunity of an education."[93]

School Funding

Because of its importance, free, publicly financed education has been paramount to the attainment of many goals promulgated in American public discourse. Of course, all public education in the United States is not equal. There is often significant disparity in the resources available and money spent for schools within any particular state as well as across states.[94] This disparity is a direct result of the local financing of public schools. Since much of public education is financed by local property taxes, and because some districts are far wealthier than others, school districts that are more affluent have far more resources to use and spend on education than do poorer school districts.

In Georgia, funding is a combination of local, state, and federal financing. For many years in the state, federal dollars accounted for about 10 percent of the total, with state funding accounting for about 50 percent, and local funding (property taxes) accounting for the remaining 40 percent. In this structure,

Georgia parallels most other states. Funding for education is shared among levels of government. Federal funds account for 5–10 percent of the education budgets of the fifty states. In the last twenty years, state governments have assumed a larger role for education funding than in the more distant past. However, education funding in Georgia by the state decreased sharply following the recession of 2008, and although there has been an upturn of state funding in the past few fiscal years, it remains well below levels in the early part of the first decade of the twenty-first century.

According to 2013 Census Bureau figures, state revenue accounted for 43.5 percent of education funding, while local revenue accounted for 46.2 percent of federal spending.[95] Federal spending constituted the balance, or slightly over 10 percent, which is within historical norms. This FY 2013 spending represented almost a 15 percent decrease in per pupil spending by the state from 2008.[96]

Although many states have decreased school funding, Georgia's decrease in spending since 2008 represented the single largest percentage decrease in education spending for any state. Much of this reduction is attributable to the decrease in state funding, although some of it was a result of a drop in property tax revenue due to decreased property values and weakness in the housing market. For example, from 2002 to 2015 "local revenue per student declined in 89 districts by an average of 20 percent in inflation-adjusted dollars. These districts enroll nearly 80 percent of public school students."[97]

As a result, for 2013 Georgia ranked thirty-eighth in per pupil expenditure of all states,[98] representing a drop in ranking from twenty-second among the states in 2002. There is significant concern over the lack of state funding, with several organizations noting that it has caused budget shortfalls in spending at the local level. According to one critic, this reduction represented a drop of $439 per student from what the students should have received based on the Quality Basic Education (QBE) formula approved by the legislature in 1985.[99] Adjusted for inflation, Georgia spends less per pupil now than it did in 2002, although more than it did in the years immediately following the Great Recession.

As figures 10.3 and 10.4 indicated, funding for Georgia's public schools and colleges remains the single largest item in the state budget, accounting for just over 50 percent of the allocated spending with more than $10 billion allocated to education. Georgia spends less per pupil ($10,370) than the U.S. average of $12,380 (see table 10.2).

Controversies over funding disparity in public education have arisen in many states, including Georgia, and have led to litigation. Initially, opponents of unequal financing sued under the Equal Protection Clause of the Fourteenth Amendment to the U.S. Constitution, arguing that using local property taxes to fund public education was a denial of the equal protection of the law because of the disparity in financing among school districts. Simply put, districts with

Table 10.2. State Spending per Pupil, by Revenue Source, Fiscal Year 2014

Rank	Elementary-Secondary Education Revenue							
	Total		*From Federal Sources*		*From State Sources*		*From Local Sources*	
	US (average)	$12,380	US (average)	$1,126	US (average)	$5,650	US (average)	$5,603
1	DC	29,427	DC	2,940	VT	16,009	DC	26,487
2	NY	22,587	AK	2,448	AK	13,025	NY	12,332
3	NJ	20,191	LA	1,832	HI	10,624	NJ	11,541
4	CT	19,519	HI	1,682	WY	9,626	CT	11,205
5	AK	19,415	NM	1,587	DE	9,471	MA	9,463
6	WY	18,498	SD	1,495	NY	8,986	PA	9,368
7	VT	18,103	MT	1,475	MN	8,464	NH	9,013
8	MA	17,315	ND	1,444	AR	8,053	RI	8,990
9	PA	16,644	MS	1,436	NJ	7,812	IL	8,063
10	RI	16,580	RI	1,418	IN	7,483	MD	8,017
11	MD	16,072	WV	1,357	CT	7,475	WY	7,632
12	DE	15,837	VT	1,283	NM	7,341	ME	7,371
13	NH	15,320	DE	1,273	WV	7,182	NE	7,292
14	IL	14,200	NY	1,268	MI	7,155	OH	6,829
15	ME	14,101	KY	1,267	MD	7,092	VA	6,325
16	ND	13,478	CA	1,262	MA	6,966	WI	5,945
17	OH	13,467	PA	1,262	WA	6,814	MO	5,462
18	MN	13,340	AZ	1,251	ND	6,784	SD	5,461
19	HI	12,621	WY	1,240	KS	6,537	ND	5,250
20	MI	12,584	NE	1,208	IA	6,243	LA	5,192
21	NE	12,514	AR	1,198	RI	6,172	CO	5,161
22	WI	12,506	MI	1,185	PA	6,014	TX	5,099
23	WV	12,309	TN	1,175	NV	5,921	DE	5,092
24	IA	12,072	TX	1,163	KY	5,782	SC	4,996
25	LA	12,045	FL	1,129	ME	5,667	IA	4,910
26	IN	11,955	SC	1,127	CA	5,660	GA	4,794
27	VA	11,846	IL	1,117	WI	5,603	MT	4,571
28	KS	11,596	AL	1,090	OH	5,571	FL	4,549
29	MT	11,566	NC	1,076	MT	5,521	OR	4,447
30	WA	11,562	GA	1,073	NH	5,435	MI	4,244
31	SC	11,412	OH	1,067	OR	5,393	AZ	4,232
32	MO	11,179	OK	1,066	NC	5,375	KS	4,198
33	NM	10,753	ME	1,064	SC	5,288	MN	4,068

Table 10.2. (*continued*)

Rank	Total		From Federal Sources		From State Sources		From Local Sources	
	US (average)	$12,380	US (average)	$1,126	US (average)	$5,650	US (average)	$5,603
34	CA	10,702	MO	997	AL	5,236	AK	3,941
35	OR	10,677	WA	992	LA	5,022	CA	3,780
36	AR	10,573	IN	977	IL	5,021	WV	3,770
37	KY	10,533	MD	964	MO	4,721	WA	3,756
38	GA	10,370	WI	958	ID	4,698	TN	3,650
39	CO	10,319	IA	919	VA	4,644	IN	3,495
40	TX	10,191	NV	908	GA	4,503	KY	3,484
41	SD	10,087	MA	886	MS	4,491	OK	3,381
42	AL	9,607	ID	877	CO	4,340	AL	3,281
43	NV	9,566	VA	877	OK	4,304	MS	3,068
44	FL	9,207	NH	873	TN	4,129	UT	2,945
45	MS	8,995	KS	861	NE	4,014	NV	2,737
46	TN	8,953	CT	839	UT	3,976	NC	2,219
47	OK	8,751	NJ	837	TX	3,928	ID	1,833
48	NC	8,670	OR	836	FL	3,528	NM	1,826
49	AZ	8,599	CO	818	SD	3,131	AR	1,322
50	UT	7,650	MN	808	AZ	3,116	VT	812
51	ID	7,408	UT	729	DC	(X)	HI	314

Source: Governing the State and Localities, http://www.governing.com/gov-data/education-data/state-education-spending-per-pupil-data.html

a larger and wealthier property-tax base could spend much more on public education than those with a poorer property-tax base. This disparity is most pronounced between rural and urban school districts and their wealthy suburban counterpart districts. For example, in Georgia, the "doughnut" around the hole—the more affluent counties of Cobb, Gwinnett, and Fayette, that surround the city of Atlanta, have a greater property-tax base than Atlanta or rural counties to the north and south. This allows these more affluent counties to spend more on education and can result in higher rated schools in many parts of these counties as compared to the rest of the state.

However, in *San Antonio Independent School District v. Rodriquez* (1973), the U.S. Supreme Court ruled that unequal financing for education did not violate the Equal Protection Clause of the U.S. Constitution.[100] That is, "the Constitution did not prohibit the government from providing different services to children in poor school districts than it did to children in wealthy school districts."[101]

This action effectively precluded any further court action at the federal level and ended the first wave of court-ordered education finance reform. However, the ruling did not stop further state court action or state legislative action. For example, one month after *Rodriguez*, the New Jersey Supreme Court, in *Robinson v. Cahill*, overturned the New Jersey educational finance system.[102] As of December 2009, forty-four states have experienced some form of state education finance litigation,[103] while a few other states have had legislative attempts to correct revenue disparities. Instead of relying on the U.S. Constitution, state litigants started to base their cases on state constitutions. Initial efforts focused on state constitutional equal protection clauses and were mostly unsuccessful; however almost all states, including Georgia, have state constitutional provisions guaranteeing a free public education. Georgia devotes an entire article of its constitution to education. Section 1, paragraph 1 states:

> Public education; free public education prior to college or postsecondary level; support by taxation. *The provision of an adequate public education for the citizens shall be a primary obligation of the State of Georgia. Public education for the citizens prior to the college or postsecondary level shall be free* and shall be provided for by taxation. The expense of other public education shall be provided for in such manner and in such amount as may be provided by law.[104]

Litigants have sued using the notion of "adequacy" to force states to equalize public financing of education. In many states, although not in Georgia, litigants have had much more success using these state education clauses to enforce the meaning of an "adequate" education on school funding. However, at the heart of the debate is the fact that more-affluent school districts do not want to subsidize education in poorer school districts, while poor school districts are increasingly looking to the state for supplemental sources of income.

Although such cases in Georgia have been unsuccessful to date, the state has not been immune from this effort. An early lawsuit found initial support from the judiciary, with a Georgia trial court finding the state's system of financing public education unconstitutional under the Equal Protection Clause. However, the state supreme court upheld the system in *McDaniel v. Thomas* in 1981.[105] The court did note that there were significant disparities in educational opportunities in Georgia and that school finance issues were justiciable; however, it upheld the state's school funding system under the equal protection and education clauses of the state constitution.

The latest attempt occurred on September 14, 2004, when, the Consortium for Adequate School Funding in Georgia (now known as the Georgia School Funding Association), a coalition of 51 of the state's 180 school districts, along with individual parents, filed a lawsuit against the state based on the education article of the Georgia Constitution. Demonstrating the split in the state, the plaintiffs were from rural school districts. Asserting that the state's school-funding system violates the education provision of the state constitution, the trial court denied the state's motion to dismiss, and the Georgia Supreme Court refused to hear the state's appeal. However, in 2008, the association withdrew the lawsuit in order to take other action. To date, there has been no successful litigation or court order to reform the educational financing system.

The issue, of course, centers on school performance. The argument is that increased spending will lead to increased school performance and better results. The issue is particularly acute in Georgia, which has seen its overall school performance lag behind many other states.

School Performance

Education is also one of those perennial issues that governors and legislatures cannot ignore. It has remained a major issue since World War II, although the controversies sparking debate have varied. Until the early 1970s, political conflict over education in Georgia was part of the larger debate over segregation. Controversies over the racial composition of school systems have subsided, but they remain a salient issue in many school systems. Recent debates over education policy have also concentrated on the performance of teachers and students. Such "reform" initiatives were not limited to Georgia but were quite visible in the South. Curriculum and symbolic issues such as school prayer also spark controversy in some areas.

Much of the impetus for reform is reflected in Georgia's history of poor performance on several indicators, although it is worth remembering that measures of educational quality are frequently topics of debate themselves. In 2014, Georgia's average SAT verbal score was 488, compared to a national average of 535; Georgia's math scores averaged 485, as opposed to a national average of 538, and the writing scores averaged 472 as compared to a national average of 518. Georgia's total combined average score of 1445 is below the national average of 1590, and ranks Georgia forty-fifth out of fifty states and the District of Columbia. Georgia did slightly better in ACT scores for 2014. The ACT is composed of math, reading, English, and science. Georgia scores for each are around the national average, and here Georgia ranks twenty-ninth out of the fifty states and the District of Columbia (see table 10.3).

This performance is in line with earlier testing in the 1990s and the early part of the new century and comes despite the implementation of accountability

Table 10.3. State SAT and ACT Scores 2014

State	SAT	ACT
Alabama	1617	19.1
Alaska	1485	21.1
Arizona	1547	19.9
Arkansas	1698	20.4
California	1504	22.5
Colorado	1735	20.7
Connecticut	1525	24.4
Delaware	1359	23.5
District of Columbia	1309	21.1
Florida	1448	19.9
Georgia	1445	21.0
Hawaii	1460	18.5
Idaho	1364	22.7
Illinois	1802	20.7
Indiana	1474	22.1
Iowa	1794	22.2
Kansas	1753	21.9
Kentucky	1746	20.0
Louisiana	1667	19.4
Maine	1387	24.2
Maryland	1468	22.7
Massachusetts	1556	24.4
Michigan	1784	20.1
Minnesota	1786	22.7
Mississippi	1714	19.0
Missouri	1771	21.7
Montana	1637	20.4
Nebraska	1745	21.5
Nevada	1458	21.0
New Hampshire	1566	24.3
New Jersey	1526	23.2
New Mexico	1617	20.1
New York	1468	23.7

Table 10.3. (*continued*)

State	SAT	ACT
North Carolina	1483	19.0
North Dakota	1816	20.6
Ohio	1652	22.0
Oklahoma	1697	20.7
Oregon	1544	21.5
Pennsylvania	1481	22.9
Rhode Island	1480	23.1
South Carolina	1443	20.4
South Dakota	1792	21.9
Tennessee	1714	19.8
Texas	1432	20.9
Utah	1690	20.2
Vermont	1554	23.5
Virginia	1530	23.1
Washington	1519	22.4
West Virginia	1522	20.8
Wisconsin	1782	22.2
Wyoming	1762	20.2

Source: Commonwealth Foundation, http://www
.commonwealthfoundation.org/policyblog/detail
/sat-scores-by-state-2014.

standards in the state that were designed to emphasize improving test scores, especially in elementary grades. Students in elementary schools are now tested yearly. State testing requires that students perform on the Criterion-Referenced Competency Test (CRCT) at grade level in grades 3 through 8 (up from just grades 3 and 5 in 2004) in order to be promoted to the next grade. Critics argue that evaluating students on the basis of a single test is inappropriate and places too much pressure on students. In 2004, 8 percent of third graders did not perform well enough to be promoted to the next grade. A decade later, the number decreased slightly to 7.7 percent.

The number of poor students in the Georgia system has risen since 2004, due much to the severity of the recession. In 2004, almost half the state's public school students were poor enough to qualify for reduced or free meals at school; by 2015, it was 60 percent.[106] Approximately one in five Georgians over the age of twenty-five do not have a high school diploma. Recent trends indicate that Georgia schools will have increasing numbers of Latino/Hispanic students. In 2004, over eighty thousand, or 4.7 percent, of the state's students were enrolled in English as a second language programs. That number rose in 2013 to over eighty-seven thousand, or 5.2 percent of the total number of students.[107]

Lottery Funds and Higher Education Funding

Proceeds from the Georgia Lottery are dedicated by law to scholarships and student loans, voluntary pre-kindergarten (pre-K), and capital improvements for education. The leading program is the HOPE (Helping Outstanding Pupils Educationally) scholarship, which finances college for all students able to maintain a B average and pays for all students in good standing who attend the state's technical schools. In all, more than $16 billion has been allocated to education since its inception, and overall more than $900 million was spent in 2014, with $423 million going to the HOPE scholarships fund.[108] A second program that is funded is pre-K. These programs are highly popular, and no Georgia politician would oppose them in the current political environment. Indeed, protection of these programs is a standard in most political rhetoric.

Another area of spending that has seen significant decreases is that of higher education. Again, Georgia is not alone among the states in this area. In Georgia spending on higher education represents a bit more than 9 percent of the state budget.[109] Adjusted for inflation, Georgia decreased spending on higher education per pupil by $2,656 between 2008 and 2014. This represented a decrease in spending on higher education of almost 25 percent.[110] It is the thirteenth largest decrease in spending per pupil of all states.

This reduction in turn has led to tuition increases for all Georgia public two-year and four-year institutions. For example, adjusted for inflation, average annual tuition at two-year colleges has increased from $2,610 in 2004 to $3,576 in 2014.[111] The increase has been greater at four-year schools. Again adjusting for inflation, tuition increased from $4,291 in 2004 to $8,094. The tuition increase is continuing, particularly for the state's four research institutions. Since 2008 alone, tuition increases have averaged almost 70 percent in Georgia, among the highest in the entire United States.[112] Tuition at the University of Georgia and Georgia Tech increased by 9 percent for 2015, while tuition for Georgia State University and Augusta University increased 5.5 percent.[113]

Debates over Curriculum

Another issue working through local school districts is the continuing debate over teaching values and promoting ideas rooted in religious beliefs. Such controversies are not limited to Georgia, however.[114] Court cases in Georgia include a successful suit to remove prayer at high school football games and controversy over student clubs that support gay or lesbian students. A controversy in Cobb County schools illustrates the degree to which parents, teachers, and school districts quickly become involved in this debate. In that case, parents petitioned the school board to have stickers placed on science textbooks. These stickers indicated that evolution was a "theory" and not a "fact." Other parents filed suit to have the stickers removed, and a federal district court agreed that the stickers unconstitutionally endorsed religion.[115] In 2006, parents and the school board reached an agreement, and the stickers were removed, but the case illustrates Georgia's continuing controversies over religion in public schools.

The Future of Education in Georgia

Georgia ranks about in the middle in teacher salaries, much of it due to increases put forth by Governor Zell Miller.[116] Georgia ranks twenty-third in teacher salaries, with an average salary of $52,880.00 in 2013. However, while Georgia does well nationally, that ranking is a decrease from its standing of sixteenth in 2000 and represents an inflation-adjusted drop in salary of almost 6 percent.[117]

Tackling education problems is seldom easy. Future policy debate will focus on funding, particularly local school systems' reliance on property taxes, differences between rich and poor districts, and the link between education and the state lottery. Debates also have grown heated over curriculum, including graduation requirements, tracking, achievements tests, and the teaching of values. None of these questions seems likely to go away, which could make for contentious sessions in the General Assembly, within the state education department, and at local school board meetings.

Social Welfare Policies

Social welfare policies are those designed to support the disadvantaged by improving their income or access to services to help them avoid poverty. Yet programs dealing with poverty seldom seem to lack controversy—in Georgia, the other forty-nine states, or nationally.

The states are heavily involved in social welfare programs, but policy tends to be made at the national level. Many of these initiatives began during President Franklin Roosevelt's New Deal during the 1930s, most notably when Congress passed the Social Security Act in 1935. Some programs are administered by the states with a combination of federal and state funds. Most of these programs experienced changes in the 1990s. The definition of who is needy, how to assist them, and how long assistance is provided are at the heart of debates about social welfare.

The Definition and Scale of Poverty

The federal government uses several measures to determine poverty. These guidelines establish who is eligible for some forms of government assistance at the state and federal level. The poverty threshold is calculated using annual income and varies with the size of households. It is based on income before taxes and does not include noncash benefits such as health care, housing, and Food Stamps. These definitions are adjusted over time for inflation. In 2015, poverty for one person under age sixty-five was $12,331; for a family of four that included two children, it was $24,036.[118]

The poverty rate is the percentage that falls below the threshold. This is often reported for the entire U.S. population, but it can be calculated by race and ethnicity, age, state, and other characteristics. The federal government also uses alternative measures. For example, if Social Security payments to the elderly and the disabled were not counted, the poverty rate in 2014 would have jumped from 14.8 to 21.6 percent of the population. On the other hand, if the value of

Figure 10.6. Percent of Population Living in Poverty: United States and Georgia, 1990–2015

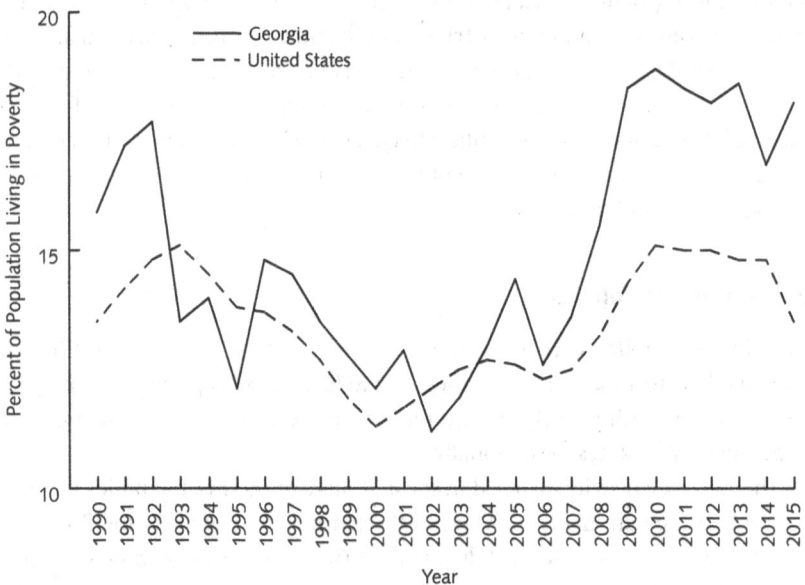

Source: U.S. Census Bureau, "Historical Poverty Tables, People and Families—1959 to 2015," tables 5 and 21, http://www.census.gov/data/tables/time-series/demo/income-poverty/historical-poverty-people .html.

Food Stamps were counted as income, poverty would have dropped from 14.8 to 13.6 percent.[119]

Figure 10.6 shows poverty rates over time for Georgia and the nation. Most noticeably, the rate tends to drop when the economy is growing steadily and rise during economic downturns, as it did during the Great Recession.[120] Following the Great Recession, the only southern states with poverty rates over 20 percent in 2014 were Kentucky, Louisiana, and Mississippi (the national high of 23.1 percent); the other three states were Arizona, New Mexico, and West Virginia. The seven states with poverty rates below 10 percent were in the North and the West. In 2015, more than 1.8 million Georgians (18.1 percent of the population) were under the poverty threshold, the fourteenth-highest percentage in the nation.[121] This rate is consistent with a pattern of poverty in Georgia being above the national level, but the gap grew during the economic problems of 2007–2012.

Overall poverty rates mask differences among various groups. An estimated 24.5 percent of Georgians under age eighteen lived in poverty in 2015. For those age sixty-five or over, however, the rate was only 9.7 percent. The poverty rate for whites was 12.5 percent, but it was 24.8 percent for blacks. Perhaps not surprisingly, for those age twenty-five or older with a bachelor's degree, only 4.9 percent were living in poverty. For those with only a high school diploma, it was 16.3 percent, but for those with less than a high school diploma, it was a staggering 28.9 percent.[122] It is worth remembering that the estimated median household income in Georgia in 2014 was $53,482.[123]

Types of Programs

Social welfare programs can be compared in terms of three general characteristics. The first is whether they provide cash or in-kind benefits. For example, Social Security pays monthly income to seniors and the disabled. Rather than direct cash payments, in-kind benefits provide goods or services. Medicare, for instance, pays for health care for seniors, while Food Stamps must be used for groceries, and housing vouchers must go for rent. The argument for in-kind support is that it forces recipients to use it for what are considered important purposes. If they were given more cash, the concern is that the money could be diverted to other expenses. Keep in mind that certain groups in addition to recipients can benefit from in-kind support, for example, landlords benefit from housing vouchers and grocery stores from Food Stamps.

The second distinction is whether a program has a "means test," which requires potential recipients to disclose their means of support because their income and assets must be below certain levels in order for them to be eligible for the program. A means test is required for programs such as subsidized school

lunches, Medicaid, subsidized housing, and college financial aid. Social Security and Medicare, on the other hand, are paid out based on age or disability no
matter what a person's income is.

The third distinguishing feature of social welfare programs is whether they
are contributory, which simply means that benefits are connected to prior contributions to a fund. For example, people have deductions from their paychecks
set aside for Social Security and Medicare. So do their employers. Unemployment compensation, which provides modest payments to workers who are laid
off, comes from a fund in each state that employers pay to support. In contrast,
people or employers do not have to pay ahead into a fund for recipients to receive Food Stamps or have children in Head Start.

Georgians eligible for assistance are aided by a number of government programs (see table 10.4). The following discussion covers programs grouped by
their general purpose: income support, health and nutrition, education and
training, and housing.

Income Support

Temporary Assistance for Needy Families (TANF). This program is the one most
often associated with welfare assistance. Originally signed into law as part of
the New Deal in the 1930s, Aid to Dependent Children provided federal support to states to aid mothers and children living without a male breadwinner. It
was later renamed Aid to Families with Dependent Children (AFDC). In 1996,
AFDC was replaced in the Personal Responsibility and Work Opportunity Reconciliation Act with a program called Temporary Assistance for Needy Families
(TANF). Much of this was in response to images of "undeserving" welfare recipients who had turned the program into a way of life and fathers who did not
meet their responsibilities to their children. The title of the law and the change
in the program name reflect that imagery and rhetoric. TANF sets income eligibility rules similar to AFDC, but it also caps the total number of years that
families will qualify for aid and requires recipients to be working and/or attending school in order to qualify.[124]

In Georgia, the legislature set a lifetime limit of forty-eight months of TANF
support, as opposed to the limit set by Congress of sixty months. States also
have flexibility in setting other eligibility and benefit levels. In addition to work
requirements for adult recipients, Georgia required teen parents to live with a
parent and remain in school or earn a high school diploma or GED, and support was not increased for recipients who had a child after receiving TANF
for ten months.[125] The program is administered by the Georgia Department of
Human Services (DHS).

Table 10.4. Major Social Welfare Programs in Georgia

Program Type and Name	Beneficiaries	Expenditures*	State Share	Federal Share
Income Support				
Temporary Assistance for Needy Families (TANF)	17,777	$66,954,227†	0.1%	99.9%
Unemployment Insurance	35,628‡	$38,762,747	10.7%	89.3%
Earned Income Tax Credit	1.1 million	$3 billion	N/A	100.0%
Social Security (OASDI)	1.1 million§	$23.7 billion§	N/A	100.0%
Health and Nutrition				
Medicaid	1,807,977	$8.87 billion†	26.2%	63.7%
PeachCare for Kids	158,537	$362,191,010	23.0%	76.5%
Medicare	1.4 million	$8.6 billion	N/A	100.0%
SNAP (food stamps)	850,628**	$2.8 billion†	0.0%	100.0%
Supplemental Nutrition for Women, Infants, and Children (WIC)	264,299	$126,957,333††	0.0%	100.0%
Education and Training				
Pre-K	80,000	$314,300,032‡‡	100.0%	N/A
Housing				
Housing Vouchers (Section 8)	16,000**	$99,000,000	0.0%	100.0%

Sources: TANF: Georgia Department of Human Services 2016, 4–5; unemployment insurance: U.S. Department of Labor, "Monthly Program and Financial Data," http://www.oui.doleta.gov/unemploy/5159report.asp; federal Earned Income Tax Credit: U.S. Internal Revenue Service, https://www.eitc.irs.gov/EITC-Central/eitcstats; Social Security: U.S. Social Security Administration 2016, section 5.J; Medicaid: Georgia Department of Community Health, "Annual Report FY 2015," https://dch.georgia.gov/sites/dch.georgia.gov/files/AnnualReport-2015.pdf; PeachCare: Georgia Department of Community Health, "Annual Report FY 2015," https://dch.georgia.gov/sites/dch.georgia.gov/files/AnnualReport-2015.pdf; Medicare: Centers for Medicare and Medicaid Services, "Medicare Geographic Variation: Public Use File, State/County Report—All Beneficiaries," https://www.cms.gov/Research-Statistics-Data-and-Systems/Statistics-Trends-and-Reports/Medicare-Geographic-Variation/GV_PUF.html; SNAP: U.S. Food and Nutrition Service, "Supplemental Nutrition Assistance Program: State Activity Report, Fiscal Year 2015," http://www.fns.usda.gov/sites/default/files/snap/2015-State-Activity-Report.pdf; WIC: annual state-level available from the U.S. Food and Nutrition Service, "WIC Program," http://www.fns.usda.gov/pd/wic-program; Section 8: Georgia Department of Community Affairs, "Housing Choice Voucher Program," https://www.dca.ga.gov/housing/RentalAssistance/programs/hcvp_program.asp.

* General Fund Appropriations, Amended Fiscal Year 2015 unless noted otherwise.

† Does not include the combined cost of determining eligibility for TANF, food stamps, and Medicaid: $106.7 million in state funds and $177.3 million in federal funds.

‡ Average number of monthly initial claims during calendar 2015.

§ Beneficiaries as of December 2014. Benefit payment total is for calendar 2014.

** Average number of households per month during federal fiscal year 2015.

†† Federal fiscal year 2015.

‡‡ These funds are generated entirely by the Georgia Lottery.

The number of people receiving monthly TANF cash assistance in Georgia has declined following the changes in the law, although some of this decline can be explained by other factors, especially economic growth in the late 1990s and early years of this century. The adult caseload dropped from more than 25,000 during 2002–2004 to under 3,000 in 2008–2009, although there was an uptick in the aftermath of the housing crisis and the Great Recession. The largest share of the caseload is children. Thus, just 2,782 of the 17,777 cases in 2015 were adults. Payments are not large, averaging $159.69 per month in 2015. The DHS also works to promote child support payments by absent parents, many of them under court orders.[126]

Unemployment Insurance. This program was also established during the 1930s and provides assistance to workers who are laid off, forced to reduce hours because of lack of work, or have lost their jobs for several other reasons. Weekly benefits in Georgia ranged from $44 to a maximum of $330 in 2016.[127] Workers are eligible for up to twenty-six weeks of payments and must seek another position after losing their job. Each state sets up its own system funded by state and federal payroll taxes paid into a trust fund by employers on a portion of each employee's wages (the first $7,000 for the federal tax and the first $9,500 for Georgia). The tax rate varies among states, among some classes of employers within a state, and according to the level of reserves available. Employers in Georgia are assigned a tax rate each year based on their history and changes in the business; a new firm is charged 2.7 percent.[128]

As one would expect, initial unemployment claims have fluctuated in Georgia in this century, partly with the recession and also on a seasonal basis. For most of 2007, fewer than fifty thousand people each month applied for benefits. Those numbers began rising as the economy worsened to over seventy thousand for all but two months between October 2008 and January 2010, including three months with over one hundred thousand claims filed. As conditions improved, initial claims dropped to under thirty thousand by mid-2016. Benefit payments varied as well, from a high of over $179 million in March 2009, when the average weekly benefit paid out was $284.28 per recipient to under $40 million from January 2015 through June 2016, when the average beneficiary received between $265 and $286.[129]

Major Federal Programs. Other programs providing income support are funded entirely by the national government. The most notable is Social Security, another program from the 1930s whose official name is Old Age, Survivors, and Disability Insurance (OASDI). It provides cash payments to retirees, survivors of those covered by the program, and the disabled. As of December 2014, over 1.1 million Georgia residents were receiving Social Security retirement payments. About 600,000 more received benefits because they were spouses, other survivors, or disabled. Payments to these individuals totaled more than $23.7 billion in 2014.[130]

Congress also created Supplemental Security Income (SSI) in 1972 to provide extra income to those sixty-five or older, blind, or disabled. Recipients must have few assets and a small monthly income, if any. In 2015, individuals could not earn more than $733 per month ($1,100 for a couple), which is the payment they would receive if they had no other income. Over 256,000 Georgia residents received SSI in December 2014 (90 percent of them disabled), and total payments to recipients in 2014 totaled just over $1.6 billion.[131]

The federal government also uses the Earned Income Tax Credit (EITC) to support the working poor by providing a refundable tax credit even if they do not owe federal taxes. For instance, in 2015, a married couple with no children would have had to earn less than $20,330 to qualify for a $503 tax credit. The income cutoff rises with the number of children, as does the credit. Qualified recipients cannot claim this benefit, however, without filing a tax return with the IRS. In Georgia, 1.1 million taxpayers qualified for the EITC in 2014, earning roughly $3 billion in tax credits, and an average of $2,752 per tax return.[132] Analysts have concluded that the EITC encourages work and helps lift households out of poverty, especially in the case of single parents.[133] Advocates argue that traditional welfare programs varied so much among the states that they encouraged people to move to get better benefits and that competition among states kept benefit levels low.[134] By 2016, the District of Columbia and twenty-six states—but not Georgia—had adopted their own EITCs.[135] Supporters of a Georgia EITC suggest that the cost of refunds would have a limited effect on state revenues compared to both other tax breaks and several ways to broaden the state's revenue sources.[136]

Health and Nutrition

Medicaid. This federal-state program was established by Congress in 1965 as Title 19 of the Social Security Act and provides health care to the poor. Thus it is a means-tested, in-kind form of support, but the states have discretion in determining eligibility. The program pays for hospital services, vaccination for children, physician services, nursing home care, and similar items. States also have the option to add prescription drugs and prosthetic devices, physical therapy, hospice care, eyeglasses, and other services. States generally pay service providers or entities such as health maintenance organizations.[137]

There are several categories of eligibility for Medicaid in Georgia, but all recipients must provide proof of citizenship. Those who qualify for SSI (see above) are eligible for Medicaid. Eligibility varies with the age of children and family income. To qualify for Low-Income Medicaid (LIM) in 2016, households with parents or caretakers having children under age nineteen faced income limits based on family size. For example, a family of three could earn no more than $6,612 per year. The income limits are somewhat higher (the federal poverty level) for those who have Medicare hospital coverage but need assistance paying premiums, coinsurance, or deductibles.[138]

During the state's 2015 fiscal year, an average of 1.8 million recipients monthly participated in Medicaid, with the typical person receiving almost $5,000 in medical care during the year. Total payments for the year reached almost $9 billion. Revenue comes from several sources. In the FY 2016 budget, for instance, the legislature appropriated $3.9 billion for Low-Income Medicaid, but two-thirds of that was federal money and 24 percent was state funds. Similarly, the Medicaid budget for the aged, blind, and disabled totaled $5.2 billion, with 64 percent coming from the federal government and 26 percent from state appropriations.[139]

The Patient Protection and Affordable Care Act (ACA), commonly known as Obamacare, included a provision for the states to expand Medicaid. In a 2012 decision, however, the U.S. Supreme Court held that Congress could not require states to expand Medicaid coverage under the law.[140] The change would cover adults without children who fell below 133 percent of the poverty level. The support was to be fully funded by the federal government for three years starting in 2014 and decline to 90 percent by 2020.[141] Left with the option, Georgia was among the nineteen states choosing not to extend Medicaid coverage as of mid-2016.

PeachCare for Kids. This program is Georgia's version of the Children's Health Insurance Program (CHIP), which was established by Congress in 1997 to provide health coverage to children whose families were not poor enough to qualify for Medicaid. In Georgia, this covers children through age eighteen whose families make no more than 247 percent of the poverty level, which was $49,623 in 2016 for a family of three.[142] During the state's 2015 fiscal year, PeachCare served more than 158,000 people, paying out almost $311 million, an average of $1,960 per participant. Participation has varied, with a recent peak of almost 274,000 during 2007, but the numbers dropped as Georgia emerged from the Great Recession and the housing crisis. The federal government contributed 94 percent of the funds in the state's 2016 budget for PeachCare, while state appropriations amounted to only 5.4 percent.[143]

Major Federal Programs. Probably the "eight-hundred-pound gorilla in the room" for health programs is Medicare, which covers people age sixty-five and older, along with the disabled and those with end-stage renal disease. This in-kind program is not means-tested but is contributory (via payroll taxes and insurance premiums). It was adopted by Congress in 1965, when poverty was much higher among seniors. It now includes hospital care (Part A), which is paid for from a trust funded by payroll taxes, and medical insurance for doctors' services and outpatient care (Part B), for which participants pay monthly premiums. In 2003, Congress added a prescription drug plan (Part D), which is also funded by monthly premiums, and allowed recipients to get services through approved private insurance companies (called Part C, or Medicare Advantage), which normally include prescription drugs. Beneficiaries pay premiums, and Medicare pays a fixed monthly amount to Medicare Advantage companies for each person enrolled.[144]

There were 1.4 million Medicare beneficiaries in Georgia during 2014. Of these, 76.6 percent were in traditional Medicare, and the remaining one-fourth used Medicare Advantage. The average beneficiary was age seventy, three-fourths of beneficiaries were non-Hispanic whites, and 20 percent were poor enough to get Medicaid, too. Total spending in Georgia exceeded $8.6 billion in 2014, and traditional Medicare paid roughly $9,000 per beneficiary.[145]

The Supplemental Nutrition Assistance Program (SNAP), commonly known as Food Stamps, is a federally funded, means-tested, in-kind program jointly administered by the U.S. Department of Agriculture and the Georgia Division of Family and Children Services (DFCS). It enables those with low incomes and limited resources to buy food.

Food Stamps began on an experimental basis, and Congress made the program permanent in 1964. It expanded and became nationwide in 1974. In the early years, recipients had to purchase Food Stamps at a percentage of their face value. The purchase requirement was eliminated in 1977, and the program eventually moved from coupons that resembled currency to a system of electronic transfers, much like a debit card. Congress gave the program its current name in 2008. Debates over the years have focused on income and resource limits for recipients, eligibility of legal aliens, work requirements and time limits for receiving benefits, links to other social welfare programs such as TANF, and the degree of flexibility to grant the states.[146]

The federal requirements to receive Food Stamps limit the program to households with gross income at or below 130 percent of the poverty level or net income at or below the poverty level. For an individual, that equals a monthly gross income up to $1,287. Maximum income levels rise with household size, for example, $2,184 for a three-person household. Resources such as a bank balance cannot exceed $2,250, but those sharing a household with someone disabled or age sixty or over could have a bank balance as large as $3,250. Various exclusions apply to these calculations, such as a person's home. Able-bodied adults must meet a work requirement; those who do not can get Food Stamps for only three months over a three-year period. Applicants must apply to DFCS, provide documentation, and be interviewed by a caseworker. The U.S. Food and

Nutrition Service reported average monthly participation in Georgia at 839,207 households. The total cost in Georgia during the federal government's 2015 fiscal year was $2.8 billion.[147] While the benefits are provided by the federal government, the state spent over $107 million during FY 2015 for staff to determine eligibility for Food Stamps, Medicaid, and TANF.[148]

Supplemental Nutrition for Women, Infants, and Children (WIC) is another federally funded, means-tested, in-kind program. It was created in 1974 and is under the U.S. Department of Agriculture (USDA). WIC provides access to a limited range of products for infants up to their first birthday, children up to their fifth birthday, and women who are pregnant and for six to twelve months after they give birth. Coverage for children in Georgia extends to those who live with foster parents. States have some flexibility in setting income limits, which cannot exceed 185 percent of the poverty level. Funding levels can also limit access to the program, which is administered in Georgia by the Department of Public Health.

USDA data indicate that the number of participants in WIC during the federal government's 2015 fiscal year was roughly 265,000, at a cost of $127 million. More recent monthly data suggest that about one-fourth of beneficiaries were women, with the remainder being infants and children.[149] The federal government provides other low-income nutrition programs that seem less visible and controversial, including school meals and milk for children not participating in federal meal programs in their schools or other institutions.[150]

Education and Training

Pre-Kindergarten. As described earlier in this chapter, Georgia devotes substantial funds to education. One initiative created after voters approved a state lottery in 1992 was a free pre-kindergarten program. Initially targeted to at-risk four-year-olds, the program was made universally available in 1995. The voluntary system of public and private pre-K providers serves over eighty thousand children across all 159 counties and is administered by the Georgia Department of Early Care and Learning (DECAL). In FY 2016, more than $321 million in state lottery funds and less than $175,000 in federal money were devoted to the state's pre-K program.[151]

Head Start and Child Care Services. These efforts rely on a different mix of state and federal money than pre-K and are administered through DECAL and the Administration for Children and Families within the U.S. Department of Health and Human Services. Head Start began in 1965 to enhance the opportunities for disadvantaged preschool children and has expanded over the years, in large part through grants to states and service providers. In Georgia, Early Head Start serves pregnant women and children up to age three, and Head Start serves children ages three to five.

The state subsidizes childcare for low-income families to support them in work, education, and training. Household income must not exceed 50 percent of the state median. Starting in 2016, DECAL also gave priority to eleven groups, including TANF households, persons experiencing domestic violence, victims of a natural disaster, and children with special needs, under child protection, or in lottery-funded pre-K.[152] In FY 2016, DECAL's child care services budget was just over $245 million, 77 percent of which was federal money.[153] There is concern, however, that the state's childcare support might reach only a small share of the low-income families who could benefit from the program.[154] DECAL is also involved in licensing, training, meal programs for service providers, and referral services.

Post-Secondary Education and Training. The creation of public colleges might be viewed as an antipoverty measure given their origins and emphasis on affordability in the 1800s. In particular, the creation of land-grant colleges beginning in 1862 aimed to provide a practical college education to those in the working class.[155] Higher education has changed substantially over the decades, although it is still viewed as an investment in upward mobility. Colleges and universities provide need-based financial assistance to individual students. This does not include the HOPE Scholarship, which dropped its income cap in 1995. Critics have focused on the growing inability of low-income students to afford the University System of Georgia and the extent to which HOPE does little to meet their needs.[156]

Georgia also provides a range of programs to enhance people's skills and access to jobs. These in-kind programs are not contributory and are generally not means-tested. They are administered by a variety of state agencies. For example, the Technical College System of Georgia's adult education programs include literacy programs and free GED preparation classes, as well as job training customized for employers. The system's budget of $768 million in FY 2016 included almost $340 million of state appropriations, a slightly larger amount of other funds (fees, tuition, and the like), and only $80 million in federal money for adult education and technical education programs.[157] Similarly, Georgia's Department of Economic Development provides training for dislocated workers and low-income adults and youth at regional centers through its Workforce Division, which was funded in FY 2016 entirely with $73 million in federal money.[158]

Federal Programs. The federal government's contribution to overall government spending on education is modest and is mostly in the form of grants to states and local school districts. It is heavily involved, though, in funding individual college students through a system of means-tested, in-kind support in the form of grants, loans, and work. For the 2014–2015 academic year, almost three hundred thousand Pell Grants were awarded to students in Georgia along with almost forty-five thousand awards for campus-based programs such as Work Study. Together, they totaled just over $1 billion. The nearly nine thousand Perkins Loans totaled $17.9 million, and the over five hundred thousand loans (including over forty-nine thousand to graduate students) reached almost $2.88 billion.[159]

Housing

State Programs. Georgia plays a limited role in housing programs for low-income populations, mainly facilitating federal programs by the Georgia Department of Community Affairs (DCA) and through enabling legislation affecting local governments. The most notable legislation historically allowed the creation of local housing authorities beginning in the 1930s. These local authorities built and operated apartment buildings with below-market rents for low-income tenants. The U.S. Department of Housing and Urban Development (HUD) stopped funding such construction during the mid-1990s, but there are other federal programs that subsidize renters and homeowners. The DCA sponsors programs for first-time homebuyers, although most of the financing comes from sources other than state appropriations.[160]

Major Federal Programs. HUD funds a system of housing vouchers commonly known as Section 8. The program is administered by the Georgia DCA and gives low-income tenants a voucher to use for a share of their rent. Participating landlords must meet certain standards and are paid directly with federal funds. The primary argument in favor of vouchers is that it gives low-income households more choices rather than being restricted to traditional government-run housing projects. To be eligible, families must have income no higher than 50 percent of the median in the metropolitan area, although HUD requires a large share of vouchers to go to those with incomes at 30 percent or less of the area median.[161] Income limits vary by family size. In 2016, the median household income in Metropolitan Atlanta was $67,500, and the income cap for a family of four to be considered low income was $33,750, while $24,300 was the maximum income to be considered "extremely" low income, which made it easier to qualify for a voucher.[162] The DCA maintains a Section 8 waiting list and reported subsidizing about sixteen thousand families per month in 2016, totaling about $99 million.[163] The DCA also administers a variety of federal programs dealing with homelessness and special-needs housing.[164]

Weatherization and Energy Assistance. The Georgia Department of Human Services administers federal funds through local agencies that help low-income residents with their utility bills or to weatherize their homes. Recipients cannot have income above 60 percent of the state median. The cap varies with household size; for example, an individual could not earn more than $21,881 in 2016. These programs cost $55.3 million in FY 2016, all of it from federal funds.[165]

The "Other" Sectors

Government is not the only service provider trying to improve conditions for disadvantaged Georgians. Nonprofits and companies are active as well. For instance, eight regional food banks are nonprofit organizations that serve all 159 Georgia counties.[166] Their work is complemented by various religious and other organizations, such as Habitat for Humanity, which helps low-income families acquire homes. Other nonprofits staff rape crisis centers, AIDS service organizations, and similar ventures. Corporate sponsors and service organizations also contribute, such as the Ronald McDonald House for children facing terminal illnesses, Lions Clubs helping people who need eyeglasses and other assistance with vision, and Georgia Power's Project SHARE, which channels company funds and donations from ratepayers to assist others with their electric bills, including about fifty thousand recipients in 2015.[167]

Continuing Debates about Social Welfare Programs

The arguments over welfare focus on several issues, particularly individual incentives, access to services, program quality, social effects, and costs. Passage of the Personal Responsibility Act in 1996 was a result of changes in direction to treat welfare benefits as short-term assistance. The debates on "dependency" led to this shift, as many believed that AFDC discouraged recipients from giving up government support to enter the labor market. Some critics have complained that the changes have shown mixed results and that states have exploited their increased flexibility in using federal money to redirect funds from recipients to other purposes.[168]

Different concerns led to enactment of the Affordable Care Act in 2010. Access to medical care in the United States generally requires insurance. Millions of Americans were not poor enough to qualify for Medicaid, lacked employer-provided insurance, and could not afford an individual health insurance policy. Others stayed in their jobs in part to keep their employer's health plan. Young, healthy people often saw little need to buy health insurance, and many poor families had to rely on free care in emergency rooms when one of their members became ill. The legislation was extremely complex, produced multiple lawsuits, and remains controversial, with opinions ranging from repealing the law to creating a universal system through the government much like Medicare and Medicaid.

Social welfare policy debates also focus on the total costs of such programs. For instance, Medicaid and PeachCare for Kids, although mainly federal money, combined for 22 percent of the state budget in 2016. Nationally, critics argue that welfare programs hinder deficit deduction.

Georgia legislators have also focused attention on ensuring that illegal immigrants are not receiving social welfare benefits, including Food Stamps, Social Security, TANF, public education, and emergency medical treatment. Still, about one in ten Georgia residents is foreign-born. One analysis has highlighted their contributions to Georgia as entrepreneurs, workers, and taxpayers—a figure likely to increase as the state continues to diversify.[169]

Questions over entitlements are at the heart of social welfare policy making, and some have started to focus on "middle-class" welfare such as Social Security, mortgage subsidies, and even veterans benefits, which are awarded without considering whether recipients are needy. Neither the welfare debate nor more general discussions of government benefits seem likely to abate soon, at the state Capitol or in Washington.

Public Safety and Security

States, along with their local governments, have long been the cornerstone in protecting the public on a daily basis. They do this through law enforcement, prosecution, corrections systems, and related efforts.

Crime

Although some crimes are strictly under the jurisdiction of the federal government, the vast majority of crimes and the vast majority of arrests and prosecutions are at the state level. In some instances, there is concurrent jurisdiction, and defendants may face charges in federal and state courts at the same time. The states differ from one another and the federal government in identifying crimes and setting penalties. In many instances, similar crimes are defined differently by various states. Differences in what constitutes criminal behavior may also vary within a state, as with myriad local laws governing alcohol purchase and consumption. Local variation can also occur when different district attorneys emphasize the prosecution of certain types of crimes over others. Police protection for citizens is usually provided by local governments, which can also maintain jails for the short-time confinement of suspects and prisoners. Prisons are generally provided by states, although there are also federal prisons.

Law Enforcement in Georgia

Counties, municipalities, state agencies, and colleges in Georgia all employ peace officers. All persons who become officers must be at least eighteen years old, hold a high school diploma, and complete a training course at a police academy.

State Agencies. Several state agencies are under the supervision of the Board of Public Safety, which is chaired by the governor. The Georgia State Patrol is the best known of all policing agencies in the state. It is a division of the Georgia Department of Public Safety (DPS) and is charged with enforcing traffic laws on Georgia highways and investigation of traffic accidents, as well as assisting in other aspects of criminal investigation and enforcement. As of the end of 2013, Georgia had 824 state troopers. The Georgia State Patrol is divided into fifty-one patrol posts within ten geographic troops and seven specialized units: Criminal Interdiction, Implied Consent, Specialized Collision Reconstruction Team (SCRT), Specialized Weapons and Tactics (SWAT), GSP Dive Team, Governor's Task Force, and the Regional K–9 Task Force. GSP officers average over five hundred thousand traffic stops and over thirteen thousand driving-under-the-influence arrests in a given year. The command officer is located at the Department of Public Safety Headquarters in Atlanta.

The Georgia Bureau of Investigation (GBI) was founded in 1937 and given its current name in 1940. In 2016, the GBI had 824 positions, and it operates in cooperation with local agencies. The GBI is divided into regional investigative offices, regional drug enforcement offices, and regional crime laboratories. It operates out of three divisions: Investigative, Forensic Sciences, and Crime Information, which deals with reporting of crimes within the state. Crimes against persons constitute 35 percent of the GBI's investigations, with drugs and property investigations the next two most significant. The GBI agents also act as crime scene specialists, perform polygraph tests, and perform drug investigations, background checks, and even bomb disposal.[170]

Other agencies with enforcement powers are the Game and Fish Division of the Georgia Department of Natural Resources, which deals with water and boating safety in addition to wildlife; the Department of Revenue's Alcohol and Tobacco unit, which deals with taxes on these specific goods; the state examining boards, which deals with licensing regulations; the State Ethics Commission, which monitors elections and lobbying; the state Fire Marshall's Office;

and the Securities Investigation Unit. More recently, the state has expanded the role of the Georgia Emergency Management Agency and its Office of Homeland Security.

Local Agencies. Much of the public safety burden in Georgia falls on county and local city and town governments. In 2014, local governments spent well over $2 billion on police and corrections. Probably the most visible local law enforcement officials are county sheriffs, who are the only elected officials to have arrest powers in Georgia. The Georgia Constitution requires each county to elect a sheriff, but the state sets few qualifications beyond a minimum age, a high school diploma or its equivalent, the lack of a criminal record, and mandatory training once in office. Georgia's sheriffs have jurisdiction only within the boundaries of their own counties, although they may execute warrants in any county in the state. Deputies are hired by the sheriffs to assist them in their duties. Georgia sheriffs have become controversial at times because of corruption, favoritism, and incompetence. Unlike judges, sheriffs are elected on a partisan ballot. Campaigns can be heated, especially when incumbents are challenged by other law enforcement officials such as one of their deputies.

Sixteen of the largest counties, including Clarke, Cobb, and Gwinnett, maintain police departments, thereby reducing the power of their sheriffs. In these instances, the county police are responsible for most law enforcement activities, and the sheriff maintains jurisdiction over courts and detention and crime reporting. Also at the local level, public college and university police departments have criminal arrest jurisdiction within a limited distance of campuses. They also enforce traffic and property laws.

Corrections

Georgia has a very large prison population. Data from 2012 showed that one in thirteen adults were under some form of correctional supervision in Georgia, and that between 1990 and 2011, Georgia's prison population more than doubled to nearly fifty-six thousand inmates.[171] By 2010, Georgia had the ninth-largest population of any state, but the state's prison population was the fifth largest in the nation.[172] Over 164,000 offenders were on probation in 2013, and the average probation sentence for an offender in Georgia is almost seven years—twice the length of the national average.[173] In total, more than 27,000 offenders were on parole in 2013.[174] The state put to death thirty-six convicts between 1977 and the end of 2004—the sixth-highest total among the states. In FY 2010, the state spent over $1 billion in prison expenditures, more than twice the amount spent in 1990, which was $492 million.[175]

At the end of FY 2014, the Georgia Department of Corrections had a budget of more than \$1.2 billion and a prison population of over fifty-three thousand prisoners, two-thirds of whom were violent offenders.[176] Sixty-one inmates, all male, are on death row, their median age is forty-nine, and slightly more than half are black or Hispanic.[177] Corrections also ran transitional, diversion, and detention centers, as well as two probation boot camps. As in other states, prison conditions have been a source of controversy in Georgia and were the subject of extended litigation in the federal courts. The issue of turning corrections over to private companies has also been debated.

Georgia's counties and cities also operate correctional facilities. Local jails are often forced to hold people who have not been convicted but are awaiting trial and cannot afford bail. Inmates at county facilities are required to work on maintenance projects while they are detained. Inmates of detention centers, while generally only short-term inmates convicted of DUI or probation offenses, are also used on community service projects. Diversion centers hold inmates only at night and permit them to hold jobs during the day. Transition centers (halfway houses) are designed to assist former prisoners in returning to normal life. Like state prisons, local facilities have also become the subject of litigation by inmates and the federal government. Complaints concentrate on inadequate security, access to legal help, and medical treatment.

Public attitudes toward crime vacillate. For instance, as the United States emerged from the recession of the early 1990s, crime replaced the economy in the Gallup Poll as the most important issue facing the county. However, domestic crime has receded as a major issue, with the significant exception of terrorism. In polls running from mid-2015 through early 2016, terrorism ranked as the second or third most important issues to those polled according to various surveys conducted by CBS News/*New York Times*, ABC News/*Washington Post*, and NBC News/*Wall Street Journal*.[178]

Similar swings in attitudes have occurred in Georgia. Somewhat surprising is the degree to which public fear about crime remained high in the mid-1990s while crime rates dropped. According to a January 2016 *Atlanta Journal-Constitution* poll, the economy and jobs are the most important issue confronting Georgians by a wide margin. However, unlike their national counterparts, Georgians do rank crime and safety as a significant concern, listing it as the third most important issue (education is second) for Georgians, with 9 percent citing it as a problem.[179]

The Federal Bureau of Investigation issues reports on crime based on reports submitted voluntarily from local police agencies around the country. The reports concentrate on seven major violent (murder and nonnegligent manslaughter, forcible rape, robbery, aggravated assault) and property (burglary,

Figure 10.7. Georgia Murder Rate, 1960–2012

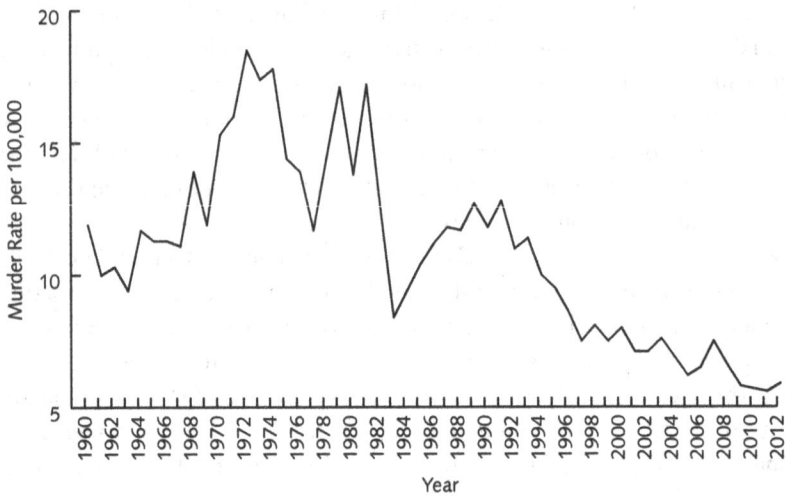

Source: Bureau of Justice Uniform Crime Reporting Statistics, http://www.bjs.gov/ucrdata
/Search/Crime/State/StatebyState.cfm.

larceny, motor vehicle theft) offenses. Because comparing total crimes for different places can be misleading, the rate at which these crimes are reported is standardized, normally as a ratio of the total reported per one hundred thousand population.

For the nation as a whole in 2013, the rate for violent crime was 366.1 offenses per one hundred thousand population—a significant drop from 684.5 percent in 1995, and these data represent a near continuous drop over this almost two-decade period.[180] Georgia's violent crime rate saw a similar drop (see figure 10.7), and the crime rate was slightly lower for 2013 at 359.7 (as compared to 657.1 in 1995). Twenty-four states had higher violent crime rates, including the neighboring states of Florida, South Carolina, and Tennessee.

Georgia's property crime rate has similarly decreased over the same period (see figure 10.8). This decrease followed a significant increase in property crimes from 1960, and the current property crime rates are well above those of five decades ago. In 2013, it stood at 3,410.6 per one hundred thousand population, a decline from 3,410.6 in 1995. However, this is an increase from 1249.1 in 1960. Even with the relatively lower figures of today, the rate is well above the rate of 3,517.1 for the nation as a whole. It was also higher than that of the neighboring states of Florida, Mississippi, and North Carolina, but below Tennessee, Louisiana, and South Carolina.[181]

Figure 10.8. Georgia Property Crime Rate, 1960–2012

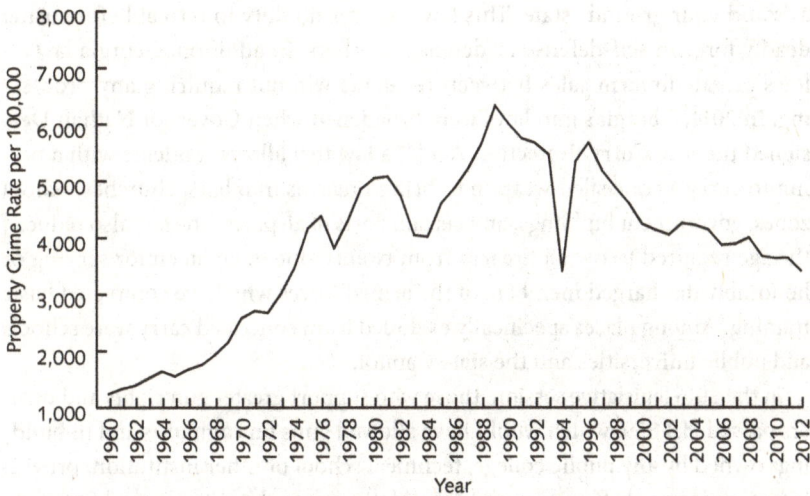

Source: Bureau of Justice Uniform Crime Reporting Statistics, http://www.bjs.gov/ucrdata/Search/Crime/State/StatebyState.cfm.

The occurrence of crimes varies across the state. In 2014, the Atlanta metropolitan area had 359 murders, more than half of the state total of 579. Of course, the Atlanta metropolitan area accounts for more than half of the total state population. Of Georgia's more than 329,000 property crimes in 2014, more than half occurred in Atlanta's suburbs.[182]

Future Issues

Perceptions of high levels of crime can prompt public officials to devote substantial resources to the criminal justice system. In many ways, it is a "no lose" political situation to look tough on crime and spend tax money. Several debates will undoubtedly continue over public safety in Georgia. Some of these relate to law enforcement and corrections, including how to keep offenders from committing additional crimes. Much of that discussion will focus on types and levels of punishment, the workload of probation and parole officials, the success of rehabilitation programs, and the adequacy of the notion of public safety.

Over the past several years, Georgia, along with several other states has loosened restrictions on private gun ownership and where one may carry a loaded weapon. The state has significantly expanded the ability and right to carry a concealed weapon into a variety of public and private spaces and locations.

Georgia, for example, offers reciprocal gun rights to those holding a permit from other states.[183] Other changes included a 2006 law when Georgia became a "stand your ground" state. This law requires no duty to retreat before using deadly force in self-defense or defense of others. In addition, Georgia law allows private firearm sales between residents without requiring any processing. In 2014, Georgia's gun laws were broadened when Governor Nathan Deal signed the Safe Carry Protection Act,[184] a law that allows residents with a permit to carry a concealed weapon to bring firearms into bars, churches, school zones, government buildings, and certain parts of airports. The law also reduced the age required to own a firearm from twenty-one to eighteen for serving or honorably discharged members of the armed forces who have completed basic training. Among places specifically excluded from concealed carry were schools and public universities and the state Capitol.

In the 2016 legislative session, those who support greater gun rights and owners passed HB 859, which would have allowed guns on campuses and in buildings owned by any public college, technical school or other institution, providing exceptions only for areas used for athletic events, dormitories, and fraternity and sorority houses.[185] Despite large support in the Republican-dominated legislature, Governor Nathan Deal vetoed the legislation, calling for stricter rules about carrying guns into offices and campus child care facilities.[186] Proponents of the legislation vowed to continue their efforts to expand the "campus carry" bill to the next legislative session.

The Future of Georgia Politics

What might Georgians expect from their political system as the state moves further into the twenty-first century? Two key factors may affect the type and rate change. One is the nature of external "shocks" to Georgia politics. Perhaps the most significant would be changes in the federal system, which would provide states with fewer resources, impose more requirements, or perhaps grant them more autonomy.

The second fundamental question is how economic and population changes, particularly migration from states outside the South and even from outside the United States, will mesh with Georgia's traditionalistic political culture. One scenario is that as Georgia becomes more diverse, it will become more like the rest of the United States. Greater diversity could also bring more competition among political parties and interest groups—and more conflict as well. Perhaps ironically, growing conflict could spur increased citizen participation in politics, including elections.

Given the rise of Georgia's Republican Party, it is unclear whether the state will remain under one-party control or whether the two political parties will compete regularly for statewide offices and a majority in the General Assembly. While Republicans and Democrats are often viewed as having a "lock" on certain areas, their geographical presence around Georgia could shift with population changes. Moreover, if Earl and Merle Black are right that southern politics will be shaped by efforts to gain the support of the white middle class, party competition in Georgia could have heavy racial and religious symbolism. If so, policy debates and election campaigns could take on a rough-edged tone that V. O. Key would recognize. The effects that these trends will have are unclear, but it is certain they will not produce a complete break with Georgia's past.

NOTES

Abbreviations

ABH *Athens Banner-Herald*
AC   *Atlanta Constitution*
AJC   *Atlanta Journal-Constitution*
NYT   *New York Times*
OCGA *Official Code of Georgia Annotated*

Chapter 1. State and Local Governments in the Federal System

1. U.S. Census Bureau 2014b.

2. See Pastor et al. 2000; Warner and Hefetz 2008; Hefetz and Warner 2012; Hilvert and Swindell 2013; International City/County Management Association 2007.

3. Chicago-Kent College of Law n.d.

4. *National Federation of Independent Business v. Sibelius*, no. 11-393 (2012).

5. International City/County Management Association 2010.

6. Misty Williams and J. Scott Trubey, "Caterpillar to Bring 1,400 Jobs to Athens," *AJC*, February 17, 2012, https://ngkfatlanta.wordpress.com/2012/02/17/caterpillar-to-build -factory-near-athens/.

7. See U.S. Census Bureau n.d.a.

8. U.S. Bureau of Economic Analysis 2013a; U.S. Bureau of Labor Statistics 2012; Labonte 2010.

9. U.S. Bureau of Labor Statistics 2013.

10. U.S. Bureau of Labor Statistics 2012.

11. "Ready to Take Off Again?" 2014.

12. U.S. Census Bureau 2012b, table 667; 2006, table 654.

13. U.S. Bureau of Economic Analysis n.d.

14. See Dhawan 2011.

15. Schoen 2016.

16. U.S. Department of Agriculture n.d.

17. J. Henderson 2012.

18. Greenblatt 2016b.

19. The U.S. Office of Management and Budget defines a metropolitan area as an urban area with a central city of fifty thousand or more residents, its county, and any surrounding counties tied to the central city economically and socially.

20. On the shifting attitudes toward city living, see Frey 2011. On the slower Sun Belt growth during the Great Recession and continued growth of suburbia in this century, see Frey 2012. More recently, however, it appears that the migration to the South and the West resumed substantially after the recession; see Frey 2017. On the creative class, see Florida 2005. On the long-term revival of central cities, see Ehrenhalt 2012; Frey 2013.

21. Glaeser 2011, 6.

22. Calculations by the authors from the Bureau of Economic Analysis's interactive regional data sets, http://bea.gov/iTable/index_regional.cfm.

23. Panek, Hinson, and Baumgardner 2013.

24. See Eisinger 1988; Altshuler and Luberoff 2003; Bartik 2005; Warner and Zheng 2013; Prillaman and Meier 2014. See also the Pew Charitable Trusts n.d.

25. Sam Howe Verhovek with Laurence Zuckerman, "Boeing, Jolting Seattle, Will Move Headquarters," *NYT*, March 22, 2001, http://www.nytimes.com/2001/03/22/us/boeing-jolting-seattle-will-move-headquarters.html?pagewanted=all&src=pm; "Denomination Moving Headquarters to Cleveland; 3rd Protestant Church Will Leave N.Y.," *Los Angeles Times*, July 8, 1989, http://articles.latimes.com/1989-07-08/local/me-2693_1_church-headquarters.

26. For a national survey of recent local economic development strategies, see International City/County Management Association 2010.

27. Burnett 2015.

28. See L. L. Martin, Levey, and Cawley 2012.

29. Steven Church, Dawn McCarty, and Margaret Cronin Fisk, "Detroit Slides from Industrial Might to Bankruptcy," *Bloomberg Personal Finance*, July 19, 2013. http://www.bloomberg.com/news/2013-07-18/detroit-becomes-biggest-u-s-city-to-file-for-bankruptcy.html.

30. Cromartie 2013.

31. U.S. Census Bureau 2012a, chaps. 1 and 2.

32. Hochschild 2012; MacManus 2012.

33. For an overview of immigration, see National Conference of State Legislatures 2016. See also the interactive map and data available at Pew Charitable Trusts 2013.

34. For a good overview of these issues, see Gray, Hanson, and Kousser 2013, chaps. 12 and 13.

35. Grovum 2014; Frey 2012; Kneebone and Berube 2013.

36. Key 1949, 673.

37. Hoyman 1997; Gerber and Phillips 2003; Wassmer and Lascher 2006; Hawkins 2011.

38. Gallagher 2013; Warner and Zheng 2013; Mallach and Vey 2011; Matt Helms, Kathleen Gray, Paul Egan, and Todd Spangler, "Orr's Detroit Bankruptcy Plan Puts Pressure on Pensioners, State, to Ante Up," *Detroit Free Press*, February 22, 2014, p. A1; see also the special issue on shrinking cities and towns, *Urban Design International* 18, no. 1 (Spring 2013).

39. Marschall, Rigby, and Jenkins 2011; National Conference of State Legislatures 2011.

40. National Center for Education Statistics 2013b.

41. National Conference of State Legislatures 2012; Al Baker, "Common Core Curriculum Now Has Critics on the Left," *NYT*, February 16, 2014, http://www.nytimes.com/2014/02/17/nyregion/new-york-early-champion-of-common-core-standards-joins-critics.html.

42. National Center for Education Statistics 2013a; Floyd Norris, "The Hefty Yoke of Student Loan Debt," *NYT*, February 20, 2014, http://www.nytimes.com/2014/02/20/business/economy/the-hefty-yoke-of-student-loan-debt.html?hpw&rref=education&action=click&module=Search&region=searchResults%230&version=&url=http%3A%2F%2Fquery.nytimes.com%2Fsearch%2Fsitesearch%2F%3Faction%3Dclick%26regio.

43. National Conference of State Legislatures 2010.

44. Berman 2001.

45. Robin Toner, "AGOP Blitz of First 100 Days Now Brings the Heavy Combat," *NYT*, April 9, 1995, sec.1, p. 1; also see Sclar 2000.

46. Included in this total are the "border" state of Kentucky (8 electoral votes) and the 11 states of the Confederacy: Alabama (9), Arkansas (6), Florida (29), Georgia (16), Louisiana (8), Mississippi (6), North Carolina (15), South Carolina (9), Tennessee (11), Texas (38), and Virginia (13). For more on the Electoral College, including election results, see its website: http://www.archives.gov/federal-register/electoral-college/about.html.

47. On partisan and ideological change in the states, see Erikson, Wright, and McIver 2006; Gaddie 2012

48. See Heilig and Mundt 1984; Welch 1990; Welch and Bledsoe 1988; Davidson and Grofman 1994.

49. Mann and Ornstein 2012; Skocpol and Williamson 2012; Jeremy W. Peters, "Tea Party Group, Celebrating Its Fifth Anniversary, Is Happy but Restless," *NYT*, February 27, 2014, http://www.nytimes.com/2014/02/28/us/politics/tea-party-group-celebrating-its-fifth-anniversary-is-happy-but-restless.html?action=click&module=Search&region=searchResults%230&version=&url=http%3A%2F%2Fquery.nytimes.com%2Fsearch%2Fsitesearch%2F%23%2Ftea%2520party%2F&_r=0.

50. Pew Research Center for the People & the Press 2013.

51. See Caress and Kunioka 2012.

52. Initiative and Referendum Institute 2017.

53. Initiative and Referendum Institute 2012.

54. Initiative and Referendum Institute 2014.

55. Nownes, Thomas, and Hrebenar 2008.

56. Cooper, Nownes, and Roberts 2005; Gerber and Phillips 2003; Hawkins 2011.

57. Among those expressing concern is the Center for Public Integrity; see, for example, Patel 2014.

58. National Conference of State Legislatures 2013.

59. Bannon et al. 2013; Ann Narayanswamy, "Donors Flooded State Level PACs with Big Checks," Sunlight Foundation blog, September 12, 2013, http://sunlightfoundation.com/blog/2013/09/12/statepacs/; McNellis and Parkinson 2012.

60. Bannon et al. 2013, 3–6.

61. Nicholas Confessore, "A National Strategy Funds State Political Monopolies," *NYT*, January 11, 2014, http://www.nytimes.com/2014/01/12/us/politics/a-national-strategy

-funds-state-political-monopolies.html?action=click&module=Search&region=
searchResults%230&version=&url=http%3A%2F%2Fquery.nytimes.com%2Fsearch
%2Fsitesearch%2F%23%2Fconfessore%2F&_r=0.

62. Fleischmann and Stein 1998.

63. Kinkaid 2012, 39.

64. *National Federation of Independent Business v. Sibelius*, no. 11–393 (2012). See the
extensive coverage of the case at https://www.oyez.org/cases/2011/11-393.

65. U.S. Department of Health and Human Services 2014; Henry J. Kaiser Family
Foundation 2016.

66. Harold Pollack, "If the Latest Obamacare Lawsuit Succeeds, Obamacare Is in Big
Trouble," *Washington Post*, February 3, 2014, http://www.washingtonpost.com/blogs
/wonkblog/wp/2014/02/03/if-the-latest-obamacare-lawsuit-succeeds-obamacare-is-in
-big-trouble/.

67. *King v. Burwell*, no. 14–114 (2015).

68. Yoshinaka 2012.

69. Lublin and Schaller 2012, 233.

70. For some critical views on the state role in dealing with local issues, see Rusk 2013;
M. Orfield 2002.

71. See Katz and Bradley 2013.

72. Boyd and Dadayan 2013; L. L. Martin, Levey, and Cawley 2012.

Chapter 2. The Setting for Contemporary Georgia Politics

1. On studying the context of state politics, see Gray 2013.

2. See Spalding 1991.

3. For a detailed account of Georgia during this period, see Coleman 1991, 71–88.

4. Evans 1972 [1898], 90–127.

5. Coleman 1991, 89–116.

6. Evans 1972 [1898], 139–140.

7. Coleman 1991, 110–113.

8. For a detailed description of antebellum Georgia, see Boney 1991.

9. On the war in Georgia, see Boney 1991.

10. On Reconstruction, see Wynes 1991, 208–224.

11. Evans 1972 [1898], 304–305.

12. See Wynes 1991, 225–237.

13. See W. F. Holmes 1991, 257–276.

14. Ibid., 319–336.

15. Blackmon 2008.

16. On lynching, see Tolnay and Beck 1995; on Forsyth County, see Phillips 2016.

17. For a detailed account of Thomas Watson's life, see Woodward 1963. Also see W. F.
Holmes 1991, 295–308.

18. For an overview of this period in Georgia, see W. F. Holmes 1991, 309–318. For an
account of how blacks in the South were controlled after Reconstruction, see Blackmon
2008.

19. For a complete review of the life of Richard Russell, see Fite 1991.

20. See Key 1949, 119–122; M. B. Hill 1994, 224–225; H. P. Henderson and Roberts 1988, 49–62.

21. On this period, see Bartley 1991.

22. On the mayoral administration of Ivan Allen, see Pomerantz 1996. For another view, see Kruse 2005.

23. On the three-governor controversy, see H. P. Henderson and Roberts 1988, 49–62; Bullock, Buchanan, and Gaddie 2015. For further reading on the postwar history of Georgia, see Bartley 1991.

24. See Fite 1991.

25. On opposition to civil rights, see Bartley 1997.

26. For a good synopsis of postwar racial change, see Bartley 1991, 361–374; 1970. On efforts to desegregate the University of Georgia, see Trillin 1991 [1963]; Pratt 2002.

27. 205 F. Supp. 248 (1962); the U.S. Supreme Court upheld the decision in *Fortson v. Toombs*, 379 U.S. 621 (1965).

28. 372 U.S. 368 (1963).

29. 376 U.S. 1 (1964).

30. See M. B. Hill 1994, 225.

31. Linda Greenhouse, "Justices in 5–4 Vote, Reject Districts Drawn with Race the 'Predominant Factor,'" *NYT*, June 30, 1995, pp. A1, A3.

32. *Shelby County v. Holder*, 12–96 (2013); see Adam Liptak, "Supreme Court Invalidates Key Parts of Voting Rights Act," *NYT*, June 25, 2013 http://www.nytimes.com/2013/06/26/us/supreme-court-ruling.html?pagewanted=all&_r=0.

33. See *Perdue v. Baker*, 277 Ga. 1: 586 S.E.2d 606 (2003); "Redistricting Proposal Just a Political Move" (editorial), *ABH*, January 15, 2006, available at www.onlineathens.com; Tom Baxter, "Changing the Map," *AJC*, March 7, 2005, p. D8.

34. Kristina Torres, "Feds Approve Voting Lines, GOP Advantage," *AJC*, December 28, 2011, http://www.ajc.com/news/news/local/feds-ok-georgia-voting-lines-gop-advantage/nQPnj/; Aaron Gould Sheinin and Kristina Torres, "Political Redistricting: Feds OK Georgia Voting Maps: State Democrats Likely to Challenge Ruling Quickly in Court. Meanwhile, Boundaries Set for 2012 Elections," *AJC*, December 24, 2011: A1. For one advocacy group's take on the plan, see the report from the Center for Voting and Democracy, http://www.fairvote.org/research-and-analysis/blog/no-more-gerrymanders-georgia/.

35. Erikson, Wright, and McIver 2006; Gaddie 2012; Hood, Kidd, and Morris 2012a; Yoshinaka 2012.

36. These changes are covered in more detail in chapters 4, 5, and 6.

37. The Census Bureau does annual estimates of population between decennial census years, which end in zero; see U.S. Census Bureau n.d.d.

38. For more information on classification of metropolitan and micropolitan statistical areas, see U.S. Census Bureau n.d.b.

39. See Fleischmann 2012, 82–86.

40. It is worth noting that the Augusta MSA includes suburbs in South Carolina, and the Columbus MSA includes suburbs in Alabama.

41. U.S. Census Bureau 1995; and tables created with an advanced search in the Bu-

reau's "American Fact Finder," http://factfinder2.census.gov/faces/tableservices/jsf/pages
/productview.xhtml?pid=DEC_10_SF1_P1&prodType=table.

42. For a general analysis of the rise of cities by a prominent economist, see Glaeser 2011.

43. Bartley 1991, 351.

44. Such changes were not peculiar to Georgia. The "Great Migration" of African
Americans to the North and the West included a large wave after World War I, which
was interrupted by the Great Depression but was followed by another wave beginning in
the 1940s. See Lemann 1991; Gregory 2007.

45. Fite 1991, 235, 244–245.

46. C. N. Stone 1989; G. Orfield and Askinaze 1991, 103–148; C. N. Stone et al. 2001;
Kruse 2005.

47. See Kruse 2005.

48. Frey 2013.

49. Shaila Dewan, "Gentrification Changing Face of New Atlanta," *NYT*, March 11,
2006, A1.

50. See Janel Davis, "Tax Breaks for Seniors: Can Counties Afford Them?," *AJC*, June 2,
2010, http://www.ajc.com/news/news/local/tax-breaks-for-seniors-can-counties-afford
-them/nQgWD/. There was some controversy over whether all people over a certain age
should benefit or just those with low incomes. Some local governments also provided such
homestead exemptions to veterans and other groups. Most local governments now list
these on their websites. See, for example, http://www.carrollcountygatax.com/#/General
Information/.

51. See L. Stone 2015.

52. See "State of Residence by State of Birth—ACS 2014 Tables," in U.S. Census Bureau
2016.

53. Data available through the Census Bureau's "American Fact Finder" search feature.
These data are derived from five-year estimates. On Georgia and Metropolitan Atlanta,
U.S. Census Bureau 2014c.

54. For annual estimates from the U.S. Census Bureau, see U.S. Census Bureau n.d.d.

55. Data on states and communities are available for various periods using the Census
Bureau's "American Fact Finder" search tool, https://factfinder.census.gov/faces/nav/jsf
/pages/index.xhtml.

56. U.S. Census Bureau 2006, table 118; 1963, table 154.

57. Data on age, race, and ethnicity are based on five-year "Demographic and Housing
Estimates" for 2010–2014 in the American Community Survey, available with the U.S. Census Bureau's "American Fact Finder" Tool, http://factfinder.census.gov/faces/tableservices
/jsf/pages/productview.xhtml?pid=ACS_14_5YR_DP05&src=pt. See also Weinberg
2005, "Poultry."

58. Fortune magazine data available at http://beta.fortune.com/fortune500/list
/filtered?hqstate=GA.

59. For more information on the state's efforts to work with international firms, see
http://www.georgia.org/business-resources/international-investment/.

60. Maria Saporta, "Losses Sting, as Leaders Reflect," *AJC*, March 8, 2006, p. C1; "Turner
Loyal to Time Warner, but Divestitures Bother Him," *AJC*, February 28, 2006, p. C1.

61. The U.S. Small Business Administration maintains brief profiles of the small business portion of the economy for the United States along with the individual states and territories; see U.S. Small Business Administration 2013.

62. Key 1949, 664.

63. See, for example, Sheryl Gay Stolberg, "As a State's Population Changes, Its Politics Begin to Shift," *NYT*, September 19, 2014, p. A1.

64. Robbie Brown, "In Georgia, Some Vote to Stay Dry on Sundays," *NYT*, November 11, 2011, http://www.nytimes.com/2011/11/12/us/georgia-or-most-of-it-ends-sunday-ban -on-alcohol-sales.html.

65. Leslie Martin 2007.

66. Knotts and Haspel 2006.

67. For a general analysis about the shifting divisions in American local politics, see Hochschild 2012.

68. Phil Kent, "Pro & Con: Should Georgia Driver's License Tests Be English-Only?," *AJC*, February 16, 2011, p. A17.

69. Owens and Brown 2014.

70. See, for example, Aaron Gould Sheinin, "Crops Old and New Fuel Georgia's Farming Boom," *AJC*, August 2, 2015, p. A1.

71. Data on foreign investment from the Georgia Department of Economic Development are available at http://www.georgia.org/business-resources/international -investment/. For the Census Bureau's international trade data by state, see U.S. Census Bureau n.d.c.

72. On political development in Georgia from the late nineteenth century through the early 1970s, see Mickey 2015, 240–280, 316–334.

73. See Black and Black 2002; Lublin 2004; Erikson, Wright, and McIver 2006; Hood, Kidd, and Morris 2012b; Yoshinaka 2012.

74. See the Pew Research Center's "Religion & Public Life Project": http://religions .pewforum.org/. For data on denominational affiliation, see Pew Research Center: Religion and Public Life Project 2015. See also Michael Lipka, "A Closer Look at Religion in the Super Tuesday States," Pew Research Center, February 25, 2016, http://www.pew research.org/fact-tank/2016/02/25/a-closer-look-at-religion-in-the-super-tuesday-states/; Michael Lipka and Benjamin Wormald, "How Religious Is Your State?," Pew Research Center, February 29, 2016, http://www.pewresearch.org/fact-tank/2016/02/29/how-religious -is-your-state/?state=georgia; Aaron Gould Sheinin, "Gun Policy Motivates Ga. Voters on Both Sides," *AJC*, September 11, 2016, p. A1.

75. Rosalind Bentley and Chris Bowling, "Race Called Key Topic for President: Poll Finds Georgians Share Priority, but Differ on How to Address It," *AJC*, August 14, 2016, p. A1.

76. See Key 1949, as well as chapters 7 and 10 of this volume.

77. Key 1949, 491–508.

78. For turnout data nationally and by state, 1980–2016, see M. McDonald 2016.

79. Key 1949, 123.

80. State Ethics Commission, "2005 Registered Lobbyists Report." The commission has been replaced by the Georgia Government Transparency and Campaign Finance

Commission, whose website includes lobbyist registration and spending reports, http://
media.ethics.ga.gov/search/Lobbyist/Lobbyist_ByName.aspx.

81. Nownes, Thomas, and Hrebenar 2008; Jeanne Cummings, "Ethics Rules Are Few
and Far Between," *AJC*, February 23, 1992, p. D1; Rhonda Cook, "Georgia's Hidden Per-
suaders," *AJC*, February 23, 1992, p. A1; Michael Hinkelman, "Developers Dole Out
Dough," *AJC*, February 26, 1990, p. A1; "Our Opinions: Ethics Not Optional" (editorial),
AJC, May, 2005, p. A18; Cynthia Tucker, "No Cash? No Love from GOP" (editorial), *AJC*,
March 8, 2006, p. A13; Ann Hardie, "The $1 Million Lobby: Largesse Up 30% during
GOP Control," *AJC*, February 2, 2006, p. F1.

Chapter 3. Georgia's Constitution

1. For one account of the amendment's history, see John Heltman, "27th Amendment
or Bust," *American Prospect*, May 30, 2012, http://prospect.org/article/27th-amendment
-or-bust.

2. *Murdock v. City of Memphis*, 87 U.S. 590 (1874).

3. *Pruneyard Shopping Ctr. v. Robins*, 447 U.S. 74, 81 (1980).

4. *Roe v. Wade*, 410 U.S. 113 (1973). For related cases, see, e.g., *Maher v. Roe*, 432 U.S.
464 (1977); *City of Akron v. Akron Center for Reproductive Health*, 462 U.S. 416 (1983);
Webster v. Reproductive Health Services, 492 U.S. 490 (1989); and *Planned Parenthood v.
Casey*, 505 U.S. 833 (1992).

5. "Why Study the Massachusetts Constitution?," http://www.mass.gov/courts/court
-info/sjc/edu-res-center/jn-adams/mass-constitution-1-gen.html.

6. "Police Power," West's Encyclopedia of American Law, 2nd ed., 2008, The Gale
Group, August 3, 2015, http://legal-dictionary.thefreedictionary.com/Police+Power.

7. *Marbury v. Madison*, 5 U.S. 137 (1803). An earlier case, *Hylton v. United States*, 3 U.S.
171 (1796), upheld the constitutionality of a federal tax on carriages. By ruling that the
tax was constitutional, the Supreme Court obviously thought it had the power of judicial
review.

8. For an interesting account of the Prohibition era, see Okrent 2010.

9. *Jacobson v. Massachusetts*, 197 U.S. 11 (1905).

10. Constitution of the State of Georgia, art. 3, sect. 9, para. 4.

11. Constitution of the State of Georgia, art. 1, sect. 6, para. 8c.

12. Constitution of the State of Georgia, art. 7, sect. 2, para. 3e.

13. Regarding the assessment of agricultural land, see Constitution of the State of
Georgia, art. 7, sect. 1, para. 3c. Regarding the exemption for disabled veterans, see Constitution of the State of Georgia, art. 1, sect. 2, para. 5.

14. Constitution of the State of Georgia, art. 7, sect. 1, para. 3d. See also M. B. Hill 1994,
152–155.

15. M. B. Hill 1994, 110.

16. *Hollinsworth v. Perry*, no. 12–144 (June 26, 2013); *United States v. Windsor*, no. 12–
307 (June 26, 2013).

17. *Obergefell v. Hodges*, no. 14–556 (June 26, 2015).

18. Grant Blankenship, "Are Georgia Courts Ready for Same Sex Marriage?," Georgia Public Broadcasting, June 22, 2015, http://www.gpb.org/news/2015/06/22/are-georgia-courts-ready-for-same-sex-marriage.

19. Constitution of the State of Georgia, art. 4; art. 8, sects. 2, 4.

20. Constitution of the State of Georgia, art. 3, sect. 6, para. 7.

21. Ibid.

22. M. B. Hill 1994, 99.

23. This section on previous constitutions draws heavily from Hill 1994. See also L. W. Hill and M. B. Hill 2016 [2002].

24. For a thorough account, see H. P. Henderson 1991, 77–96.

25. M. B. Hill 1994, 20–22.

26. Ibid., 14–15.

27. Fleischmann and Custer 2004.

28. Bill Montgomery, "New Constitution in Hands of Voters," *AC*, November 2, 1982, p. A9; M. B. Hill 1994, 21.

29. M. B. Hill 1994, 15–17.

30. Bill Shipp, "Adopting a New Constitution and Dancing with a Grizzly Bear," *AC*, January 1, 1981, p. B2.

31. "A Constitutional Mess," *AC*, August 28, 1981, p. A4.

32. Rosenthal 1990, 87.

33. Bill Shipp, "Do the State a Favor: Forget the New Constitution," *AC*, August 15, 1981, p. B2; H. P. Henderson and Roberts 1988, 267–269.

34. "Streamlined State Constitution," *AC*, June 30, 1983, p. A22; "New State Constitution Deserves Ratification" (editorial), *AC*, October 24, 1982, p. C2.

35. Duane Stafford, "Voters Left Some Blanks Unfilled," *AJC*, November 7, 2004, p. JJ6.

36. The Georgia Secretary of State's Elections Division includes information on proposed amendments, including wording and the outcome, http://sos.ga.gov/index.php/?section=elections.

37. M. B. Hill 1994, 70.

38. Constitution of the State of Georgia, art. 3. For an interesting comparison of Congress and state legislatures, see Squire and Hamm 2005.

39. Constitution of the State of Georgia, art. 5, sect. 3.

40. Constitution of the State of Georgia, art. 6, sect. 7.

41. Constitution of the State of Georgia, art. 8, sects. 5–6; art. 9.

42. Constitution of the State of Georgia, art. 10. On ratification procedures and recent actions in other states, see Council of State Governments 2014, chap. 1.

43. Constitution of the State of Georgia, art. 3, sects. 5, 7, 9.

44. Constitution of the State of Georgia, art. 1, sect. 1, para. 1; M. B. Hill 1994, 30–33.

45. *Suber v. Bulloch County Board of Education*, 722 F.Supp. 736 (S.D. Ga., 1989).

46. *Stephens v. State*, 265 Ga. 356, 456 S.E.2d 560, cert. denied 516 U.S. 849 (1995).

47. *Kelo v. New London*, 545 U.S. 469 (2005).

48. Constitution of the State of Georgia, art. 1, sect. 1, para. 2; M. B. Hill 1994, 33–36.

49. *Grissom v. Gleason*, 262 Ga. 374, 418 S.E.2d 27 (1992).

50. *Tolbert v. Mitchell*, 253 Ga. 566, 322 S.E.2d 487 (1984).

51. *American Subcontractors Association v. City of Atlanta*, 259 Ga. 14, 376 S.E.2d 662 (1989).

52. Douglas A. Blackmon and Holly Morris, "Court Gives Split Ruling on Gay Rights," *AC*, March 15, 1995, p. E1.

53. Cameron McWhirter, "Atlanta Halts Effort to Fine Club," *AJC*, November 6, 2005, p. E4.

54. On the right to vote, see L. McDonald, Binford, and Johnson 1994.

55. For a thorough discussion, see C. N. Stone 1989.

56. W. F. Holmes 1991.

57. For a good synopsis of postwar racial change, see Bartley 1991.

58. *Stell v. Savannah-Chatham County Board of Education*, 333 F.2d 55 (1964).

59. *Regents of the University of California v. Bakke*, 438 U.S. 265 (1978).

60. The Supreme Court's position on affirmative action programs has remained consistent since Justice Powell's majority opinion in *Regents of University of California v. Bakke*, 438 U.S. 265 (1978). In *Gratz v. Bollinger*, 539 U.S. 244 (2003), and *Grutter v. Bollinger*, 539 U.S. 306 (2003), the court affirmed the use of strict scrutiny for any race-based admission standard but upheld the University of Michigan's program as premised on the compelling state interest of diversity first enunciated in Bakke. The most serious challenge to this holding occurred in *Fisher v. University of Texas*, 57 U.S. ___ (Fisher I, 2013), https://www.supremecourt.gov/opinions/12pdf/11-345_15gm.pdf. In this case, a white woman who was denied admission to the University of Texas challenged the undergraduate admissions system. The system includes two components. First, it offers admission to any students who graduate from a Texas high school in the top 10 percent of their class. It then fills the remainder of its incoming freshman class, some 25 percent, by combining an applicant's "Academic Index"—the student's SAT score and high school academic performance—with the applicant's "Personal Achievement Index," a holistic review encompassing numerous factors, including race. In Fischer I, the court remanded the case to the lower court for additional review and further action. Following the lower court's upholding of the race-conscious system, Fisher again appealed to the Supreme Court. This time the court decided in favor of the state of Texas, *Fisher v. University of Texas at Austin* (Fisher II), U.S. Supreme Court Docket No. 14-981 (2016). The vote was 4–3 with Justice Kennedy writing the majority opinion. The court upheld the race-conscious admission standard. For the University of Georgia's admissions policies, see Doug Cumming, "Applicants Nervously Await Decisions," *AC*, March 25, 1998, C5; *Wooden v. Board of Regents*, 247 U.S. F3d 1262 (2001).

61. See *Wesberry v. Sanders*, 376 U.S. 1 (1964).

62. M. B. Hill 1994, 225.

63. Linda Greenhouse, "Justices, in 5–4 Vote, Reject Districts Drawn with Race the 'Predominant Factor,'" *NYT*, June 30, 1995, p. A1.

64. *Shelby County v. Holder*, no. 12–96 (June 25, 2013).

65. This liberty is discussed in Constitution of the State of Georgia, art. 1, sect. 1, paras. 3 and 4; M. B. Hill 1994, 36–38.

66. Constitution of the State of Georgia, art. 1, sect. 1, para. 4.

67. *Coleman v. City of Griffin*, 55 Ga. App. 123, 189 S.E. 427 (1936).

68. *Spillers v. State*, 145 Ga. App. 809, 245 S.E.2d 54 (1978).

69. For example, Doug Cumming, "Bowers: Education on Origin Theories Must Avoid Religion," *AC*, March 13, 1996, p. C1; Kristina Torres, "Final Plea Heard in Evolution Case," *AJC*, November 13, 2004, p. B1.

70. Freedom of speech and press is discussed in Constitution of the State of Georgia, art. 1, sect. 1, para. 5; M. B. Hill 1994, 38–40.

71. *K. Gordon Murray Productions, Inc. v. Floyd*, 217 Ga. 784, 125 S.E.2d 207 (1962).

72. *State v. Café Erotica*, 269 Ga. 486, 500 S.E.2d 547 (1998).

73. *Hirsch v. City of Atlanta*, 261 Ga. 22, 401 S.E.2d 530 (1991).

74. *State v. Miller*, 260 Ga. 669, 398 S.E.2d 547 (1990).

75. *Vaughn v. State*, 259 Ga. 325, 381 S.E.2d 30 (1989).

76. See *OCGA*, title 24, chap. 9, sect. 30.

77. *Statesboro Publishing Co. v. City of Sylvania*, 271 Ga. 92, 516 S.E.2d 926 (1999).

78. *Cunningham v. State*, 260 Ga. 827, 400 S.E.2d 916 (1991).

79. The amendment on nude dancing became art. 3, sect. 6, para. 7 of the Georgia Constitution, which deals with the legislature's "Exercise of Powers." The amendment's application was upheld in *Goldrush II v. City of Marietta*, 267 Ga. 683, 482 S.E.2d 347 (1997).

80. Constitution of the State of Georgia, art. 1 sect. 1, paras. 11–24; M. B. Hill 1994, 42–51

81. On whipping and banishment, see Constitution of the State of Georgia, art. 1, sect. 1, para. 21; on imprisonment for debt, see art. 1, sect. 1, para. 23; on "abused in being arrested," see art. 1, sect. 1, para. 17.

82. *Bergman v. McCullough*, 218 Ga. App. 353, 461 S.E.2d 544 (1995), cert. denied 517 U.S. 1141 (1996).

83. *Crutchfield v. State*, 218 Ga. App. 360, 461 S.E.2d 555 (1995).

84. *Fleming v. Zant*, 259 Ga. 687, 386 S.E.2d 339 (1989). The U.S. Supreme Court case was *Atkins v. Virginia*, 536 U.S. 304 (2002).

85. Sandra Eckstein, "Ruling: Prosecutors Bear Racial Onus in Drug Cases," *AJC*, March 18, 1995. p. C4; "Supreme Court's Flip Flop" (editorial), *AC*, April 3, 1995, p. A6.

86. Constitution of the State of Georgia, art. 1, sect.1, para. 1b.

87. *Pavesich v. New England Life Insurance Co.*, 122 Ga. 190, 50 S.E. 68 (1904).

88. *Powell v. State of Georgia*, 270 Ga. 327, 510 S.E.2d 18 (1998)

89. *Christensen v. State*, 266 Ga. 474, 464 S.E.2d 188 (1996).

90. *Powell v. State*, 270 Ga. 327, 510 S.E.2d 18 (1998).

91. *Morrison v. State*, 272 Ga. 129, 526 S.E.2d 336 (2000).

92. *Lawrence v. Texas*, 539 U.S. 558 (2003). For a history of this case, see Carpenter 2012.

93. For the U.S. Supreme Court's view of assisted suicide and the right to privacy, see *Washington v. Glucksberg*, 521 U.S. 702 (1997), and *Vacco v. Quill*, 521 U.S. 793 (1997). On the Oregon conflict, see *Gonzales v. Oregon*, 546 U.S. 243 (2006).

94. See Mark Curriden, "Is Naming Judges Serving Justice?," *AJC*, November 29, 1992,

p. G1; Andrew Kull, "The Slow Death of Colorblind Justice," *AJC*, November 29, 1992, p. H1; Mark Curriden, "Road to a Judicial Appointment Not Clear—Even to State's Judges," *AC*, December 21, 1992, p. C3.

95. Constitution of the State of Georgia, art. 7, sect. 1, para. 3e.

96. Constitution of the State of Georgia, art. 8, sect. 5, paras. 2 and 3.

97. Nancy Badertscher and Sonji Jacobs, "Some Bills Made It; Others Didn't," *AJC*, March 15, 2006, p. B4.

Chapter 4. Voting and Elections

1. See Holbrook and LaRaja 2013, 63–104.

2. Ibid., 84–85.

3. *OCGA*, title 21, chap. 2, sects. 195 and 196.

4. The other states with runoffs are Alabama, Arkansas, Louisiana, Mississippi, North Carolina, Oklahoma, South Carolina, South Dakota, and Texas. Vermont has a provision for a runoff election but only in the extremely rare event of a tied vote. North Carolina requires the leading candidate to get at least 40 percent of the vote to avoid a runoff (National Council of State Legislators 2014).

5. L. McDonald, Binford, and Johnson 1994, 72–74.

6. Bullock and Johnson 1992, 1–8, 93–118.

7. Ibid., 135–177; Haeberle 1993.

8. *Brooks v. Miller*, 158 F.3d 1230 (1998); *Brooks v. Barnes*, no. 98–1521, cert., denied May 24, 1999; Kathey Pruitt, "Majority Vote Still Needed in Primaries," *AC*, May 25, 1999, p. B3.

9. Bullock and Johnson 1992, 38–39, 51–53, 115–117.

10. Engstrom and Engstrom 2008, 407–416.

11. Initiative and Referendum Institute 2017.

12. Charles Walston, "Public initiative on Hold for Now," *AJC*, March 4, 1995, p. C2.

13. Ballotpedia n.d.a.

14. Ballotpedia, 2016 Ballot Measures, https://ballotpedia.org/2016_ballot_measures.

15. Council of State Governments 2016, 331–333.

16. *OCGA*, title 21, chap. 4.

17. Blake Aued, "Petition to Recall Denson Thrown Out," *ABH*, February 27, 2012, http://onlineathens.com/local-news/2012–02–27/petition-recall-denson-thrown-out/.

18. Fox 31 News Team, "Recall in Warwick Dismissed by Judge," December 9, 2014, WFXL Fox 31, http://wfxl.com/news/local/recall-in-warwick-dismissed-by-judge?id= 1133601#.VIeDfDHF-mE; Mike Morrison, "Judge Throws out Effort to Recall McIntosh Commission Chairwoman," January 12, 2012, *Florida Times-Union*, http://jacksonville.com /news/georgia/2012–01–12/story/judge-throws-out-effort-recall-mcintosh-commission -chairwoman#ixzz1jNdgvn18.

19. Coleman 1991, 92, 279, 392; H. P. Henderson and Roberts 1988, 34–38; L. McDonald, Binford, and Johnson 1994, 64–75.

20. Key 1949, 536.

21. Ibid., 531–663.

22. *Smith v. Allwright*, 321 U.S. 649 (1944).

23. *King v. Chapman*, 154 F.2d 450 (1946). See Key 1949, 619–643; L. McDonald, Binford, and Johnson 1994, 69–72; C. N. Stone 1989, 25–50; W. F. Holmes 1991, 279; Kruse 2005.

24. W. F. Holmes 1991, 280.

25. Ibid., 279–280; Key 1949, 569–570; L. McDonald, Binford, and Johnson 1994, 69–70.

26. Bositis 2002.

27. *Shelby County v. Holder*, 570 U.S. ___ (2013).

28. Coleman 1991, 306–307, 392; H. P. Henderson 1991, 55–60.

29. *Baker v. Carr*, 296 U.S. 186 (1962).

30. For an interesting account of a Georgia campaign in the early days of "one person, one vote," see Carter 1992.

31. See *Perdue v. Baker*, 277 Ga. 1: 586 S.E.2d 606 (2003).

32. Gary Hendricks, "House Divided Will Be Boon to Blacks, GOP," *AJC*, August 4, 1991, p. C1.

33. Doug Nurse, "Redistricting: New Maps Yield Tight, Single-Member Units," *AJC*, April 1, 2004, p. JJ5.

34. See "Legislature 2005: In Brief," *AJC*, March 16, 2005, p. B3; Tom Baxter, "Changing the Map," *AJC*, March 7, 2005, p. D8.

35. Care should be taken when interpreting voter turnout. In many instances, turnout is calculated as a percentage of registered voters. Data throughout this chapter, unless otherwise noted, reflect voter turnout as a percentage of the voting age population of a jurisdiction.

36. U.S. Census Bureau 2010, table 397. There are ongoing debates about measuring turnout, including biases in surveys and whether to use total voting-age population in calculations even though some residents are not eligible to register. See reports of the United States Election Project at George Mason University, http://elections.gmu.edu.

37. M. McDonald 2016.

38. Atkenson and Partin 1995; Squire and Fastnow 1994.

39. C. Wood 2002; Hajnal and Lewis 2003.

40. More information on these differences is available from the U.S. Election Assistance Commission, https://www.eac.gov.

41. Council of State Governments 2016, 300–301.

42. Council of State Governments 1996, 162–163; D. Lewis 2005. See also the activities and reports of the National Association of Election Officials, http://www.electioncenter .org.

43. Carlos Campos, "Voter ID Bill Approved; Opponents Vow to Continue Fight," *AJC*, January 26, 2006, p. A1; Nancy Badertscher and Sonji Jacobs, "Legislature 2006: Voter ID Costs Still Debated," *AJC*, January 28, 2006, p. E1.

44. *OCGA*, title 21, chap. 2. sect. 417.1

45. See Dan Tokaji, "Early Returns on Election 2004," http://moritzlaw. osu.edu/blogs /tokaji/2004_12_01_equalvote_archive.html, December 24.

46. Cathy Cox, "Elections System's Safeguards Effective," *AJC*, March 10, 2005, p. A23; Bullock, Hood, and Clark 2005.

47. Bill Osinski, "Voting Irregularities Alleged," *AC*, August 7, 1992, p. D3; Bill Osinski, "Early-Ballot System May Replace Ga. Absentee Voting," *AJC*, October 17, 1993, p. F7; Alan Judd, "Absentee Voter Fraud Untouched by ID Law," *AJC*, January 29, 2006, p. A1; http://www.politifact.com/georgia/statements/2014/jun/04/brian-kemp/early-voting -grows-popularity/.

48. Key 1949, 491–508.

49. Black and Black 1987, 175–179.

50. "Voter Turnout, National Turnout Rates 1787–2016," United States Election Project, http://www.electproject.org/home/voter-turnout/voter-turnout-data. An alternative measure would be to calculate turnout with total ballots cast as the numerator, but there are gaps in the U.S. and Georgia data throughout the 1980–2014 period.

51. On primaries, see Flanigan and Zingale 2014, 70–77, 81–82, 171–176; see also James Salzer and Nancy Badertscher, "Parties Spin Vote Their Way; Perdue's Coattails Run Short, but Democrats Outnumbered," *AJC*, July 22, 2004, p. A1.

52. See Key 1949, 107–127; W. F. Holmes 1991, 296–305, 311–318; Anderson 1975; Carter 1992.

53. Beyle 1996, 213–218.

54. All data on campaign expenditures in this section are from the Georgia Secretary of State, http://www.sos.state.ga.us. However, the responsibility for maintaining such data was transferred to the State Ethics Commission in January 2006, http://ethics .ga.gov/.

55. Institute on Money in State Politics 2006.

56. Jim Galloway, "Perdue Raises More Than Rivals Combined," *AJC*, January 11, 2006, p. B5.

57. Institute on Money in State Politics, "Overview of Georgia 2014 Elections," https:// www.followthemoney.org/election-overview?s=GA&y=2014.

58. See http://media.ethics.ga.gov/references/pdf/CF_Act_2010.pdf.

59. Patrick Milsaps, December 2, 2010, State Ethics Commission, "Contribution Limits," www.ethics.georgia.gov.

60. Frances Schwartzkopff, "Skirting New Ethics," *AC*, April 6, 1992, p. D1; Ben Smith, "Homemakers Generous Campaign Givers," *AJC*, June 5, 2005, p. C1.

61. Mark Sherman, "Critics Say Ethics Law Has Loophole Big Enough to Drive Lots of Cash Through," *AJC*, January 23, 1993, p. B1.

62. Alan Judd, "2 Speaker Candidates Funnel Bucks to Legislators," *AJC*, January 12, 2003, p. A1.

Chapter 5. Political Parties and Interest Groups

1. Madison 1787.

2. On the organization and operation of political parties, see Hershey 2015.

3. For post-1970 changes in the South as an example of such variation, see Black and Black 2002; Hood, Kidd, and Morris 2012b.

4. This was especially true in the 1990 U.S. Senate race between Wyche Fowler and Paul Coverdell, in which a Libertarian candidate's portion of the vote forced a runoff and

changed the outcome of the election. Fowler achieved the plurality of the vote in the general election, but Coverdell was the victor in the runoff. See chapter 4 for a more detailed discussion. See also Elliott, Gryski, and Reed 1990.

5. Black and Black 1992, 141–210; Erikson, Wright, and McIver 2006; Gaddie 2012.

6. Key 1964, 315.

7. W. F. Holmes 1991, 295–308.

8. For more on Henry Grady, see Bartley 1990, 82–85.

9. Key 1949, 106–107; H. P. Henderson 1991; Bullock, Buchanan, and Gaddie 2015.

10. See Rae 1992; Black and Black 1987, 3–22, 232–256.

11. Black and Black 1992, 243.

12. Black and Black 2002; Lublin 2004; Erikson, Wright, and McIver 2006.

13. James Salzer and Sonji Jacobs, "Candidates Emphasize Black Vote; Democrats Look for Governorship Backing," *AJC*, December 2, 2005, p. E1.

14. April Hunt, "Is Most of Georgia's Population Growth from Minorities?," *PolitiFact Georgia*, June 17, 2014, http://www.politifact.com/georgia/statements/2014/jun/17/stacey -abrams/most-georgias-population-growth-minorities/.

15. Kristina Torres, "Minority Voters on the Rise," *AJC*, October 22, 2014, p. A1.

16. See Yoshinaka 2012.

17. Gallup tracking poll, January 16, 2016, http://www.gallup.com/.

18. See H. P. Henderson and Roberts 1988, 193–200; Bass and DeVries 1976, 141–143.

19. The Georgia secretary of state maintains extensive records of election results. Those for 2006 can be found at http://www.sos.state.ga.us/elections/election_results /2006_1107/default.htm.

20. Scher 1992.

21. Gary Boulard, "Seismic Shift in the South," *State Legislatures*, January 1995, 5, 16–21, http://go.galegroup.com/ps/i.do?p=AONE&sw=w&u=lom_emichu&v=2.1&id= GALE%7CA16352147&it=r&asid=30beb561376ed2c2a0b5d2149a2d3b26.

22. Council of State Governments 2004, 82.

23. James Salzer, "Stripped of Power, Caucus Aims to Pull Party to the Middle," *AJC*, December 23, 2004, p. A1; Jim Tharpe, "Parties Take Stock: Flattened Democrats Seek to Regain Footing," *AJC*, November 7, 2004, p. E12.

24. Mike Christensen, "Anti-Talmadge Vote Was Gone—and So Was Mack Mattingly," *AJC*, November 9, 1986, p. A1; Lamis 1990, 101–103.

25. Tom Baxter and Jim Galloway, "Legislature 2005: More Blacks Register to Vote," *AJC*, February 10, 2005, p. C5.

26. See Gary Boulard, "Seismic Shift in the South," *State Legislatures*, January 1995, 16–21, http://go.galegroup.com/ps/i.do?p=AONE&sw=w&u=lom_emichu&v=2.1&id= GALE%7CA16352147&it=r&asid=30beb561376ed2c2a0b5d2149a2d3b26.

27. Teixeira, Frey, and Griffin 2015.

28. Hrebenar and Scott 1990, 29–35.

29. Ibid., 10–29.

30. For a discussion of the many forms that lobbying takes and the different types of lobbyists, see Hrebenar and Scott 1990, 69–165; 214–239; Hrebenar and Thomas 1992, 10–12.

31. National Conference of State Legislatures, "2015–2016 Election Cycle: State Limits on Contributions to Candidates," July 12, 2016, http://www.ncsl.org/Portals/1/documents /legismgt/elect/ContributionLimitstoCandidates2015-2016.pdf.

32. Epstein 1994.

33. Lynch 2004.

34. Thomas and Hrebenar 1996, 123–158.

35. Nownes, Thomas, and Hrebenar 2008.

36. Gilens and Page 2014.

37. Hrebenar and Thomas 2004.

38. Wolak et al. 2002.

39. Hrebenar and Thomas 1992, 17–26.

40. Key 1949, 123–124, 467–468, 475.

41. Main, Epstein, and Elovich 1992, 231–248.

42. Hunter 1963; Main, Epstein, and Elovich 1992.

43. Main, Epstein, and Elovich 1992, 235–248.

44. Georgia Government Transparency and Campaign Finance Commission n.d.

45. For a comparative analysis, see Opheim 1991; Newmark 2005.

46. Jeanne Cummings, "Ethic Rules Few and Far Between in Georgia," *AJC*, June 23, 1991, p. D1; Mark Sherman, "Cleland Panel Finalizes Tough Ethics Proposals," *AC*, December 6, 1991, p. A1.

47. *OCGA*, title 21, chap. 5, sects. 71–73.

48. Rhonda Cook, "Reports Don't Tell Lobbying Secrets," *AJC*, April 25, 1993, p. D1.

49. Chris Joyner, "Ethics Backlog Undermines Transparency," *AJC*, September 26, 2014, http://www.myajc.com/news/news/ethics-backlog-undermines-transparency/nhT8F/.

50. The figures are taken from the Institute on Money in State Politics (http://www. followthemoney.org), which provides summaries from the databases of the Georgia Secretary of State and the Georgia Government Transparency and Campaign Finance Commission. These data are for all donations and contributions reported for elections held in 2016. Local races are not included in these data.

51. Ibid.

52. Main, Epstein, and Elovich 1992, 236–240.

53. Ann Hardie, "Lobbyists Stand Ground," *AJC*, January 19, 2006, p. A1.

54. Ann Hardie, "The $1 Million Lobby," *AJC*, February 2, 2006, p. F1.

55. Frank LoMonte, "Lobbyists Play, Pay Power Game," *Athens Daily News/Banner Herald*, March 10, 1991, p. D1; Rhonda Cook, "Oink if You Know the Secret Menu for Legislature's Wild Hog Supper," *AJC*, January 10, 1993, p. A1; Melissa Turner, "More than 200 Politicians Take Olympic Ticket Offer," *AJC*, August 5, 1995, p. A1; Ben Smith III, "Who Leases Ga. Power's Lots? Not Just Anyone," *AJC*, May 5, 1991, p. A1; Rhonda Cook, "Legislators Being Feted in Daytona," *AJC*, February 13, 1993, p. A1; Mark Sherman, "Lobbyists Ply Lawmakers with Food," *AC*, August 9, 1995, p. E3; Mark Sherman, "Lobbyist-Paid Trips Are Common," *AC*, August 9, 1995, p. B1; Jill Young Miller, "Free Doctoring a Legislative Perk," *AJC*, February 19, 2006, p. E1.

56. The figures are from the database of the State Ethics Commission (http://www .ethics.state.ga.us) in January 2006.

57. Mark Sherman, "How NRA's Allies Outflanked Foes," *AC*, March 16, 1995, p. B4; Ben Smith III, "'Christian Right' Grows in Influence," *AJC*, October 9, 1994, p. D1.

58. Jill Vejnoska, "Interest-Cap Unlikely to Get to Ga. Senate Floor," *AJC*, February 14, 1993, p. A1.

59. Abney 1988.

60. Steve Janus, letter to the editor, *AC*, August 11, 1995, p. A16.

61. Betsy White, "Schrenko Gives Priority to Contributors," *AJC*, February 24, 1996, p. C4.

62. Rhonda Cook, "Firms Gave Thousands to Ryles in '92," *AJC*, January 30, 1993, p. C1; Mark Sherman, "Politicians Cash in on Campaign Leftovers," *AC*, August 5, 1993, p. D1; Institute of Money in State Politics, http://www.followthemoney.org.

63. Chris Joyner, "Speaker Has Secret Political Fund," *AJC*, May 13, 2016, p. B1.

64. Alan Judd, "Unregulated Donations Build Richardson Fund," *AJC*, February 24, 2006, p. A1; Jim Galloway, "GOP Not First with Lobby Fund," *AJC*, February 25, 2006, p. B1.

65. Richard Whitt, "'90 Timber Tax Cut Goes Awry," *AJC*, December 27, 1992, p. A1.

66. For background, see "Georgia Sales Tax to Fund Transportation Projects, Referendum 1 (July 2012)," Ballotpedia, https://ballotpedia.org/Georgia_Sales_Tax_Increase _to_Fund_Transportation_Projects,_Referendum_1_(July_2012).

67. Jim Tharpe, "Gay Union Battle Brews: Same Sex Marriage; Proposed Ban's Friends, Foes Prepare Campaigns," *AJC*, May 12, 2004, p. B1.

68. Bartley 1991.

69. Scott Bronstein, "Ga.'s Workers' Comp Law Protested," *AC*, March 3, 1992, p. C4.

Chapter 6. The Legislature

1. Comparisons in this section are based on Council of State Governments 2005, chap. 3.

2. For a discussion of the different types of legislatures, see Hamm and Moncrief 2004, 157–160; Squire 2000, 1988; Squire and Hamm 2005.

3. Maddox 2004.

4. Kurtz 2015.

5. See Jackson and Stakes 1988a, 1–10.

6. Rhonda Cook, "Attorney General's Authority Upheld," *AJC*, September 5, 2003, p. A1.

7. Requirements are delineated in Constitution of the State of Georgia, art. 2, sect. 2, paras. 3, 4.

8. *Chandler v. Miller*, 520 U.S. 305 (1997).

9. Rules regarding legislative sessions are delineated in Constitution of the State of Georgia, art. 5, sect. 2, para. 7.

10. Constitution of the State of Georgia, art. 2, sect. 4, para. 6; Council of State Governments 2016, 66–67.

11. National Conference of State Legislatures, "2016 Survey: State Legislative Compensation," http://www.ncsl.org/Portals/1/Documents/legismgt/2016_Leg_Comp_Session _Per%20Diem_Mileage.pdf.

12. Moncrief et al. 1992.

13. Story 2003.

14. Council of State Governments 2015, 70–72.

15. Moncrief et al. 1992.

16. National Conference of State Legislatures, "Legislator Demographics: Table for Gender," September 4, 2015. http://www.ncsl.org/Portals/1/Documents/About_State_Legislatures/Gender.pdf.

17. National Conference of State Legislatures, "Legislator Demographics: Table for Occupations," 2017, http://www.ncsl.org/Portals/1/Documents/About_State_Legislatures/Occupations.pdf.

18. Nancy Badertscher and James Salzer, "GOP Flexes Muscle," *AJC*, November 11, 2004, p. B1; Thomas Stinson, John Kessler, Andrea Jones, Mary Macdonald, Matt Kempner, Michelle Hiskey, Gayle White, John Blake, Bo Emerson, Thomas Stinson, and Dave Hirschman, "Reddest of the Red: State Bucks National Trend, Remains Republican Fortress," *AJC*, November 12, 2006, A1; James Salzer, "GOP Secures Georgia," *AJC*, November 8, 2006, D1. On party switching in the South, see Yoshinaka 2012.

19. Constitution of the State of Georgia, art. 3, sect. 3.

20. Hurst 2004.

21. Jewell and Whicker 1994, 63–76.

22. James Salzer and Rhonda Cook, "Rural Leadership Chosen," *AJC*, November 13, 2002, p. B1; James Salzer, "Johnson: Partisan Days Are Ending," *AJC*, November 17, 2002, p. F4; Jim Galloway, "Coleman: Change of Direction Is Needed," *AJC*, November 17, 2002, p. F4.

23. Rhonda Cook, "'A New Day in Georgia': Coleman Wins Speaker's Race; In Senate, GOP Strips Taylor of Most Power," *AJC*, January 14, 2003, p. D1; Tom Baxter and Jim Galloway, "Legislature 2005: Democrat Denied Ceremonial Role," *AJC*, January 13, 2005, p. C8.

24. Council of State Governments 2004, 124–127; National Conference of State Legislatures 2003.

25. National Conference of State Legislatures 2009; Rhonda Cook and Nancy Badertscher, "General Assembly Leaders Add Staff," *AJC*, September 28, 2003, p. C1.

26. Council of State Governments 2016, 113–114.

27. *Rules, Ethics and Decorum of the House of Representatives* [2005 session], Rules 11.1, 11.3, 11.8; Nancy Badertscher, "GOP's 'Hawks' Ruffle Democratic Feathers," *AJC*, January 17, 2005, p. B1.

28. *Rules of the Georgia State Senate, 2005 Session* (adopted January 10, 2005), sec. 2, part 1.1.

29. Information on the membership of House and Senate committees, as well as biographies and district maps for individual members, is available at the General Assembly's website, http://www.legis.state.ga.us/.

30. For the constitutional requirements on lawmaking, see Constitution of the State of Georgia, art. 3, sect. 5.

31. Constitution of the State of Georgia, art. 3, sect. 5, para. 8.

32. Council of State Governments 2016, 105–106.

33. On the adoption of legislation, see Constitution of the State of Georgia, art. 3, sect. 5.

34. Constitution of the State of Georgia, art. 3, sect. 6.

35. Constitution of the State of Georgia, art. 3, sect. 4, para. 11.

36. Gary Pomerantz, "The State Capitol's Wily Wizard of Oz," *AC*, March 8, 1992, p. A1.

37. "Rules of the Georgia State Senate, 2015–2016 Term," Rule 3–1.5, http://www.senate .ga.gov/sos/Documents/senaterules2015.pdf. See also "Rules, Ethics, and Decorum of the House of Representatives: 2015–2016 Biennium," Rule 150, http://www.house.ga.gov /Documents/Information/HouseRules2016.pdf; Sonji Jacobs and Nancy Badertscher, "Bills Race Clock for Today's Deadline: Republicans Expect Smooth 'Crossover,'" *AJC*, March 13, 2006, p. C1.

38. Constitution of the State of Georgia, art. 3, sect. 5, paras. 11–13.

39. Council of State Governments 2016, 163–164.

40. Greg Bluestein and James Salzer, "Gov. Deal Faces New Challenges in 'Post-Veto' Era," *AJC*, April 3, 2016, p. A1; Aaron Gould Sheinin and Kristina Torres, "Poll: Voters Split on Deal's Veto Decisions," *AJC*, May 16, 2016, p. A1.

41. Steve Harvey, "Georgia Funds Allocated Secretly," *AC*, May 9, 1992, p. A1.

42. Mark Sherman, "Governor OKs Strict Ethics Law," *AC*, April 7, 1992, p. A1.

43. Main, Epstein, and Elovich 1992.

44. Abney 1988.

45. Jim Tharpe and Nancy Badertscher, "Legislature '05: Lobbies Spend a Million in 2004," *AJC*, February 2, 2005, p. B1; James Salzer, "Legislature 2005: On the House; Lobbyist for Stores Dispenses Goodies to Lawmakers," *AJC*, March 26, 2005, p. F5; Nancy Badertscher and Sonji Jacobs, "Legislature '05: The Big Issues; Open Season for Lobbying at Gold Dome," *AJC*, December 20, 2004, p. D1; Sonji Jacobs, "Legislature '05: The Big Issues; Abortion Foes to Push Limits," *AJC*, December 12, 2004, p. D1.

46. Mark Sherman, "Cleland Panel Finalizes Tough Ethics Proposals," *AC*, December 6, 1991, p. A1; Peter Mantius, "BCCI Tied to Change in State Law," *AC*, September 27, 1991, p. A1; Mark Sherman, "Governor OKs Strict Ethics Law," *AC*, April 7, 1992, p. A1.

47. Newmark 2005.

48. James Salzer, "Legislature '05: Lobbyists May Face New Rules," *AJC*, February 13, 2005, p. A1; James Salzer, "Lobbyists Cozy Up to Party in Power," *AJC*, January 14, 2005, p. A1.

49. See Jackson and Stakes 1988a.

50. Steve Harvey, "Two Who Bucked Murphy Lose Committee Posts," *AJC*, December 22, 1992, p. C5.

Chapter 7. The Executive Branch

1. Council of State Governments 2015, 183–188.

2. On these changes, see Teaford 2002.

3. Beyle 2003; Beyle and Ferguson. 2008. There are clearly limitations with Beyle's scoring, particularly the inclusion of items such as party control of the legislature in formal authority. Beyle's last contribution to this analysis prior to retirement was in the

9th edition of the reader that long included his chapter on governors and the executive branch. The 10th edition, however, incorrectly codes the budgetary and veto power of Georgia's governor. See Gray, Hanson, and Kousser 2013, 225–226.

4. Ferguson 2006.

5. Council of State Governments 2014, 149–150.

6. Constitution of the State of Georgia, art. 5, sect. 1. For a brief history of Georgia's governorship, see Jackson and Stakes 1988b, 38–45.

7. *Clinton v. New York*, 524 U.S. 417 (1998).

8. Constitution of the State of Georgia, art. 3, sect. 5.

9. Beyle 2003, 212–215; Constitution of the State of Georgia, art. 3, sect. 9; Lauth 1986.

10. Beyle 2003, 210–214.

11. Jay Bookman, "Governor Deal and the Concentration of Power," *AJC*, May 4. 2015; Tom Crawford, "A State Representative Accused Gov. Nathan Deal of Being a King," *Flagpole*, March 25, 2015.

12. James Salzer, "Carter Vows to Release Donor Information on Appointees," *AJC*, August 22, 2014.

13. Maureen Downey, "NAACP Calls for Halt to Privately Managed Charter Schools: Will That Hurt or Help Kids?," *AJC*, August 22, 2016.

14. Stacey Shelton, "Perdue Swears In 24 Environmental Advisers," *AJC*, June 9, 2005, p. C3.

15. Bill Rankin, "Perdue's Court Pick Historic," *AJC*, June 9, 2005, p. A1.

16. See Key 1949.

17. Neustadt 1990.

18. Alicia Parlapiano, "Pence Ranks Low in Approval, but Not as Low as Trump and Clinton," *NYT*, July 15, 2016, http://www.nytimes.com/interactive/2016/07/14/us/politics/mike-pence-approval-rating-governors.html.

19. Louis Jacobson, "The Best of Times, the Worst of Times: A Ranking of State Economies," Governing: The State and Localities, August 22, 2016, http://www.governing.com/topics/politics/gov-state-economic-rankings-governor-ratings.html.

20. See Dilger 1995, 118–126.

21. For a discussion of gubernatorial roles, see Rosenthal 1990, 20; Beyle 2003, 218–227; Bowman and Kearney 2011, chap. 7.

22. See Beyle 2003, 219–226; Bowman and Kearney 2011, chap. 7.

23. Lauth 1990.

24. Eisinger 1988.

25. Lufken 2012.

26. Derek Willis, "Narendra Modi, the Social Media Politician," *NYT*, September 25, 2014, https://www.nytimes.com/2014/09/26/upshot/narendra-modi-the-social-media-politician.html.

27. *Near v. Minnesota*, 283 U.S. 697 (1931).

28. On governors and the media generally, see Beyle 2003, 224–226.

29. David Beasley, "Land-Use Plan May Change Face of Rural Georgia," *AJC*, October 30, 1988, p. 1C; David Beasley, "State Land-Use Plan: Hardest Part Is Yet to Come," *AC*, April 17, 1989, p. 3E.

30. Ken Foskett, "State Privatization Moving Too Fast, Critics Say," *AJC*, November 25, 1995, p. B6; Shelly Emling and Ken Foskett, "Privatization Proposals Win OK," *AC*, February 16, 1996, p. B4.

31. Nancy Badertscher, "Task Force to Evaluate Topics: Governor Names Pair to Co-Chair New Board," *AJC*, May 28, 2003, p. B3.

32. Office of the Governor 2015.

33. Kousser and Phillips 2009.

34. Thompson and Boyd 1994.

35. Rosenthal 1990, 20.

36. Beyle 1996, 209–213.

37. Kousser and Phillips 2009.

38. Ibid.

39. See Henderson and Roberts 1988; H. P. Henderson 1991.

40. See Rosenthal 1990, 22–24.

41. Ibid., 13–17.

42. See, for example, Dick Pettys, "Miller Isn't Shy in Touting Grants of $4 Million-Plus," *AC*, July 13, 1993, p. B3.

43. Ken Foskett, "Plan Spreads Lotto Green across State," *AC*, January 5, 1994, p. D1; Ben Smith III, "Miller Tax Plan Hailed as a Good Political Move," *AJC*, December 18, 1993, p. B1; Ken Foskett, "Lawmakers Give Miller Agenda Cooler Reception," *AC*, March 20, 1995, p. B1.

44. Rosenthal 1990, 35–36.

45. Bowman and Kearney 2012, 181–183, 194–195.

46. Conant 1992.

47. Council of State Governments 2014, 218–219.

48. Betsy White, "Battle Weary," *AC*, October 3, 1996, p. B4; James Salzer, "Perdue Asks Resignations of 4 on State School Board," *AJC*, January 10, 2003, p. C3; Joey Ledford, "DOT's Reynolds: Perdue Forced Exit," *AJC*, August 22, 2003, p. C1; Nancy Badertscher and Jim Galloway, "Perdue Ousts DHR's Chief," *AJC*, September 17, 2003, p. A1.

49. Bartley 1991, 361–370; C. N. Stone 1989, 25–76.

50. "Carter Plans Trip to Latin America," *AC*, February 19, 1972, p. 6B; "Carter Leaves Desk for 9-City Air Tour," *AC*, December 9, 1972, p. 12B; "Carter Flies from Paris to Israel," *AC*, May 25, 1973, p. 7A; "Busbee Arrives in South Korea," *AC*, October 27, 1975; Beau Cutts, "Ga. Leaders to Go to NYC to Lure Business, Tourism," *AJ*, March 21, 1983, p. 7B; Elizabeth Kurylo, "Miller Going to Russia, May Talk with Yeltsin," *AC*, December 5, 1991, p. A4; James Salzer, "'Growing Jobs' No Snap: Perdue Finds Task Easier Said than Done," *AJC*, August 10, 2005, p. C1.

51. Office of the Governor 2014b.

52. Greg Bluestein, "Deal to Talk Trade in Brazil," *AJC*, June 12, 2015, p. A1.

53. Constitution of the State of Georgia, art. 5, sect. 3.

54. Constitution of the State of Georgia, art. 5, sect. 4.

55. *OCGA*, title 45, chap. 15; Jackson and Stakes 1988b, 63–69.

56. Rhonda Cook, "Oink If You Know the Secret Menu for Legislature's Wild Hog Supper," *AJC*, January 10, 1993, p. A1.

57. Peter Mantius, "Weak Regulatory Setup Lets Insurers Call the Shots," *AJC*, November 20, 1988, p. 1A; Rhonda Cook, "Firms Gave Thousands to Ryles in '92," *AJC*, January 30, 1993, p. C1.

58. Analysis based on data from the National Institute on Money in State Politics, http://followthemoney.org/show-me?f-core=1&c-t-eid=12999137#[{1|gro=c-t-id{1|gro=y,d-cci. Data can be sorted for candidates by individual donors, industries, zip codes, and other categories.

59. National Institute on Money in State Politics, http://followthemoney.org/show-me?c-t-eid=6667029&c-t-id=175094#[{1|gro=y,d-cci.

60. Shelley Emling, "Insurance Chief Agrees to Collect Tax," *AC*, August 18, 1995, p. C2.

61. J. Lewis n.d.

62. See Anderson 1975, 195–204.

63. Jackson and Stakes 1988b, 96–99.

64. Hal Strauss, "Work of State Licensing Boards Limited," *AJC*, September 2, 1984; Frank LoMonte, "Consultants Costing Ga. Big Bucks," *ABH*, August 25, 1991, p. 1A; Mark Sherman, "DOT Board Had $88,000 in Expenses," *AC*, August 12, 1993, p. C1; "DNR Board Out of Balance" (editorial), *AC*, August 31, 1993, p. A18; Carrie Teegardin and Ann Hardie, "Auto Deal Gone Sour? Don't Count on Help from State's Consumer Agencies," *AJC*, October 24, 2005, p. A1.

65. See Walters 1997.

66. Governor's Commission on Effectiveness and Economy in Government 1992, 48.

67. Jackson and Stakes 1988b.

68. Andy Miller, "PeachCare for Kids Kicks Off Blitz for New Health Insurance," *AJC*, July 15, 1998, p. C3; Andy Miller, "Legislators OK New Agency," *AJC*, March 21, 1999, p. D6; Peter Mantius, "Health Agency Created as Barnes Combines Divisions," *AJC*, April 20, 1999, p. C2; Kathey Pruitt, "New Czar for Health Dismisses 19 Staffers," *AJC*, July 15, 1999, p. E2; Andy Miller, "Barnes Names Members of New Health Department's Board," *AJC*, August 5, 1999, p. G2, https://dch.georgia.gov/.

69. On the problems of assessing the work of government, see Jones 1982; Osborne and Gaebler 1992.

70. See Abney and Lauth 1986.

71. Betsy White, "Miller to Nix School-Grant Allocations," *AC*, February 8, 1994, p. C1; James Salzer, "Legislature '05: House Serves Up 'Pork' for Suburbia," *AJC*, March 19, 2005, p. C1; James Salzer, "Legislature 2005: Pork Clogs Budget Path," *AJC*, March 29, 2005, p. B3.

72. See Osborne and Gaebler 1992.

73. Pew Charitable Trust, "Measuring Performance: The State Management Report Card for 2008," February 29, 2008, http://www.pewtrusts.org/en/research-and-analysis/reports/2008/02/29/measuring-performance-the-state-management-report-card-for-2008.

74. David C. King, Richard J. Zeckhauser, and Mark T. Kim. "The Management Performance of U.S. States," July 30, 2002, https://www.hks.harvard.edu/fs/rzeckhau/GradingStatesv1.pdf.

75. Wilson 1989, 376.

Chapter 8. The Legal System

1. Ducat 2009, 334.

2. See Glick 2004; Jacob 1995, 26–36.

3. *Erie Railroad Co. v. Tompkins*, 304 U.S. 64 (1938).

4. Georgia Office of Planning and Budget 2016a

5. Bill Raftery, "Georgia: Judicial Omnibus Bill Includes 3 New Court of Appeals Judges, Salary Increases, Judicial Compensation Commission," *Gavel to Gavel* (blog), April 15, 2015, http://gaveltogavel.us/2015/04/15/georgia-judicial-omnibus-bill-includes-3-new-court-of-appeals-judges-salary-increases-judicial-compensation-commission/.

6. 1967 Ga. Laws, p. 538.

7. Court of Appeals of Georgia n.d.

8. "Deal Signs Legislation Adding Two Members To Georgia's Supreme Court," *Times Free Press*, March 3, 2016, http://www.timesfreepress.com/news/politics/state/story/2016/may/03/deal-signs-legislation-adding-two-members-georgias-supreme-court/363713/.

9. Greenblatt 2016a.

10. Brace, Langer, and Hall 2000.

11. See Berry et al. 1998.

12. Judicial Council of Georgia: Administrative Office of the Courts, Annual Reports Georgia Courts FY 2014, http://www.georgiacourts.org/sites/default/files/Annual%20Reports/FY_14%20Report.pdf.

13. Sentell 2004, 82–84.

14. Ibid., 53–59.

15. Eisenberg and Miller 2004.

16. For more detail, see Administrative Office of the Courts, "Judicial Branch of Georgia," http://www.georgiacourts.org/.

17. Judicial Qualifications Commission, State of Georgia, "Functions and Procedures," 2017, http://www.gajqc.com.

18. Ibid.

19. Bill Rankin, "Georgia Judges Ousted, Some in Handcuffs," *AJC*, July 30, 2015, p. A1.

20. Nancy Badertscher, "Georgia House Votes to Create Panel to Investigate Judicial Watchdog," *AJC*, February 24, 2016, http://www.myajc.com/news/news/state-regional-govt-politics/georgia-house-votes-to-create-panel-to-investigate/nqXXy/.

21. Georgia Legislative Navigator, 2016, "Bill to Create New Judicial Qualifications Commissions," *AJC*, https://www.documentcloud.org/documents/3250731-HB-808.html

22. The leading case here is *Gideon v. Wainwright*, 372 U.S. 335 (1963).

23. Judicial Council of Georgia: Administrative Office of the Courts n.d.a; Bill Rankin, "Three Systems: Is One Superior?," *AJC*, April 21, 2002, p. A21; Bill Rankin, "A Cheap Dose of Due Process in Dodge," *AJC*, April 22, 2002, p. A1; Bill Rankin, "Other States Offer Lessons in Reform," *AJC*, April 23, 2002, p. A1.

24. Nancy Badertscher, "Indigent Defense Measure Now Law," *AJC*, June 16, 2004, p. D1; Bill Rankin, "Counties' Legal Plans Rejected; Indigent Protection Cited," *AJC*, October 30, 2004, p. B1; Bill Rankin, "Legislature '05: Defender System Gets Early Praise; State Indigent Program Off to Quiet Start," *AJC*, February 6, 2005, p. F1.

25. A. G. Sulzberger, "Ouster of Iowa Judges Sends Signal to Bench," *NYT*, November 4, 2010, p. A1.

26. See Judicial Selection in the States, National Center for State Courts, 2017, http://www.judicialselection.us/.

27. Glick 1993.

28. Spill and Bratton 2002.

29. Hall 2001.

30. M. D. Holmes et al. 1993.

31. Steffensmeier and Britt 2001.

32. Gorton and Boies 1999.

33. Hall 1992; Hall and Brace 1994.

34. William Glaberson, "A Spirited Campaign for Ohio Court Puts Judges in New Terrain," *NYT*, July 7, 2000, p. A11; William Glaberson, "States Taking Steps to Rein In Excesses of Judicial Politicking," *NYT*, June 15, 2001, p. A1; Adam Liptak, "Judicial Races in Several States Become Partisan Battlegrounds," *NYT*, October 24, 2004, sec. 1, p. 1; Rothman and Schotland 2005.

35. Bonneau 2005.

36. On judicial qualifications, see Constitution of the State of Georgia, art. 6, sect. 7. See also http://www.georgiaencyclopedia.org/articles/government-politics/judicial-branch-overview.

37. Peter Mantius, "Campaign Ad Draws Official Rebuke," *AC*, July 3, 1996, p. C5; Georgia Judicial Qualifications Commission, "Code of Judicial Conduct, State of Georgia," http://www.gasupreme.us/wp-content/uploads/2016/09/Code_of_Judicial_Conduct_09_22_16.pdf.

38. Constitution of the State of Georgia, art. 6, sect. 7, paras. 3 and 4; Office of the Governor 2003.

39. Georgia Supreme Court Commission on Racial and Ethnic Bias in the Court System 1995, 52–54.

40. Alan Judd, "Judgeships Often Go to Donors to Barnes," *AJC*, October 13, 2002, p. A1.

41. Randy Evans, "Newest Justice Sure to Make a Difference," *AJC*, June 13, 2005, p. A9.

42. *OCGA*, title 15, chap. 12, art. 40.

43. *Smith v. the State*, 275 Ga. 715, 571 S.E.2d 740 (2002).

44. Glick 1993, 252–261, 265–269.

45. This requirement was imposed on the states in *Duncan v. Louisiana*, 391 U.S. 145 (1968).

46. Glick 1993, 270–271; *Williams v. Florida*, 399 U.S. 78 (1970); *Ballew v. Georgia*, 435 U.S. 223 (1978); *Apodaca v. Oregon*, 406 U.S. 404 (1972); *Burch v. Louisiana*, 441 U.S. 130 (1979).

47. See *OCGA*, titles 15 and 17 generally.

48. See *OCGA*, sect. 15–12–132.

49. See *Foster v. Chapman*, 578 U.S. ___ (2016), Supreme Court no. 14-8349, https://www.supremecourt.gov/opinions/15pdf/14-8349_6k47.pdf; Ariane de Vogue, 2016. "Supreme Court Sides with Death Row Inmate in Racial Discrimination Case," http://

www.cnn.com/2016/05/23/politics/supreme-court-racial-discrimination/; see also Linda Greenhouse, "High Court Bars Sex as Standard in Picking Jurors," *NYT*, April 20, 1994, p. A1.

50. Hafetz and Pellettieri 1999; see also Tobin 2014.

51. American Bar Association 2016.

52. American Bar Association 2015a.

53. American Bar Association 2015b.

54. See Glick 1993, 86–91.

55. Ibid.

56. The State Bar of Georgia's provides information on mandatory continuing legal education, https://www.gabar.org/membership/cle/. See also the Institute for Continuing Legal Education in Georgia, http://www.iclega.org/.

57. See also Kauffman 2015.

58. State Bar of Georgia, 2013 Report of the Office of the General Counsel, https://www.gabar.org/barrules/ethicsandprofessionalism/upload/2012-13_OGC_Annual_Report.pdf.

59. State Bar of Georgia, Committees, Programs, and Sections, Consumer Assistance Program (CAP), https://www.gabar.org/committeesprogramssections/programs/consumer assistanceprogram/.

60. Saad 2011.

Chapter 9. Local Government and Politics

1. For a description and listing of local governments in Georgia, see U.S. Census Bureau 2013a, 66–73.

2. *OCGA*, title 36, chap. 86; Georgia Department of Community Affairs 1993; Bill Osinski, "Law Has Towns Fighting Oblivion," *AC*, March 28, 1994, p. B1; Don Melvin, "Who Needs a Charter?," *AJC*, July 1, 1995, p. C2.

3. See Nice 1987, 137–145; Richardson 2011.

4. The General Assembly even commissioned a study of the costs and benefits of creating Milton County. The results were published in early 2009 by the University of Georgia's Carl Vinson Institute of Government; see Ertas et al. 2009.

5. M. B. Hill 1994, 184–200.

6. U.S. Advisory Commission on Intergovernmental Relations 1993, 7–9–17–22.

7. See Jackson and Stakes 1988b, 79–90.

8. Constitution of the State of Georgia, art. 9, sect. 4.

9. Mary Williams Walsh, "Cracks Starting to Appear in Public Pensions' Armor," *NYT*, February 25, 2015, http://www.nytimes.com/2015/02/26/business/dealbook/public-pensions-once-unassailable-start-to-look-vulnerable.html; Mary Williams Walsh, "A Municipal Bankruptcy May Create a Template," *NYT*, November 19, 2013, http://dealbook.nytimes.com/2013/11/19/a-municipal-bankruptcy-may-create-a-template/; Nathan Bomey, John Gallagher, and Mark Stryker, "How Detroit Was Reborn: The Inside Story of Detroit's Historic Bankruptcy Case," *Detroit Free Press*, November 9, 2014, http://www.freep.com/story/news/local/detroit-bankruptcy/2014/11/09/detroit-bankruptcy-rosen-orr-snyder/18724267/.

10. Jim Galloway, "Counties Have Grown like Kudzu during Georgia's History," *AJC*, April 28, 1985, p. 13A; Lucy Soto, "Paying Up . . . and Up," *AC*, May 17, 1996, p. D9.

11. *OCGA*, title 36, chaps. 31 and 35.

12. David Segal, "A Georgia Town Takes the People's Business Private," *NYT*, June 23, 2012, http://www.nytimes.com/2012/06/24/business/a-georgia-town-takes-the-peoples-business-private.html?_r=0.

13. For a list of incorporation votes, see Georgia General Assembly 2014, 265A–365A. On Atlanta see https://www.atlantaga.gov/government/departments/planning-community-development/office-of-zoning-development/annexation-information.

14. Mark Niesse, "Investigators: DeKalb Is 'Rotten' to the Core," *AJC*, August 8, 2015, p. A1.

15. Katie Leslie, "Passions Run High in Debate on Annexation," *AJC*, March 19, 2015, p. B1; Bill Banks, "DeKalb Cities' Plans to Grow Falling Short," *AJC*, April 3, 2015, p. B1; Mark Niesse, "Tucker Wins Cityhood; LaVista Hills Loses Vote," *AJC*, November 4, 2015, p. A1; Mark Niesse, "Narrow Defeat of LaVista Hills Stands," *AJC*, November 15, 2015, p. B1; Mark Niesse, "Tucker's 1st Mayor, Council Elected," *AJC*, March 3, 2016, p. B2; Arielle Kass, "South Fulton Cityhood Stalls Again," *AJC*, March 11, 2016, p. B2; Mark Niesse and Arielle Kass, "Has Cityhood Drive Peaked?," *AJC*, March 31, 2016, p. A1.

16. Special districts are covered very briefly in Constitution of the State of Georgia, art. 9, sect. 2, para. 6. For additional information, see Constitution of the State of Georgia, sects. 6 and 7, and *OCGA*, title 36, chaps. 41–43, 62, 63.

17. *OCGA*, title 36, chap. 36; Georgia Municipal Association 2014.

18. *OCGA*, title 36, chap. 68; Donna Williams Lewis, "Conyers Voters Kill Rockdale Merger," *AC*, November 15, 1989, p. B2.

19. Leland and Thurmaier 2004, esp. chaps. 3, 6, 10; Fleischmann 2000; Fellows 2011; Mike Stucka, "Macon-Bibb County Consolidation Wins with Strong Majorities," *Macon Telegraph*, July 31, 2012, http://www.macon.com/news/politics-government/election/article3010974.html.

20. Carr and Feiock 2004; Fleischmann 1986; Wayne Partridge, "Merger Could Put Augusta on the Map," *Augusta Chronicle*, June 23, 1995, p. 1A; "A Brighter Future" (editorial), *Augusta Chronicle*, June 22, 1995, p. 4A; Susan Laccetti, "Panel: N. Fulton Should Incorporate," *AJC*, December 16, 1995, p. F1; Carlos Campos, "Government Consolidation Plan Shelved," *AC*, November 15, 1996, p. F1; Eva C. Galambos, "Sandy Springs, Birth of a City: Inaugural Address," *AJC*, December 1, 2005, p. JH2; Doug Nurse, "New City Bets Millions on Privatization," *AJC*, November 12, 2005, p. B1; Arlinda Smith Broady, "Drive for New Cities Began in Sandy Springs," *AJC*, June 18, 2015, p. B5; Arielle Kass, "Atlanta, Fulton Spar over Annexation, *AJC*, July 5, 2016, p. B1; Mark Niesse, "Emory Annexation Plan with Atlanta Concerns Neighbors," *AJC*, August 24, 2016, p. A1.

21. *OCGA*, title 21, chaps. 2 and 3.

22. See *OCGA*, title 36, chaps. 20 and 45.

23. *OCGA*, title 45, chap. 16.

24. *OCGA*, title 36, chap. 1, sect. 24, and chap. 45, sect. 20.

25. *OCGA*, title 36, chap. 32.

26. Mark Niesse, "Dunwoody HOA Mandate on Hold," *AJC*, June 27, 2016, p. B1. On

zoning in Metropolitan Atlanta, see Fleischmann 1989; Fleischmann and Pierannunzi 1990.

27. *OCGA*, title 35, chap. 8; title 25, chap. 4.

28. *OCGA*, title 17, chap. 2.

29. *OCGA*, title 36, chap. 81, sect. 3b.

30. Shelley Emling and Lucy Soto, "November Ballot Will Have 5 Amendments," *AJC*, March 24, 1996, p. H5; Doug Cumming and Marcus Franklin, "Ready, Set, Build: 63 School Districts Plan Construction," *AC*, March 20, 1997, p. C4.

31. *OCGA*, title 36, chaps. 5, 7, and 8.

32. Reinagel 2012.

33. See *OCGA*, title 36, chap. 81; Hudson and Hardy 2002, 2005.

34. *OCGA*, title 50, chap. 14, title 36, chap. 66, sect. 4; Charmagne Helton, "Retreats Often Stray into Illegal Territory," *AC*, August 15, 1995, p. C3; Duane D. Stanford, "Gwinnett Ends Secret Land Deals," *AJC*, November 1, 2005, p. B1; "Let Sun Shine on Gwinnett Schools" (editorial), *AJC*, November 2, 2005, p. A14.

35. *OCGA*, title 50, chap. 18, art. 4.

36. *OCGA*, title 21, chap. 5, art. 3.

37. *OCGA*, title 35, chap. 67A.

38. *OCGA*, title 36, chap. 71, sect. 5b.

39. *OCGA*, title 36, chap. 30, sect. 4.

40. *OCGA*, title 36, chap. 62, sect. 5, and chap. 62A, sect. 1.

41. See Bridges and Kronick 1999; C. Wood 2002; Oliver 2012, chaps. 2, 4; Krebs 2014.

42. Tammy Joyner, "Voting Rights Feud: A Petri Dish of Social Change," *AJC*, November 22, 2015, p. A1; Tammy Joyner, "Voting Fight Comes to an End," *AJC*, January 16, 2016, p. B1.

43. See Welch 1990; L. McDonald, Binford, and Johnson 1994; Fleischmann and Stein 1987; Trounstine and Valdini 2008; Marschall, Ruhil, and Shah 2010.

44. Ken Foskett, "The Privileges of the Powerful," *AJC*, April 26, 1992, p. F1; "Deadwood on the Ballot" (editorial), *AC*, November 11, 1996, p. A12.

45. For a list of Georgia's 159 counties along with their government structure, see Association County Commissioners of Georgia n.d. *Holder v. Hall*, 512 U.S. 874 (1994); Steve Goldberg, "One-Man Rule: Power Is Enormous," *AC*, July 5, 1990, p. C2; Bill Torpy, "Sole-Commission System Fades," *AJC*, July 5, 1992, p. A1; Dan Chapman, "The Heart and 'Sole' of Running a County," *AJC*, November 25, 2000, p. G1; Clint Williams, "Solo Rule Cool in Bartow," *AJC*, July 16, 2000, p. C5; "Bartow Treads on People's Rights" (editorial), *AJC*, April 13, 2004, p. A10; Cameron McWhirter, "Can One Man Run a County? Yes, but It's Not Easy," *AJC*, January 22, 2006, p. A1; Willis 2014.

46. On the difference between county administrators and county managers, see Ammons and Campbell 1992.

47. DeKalb voters approved this form of government in 1982, with the first officials elected in 1984; see *Georgia Laws 1981*, vol. 2: *Local and Special Acts and Resolutions*, pp. 4304–4331.

48. For background on municipal government, see Georgia Municipal Association 2012. This online guide was produced in collaboration with the University of Georgia's

Carl Vinson Institute of Government, which published the previous editions in hard copy.

49. Thanks to Mara Register of UGA's Vinson Institute of Government and Korey Dickens of the Georgia Municipal Association for providing these data. For the form used in DCA's Government Management Indicators Survey, see http://www.dca.ga.gov /development/research/programs/documents/GOMI_2014_SurveyForm.pdf. See also U.S. Census Bureau 2013a, 66; International City/County Management Association 2011.

50. International City/County Management Association 2011, 5.

51. Constitution of the State of Georgia, art. 8, sect. 5, paras. 2 and 3. On former methods of choosing boards and superintendents, see Bachtel and Boatright 1992, 66–70; L. McDonald, Binford, and Johnson 1994, 68.

52. For a detailed list, see U.S. Census Bureau 2013a, 66–73. See also Wells and Scheff 1992; Steve Visser, "A Taxing Decision: Property-Owner Organizations Could Be Key to Controlling Sprawl," AJC, June 14, 1999, p. E7; Janet Frankston, "Self-Taxing Districts Gain Traction," AJC, January 13, 2003, p. E1; David Pendered, "Beltline on Fast Forward," AJC, December 22, 2005, p. A1.

53. For an excellent analysis of local elections, see Oliver 2012, including his argument that low turnout might not be such a problem (pp. 82–86). See also Krebs 2014; Baybeck 2014; Hajnal and Lewis 2003; Gerber and Phillips 2003. For a good overview of citizen contacting, see Hirlinger 1992. On citizen contacting in Atlanta, see J. C. Thomas and Melkers 1999.

54. Oliver 2012, 64–65.

55. Hajnal and Lewis 2003. Also see Krebs 2014, 190–193; Baybeck 2014, 102–104.

56. Oliver 2012, 66–76.

57. Data are available at Athens-Clarke County, https://athensclarkecounty.com/Archive .aspx?AMID=36.

58. Election data for Atlanta are available from the Fulton County Department of Registration and Elections, http://www.fultoncountyga.gov/elections-documents. See also Katie Leslie, "Voters Favor $250M Infrastructure Fix," AJC, March 18, 2015, p. B1.

59. Data are available from the Chatham County Board of Elections, http://elections. chathamcounty.org/.

60. Fleischmann and Stein 1998; official disclosure reports of "Atlantans for Maynard Jackson," October 17, 1989, and January 3, 1990 (records maintained by the Atlanta municipal clerk); "Incumbency Provides Big Boost to Lomax's Campaign Financing," AJC, April 29, 1989, p. A1; Mark Sherman, "Ethics of Council Donations Questioned," AJC, April 15, 1990, p. A1.

61. Gurwitt 2001; Colin Campbell, "Negative Polling, Ads Mar Mayoral Campaign, AJC, October 14, 2001, p. 6D.

62. Ernie Suggs, "Watchdog Group Calls War Chests Excessive," AJC, October 20, 2005, p. C1.

63. Eric Stirgus and Cameron McWhirter, "Norwood Far Outspent Mayoral Rivals in October," AJC, October 30, 2009, http://www.ajc.com/news/news/local/norwood-far-outspent-mayoral-rivals-in-october/nQYp6/.

64. Susanna Capolouto and John Sepulvado, "Barnes Backs Fellow Democrat for ATL Mayor," Georgia Public Broadcasting, November 12, 2009, http://www.gpb.org /news/2009/11/12/barnes-backs-fellow-democrat-for-atl-mayor. For an overview and analysis of the 2009 mayoral election, see Owens and Brown 2014.

65. Campaign finance data are available at Columbus, Georgia, Elections & Registration Office, http://www.columbusga.org/elections/formsPubs.htm.

66. This discussion is based in part on reports filed with city and county election officials. See also Lucy Soto, "More Seats than Candidates," *AJC*, September 25, 1995, p. C1; Don Plummer, "'No Contest' at Polls for District Attorneys," *AC*, November 8, 1996, p. E5.

67. Laura Kinsler, "It's Horton over Hunter in Oconee BOE," *ABH*, July 10, 1996, p. 1.

68. Mark Niesse, "Incumbents Face Fight amid Scandals," *AJC*, May 12, 2016, p. A1; Mark Niesse, "DeKalb County Voters Oust DA James," *AJC*, May 15, 2016, p. A1; DeKalb County 2016b, 2016a.

69. Greg Bluestein, "Crime Brings Shift in Savannah Politics," *AJC*, December 29, 2015, p. A1.

70. This discussion of Atlanta is based on Murray and Vedlitz 1978; Bullock and Campbell 1984; Bullock 1985; Abney and Hutcheson 1981; C. N. Stone 1989; Pierannunzi and Hutcheson 1991; Tankersley and Custer 2004; Fleischmann 2004; Kruse 2005. For a less flattering view about racial transition in Atlanta and efforts throughout Georgia to restrict participation, particularly in South Georgia, see Mickey 2015, 119–129, 316–333.

71. U.S. Census Bureau 2008, table 402. Data on minority representation are difficult to come by since the Joint Center for Political and Economic Studies ceased publishing an annual update, on which the Census Bureau relied.

72. Association County Commissioners of Georgia 2015. These data on the composition of county boards of commissioners were provided in a spreadsheet format by Michele NeSmith of the Association County Commissioners of Georgia.

73. Center for American Women and Politics 2015.

74. Association County Commissioners of Georgia 2015.

75. Ibid. Counties with all-Republican commissions as of May 2015 (30): Banks, Berrien, Bryan, Camden, Catoosa, Cherokee, Dade, Dawson, Effingham, Fannin, Floyd, Forsyth, Gilmer, Gwinnett, Habersham, Hall, Houston, Jackson, Lee, Lumpkin, Madison, Oconee, Oglethorpe, Paulding, Pickens, Pierce, Pike, Stephens, White, Whitfield. Barrow County is not included because one seat was vacant. All-Democrat county commissions (17): Baker, Clayton, Decatur, Jenkins, Liberty, Long, Macon, Miller, Rockdale, Stewart, Talbot, Taliaferro, Treutlen, Warren, Washington, Wilkes, Wilkinson. Counties with all Republicans except for one commissioner (25): Bacon, Brantley, Carroll, Cobb, Columbia, Coweta, Emanuel, Fayette, Franklin, Glynn, Gordon, Greene, Haralson, Harris, Hart, Heard, Henry, Jasper, Lamar, McIntosh, Rabun, Toombs, Troup, Walton, Ware. Counties with all Democrats except for one commissioner (15): Brooks, Calhoun, Dooly, Grady, Hancock, Jefferson, Johnson, Marion, Mitchell, Seminole, Tattnall, Taylor, Terrell, Turner, Twiggs.

76. David Wickert, "Democrats Poised to Gain Ground," *AJC*, March 20, 2016, p. B1.

77. Bullock 1993, 3–5.

78. These data are derived from county returns available from the Georgia Secretary of State, http://sos.ga.gov/index.php/Elections/current_and_past_elections_results. The analysis covers the metropolitan area that existed for the 2012 elections; Morgan County became the twenty-ninth county in the Atlanta MSA in December 2013. See also Jeremy Redmon, "Large Racial Shifts Transform Counties," *AJC*, May 26, 2015, p. A1.

79. Bullock 1993, 3–7.

80. The 2012 and 2014 county commission results are available from the Georgia Secretary of State, http://sos.ga.gov/index.php/Elections/current_and_past_elections_results.

81. Georgia General Assembly 2014, 310A–365A.

82. "Sales Tax Sustains 75% Success Rate," *Georgia County Government*, December 1985, pp. 10–11.

83. Richard Whitt, "Cobb Drivers See Relief in Tax Hike: Penny Increase per Dollar Barely Squeaks Through," *AJC*, September 22, 2005, p. A1; Mike King, "End Tax Votes in Special Elections" (editorial), *AJC*, September 29, 2005, p. A15. On controversies over tax elections in Fayette County, see Kevin Duffy, "County OKs First 5-year Tax Increase: Slim Margin to Fund Roads," *AJC*, November 11, 2004, p. JM1.

84. Peter Scott, "A Wet Tide Pouring over the State," *AJC*, November 2, 1996, p. D6; Peter Scott, "Drys Put Cork in More Liquor Sales," *AC*, November 7, 1996, p. C10; Clint Williams, "Election 2005: Sunday Liquor Sales in Canton," *AJC*, November 17, 2005, p. JQ1; Robbie Brown, "In Georgia, Some Vote to Stay Dry on Sundays," *NYT*, November 11, 2011, http://www.nytimes.com/2011/11/12/us/georgia-or-most-of-it-ends-sunday-ban-on-alcohol-sales.html.

85. *OCGA*, title 21, chap. 4.

86. Cox, Daley, and Pajari 1991.

87. Athens Life Unleashed, http://www.visitathensga.com/about-us/.

88. Maria Saporta, "The Myriad Business Voices," *AC*, January 9, 1989, p. 1B.

89. Greg Bluestein and J. Scott Trubey, "Mercedes Unveils Sandy Springs HQ Location," *AJC*, February 3, 2015, http://www.ajc.com/news/business/mercedes-unveils-sandy-springs-hq-location/nj32y/.

90. Ben Smith, "Show Me the Money: Beaudreau Did Accept Money from Developers," *AJC*, May 20, 2005, p. JJ1; Ben Smith and Duane D. Stafford, "King of the Deal," *AJC*, November 13, 2005, p. A1; Scott Trubey, "Fort McPherson Sale to Filmmaker Wins OK," *AJC*, June 27, 2015, p. B1.

91. Matt Kempner, "Big Apple Chomps on Ted's Legacy," *AJC*, May 22, 2015, p. A11.

92. Shelley Emling, "DeKalb Homeowners Unite for Political Clout," *AJC*, November 27, 1992, p. D12; Frances Schwartzkopff, "No Place like a Homeowners' Group to Take on Government," *AJC*, February 9, 1991, p. A1; Lucy Soto, "Discovering Strength in Numbers," *AJC*, June 18, 1995, p. G1; Chandler Brown, "Homeowners Groups Wield Clout: More than Zoning on Their Plates," *AJC*, December 2, 2004, p. JF2; Faga 2014.

93. Most of the governments not responding were very small. Seven of the eight nonresponding counties had fewer than 15,000 residents; the other county was Fulton, with almost a million residents. The largest nonresponding cities were Marietta (60,000), Brunswick (roughly 16,000), and Jefferson (about 10,000). Another five cities had populations between 3,000 and 7,500; the remaining thirty-seven communities were under 2,000 population, including many with only a few hundred residents.

94. Georgia Department of Community Affairs 2015a, sect. 2.

95. Ibid.; 2015c, sect. 2.

96. Toulmin 1988.

97. Dan Klepal, "Cobb Skimming Water Revenue," *AJC*, December 13, 2015, p. B1.

98. Georgia Department of Community Affairs 2015b.

99. Eplan 2014.

100. Hutcheson and Prather 1988; Fleischmann 1989; Fleischmann and Pierannunzi 1990.

101. Such efforts extend beyond the major events in Atlanta. See, for example, campaigns to promote Athens (http://www.visitathensga.com/), Savannah (http://visitsavannah .com/), the Georgia mountains (http://georgiamountains.org/), and extending to smaller communities like Colquitt-Miller County (http://swampgravy.com/).

102. See Georgia Department of Community Affairs, "2015 Directory of Registered Local Government Authorities," http://www.dca.ga.gov/development/Research/programs/RASearch/RASearch.asp.

103. Misty Williams and J. Scott Trubey, "Caterpillar Plant to Bring 1,400 Jobs to Athens," *AJC*, February 17, 2012, http://www.ajc.com/news/business/caterpillar-plant-to -bring-1400-jobs-to-athens/nQRP7/.

104. J. Scott Trubey, "Project Pitched near Old GM Site," *AJC*, June 12, 2015, p. A7; Andria Simmons, "MARTA Villages Plan Grows," *AJC*, May 6, 2015, p. A1.

105. Dan Klepal, "Cobb Diverts Tax to Braves," *AJC*, April 8, 2015, p. A1; Dan Klepal, "Stadium 'Bricks and Sticks' to Cost $462 Million," *AJC*, May 27, 2015, p. B1; J. Scott Trubey, "Developer Shops Ballpark to 35,000 Retail Big Shots," *AJC*, May 20, 2015, p. A1; Jim Galloway, "Braves, Mass Transit and Cobb's Wariness," *AJC*, June 28, 2015, p. B1; Dan Klepal, "Cobb Gets OK to Sell Bonds," *AJC*, June 30, 2015, p. A1.

106. David Wickert and Meris Lutz, "Challenger Ousts Cobb Chairman," *AJC*, July 27, 2016, p. A1.

107. Georgia Government Transparency and Campaign Finance Commission, "2015 Docket of Legislative Appearance in Alphabetical Order Listed by Lobbyist," which is generated from the menu at the commission's website, http://media.ethics.ga.gov/search /Lobbyist/Lobbyist_Menu.aspx.

108. Johnny Edwards, "Fulton Board Eliminates Top Lobbyist's Job," *AJC*, January 9, 2013, http://www.ajc.com/news/news/local/fulton-board-eliminates-top-lobbyists-job /nTrYb/.

109. Expenditure data are available at the commission website by group or lobbyist, http://media.ethics.ga.gov/search/Lobbyist/Lobbyist_Groupsearchresults.aspx?& Year=2006%20and%20Newer&GroupName=&GroupNameContains=association%20 county%20commissioners.

110. Walter C. Jones, "Georgia House Defeats Bill Preventing Plastic Bag Bans," *ABH*, March 29, 2015, http://onlineathens.com/local-news/2015-03-27/georgia-house-defeats -bill-preventing-plastic-bag-bans; Jessica Leigh Lebos, "Tybee One Step Closer to Being Banned from Banning Plastic Bags," *Connect Savannah*, March 4, 2015 http://www.connect savannah.com/savannah/tybee-one-step-closer-to-being-banned-from-banning-plastic -bags/Content?oid=2534413.

111. Rhonda Clark, "Jail's Oversight Lifted," *AJC*, April 24, 2015, p. A1.

112. J. Scott Trubey, "NCR Could Add Jobs, Get More Credits," *AJC*, May 29, 2–15, p. A6.

113. On regional cooperation, see Fleischmann 2000.

114. On GRTA, see http://www.grta.org/index.php. See also Georgia Department of Community Affairs n.d.; D. L. Bennett, "Cities, Counties Go Toe-to-Toe in Talks," *AC*, November 15, 1999, p. D4.

115. Rhonda Cook, "Jail's Oversight Lifted," *AJC*, April 24, 2015, p. A1.

116. See the analysis, discussion, and comparisons to other metropolitan areas in two series of articles: "Our Future: Boom or Bust?," *AJC*, April 12, 2015 p. A1ff; "Regionalism: Big Government or Best Government?," *AJC*, May 31, 2015, p. A13ff.

Chapter 10. Public Policies

1. For general descriptions of this process, see Kingdon 1995; Baumgartner and Jones 1993; Peters 2016, chaps. 3 and 4. For factors influencing policy making at the state level and differences among state policies, see Gray 2013; Lowry 2014; Schneider and Jacoby 2014.

2. Key 1949, 664.

3. Ibid., 671–675; Black and Black 2002, 1987; Hood, Kidd, and Morris 2012b.

4. For a discussion of the "problem environment," see Nice 1994, 20–25.

5. See Squire 1992; Ben Smith III, "Political Tremors at the Capitol," *AJC*, March 27, 1994, p. G3.

6. Pew Research Center 2014.

7. Ibid., 29.

8. Rhonda Cook, "A Year Later, How Cheating Trial Is Still Epic," *AJC*, April 2, 2016, p. A1; "Keep Scrubbing DeKalb" (editorial), *AJC*, May 31, 2015, p. A19.

9. For more about Morris Communications, see http://www.morris.com/; on Morris News Service, see http://morrisnewsservice.com/.

10. American Legislative Exchange Council, http://www.alec.org/. Also see Mike McIntire, "Conservative Nonprofit Serves as Stealth Business Lobbyist," *NYT*, April 21, 2012, p. A1; Tom Hamburger, Joby Warrick, and Chris Mooney, "This Conservative Group Is Tired of Being Accused of Climate Denial—and Is Fighting Back," *Washington Post*, April 5, 2015, http://www.washingtonpost.com/news/energy-environment/wp/2015/04/05/this -conservative-group-is-tired-of-being-accused-of-climate-denial-and-is-fighting-back/.

11. Walker 1969; Gray 1973. For a synopsis on diffusion, see Shipan and Volden 2012.

12. Glick and Hays 1991.

13. Shipan and Volden 2006; Bergal 2015; Greenblatt 2016c.

14. For a general discussion, see Hamm and Moncrief 2004, 188–189.

15. For a general discussion of courts in the political system, see Baum 2013.

16. See a discussion of alternatives to government production of services, see Osborne and Gaebler 1992.

17. See Governor's Local Governance Commission 1992; "National Unfunded Mandates Day a Success," *Georgia's Cities*, November 30, 1993, p. 1; Association County Commissioners of Georgia, *ACCG 2015–2016 County Platform*, http://www.accg.org/library/county _platform.pdf.

18. For an overview, see Governor's Office of Planning and Budget, "The Budget Process," https://opb.georgia.gov/budget-process. See also Lauth 1986.

19. Governor's Office of Planning and Budget 2016a, 21, 24.

20. See Main, Epstein, and Elovich 1992, 237; Lauth 1990.

21. Governor's Office of Planning and Budget 2016a, 5.

22. Ibid., 250.

23. See the changes laid out in the Governor's Office of Planning and Budget 2016b, 34. For example, as economic conditions worsened in 2010, the legislature cut an additional $1.5 billion from the budget it had approved less than a year earlier. On the flip side, as conditions improved a bit, it added $174 million to the FY 2011 budget.

24. See U.S. Bureau of Labor Statistics, "CPI Inflation Calculator," http://data.bls.gov/cgi-bin/cpicalc.pl.

25. Governor's Office of Planning and Budget 2016b, 32–33.

26. Ibid., 18–19.

27. Governor's Office of Planning and Budget 2016b, 28–29, 257–266.

28. Ibid., 22.

29. Council of State Governments 2016, 394–395, 420–421.

30. For a comparison of state income taxes, see Council of State Governments 2016, 394–395.

31. Steve Harvey, "Panel Says State Must Revise Taxes," AJC, July 25, 1992, p. A1; Richard Whitt, "Study: Eliminating Sales Tax on Food Would Require Increase in Tax Rate," AJC, September 18, 1993, p. D5; Frank LoMonte, "Economists Question the Wisdom of Zell Miller's Tax Relief Plans," ABH, February 20, 1994, p. 1A; James Salzer and Nancy Badertscher, "Sales Taxes May Fund Schools," AJC, August 28, 2005, p. A1; Melody Harrison, "Small Business Backs Sales Tax," AJC, October 7, 2005, p. A19. See also Georgia Budget and Policy Institute 2011.

32. For an overview of Georgia's property tax system, see Sjoquist and Warner 2016.

33. Fiscal Research Center, Georgia State University 2015. For more detail on the film industry, see Small and Wheeler 2016.

34. Prillaman and Meier 2014.

35. For one view on modifying the state's tax system, see Tharpe 2015.

36. Witko and Newmark 2005.

37. The advocacy group Good Jobs First, which was founded in 1998, conducts research and tracks economic development subsidies, http://www.goodjobsfirst.org/. Also see Elaine S. Povich, "States Questioning Breaks for Film Industry," AJC, May 26, 2015, p. A7; Prillaman and Meier 2014.

38. Cobb 1993; Eisinger 1988; Cortright and Mayer 2004; Jolley, Lancaster, and Gao 2015. For differences in one major state program, see Dalehite, Mikesell, and Zorn 2005.

39. Liz Farmer, "The Fight for Jobs Intensifies between Kansas and Missouri," Governing, May 12, 2016, http://www.governing.com/topics/finance/gov-fight-for-jobs-intensifies-between-kansas-missouri.html?utm_term=1%20City%2C%202%20States%20and%20a%20Fight%20for%20Jobs&utm_campaign=A%20History%20of%20Insurgent%20Candidates%27%20Impact%20on%20Down-Ballot%20Races&utm_content=email&utm_source=Act-On+Software&utm_medium=email.

40. Nancy Nethery, "Quick Start Gets Companies Up and Running," AC, October 20,

1992, p. C1; Matthew C. Quinn, "Quick Start: Job Program Helps Bring in the Business," *AC*, April 9, 1996, p. E2; Maria Saporta, "Commitment to Columbus," *AC*, March 8, 1996, p. H1; Matthew C. Quinn, "Major Improvements Boost Savannah's Port," *AC*, June 27, 1995, p. D1; Tamar Hallerman, "Backers Optimistic about Savannah Harbor Funds," *AJC*, April 16, 2016, p. B1; Greg Bluestein, "Ga.'s New Inland Port to Ease Truck Traffic," *AJC*, July 29, 2015, p. A7; Curtis Foltz, "Ga. Ports Set Records, Eye Future," *AJC*, August 5, 2015, p. A12.

41. Georgia.org. n.d.

42. Greg Bluestein, "Deal to Talk Trade in Brazil," *AJC*, June 12, 2015, p. A1.

43. Walter Woods, "Daimler Talks: 2 Sides Apart by $22 Million," *AJC*, April 16, 2005, p. F1.

44. Walter Woods, "$160,000 per Job to Land Kia," *AJC*, March 14, 2006, p. A1.

45. J. Scott Trubey, "State Leaders React to Volvo Snub," *AJC*, May 12, 2015, p. A1; J. Scott Trubey, "GE May Tour Atlanta for HQ Site," *AJC*, September 30, 2015, p. A9.

46. J. Scott Trubey, "NCR Could Add Jobs, Get More Credits," *AJC*, May 29, 2015, p. A6; J. Scott Trubey, "NCR in Deal with Cousins for Midtown HQ," *AJC*, July 16, 2015, p. A9.

47. J. Scott Trubey, "CNN Has Big Plans for Atlanta Campuses," *AJC*, May 14, 2016, p. A1; J. Scott Turbey, "MGM Leads Push for Casino," *AJC*, July 20, 2015, p. A1; Greg Bluestein, "Deal Offers Opening for Casinos," *AJC*, July 28, 2015, p. B1; Kristina Torres, "Lawmakers to Study Gambling," *AJC*, September 14, 2015, p. A1.

48. Michael E. Kanell, "Newell HQ Headed to Hoboken, N.J.," *AJC*, May 14, 2016, p. A11.

49. Georgia Budget and Policy Institute 2005; Tharpe 2013.

50. Eisinger 1988, 220–224; Skoro 1988; Brace 1993; Prillaman and Meier 2014; Jolley, Lancaster, and Gao 2015.

51. Georgia has seaports in Brunswick and Savannah and has inland operations in Bainbridge and Columbus. See Georgia Department of Economic Development 2014.

52. Georgia Department of Transportation 2013.

53. Toon 2016 [2014].

54. Erika Rawes, "8 States with the Longest Commute Times," *USA Today*, October 19, 2014, http://www.usatoday.com/story/money/business/2014/10/19/cheat-sheet-states -longest-commutes/17428945/.

55. Mandi Albright, "Atlanta Tops in Typical Commute Distance," *AJC*, March 25, 2015, http://www.ajc.com/news/news/local-govt-politics/atlanta-tops-typical-commute -distance/nkd7M/.

56. Tim Harlow, "The Drive: More of Us Are Driving to Work Solo," *Minneapolis Star Tribune*, November 11, 2013, http://www.startribune.com/the-drive-more-of-us-are -driving-to-work-solo/231370801/.

57. Hartsfield-Jackson Atlanta International Airport. n.d.a.

58. Hartsfield-Jackson: Atlanta International Airport. n.d.b.

59. Kelly Yamanouchi, "Hartsfield-Jackson to Begin $6 Billion Expansion Plan," *AJC*, March 9, 2016, p. A1.

60. The Georgia Ports Authority operates state ports, but GDOT is charged with

much of the planning and financial oversight of these facilities. Local boards also have jurisdiction over public transportation systems, such as the MARTA board in Fulton, DeKalb, and Clayton Counties.

61. Georgia Department of Transportation 2014.

62. Data on intersections showing the average number of vehicles is available on the DOT website, http://geocounts.com/gdot/. Collecting such information is part of the Georgia State Traffic and Report System (STARS) of the GDOT.

63. See, e.g., GDOT 511, http://www.511ga.org/#Variable_Speed_control&zoom=3&lat=3990785.92806&lon=-9392690.23602 and http://www.wsbtv.com/traffic.

64. Georgia Department of Transportation 2015.

65. Georgia General Assembly, Joint Committee on Critical Transportation Infrastructure Funding 2014, p. 7.

66. "Georgia's Tanking Transportation" (moderated by Tom Sabulis), *AJC*, November 24, 2014, http://atlantaforward.blog.ajc.com/2014/11/24/georgias-tanking-transportation/.

67. Governor's Office of Planning and Budget 2010.

68. Andria Simmons, "MARTA Legislation Wraps Up Session," *AJC*, March 25, 2016, p. A1.

69. Douglas Sams, "How Metro Atlanta Voted for TSPLOST," *Atlanta Business Chronicle*, August 6, 2012, http://www.bizjournals.com/atlanta/real_talk/2012/08/how-tplost-vote-fared-by-region.html?s=image_gallery.

70. Matthew Yglesias, "Atlanta Is a Regional Transportation Planning Disaster," *Slate.com*, January 29, 2014, http://www.slate.com/blogs/moneybox/2014/01/29/atlanta_traffic_nightmare_terrible_regional_planning.html.

71. National Association of State Budget Officers, "2014 Small Business Profiles for the States and Territories," February 4, 2015, https://www.sba.gov/advocacy/small-business-profiles-states-and-territories-2014.

72. Environmental Council of the States n.d.

73. For the Georgia Environmental Protection Division, see http://epd.georgia.gov/. For the Georgia Department of Natural Resources, see http://www.gadnr.org/.

74. The provisions of the Clean Air Acts of 1990 and 1997 are covered in this section.

75. See Georgia's Clean Air Force, http://www.cleanairforce.com/.

76. Georgia Department of Community Affairs 1989.

77. Southeast Green 2012.

78. Ibid.

79. See Atlanta BeltLine, http://beltline.org/.

80. *Berman v. Parker*, 348 U.S. 26 (1954).

81. *Kelo v. New London*, 545 U.S. 469 (2005).

82. Utt 2007.

83. Dan Chapman, "Tipping Point in Water War? Georgia Optimistic about Long Legal Battle, but Judge Warns of a Decision That Will Make Both Sides Unhappy," *AJC*, http://specials.myajc.com/georgia-water-war/.

84. Office of the Governor 2014a.

85. Greg Bluestein, "Water Program Short of Its Goal," *AJC*, November 23, 2015, p. A1.

86. The city also increased water rates and undertook several major construction projects (see Clean Water Atlanta, http://www.cleanwateratlanta.org/default.htm). The major party bringing the lawsuit was the Upper Chattahoochee Riverkeeper (see http://www.cleanwateratlanta.org).

87. The Georgia Water Planning and Policy Center has several working papers on this issue, including Rowles and Thompson 2005.

88. Harold Reheis, "Equal Time: Water Transfers Prove Useful and Cost Effective" (editorial), *AJC*, July 10, 2003, p. A15.

89. Bob Hanner, "Water Resource Management: Critics of House Bill Lob Many False Claims" (editorial), *AJC*, April 9, 2003, p. A23.

90. "Growing Old and Polluting the Air: Air Quality Laboratory Monitors Emissions of an Aging Vehicle Fleet," Georgia Institute of Technology Research News, press release, May 1999, http://gtresearchnews.gatech.edu/newsrelease/EMISSION.html.

91. Hepburn 2010; McCutchen 1994.

92. Madison 1810.

93. *Brown v. Board of Education I*, 347 US 483 (1954), p. 493.

94. Evans, Murray, and Schwab 1997; B. D. Wood and Theobald 2000.

95. U.S. Census Bureau 2013d.

96. *Governing* n.d.

97. Suggs 2014.

98. U.S. Census Bureau 2013d.

99. Suggs 2014, 1.

100. *San Antonio Independent School District v. Rodriquez*, 411 U.S. 1 (1973),

101. Van Slyke, Tan, and Orland 1994.

102. *Robinson v. Cahill*, 62 N.J. 473 (1973).

103. The six states where the courts have not ruled on education finance litigation are Delaware, Hawaii, Mississippi, Nevada, Utah, and Iowa. No litigation been filed in the first five, while in Iowa there has been no been court decision (National Access Network, http://www.schoolfunding.info). Hawaii has a statewide unified school district and therefore no variation across districts. In addition, New Mexico has not had a high court decision.

104. Constitution of the State of Georgia, art. 8, sect. 1, para. 1, emphasis added.

105. *McDaniel v. Thomas*, 285 S.E.2d 156 (Ga. 1981).

106. Rich Motoko, "Percentage of Poor Students in Public Schools Rises," *NYT*, January 16, 2015, p. A13.

107. National Center for Education Statistics 2014.

108. Georgia Lottery, https://www.galottery.com/en-us/home.html.

109. Georgia Public Policy Foundation 2014.

110. Michael Mitchell, Vincent Palacios, and Michael Leachman 2014.

111. CollegeBoard. n.d.

112. Fox 2015.

113. Dave Williams, "Georgia's Public Universities Raising Tuition up to 9 Percent," *Atlanta Business Chronicle*, April 14, 2015, http://www.bizjournals.com/atlanta/news/2015/04/14/georgia-s-public-universities-raising-tuition-up.html.

114. See Gibson 2004.

115. Bill Rankin, "Petitions Key in Cobb Sticker Case: School Board's Attorney Doubts Documents Exist," *AJC*, January 5, 2006, p. C1.

116. These data are from the National Education Association database, http://www.nea.org/home/38465.htm.

117. National Center for Education Statistics n.d.

118. *Federal Register*, vol. 69, no. 30, February 13, 2004, pp. 7336–7338.

119. U.S. Census Bureau, "Income and Poverty in the United States: 2014," https://www.census.gov/content/dam/Census/library/publications/2015/demo/p60-252.pdf.

120. U.S. Census Bureau, "Historical Poverty Tables: People and Families—1980 to 2015," table 13, September 1, 2016, https://www.census.gov/data/tables/time-series/demo/income-poverty/historical-poverty-people.html.

121. Ibid., table 21.

122. Data available from the Census Bureau's "American Fact Finder" portal searching by state, "Poverty Status in the Past 12 Months: 2015 American Community Survey 1-Year Estimates," https://factfinder.census.gov/faces/tableservices/jsf/pages/productview.xhtml?pid=ACS_15_1YR_S1701&prodType=table.

123. See the Census Bureau's "American Fact Finder" for details from the American Community Survey, 2010–2014, http://factfinder.census.gov/faces/tableservices/jsf/pages/productview.xhtml?pid=ACS_14_5YR_DP03&src=pt.

124. For a history and analysis of means-tested programs, see Moffitt 2003, esp. chap. 5, which covers TANF.

125. Georgia Division of Family and Children Services 2013, iii–v.

126. Georgia Department of Human Services 2016, 4–5.

127. Georgia Department of Labor, "Unemployment Insurance: Claimant Handbook," http://dol.georgia.gov/sites/dol.georgia.gov/files/related_files/document/dol414.pdf.

128. For a general description and history of unemployment compensation, see U.S. Social Security Administration 2016, 65–67. For details, see U.S. Department of Labor, Employment & Training Administration, "Comparison of State Unemployment Laws," chap. 2, http://www.unemploymentinsurance.doleta.gov/unemploy/comparison2016.asp; Georgia Department of Labor, "Information about Unemployment Insurance for Employers: Tax Reporting and Liability," http://dol.georgia.gov/sites/dol.georgia.gov/files/related_files/document/dol4e.pdf.

129. U.S. Department of Labor, Employment & Training Administration, "Monthly Program and Financial Data," http://www.oui.doleta.gov/unemploy/5159report.

130. U.S. Social Security Administration 2016, section 5.J, "OASDI Current-Pay Benefits: Geographic Data."

131. For a history and description of SSI, see U.S. Social Security Administration 2016, 20–36, with data on recipients and payments in table 7.B1.

132. Background and statistics are available from the U.S. Internal Revenue Service, "EITC Central," https://www.eitc.irs.gov/?_ga=1.39534883.1445165383.1475510144.

133. For an overview, see Center on Budget and Policy Priorities, "Policy Basics: The Earned Income Tax Credit," January 25, 2016, https://www.eitc.irs.gov/?_ga=1.39534883.1445165383.1475510144.

134. See, for example, Gary S. Becker, "How to End Welfare as We Know It" (editorial), *Business Week*, June 3, 1996, p. 22.

135. For a map and summary, see Center on Budget and Policy Priorities, "Policy Basics: State Earned Income Tax Credits," June 17, 2016, http://www.cbpp.org/research/state -budget-and-tax/policy-basics-state-earned-income-tax-credits?fa=view&id=2506.

136. Wesley Tharpe, "Georgia Work Credit an Ambitious yet Affordable Investment," Georgia Budget & Policy Institute, September 20, 2016, https://gbpi.org/2016/georgia-work -credit-ambitious-yet-affordable-investment/.

137. U.S. Social Security Administration 2016, 58–64.

138. Georgia Department of Community Health, "Medicaid Income and Resource Limits," February 2, 2016, http://dch.georgia.gov/sites/dch.georgia.gov/files/2016%20ABD %20and%20FM%20Income%20Limits%20%20revised%2021516.pdf.

139. Georgia Department of Community Health, "Annual Report FY 2015," pp. 6–9, https://dch.georgia.gov/sites/dch.georgia.gov/files/AnnualReport-2015.pdf; Governor's Office of Planning and Budget 2016, 107.

140. *National Federation of Business v. Sebelius*, 132 S.Ct. 2566 (2012).

141. U.S. Centers for Medicare and Medicaid Services, "Affordable Care Act Provisions," https://www.medicaid.gov/affordable-care-act/index.html.

142. Georgia Department of Health, "PeachCare for Kids Eligibility Criteria," https:// dch.georgia.gov/eligibility-criteria.

143. Georgia Department of Community Health, "Annual Report FY 2015," p. 10, https://dch.georgia.gov/sites/dch.georgia.gov/files/AnnualReport-2015.pdf; Governor's Office of Planning and Budget 2016," p. 107.

144. See U.S. Centers for Medicare and Medicaid Services, "History," https://www.cms .gov/About-CMS/Agency-Information/History/index.html?redirect=/history/. For more detail on the different types of coverage, see "About Medicare Health Plans," https:// www.medicare.gov/sign-up-change-plans/medicare-health-plans/different-types-of -medicare-health-plans.html.

145. CMS provides relatively current data on the number of Medicare enrollees, but spending data lag somewhat. State and county data reported here for 2014 are available at Centers for Medicare and Medicaid Services, "Medicare Geographic Variation: Public Use File, State/County Report—All Beneficiaries," https://www.cms.gov/Research-Statistics -Data-and-Systems/Statistics-Trends-and-Reports/Medicare-Geographic-Variation/GV _PUF.html.

146. See U.S. Department of Agriculture, "A Short History of SNAP," http://www.fns .usda.gov/sites/default/files/History_of_SNAP.pdf.

147. U.S. Department of Agriculture, Food and Nutrition Service, "Supplemental Nutrition Assistance Program (SNAP): Eligibility," March 21, 2017, http://www.fns.usda .gov/snap/eligibility; and "Supplemental Nutrition Assistance Program: State Activity Report, Fiscal Year 2015," August 2016, http://www.fns.usda.gov/sites/default/files /snap/2015-State-Activity-Report.pdf; Georgia Division of Family and Children Services, "Supplemental Nutrition Assistance Program—SNAP (Food Stamps)," November 2015, http://dfcs.georgia.gov/sites/dfcs.georgia.gov/files/47-1.2016.pdf.

148. Georgia Office of Planning and Budget 2016a, 156, 161.

149. See the U.S. Department of Agriculture's monthly data on the WIC program, which are available in Excel spread sheets at http://www.fns.usda.gov/pd/wic-program.

150. U.S. Department of Agriculture, Food and Nutrition Service, "School Meals," http://www.fns.usda.gov/school-meals/child-nutrition-programs; and "Special Milk Program," http://www.fns.usda.gov/smp/special-milk-program.

151. Georgia Office of Planning and Budget 2016a, 35.

152. For more detail on eligibility, see DECAL's Childcare and Parent Services Policies, http://www.caps.decal.ga.gov/en/Policy/.

153. Georgia office of Planning and Budget 2016a, 120–122.

154. Melissa Johnson, "Help Needed to Meet Georgia's Laudable Child Care Goals," Georgia Budget & Policy Institute, July 2016, https://gbpi.org/wp-content/uploads/2016/07/Funding-Georgia-Child-Care-Plan.pdf.

155. Association of Public and Land-Grant Universities, "The Land-Grant Tradition" (2012), http://www.aplu.org/library/the-land-grant-tradition/file.

156. Claire Suggs, "Troubling Gaps in HOPE Point to Need-Based Aid Solutions," Georgia Budget & Policy Institute, September 2016, https://gbpi.org/wp-content/uploads/2016/09/Troubling-Gaps-in-HOPE-Point-to-Need-based-Aid-Solutions.pdf.

157. Georgia Office of Planning and Budget 2016b, 243–245. See the system website for more detail on programs, https://tcsg.edu/index.php.

158. Georgia Office of Planning and Budget 2016b, 126–127. For more detail on programs, see Georgia Department of Economic Development, Workforce Division, http://www.georgia.org/competitive-advantages/workforce-division/.

159. National Association of Independent Colleges and Universities, "Federal Student Aid Programs, 2014–2015: Georgia," 2016, https://www.naicu.edu/special_initiatives/page/federal-student-aid-awarded-in-georgia-state-wide-and-by-congressional-district.

160. Georgia Department of Community Affairs, "Georgia Dream Ownership Program," https://www.dca.ga.gov/GeorgiaDream/gadream.asp; Georgia Office of Planning and Budget 2016b, 93–96.

161. U.S. Department of Housing and Urban Development, "Housing Vouchers Fact Sheet," http://portal.hud.gov/hudportal/HUD?src=/topics/housing_choice_voucher_program_section_8.

162. Data are available by county at HUD's "FY 2016 Income Limitations Documentation System," https://www.huduser.gov/portal/datasets/il/il2016/select_Geography.odn.

163. Georgia Department of Community Affairs, "Housing Choice Voucher Program," https://www.dca.ga.gov/housing/RentalAssistance/programs/hcvp_program.asp.

164. Georgia Department of Community Affairs, "Homeless and Special Needs Housing," https://www.dca.ga.gov/housing/SpecialNeeds/index.asp.

165. Benefits.gov, "Georgia Energy Assistance Program," https://www.benefits.gov/benefits/benefit-details/1554; Georgia Division of Family and Children Services, "Energy Assistance," http://dfcs.dhs.georgia.gov/energy-assistance; Georgia Office of Planning and Budget 2016a, 161.

166. See Georgia Food Bank Association, http://georgiafoodbankassociation.org/.

167. Georgia Power, "Project SHARE," https://www.georgiapower.com/residential/payment-options/project-share-assistance.cshtml.

168. Center on Budget and Policy Priorities, "TANF at 20," https://www.cbpp.org /tanf-at-20.

169. Wesley Tharpe, "Immigrants Help Chart Georgia's Course to Prosperity," Georgia Budget & Policy Institute, December 2015, https://gbpi.org/wp-content/uploads/2015/12 /Immigrants-Help-Chart-Course-to-Prosperity.pdf.

170. Georgia Bureau of Investigation 2016.

171. Pew Center for the States 2012.

172. Vera Institute of Justice, "The Price of Prisons: Georgia" (fact sheet), January 2012, http://archive.vera.org/files/price-of-prisons-georgia-fact-sheet.pdf.

173. For number of offenders on probation, see Georgia Department of Corrections, "Annual Statistical Reports," http://www.dcor.state.ga.us/Research/Annual. For average probation sentence, see Georgia General Assembly Report 2011.

174. Georgia Center for Opportunity, "State of Corrections Fact Sheet," http://georgia opportunity.org/assets/2014/10/GCO-prisoner-reentry-fact-sheet-2014.pdf.

175. Vera Institute of Justice, "The Price of Prisons: Georgia" (fact sheet), January 2012, http://archive.vera.org/files/price-of-prisons-georgia-fact-sheet.pdf.

176. Georgia Department of Corrections 2015.

177. Georgia Department of Corrections 2016.

178. See Polling Report 2016.

179. *AJC* Poll, January 2016, http://media.cmgdigital.com/shared/news/documents/2016 /01/09/30401_GA_Poll_Banners.pdf.

180. U.S. Department of Justice 2014.

181. U.S. Department of Justice, "Uniform Crime Reporting Statistics," January 26, 2017, http://www.ucrdatatool.gov/Search/Crime/State/RunCrimeOneYearofData.cfm.

182. Georgia Bureau of Investigation 2014.

183. Handgunlaws.us. n.d.

184. Megan Fitzpatrick, "Georgia's 'Guns Everywhere' Bill Celebrated by Pro-gun Lobby," April 4, 2014, *CBCnews*, http://www.cbc.ca/news/world/georgia-s-guns-everywhere -bill-celebrated-by-pro-gun-lobby-1.2597232.

185. Chappell 2016.

186. Ibid.

REFERENCES

Abney, Glenn. 1988. "Lobbying by the Insiders: Parallels of State Agencies and Interest Groups." *Public Administration Review* 48 (September/October): 911–917.

Abney, Glenn, and John D. Hutchenson Jr. 1981. "Race, Representation, and Trust: Changes in Attitudes after the Election of a Black Mayor." *Public Opinion Quarterly* 45 (Spring): 91–100.

Abney, Glenn, and Thomas P. Lauth. 1986. *The Politics of State and City Administration*. Albany: State University of New York Press.

Altshuler, Alan, and David Luberoff. 2003. *Mega-projects: The Changing Politics of Urban Public Investment*. Washington: Brookings Institution Press.

American Bar Association. 2016. "ABA National Lawyer Population Survey Historical Trend in Total National Lawyer Population 1878–2016." http://www.americanbar.org /content/dam/aba/administrative/market_research/total-national-lawyer-population -1878-2016.authcheckdam.pdf.

———. 2015a. "Lawyer Demographics." http://www.americanbar.org/content/dam/aba /administrative/market_research/lawyer-demographics-tables-2015.authcheckdam .pdf.

———. 2015b. "2015 Law Graduate Employment Data." http://www.americanbar.org /content/dam/aba/administrative/legal_education_and_admissions_to_the_bar /reports/2015_law_graduate_employment_data.authcheckdam.pdf.

Ammons, David N., and Richard W. Campbell. 1992. "Does Your County Have Professional Management . . . or Just Limited Professional Assistance?" *Georgia County Government*, July: 24–27.

Anderson, William. 1975. *The Wild Man from Sugar Creek: The Political Career of Eugene Talmadge*. Baton Rouge: Louisiana State University Press.

Association County Commissioners of Georgia. 2015. "Demographic and Partisan Information on County Commissioners." Data provided to the authors by ACCG.

———. 2014. *2015–2016 County Platform*. http://www.accg.org/library/county_platform. pdf.

———. n.d. "Form of Government." http://www.accg.org/library/Forms_of_Government _Table.pdf.

Atkenson, Lonna Rae, and Randall W. Partin. 1995. "Economic and Referendum Voting: A Comparison of Gubernatorial and Senatorial Elections." *American Political Science Review*. 89, no. 1: 99–107.

Bachtel, Douglas C., and Laura Boatright, eds. Annual. *The Georgia County Guide*. Athens: Cooperative Extension Service, University of Georgia.

Ballotpedia. n.d.a. "2014 ballot measures." https://ballotpedia.org/2014_ballot_measures.

———. n.d.b. "2015 ballot measures." https://ballotpedia.org/2015_ballot_measures.

Bannon, Alicia, Eric Velasco, Linda Casey, and Lianna Reagan. 2013. *The New Politics of Judicial Elections 2011–12: How New Waves of Special Interest Spending Raised the Stakes for Fair Courts*. Washington, D.C.: Brennan Center for Justice and the National Institute on Money in State Politics. https://www.brennancenter.org/sites/default/files/publications/New%20Politics%20of%20Judicial%20Elections%202012.pdf.

Barnett, Katherine, and Richard Greens. 1999. "Grading the States." *Governing*, February 17–18.

Bartik, Timothy J. 2005. "Solving the Problems of Economic Development Incentives." *Growth and Change* 36, no. 2 (Spring): 139–166.

Bartley, Numan V. 1997. *The Rise of Massive Resistance: Race and Politics in the South During the 1950's*. Baton Rouge: Louisiana State University Press.

———. 1991. "Part Six: 1940 to the Present." In *A History of Georgia*, 2nd ed., edited by Kenneth Coleman, 337–407. Athens: University of Georgia Press.

———. 1990. *The Creation of Modern Georgia*. 2nd ed. Athens: University of Georgia Press.

———. 1970. *From Thurmond to Wallace: Political Tendencies in Georgia, 1948–1968*. Baltimore: Johns Hopkins University Press.

Bass, Jack, and Walter DeVries. 1976. *The Transformation of Southern Politics: Social Change and Political Consequence since 1945*. New York: Basic Books.

Baum, Lawrence. 2013. *American Courts: Process and Policy* 7th ed. Boston: Cengage.

Baumgartner, Frank R., and Bryan D. Jones. 1993. *Agendas and Instability in American Politics*. Chicago: University of Chicago Press.

Baybeck, Brady. 2014. "Local Political Participation." In *The Oxford Handbook of State and Local Politics*, edited by Donald P. Haider-Markel, 95–111. New York: Oxford University Press.

Bergal, Jenni. 2015. "Many Cities Are Creating Policies Apart from Their States." *Governing*, January 25. http://www.governing.com/topics/urban/many-cities-are-creating-policies-apart-from-their-states.html.

Berman, David. 2001. "State-Local Relations: Authority, Finances, Partnerships." In *Municipal Yearbook 2001*, 61–76 Washington, D.C.: ICMA.

Berry, William D., Evan J. Ringquist, Richard C. Fording, and Russell L. Hanson. 1998. "Measuring Citizen and Government Ideology in the American States, 1960–93." *American Journal of Political Science* 42, no. 1 (January): 327–348.

Beyle, Thad. 2003. "The Governors." In *Politics in the American States: A Comparative Analysis*, 8th ed., edited by Virginia Gray and Russell L. Hanson, 194–231. Washington, D.C.: Congressional Quarterly Press.

———. 1996. "Governors: The Middlemen and Women in Our Political System." In *Pol-

itics in the American States: A Comparative Analysis, 6th ed., edited by Virginia Gray and Herbert Jacob, 207–252. Washington, D.C.: Congressional Quarterly Press.

Beyle, Thad, and Margaret Ferguson. 2008. "Governors and the Executive Branch." In *Politics in the American States: A Comparative Analysis*, 9th ed., edited by Virginia Gray and Russell L. Hanson, 192–228. Washington, D.C.: Congressional Quarterly Press.

Black, Earl, and Merle Black. 2002. *The Rise of Southern Republicans*. Cambridge: Belknap Press of Harvard University.

———. 1992. *The Vital South: How Presidents Are Elected*. Cambridge: Harvard University Press.

———. 1987. *Politics and Society in the South*. Cambridge: Harvard University Press.

Blackmon, Douglas A. 2008. *Slavery by Another Name: The Re-Enslavement of Black Americans from the Civil War to World War II*. New York: Anchor Books.

Boney, F. N. 1991. "Part Three: 1820–1865." In *A History of Georgia*, 2nd ed., edited by Kenneth Coleman, 127–204. Athens: University of Georgia Press.

Bonneau, Chris W. 2005. "What Price Justice(s)? Understanding Campaign Spending in State Supreme Court Elections." *State Politics and Policy Quarterly* 5 (Summer): 107–125.

Bositis, David. 2002. *Black Elected Officials: A Statistical Summary, 2000*. Washington D.C.: Joint Center for Political and Economic Studies.

Bowman, Ann. O'M., and Richard C. Kearney. 2011. *State and Local Government*. 8th ed. Boston: Wadsworth, Cengage.

Bowser, Jennifer Drage, Keon S. Chi, and Thomas H. Little. *Coping with Term Limits: A Practical Guide*. Denver: National Conference of State Legislatures, 2006.

Boyd, Dan, and Lucy Dadayan. 2013. "The State Budget Crisis Task Force and Fiscal Challenges Ahead." In *The Book of the States 2014*, 341–349. Lexington, Ky.: Council of State Governments.

Brace, Paul. 1993. *State Government and Economic Performance*. Baltimore: Johns Hopkins University Press.

Brace, Paul, Laura Langer, and Melinda Gann Hall. 2000. "Measuring the Preferences of State Supreme Court Judges." *Journal of Politics* 62, no. 2 (May): 387–413

Bridges, Amy, and Richard Kronick. 1999. "Writing the Rules to Win the Game: The Middle-Class Regimes of Municipal Reformers." *Urban Affairs Review* 34 (May): 691–706.

Bullock, Charles S., III. 1993. *The Partisan, Racial, and Gender Makeup of Georgia County Offices*. Athens: Carl Vinson Institute of Government.

———. 1985. "Aftermath of the Voting Rights Act: Racial Voting Patterns in the Atlanta-Area Elections." In *The Voting Rights Act: Consequences and Implications*, edited by Lorn S. Foster, 185–208. New York: Praeger.

Bullock, Charles S., III, Scott E. Buchanan, and Ronald Keith Gaddie. 2015. *The Three Governors Controversy: Skullduggery, Machinations, and the Decline of Georgia's Progressive Politics*. Athens: University of Georgia Press.

Bullock, Charles S., III, and Bruce A. Campbell. 1984. "Racist or Racial Voting in the 1981 Municipal Elections." *Urban Affairs Quarterly* 20 (December): 149–164.

Bullock, Charles S., and Loch K. Johnson. 1992. *Runoff Elections in the United States.* Chapel Hill: University of North Carolina Press.

Bullock, Charles S., III, M. V. Hood III, and Richard Clark, 2005. "Punch Cards, Jim Crow, and Al Gore: Explaining Voter Trust in the Electoral System in Georgia, 2000." *State Politics and Policy Quarterly* 5 (Fall): 283–294.

Burke, Brendan F., and Deil S. Wright. 2002. "Reassessing and Reconciling Reinvention in the American States: Exploring State Administrative Performance." *State and Local Government Review* 34 (Winter): 7–19.

Burnett, Jennifer. 2015. "State Overseas Trade and Investment Offices, 2015." *Council of State Governments*, November. http://knowledgecenter.csg.org/kc/system/files/CR_overseas_trade.pdf.

Caress, Stanley M., and Todd T. Kunioka. 2012. *Term Limits and Their Consequences: The Aftermath of Legislative Reform.* Albany: State University of New York Press.

Carpenter, Dale. 2012. *Flagrant Conduct: A Story of Lawrence v. Texas.* New York: W. W. Norton.

Carr, Jered B., and Richard C. Feiock, eds. 2004. *City-County Consolidation and Its Alternatives: Reshaping the Local Government Landscape.* Armonk, N.Y.: M. E. Sharpe.

Carter, Jimmy. 1992. *Turning Point: A Candidate, a State, and a Nation Come of Age.* New York: Times Books.

Center for American Women and Politics. 2015. "Women as Mayors 2015." Rutgers University, February 1. http://www.cawp.rutgers.edu/levels_of_office/local.

Chappell, Bill. 2016. "'Campus Carry' Gun Bill Is Vetoed in Georgia, With a Lengthy Explanation." NPR, May 4. http://www.npr.org/sections/thetwo-way/2016/05/04/476725918/-campus-carry-gun-bill-is-vetoed-in-georgia-with-a-lengthy-explanation.

Chicago-Kent College of Law. n.d. "The Affordable Care Act Cases." http://www.oyez.org/cases/2010-2019/2011/2011_11_400.

Clean Water Atlanta. n.d. "The Goal of Clean Water Atlanta." *City of Atlanta.* http://www.cleanwateratlanta.org/default.htm.

Cobb, James C. 1993. *The Selling of the South: The Southern Crusade for Industrial Development, 1936–1990.* 2nd ed. Urbana: University of Illinois Press.

Coleman, Kenneth. 1991. "Part Two: 1775–1820." In *A History of Georgia*, 2nd ed., edited by Kenneth Coleman, 69–126. Athens: University of Georgia Press.

CollegeBoard. n.d. "Tuition and Fees by Sector and State Over Time." https://trends.collegeboard.org/college-pricing/figures-tables/tuition-fees-sector-state-over-time.

Conant, James K. 1992. "Executive Branch Reorganization: Can It Be an Effective Antidote for Fiscal Stress in the States?" *State and Local Government Review* 24 (Winter): 3–11.

Cooper, Christopher A., Anthony J. Nownes, and Steven Roberts. 2005. "Perceptions of Power: Interest Groups in Local Politics." *State and Local Government Review* 37 (Fall): 206–216.

Cortright, Joseph, and Heike Mayer. 2004. "Increasingly Rank: The Use and Misuse of Rankings in Economic Development." *Economic Development Quarterly* 18 (February): 34–39.

Council of State Governments. Annual. *The Book of the States*. Lexington, Ky.: Council of State Governments.

Court of Appeals of Georgia. n.d. "History of the Court of Appeals." http://www.gaappeals.us/history/.

Cox, George H., John H. Daley, and Roger N. Pajari. 1991. "Local Government Support of Economic Development." *Public Administration Quarterly* 15 (Fall): 304–327.

Cox, George, and Raymond Rosenfeld. 2001. *State and Local Government*, Boston: Wadsworth Thomson Learning.

Crawford, Tom. 2015. "A State Representative Accused Gov. Nathan Deal of Being a King." *Flagpole*, March 25.

Cromartie, John. 2013. "How Is Rural America Changing?" PowerPoint for C-SPAN. *Economic Research Service, U.S. Department of Agriculture*, May 24. http://www.census.gov/newsroom/cspan/rural_america/20130524_rural_america_slides.pdf.

C-SPAN.org. n.d. "109th Congress A Profile." https://www.c-span.org/congress/members/?congress=109&chamber=House&visual=&find-name=all&find-state=all&find-party=all&freshman=0&sort-names=name.

Dalehite, Esteban G., John L. Mikesell, and C. Kurt Zorn. 2005. "Variation in Property Tax Abatement Programs among States." *Economic Development Quarterly* 19 (May): 157–173.

Davidson, Chandler, and Bernard Grofman. 1994. *Quiet Revolution in the South*. Princeton: Princeton University Press.

DeKalb County. 2016a. "Election Summary Report, DeKalb County: State of Georgia Primary and Special Election Runoff, July 26, 2016." August 1. https://www.dekalbcountyga.gov/sites/default/files/user18/Result_07262016.pdf.

———. 2016b. "Election Summary Report, DeKalb County: State of Georgia Primary and Nonpartisan General Election, May 24, 2016." May 27. https://www.dekalbcountyga.gov/sites/default/files/Result_05242016_0.pdf.

Dhawan, Rajeev. 2011. "A Confounding Regional Recovery." Economic Forecasting Center, Georgia State University, February. http://www.rdhawan.com/booklets/Ga&ATL_Booklet_Feb11_press.pdf.

Dilger, Robert Jay. 1995. "A Comparative Analysis of Gubernatorial Enabling Resources." *State and Local Government Review* 27 (Spring): 118–126.

Ducat, Craig. 2009. *Constitutional Law: Powers of Government Volume 1*. Boston: Wadsworth.

Ehrenhalt, Alan. 2012. *The Great Inversion and the Future of the American City*. New York: Alfred A. Knopf.

Eisenberg, Theodore, and Geoffrey P. Miller. 2004. "Reversal, Dissent, and Variability in State Supreme Courts: The Centrality of Jurisdictional Source." *Boston University Law Review* 89: 1451

Eisinger, Peter K. 1988. *The Rise of the Entrepreneurial State: State and Local Economic Development Policy in the United States*. Madison: University of Wisconsin Press.

Elliott, Euel, Gerald S. Gryski, and Bruce Reed. 1990. "Minor Party Support in State Legislative Elections." *State and Local Government Review*. 22 (Fall): 123–131.

Engstrom, Richard L., and Richard N. Engstrom. 2008. "The Majority Vote Rule and Runoff Primaries in the United States." *Electoral Studies* 27, no. 3: 407–416.

Environmental Council of the States. n.d. https://www.ecos.org/wp-content/uploads /2017/03/Budget-Report-FINAL-3_15_17-Final-4.pdf.

Eplan, Leon S. 2014. "The Genesis of Citizen Participation in Atlanta." In *Planning Atlanta*, edited by Harley F. Etienne and Barbara Faga, 94–102. Chicago: Planners Press.

Epstein, Lee. 1994. "Exploring the Participation of Organized Interests in State Court Litigation." *Political Research Quarterly* 47 (June): 335–351.

Erikson, Robert S., Gerald C. Wright, and John P. McIver. 2006. "Public Opinion in the States: A Quarter Century of Change and Stability." In *Public Opinion in State Politics*, edited by Jeffrey E. Cohen, 229–253. Stanford, Calif.: Stanford University Press.

Ertas, Nevbahar, Jungbu Kim, John Matthews and Laura Wheeler. Carl Vinson Institute of Government and Andrew Young School of Policy Studies. 2009. "Creating a New Milton County." http://cslf.gsu.edu/files/2014/06/Report_1_Costs_Revenue _Milton_3-03-09.pdf.

Evans, Lawton B. 1972 [1898]. *History of Georgia*. New York: American Book Company.

Evans, William, Sheila Murray, and Robert Schwab. 1997. "Schoolhouses, Courthouses, and Statehouses after Serrano." *Journal of Policy and Management* 10: 10–31.

Faga, Barbara. 2014. "Freedom Park: A Modern Day Battle." In *Planning Atlanta*, edited by Harley F. Etienne and Barbara Faga, 103–110. Chicago: Planners Press.

Fellows, Matthew. 2011. "City-County Consolidation through 2010." National Association of Counties. June 9. http://www.naco.org/sites/default/files/documents/City%20 County%20Consolidations.01.01.2011.pdf.

Ferguson, Margaret R. 2006. "Introduction to State Executives." In *The Executive Branch of State Government: People, Process and Politics*, edited by Margaret R. Ferguson, 208–249. Santa Barbara, Calif.: ABC-CLIO.

Fiscal Research Center, Georgia State University. 2015. "Georgia Tax Expenditure Report for FY2017." *Governor's Office of Planning and Budget*, December 1. http://opb.georgia .gov/sites/opb.georgia.gov/files/related_files/site_page/TER%202017%20Final%20 Deliverable%20-Second%20Version-12-14-2015.pdf.

Fite, Gilbert Courtland. 1991. *Richard B. Russell, Jr., Senator from Georgia*. Chapel Hill: University of North Carolina Press.

Flanigan, William, and Nancy H. Zingale. 2014. *Political Behavior of the American Electorate*. 13th ed. Washington, D.C.: Congressional Quarterly Press.

Fleischmann, Arnold. 2012. "Urbanization of the South." In *The Oxford Handbook of Southern Politics*, edited by Charles S. Bullock III and Mark J. Rozell, 80–102. New York: Oxford University Press.

———. 2004. "Regionalism and City-County Consolidation in Small Metro Areas." *State and Local Government Review* 32 (Fall): 213–226.

———. 2000. "Regionalism and City-County Consolidation in Small Metro Areas." *State and Local Government Review*. 32 (Fall): 213–226.

———. 1989. "Politics, Administration, and Local Land-Use Regulation: Analyzing Zoning as a Policy Process." *Public Administration Review* 49 (July–August): 337–352.

———. 1986. "The Goals and Strategies of Local Boundary Changes: Government Organization or Private Gain?" *Journal of Urban Affairs* 8 (Fall): 63–76.

Fleischmann, Arnold, and Jennifer Custer. 2004. "Goodbye, Columbus." In *Case Studies of City-County Consolidation: Reshaping the Local Government Landscape*, edited by Suzanne M. Leland and Kurt Thurmaier, 46–59. New York: M. E. Sharpe.

Fleischmann, Arnold, and Carol Pierannunzi. 1990. "Citizens, Development Interests, and Local Land-Use Regulations." *Journal of Politics* 52 (August): 838–853.

Fleischmann, Arnold, and Lana Stein. 1998. "Campaign Contributions in Local Elections." *Political Research Quarterly* 51 (September): 673–689.

———. 1987. "Minority and Female Success in Municipal Runoff Elections." *Social Science Quarterly* 68 (June): 378–385.

Florida, Richard. 2005. *Cities and the Creative Class*. New York: Routledge.

Fox, Emily Jane. 2015. "Where Public University Tuition Has Skyrocketed." CNN, May 13. http://money.cnn.com/2015/05/13/pf/college/public-university-tuition-increase/.

Frey, William H. 2017. "Census Shows a Revival of Pre-recession Migration Flows." *The Avenue* (blog), Brookings Institution, March 30. https://www.brookings.edu/blog/the-avenue/2017/03/30/census-shows-a-revival-of-pre-recession-migration-flows/.

———. 2013. "A Big City Growth Revival?" (opinion column). Brookings Metropolitan Policy Program, May 28. http://www.brookings.edu/research/opinions/2013/05/28/city-growth-frey.

———. 2012. "Population Growth in Metro America since 1980: Putting the Volatile 2000s in Perspective." Brookings Metropolitan Policy Program, March. http://www.brookings.edu/research/population-growth-in-metro-america-since-1980-putting-the-volatile-2000s-in-perspective.

———. 2011. "Melting Pot Cities and Suburbs: Racial and Ethnic Change in Metro America in the 2000s." Brookings Metropolitan Policy Program, May. https://www.brookings.edu/wp-content/uploads/2016/06/0504_census_ethnicity_frey.pdf.

Gaddie, Ronald Keith. 2012. "Realignment." In *The Oxford Handbook of Southern Politics*, edited by Charles S. Bullock III and Mark J. Rozell, 289–313. New York: Oxford University Press.

Gallagher, John. 2013. *Revolution Detroit: Strategies for Urban Reinvention*. Detroit: Wayne State University Press.

Georgia Budget and Policy Institute. 2011. "Advancing Georgia's 1930s Tax System to the Modern Day: Fair and Adequate Tax Reform for 21st Century Georgians." August. https://gbpi.org/wp-content/uploads/2011/10/20100825_AdvancingGeorgias1903sTaxSystemToTheModernDay.pdf.

———. 2005. "Don't Tax and They Will Come? The Questionable Link between State Corporate Income Taxes and Economic Development." July 18. http://www.gbpi.org/pubs/20050718report.pdf.

Georgia Bureau of Investigation. 2016. "Georgia Bureau of Investigation: March Monthly Report FY2016." http://gbi.georgia.gov/sites/gbi.georgia.gov/files/related_files/site_page/May%202016%20Statistical%20Report.pdf.

———. 2014. "2014 Summary Report: Uniform Crime Reporting (UCR) Program." Georgia Crime Information Center. https://gbi.georgia.gov/sites/gbi.georgia.gov/files/related_files/site_page/2014CrimeStatisticsSummaryReport.pdf.

Georgia Department of Community Affairs. 2016. "2016 Government Management Indicators Survey." Prepublication data provided to the authors, October 2016.

———. 2015a. *County Government Information Catalog* (October). Atlanta: Georgia Department of Community Affairs.

———. 2015b. *Georgia Local Government Finance Highlights: Local Government Data for Fiscal Years Ended in 2013* (December). Atlanta: Georgia Department of Community Affairs.

———. 2015c. *Municipal Government Information Catalog* (October). Atlanta: Georgia Department of Community Affairs.

———. 1993. *Local Government Efficiency Grant General Program Guidelines*. Atlanta: Georgia Department of Community Affairs.

———. 1989. "The Georgia Planning Act 1989." http://www.dca.state.ga.us/development/ PlanningQualityGrowth/DOCUMENTS/Laws.Rules.Guidelines.Etc/GAPlanningAct.pdf.

———. n.d. "Service Delivery Strategy." http://dca.ga.gov/development/PlanningQualityGrowth/programs/servicedelivery.asp.

Georgia Department of Corrections. 2016. "Inmate Statistical Profile: Under Death Sentence." May 1. http://www.dcor.state.ga.us/sites/all/themes/gdc/pdf/Profile_death_row _2016_04.pdf.

———. 2015. "2015 Fiscal Year Report." https://www.joomag.com/magazine/mag /0959351001458589032.

Georgia Department of Economic Development. 2014. "Gateway to the World." *Georgia.org*. http://www.georgia.org/wp-content/uploads/2014/03/Logistics-Brochure-Update.pdf.

Georgia Department of Human Services. 2016. "Georgia Department of Human Services Quick Facts." January. https://dhs.georgia.gov/sites/dhs.georgia.gov/files/DHS%20 Quick%20Facts%20Book42016.pdf.

Georgia Department of Transportation. 2015. "Georgia Department of Transportation: Amended FY 2016 & FY 2016 Budget Update." Atlanta: Georgia Department of Transportation.

———. 2014. "Georgia Department of Transportation Factbook." http://www.georgia.org/wp -content/uploads/2014/03/Logistics-Brochure-Update.pdf.

Georgia Division of Family and Children Services. 2013. "Welfare Reform in Georgia, 2012: Senate Bill 104." http://dfcs.dhs.georgia.gov/sites/dfcs.dhs.georgia.gov/files/related _files/document/WelfareReform2012.pdf.

Georgia General Assembly. 2014. *Acts and Resolutions of the General Assembly of the State of Georgia: 2014*. Vol. 3, *Local and Special Acts and Resolutions*. Atlanta: Georgia General Assembly.

———. 2011. "Report of the Special Council on Criminal Justice Reform for Georgians." November 1. http://www.legis.ga.gov/Documents/GACouncilReport-FINALDRAFT .pdf.

———. 1981. *Acts and Resolutions of the Georgia General Assembly: 1981*. Vol. 2, *Local and Special Acts and Resolutions*. Atlanta: Georgia General Assembly.

Georgia General Assembly, Joint Committee on Critical Transportation Infrastructure Funding. 2014. *Final Report* (December). http://www.metroatlantachamber.com/docs

/default-source/pp_transportation-/transportation_study_committee_final_report _2014.pdf?sfvrsn=2.

Georgia Government Transparency and Campaign Finance Commission. n.d. http:// ethics.ga.gov/.

Georgia Governor's Commission on Effectiveness and Economy in Government. 1992. *Final Report* (January). Atlanta: Governor's Commission on Effectiveness and Economy in Government.

Georgia Municipal Association. 2014. *Growing Cities, Growing Georgia: A Guide to Georgia's Annexation Law* (January). 6th ed. Atlanta: Georgia Municipal Association.

———. 2012. *Handbook for Georgia Mayors and Councilmember,* 5th ed. Atlanta: Georgia Municipal Association. http://www.gmanet.com/GMASite/media/PDF/handbook /handbook_complete.pdf.

Georgia Public Policy Foundation. 2014. "Analyzing Education Spending." January 27. http://www.georgiapolicy.org/2014/01/analyzing-education-spending/.

Georgia Secretary of State. 2016. "General Primary Turnout Demographics." May 24. http://sos.ga.gov/index.php/elections/general_primary_turnout_demographics.

———. 2006. "Georgia Election Results: Official Results of the Tuesday, November 6, 2006 General Elections." November 7. http://sos.ga.gov/elections/election_results /2006_1107/default.htm.

———. 2005. "Secretary of State News." www.sos.ga.us/pressrel/111804.htm. Page no longer available.

Georgia Student Finance Commission. 2015. "Programs and Regulations." http://gsfc. georgia.gov/hope.

Georgia.org. n.d. "International Representatives." http://www.georgia.org/business -resources/international-trade/representatives/.

Georgia Supreme Court Commission on Racial and Ethnic Bias in the Court System. 1995. *Let Justice Be Done: Equally, Fairly, and Impartially.* Final report. Atlanta: Georgia Supreme Court Commission on Racial and Ethnic Bias in the Court System.

Gerber, Elizabeth R., and Justin H. Phillips. 2003. "Development Ballot Measures, Interest Group Endorsements, and the Political Geography of Growth Preferences." *American Journal of Political Science* 47 (October): 625–639.

Gibson, M. Troy. 2004. "Culture Wars in State Education Policy: A Look at the Relative Treatment of Evolutionary Theory in State Science Standards." *Social Science Quarterly* 85 (December): 1129–1149.

Gilens, Martin, and Benjamin I. Page. 2014. "Testing Theories of American Politics: Elites, Interest Groups, and Average Citizens." *Perspectives in Politics* 12, no. 3: 564– 581.

Glaeser, Edward L. 2011. *The Triumph of the City: How Our Greatest Invention Makes Us Richer, Smarter, Greener, Healthier, and Happier.* New York: Penguin Press.

Glick, Henry R. 2004. "Courts: Politics and the Judicial Process." In *Politics in the American States: A Comparative Analysis,* 8th ed., edited by Virginia Gray and Russell L. Hanson, 232–260. Washington, D.C.: Congressional Quarterly Press.

———. 1993. *Courts, Politics and Justice* 3rd ed. New York: McGraw Hill.

Glick, Henry B., and Scott P. Hays. 1991. "Innovation and Reinvention in State Policy-making: Theory and the Evolution of Living Will Laws." *Journal of Politics* 53, no. 3 (August): 835–850.

Gorton, Joe, and John L. Boies. 1999. "Sentencing Guidelines and Racial Disparity across Time: Pennsylvania Prison Sentences in 1977, 1983, 1992, and 1993." *Social Science Quarterly* 80 (March): 37–54.

Governing. n.d. "Education Spending per Student by State." http://www.governing.com/gov -data/education-data/state-education-spending-per-pupil-data.html.

Governor's Local Governance Commission. 1992. *A Platform for Local Governance Change.* Final report (November). Atlanta: Governor's Local Governance Commission.

Governor's Office of Planning and Budget. 2016a. *Budget in Brief: Amended Fiscal Year 2015 and Fiscal Year 2016.* http://opb.georgia.gov/sites/opb.georgia.gov/files/related_files /site_page/State%20of%20Georgia%20BIB%20AFY%202015-FY%202016.Final UPDATED08282015.pdf.

———. 2016b. *The Governor's Budget Report: Amended Fiscal Year 2017.* http://opb.georgia .gov/sites/opb.georgia.gov/files/related_files/site_page/AFY%2017%20State%20of %20Georgia%20Budget.pdf.

———. 2015. Governors Office of Planning and Budget: Budget Documents. https://opb .georgia.gov/budget-information.

———. 2010. "Georgia 2030: Population Projections." March 12.

Gray, Virginia. 2013. "The Socioeconomic and Political Context of States." In *Politics in the American States: A Comparative Analysis,* edited by Virginia Gray, Russell L. Hanson, and Thad Kousser, 1–29. Thousand Oaks, Calif.: Congressional Quarterly Press.

———. 1973. "Innovations in the States: A Diffusions Study." *American Journal of Political Science* 67 (December): 1174–1185.

Gray, Virginia, Russell L. Hanson, and Thad Kousser, eds. 2013. *Politics in the American States: A Comparative Analysis.* 10th ed. Thousand Oaks, Calif.: Congressional Quarterly Press.

Greenblatt, Alan. 2016a. "Does Size Matter? The Latest Battle over State Supreme Courts." *Governing: States and Localities,* May 12. http://www.governing.com/topics/politics/gov -georgia-arizona-supreme-court-expansion.html?utm_term=Does%20Size%20 Matter%20The%20Latest%20Battle%20Over%20State%20Supreme%20Courts&utm _campaign=Does%20Size%20Matter%20The%20Latest%20Battle%20Over% 20State%20Supreme%20Courts%20&utm_content=email&utm_source=Act-On+ Software&utm_medium=email.

———. 2016b. "Stuck in the Middle: In Rural America, Middle-Class Workers Seem to Be Stuck in an Endless Recession." *Governing* (August): 24–30.

———. 2016c. "Beyond North Carolina's LGBT Battle: States' War of Cities." *Governing,* March 25. http://www.governing.com/topics/politics/gov-states-cities-preemption -laws.html.

Gregory, James N. 2007. *The Southern Diaspora: How the Great Migrations of Black and White Southerners Transformed America.* Chapel Hill: University of North Carolina Press.

Grovum, Jake. 2014. "Uneven Gains for States after 50 Years of the War on Poverty." *Stateline: The Daily News Service of the Pew Charitable Trusts,* January 30. http://www

.pewstates.org/projects/stateline/headlines/uneven-gains-for-states-after-50-years-of
-the-war-on-poverty-85899536709#.

Gurwitt, Rob. 2001. "Shirley Franklin: Old Hand, Fresh Appeal." *Governing*, December, 64.

Haeberle, Steven H. 1993. "Divisive Competition in Runoff Primaries." *Southeastern Politics Review* 21 (Winter): 79–98.

Hafetz, Frederick P., and John M. Pellettieri. 1999. "Time to Reform the Grand Jury." *The Champion*, National Association of Criminal Defense Attorneys, January/February 1999, 12. https://www.nacdl.org/Champion.aspx?id=648.

Hajnal, Zoltan L., and Paul G. Lewis. 2003. "Municipal Institutions and Voter Turnout in Local Elections." *Urban Affairs Review* 38 (May): 645–668.

Hall, Melinda Gann. 2001. "State Supreme Courts in American Democracy." *American Political Science Review* 95 (June): 315–330.

———. 1992. "Electoral Politics and Strategic Voting in State Supreme Courts." *Journal of Politics* 54 (May): 427–446.

Hall, Melinda Gann, and Paul Brace. 1994. "The Vicissitudes of Death by Decree: Forces Influencing Capital Punishment Decisionmaking in State Supreme Courts." *Social Science Quarterly* 75 (March): 136–151.

Hamm, Keith, and Gary Moncrief. 2004. "Legislative Politics in the States." In *Politics in the American States: A Comparative Analysis*, 8th ed., edited by Virginia Gray, and Russell L. Hanson, 157–193. Washington: Congressional Quarterly Press.

Handgunlaws.us. n.d. "Georgia." http://www.handgunlaw.us/states/georgia.pdf.

Hartsfield-Jackson: Atlanta International Airport. n.d.a. "Operation Statistics." *City of Atlanta.*

———. n.d.b. "ATL Fact Sheet." *City of Atlanta.*

Hawkins, Christopher. 2011. "Electoral Support for Community Growth Management Policy." *Social Science Quarterly* 92 (March): 268–284.

Hefetz, Amir, and Mildred Warner. 2012. "Contracting or Public Delivery? The Importance of Service, Market, and Management Characteristics." *Journal of Public Administration Research and Theory* 14, no. 2 (April): 289–317.

Heilig, Peggy, and Robert Mundt. 1984. *Your Voice at City Hall: The Politics, Procedures, and Policies of District Representation*. Albany: State University of New York Press.

Heltman, John. 2012. "27th Amendment or Bust." *The American Prospect*, May 30. http://prospect.org/article/27th-amendment-or-bust.

Henderson, Harold P. 1991. *The Politics of Change in Georgia: A Political Biography of Ellis Arnall*. Athens: University of Georgia Press.

Henderson, Harold P., and Gary L. Roberts. 1988. *Georgia Governors in an Age of Change: From Ellis Arnall to George Busbee*. Athens: University of Georgia Press.

Henderson, Jason. 2012. "Rebuilding Rural Manufacturing." *Main Street Economist*, no. 2. http://www.kansascityfed.org/publicat/mse/mse_0212.pdf.

Henry J. Kaiser Family Foundation. 2016. "Status of State Individual Marketplace and Medicaid Expansion, 2014." January 1, http://kff.org/health-reform/slide/current-status
-of-state-individual-marketplaces-and-medicaid-expansion-decisions/.

Hepburn, Cameron. 2010. "*Environmental Policy, Government, and The Market.*" *Oxford Review of Economic Policy* 26, no. 2: 117–136.

Hershey, Marjorie Randon. 2015. *Party Politics in America.* 16th ed. New York: Routledge.

Hill, Laverne W., and Melvin B. Hill. 2017 [2002]. "Government and Politics, Constitutional History, Georgia Constitution." *New Georgia Encyclopedia.* http://www.georgia encyclopedia.org/articles/government-politics/georgia-constitution.

Hill, Melvin B., Jr. 1994. *The Georgia State Constitution: A Reference Guide.* Westport, Conn.: Greenwood Press.

Hilvert, Cheryl, and David Swindell. 2013. "Collaborative Service Delivery: What Every Local Government Manager Should Know." *State and Local Government Review* 45, no. 4 (December): 240–254.

Hirlinger, M. W. 1992. "Citizen-Initiated Contacting of Local Government Officials: A Multivariate Explanation." *Journal of Politics* 54, no. 2: 553–564.

Hochschild, Jennifer. 2012. "Race and Cities: New Circumstances Imply New Ideas." *Perspectives on Politics* 10, no. 3 (September): 647–658.

Holbrook, Thomas M., and Raymond J. LaRaja. 2013. "Parties and Elections." In *Politics in the American States*, 10th ed., edited by Virginia Gray and Russell L. Hanson, 63–104. Washington D.C.: Congressional Quarterly Press.

Holmes, Malcolm D., Harmon M. Hosch, Howard C. Daudistel, Dolores A. Perez, and Joseph B. Graves. 1993. "Judges' Ethnicity and Minority Sentencing: Evidence Concerning Hispanics." *Social Science Quarterly* 74 (September): 496–506.

Holmes, William F. 1991. "Part Five: 1890–1940." In *A History of Georgia*, 2nd ed., edited by Kenneth Coleman, 255–336. Athens: University of Georgia Press.

Hood, M. V., III, Quentin Kidd, and Irwin L. Morris. 2012a. *The Rational Southerner: Black Mobilization, Republican Growth, and the Partisan Transformation of the American South.* New York: Oxford University Press.

———. 2012b. "The Republican Party in the American South: From Radical Fringe to Conservative Mainstream." In *The Oxford Handbook of Southern Politics*, edited by Charles S. Bullock III and Mark J. Rozell, 330–354. New York: Oxford University Press.

Hoyman, Michele. 1997. *Power Steering: Global Automakers and the Transformation of Rural Communities.* Lawrence: University Press of Kansas.

Hrebenar, Ronald J., and Ruth K. Scott, 1990. *Interest Group Politics in America.* 2nd ed. Englewood Cliffs, N.J.: Prentice Hall.

Hrebenar, Ronald J., and Clive S. Thomas, eds. 1992. *Interest Group Politics in the Southern States.* Tuscaloosa: University of Alabama Press.

Hudson, Betty J., and Paul T. Hardy, eds. 2005. *Handbook for Georgia Mayors and Councilmembers*, 4th ed. Athens: Carl Vinson Institute of Government, University of Georgia.

———. 2002. *Handbook for Georgia County Commissioners.* 4th ed. Athens: Carl Vinson Institute of Government, University of Georgia.

Hunter, Floyd. 1963. *Community Power Structure: A Study of Decision Makers.* Garden City, N.Y.: Doubleday.

Hurst, Julia Nienaber. 2004. "Lieutenant Governors: Powerful in Two Branches." In *The Book of the States 2004*, 187–188. Lexington, Ky.: Council of State Governments.

Hutcheson, John D., and James E. Prather. 1988. "Community Mobilization and Participation in the Zoning Process." *Urban Affairs Quarterly* 23 (March): 346–368.

Initiative and Referendum Institute. 2017. "Overview of Initiative Use, 1900–2016." *Initia-*

tive Use. February. http://www.iandrinstitute.org/docs/IRI%20Initiative%20Use%20 (2017-1).pdf.

———. 2014. "Election Results 2014: Yes on Marijuana and Minimum Wage; No on Taxes." *Ballotwatch* no. 2, November 5. http://www.iandrinstitute.org/docs/BW%202014-2%20 Election%20results%20(v1)%202014-11-04.pdf.

———. 2012. "Election Results 2012: Breakthrough Wins for Marijuana and Same-Sex Marriage." *Ballotwatch* no. 3, November 8. http://www.iandrinstitute.org/docs/BW%202012 -3%20Election%20results%20v1.pdf.

Institute on Money in State Politics. 2014. "Election Overview: Georgia 2014." http:// www.followthemoney.org/election-overview?s=GA&y=2014.

———. 2006. January. http://followthemoney.org/tools/election-overview/?s=GA&y= 2006.

International City/County Management Association (ICMA). 2011. "Municipal Form of Government, 2011." Washington, D.C.: ICMA.

———. 2010. "Economic Development 2009 Survey Summary." Washington, D.C.: ICMA. http://icma.org/en/icma/knowledge_network/documents/kn/Document /107026/ICMA_2009_Economic_Development_Survey_Summary.

———. 2007. "ICMA Profile of Local Government Service Delivery Choices, 2007." https://icma.org/sites/default/files/101785_asd2007_2008web.pdf.

Jackson, Edwin L., and Mary E. Stakes, 1988a. *Handbook for Georgia Legislators*. 10th ed. Athens: Carl Vinson Institute of Government, University of Georgia.

———, 1988b. *Handbook for Georgia State Agencies*. 2nd ed. Athens: Carl Vinson Institute of Government, University of Georgia.

Jacob, Herbert. 1995. *Law and Politics in the United States*. 2nd ed. New York: Harper-Collins.

Jacobsen, Louis. 2016. "The Best of Times, the Worst of Times: A Ranking of State Economies." *Governing*, August 22. http://www.governing.com/topics/politics/gov-state-economic -rankings-governor-ratings.html.

Jewell, Malcolm E., and Marcia Lynn Whicker. 1994. *Legislative Leadership in the American States*. Ann Arbor: University of Michigan Press.

Jolley, G. Jason, Mandee Foushee Lancaster, and Jang Gao. 2015. "Tax Incentives and Business Climate: Executive Perceptions from Incented and Nonincented Firms." *Economic Development Quarterly* 29, no. 2 (May): 180–186.

Jones, Bryan D. 1982. "Assessing the Products of Government." In *Analyzing Urban-Service Distributions*, edited by Richard C. Rich, 155–169. Lexington, Mass.: Lexington Books.

Judicial Council of Georgia: Administrative Office of the Courts. Annual. "Caseload Reports." February 2, 2017. http://www.georgiacourts.org/content/caseload-reports.

———. n.d.a. "Indigent Defense Reports." http://www.georgiacourts.com/aoc/press/idc/idc .html.

———. n.d.b. "Code of Judicial Conduct, State of Georgia." http://www.georgiacourts .org/sites/default/files/GEORGIA%2520CODE%2520OF%2520JUDICIAL%2520 CONDUCT%2520-%252009_23_11.pdf.

Judicial Qualifications Commission State of Georgia. n.d. "The Judicial Qualifications Commission State of Georgia." http://www.gajqc.com/.

Katz, Bruce, and Jennifer Bradley. 2013. *The Metropolitan Revolution: How Cities and*

Metros Are Fixing Our Broken Politics and Fragile Economy. Washington, D.C.: Brookings Institution Press.

Kauffman, Robert. 2015. "Seeking a More Efficient Disciplinary Process." *State Bar of Georgia*. December 15. https://www.gabar.org/aboutthebar/presidentspage_dec15.cfm

Kelly, Katie P., Lindsey Needham, and Sheahan Virgin. 2011. "No More Gerrymanders: Georgia's Partisan Plan versus the Fair Voting Alternative." *Fair Vote*. October 31. http://www.fairvote.org/no-more-gerrymanders-georgia.

Key, V. O., Jr. 1964. *Parties, Politics, and Pressure Groups*. New York: Crowell.

———. 1949. *Southern Politics in State and Nation*. New York: Knopf.

Kingdon, John W. 1995. *Agendas, Alternatives, and Public Policies*. 2nd ed. New York: Harper Collins.

Kinkaid, John. 2012. "State-Federal Relations: Revolt against Coercive Federalism." In *The Book of the States 2012*, 39–50. Lexington, Ky.: Council of State Governments.

Kneebone, Elizabeth, and Alan Berube. 2013. *Confronting Suburban Poverty in America*. Washington, D.C.: Brookings Institution Press.

Knotts, H. Gibbs, and Moshe Haspel. 2006. "The Impact of Gentrification on Voter Turnout." *Social Science Quarterly* 87 (March): 110–121.

Kousser, Thad, and Justin H. Phillips. 2009. "Who Blinks First? Legislative Patience and Bargaining with Governors." *Legislative Studies Quarterly* 34, no. 1: 55–86.

Krebs, Timothy B. 2014. "Local Campaigns and Elections." In *The Oxford Handbook of State and Local Government*, edited by Donald P. Haider-Markel, 189–211. New York: Oxford University Press.

Kruse, Kevin M. 2005. *White Flight: Atlanta and the Making of Modern Conservatism*. Princeton: Princeton University Press.

Kurtz, Karl. 2015. "Who We Elect: The Demographics of State Legislatures." *National Conference for State Legislatures*. December 1. http://www.ncsl.org/research/about-state-legislatures/who-we-elect.aspx.

Labonte, Marc. 2010. *The 2007–2009 Recession: Similarities to and Differences from the Past*. Washington, D.C.: Congressional Research Service. October 10. http://www.au.af.mil/au/awc/awcgate/crs/r40198.pdf.

Lamis, Alexander P. 1990. *The Two-Party South*. 2nd ed. New York: Oxford University Press.

Lauth, Tom. 1990. "The Governor and the Conference Committee in Georgia." *Legislative Studies Quarterly* 15 (August): 441–453.

———. 1986. "The Executive Budget in Georgia." *State and Local Government Review* 18 (Spring): 56–64.

Leland, Suzanne, and Kurt Thurmaier, eds. 2004. *Case Studies of City-County Consolidation: Reshaping the Local Government Landscape*. Armonk, N.Y.: M. E. Sharpe.

Lemann, Nicholas. 1991. *The Promised Land: The Great Black Migration and How It Changed America*. New York: Vintage Books.

Lewis, Doug. 2005. "2004 Election Success and State Initiatives." In *The Book of the States 2005*, 346–349. Lexington, Ky.: Council of State Governments.

Lewis, John. n.d. "Understanding the Highway Trust Fund." https://johnlewis.house.gov/legislative-work/issues/transportation/understanding-highway-trust-fund.

Lowry, Robert C. 2014. "The Context of State Policy Policymaking." In *The Oxford Handbook of State and Local Government,* edited by Donald P. Haider-Markel, 534–560. New York: Oxford University Press.

Lublin, David. 2004. *The Republican South: Democratization and Partisan Change.* Princeton: Princeton University Press.

Lublin, David, and Thomas F. Schaller. 2012. "Gerrymandering and the Republican Conversion of Southern State Legislatures." In *The Oxford Handbook of Southern Politics,* edited by Charles S. Bullock III and Mark J. Rozell, 216–234. New York: Oxford University Press.

Lufken, Matthias. 2012. "Tweet Me to Your Leader: How the World's Big Shots Use Social Media." *Atlantic,* October 18, https://www.theatlantic.com/international/archive/2012/10/tweet-me-to-your-leader-how-the-worlds-big-shots-use-social-media/263752/.

Lynch, Kelly J. 2004. "Best Friends? Supreme Court Law Clerks on Effective Amicus Curiae Briefs." *Journal of Law and Politics.* 33 (Winter): 33–75.

MacManus, Susan A. 2012. "The South's Changing Demographics." In *The Oxford Handbook of Southern Politics,* edited by Charles S. Bullock III and Mark J. Rozell, 47–79. New York: Oxford University Press.

Maddox, H. W. Jerome. 2004. "Working outside of the State House (and Senate): Outside Careers as an Indicator of Professionalism in American State Legislatures." *State Politics and Policy Quarterly* 4 (Summer): 211–226.

Madison, James. 1810. "State of the Union Address." http://www.infoplease.com/t/hist/state-of-the-union/22.html.

———. 1787. "*The Federalist,* no 10." In *The Federalist Papers* by Alexander Hamilton, James Madison, and John Jay. Gutenberg.org, https://www.gutenberg.org/files/1404/1404-h/1404-h.htm#link2H_4_0010.

Main, Eleanor C., Lee Epstein, and Debra L. Elovich. 1992. "Georgia: Business as Usual." In *Interest Group Politics in the Southern States,* edited by Ronald J. Hrebenar and Clive S. Thomas, 231–248. Tuscaloosa: University of Alabama Press.

Mallach, Alan, and Jennifer S. Vey. 2011. "Recapturing Land for Economic and Fiscal Growth." *Rockefeller-Brookings Project on State and Metropolitan Innovation,* May. https://www.brookings.edu/wp-content/uploads/2016/06/0503_land_value_mallach_vey.pdf.

Mann, Thomas E., and Norman J. Ornstein. 2012. *It's Even Worse Than It Looks: How the American Constitutional System Collided with the New Politics of Extremism.* New York: Basic Books.

Marschall, Melissa J., Elizabeth Rigby, and Jasmine Jenkins. 2011. "Do State Policies Constrain Local Actors? The Impact of English Only Laws on Language Instruction in Public Schools." *Publius: The Journal of Federalism* 41 (October): 586–609.

Marschall, Melissa J., Anirudh V. S. Ruhil, and Paru R. Shah. 2010. "The New Racial Calculus: Electoral Institutions and Black Representation in Local Legislatures." *American Journal of Political Science* 54, no. 1 (January): 107–124.

Martin, Lawrence L., Richard Levey, and Jenna Cawley. 2012. "The 'New Normal' for Local Government." In 'The New Normal: Local Governments after the Great Recession," supplement, *State and Local Government Review* 44: 17–28.

Martin, Leslie. 2007. "Fighting for Control: Political Displacement in Atlanta's Gentrifying Neighborhoods." *Urban Affairs Review* 42 (May): 603–628.

Massachusetts Court System. n.d. "Why Study the Massachusetts Constitution." http://www.mass.gov/courts/court-info/sjc/edu-res-center/jn-adams/mass-constitution-1-gen.html.

McDonald, Laughlin, Michael B. Binford, and Ken Johnson. 1994. "Georgia." In *Quiet Revolution in the South: The Impact of the Voting Rights Act, 1965–1990*, edited by Chandler Davidson and Bernard Grofman, 67–102. Princeton: Princeton University Press.

McDonald, Michael. 2016. "United States Elections Project." May 1. http://www.electproject.org/home/voter-turnout/voter-turnout-data.

McNellis, Kevin, and Robin Parkinson. 2012. "Independent Spending's Role in State Elections, 2006–2010." National Institute on Money in State Politics, March 15. http://www.followthemoney.org/press/ReportView.phtml?r=481.

Mickey, Robert. 2015. *Paths out of Dixie: The Democratization of Authoritarian Enclaves in America's Deep South, 1944–1972*. Princeton: Princeton University Press.

Mitchell, Michael, Vincent Palacios, and Michael Leachman. 2014. "States Are Still Funding Higher Education below Pre-recession Levels." *Center on Budget and Policy Priorities*, May 1. http://www.cbpp.org/research/states-are-still-funding-higher-education-below-pre-recession-levels.

Moffitt, Robert A. 2003. *Means-Tested Transfer Programs in the United States*. Chicago: University of Chicago Press.

Moncrief, Gary F., Joel A. Thompson, Michael Haddon, and Robert Hoyer. 1992. "For Whom the Bell Tolls: Term Limits and State Legislatures." *Legislative Studies Quarterly* 17 (February): 37–47.

Murray, Richard, and Arnold Vedlitz. 1978. "Racial Voting Patterns in the South: An Analysis of Major Elections from 1960 to 1977." *Annals of the American Academy of Political and Social Science*, no. 439 (September): 29–39.

National Center for Education Statistics. 2015. "Table 204.20: Number and Percentage of Public School Students Participating in Programs for English Language Learners, by State." March 1. http://nces.ed.gov/programs/digest/d14/tables/dt14_204.20.asp?current=yes.

———. 2013a. "Postsecondary Revenues by Source." May. http://nces.ed.gov/programs/coe/indicator_cud.asp.

———. 2013b. "Public School Revenue Sources." May. http://nces.ed.gov/programs/coe/indicator_cma.asp.

———. n.d. "Table 211.60: Estimated Average Salary of Teachers in Public Elementary and Secondary Schools, by State." March 1. https://nces.ed.gov/programs/digest/d13/tables/dt13_211.60.asp.

National Conference of State Legislatures. 2016. "Snapshot of U.S. Immigration 2016." February 24. http://www.ncsl.org/research/immigration/us-immigration-snapshot-2011.aspx.

———. 2015. "Incumbent Reelection Rates in 1994 State Legislative Elections." May 15. https://ballotpedia.org/Competitiveness_in_State_Legislative_Elections:_1972-2014.

———. 2014. "Primary Runoffs." July 15. http://www.ncsl.org/research/elections-and
-campaigns/primary-runoffs.aspx.

———. 2013. "State Limits on Contributions to Candidates." October. http://www.ncsl.org
/Portals/1/documents/legismgt/Limits_to_Candidates_2012-2014.pdf.

———. 2012. "Overview of the Common Core State Standards." May 1. http://www.ncsl.org
/research/education/common-core-state-standards-overview.aspx.

———. 2011. "In-State Tuition and Unauthorized Immigrant Students." February 19. http://
www.ncsl.org/research/immigration/in-state-tuition-and-unauthorized-immigrants
.aspx.

———. 2010. "Improving College Completion: Actions Steps for Legislators." November 1.
http://www.ncsl.org/research/education/improving-college-completion-action
-steps-for-le.aspx.

———. 2009. "Size of State Legislative Staff." June 1. http://www.ncsl.org/research/about
-state-legislatures/staff-change-chart-1979-1988-1996-2003-2009.aspx.

———. 2007. "Total Legislative Turnover 1994–96." February 1. http://www.ncsl.org
/documents/legisbriefs/07LBFeb_TermLimits.pdf.

———. 2005. "Women in State Legislatures 2005." February 1. www.ncsl.org/programs/wln
/2004electioninfo.htm.

———. 2003. "50 State Staff Count." February 1. www.ncsl.org/programs/legman/about
/staffcount2003.htm.

Neustadt, R. E. 1990. *Presidential Power and the Modern Presidents: The Politics of Leadership from Roosevelt to Reagan*. New York: Free Press.

Newmark, Adam J. 2005. "Measuring State Legislative Lobbying Regulation, 1990–2003."
State Politics and Policy Quarterly 5 (Summer): 182–191.

Nice, David C. 1994. *Policy Innovation in State Government*. Ames: Iowa State University Press.

———. 1987. *Federalism: The Politics of Intergovernmental Relations*. New York: St. Martin's.

Nownes, Anthony J., Clive S. Thomas, and Ronald J. Hrebenar. 2008. "Interest Groups in
the States." In *Politics in the American States: A Comparative Analysis*, 9th ed., edited
by Virginia Gray and Russell L. Hanson, Kousser, 98–126. Washington, D.C.: Congressional Quarterly Press.

Office of the Governor. 2015. "Press Release: Deal Names Education Reform Commission Members." January 21. http://gov.georgia.gov/press-releases/2015-04-17/deal
-names-education-reform-commission-members.

———. 2014a. "Deal Bolsters State Team in Preparation for Supreme Court Water Case." December 11. https://gov.georgia.gov/press-releases/2014-12-11/deal-bolsters-state-team
-preparation-supreme-court-water-case.

———. 2014b. "Press Release: Deal: Film Industry Generates $5.1 Billion in Economic Impact." August 5. http://gov.georgia.gov/press-releases/2014-08-05/deal-film-industry
-generates-51-billion-economic-impact.

———. 2003. "Governor Perdue Announces Formation of the Judicial Nominating Commission." June 11. http://www.gov.state.ga.us/press/2002_2003/press141.shtml.

Okrent, Daniel. 2010. *Last Call: The Rise and Fall of Prohibition*. New York: Scribner.

Oliver, J. Eric. 2012. *Local Elections and the Politics of Small-Scale Democracy*. Princeton: Princeton University Press.

Opheim, Cynthia. 1991. "Explaining Differences in State Lobby Regulation." *Western Political Quarterly* 44 (June): 405–421.

Orfield, Gary, and Carole Ashkinaze. 1991. *The Closing Door: Conservative Policy and Black Opportunity*. Chicago: University of Chicago Press.

Orfield, Myron. 2002. *American Metropolitics: The New Suburban Reality*. Washington, D.C.: Brookings Institution Press.

Osborne, David, and Ted Gaebler. 1992. *Reinventing Government: How the Entrepreneurial Spirit Is Transforming the Public Sector*. Boston: Addison Wesley.

Owens, Michael Leo, and Jacob Robert Brown. 2014. "Weakening Strong Black Political Empowerment: Implications from Atlanta's 2009 Mayoral Election." *Journal of Urban Affairs* 36, no. 4 (October): 663–681.

Panek, Sharon D., Jacob R. Hinson, and Frank T. Baumgardner. 2013. "Gross Domestic Product by Metropolitan Area: Advance Statistics for 2012 and Rived Statistics for 2001–2011." U.S. Bureau of Economic Analysis. *Survey of Current Business*, October, 105–141. http://bea.gov/scb/pdf/2013/10%20October/1013_gpd_by_metropolitan_area.pdf

Pastor, Manuel, Jr., Peter Drier, J. Eugene Grisby III, and Marta Lopez-Garza. 2000. *Regions That Work: How Cities and Suburbs Work Together*. Minneapolis: University of Minnesota Press.

Patel, Julie. 2014. "Nonprofits' Failure to Report Political Activity to IRS Raises Questions." *The Center for Public Integrity*. February 27. https://www.publicintegrity.org/2014/02/27/14295/nonprofits-failure-report-political-activity-irs-raises-questions.

Peters, B. Guy. 2016. *American Public Policy: Promise and Performance*. 10th ed. Thousand Oaks, Calif.: Sage.

Pew Center for the States. 2012. "2012 Georgia Public Safety Reform." Public Safety Performance Project, July. http://www.pewtrusts.org/~/media/legacy/uploadedfiles/pcs_assets/2012/pewgeorgiasafetyreformpdf.pdf.

Pew Charitable Trusts. 2013. "U.S. Immigration: National and State Trends and Actions." *State and Consumer Initiatives*. September 6. http://www.pewstates.org/research/data-visualizations/us-immigration-national-and-state-trends-and-actions-85899500037.

———. n.d. "Economic Development Tax Incentives Project." http://www.pewstates.org/projects/economic-development-tax-incentives-project-329163.

Pew Research Center. 2014. "Key Indicators in Media & News." March 26. http://www.journalism.org/2014/03/26/state-of-the-news-media-2014-key-indicators-in-media-and-news/.

Pew Research Center for the People & the Press. 2013. "State Government Viewed Favorably as Federal Rating Hits New Low." April 15. http://www.people-press.org/2013/04/15/state-govermnents-viewed-favorably-as-federal-rating-hits-new-low/.

Pew Research Center: Religion and Public Life. 2015. "Religious Landscape Study: Adults in Georgia." http://www.pewforum.org/religious-landscape-study/state/georgia/.

———. n.d. "U.S. Religious Landscape Survey." http://www.pewforum.org/religious-landscape-study/.

Phillips, Patrick. 2016. *Blood at the Root: A Racial Cleansing in America*. New York: W. W. Norton.

Pierannunzi, Carol, and John D. Hutchenson Jr. 1991. "Deracialization in the Deep South: Mayoral Politics in Atlanta." *Urban Affairs Quarterly* 27 (December): 192–201.

"Police Power." 2008. In *West's Encyclopedia of American Law*, 2nd ed. *The Gale Group*. http://legal-dictionary.thefreedictionary.com/Police+Power.

Polling Report. 2016. "Problems and Priorities." April 8. http://www.pollingreport.com /prioriti.htm.

Pomerantz, Gary M. 1996. *Where Peachtree Meets Sweet Auburn: The Saga of Two Families and the Making of Atlanta*. New York: Scribner.

Pratt, Robert A. 2002. *We Shall Not Be Moved: The Desegregation of the University of Georgia*. Athens: University of Georgia Press.

Prillaman, Soledad Artiz, and Kenneth J. Meier. 2014. "Taxes, Incentives, and Economic Growth: Assessing the Impact of Pro-business Taxes on U.S. State Economies." *Journal of Politics* 76, no. 2 (April): 364–379.

Rae, Nicol C. 1992. "The Democrats' 'Southern Problem' in Presidential Politics." *Presidential Studies Quarterly* 22 (Winter): 135–151.

"Ready to Take Off Again?" 2014. *Economist*, January 4, 23–25.

Reinagel, Tyler P. 2012. "Divvying the Dollars: Local Option Sales Tax Distribution Negotiations in Georgia Cities and Counties." *State and Local Government Review* 45, no. 1 (March): 25–35.

Richardson, Jesse J., Jr. 2011. "Dillon's Rile Is from Mars, Home Rule Is from Venus: Local Government and the Rules of Statutory Construction." *Publius* 41, no. 1 (October): 662–685.

Rosenthal, Alan. 1990. *Governors and Legislatures: Contending Powers*. Washington D.C.: Congressional Quarterly Press.

Rothman, David B., and Roy A. Schotland. 2005. "2004 Judicial Elections." In *The Book of the States 2005*, 305–308. Lexington, Ky.: Council of State Governments.

Rowles, Kristin, and Ben Thompson. 2005. "Water Quality Trading: Legal Analysis for Georgia Watersheds." Working paper. Georgia Water Planning and Policy Center. June. http://www.h2opolicycenter.org/researchpapers/WaterQualityTrading_Legal.pdf.

Rusk, David. 2013. *Cities without Suburbs: A Census 2010 Perspective*. 4th ed. Washington, D.C.: Woodrow Wilson Center Press.

Saad, Lydia. 2011. "Americans Express Mixed Confidence in Criminal Justice System." *Gallup*. July 11. http://www.gallup.com/poll/148433/americans-express-mixed-confidence -criminal-justice-system.aspx.

Scammon, Richard M., and Alice V. McGillivray, 1993. *America Votes: A Handbook of Contemporary American Election Statistics: 1992*, Washington, D.C.: Congressional Quarterly Press.

Scher, Richard K. 1992. *Politics in the New South: Republicanism, Race, and Leadership in the Twentieth Century*. New York: Paragon House.

Schneider, Sandra K., and William J. Jacoby. 2014. "State Policy and Democratic Representation." In *The Oxford Handbook of State and Local Government*, edited by Donald P. Haider-Markel, 561–583. New York: Oxford University Press.

Schoen, John W. 2016. "Painful Transition of Energy States as Oil Revenues Evaporate." *CNBC News*. April 22. http://www.cnbc.com/2016/04/18/painful-transition-for-energy -states-as-oil-revenues-evaporate.html.

Sclar, Elliott D. 2000. *You Don't Always Get What You Pay For: The Economics of Privatization*. Ithaca: Cornell University Press.

Sentell, R. Perry Jr. 2004. *Essays on the Supreme Court of Georgia*. Athens: Carl Vinson Institute of Government, University of Georgia.

Shipan, Charles R., and Craig Volden. 2012. "Policy Diffusion: Seven Lesson for Scholars and Practitioners." *Public Administration Review* 72, no. 6 (December): 788–796.

———. 2006. "Bottom-Up Federalism: The Diffusion of Antismoking Policies from U.S. Cities to States." *American Journal of Political Science* 50, no. 4 (October): 825–843.

Sjoquist, David. L., and Nicholas Warner. 2016. "Georgia's Property Taxes by the Numbers." Fiscal Research Center, Georgia State University. March 8. http://frc.gsu.edu/files /2016/03/Georgia-Property-Taxes-By-the-Numbers-March-2016.pdf.

Skocpol, Theda, and Vanessa Williamson. 2012. *The Tea Party and the Remaking of Republican Conservatism*. New York: Oxford University Press.

Skoro, Charles L. 1988. "Rankings of State Business Climates: An Evaluation of Their Usefulness in Forecasting." *Economic Development Quarterly* 2 (May): 138–152.

Small, Oronde, and Laura Wheeler. 2016. "A Description of the Film Tax Credit and Film in Georgia." *Fiscal Research Center, Georgia State University*. February. http://frc.gsu.edu /files/2016/02/Georgia-Film-Tax-Credit-February-2016.pdf.

Southeast Green. 2012. "Solid Waste Trust Fund for Georgia Being Protected By New Legislation." http://www.southeastgreen.com/index.php/news/georgia/5542-solid-waste -trust-fund-for-georgia-being-threatened-by-new-legislation.

Spalding, Phinizy. 1991. "Part One: Colonial Period." In *A History of Georgia*, 2nd ed., edited by Kenneth Coleman, 7–67. Athens: University of Georgia Press.

Spill, Rorie L., and Kathleen A. Bratton. 2002. "Clinton and Diversification of the Federal Judiciary," *Judicature* 84: 256.

Squire, Peverill. 2000. "Uncontested Seats in State Legislative Elections." *Legislative Studies Quarterly* 25 (February): 131–146.

———. 1992. "Legislative Professionalism and Membership Diversity in State Legislatures." *Legislative Studies Quarterly* 17 (February): 69–79.

———. 1988. "Member Career Opportunities and the Internal Organization of Legislatures." *Journal of Politics* 50: 726–744.

Squire, Peverill, and Christina Fastnow. 1994. "Comparing Gubernatorial and Senatorial Elections." *Political Research Quarterly* 47, no. 3: 705–720.

Squire, Peverill, and Keith E. Hamm. 2005. *101 Chambers: Congress, State Legislatures, and the Future of Legislative Studies*. Columbus: Ohio State University Press.

Steffensmeier, Darrell, and Chester L. Britt. 2001. "Judges' Race and Judicial Decision Making: Do Black Judges Sentence Differently?" *Social Science Quarterly* 82 (December): 749–764.

Stone, Clarence N. 1989. *Regime Politics: Governing Atlanta, 1946–1988*. Lawrence: University Press of Kansas.

Stone, Clarence N., Jeffrey R. Henig, Bryan D. Jones, and Carol Pierannunzi. 2001. *Build-*

ing Civic Capacity: The Politics of Reforming Urban Schools. Lawrence: University Press of Kansas.

Stone, Lyman. 2015. "Mapping Migration in Atlanta: Visualizing Local Migration Trends in the South's Biggest City." *Medium*, January 7. https://medium.com/migration-issues/mapping-migration-in-atlanta-4632a4c6ff6e.

Story, Tim. 2003. "2002 State Legislative Elections." In *The Book of the States 2003*, 81–86. Lexington, Ky.: Council of State Governments.

Suggs, Claire. 2014. "The Schoolhouse Squeeze 2014." Georgia Budget & Policy Institute. September. https://gbpi.org/wp-content/uploads/2014/09/Schoolhouse-Squeeze-2014.pdf.

Tankersley, Holley, and Jennifer Custer. 2004. "The End of a Regime? The Election of Shirley Franklin as Atlanta's First Female Mayor." Paper presented at the annual meeting of the Western Political Science Association, Portland, Ore., March 11–13.

Teaford, Jon C. 2002. *The Rise of the States: The Evolution of American State Government*. Baltimore: Johns Hopkins University Press.

Teixeira, Ruy, William H. Frey, and Rob Griffin. 2015. *States of Change: The Demographic Evolution of the American Electorate, 1974–2060*. February 24. https://www.americanprogress.org/issues/democracy/reports/2015/02/24/107261/states-of-change/.

Tharpe, Wesley. 2015. "A Tax Blueprint to Strengthen Georgia: Georgia's Tax System Can Help Working Families and Protect the State's Investment." *Georgia Budget and Policy Institute*. October. https://gbpi.org/wp-content/uploads/2015/10/A-Tax-Blueprint-to-Strengthen-Georgia.pdf.

———. 2013. "Tax Shift Plans Threaten Georgia's Future." Georgia Budget and Policy Institute. October. https://gbpi.org/wp-content/uploads/2013/08/Tax-Shift-Plans-Threaten-Georgias-Future1.pdf.

Thomas, Clive S., and Ronald J. Hrebenar. 1996. "Interest Groups in the States." In *Politics in the American States: A Comparative Analysis*, 6th ed., edited by Virginia Gray and Herbert Jacob, 122–158. Washington, D.C.: Congressional Quarterly Press.

Thomas, John C., and Julia Melkers. 1999. "Explaining Citizen-Initiated Contacts with Municipal Bureaucrats Lessons from the Atlanta Experience." *Urban Affairs Review* 34, no. 5: 667–690.

Thompson, Pat, and Steven R. Boyd. 1994. "Use of the Item Veto in Texas, 1940–1990." *State & Local Government Review* 26, no. 1 (Winter); 38–45.

Tolnay, Stuart E., and E. M. Beck. 1995. *A Festival of Violence: An Analysis of Southern Lynchings, 1882–1930*. Urbana: University of Illinois Press.

Tobin, Jeffrey. 2014. "How Not to Use a Grand Jury." *New Yorker*. November 25. http://www.newyorker.com/news/news-desk/use-grand-jury.

Toon, John D. 2016 [2004]. "Georgia Department of Transportation." *New Georgia Encyclopedia*. Updated by NGE staff, October 12, 2016. http://www.georgiaencyclopedia.org/articles/government-politics/georgia-department-transportation.

Toulmin, Llewellyn M. 1988. "Equity as a Decision Rule in Determining the Distribution of Urban Public Services." *Urban Affairs Quarterly* 23 (March): 389–413.

Trillin, Calvin. 1991 [1963]. *An Education in Georgia: Charlayne Hunter, Hamilton Holmes, and the Integration of the University of Georgia*. Athens: University of Georgia Press.

Trounstine, Jessica, and Melody E. Valdini. 2008. "The Context Matters: The Effects of District versus At-Large Districts on City Council Diversity." *American Journal of Political Science* 52, no. 3 (July): 554–569.

U.S. Advisory Commission on Intergovernmental Relations. 1993. *State Laws Governing Local Government Structure and Administration.* Report M-186. Washington, D.C.: Government Printing Office.

U.S. Bureau of Economic Analysis. 2013a. "National Economic Accounts." http://bea.gov/national/index.htm#gdp.

———. 2013b. "Current Dollar and 'Real' GDP." http://bea.gov/national/index.htm#gdp.

———. n.d. "Regional Data: GDP & Personal Income, Gross Domestic Product by State." http://bea.gov/iTable/iTable.cfm?reqid=70&step=1&isuri=1&acrdn=1#reqid=70&step=10&isuri=1&7007=-1&7093=levels&7003=200&7035=-1&7036=-1&7001=1200&7002=1&7090=70&7004=naics&7005=101&7006=xx.

U.S. Bureau of Labor Statistics. 2013. "Databases, Tables & Calculators by Subject." May 1. https://www.bls.gov/data/.

———. 2012. "Employment Projections: Fastest Growing Occupations." February. http://data.bls.gov/cgi-bin/print.pl/emp/ep_table_103.htm.

U.S. Census Bureau. 2016. "State of Residence by State of Birth—ACS 2014." November 15. https://www.census.gov/data/tables/time-series/demo/geographic-mobility/state-of-residence-place-of-birth-acs.html.

———. 2014a. *Metropolitan and Micropolitan Statistical Areas Main.* "Historical Statistical Area Delineations." May 1. http://www.census.gov/population/metro/data/pastmetro.html

———. 2014b. "Annual Survey of School System Finances." June 9. https://www.census.gov/library/publications/2016/econ/g14-aspef.html.

———. 2014c. "Selected Social Characteristics in the United States." May 1. https://factfinder.census.gov/faces/tableservices/jsf/pages/productview.xhtml?pid=ACS_15_5YR_DP02&src=pt.

———. 2014d. "ACS Demographics and Housing Estimates 2010–2014." May 1. http://factfinder.census.gov/faces/tableservices/jsf/pages/productview.xhtml?pid=ACS_14_5YR_DP05&src=pt.

———. 2013a. *Lists and Structures of Governments: Number of Governments.* May 1. https://www.census.gov/govs/go/index.html.

———. 2013b. *2012 Census of Governments.* "Organization Tables: Final." September 26. http://www2.census.gov/govs/cog/g12_org.pdf.

———. 2013c. "State and Local Government Finances by Level of Government and by State: 2013." May 1. http://factfinder.census.gov/faces/tableservices/jsf/pages/productview.xhtml?pid=SLF_2013_SLF003&prodType=table.

———. 2013d. "Public Elementary-Secondary Education Finance Data." June 1. http://www.census.gov/govs/school.

———. 2012a. *Patterns of Metropolitan and Micropolitan Population Change: 2000 to 2010.* 2010 Census Special Reports, C2010SR-01, (September). https://www.census.gov/library/publications/2012/dec/c2010sr-01.html.

———. 2012b. *Statistical Abstract of the United States: 2012*. Washington, D.C.: U.S. Census Bureau.

———. 2011. *Statistical Abstract of the United States: 2011*. https://www.census.gov/library/publications/2010/compendia/statab/130ed/state-local-govt-finances-employment.html.

———. 2010. *Statistical Abstract of the United States: 2010*. Washington, D.C.: U.S. Census Bureau.

———. 2008. *Statistical Abstract of the United States: 2008*. Washington, D.C.: U.S. Census Bureau.

———. 2006. *Statistical Abstract of the United States: 2006*. Washington, D.C.: U.S. Census Bureau.

———. 1995. "Georgia: Population of Counties by Decennial Census: 1900 to 1990." https://www.census.gov/population/www/censusdata/cencounts/files/ga190090.txt.

———. 1963. *Statistical Abstract of the United States: 1963*. Washington D.C.: U.S. Census Bureau.

———. n.d.a. "Annual Survey of Public Employment & Payroll." http://www.census.gov/govs/apes/.

———. n.d.b. "Metropolitan and Micropolitan Statistical Area Reference Files: Delineation Files." https://www.census.gov/geographies/reference-files/time-series/demo/metro-micro/delineation-files.html.

———. n.d.c. "Foreign Trade: State by 6-Digit HS Code and Top Countries." http://www.census.gov/foreign-trade/statistics/state/data/index.html.

———. n.d.d. "American Community Survey." https://www.census.gov/programs-surveys/acs/.

U.S. Department of Agriculture. n.d. "Farm Numbers Fact Sheet." *2007 Census of Agriculture*. http://www.agcensus.usda.gov/Publications/2007/Online_Highlights/Fact_Sheets/Farm_Numbers/farm_numbers.pdf.

U.S. Department of Health and Human Services. 2014. "Health Insurance Marketplace: February Enrollment Report." *ASPE Issue Brief*, February 12. http://aspe.hhs.gov/health/reports/2014/MarketPlaceEnrollment/Feb2014/ib_2014feb_enrollment.pdf.

U.S. Department of Justice. 2014. "2014 Crime in the United States." *Federal Bureau of Investigation*. https://ucr.fbi.gov/crime-in-the-u.s/2014/crime-in-the-u.s.-2014/tables/table-1.

U.S. Office of Management and Budget. 2010. "2010 Standards for Delineating Metropolitan and Micropolitan Statistical Areas; Notice." *Federal Register*, June 28, 75(123). https://www.whitehouse.gov/sites/default/files/omb/assets/fedreg_2010/06282010_metro_standards-Complete.pdf. February 4. https://www.sba.gov/advocacy/small-business-profiles-states-and-territories-2014.

U.S. Social Security Administration. 2016. "Annual Statistical Supplement, 2015" (April). October 3. https://www.ssa.gov/policy/docs/statcomps/supplement/index.html.

Utt, Ronald D. 2007. "States Vote to Strengthen Property Rights." *The Heritage Foundation*. February 1. http://www.heritage.org/research/reports/2007/02/states-vote-to-strengthen-property-rights.

Van Slyke, Dore, Alexandra Tan, and Martin E. Orland. 1994. "School Finance Litigation: A Review of Key Cases." Report prepared for the Education Finance Project.

Vogue, Ariania de. 2016. "Supreme Court Sides with Death Row Inmate in Racial Discrimination Case." CNN. May 23. http://www.cnn.com/2016/05/23/politics/supreme-court-racial-discrimination/.

Walker, Jack L. 1969. "The Diffusion of Innovations among the American States." *American Journal of Politics Science* 63 (September): 880–899.

Walters, Jonathan. 1997. "Who Needs Civil Service?" *Governing* 10, no. 11: 17–21.

Warner, Mildred E., and Amir Hefetz. 2008. "Managing Markets for Public Service: The Role of Mixed Public-Private Delivery on City Services." *Public Administration Review* 68, no. 1 (January/February): 155–166.

Warner, Mildred E., and Lingwen Zheng. 2013. "Business Incentive Adoption in the Recession." *Economic Development Quarterly* 27, no. 2 (May): 90–101.

Wassmer, Robert W., and Edward L. Lascher Jr. 2006. "Who Supports Local Growth and Regional Planning to Deal with Its Consequences?" *Urban Affairs Review* 41 (May): 621–645.

Weinberg, Carl. 2005. "Poultry." *New Georgia Encyclopedia*. http://www.georgiaencyclopedia.org/articles/business-economy/poultry.

Welch, Susan, 1990. "The Impact of At-Large Elections on Black and Hispanic Representation." *Journal of Politics* 52 (November): 1050–1076.

Welch, Susan, and Tim Bledsoe. 1988. *Urban Reform and Its Consequences: A Study in Representation*. Chicago: University of Chicago Press.

Wells, Donald T., and Richard Scheff. 1992. "Performance Issues for Public Authorities in Georgia." In *Public Authorities and Public Policy: The Business of Government*, edited by Jerry Mitchell, 167–176. New York: Greenwood.

Willis, Dave. 2014. "Government: Contemplating the Future." *Georgia County Government* (Fall): 39–47

Wilson, James Q. 1989. *Bureaucracy: What Government Agencies Do and Why They Do It*. New York: Basic Books.

Witko, Christopher, and Adam J. Newmark. 2005. "Business Mobilization and Public Policy in the U.S. States." *Social Science Quarterly* 86 (June): 356–367.

Wolak, Jennifer, Adam J. Newmark, Todd McNoldy, David Lowery, and Virginia Gray. 2002. "Much of Politics Is Still Local: Multi-State Lobbying in State Interest Communities." *Legislative Studies Quarterly* 27, no. 4: 527–555.Wood, Curtis. 2002. "Voter Turnout in City Elections." *Urban Affairs Review* 38 (November): 209–231.

Wood, B. Dan, and Nick A. Theobald. 2000. "Equity, Efficiency, and Politics in State Education Finance." Paper presented at the Annual Meeting of the Midwest Political Science Association, Chicago, April 29.

Woodward, C. Vann. 1963. *Tom Watson: Agrarian Rebel*. New York: Oxford University Press.

Wynes, Charles E. 1991. "Part Four: 1865–1890." In *A History of Georgia*, 2nd ed., edited by Kenneth Coleman, 205–254. Athens: University of Georgia Press.

Yoshinaka, Antoine. 2012. "Party Building in the South through Conversion." In *The Oxford Handbook of Southern Politics*, edited by Charles S. Bullock III and Mark J. Rozell, 355–381. New York: Oxford University Press.

INDEX

Abramoff, Jack, 137
absentee ballots, 109–110
activism: grassroots, 146, 177; political, 22–23, 137
ACT scores, 313–315
administration floor leader, House, 161, 162, 193, 286
Administrative Office of the Courts, 233
adult and technical education, 167, 327
advisory opinions, of Georgia attorney general, 82
affirmative action, 87, 348n60
Affordable Care Act (ACA), 3, 20, 25, 324, 329
Aflac, 51
agriculture, 9, 11, 43, 49, 54; water use and, 307
Aid to Families with Dependent Children (AFDC), 321. See also social welfare policy
air protection, 304–305
Ali v. Federal Bureau of Prisons, 95
Allen, Ivan, 37
amending state constitutions, procedures for, 83
amendments to Georgia Constitution, 57, 59, 65, 66, 77–80, 98, 146, 168, 187; proposed by legislature, 79, 82
amendments to state constitutions, 64
amendments to U.S. Constitution, 57, 59, 61; Eighteenth, 66, 68; Eighth, 96; Fifth, 84, 305; First, 90–92; Fourteenth, 2, 33, 36, 38, 83, 85–89, 309; Fourth, 94; Nineteenth, 106; Seventeenth, 61; Sixth, 94–95; Tenth, 59, 63; Thirteenth, 33; Twenty-First, 66, 68; Twenty-Fourth, 86; Twenty-Seventh, 59; Twenty-Sixth, 64
American Association of Retired Persons (AARP), 147

American Bar Association, 240–242
American Civil Liberties Union (ACLU), 161–162; in redistricting, 107
American Revolution, 29–30, 58; in Georgia, 29–30
Americans with Disabilities Act of 1990, 86, 88
amicus curiae briefs, 137
annexation, 246, 250–253
antebellum Georgia, 31–32, 125
antigovernment hostility, 23
Anti-Mask Act, 90
appellate courts, 211, 213, 236, 286; workloads of, 229
Arnall, Ellis, 36, 37, 75, 77, 86, 105, 126
Article 1 (U.S. Constitution), 2, 57, 60
Article 2 (U.S. Constitution), 60
Article 3 (U.S. Constitution), 60
Article 6 (U.S. Constitution), 2, 57, 58
Article 7 (U.S. Constitution), 66
Articles of Confederation, 30, 58–59, 72
Association County Commissioners of Georgia (ACCG), 279
at-large representation, 22, 257, 258, 265
attorney general, Georgia, 82, 108, 152–153, 198–199; qualifications for, 235
auto emissions standards, 308

Baker, Thurbert, 108, 153
Baker v. Carr, 107
Ballew v. Georgia, 94, 95
banking crisis, 9
Barnes, Roy, 39, 117, 119, 120, 130, 226; judicial appointments, 238; legislative agenda, 195
Beltline Park, 305
Beyle, Thad, 183–190; gubernatorial scoring system by, 183

403

Bill of Rights: Georgia, 83–98; U.S., 2
black enfranchisement, 74, 85–86, 105, 109,
    111, 127
black people: on death row, 333; elected to
    office, 45, 74, 106–108, 127, 151, 156–157,
    180, 267; in elections by district, 258;
    officeholders during Reconstruction, 33;
    percent of lawyers, 240; voting power of,
    33, 102, 127, 133, 240, 267, 281
Board of Education, State, 187, 200
Board of Public Safety, 331
Board of Regents, University System of
    Georgia, 126, 144, 187, 200
boards and commissions, state, 69, 81, 187,
    200–202
bonds: general obligation, 269; revenue,
    248–249, 276, 296–298
Borders, Lisa, 266
Bourbon Democrats, 34, 75, 126
Bowers, Michael, 199
Bowers v. Hardwick, 96–97
Braves, Atlanta, 278
briefs, amicus curiae, 137
Brown, Joseph, 33, 126
Brown v. Board of Education, 87, 308
Buckner, Gail, 130
budget: balanced, 176, 255, 293; power, 183, 184,
    186, 190, 192, 193, 286, 287–289; process,
    164, 168, 195; regulation of, 256
bureaucracy, state, 192, 197, 202–207
Busbee, George, 76–78
Bush, George W., 19, 20, 129

Cagle, Casey, 130
Calhoun, John C., 32
Callaway, Howard "Bo," 130, 133
campaign contribution limits, 117–118, 142,
    145, 177
campaign costs, 116–117
Carmichael, James, 37
carpetbaggers, 74
Carter, Jason, viii, 117, 120
Carter, Jimmy, 112, 128, 189, 198, 214
Carter Presidential Center, 272
certiorari, 220, 232
Chambliss, Saxby, 40, 55
Chandler v. Miller, 94, 95
Chattahoochee River, 306–307
Cherokees, 28, 32
Christensen v. State, 97
Citizens United v. Federal Elections
    Commission, 24
city-county consolidation, 251–252

city governments, Georgia, 249, 253, 261–262
civil law, 210
civil liberties, 61
civil rights, 125, 127, 147
Civil Rights Act of 1964, 38, 39, 54, 86, 87, 88,
    283
civil rights movement, 38, 39, 111, 258
civil service system, 202, 254
Civil War, 32–34, 39
Clark, John, 31–32
Clean Air Act, 304
Cleland, Max, 141, 177
Clinton, Bill, 128, 129
Clinton, Hillary Rodham, viii, ix, 100, 120
closed primaries, 100
Cobb, T. R. R., 73
Coca-Cola Company, 51, 177
Coker v. Georgia, 95, 96
Coleman, Terry, 160
colonial Georgia, 28–29, 70–72
Colquitt, Alfred, 126
Commission for a New Georgia, 192
committees, legislative, 132, 176, 286
common law, 209
Community Affairs, Department of, 205, 256,
    305, 328
Community Health, Department of, 205
commutes, 11, 299, 301
competition, 3–4, 278–279; partisan, 111, 125,
    126, 148
Confederacy, 33, 73, 74, 125, 132
Confederate Constitution, 33, 73
confederation, 1
consolidation, 245, 246, 250–253; city-county,
    251–252
Constitution, Georgia, 64–65, 76–88;
    adoption of, 77–80; amendment of,
    66, 67, 82; Article 3, 70; Articles 1–6,
    64–65; bill of rights, 83–98; home rule
    in, 247; local government and, 247;
    Miscellaneous Provisions article, 64;
    previous constitutions, 70–76; proposed
    amendments to, 79. See also amendments
    to Georgia Constitution
Constitution, U.S., 2, 57–64, 72, 122; Article
    1, 2, 57–58, 60; Article 2, 60; Article 3, 60;
    Article 6, 58; Article 7, 66; framework
    created by, 209. See also amendments to
    U.S. Constitution
constitutional officers, 198–199, 247, 258
constitutions, state, 2, 83, 149–150;
    amendments to, 103, 106, 146, 168; equal
    protection and, 312; federal government

and, 70; of Georgia, 30–36, 57, 64–70, 70–83; table of, 62
Consumer Affairs, Office of, 204
cooperation, 2–3, 122, 279–280
corrections, 8, 332–335
Corrections, Department of, 176, 211, 333
cotton, 31, 34
Council for the Arts, 204
Council of Safety, 29
Council of Superior Court Judges, 233
counties, Georgia, 4, 258–261; map of county government structures, 260
county-unit system, 38, 75, 88, 89, 107, 116, 249, 283
Court of Appeals, Georgia, 212–216; judges serving on, 215–217; percent of female members, 217–218; percent of minority members, 217–218; percent of Republicans, 219
court system, Georgia, 211–233; appellate courts, 229–230; juvenile courts, 212–213, 228; probate courts, 212, superior courts, 229; trial courts, 211–213, 228. *See also* Court of Appeals, Georgia; magistrate courts; Supreme Court, Georgia
Coverdell, Paul, 132–133
Cox, Cathy, 130
Cox Broadcasting Corp. v. Colin, 92
creative class, 11
Creek nation, 28–29, 32
crime, 93, 267, 330–335
criminal law, 210
Criterion-Referenced Competency Test (CRCT), 315
crossover day, 174
cruel and unusual punishment, in Georgia, 93
CSX Railroad, 300

Deal, Nathan, ix, 119, 183, 187–189, 193; campaigns of, 117, 120; film industry and, 198; judiciary and, 214, 220; partisan change, 119, 128; social media use of, 191; veto use of, 175, 195, 289
Dean v. United States, 95
death penalty in Georgia, 93–96
Debs, Eugene, 36
Declaration of Independence, 29–30, 72
Delta Air Lines, 51
Democratic Party, 26, 36, 86, 100, 105, 124–127, 148, 228; black voters and, 22, 54, 127–128, 214; coalitions, 127; decline of, in Georgia, 119; dominance of, in Georgia, 35, 39, 124, 219, 225–226; factions of, 75, 125–126.

See also Bourbon Democrats; one-party politics
demographic changes: in Atlanta, 267; in Georgia, vii, ix, 112, 134, 136, 148, 158, 214, 223
Department of Adult and Technical Education, 167
Department of Community Affairs (DCA), 205, 256, 305, 328
Department of Community Health, 205
Department of Corrections, 176, 211, 333
Department of Driver Services, 205
Department of Early Care and Learning (DECAL), 326–327
Department of Economic Development, 296, 327
Department of Housing and Urban Development (HUD), U.S., 328
Department of Natural Resources, Georgia, 253, 304, 331
Dillon's Rule, 246
discrimination. *See* equal protection
Disenfranchisement Act of 1908, 86–87
doctor-assisted suicide, 97
Doe v. Bolton, 96, 97
Driver Services, Department of, 205
due process, 2, 84
Dukakis, Michael, 128

earmarks, 67, 200, 289, 301
Earned Income Tax Credit (EITC), 323
economic cycles, 8
economic development, 12, 176, 191, 277–278, 295–299; state policies and, 297
Economic Development, Department of, 296
education: adult, 167, 327; challenges, 13, 17; legal, 241; levels in Georgia, 46–47, 48; policy, 18–19, 65, 308–317; public, 35, 66, 74, 308–312; spending, 6–8, 291–292, 309–312, 327
Education, State Board of, 187, 200
Eighteenth Amendment to U.S. Constitution, 66, 68
eighteenth-century constitutions of Georgia, 70–73
Eighth Amendment to U.S. Constitution, 96
elastic clause, 2, 58, 60–61
election, presidential, 109, 118–119; in 2008, 118–119, 120; in 2012, 118–119, 120; in 2016, 112, 120–121; 2016 presidential primary, 100–101
election procedures: in Georgia, 104–106; U.S., 109

elections: city, 25; delegate selection, 101; general, 55, 100, 111–114; General Assembly and election procedures, 65; in Georgia, 99–111; local, 263–269; money in, 26; municipal, 109, 263, 264; presidential, 109, 118–119; results of, 110; role of federal government in, 38; role of "independent spending" in, 24; rules in Article 2 of Georgia Constitution, 64; special, 104; timing of, 109; voting and, 99–121. *See also* primary elections; runoff elections; voter turnout

Electoral College, 21, 59, 61, 118–119, 134

eminent domain, 84, 305–306

employment, 9, 50; Great Recession and, 49; postwar, 37; public, 8, 69

enterprise funds, 274, 276

entitlement programs, 8, 330. *See also* Medicaid; Medicare; Social Security

enumerated powers, 2, 58, 60

environmental policy, 303–308

Environmental Protection Agency (EPA), 303, 304

environmental quality, services affecting, 253

equal protection, 2, 38, 78, 309–313; in Georgia's constitution, 85–89

Equal Protection Clause, 309–313

equal representation, 88–89

Erie Railroad Co. v. Tompkins, 209

Ethics Commission, 331

European settlement of Georgia, 28–29

executive branch: of Georgia government, 81, 181–207; lieutenant governor, 81, 159; in states, 181–182. *See also* governor

executive orders, 60, 197, 209

executive powers, 60, 181; limits on, 206–207

Federal Clean Air Act, 304

federalism, 1, 4, 19–20, 207, 208; "coercive," 24–25; "new," 19

Federalist Papers, 59, 60

Fifth Amendment to U.S. Constitution, 84, 305

finances, government, in 2014, 6

First Amendment to U.S. Constitution, 90–92

Fisher v. University of Texas, 87

Forsyth County, Georgia v. Nationalist Movement, 92

Fortson v. Toombs, 38, 88, 89

Fourteenth Amendment to U.S. Constitution, 2, 33, 36, 38, 83, 85–89, 309

Fourth Amendment to U.S. Constitution, 94

Fowler, Wyche, 132

Franklin, Shirley, 265–266, 268

freedom of press, in Georgia, 90–91, 92

freedom of religion, in Georgia, 90

freedom of speech, in Georgia, 90–93

Furman v. Georgia, 94, 95

gay and lesbian voters, 267

gay rights, 85, 147; same-sex marriage, 68–69, 80

General Assembly, Georgia. *See* Georgia General Assembly

general obligation bonds, 269, 296

gentrification, 45, 53

Georgia Bureau of Investigation (GBI), 331

Georgia Chamber of Commerce, 194

Georgia Court of Appeals. *See* Court of Appeals, Georgia

Georgia Department of Corrections, 176, 211, 333

Georgia Department of Natural Resources, 253, 304; Game and Fish Division of, 331

Georgia Department of Public Safety, 331

Georgia Department of Transportation (GDOT), 200, 289, 300–303

Georgia General Assembly, 55, 65, 78, 80, 127, 128, 130–132, 149; anti-desegregation efforts by, 38–39, 44, 87; budget, 287; campaign rules, 117; characteristics of members, 154–159; committees, 163–167; constitutional provisions, 151–154; lawmaking, 170–175; leadership, 159–164; legislation, types of, 167–170; legislative norms, 178–180; lobbying of, 176–178; partisan composition, 158–159; redistricting, 107–108; staff, 162–163; terms, 109

Georgia Government Transparency and Campaign Finance Act of 2010, 117

Georgia Municipal Association (GMA), 144, 279

Georgia Ports Authority, 302

Georgia Regional Transportation Authority, 280, 302

Georgia School Funding Association, 313

Georgia State Patrol, 331

Georgia Trial Lawyers Association, 143

Georgia v. Ashcroft, 89

Georgia v. Randolph, 95

gerrymandering, 25, 107

Gingrich, Newt, 133

global economy, Georgia in, 51, 54

globalization, 9–10, 13

Goldwater, Barry, 39, 130, 158

Gordon, John, 126

Government Performance Project, Pew, 206
governor, 182–183; agenda setting and, 284;
    Article 5 and, 65; budget process and, 186,
    287–289; colonial, 29; Confederate, 74;
    informal powers of, 81; institutional powers
    of, 183–184; legislative agenda of, 161,
    193–197; as manager of executive branch,
    197; military and, 33; party control by, 188;
    personal powers of, 188; policy making
    and, 190; popular election of, 71; power
    of, 152, 186; role in executive branch, 81,
    181–198; role in legislative process, 174–175,
    193–197; royal, 30; special sessions and, 153;
    succession rules, 160; symbolic leadership
    of, 198; terms and term limits of, 71, 109,
    183; veto power of, 174–175, 185–186. See
    also entries for specific governors
Governor's Office of Planning and Budget
    (OPB), 186, 287–288
Grady, Henry, 126
grand juries, 238, 240
grants, 19–20, 285, 327, 328
grassroots activism, 146, 177
Gray v. Sanders, 38, 88, 89
Great Recession, 9–12, 17, 26, 49, 191, 249, 293
Gregg v. Georgia, 94, 95
Griffin, Marvin, 198
gross domestic product (GDP) of Georgia,
    49, 51
Growth Strategies Commission, 192
gubernatorial campaigns, recent Georgia,
    119–120
gubernatorial vote distribution (1966–2014),
    131
gun laws, 335–336

Hamilton, Alexander, 59, 61
Handel, Karen, 120, 130
Harris, Joe Frank, 192
Hartsfield-Jackson Atlanta International
    Airport, 299, 300
Head Start, 326–327
Heart of Atlanta Motel v. United States, 86, 88
Helping Outstanding Pupils Educationally
    (HOPE) scholarships, 98, 167, 316, 327
highways, interstate, 45, 300
Hispanics, ix, 45, 46, 47; on death row, 333;
    on juries, 238; lawyers, 240; student
    populations, 316; voting, 112–114. See also
    Latinos
Hollingsworth v. Perry, 68
Home Depot, 51
home rule, 71, 76, 247–248

House committees, 164–166
House Higher Education Committee, 167
House of Representatives, U.S., changes in
    seats (1990–2010), 21
housing, 328; bubble, 9; crisis, 11
Housing and Urban Development (HUD),
    U.S., Department of, 328
Hunstein, Carol, 224

ideology: of Georgia Supreme Court, 226; of
    political parties, 32, 124, 125
immigration, vii, 11, 17, 18, 53, 180, 330
incentives, 3, 296–298
income tax, 7, 293–295, 298
incorporation, 250
indigent defense, 234, 241
infrastructure, 11, 12, 26, 146, 296, 301
initiatives, ballot, 103
Institute of Continuing Judicial Education, 233
Institute of Continuing Legal Education, 241
integration, 38, 44, 87, 200
interbasin water transfers, 307
interest groups, 122, 136; agenda setting, 285;
    alliances and relationships, 144; campaigns
    and, 145; classification of, 138–140; courts,
    use of, 137, 147; donations from, 137; favors
    by, 143; in Georgia, 56, 140; grassroots
    pressure by, 146; impact of, 139; influence
    on budget, 288; lobbying, 136–137, 143; in
    local politics, 270–272; protests by, 137–138,
    147; regulation of, 141–143, in states,
    138. See also lobbying; political action
    committees
intergovernmental relations, 1–4, 278–280
intergovernmental revenue, 6–7
interstate commerce, 2, 58
interstate highways, 45, 300
Isakson, Johnny, 8, 40, 55, 121, 130, 133

Jackson, Maynard, 38, 265, 267
Jacobson v. Massachusetts, 66
Jefferson, Thomas, 149
Jim Crow laws, 38, 87
Johnson, Gary, 8, 120
Johnson, Lyndon, 19, 39
judges, 235; qualifications and selection of,
    235–238
judicial branch of government, 65, 81–82, 247;
    agencies, 233–235; judicial qualifications
    and selection, 235–238
Judicial Council, 233
Judicial Nominating Commission, 237
Judicial Qualifications Commission, 234

juries, 235, 238–240; grand, 238, 240; trial, 238–239
jury pools, 238, 239
juvenile courts, Georgia, 212–213, 228

Kelo v. City of New London, 84
Kerry, John, 129
Key, V. O., Jr., 18, 52–56, 105, 124–126, 134, 140, 148, 283, 337
King v. Chapman, 86, 105
Ku Klux Klan, 38, 90, 92

Land Conservation Council, Georgia, 305
Latinos, 17, 46, 54, 55, 112, 133; student population, 316. *See also* Hispanics
law enforcement, Georgia, 331–332
lawmaking, Georgia, 82. *See also* Georgia General Assembly
Lawrence v. Texas, 97
law schools, 241
lawyers, 240–241; minorities as, 240
legal system, 208–242; Georgia, 211–242; U.S., 208–211
legislative districts, Georgia, redrawing, 151–153
legislative norms, 178–180
legislative sessions, Georgia, 153
legislative staff, 162
legislators: compensation of, 154; qualifications of, 153; typical, 151
Legislature, Georgia. *See* Georgia General Assembly
legislatures: state, 149–151; term limits of, 155; turnover in, 154–155
legitimacy, 99
LGBT rights. *See* gay rights
Libertarian Party, viii, 94, 118, 119, 120, 124, 132
Lincoln, Abraham, 33, 39
line-item veto, 82, 175, 185, 193–195
literacy tests, 87, 88, 105–106, 111
lobbying: by interest groups, 136–137, 143–144, 176; in local government, 279; regulation of, 177; "revolving door," 177. *See also* interest groups; political action committees
lobbyists, 56, 140–143, 176–178
Local Governance Commission, 281
local governments, 82; appointed officials of, 254; creating new, 249; economic challenges of, 8–13; economic development and, 277–278, 298; elected officials of, 254; federalism and, 4–8; finances of, 255, 274–275; foundations of, 243; future of,

280–281; Georgia Constitution and, 247; Georgia law and, 249; in legal system, 211; number of, 4, 5, 244–245; organization and authority of, 247; political challenges of, 19–26; procedures of, 257; public employees of, 254–255; public safety and, 332; regulation by, 276–277; social challenges of, 13–19; state methods for limiting, 246; structure of, 257–258; U.S. Constitution and, 245
local policy process, 272
local politics, 263; campaigns, 265; racial polarization in, 267; voter turnout, 263–265; voting patterns of, 267
lottery, 67, 68, 98, 290, 316, 326
lynching, 35

Maddox, Lester, 130, 196
Madison, James, 59–61, 122, 308
magistrate courts, 212, 213, 228, 239
magistrates, 237
Majette, Denise, 133
majority leader, Georgia General Assembly, 161, 166
manufacturing, 9, 34, 43; decline of, 11; rural, 49; shift from farming to, 37
Marbury v. Madison, 64
marriage, same-sex, 68–69, 80
Marshall, John, 59
Martin, Jim, 130
Mattingly, Mack, 40, 132
Maynard H. Jackson Jr. International Terminal, 300
McCain, John, 118–119
McCleskey v. Kemp, 95, 96
McDaniel v. Thomas, 312
McKinney, Cynthia, 118, 179
Medicaid, 70, 205, 323–326, 330; expansion of, 20, 25
Medical Assistance, Department of, 205
Medical Association of Georgia, 288
Medicare, 7, 319, 321, 324–325
metropolitan areas in Georgia, 15, 41–44
Metropolitan Atlanta Rapid Transit Authority (MARTA), 250, 262, 301–302
micropolitan areas in Georgia, 16, 41–44
migration. *See* immigration
Miller, Zell, 39, 68, 130, 132, 184, 189, 192, 196, 198, 226, 317; veto by, 175
Miller v. Johnson, 89
Milner, Guy, 130
minority leader, Georgia General Assembly, 161

Missouri Compromise, 32
Moncrieffe v. Holder, 95
Monroe, James, 32
Morris Communications, 285
motor fuel taxes, 67, 200
multimember boards and commissions, 81, 181, 200, 259
multimember districts, 108, 152
municipal bankruptcy, 13
municipal courts, 211, 212, 228, 237
municipalities, 249, 251, 261–262; structure of government, 262
murder rate, 334
Murdock v. City of Memphis, 61, 220
Murphy, Tom, 77–78, 158, 160, 161

NAACP, in redistricting, 107
National Highway Traffic Safety Administration, 295
National Rifle Association, 160
Native Americans, 28–29, 32
Natural Resources, Georgia Department of, 253, 304, 331
Near v. Minnesota, 191
neighborhood organizations, 271–272
Neill Primary Act of 1917, 36, 75
New Deal policies, 124, 127, 317, 321
Nineteenth Amendment to U.S. Constitution, 106
Nixon administration, 19
No Child Left Behind Act of 2002, 19, 20
nonattainment zones, 304
Norfolk Southern Railroad, 300
Norwood, Mary, 266
nude dancing, 69–70, 91

Obama, Barack, 112, 118–119, 129
Obamacare (Affordable Care Act), 3, 20, 25, 324, 329
Obergefell v. Hodges, 69, 148
obscenity, 91–92
Office of Consumer Affairs, 204
Office of Planning and Budget (OPB), Governor's, 186, 287–288
Oglethorpe, James, 28–29
Olmstead v. L. C., 86, 88
one-party politics, 34, 37, 39, 54, 101–102, 134, 148, 193, 214, 336
open primaries, 100, 116
Oxendine, John, 199

PAJID scores, 226
Paris Adult Theatre I v. Slaton, 91

parties, political: coalitions, 127–128; definition of, 123; development of, 30, 32; dynamics of, 124; gridlock, 22; history of, 32, 122; ideology and, 54; partisan change, 25, 40, 125, 128, 158; Populist Party, 35–36, 124, 126; States' Rights Party, 32, 127; Union Party, 32; Whig Party, 30, 32, 125. *See also* Democratic Party; Libertarian Party; Republican Party
party caucuses, 160
party identification, 123
party politics in Georgia, future of, 134, 336–337
PeachCare for Kids, 324, 330
Perdue, David, viii, 40
Perdue, Sonny: budgets of, 288; campaigns of, 39, 117, 130, 189; ethics legislation and, 178; as first Republican governor since Reconstruction, 188; judicial appointments, 128, 188; legislative agenda, 195; partisan change, 25, 119, 128; redistricting controversy and, 152–153
Personal Responsibility and Work Opportunity Reconciliation Act of 1996, 321, 329
Pew Government Performance Project, 206
Planning and Budget, Office of, 186, 287–288
plural executives, 182
police power, 63, 66, 208
policy adoption, 286–287
policy implementation, 287
policy making, 282–287; citizens' role in, 243; education, 18–19, 65, 308–317; environmental, 303–308; in Georgia, 282–289; gubernatorial power and, 187; interest groups and, 138–140; limits on, 69; media role in, 284–286; municipal, 261; process of, 282–284; public safety, 330–336; social welfare, 2, 176, 317–330; in special districts, 262; transportation, 302
political action committees (PACs), 117, 137, 142–143. *See also* interest groups; lobbying
political culture, in Georgia, 28, 31, 33, 59, 72, 336
political parties. *See* parties, political
poll tax, 76, 85–86, 104–105, 111, 126
population: of Atlanta, 302; change in Georgia, 13–14, 17, 27, 40, 127, 134, 152, 203, 301, 336; dependent, 17; distribution of Georgia's, 44; drawing districts and, 22, 38, 88, 107, 151; effects of changes in, 18; foreign-born, 17; of Georgia, 41, 46, 48, 152; growth of, 40–48; immigrant, vii; trends, 20, 26, 53; urbanization of, 16, 40–41

population bills, 171
Populist Party, 35–36, 124, 126
pork-barrel legislation, 166, 206, 285
poverty, 17, 317, 318, 323; rural, 27, 34
poverty rate, 17, 46, 318–319
Powell v. State of Georgia, 96, 97
pre-kindergarten programs, 316, 326–327
presidential primary, 116; in 2016, 100–101
presidential vote distribution, Georgia
  (1956–2012), 129
president pro tempore, 159, 162
primary elections, 100, 104, 111, 114, 116; black
  turnout in, 127; contribution limits, 117,
  142; runoffs, 101–102; turnout in, 115. *See
  also* elections; runoff elections
prison population, 332–333
privacy, right to, 92, 96–97, 147
privatization, 192
probate courts, 212, 228, 237
Progressive Era, 257–258
property rights, 305–306
property taxes, 45, 65, 225, 295, 308–309, 317
Public Defender Standards Council, 234
public employees, 8, 24, 140, 202–203, 254–255
public-private partnerships, 12
public safety, 330–336
Public Service Commission, 81, 130, 187, 200

race: Census Bureau definitions of, 46;
  identification of, 47
railroads, 31, 33, 34, 296, 300
Reagan, Ronald, 19–20
Recall Act of 1989, 238
recalls, 64, 103–104, 238, 270
Reconstruction, 32–34, 125
redistricting, 38–39, 89, 106–109, 152–153, 156
Reed, Kasim, 264, 266
referenda, 103, 117, 146, 269
Regents of the University of California v. Bakke,
  87, 348n60
Regional Transportation Authority, Georgia,
  280, 302
regressive taxation, 293–294
regulation, 2, 85, 209, 296; environmental,
  304–307; of interest groups, 141; of legal
  profession, 241–242; of lobbyists, 177–178;
  local, 276–277
religion, freedom of, 90, 266, 317
religion in schools, 90, 147, 266, 313, 316–317
republican government, 60
Republican Party, 26, 100; black voters and,
  128; in Congress, 132–133; dominance in
  Georgia politics, vii–ix, 22, 27, 39–40,

54–55, 112, 124, 128, 130, 134, 156, 187;
  fundraising, 118; future of, 148; in General
  Assembly, 180; on Georgia Court of
  Appeals, 219; on Georgia Supreme
  Court, 225–226; in local offices, 133,
  268–269; partisan change and, 25, 128, 214;
  postbellum, 34, 39, 75, 105, 125; presidential
  elections, 118–119, 120, 125, 128, 134–156;
  redistricting and, 107–108, 153; rise of, 107,
  116, 119, 131, 158–159; in statewide offices,
  130–133; Tea Party and, 23; in 2016 primary,
  100–101; in U.S. offices, 129, 132
resolutions, 168, 251
revenue bonds, 248–249, 276, 296–298
revenue sources, Georgia, 293–294
Revolutionary War, 29–30, 58
Richardson, Glenn, 145, 166
rights of accused and convicted, 93–96
right to life, liberty, and property, 84
right to privacy, 92, 96–97, 147
Robinson v. Cahill, 312
Roe v. Wade, 63, 96
Romney, Mitt, 119
Roosevelt, Franklin, 124, 140, 317
Roosevelt, Theodore, 124
Rules and Regulations of 1776, 70–72, 90
Rules Committee of the House, 160, 166,
  172–173, 286
runoff, water, 307
runoff elections, 101–102; campaign
  contribution limits in, 117; minority
  representation and, 258; in special
  elections, 104; turnout in, 116, 264
rural bias in Georgia politics, 18, 22, 36
rural decline, 9, 11, 13, 35, 140, 281
rural poverty, 27, 34
rural voters, 116, 119, 120, 126, 132, 133
Russell, Richard, 36, 44, 204

Safe Carry Protection Act, 336
sales tax, 7
same-sex marriage, 68–69, 80
*San Antonio Independent School District v.
  Rodriquez*, 311–312
SAT scores, 313–315
school: boards, 262; curricula, 316–317;
  funding, 308–313; performance, 313–316;
  prayer, 147, 313, 317; religion in, 90, 147,
  266, 313, 316–317
Schrenko, Linda, 145, 198
searches and seizures, protection from
  unreasonable, in Georgia, 93, 94
secession, 32, 33, 54, 73, 74

security, state spending on, 6–7

segregation, 35–36, 53, 54, 85, 125; of public facilities, 2, 38, 87

Senate, Georgia: leadership, 161–162; role of lieutenant governor in, 161–162, 166

Senate committees, 163, 164–166

service providers, 329

services, local government, 253, 272–274

service sector, 9, 12, 43, 49

set-aside programs, 85

Seventeenth Amendment to U.S. Constitution, 61

sharecropping, 34, 43–44

Shelby County v. Holder, 39, 89, 258

Silver Comet Trail, 305

Sixth Amendment to U.S. Constitution, 94–95

slavery, 29, 31; abolition of, 33, 74; on plantations, 31; Whig Party and, 32

slave trade, 73

small businesses in Georgia, 52

Social Security, 7, 318, 319, 320, 321–323, 330

Social Security Act of 1935, 317, 323

social welfare policy, 2, 176, 317–330

Solid Waste Trust Fund, 305

Southern Company, 51

sovereign immunity, 95

speaker of the House, Georgia, 160

speaker pro tempore, 159, 161

special districts, 4, 25, 243, 245, 249–250, 262–263, 280

special elections, 104, 116, 151, 270

specialized courts, 212

special purpose local option sales tax (SPLOST), 255, 269, 303

special session, 155, 193

speech, freedom of, 74, 90–93

spending, Georgia, 4; patterns for, 289–293

standing committees, 163–166, 173

Stanley v. Georgia, 91–92

state agencies, 140, 144, 203–206, 278, 287; law enforcement and, 331

state boards and commissions, 69, 81, 187, 200–202

state constitutions. *See* constitutions, state

State Court: decisions of, 69–70; of Georgia, 212

state legislature, Georgia. *See* Georgia General Assembly

state legislatures, 65, 154; committees in, 163–167; overview of fifty, 149–151; redistricting and, 106–107; staffing of, 162–163

state patrol, Georgia, 331

states' rights, 32–34, 74, 125

States' Rights Party, 32, 127

Stephens, Alexander, 33

subnational government, 2–27

sunshine laws, 172

Superior Court, Georgia, 212

superior courts, 65, 213, 228

Supplemental Nutrition Assistance Program (SNAP), 325–326

Supplemental Nutrition for Women, Infants, and Children (WIC), 326

Supplemental Security Income (SSI), 323

supremacy clause, 2, 63, 209

Supreme Court, Georgia, 65, 69, 212–213, 219–233, 237, 287; female percentage of justices, 225; ideology of, 226–228; justices of, 221–223; minority percentage of justices, 224; Republican percentage of justices, 226; workload of, 231–232

Supreme Court, U.S., 59–61, 233, 286

Swindall, Pat, 133

Talmadge, Eugene, 36–37, 52, 116, 126, 200

Talmadge, Herman, 37, 126, 196

taxation, regressive, 293–294

taxes, 6, 255–256, 274–275, 293–295; breaks, 67; credits and incentives, 3, 296–298; income, 7, 293–295, 298; motor fuel, 67, 200; payroll, 324–325; poll, 76, 85–86, 104–105, 111, 126; property, 45, 65, 225, 295, 308–309, 317; sales, 7, 225

Taylor, Mark, 119, 130, 162, 166

Temporary Assistance for Needy Families (TANF), 320–322

tenant farming, 34, 43–44

Tenth Amendment to U.S. Constitution, 59, 63

Thirteenth Amendment to U.S. Constitution, 33

Thompson, M. E., 37

Transportation, Georgia Department of (GDOT), 200, 289, 300–303

Transportation Board, 200

transportation policy, 302

transportation system, Georgia, 299–300

Treaty of Paris of 1763, 29, 30

trial courts, Georgia, 211–213, 228

trial juries, 238–239

Trial Lawyers Association, Georgia, 143

Troup, George, 31–32

Truman, Harry, 127

Trump, Donald, viii, ix, 101, 114, 120

Twenty-First Amendment to U.S. Constitution, 66, 68

Twenty-Fourth Amendment to U.S. Constitution, 86

Twenty-Seventh Amendment to U.S. Constitution, 59
Twenty-Sixth Amendment to U.S. Constitution, 64

unemployment, 9, 49; compensation, 321; insurance, 322
unfunded mandates, 2, 287
Union, readmission to, 74
Union Party, 32
unitary political system, 1
United Parcel Service, 4, 51, 279
United States v. Georgia, 86
United States v. Windsor, 68–69
urbanization, 40–46
U.S. Constitution. *See* Constitution, U.S.
U.S. House of Representatives, changes in seats (1990–2010), 21

vaccinations, 66
veto, 174–175, 183, 185–186, 193–195; line-item, 82, 175, 185, 193–195; mayoral, 261
voter ID laws, 110
voter registration, 65, 104, 110, 134, 217; purging of rolls, 87, 106
voter turnout, 55–56, 104, 109–115, 258, 284;

of blacks, 127; in Georgia elections, 99, 111–121; in local elections, 263–267; for referenda, 269
Voting Rights Act of 1965, 22, 38–39, 54, 88–89, 106, 258–259, 267, 283

Wallace, George, 126
water quality, 306–307
Watson, Thomas E., 35–36, 116
welfare policy, 2, 176, 317–330
Wesberry v. Sanders, 38
Whig Party, 30, 32, 125
white flight, 45
white primary, 85, 86, 105, 267
white supremacy, 36–38, 75, 125, 126
Wild Hog Supper, 143
women: holding political office, 151, 180, 267–268; as lawyers, 240; property rights of, 74; public life of, 35; voting rights for, 106
World War II, 37

Yazoo Land Deal, 30–31, 73

zoning, 247, 257, 274–277

www.ingramcontent.com/pod-product-compliance
Lightning Source LLC
Chambersburg PA
CBHW010114270326
41929CB00023B/3345